# Countries, Peoples & Cultures

## North America &
## The Caribbean

# Countries, Peoples & Cultures

## North America & The Caribbean

First Edition

Volume 8

Editor

**Michael Shally-Jensen, PhD**

SALEM PRESS
A Division of EBSCO Information Services, Inc.
Ipswich, Massachusetts

Grey House
Publishing

Publisher's Cataloging-In-Publication Data
(Prepared by The Donohue Group, Inc.)

North America & the Caribbean / editor, Michael Shally-Jensen, PhD. –
  First edition.

  pages : illustrations, maps ;  cm. – (Countries, peoples & cultures ; v. 8)

  Includes bibliographical references and index.
  ISBN: 978-1-61925-786-3 (v.8)
  ISBN: 978-1-61925-800-6 (set)

  1. North America–History.  2. Caribbean Area–History.  3. North America–Economic conditions.  4. Caribbean Area–Economic conditions.  5. North America–Social life and customs.  6. Caribbean Area–Social life and customs.  I. Shally-Jensen, Michael.  II. Title: North America and the Caribbean  III. Series: Countries, peoples & cultures ; v. 8.

E38 .N67 2015
970

# Contents

# Publisher's Note

*Countries, Peoples & Cultures: North America & The Caribbean* is the eighth volume of a new 9-volume series from Salem Press. *Countries, Peoples & Cultures* offers valuable insight into the social, cultural, economic, historical and religious practices and beliefs of nearly every country around the globe.

Following the extensive introduction that summarizes this politically and physically complex part of the world, this volume provides 20-page profiles of the 22 countries that make up North America and the Caribbean. Each includes colorful maps—one highlighting the country's location in the world, and one with its major cities and natural landmarks—and a country flag, plus 10 categories of information: General Information; Environment & Geography; Customs & Courtesies; Lifestyle; Cultural History; Culture; Society; Social Development; Government; and Economy. Each profile also includes full color photographs, valuable tables of information including fun "Do You Know?" facts, and a comprehensive Bibliography.

Each country profile combines must-have statistics, such as population, language, size, climate, and currency, with the flavor and feel of the land. You'll read about favorite foods, arts & entertainment, youth culture, women's rights, health care, and tourism, for a comprehensive picture of the country, its people, and their culture.

Appendix One: World Governments, focuses on 21 types of governments found around the world today, from Commonwealth and Communism to Treaty System and Failed State. Each government profile includes its Guiding Premise, Structure, Citizen's Role, and modern-day examples.

Appendix Two: World Religions, focuses on 10 of the world's major religions from African religious traditions to Sikhism. Each religion profile includes number of adherents, basic tenets, major figures and holy sites, and major rites and celebrations.

The nine volumes of *Countries, Peoples & Cultures* are: *Central & South America; Central, South & Southeast Asia; Western Europe; Eastern Europe; Middle East & North Africa; East & Southern Africa; West & Central Africa; North America & the Caribbean;* and *East Asia & the Pacific.*

# Introduction

Describing the history, peoples, and cultures of any large region of the world is inevitably difficult, if not impossible. The present case, concerning North America and the Caribbean, is no exception. Although the histories of the countries of this region share certain aspects because of their involvement in the early growth and development of the New World and their subsequent emergence as modern nations, they also display profound differences. Thus, we will attempt no grand synthesis here in this introduction, but instead will consider the larger nations—Canada, Mexico, and the United States—individually, and the Caribbean island nations together as a whole.

## Canada

Canada covers some 3,854,000 square miles (9,985,000 sq km) and is home to nearly 36 million people. More than half of the population is of British or French descent, but it also includes sizeable minorities of German, Italian, Indian, Chinese, Ukrainian, American Indian, and Inuit (Eskimo) descendents. The two official languages in Canada are English and French and the main religions are Roman Catholicism and Protestantism (United Church of Canada, Anglican Church of Canada). Nearly a quarter of the population, however, declares no religious affiliation.

Canada is made up of a few different geographic regions. Hudson Bay forms the center of a vast interior basin that occupies nearly four-fifths of the country. The basin area consists of boreal forest (underlain by the Canadian Shield), the interior plains, and the Great Lakes–St. Lawrence lowlands. Edging the basin are highland regions, including the Arctic Archipelago in the north. Major mountain ranges include the Rocky Mountains, the Coast Mountains (western edge), and the Laurentian Mountains (St. Lawrence region). The largest rivers in Canada are the St. Lawrence, the Mackenzie, the Yukon, the Fraser, and the Nelson. The largest lakes, apart from Lakes Superior and Huron (both of which are shared with the United States) are the Great Bear and Great Slave lakes; there are thousands of smaller lakes. The country also contains several large islands, including Baffin, Ellesmere, Victoria, Newfoundland, and Melville, along with thousands of small islands and islets.

There are ten Canadian provinces and three territories. Canada's border with the United States, extending nearly 4,000 miles (6,400 km), represents the longest demilitarized border in the world. Featuring a modern market economy based on exports and development of natural resources, Canada is one of the world's most prosperous countries. Its government, located in Ottawa, is a parliamentary one with two legislative houses (Senate and House of Commons). As a constitutional monarchy, its formal chief of state is, formally, the British monarch; the head of government, however, is the prime minister. The main political parties of Canada are the Liberal Party, the Conservative Party, and the social-democratic New Democratic Party.

Originally inhabited by American Indians and Inuit, Canada was visited in 1000 CE by Norse explorers, who resided briefly in Newfoundland. The French presence in Canada began in 1534, when Jacques Cartier entered the Gulf of St. Lawrence. A small French settlement in Nova Scotia (Arcadia) was erected in 1605, and three years later Samuel de Champlain founded Quebec (city). The main drivers of early colonization were the search for the Northwest Passage, the fur trade, and, to a lesser extent, missionary activities. In response to French operations, the English formed the Hudson's Bay Company in 1670. For the next century the British-French rivalry for control of the region largely defined Canada's development. The French experienced the loss of Nova Scotia and Newfoundland to Britain in 1713, at the conclusion of Queen Anne's War (War of the Spanish Succession, 1702–1713). Fifty years later, following the Seven Years' War (French and Indian War, 1754–1763), the French were expelled from North America, although they left behind a substantial population of French-speaking descendents. After the American Revolution, Canada's population was augmented by loyalists (monarchists) fleeing the United States. The number of new arrivals landing in Quebec caused the British to divide the colony into Upper and Lower Canada in 1791; the two provinces were reunited in 1841.

A move for confederation, or the establishment of a Dominion of Canada, gained hold in the mid-nineteenth century, and in 1867 the Dominion was created through the confederation of Nova Scotia, New Brunswick, Quebec, and Ontario. Other provinces were added as a result of westward expansion and further territorial development in the east.

Canada entered World War I in 1914. The Statute of Westminster (1931) recognized Canada as an equal partner of Great Britain. The country entered World War II in 1939 and signed an agreement with the United States on joint air defense after the war. With the Canada Act of 1982, Canada was given total control over its constitution and severed its remaining legal connections with Britain while still remaining within the British Commonwealth. A movement for Quebec independence took hold in the late twentieth century and caused serious friction between the English and French communities. Nonetheless, referendums for autonomy for Quebec were rejected in 1980 and 1995. In 2006, the House of Commons passed a motion recognizing "Québécois as a nation within a united Canada." Canada partnered with the United States during several US-led overseas military operations in the 1990s and 2000s.

## The Caribbean

The Caribbean region is an island area defined by the Caribbean Sea in its southern reaches and the Atlantic Ocean in the north. The region as a whole occupies more than one million square miles (2.75 sq km), though its total land area is far smaller, consisting of 92,000 square miles (240,000 sq km). The region's population is over 39 million. Most of the original American Indian inhabitants were replaced early in its history by European settlers and African slaves. The Spaniards mixed with the Africans more so than did the British and the French; however, the latter settlers, as well as the Spaniards, generated descendants of mixed race and ethnicity. Dutch settlers and others, including South Asians also have descendants throughout the region. Religion in the islands is predominantly Roman Catholic with an overlay of folk tradition (spiritism). Haiti is known for its Vodou (Voodoo) tradition.

The heart of the region is the archipelago known as the Antilles or West Indies, forming a broken arc of land from Cuba to Venezuela. The Greater Antilles is made up of Cuba, Jamaica, Hispaniola (Haiti and the Dominican Republic), and Puerto Rico; the Lesser Antilles consists of numerous smaller islands, including Curaçao, Aruba, and Trinidad. The Bahamas represent the northernmost section of the Caribbean. Tourism is one of the major industries in the region, along with the production of sugar, coffee, tropical fruits, and spices. Politically, the region is diverse, ranging from communist Cuba to various democratic republics. Some of the islands, such as Haiti, have endured harsh dictatorships in the past.

Christopher Columbus made his first landfall in the West Indies. The Spaniards continued to explore the Caribbean and soon settled the Greater Antilles, displacing or eliminating native Arawaks, Caribs, and Taino. Santo Domingo, in the Dominican Republic, is considered the oldest city in the Americas. By the seventeenth century, the French, Dutch, English, and Danish began to compete for territory. Spices and valuable sugar plantations transformed the West Indies into an engine of economic expansion for the European powers. That situation persisted, to varying degrees, for nearly two centuries. In the Spanish-American War (1898), the United States took Cuba and Puerto Rico from Spain. Cuba; Haiti, and the Dominican Republic struggled as independent countries in the first half of the twentieth century and beyond, swerving between revolutionary anarchy and bloody dictatorship. Under Fidel Castro, Cuba became an ally of the Soviet Union in the 1960s, at a time when most of the other Caribbean colonies achieved their own independence. Since then the region (with individual exceptions) has remained relatively stable, with most of its constituent nations linked together in the Caribbean Community (CARICOM) economic union.

## Mexico

Mexico is separated from the United States by the Río Brava (Río Grande in the U.S.) along its northeastern boundary and by a land border along its northwestern boundary. It occupies nearly 758,500 sq mi (1,964,400 sq km) and has a population of close to 120 million. About three-fifths of its people are mestizos, about one-fifth are American Indians, and most of the rest are of European ancestry. Its principal language is Spanish, although there are dozens of Indian languages in use locally. The dominant religion is Roman Catholicism; Protestantism, especially evangelical Protestantism, has grown in recent decades. Folk tradition (spiritism) colors the practice of both of these religions in Mexico.

The geography of Mexico is varied. At the core of the country lies the high Mexican Plateau, which is enclosed by mountain ranges— the Sierra Madre Occidental, to the west; the Sierra Madre Oriental, to the east; and the Sierra Nevada (Cordillera Neo-Volcánica) to the south. Mexico has two major peninsulas: the lowland Yucatán Peninsula in the southeast and the rugged Baja California peninsula in the northwest.

Mexico has a mixed economy based on agriculture, manufacturing, and the mining of oil and natural gas. Mexico is the world's largest producer of silver and bismuth, among other minerals. Manufactured goods include textiles, chemicals, processed food, vehicles, and machinery. Mexico is a federal republic with a president, two legislative houses (Senate and Chamber of Deputies), and a judiciary. The country consists of 31 states and one federal district, Mexico City. The main political parties are the Institutional Revolutionary Party (PRI), the National Action Party (PAN), and the Party of the Democratic Revolution (PRD).

Mexico was settled perhaps 30,000 or 40,000 years ago. The first great civilization in the region was the Olmec, followed by the Toltec, the Mayan, and the Aztec. The latter was confronted with the Spanish explorer Hernán Cortés in 1521; Cortés established Mexico City on the site of the Aztec capital, Tenochtitlán. Shortly thereafter Mexico became part of the Viceroyalty of New Spain. In 1821 rebels succeeded in gaining Mexico's independence from Spain, and two years later the nation was declared a republic. In 1845 the United States moved to annex Texas, launching the Mexican War (1846–1848). Under the Treaty of Guadalupe Hidalgo (1848) and the Gadsden Purchase (1853), Mexico ceded a vast territory in what is now the southwestern United States. The late nineteenth and early twentieth centuries saw the eruption of several rebellions and civil wars in Mexico, along with incursions by Spain, Great Britain, and France. Between 1876 and 1911, the country was in the grip of a dictatorship under Porfirio Díaz. During World War I, Germany briefly sought an alignment with Mexico against the United States, but the plan failed. Foreign oil holdings were expropriated in 1936 and the industry was nationalized. During World War II Mexico declared war on the Axis powers. It joined the Organization of American States in 1948. In the 1940s and 1950s Mexican laborers were recruited to the United States under the bracero program, and since then Mexican-U.S. immigration has remained a political topic in the United States, particularly in recent years. In 1993 Mexico ratified the North American Free Trade Agreement. The election of Vicente Fox to the presidency in 2000 ended over 70 years of rule by the Institutional Revolutionary Party, or PRI. More recently, after several years of rule by the National Action Party, or PAN, leadership again reverted to the PRI. In recent decades the Mexican government has struggled to contain the country's powerful illegal drug cartels, a conflict that has produced heavy violence and thousands of deaths.

## United States

The territory that is now the United States, representing over 3.5 million square miles (9.2 million sq km), was originally inhabited by American Indian peoples. Beginning in the sixteenth century, European exploration and settlement started displacing the Indians. Spanish settlements took root in Florida and the southwest (New Spain), while British settlers landed in Jamestown, Virginia (1607), Plymouth, Massachusetts (1620), Maryland (1632), and elsewhere. The Dutch held New York, New Jersey, and Delaware until 1664, when these lands were ceded to the British. The Dutch also settled parts of Pennsylvania but yielded them to Britain in 1674. A long contest between the French and the British in the region ended in 1763 with France's defeat and Britain's cementing of its control over the thirteen American colonies.

Today, the United States is demographically diverse while also reflecting the patterns of settlement and immigration linked to its past. Most of the population, which stands at over 320 million, is of European descent; but there are sizeable minorities of Hispanics (over 15 percent), African Americans (13 percent), Asian Americans (over 5 percent), American Indians (1.2 percent), and others. The United States is a federal republic with two legislative houses (Senate and House of Representatives), a judiciary, and a chief executive (president). There are fifty states and over a dozen dependencies, including Puerto Rico, the U.S. Virgin Islands, and Guam. Christianity, primarily Protestantism, is the majority religion; about a quarter of the population identifies as Roman Catholic. A number of other religions are represented, as well.

The constraints of British colonial policy led to the American Revolution (1775–83) and the Declaration of Independence (1776). The new country, its boundaries reaching the Mississippi River (excluding Spanish Florida), was first organized under the Articles of Confederation (1781) and subsequently as a federal republic under the Constitution (1787). In 1803 land acquired from France (the Louisiana Purchase) nearly doubled the country's territory. The United States fought the War of 1812 with the British and obtained Florida from Spain in 1819. In 1830 it authorized removal of American Indians to lands west of the Mississippi River. By the mid-nineteenth century, settlement had expanded to the West Coast. In the wake of the Mexican War (1846–48), the territory of seven additional future states (including California and Texas) came into U.S. possession. The northwestern boundary was set by an 1847 treaty with Great Britain, and southern Arizona was acquired from Mexico through the Gadsden Purchase (1853).

The nation experienced much internal disharmony over African American slavery in the South and the question of whether the new states would be slave or free states in the lead up to the Civil War (1861-1865). Although the North was victorious and slavery abolished under the 13th Amendment, discrimination against former slaves and their descendants remained. Amid postwar reconstruction, the United States experienced rapid growth, industrial development, urbanization, and further immigration from Europe. A great series of Indian wars was fought in the western region, as rail lines were laid and whites were encouraged to migrate; Indian populations were decimated and their territorial claims virtually erased, as a result. Near the end of the nineteenth century, the nation acquired a number of outlying territories, including Alaska, the Hawaiian Islands, Midway Island, the Philippines, Guam, Wake Island, American Samoa, Puerto Rico, the Panama Canal Zone, and the Virgin Islands. Its economy expanded greatly as foreign trade grew.

World War I saw the late entry (1917) of the United States in the conflict, as isolationist tendencies predominated. Women were given the vote in 1920, and citizenship was granted to American Indians in 1924. A speculative bubble and other causes created the stock market crash of 1929 and Great Depression of the 1930s. Following the Japanese bombing of Pearl Harbor (December 1941), the United States entered World War II. The first use of the atomic bomb, against Japan, in 1945 brought an end to the war and established the United States as a world military power. After the war the United States led the reconstruction of Europe and Japan and became enmeshed in the Cold War against the Soviet Union. It participated in the Korean War (1950-1953), granted commonwealth status to Puerto Rico (1952), and made Alaska and Hawaii states (1959). It also declared racial segregation in schools unconstitutional (1954) and, in the wake of protests, passed major civil rights legislation (1964, 1965).

After first sending only advisers, the United States intervened militarily in the Vietnam War in 1964 and remained in the conflict until 1973. The war years brought widespread civil disorder in the form of antiwar demonstrations and ongoing racial tensions. The first ever manned lunar landing was achieved by U.S. aerospace teams in 1969. The 1970s saw the opening of relations with China, the resignation of a U.S. president (Nixon) in the wake of a scandal, various "small wars" and conflicts abroad, and a stagnating economy. The economy revived, even as military conflicts (in El Salvador, Angola, and elsewhere) and another major presidential scandal (Iran-Contra) erupted under President Ronald Reagan. The United States led a coalition of forces against Iraq in the Persian Gulf War (1991), sent troops to Somalia (1992), and supported NATO forces in the former Yugoslavia (1995, 1999). Following terrorist attacks against targets in New York City and Washington, D.C., on December 11, 2001, a U.S.-led coalition invaded Afghanistan (2001) and Iraq (2003) to respond to the threat. The Iraq invasion was subsequently found to have been based on faulty information. After over 10 years in those two countries, the U.S. military presence was scaled back. A severe recession, caused by shaky investment products and other factors, hit the country in 2008-2009. Within a few years the economy had improved, but caution in economic, military, and other affairs remained the watchword.

*Michael Shally-Jensen, PhD*

**Bibliography**

Bothwell, Robert. *The Penguin History of Canada*. Toronto: Penguin Canada, 2006.

Buchenau, Jurgen. *Mexican Mosaic: A Brief History of Mexico*. Malden, MA: Wiley-Blackwell, 2012.

Jenkins, Philip. *A History of the United States*. New York: Palgrave Macmillan, 2012.

Palmié, Stephen and Francisco A. Scarano. *The Caribbean: A History of the Region and Its Peoples*. Chicago: University of Chicago Press, 2011.

Remini, Robert V. *A Short History of the United States*. New York: Harper Perennial, 2009.

# NORTH AMERICA

*Banff Park in western Canada is home to elk and other animals. iStock/Roberto A Sanchez*

CANADA

# Introduction

Canada is located on the North American continent, directly north of the United States of America. Canada is rich in land and natural resources, and is divided into ten provinces and three territories. It is the second-largest country in the world.

Canadian culture reflects respect for its ethnic, religious, and social diversity. The country's artistic and cultural life has roots in the cultures of the native peoples that have occupied the region since ancient times, and in its history as a colonial and commonwealth territory managed by European powers.

Ottawa is the capital and the technological, political, and cultural center of Canada. Ottawa is part of the national capital region in eastern Ontario and as the fourth largest city in Canada, it has an unusual charm associated with its status as a major city within a rural landscape.

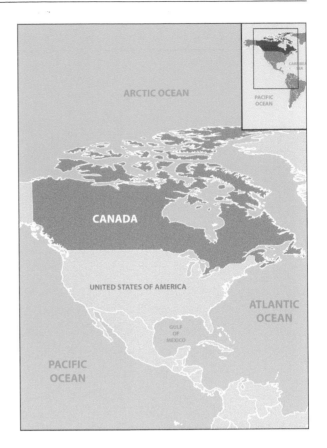

## GENERAL INFORMATION

**Official Language(s):** English, French
**Population:** 35,099,836 (2015 estimate)
**Currency:** Canadian dollar (CAD)
**Coins:** Canadian coins come in seven denominations: the toonie, the loonie, 50, 25, 10, and 5 (1 or penny no longer distributed starting in 2013).
**Land Area:** 9,093,507 square kilometers (3,854,085 square miles)
**Water Area:** 891,163 square kilometers (344,089 square miles)
**National Anthem:** "O Canada"

**Capital:** Ottawa
**Time Zone(s):** Canada encompasses six times zones: Pacific Standard Time (GMT -8); Mountain Standard Time (GMT -7); Central Standard Time (GMT -6); Eastern Standard Time (GMT -5); Atlantic Standard Time (GMT -4); Newfoundland Standard Time (GMT -3).
**Flag Description:** The Canadian flag consists of a white square flanked by a band of red on either side. In the center of the white square is a red eleven-point maple leaf. Red and white are the national colors of Canada.

## Population

Canada is one of the world's most sparsely populated countries and features one of the lowest population densities, as well: 3.41 people per square kilometer (8.3 people per square mile) in 2011. Most of the population lives within 160 kilometers (100 miles) of the United States border as the climate in northern Canada is too cold to sustain high populations.

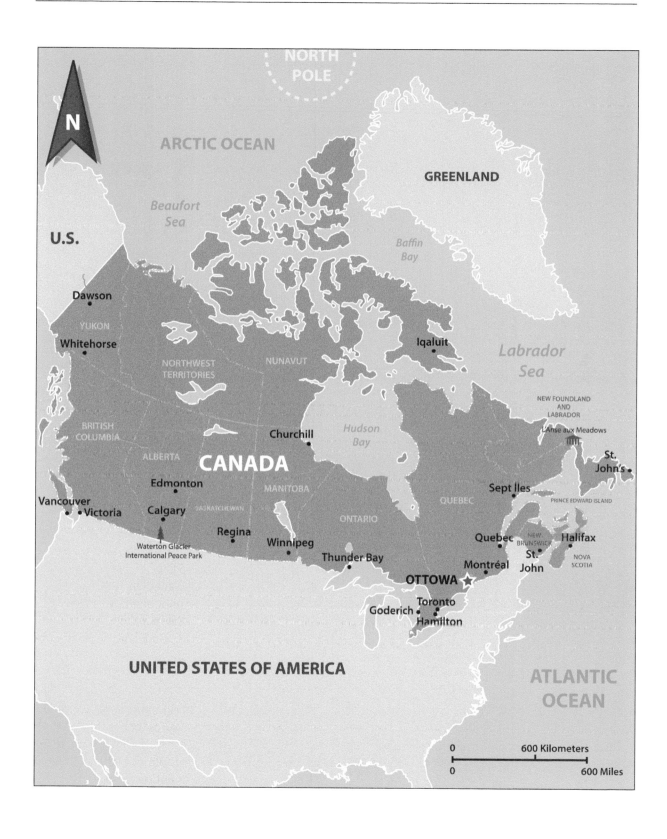

## Principal Cities by Population (2015):

- Toronto (5,993,000)
- Montreal (3,981,000)
- Vancouver (2,485,000)
- Calgary (1,337,000)
- Ottawa (1,326,000)
- Edmonton (1,272,000)
- Mississauga (668,549)
- North York (636,000)
- Scarborough (600,000)
- Québec City (528,595)

The greatest population density is between the Great Lakes and the Gulf of St. Lawrence. The most densely populated provinces, however, are Prince Edward Island and Nova Scotia in Atlantic Canada. The country is nearly empty above 60 degrees north latitude.

More than three-quarters of the people live in urban areas, especially Toronto, with a population of more than 5.9 million in its metropolitan area. Other large Canadian cities include Montreal, with more than 3.9 million people; Vancouver, with over 2.5 million; and Ottawa, with 1.3 million. According to Statistics Canada, almost 40 percent of Canadians live in the province of Ontario (2011).

## Languages

Approximately 59 percent of the population speaks English, and 22 percent speaks French. After these official languages, Punjabi is the most commonly spoken language.

## Native People & Ethnic Groups

In 2011, Canada had an aboriginal population of 1.4 million, composed of North American Indians, Métis, and Inuit. These native peoples are referred to as First Nations. In 1985, legislation was passed that mandated legal recognition of aboriginal peoples in Canada. Status Indians are entitled to certain legal rights and social services. In addition, they do not pay taxes on personal property on a reserve (reservation), including any income that is earned on it. However, disputes over land ownership for aboriginals continue. Inuit land claims were settled in 2005 by the Labrador Inuit Land Claims Agreement.

Today, the First Nations people live throughout Canada, but mostly in the territories and Prairie Provinces. Most of the communities on reserves are small, with fewer than 500 residents. Unemployment and poverty are higher among First Nations people than among other Canadians.

Throughout history, numerous societies have existed in what is now Canada. The Thule (Inuit) cultures lived in the arctic regions of the country. The Thule were organized into bands of related families who worked together to hunt and fish. They are noted for their carvings in ivory. In 2011, there were approximately 60,000 Inuit living in Canada, comprising roughly four percent of Canada's total aboriginal population. The vast majority of Inuit in Canada live in northern Québec, the Northwest Territories, Nunavut, and Labrador. These Inuit regions are known collectively as Inuit Nunangat. The Inuit speak Inuktitut, an umbrella term for Inuit traditional language variants in Canada that is recognized as an official language in both the Northwest Territories and Nunavut.

In 2011, there were approximately 452,000 Métis living in Canadian provinces such as British Columbia, Manitoba, Alberta, Saskatchewan, Nova Scotia, and Ontario. The Métis are a group of mixed European and First Nations ancestry who comprise 32 percent of Canada's aboriginal population. Some Métis are French and Indian, while others are Scottish and Indian. These descendants of early fur traders and Indian women combine elements of both native and European cultures. The Métis speak Métis French, in addition to English and/ or French.

The Métis are considered separate cultural groups, but the vague legal definition has caused problems. While researchers have identified poor housing, transportation needs, a lack of home care, and accessibility barriers, there is a lack of government funds to remedy these conditions. Métis are demanding the same hunting and other rights as other First Nations groups. In some places, the Métis have sued for land rights.

North American Indians comprise 61 percent of Canada's aboriginal population (2011). The area that is now Québec, Ontario, most of Alberta, and the northern part of Saskatchewan was home to the Athabascan and Algonquian groups. These were small family groupings of hunters and gatherers. These people moved to and from seasonal camps using dog sleds.

The Mi'kmaq (Micmac), Maliseet, and Beothuk lived in the Atlantic and Gulf region. These peoples lived primarily by hunting, fishing, and gathering. They sometimes moved inland for a season. Sioux (Dakota), Blackfoot, Gros Ventre, and Assiniboine were the nomads of the Great Plains. Seasonal camps of up to 100 people followed the buffalo.

Various tribes of the Iroquoian and Algonquian groups inhabited the Great Lakes and St. Lawrence lowlands. Extended families lived together in longhouses, with up to fifty longhouses and 1,500 people in a village. They raised crops in an area until the soil was depleted and then moved on.

Semi-nomadic peoples such as the Kootenay and Chilcotin lived on the plateau west of the Rocky Mountains, in present-day British Columbia. They lived in multi-family lodges made of poles, bark, and earth. They hunted deer and other large mammals and fished, especially for salmon.

Complex cultures, such as the Tsimshian and Salish, lived west of the Rockies and north of the plateau. These peoples settled on the edge of bays and inlets in permanent villages of between 200 and 700 inhabitants. They caught fish in the ocean and rivers, and harpooned whales.

Canada's other major ethnic groups include British (19.8 percent of the population), French (15.5 percent), Scottish/Irish (27 percent), other Europeans (14 percent), and Native American (4.2 percent). There are also small populations of Asians, Africans, and Arabs.

## Religions

The majority of the population (approximately 41 percent) professes the Catholic faith, with 20 percent of the population adhering to Protestant denominations, 15 percent professing other faiths, and 24 percent that adhere to none (2011 estimate).

## Climate

Canada's mostly continental climate features frigid winters, especially inland, with heavy snow and light-to-moderate rainfall. Southern and Pacific coastal areas experience more temperate and humid conditions. Permafrost and drought are common on the arctic tundra.

In Ottawa, the average temperature in January is 11° Celsius (52° Fahrenheit), but winters are generally very cold. Temperatures rise to an average of 20° Celsius (68° Fahrenheit) in July. In Vancouver, the average winter temperature is 2° Celsius (36° Fahrenheit), and the average summer temperature is 17° Celsius (64° Fahrenheit). Yellowknife experiences an average temperature of –26° Celsius (–15° Fahrenheit) during winter, and 16° Celsius (61° Fahrenheit) during the summer.

Annual precipitation also varies. The arctic region receives the least rain, only about 30 centimeters (12 inches). The Plains receive about 30 to 50 centimeters (12–20 inches). Areas that experience heavier rainfall include the Atlantic Provinces (150 centimeters/60 inches), and the Pacific coast receives up to 200 centimeters (80 inches).

## ENVIRONMENT & GEOGRAPHY

## Topography

Canada is the second-largest country in the world, after Russia. It constitutes the northern part of North America (except for Alaska), extending from the Atlantic to the Pacific. Canada's only national boundary is with the United States, to the south. The St. Lawrence Seaway and the Great Lakes form part of this boundary.

The country consists mostly of plains, with mountains in the west and lowlands in the east.

The highest point is at the top of Mount Logan, in the Yukon Territory, at 5,959 meters (19,550 feet).

The topographical areas of Canada are the Canadian Shield in the northeast; the Interior Plains (or Great Plains or Prairies), with numerous lakes and rivers, stretching northwest to southeast; the Canadian Rockies, consisting of several ranges stretching from the western part of the country to the Pacific coast; and four of the five Great Lakes.

The country's largest urban areas are Montreal and Toronto. Toronto, the capital of Ontario, began as an Indian village and became a city in 1834. Montreal stands on the Island of Montreal in Québec. It began as the home of the Iroquois Indians.

## Plants & Animals

Flora and fauna vary with the geography throughout Canada. In the arctic tundra and in high mountains, dwarfed trees and lichens are common. Coniferous forests dominate the landscape south of Hudson Bay. Conifers also grow on the Rockies, along with beech and other cold-weather trees. Deciduous trees such as maple, ash, and linden grow on the lower slopes, across the central plains and around the Great Lakes. On slopes facing the Pacific, hemlock, cypress, and cedar dominate.

A wide variety of wildflowers thrive in Canada, including skunk cabbage, wintergreen, prickly pear cactus, asters, columbines, sedges, thistles, wild roses, saxifrages, and various wild berries.

Perhaps Canada's most famous animal is the polar bear. Other large mammals found in Canada include the grizzly bear, the American black bear, elk, wapiti, caribou, and musk ox. Canada is also home to many fur-bearing animals such as the arctic fox, ermine, beaver, and mink. Sea animals such as whales, walrus, and seal are native to Canada's waters.

More than 450 species of birds live in Canada, and many others migrate there. Only Harris' sparrow is endemic. Typical birds found in Canada include puffins, eagles, vultures, hawks, American white pelicans, bitterns, egrets, herons, canvasback ducks, and terns.

## CUSTOMS & COURTESIES

### Greetings

A firm handshake is the typical greeting most Canadians exchange when meeting for the first time. It is also important to give complete attention to the person one is meeting. As such, speaking on a cell phone, not making eye contact, or appearing disinterested is considered rude in most situations. In formal or business meetings, introducing someone by their title is generally expected. Until invited to use a person's first name, it is customary to address someone by his or her appropriate title and last name.

In Québec, and in many other francophone communities throughout Canada, it is customary to greet someone with a hug or an affectionate hand squeeze, while placing a kiss on both cheeks (left cheek first). The same ritual is also repeated when saying goodbye. This gesture is often exchanged at the end of a first meeting rather than at the beginning, and men do not usually exchange cheek kisses with other men.

In many aboriginal communities formal greetings are usually reserved for strangers. Traditionally, aboriginal people introduce their clan, totem (tribal symbol) and/or band when greeting people, and visitors are also expected to introduce their ethnic background. There are also numerous traditions confined to certain tribes. For example, the Inuit traditionally make a slow circle over their heart when greeting someone. In addition, a gesture known as the kunik, where one person presses their nose and upper lip against the other person's cheek or forehead and inhales deeply, is also commonly exchanged between members of Inuit communities. In most aboriginal languages, including Ojibwa and Mi'kmaq, there are no words for goodbye. However, English or French greetings are now more commonly exchanged in place of more traditional greetings.

## Gestures & Etiquette

Canadians have a reputation for being polite, helpful, and reserved with their emotions and extremely sensitive to the feelings of others. Political correctness is generally expected, even if it does not reflect a person's true opinion. With the diversity of ethnicities, religions, and political beliefs in the country, this caution serves as a way to avoid unintentionally offending someone. Canadians generally try to avoid conflict, especially in public. Additionally, asking someone about their salary, the price of their large purchases, their weight, or other personal matters, is considered rude, even among friends. Generally, Canadians also expect a certain amount of personal space to be maintained.

Each province and territory has its own set of etiquette, as well as its own stereotypes. For example, it is offensive for visitors to address people by their colloquial titles, such as referring to Newfoundlanders as "Newfies." In northern parts of the country, and in most rural or remote areas, drivers will customarily stop to help stranded drivers, as road assistance may be very long in coming and cell phone reception is typically not reliable. It is also common for people living in small towns in the prairies or in the north to leave their car doors unlocked in the winter, lest someone should be in need of emergency shelter. Additionally, the Québécois (French-speaking natives or residents of Québec) prefer to speak French rather than English, In general, French Canadians engage in more physical contact when in conversation than English Canadians.

## Eating/Meals

Generally, eating habits in Canada vary considerably between people of different ethnic backgrounds, as well as between people living in urban and rural areas. Typically, Canadians eat three meals a day. Coffee and tea are morning staples, and are commonly accompanied by traditional staples such as a pastry or muffin. Additionally, cereal, eggs, toast, fruit and yogurt remain popular choices.

Lunch in Canada is often eaten outside the home. Business lunches can last up to two hours, and the food is typically heavier, often resembling a light dinner. The midday meal is usually spent with coworkers or classmates. Cafés and cafeterias are popular lunch stops, as are market and street vendors. International fare is becoming increasingly popular and widespread in urban centers. In addition, brunch remains a popular weekend tradition, and commonly includes staples such as omelets, pancakes, French toast and eggs benedict (a dish that typically features an English muffin topped with ham, poached eggs, and hollandaise sauce).

Dinner is typically the one meal that many Canadians share with their families. However, eating dinner as a family varies considerably between rural and urban populations. For example, it is more common for families in small or rural communities to sit down together for dinner early in the evening. In urban areas, where parents might work longer hours, the family might not eat dinner until eight or nine in the evening. It is also more common for urban families to eat dinner separately, particularly as children grow older.

## Visiting

When visiting in Canada, punctuality is relaxed, and it is customary to arrive late rather than early. However, if guests expect to be more than fifteen minutes late, it is courteous to notify the host. Canadians usually offer a small host gift when visiting, such as wine, chocolate, or flowers. Guests typically avoid bringing red roses, as they are associated with romantic intentions, and white lilies, as they are traditionally reserved for mourning or funerals. Additionally, removing one's shoes at the door is expected. It is also common for guests to bring their own slippers or indoor footwear.

There are also many practices and traditions when visiting that are unique to certain areas. For example, in rural areas, if the weather is bad or the drive home is long, dinner guests are encouraged to spend the night. At a ceilidh, a kitchen party commonly held on the east coast, people typically gather around the kitchen stove and engage in activities such as storytelling, dancing, and listening to Celtic music. Traditionally, a person kisses a cod upon joining the party. However, because cod has been fished to near extinction, a wooden or plastic fish is now used. In addition, it is acceptable to drop by to visit someone unannounced in many small or rural communities. In many aboriginal communities, guests do not knock on the door before entering a house, though most make plans to visit in advance.

## LIFESTYLE

### Family

The Canadian family has become extremely diversified in the 21st century. The nuclear family—traditionally a mother, father, and their children—is but one of many kinds of families that exist in the country. In 2005 Canada approved Bill C-38 (the Civil Marriage Act) to become the fourth country in the world to legalize same-sex marriage. The number of same-sex couples and same-sex parents increased dramatically after the bill's passage. It is also becoming more common for families to be separated by large distances, particularly as more Canadians are finding work in other provinces.

In 2001, the average family consisted of three children per household. The number of childless couples has increased steadily and, as of 2011, there were more couples without children than with children. Additionally, many couples are choosing not to get married, with 2011 numbers showing that the number of common-law couples increased while marriages declined. Divorce rates are also high in Canada, and single parent households are becoming commonplace.

### Housing

Historically, Canada has a low population density, which has resulted in housing that is much larger than in other countries. In small towns and rural areas, most families live in a house with a backyard or considerable land. A-frame houses,

which characteristically have a triangular shape and steeply angled roofs, are common in the snowier and rural regions of the country. Until the early 21st century, many Canadians also had a lakeside cottage, or "camp," that families and friends retreat to on the weekends or throughout the summer. Apartment or condominium living is becoming increasingly more common in large cities and urban areas.

Government subsidized housing and social services such as the Housing Services Corporation (HSC) have helped low-income citizens access safe and affordable housing. Landlords also took initiatives, capping rents in order to keep living expenses affordable. However, affordable housing, on which a homeowner spends less than 30 percent of their monthly income, became increasingly rare in major cities after 2002, even for people with full-time jobs and steady salaries.

### Food

Canadian national cuisine is reflective of the country's environment and cultural makeup, and varies from region to region. In general, Canadian food has distinct British and French influences, while western Canada has more Eastern European influences, namely Polish, Scandinavian, and Russian. The culinary traditions of the First Nations, such as the use of fruits, wild game, and other indigenous foodstuffs, have also blended into the national cuisine. Seafood is also a particularly important part of the Canadian diet in the coastal regions.

Maple syrup, first harvested by the aboriginal peoples living in Québec and Ontario, is a signature Canadian food. It is used for topping crêpes (thin pancakes) and pancakes, and is also used to sweeten or flavor a variety of drinks and dishes. Maple is also popular ingredient for smoking meat and fish. Poutine, which consists of french fries covered in gravy and cheese curds, was made popular in Québec. Meat pies, or tourtière, are also a special French-Canadian dish, usually reserved for the winter months. The east coast is famous for its lobster and the west coast is known for its multitude of salmon dishes. Saskatchewan, Manitoba, and Alberta are also known for their

Eastern European cuisine, passed down from the first European settlers in the area. Saskatchewan also boasts outstanding Syrian cuisine thanks to the significant Syrian population that settled in the area.

Produce from Canada's fertile Niagara region in southern Ontario, and the Okanogan Valley in British Columbia, is renowned for its quality. Since 2000, there has been a big push throughout the country to eat locally grown produce rather than imported fruit and vegetables. Traditional meat and fish, such as moose, beaver, bear, deer, whale, and seal, have also made a comeback. The socio-environmental movement to eat locally grown and harvested foods has chefs in major cities reintroducing many old dishes to their restaurants.

**Life's Milestones**

Canadian milestones traditionally follow Christian practices of baptism, marriage, and funerals. However, as a result of increased secularism, atheism, and agnosticism, many of these traditions are practiced omitting the religious ceremonies. Immigrant communities have also introduced many new traditions surrounding major life events.

Prior to the birth of their child, most mothers typically have a baby shower, receiving gifts for the unborn child. It is common that another small party follows the birth for friends and family to meet the baby. Generally, graduation, independent living, and marriage are associated with coming of age. Initiation rites testing physical and mental strength and marking the transition from childhood to adulthood do exist in Canada, though many are contemporary inventions. For example, tree planting in Alberta, British Columbia, and Ontario is considered a rite of passage for young adults to prove their hardiness in Canada's backcountry. Tree planting is also considered a rite of passage because tree planters are able to independently afford other coming of age activities, such as travel and higher education.

Ceremonies surrounding death and funerals remain similar to those found in other Western cultures, and typically involve visitation, funeral, and burial. Eulogies in praise of the deceased's life and achievements are commonly delivered. In recent years many Canadians have modified funeral rites in order to make them reflective of the beliefs and characteristics of the deceased.

## CULTURAL HISTORY

**Art**

Canada's visual arts have their roots in the cultures of the aboriginal peoples that occupied the region since ancient times. Each group developed distinct visual art forms and specialized in different media. The best-known aboriginal art includes Ojibwa and Cree petroglyphs (rock carvings) and paintings, and the totem poles and masks created by many of the peoples living on Canada's Pacific Coast. In the arctic and subarctic areas, the Inuit made detailed carvings of spirits, animals, and figures from a variety of available resources, most notably the bones of sea mammals, ivory, soapstone, and antlers. Generally, most aboriginal peoples engaged in handicrafts such as beadwork and embroidery, as well as functional arts such as Mi'kmaq basket weaving. In addition, many artistic creations carried spiritual meaning, and aboriginal communities still consider many artistic works to be sacred.

During the 19th century, largely as a reaction to the swelling European population, art in aboriginal communities took on an increasingly important cultural role. For example, aboriginal art forms that were believed to have healing powers, such as the ritualistic false face masks of the Six Nations (an umbrella term describing the six tribes of the Iroquois), began to be used to treat the ills introduced by Europeans, such as alcoholism and depression. In addition, aboriginal artist Norval Morriseau (1932–2007) became famous for a style of painting known as "medicine painting," also known as the Woodlands school of painting.

Art continues to help aboriginal people retain their cultural identity. Aboriginal artists such as

Bill Reid (1920–1998) and Roy Vickers (1946– ) are among Canada's internationally recognized artists. Their works not only serve to help Canadians and the world understand aboriginal cultures, they also bring much needed attention to the ongoing struggle of many aboriginal people throughout the country, most notably their struggles against poverty, land claim issues, and historical abuses.

French traders, merchants, and businessmen were the first non-Native artists in Canada. The Canadian landscape and aboriginal people were reoccurring subjects in these early works. However, it was not until the early 20th century that artists moved away from traditional European techniques and established a distinctly Canadian style. During the early 20th century, Canadian painter Tom Thomson (1877–1917) and a group of landscape painters known as the Group of Seven (Franklin Carmichael, Lawren Harris, A.Y. Jackson, Frank Johnston, Arthur Lismer, J.E.H. MacDonald, and Frederick Varley) emerged on the Canadian art scene.

This group, largely influenced by 19th-century impressionism and by Thomson himself, was renowned for their passionate paintings of landscapes, ranging from Québec, Ontario, to the arctic regions and Canada's west coast. Painter Emily Carr (1871–1945), from western Canada, was also associated with the Group of Seven. She eventually became the best-known female artist from this era, receiving national and international praise for her paintings of Haida Gwai and other coastal locations. The Group of Seven and their contemporaries became immensely popular, and are considered the foundation of non-Native art in Canada. Throughout the 1930s and 1940s, numerous art schools opened across the country, and many new artists began to contribute to Canada's emerging national culture.

Generally, art took on more importance in Canadian culture after the First World War, particularly as Canadians developed their national identity after gaining more independence from Britain. Considering the loss of soldiers, nurses, and other military personnel during the two world wars, some of the first major works of national art commissioned by the Canadian government were commemorative pieces. During and after the Great Depression of the 1930s, Canadian art depicted the struggles of farmers and new immigrants.

In addition, art as therapy became standardized during the 1940s as part of the treatment of patients in mental institutions. This led to the establishment of the Art Therapy Association of Canada in 1977. Art therapy is used in many different facilities, from Canada's correctional institutions to rehabilitation centers for children recovering from trauma and abuse. Since the mid-1950s, sculptures, murals, mosaics, and architecture have been used as a way for the Canadian population to mourn its losses, celebrate its achievements, and caution against its mistakes.

## Drama

Throughout the 17th century, theater in Nouvelle France (French Canada) consisted of amateur actors performing popular European drama, as well as small plays reflecting life in the new country. It was not until 1825 that the first theaters were built in Canada: Théatre Royale in Montréal and the Royal Circus in Québec. These theaters typically hosted European productions and actors. However, by the end of the 19th century, a number of Canadian plays began to be performed and produced. The first established playwrights typically followed European writing styles, but often centered their works on Canadian experiences and characters.

## Music

Canada's aboriginal population developed a variety of unique musical styles and instruments some ten thousand years ago. Traditionally, much of the music performed by Canada's aboriginal peoples was vocal, typically accompanied by percussion instruments such as rattles and drums. Songs were customarily believed to be the property of the person who received them, either in a dream or as a gift from another singer. One particularly renowned and unique aboriginal musical tradition is Inuit throat singing, largely practiced by women in Inuit communities throughout northern Canada, and not heard anywhere else in the world.

When European settlers began to arrive in the early 17th century, they brought with them many European musical traditions. Fur traders, lumberjacks, and other early immigrants wrote new songs describing their lives in the new country, accompanied by traditional instruments such as wooden spoons, fiddles, guitars, flutes, and drums. This early Euro-Canadian music influenced numerous 20th century Canadian folk and country musicians, including Félix Leclerc (1914–1988), Gilles Vigneault (1928– ), Hank Snow (1914–1999) and Stan Rogers (1949–1983). During the 1960s and 1970s, Canadian folk music was further highlighted by the international prominence of artists such as Joni Mitchell (1943– ), Leonard Cohen (1934– ), and Gordon Lightfoot (1938– ).

## Literature

Canadian literature is rooted in the rich oral traditions of Canada's aboriginal peoples, who practiced the art of storytelling for thousands of years. Gradually, these historical and mythological narratives made their way into modern Canadian literature. Euro-Canadian literature emerged with Nova Scotian businessman and judge Thomas Chandler Haliburton (1796–1865), who wrote popular comic novels. The first French-Canadian novel, *L'influence d'un livre*, was published in 1837, written by Philippe-Ignace-Francois Aubert de Gaspé (c. 1814–1841). However, the first Canadian author to gain international recognition was John McCrae (1872–1918), a surgeon and poet from the First World War who penned the famous poem "In Flander's Fields."

By the turn of the 20th century, women increasingly found a prominent voice within Canadian literature. Lucy Maude Montgomery (1874–1942) became a Canadian icon for her *Anne of Green Gables* series, set in Prince Edward Island. In addition, francophone author Gabrielle Roy (1909–1983) earned international acclaim from her books set in Montréal and Manitoba during World War II, which describes the lives of the French-Canadian and immigrant working-class populations.

After the Second World War, Canada's literary culture became more diversified, and a new generation of Canadian writers emerged. Some of the most celebrated authors of this era include Margaret Atwood (1939– ), Timothy Findley (1930–2002), Mordecai Richler (1931–2001), Robertson Davies (1913–1995), Farley Mowat (1921–2014), Alice Munro (1931– ), and Carol Shields (1935–2003). Additionally, francophone authors of international acclaim include Antonine Maillet (1929– ), Yves Thériault (1915–1983) and Roch Carrier (1937– ) whose short story *Le chandail de hockey* (*The Hockey Sweater*) was commemorated on Canada's five-dollar bill.

## CULTURE

## Arts & Entertainment

Beginning in the late 1990s, Canada's alternative music scene emerged as one of the most acclaimed in the world. Alternative bands and musicians such as Arcade Fire, Billy Talent, Feist, and Broken Social Scene surprised the international music scene with the quality and originality of their work. Many contemporary aboriginal musicians, such as Buffy Sainte-Marie (1941– ) and Susan Aglukark (1967– ), also began to incorporate traditional music with mainstream styles. Additionally, Canadian jazz artists such as Diana Krall (1964– ) and Michael Bublé (1975– ) have made significant contributions to their genre, while contemporary Canadian country artists such as Shania Twain (1965– ), Corb Lund, and Kathleen Edwards (1978– ) have also achieved widespread success.

Many Canadian theaters and festivals continue to spotlight dramatic works from Europe and the United States. Annual theater festivals, such as the Magnetic North Theater Festival and fringe festivals hosted in Canada's major cities, devote themselves to Canadian works, as do a number of theaters across the country. Additionally, Canada hosts numerous literary festivals, and the country's new immigrant population has produced a number of notable works, including *Life of Pi* (2001) by Yann Martel (1963– ) and *The English Patient* (1992) by Michael Ondaatje (1943– ). Works from Chinese author Wayson Choy (1939– ) and Indian author Rohinton Mistry (1952– ) have also garnered much praise.

According to the Canadian Council of the Arts in 2003, Canadians spent over $250 million USD on art supplies to pursue their creative habits. Additionally, over 50,000 Canadians volunteer for visual arts organizations every year, and another 200,000 support the arts as members of galleries or as individual sponsors. The Canada Council for the Arts also stated that, in the early 21st century, there was an estimated 600,000 jobs in Canada's art and culture sector, which is roughly the equivalent of the combined jobs in agriculture, forestry and fishing, mining, and the oil and gas industries. In 2007, the cultural sector was responsible for $46 billion USD in revenue, which is approximately 3.8 percent of Canada's gross domestic product (GDP).

In 2008, Canadian Prime Minister Stephen Harper's Conservative Party managed to secure only a minority government during the October elections, despite predictions to the contrary. Many critics blame Harper's failure to achieve a majority on his $45-million cut to arts and culture funding as well as on his condescending remarks about art appreciation in Canada, including his statement that "ordinary folks don't care about the arts." During his 2008 election, campaign rallies and protests were staged across the country against the cuts, and Harper lost key ridings (electoral divisions) and alienated many supporters because of what many Canadians felt was a grave threat to arts and culture in the country. In 2015, the leader of the Liberal Party of Canada, Justin Trudeau, released a platform for the arts and culture industries that included reinvestment and increased funding in order to create jobs, grow local economies, and help Canadian artists.

Ice hockey is Canada's national sport. The country regularly ices "a medal-contending Olympic team and has three national leagues and numerous local and regional leagues. Some of Canada's most famous hockey players include Bobby Hull, Bobby Orr, and Bobby Clarke.

Basketball is also popular. Since 1936, Canada has had an Olympic basketball team. The first National Basketball Association (NBA) game was played in Toronto in 1946. Canadians also love baseball. Jackie Robinson broke the color barrier in baseball when he played with the Montreal Royals. The 1877 Tecumsehs and the 1994 Toronto Blue Jays won the World Series.

## Cultural Sites & Landmarks

Canada's oldest cultural sites date back to the Pleistocene Epoch (which began 1.65 million years ago) when the Beringia Land Bridge allowed ancient populations to travel from continental Europe to North America. Evidence of the early peoples have been found throughout the Yukon and the Northwest Territories, along with the remains of mammoths, mastodons, giant sloths, saber-tooth tigers, and various species of flora and fauna. The history and archaeological discoveries of the area are showcased in the Yukon Beringia Interpretive Centre in the Yukon.

The traces of ancient cultures are still evident in numerous sites across the country. In fact, many of these were designated as World Heritage Sites by the United Nations Educational, Scientific and Cultural Organization (UNESCO). There are seventeen such sites throughout Canada. At Head-Smashed-In Buffalo Jump in southern Alberta—designated as a World Heritage Site in 1981—the remains of the buffalo herds driven off cliffs by the Blackfoot, along with the meat-preparation camps, can still be seen. Gwaii Haanas, an island in the Haida Gwaii archipelago on the northern coast of British Columbia, hosts massive totem poles and long houses constructed by the Haida Nation. This heritage site was named a national park and designated as a World Heritage Site in 1988.

The first European settlement in Canada is a Viking encampment in Newfoundland from the 11th century called L'Anse aux Meadows. The archaeological site was designated as a World Heritage Site in 1978. Early colonial settlement sites include Fort William, located near Thunder

Bay, a major trade post during the height of the Canadian fur trade period. The Red Bay Basque Whaling Station, established by Basque mariners in the 16th century, was designated in 2013. The station was used for 70 years, starting in the 1530s, and is the best preserved and most complete archaeological site of the European whaling tradition. In addition, the Historic District of Old Québec (founded by the French in 1608) and Old Town Lunenburg in Nova Scotia (founded by the British in the late 18th century) are both World Heritage Sites.

Other important cultural and historic sites include Dawson City, in the Yukon Territory. Dawson City was a bustling city of 40,000 during the Klondike Gold Rush of the late 19th century. In particular, the Klondike-era architecture of the town has been largely preserved.

Canada's most famous landmark is perhaps its spectacular natural landscape. Many natural sites have been named UNESCO World Heritage Sites, including the Rocky Mountain Parks (1984), Nahanni National Park (1978), Waterton-Glacier International Peace Park (1995), Joggins Fossil Cliffs (2008), and Wood Buffalo National Park (1983). In addition, Canada is home to numerous significant paleontological sites, such as Dinosaur Provincial Park in Alberta. The Bay of Fundy in Nova Scotia and the Bay of Ungava in Québec are renowned for having the highest tidal ranges in the world.

## Libraries & Museums

Halifax's Pier 21 is considered one of the most important sites in Canada. Pier 21 was the most active port of departure for Canadian troops during World War II. Further, between 1928 and 1971 over one million immigrants, 100,000 refugees, and thousands of war brides and war orphans arrived in Canada at this pier. It is the home to the Canadian Museum of Immigration, which is one of the six National museums of Canada (NMC). The others are the National Gallery of Canada, the National Museum of Science and Technology, the Canadian Museum of Civilization, the Canadian Museum for Human Rights, and the Canadian Museum of

Nature. There are over 2,400 Canadian museums in all.

Canada's national repositories include the Library and Archives Canada (Bibliothèque et Archives Canada) and the Canada Institute for Scientific and Technical Information (NRC–CISTI).

## Holidays

Official holidays observed in Canada include Victoria Day, the Queen's birthday (May 23), Canada Day (July 1), Thanksgiving (second Monday in October), Remembrance Day (November 11), and Boxing Day (December 26).

## Youth Culture

In general, Canadian youth have a great degree of freedom and independence. There are numerous services and programs geared toward young people, such as the federal Jeunesse Canada Monde, or Canada World Youth (CWY), which provides international educational initiatives and programs for youth ages fifteen to thirty-five. In addition, more Canadians between the ages of 20 and 30 are choosing to live with their parents. This trend is due in large part to the housing boom and increased living costs in most major cities across the country.

Canadian youth typically spend a great deal of time on the Internet, and social networking sites (SNS) such as Facebook and Twitter are popular. Additionally, a large part of Canada's vibrant youth culture is linked to the natural landscape. As such, recreational activities such as snowboarding, skiing, downhill mountain biking, kayaking, hockey, and winter surfing are very popular in Canada, and also attract young visitors from around the world.

## SOCIETY

## Transportation

Speeds and distances for roadways in Canada are shown in kilometers. Roads signs may be in either French or English, depending on the province or territory. (In French-speaking Québec, signage is typically in French.) Drivers drive on the right side of the road in Canada, and seat belts are required by law, as are car seats for children. The legal speed limit for drivers is usually around 80 kilometers/hr on highways (approximately 49 mph) and 50 kilometers/hr (approximately 31 mph) in or near cities. Laws regarding radar detectors in automobiles and cell phone usage while driving vary across the provinces and territories.

The majority of Canada's large urban cities have efficient and modern public transportation systems. In Vancouver, for example, the skytrain, seabus, and bus system link the city center to the greater metropolitan areas. Generally, using public transportation is encouraged in urban centers. Additionally, most major cities also host bike lanes and bike routes, while pedestrian paths, overhead bridges, and tunnels are also growing in number.

Outside the major cities and urban centers, however, life without a car can be difficult. Winter weather coupled with underdeveloped public transportation in small cities and rural areas forces most people to own a car. In the far north, for example, where snow can cover the ground for four to eight months, snowmobiles, snowshoes, cross-country skies and sleds are often more efficient modes of transportation than vehicles. In coastal areas, in the Boundary Lakes region in northern Ontario, and in the arctic regions, canoes, kayaks, and motor boats are still commonly used. Remote regions in the north and on the west coast can only be accessed by floatplane (a type of seaplane) or helicopter.

Canada is also home to the infamous ice roads of the northern territories of Yukon, Northwest Territories, and Nunavut. The roads are constructed annually over bogs and waterways, and serve as supply links between communities, in addition to being heavily used by mining and oil companies.

### Transportation Infrastructure

Canada's National Highway System (NHS) was established in 1988 by the Council of Ministers Responsible for Transportation and Highway

Safety, and by 2013, the NHS comprised over 38,000 kilometers of highway. Over 95 percent of the NHS is owned and operated by provincial and territorial authorities. In 2011, approximately 25,000 km of NHS pavement was categorized as "good," which was a 4.3 percent increase over the previous year. Usage of the NHS by vehicles increased by eight percent from 2005 to 2011, and truck travel increased three percent in that same period. There are approximately 8,900 bridges in the NHS, with about 1,350 that are less than 10 years old. Since 2007 approximately 950 bridges have undergone rehabilitation or are new. Canadian governments in the 2011–2012 fiscal year invested $3.4 billion CAN in the NHS.

According to Transport Canada, there are 26 airports in the country's National Airport System (NAS), which handle 94 percent of air travel in Canada. In addition, there are 1,467 airports, 523 with paved runways (2013).

### Media & Communications

Canadian media includes over 2,000 radio stations, 150 television stations, and at least one major newspaper in each city. Maintaining a plurality of opinions and representing Canada's religions, cultures, and political positions is an important stipulation in Canadian media, as is providing news and entertainment in a diversity of languages. The government-funded Canadian Broadcasting Corporation (CBC) airs predominantly Canadian programs, and is one of the most popular news and cultural sources in the country. CanWest Global Communications was a company that prior to 2009 controlled 14 of Canada's major newspapers, and the largest television network. The publishing properties of CanWest were acquired by Postmedia Network in 2010, and in 2015 approval was given for additional acquisition by Postmedia of several SunMedia English-language properties.

Radio and television is heavily subsidized by the Canadian government. Imported cultural programming from the United States has overshadowed Canadian programs for decades. The Canadian Radio-Television and Telecommunications Commission (CRTC) has made rulings in order to nurture better quality Canadian television programs by reducing the number of hours when they must be broadcast while giving greater freedom to broadcasters on the remainder of the daily schedule.

As of 2014, 92.9 percent of the Canadian population were Internet users. Wireless Internet access is available in every province and territory, including in some of the most remote towns in the Nunavut and the Northwest Territories. Additionally, approximately 85 percent of Canadians have a cell phone.

## SOCIAL DEVELOPMENT

### Standard of Living
In 2014, the Human Development Index (HDI) ranking of Canada was eight (out of 187 countries).

### Water Consumption
Canada contains approximately 6.5 percent of the world's renewable freshwater, giving it the third largest supply in the world. In addition, Canada has more lakes than any other country in the world—they cover around nine percent of the country. Two percent of Canada is covered by glaciers and ice fields (2013). In the early 21st century, approximately 8.5 million Canadians got their drinking water from the Great Lakes.

While the majority of Canadians live close to the US border, 60 percent of the country's freshwater drains to the north, which has raised concerns about water shortages, as well as water contamination. Canada is one of the highest per capita users of water in the world. According to Environment Canada, approximately 8 million citizens use groundwater for drinking and household use, while the majority relies on municipal water sources.

In 2015, the Canadian government pledged $375 million to improving clean water access in First Nations communities. In 2006, the Clean Water Act was passed in Ontario, Canada. The act mandates that communities create and implement

strategies to protect their municipal water supplies and to protect water sources.

### Education
Canadian education policy is determined by the provinces, so compulsory education requirements vary. In general, primary education begins at age five or six and continues to age thirteen or fourteen. High school typically lasts for five years.

There are nearly 100 universities throughout Canada. McGill University is an English-language institution in Montreal, while the University of Montreal is a French-language university. The University of King's College, founded in Nova Scotia in 1789, is the oldest in Canada. The university was established by British loyalists who moved to Canada after the American Revolution. The University of Toronto has the country's largest enrollment and has three campus locations.

The average literacy rate in Canada is approximately 97 percent. In 2013, the Council of Ministers of Education released its Pan-Canadian Assessment Program report, which stated that, among Canadian students in Grade 8/Secondary II, there continued to be a gender difference in reading, with girls outperforming boys. The report also found that the gender gap in mathematics and science performance had closed, with male and female students performing relatively equally.

In 1971, 68 percent of university graduates between the ages of 25 and 29 were men; however, by 2006, 60 percent of university graduates in this age bracket were women.

### Women's Rights
The 2008 International Women's Day in Canada marked the significant advancements that have been made concerning women's rights in Canada. Women gained the right to vote in 1917. In 1929, the Supreme Court of Canada recognized women as "qualified persons," enabling them to serve in the Senate. In 1967, Prime Minister Lester B. Pearson instituted the Royal Commission on the Status of Women in

Canada (RCSM) in order to improve conditions for women. Additionally, the right to have an abortion was legally recognized in 1969, and perpetrators of sexual and verbal harassment are prosecuted under Canadian law.

Despite the dramatic improvements in women's rights, Canada came under harsh international reprimand in the 1970s for the Indian Act. Under a particular article in the act, aboriginal women and their children lost their aboriginal status after marrying a non-aboriginal man. However, the article allowed a non-aboriginal woman to claim status after marrying an aboriginal man. The case was tried in the Supreme Court of Canada as well as by the UN. As a result of these cases, Bill C-31 was introduced in 1985, reversing the loss of status for aboriginal women. The status of aboriginal children in Canada is still determined paternally.

Poverty remains an issue for many Canadian women, especially single mothers and aboriginal, immigrant, and disabled women. As of 2003, Canadian-born and immigrant women working full time were underpaid in comparison to their male counterparts. Additionally, according to 2005 statistics, over 50 percent of Canadian women experienced violence in the home and in society, with low-income, aboriginal and immigrant women the most likely victims. The government's statistical agency reported there were approximately 600 shelters and transition homes providing services to abused women.

Following the 2005 election, drastic cuts were made to the Status of Women Canada (SWC), a federal organization that promotes the participation and equality of women in society. The organization also works with other countries and international organizations on domestic and foreign policies. SWC is a particularly strong supporter of the rights and participation of gay women in Canada. Because of the cuts, SWC was forced to change its mandate by dropping the word "equality" from its statement of purpose. In addition, projects that involved advocacy work, lobbying of the government or general research lost funding.

## Health Care

The Canadian health care system, known as "Medicare," provides universal coverage for physician visits and hospital services. The federal government, provinces, and territories cooperate in a system that is being constantly reformed in response to societal changes.

The federal government, through the Canada Health Act, administers national aspects of the system such as public health programs and health research. It also helps to fund provincial and territorial health care services. In addition, the federal government provides services to specific groups such as First Nations, Inuit, and veterans.

The provinces and territories administer and deliver services locally. They also provide supplemental benefits, such as prescription drug coverage, to certain groups. This coverage varies in the different jurisdictions.

Canadians enjoy a long average life expectancy of almost 82 years (79 for men and 85 for women). The country has roughly two doctors for every 1,000 people. Health expenditures made up 10.9 percent of the GDP in 2013.

## GOVERNMENT

### Structure

Canada is a federal parliamentary democracy, with universal suffrage for adults 18 years and older. The confederation consists of 10 provinces (Alberta, British Columbia, Saskatchewan, Ontario, Nova Scotia, Manitoba, Québec, New Brunswick, Prince Edward Island, Newfoundland, and Labrador) and three territories (Yukon, Northwest Territories, and Nunavut).

The official chief of state is the monarch of England, who is represented in Canada by the governor general. The monarch appoints the governor general to a five-year term. After elections for Parliament, the governor general appoints the leader of the majority party as prime minister (PM). The prime minister appoints the cabinet from the prime minister's party in Parliament.

Canada's Parliament is bicameral, with a Senate of 105 senators, appointed by the governor general; and a House of Commons, whose 308 members are elected by popular vote. The Senators serve until age 75. Members of Parliament (MPs) serve for up to five years, but Parliament may be dissolved by a vote of no confidence.

Supreme Court judges are appointed by the prime minister and confirmed by the governor general.

## Political Parties

The following parties were represented in the 2015 House of Commons: Bloc Québécois (BQ); the Conservative Party of Canada; the Green party of Canada; the Liberal Party of Canada; and the New Democratic Party.

Bloc Québécois, generally referred to as the Bloc or BQ, is a social democratic Québec nationalist party that formed in 1991. BQ is concerned with protecting the interests and sovereignty of Québec, and its members are usually referred to as Bloquistes. In the 2015 federal elections, the BQ won 4.7 percent of the popular vote and 10 seats in the House of Commons.

The Conservative Party leans right on the Canadian political spectrum and is sometimes referred to as the Tories. It formed in 2003 as a result of the merging of the Canadian Alliance Party and the Progressive Conservative Party. In its first decade of existence, the Conservative Party has supported increased military spending, reduced taxes, decentralization of the federal government, and election reform. In the 2015 federal election, the Conservative Party won 99 House of Common seats and almost 40 percent of the popular vote.

The Green Party, formed in 1983, aims to rescue grassroots democracy with the goal of ensuring that the planet survives and thrives for generations to come. The Green Party won one seat in the House of Commons and 3.4 percent of the popular vote.

The Liberal Party of Canada, also known as the Grits, is a center-left party that formed in 1867. The party has supported issues that span the traditional political spectrum, such as increased military spending and the provision of national childcare services. At certain points in its recent history, the party has supported a reduction in social assistance programs in favor of deficit reduction (2005). The Liberal Party won 184 House of Common seats in the 2015 federal election and just over 39 percent of the popular vote.

The New Democratic Party formed in 1961 and grew out of the Co-operative Commonwealth Federation, a party formed in 1932 to represent farmers and other workers. The New Democratic Party leans left on the Canadian political spectrum and represents, generally, the ideals of social democracy through its support of social assistance programs, equal rights, and poverty reduction. In the 2015 federal elections, the New Democratic Party won 44 seats in the House of Commons and 19.7 percent of the popular vote.

## Local Government

Canada has three levels of government: federal, provincial, and local, or municipal government. Municipal governments derive their power from provincial governments and are sometimes referred to as "creatures of the provinces." Municipal governments have limited authority on fiscal and policy-related issues. There are approximately 3,700 municipal governments in Canada that employ approximately 368,000 people (2011). Municipal governments are largely funded by property taxes, business taxes, and "user fees" such as parking tickets.

The structure of municipal government varies across the territories, with some featuring tiered systems that include regional, county, and municipal governments. In the early 21st century, municipal governments in Canada sought out increased constitutional power to increase their revenue bases. Municipal governments are responsible for services such as police, fire, animal control, library, tax collection, and parks and recreation.

## Judicial System

The highest court is the Supreme Court, to which nine judges from the five major areas of Canada are appointed. Other courts established by the federal government are the Tax Court, the Federal Court of Appeal, and the Federal Court.

Court names vary among the territories, but the system is basically the same across the country, with there being two levels of courts: provincial, in which judges are appointed by the territory, and superior, in which the judge is appointed by the federal government. Each territory also has appellate courts.

Federally appointed judges are required to retire at the age of 75, while judges appointed by provincial and territorial governments may be required to retire at the age of 70. In order to be appointed a judge in a superior, federal or supreme court, the person must have at least ten years of experience as a lawyer.

## Taxation

Approximately 70 percent of the Canadian government's income is derived from taxation. The Canada Revenue Agency (CRA) collects federal taxes. Income taxes are imposed by both the federal and territorial/provincial governments and account for over 50 percent of tax revenue. Income tax is "progressive," meaning the amount paid is based on an individual's income; therefore, those with higher incomes pay higher taxes.

Sales taxes are imposed by both the federal and territorial/provincial governments. Federal sales taxes are known as the Goods & Services Tax (GST) and the Harmonized Sales Tax (HST). (Alberta does not levy a provincial sales tax.) Other taxes in Canada include property taxes, excise taxes, payroll taxes, and estate taxes.

## Armed Forces

Canada's military is known as the Canadian Forces (CF), which is comprised of the Canadian Army, Royal Canadian Navy (RCN), and Royal Canadian Air Force (RCAF), as well as the Canadian Joint Operations Command, which includes responsibility for homeland security. There are also branches of reserve forces, such as the Primary and Supplementary Reserves, as well as the Canadian Rangers.

## Foreign Policy

Despite being considered one of the world's middle powers, Canadian foreign policy reflects its position as a leader in world affairs. Following the Second World War, Canada began to act independently of Britain, and its involvement in foreign affairs expanded exponentially. Canada gained its reputation as a peacekeeping nation during the first UN mission to Korea in 1950, and quickly became one of the world's leading diplomatic voices. As one of the founding members of the North Atlantic Treaty Organization (NATO), Canada has participated in over 50 peace operations around the world, including operations in Bosnia, Sudan, Haiti, and Croatia. In addition, Canada garnered much attention as the only peacekeepers serving in Rwanda during the 1996 genocidal conflict between the Hutu and Tutsis. In 2002, Canada prioritized the rebuilding of Afghanistan and, despite the disapproval of most Canadians, made a long-term commitment of maintaining a peacekeeping force in Afghanistan until 2011.

Since 1976, Canada has been a member of the international Group of Eight (G8) (currently the Group of Seven-G7) industrialized nations, which also includes France, Germany, Italy, Japan, Russia (suspended), the United Kingdom and the United States along with the European Union. These nations dominate global economics and hold most of the world's military and nuclear power. Canada's activities and programs abroad as part of the forum include humanitarian concerns, disarmament, health care, the environment and international security.

Canada has also developed one of the strongest trade economies in the world. The Department of Foreign Affairs and International Trade, run by the minister of foreign affairs, was developed in the 1980s to deal with Canada's growing involvement in international trade. The prime minister retains a key role in foreign affairs decisions. However, Canada's provinces and territories have a high level of freedom to operate internationally. For example, the provinces of Québec, Ontario, and Alberta all have independent foreign operations.

Canada's relationship with the United States is regarded as its most important. However, there remains debate over the maritime boundaries between Canada and the United States on the east and west coasts. Canada maintains important trade relations with Europe and British Commonwealth nations, as well as with communist countries, including Cuba and China. Canada also has many investments in South America and the Caribbean.

Canada is involved in a territorial dispute with Denmark over Hans Island and the Kennedy Channel near Greenland. In 2014, although the status of Hans Island was still uncertain, the cooperation between the two countries increased. The recent melting of polar ice has also heightened disputes over sovereignty of the Arctic, and increased accessibility to the Northwest Passage and surrounding waters has revealed large oil and mineral deposits at the bottom of the Beaufort Sea. Canada has asserted control over the Northwest Passage and the Beaufort Sea, while the United States and other neighboring countries have challenged this assertion.

**Human Rights Profile**

International human rights law insists that states respect civil and political rights, and also promote an individual's economic, social, and cultural rights. The United Nations (UN) Universal Declaration on Human Rights (UDHR) is recognized as the standard for international human rights. Its authors sought the counsel of the world's great thinkers, philosophers, and religious leaders, and were careful to create a document that reflects the core values shared by every world culture. (To read this document or view the articles relating to cultural human rights, go to: http://www.un.org/en/documents/udhr/.)

Canada's Human Rights Act (1977) and the Canadian Charter of Rights and Freedoms (1982) serve as the legislative authority protecting the political and civil rights of individuals. Canada's human rights record is regarded as good, and the country has set precedents with groundbreaking human rights legislation, including patients' rights, minority rights, and legalization of same-sex marriage. Nevertheless, Canada's international reputation as a model for human rights has been tainted by the country's historical and contemporary treatment of aboriginal people, African immigrants, and visible minorities. From 1928 to 1972, compulsory sterilization programs were in place in Alberta and British Columbia with the aim of preventing aboriginal people, the mentally and physically disabled, minorities, and troubled youth from reproducing. Canada also violated the rights of other Canadian citizens on several occasions such as the internment of Ukrainians during World War I and the Japanese during World War II.

Canada's violation of the human rights of aboriginal people remains its most notorious legacy. Beginning in the 19th century, Canada implemented the residential school system, a joint effort between the church and the government to assimilate aboriginal children. Under this system, aboriginal parents were forced to send their children to schools or face fines or imprisonment. At these schools, the children were forbidden from speaking their native languages, and were taught that their cultures were barbaric and wrong. In certain schools, over 70 percent of the children died from disease, malnutrition, and neglect. In fact, nearly 100 percent of the children who attended residential schools suffered sexual and/or physical abuse.

The last residential school closed in 1998, and the oppressive system is largely regarded as the most significant culprit for the loss of the majority of Canada's aboriginal languages, as well as ongoing problems of abuse, addiction, mental illness, and poverty that are now widespread among aboriginal peoples. In 2008 the Truth and Reconciliation Commission was established to uncover some of the truth of what happened and to provide reconciliation to the victims. In 2015 the commission held its closing events. Canada's contemporary treatment of its aboriginal population continues to cause alarm in the UN and in members of the international community, particularly in regard to the high number of aboriginal deaths while in police custody, the poor sanitary state of many of the country's reserves, as well as unresolved land and resource issues.

In a 2013 examination of Canada's human rights profile, the UN challenged Canada's lack of investment in social programs. It was reported that while there had been "notable efforts" by the government to improve the social and economic well-being of women, aboriginal peoples, people with disabilities, immigrants, and visible minorities, there had been little progress since the previous review in 2004. Generally, life in Canada for underprivileged people is considered to have worsened since 1998. Canada's profile abroad has also caused alarm, particularly in its resource extractions activities. Reports of gross human rights abuses by Canadian mining companies in West Africa and South America have resulted in protests from local communities and governments. However, little has been done nationally to address the violations.

## ECONOMY

### Overview of the Economy
Canada's modern industrial economy resembles that of the United States. Trade between the two countries has increased since 1994, due to the North American Free Trade Agreement (NAFTA).

In 2014, Canada's gross domestic product (GDP) was estimated to be around $1.592 trillion USD. The per capita GDP was roughly $44,800 USD. As of 2015, the unemployment rate was 7.1 percent of a skilled work force of more than 18 million.

### Industry
Canada's primary industries include the manufacture of chemical products, paper products, petroleum and coal products, and transportation equipment. Other important industries include mining, agriculture, and fishing.

Exports of motor vehicles, industrial machinery, chemicals, plastics, aircraft, fertilizers, telecommunications equipment, wood pulp and timber, electricity, aluminum, and natural gas earned around $465.1 billion USD in 2014.

Ottawa is a major technological center; over 90 percent of Canada's telecommunications developments occur there. The city is home to numerous technology firms that specialize in telecommunications and software. According to Statistics Canada, 65,200 people were employed by the city's technology sector in 2014.

The other major employer in Ottawa is the federal government. Ottawa is home to Canada's Parliament, Senate, and the Supreme Court. Ottawa is also a major education and science center, and houses many academic institutions. Significant portions of the $40 billion Ottawa contributes to Canada's gross domestic product stems from the aforementioned industries and governmental operations.

### Labor
In 2014, Canada had a labor force of roughly 19.2 million people and an unemployment rate of seven percent.

### Energy/Power/Natural Resources
Canada is one of the largest energy producers in the world, most notably natural gas and petroleum. A great deal of this energy is exported to the United States, which receives more oil from Canada than it does from any other country.

Air pollution, resulting in acid rain, is a growing problem, severely affecting lakes and forests. Pollution has also hurt both agriculture and forestry. In addition, the side-effects of agriculture, industry, mining, and forestry are contaminating the oceans surrounding Canada.

### Fishing
Canada's fishing industry brings in approximately $5 billion CAD a year and accounts for 80,000 jobs, according to the Department of Fisher and Oceans (2014). Canada's five most valuable exports in 2014 by species were lobster, snow or queen crab, shrimp, Atlantic salmon, and scallop.

### Forestry
According to Natural Resources Canada, the forestry industry contributed approximately 1.25 percent to the country's GDP in 2013 and directly

employed 216,500 people. Canada is one of the leading exporters of wood products, including softwood lumber, wood pulp, and newsprint.

## Mining/Metals

Canada is rich in mineral resources, with large deposits of iron ore, nickel, copper, zinc, lead, gold, potash, rare earth elements, molybdenum, diamonds, silver, and coal.

## Agriculture

Less than five percent of Canada's land is arable; most of this land is in the Prairie Provinces, where grain, livestock and forest products are produced. Canada is a leading producer of wheat and oats. Rye, barley, and corn are also grown on the prairies.

Farmers in the Atlantic Provinces raise flax, soybeans, rapeseed, sugar beets, and tobacco, with some fruit and vegetables. Along the west coast, farmers primarily raise livestock and produce meat, butter and dairy foods.

Natural hazards to agriculture include continuous permafrost in the north and cyclonic storms east of the Rocky Mountains.

## Animal Husbandry

Fur farming is big business in Canada, with more than 2,000 companies raising beavers, mink, otters, chinchilla, and silver fox.

## Tourism

Canada has a large tourist industry, with more than 16.6 million international visitors annually; 3 out of 4 visitors are from the United States. The country remains among the top twenty most visited countries in the world. Overnight visitors to Canada spent an estimated $12.27 billion dollars in 2012.

Tourist sites include the country's thirty-nine national parks natural regions, with a combined area of more than 250,000 square kilometers (96,000 square miles), and hundreds of provincial parks. Many popular tourist destinations also appear on the United Nations Educational, Scientific and Cultural Organization (UNESCO) list of World Heritage sites. These include Head-Smashed-In Buffalo Jump, the L'Anse aux Meadows Viking village, the Canadian Rocky Mountain Parks, and the Historic District of Québec.

*Gabrielle Parent, Ellen Bailey, Amanda Wilding*

## DO YOU KNOW?

- Dr. James Naismith, the inventor of basketball, was Canadian, and so were ten of the players in the first game.

- Poutine, invented in 1957 by a Montreal restaurant owner, is a favorite Québec junk food. The dish consists of French fries topped with cheese curds (bits of fresh cheddar before it is pressed into blocks and aged) and gravy.

- Ottawa's motto is "Advance-Ottawa, En Avant" ("Advance Ottawa Forward"). It is a bilingual slogan, representing the bilingual nature of the city's population.

- Ottawa is home to the Ottawa Senators, a National Hockey League team.

- Behind the Parliament building is a hill that was home to hundreds of cats, squirrels, raccoons, and other small animals. The hill, appropriately named "Cat Hill," had a caretaker who fed the animals every day. The sanctuary for the cats was closed in 2013 after all remaining felines were adopted into homes.

## Bibliography

Bumsted, J.M. A History of the Canadian Peoples. Don Mills, ON: Oxford University Press, 2011.

Conrad, Margaret. A Concise History of Canada. New York: Cambridge University Press, 2012.

Dowbiggin, Bruce. The Meaning of Puck: How Hockey Explains Modern Canada. Toronto: Key Porter Books, 2008.

Holloway, Steven Kendall. Canadian Foreign Policy: Defining the National Interest. Toronto: University of Toronto Press, 2006.

Milloy, John S. *A National Crime: The Canadian Government and the Residential School System 1879–1986*. Manitoba: University of Manitoba Press, 1999.

New, William H. *A History of Canadian Literature*. Kingston-Montréal: McGill-Queen's Press, 2003.

Thomas, David M. and David N. Biette, eds. *Canada and the United States: Differences that Count*. Toronto: University of Toronto Press, 2014.

Timpson, Annis May, ed. *First Nations, First Thoughts: The Impact of Indigenous Culture in Canada*. Vancouver, BC: University of British Columbia Press, 2009.

Tomlin, Brian W., Norman Hillmer, and Fen Osler Hampson. *Canada's International Policies: Agendas, Alternatives and Politics*. Don Mills, ON: Oxford University Press, 2011.

Vance, Jonathan F. *A History of Canadian Culture*. Don Mills, ON: Oxford University Press, 2009.

## Works Cited

"At Least 4,000 Aboriginal Children Died in Residential Schools, Commission Finds." *Ottawa Citizen*. Canada. com. 3 January 2014: http://o.canada.com/news/national/at-least-4000–aboriginal-children-died-in-residential-schools-commission-finds

Canada Revenue Agency: http://www.cra-arc.gc.ca/menu-eng.html

Canada-UNESCO World Heritage List: http://whc.unesco.org/en/statesparties/ca

Canada's National Highway System Annual Report 2012. Council of Ministers Responsible for Transportation and Highway Safety: http://www.comt.ca/english/NHS%20Annual%202012.pdf

Canadian First World War Internment Recognition Fund: http://internmentcanada.ca/

2015 Canadian Social Media Usage Statistics: http://canadiansinternet.com/2015–canadian-social-media-usage-statistics/

*CIA World Factbook*. "Canada." https://www.cia.gov/library/publications/the-world-factbook/geos/ca.html

City Population Data from 2006 Census: http://census2006.ca/census-recensement/2006/dp-pd/prof/92-591/index.cfm?Lang=E

Council of Ministers Responsible for Transportation and Highway Safety. "Canada's National Highway System Condition Report." http://www.comt.ca/english/NHS-Condition09.pdf.

CRTC Rewrites Canadian Content Quotas on Television. The Globe and Mail. 12 March 2015: http://www.theglobeandmail.com/report-on-business/crtc-to-relax-canadian-content-rules-on-television/article23420352/

Health Canada: http://www.hc-sc.gc.ca/index-eng.php

Human Resources & Skills Development Canada. "Canadians in Context: Aboriginal Populations." http://www4.hrsdc.gc.ca/.3ndic.1t.4r@-eng.jsp?iid=36

Industry Canada: http://www.ic.gc.ca/ic_wp-pa.htm

Major Cities in Canada Population 2015: http://worldpopulationreview.com/countries/canada-population/major-cities-in-canada/#

Parliament Hill Cat Sanctuary Shutting Down for Good: http://www.cbc.ca/news/canada/ottawa/parliament-hill-cat-sanctuary-shutting-down-for-good-1.1304368

PCAP 2013 http://www.cmec.ca/Publications/Lists/Publications/Attachments/337/PCAP-2013–Public-Report-EN.pdf

The State of Canada's Birds: http://www.stateofcanadasbirds.org/overview.jsp

Statistics Canada: http://www.statcan.gc.ca/start-debut-eng.html

Transport Canada: http://www.tc.gc.ca/eng/menu.htm

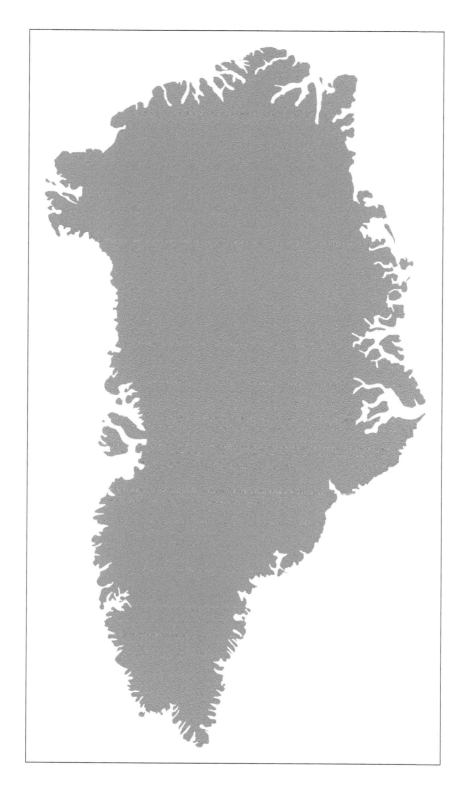

GREENLAND

## Introduction

Greenland is the world's largest island. More than 80 percent of the island is covered in ice, and the country is sparsely populated. Greenland's residents claimed their national independence from Denmark after a 1979 vote of the Danish Parliament. In 2009 when the Act on Greenland Self-Government was signed, increased self-rule was established.

## GENERAL INFORMATION

**Official Language(s):** Kalaallisut (Greenlandic) and Danish

**Population:** 57,733 (2015 estimate)

**Currency:** Danish krone

**Coins:** 100 øre are equal to one krone. Øre are only issued in denominations of 50. Krone coins come in denominations of 1, 2, 5, 10, and 20 krone.

**Land Area:** 2,166,086 square kilometers (836,330 square miles)

**Ice-free Area:** 410,449 square kilometers (158,475 square miles)

**National Anthem:** "Nunarput utoqqarsuanngoravit" ("You, Our Ancient Land")

**Capital:** Nuuk (formerly Godthåb)

**Time Zone(s):** GMT -3 (Greenland Standard Time)

**Flag Description:** Greenland's flag, a fairly modern design, consists of two equal horizontal bands of red (bottom) and white (top). A circle, set slightly off-center to the left, is offset with transposed colors, red on the top and white on the bottom. The red circle symbolizes the setting sun and its reflection on the water and ice.

### Population

Greenlanders have an average life expectancy of 72 years; almost 75 for women and 69 years for men (2015 estimate). Infant mortality averages at about nine deaths for every 1,000 live births. At about 14 births per 1,000 people, Greenland's birth rate is almost twice the death rate, which is approximately 8.5 per 1,000 (2015 estimate).

Because most of the land mass is covered in ice, the majority of Greenland's population (86 percent as of 2015) lives in the towns and larger settlements, such as Nuuk and Ilulissat, which are located on the southern region of island's western coastline. Taasiliq (formerly called Ammassalik), Daneborg, and Kulusuk account for the only significant towns on the eastern coast. A small portion of Greenlanders live in outlying areas

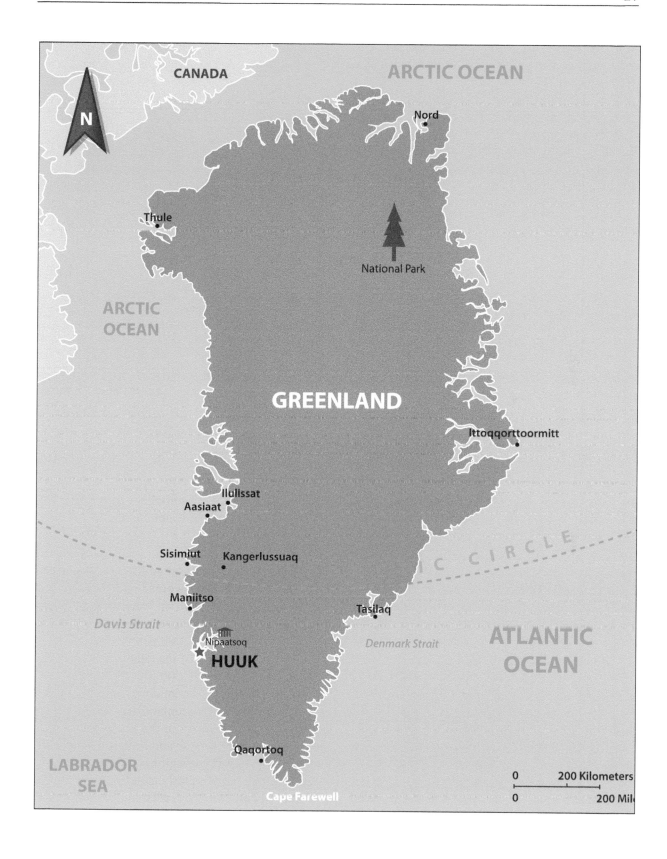

**Principal Cities by Population (2014):**

- Nuuk (16,818)
- Sisimiut (5,524)
- Ilulissat (4,530)
- Qaqortoq (3,248)
- Aasiaat (3,102)

where they survive by means of sheep farming or migratory hunting.

## Languages

In addition to the official languages of Danish and Kalaallisut (or Greenlandic, a form of Inuit), English is also spoken widely among Greenlanders.

## Native People & Ethnic Groups

The Thule are the first well-documented group to inhabit Greenland. They arrived on the island sometime around the tenth century, and Greenland's Inuit populations trace their ancestry to them. Traditional Greenlanders currently recognize three cultural categories: the Kitaamiut (West Greenlanders), the Tunumiut (East Greenlanders), and the Inughuit (Polar Inuit in North Greenland. Inuit populations in Greenland are closely related, historically and linguistically, to those in Canada, Alaska, and Siberia.

Greenland's modern ethnic profile blends native Inuit influences with European influences, particularly those of the Danes, Norwegians, and the Icelanders brought in to colonize the country under the leadership of Eric the Red. Greenland's population statistics only refer to native-born Greenlanders and those born out of the country. About 88 percent of Greenland's population is native-born, including those of Inuit and non-Inuit ancestry. The remaining 12 percent are mostly Danish, with a small mixture of other nationalities.

## Religions

The overwhelming majority of Greenlanders who profess to practice a religion belong to the Evangelical Lutheran Church. Traditional Inuit spiritual beliefs are also still held. There are other religious communities, which include the Catholic Church, Jehovah's Witnesses, Bahai, and Pentecostal.

## Climate

Greenland's climate ranges from high arctic in the north to sub-arctic in the southern portion of the island, although conditions also vary considerably between the coast and the interior.

During the sunlit months of the year, from January to July, temperatures on the southern coast range between 7° and 10° Celsius (18° to 50° Fahrenheit), as opposed to –22° to 5° Celsius (–8° to 41° Fahrenheit) on the northern coastline. The particularly brutal inland temperatures generally range from about –47° to –12° Celsius (–53° to 10° Fahrenheit) between February and July. Temperatures can rise to more than 20° Celsius (68° Fahrenheit) in June, July, or August in the southern part of the country and the innermost parts of the long fjords.

The northern part of the island receives only 20 centimeters (8 inches) of rainfall each year, compared with an average 89 centimeters (35 inches) in the south.

---

## ENVIRONMENT & GEOGRAPHY

## Topography

Greenland lies in the farthest reaches of North America, between the Arctic Ocean and the northern Atlantic. Its capital, Nuuk, is located in the southwest portion of the island.

About 81 percent of Greenland is covered in ice at any time of year, making its ice sheet the largest in the world, second only to Antarctica's. Like a mountain range, however, the ice has its own varying elevation. Satellite images have demonstrated that Greenland's icy cover creates a vast ridge cutting straight down the length of the island. In the east-central interior of the island, the ridge's elevation reaches more than 3,200 meters (about 10,500 feet). The ridge descends gradually to the sea on the western side of the island and drops more dramatically to sea level to the east. Mountainous rivers and streams cut channels through the barren landscape to the rugged coastline.

Greenland's frozen landscape is constantly producing icebergs. The island's fast moving glaciers produce about 160 cubic kilometers (100 cubic miles) worth of icebergs every year.

## Plants & Animals

Carved out of the northeastern portion of the island, Greenland National Park is a vast 972,000 square kilometers (375,400 square miles) of protected conservation area. In spite of its size, the forbidding arctic landscape of the park can accommodate only the stoutest of animal or plant species.

Greenland's entire landscape is rocky, barren, and treeless, though the summer months bring a proliferation of wild grasses, wild flowers, and life-sustaining lichen, particularly in the sub-arctic zone to the south. Small mammals like moles, lemmings, and arctic hare have adapted to the barren landscape. More famous among tourists and hunters, however, are the caribou, musk ox, polar bear, and arctic wolf.

Greenland's marine life is far richer than its terrestrial life and includes shrimp, cod, halibut, ringed seals, harp seals, and several species of whale.

## CUSTOMS & COURTESIES

## Greetings

In general, Greenlanders have a reputation for being extremely friendly. In fact, Greenland's foremost author and explorer, Knud Rasmussen, once wrote that the intense joy Inuit people display that often surprises foreigners is the result of living in such a harsh environment. Up until very recently, Inuit communities existed solely on subsistence hunting and fishing, and a poor hunting season meant that the threat of starvation was severe. Thus, according to Rasmussen, the memory of the harsh lives of the Inuit people has led to an overall greater appreciation of daily

life in the country, and Greenlanders are not shy about sharing this joy with strangers.

When greeting someone in Greenlandic, a common phrase is "Aluu" ("Hello"). However, this was probably introduced to Greenland by American soldiers during World War II. Danish cultural norms are also standard—roughly 12 percent of Greenland's population is of Danish origin—and it is common to greet by shaking hands in Danish culture. It is considered polite to shake hands with women first, and one should also shake hands again before leaving. Additionally, the common expression "Hej" ("Hello") is used in greeting.

## Gestures & Etiquette

Greenlandic culture is generally very relaxed. Unless the situation is very formal, casual clothes are usually fine. In Danish culture, privacy is very important, and asking detailed questions about a person's private life, such as marriage status or income, should be avoided.

One important cultural note is that Greenlandic attitudes toward animals may vary from those of other cultures. As hunting is a central part of Greenlandic culture, gutting fish or butchering reindeer, oxen or seals in public is not considered unusual, and it is common for houses to drape freshly removed animal skins in their front lawn to dry. Another cultural difference is the treatment of dogs, which are largely considered work animals, and not domestic pets. Because of this, it is not polite to pet a dog unless the owner gives permission. In addition, dogs are commonly kept outside throughout the year in large lots, even during the winter. As many hunters have between 15 and 30 sled dogs, it is unfeasible to keep them inside the home. A strict series of laws ensures the proper care and feeding of sled dogs, such as mandating that pregnant dogs are provided with a kennel for shelter.

An additional point to note is that Greenpeace has been very active in rigorously promoting fishing and whaling restrictions on Greenlandic hunting practices. As a result, bringing cameras into marketplaces and taking pictures of the day's catch is unadvisable, as it may make the fishmongers nervous.

## Eating/Meals

Greenlandic meals feature an abundance of meat, because large doses of protein are necessary to provide the energy for hunting and living in a harsh Arctic climate. Traditionally, members of the same community hunt together, and their catch is shared among the various families. Because of this, mealtime is an important symbol of social cooperation and solidarity in Inuit culture, as well as a nexus of communal life. Greenlandic families eat together and will often invite guests to share their meal. During the summer, it is popular for a family to eat their meal outdoors, cooking meat or fish over an open fire and eating off flat stones.

Greenlandic buffets are a popular variation on the Scandinavian buffet. They feature spreads of seal, reindeer, whale, fish, and even polar bear meat prepared in a variety of ways, such as cooked, smoked, fried, and raw. Greenlandic buffets are usually served in restaurants and hotels.

Today, meals are a central part of Greenlandic hospitality. If invited to eat a meal with a Greenlandic family, it is polite to try everything on one's plate.

## Visiting

Visitors to Greenland may be invited to a kaffemik, which literally means "coffee-milk." Kaffemiks are gatherings in a host's home, where guests are traditionally served coffee, tea, candy, whale blubber, and many kinds of cake (the traditional number is seven). Kaffemiks are often held to celebrate specific occasions, such as birthdays, weddings, confirmations, or the first time a child catches a seal. However, they can also be held as a chance to just catch up with friends, exchange local news, or show hospitality.

If invited to a kaffemik, one should accept the invitation. Before entering the home, visitors should remove their shoes so as not to track in mud or snow. Additionally, visitors should make sure to keep an eye on the other guests, to make sure there is enough food left for everyone. Some

large towns in Greenland will even help tourists book a kaffemik with a local host family as a way to acquaint them with Greenlandic culture.

## LIFESTYLE

## Family

Kinship groups are extremely important in Greenlandic communities. One's circle of acquaintances is usually separated into two groups: a close kindred group and an acquaintance group. Close kindred, called "ilaqutariit", may be blood relations, close friends, or even people who share one's name or birthday. People with whom one is not very close are called "eqqarleq". This group may include casual acquaintances or even blood relatives, if relations with them are not especially close or friendly. Ilaqutariit are called by their kinship names (such as "illoq", or "cousin"), but eqqarleq are called by their first names, which is considered more formal.

Kinship groups are the basis for social organizing and social activities, such as fishing or hunting. Members of the same kin may share hunting equipment or other communal property, and must distribute portions of their catch among their kin members. Kinship relations are also transformable; for instance, a member of one's kin can be changed from ilaqutariit to eqqarleq if one finds the relationship unsatisfactory, though this is not acceptable with regard to close blood relatives such as parents or siblings. A close friend can likewise become an ilaqutariit, and afterward be addressed by a kinship name expressing the degree of the relationship instead of their personal name.

Additionally, children are often named for a deceased member of a kinship group in order to honor the person's name. In this way, the child also becomes a member of the deceased person's kinship group.

## Housing

One traditional form of Inuit housing was a sealskin tent with a driftwood frame. Easily portable, these tents were used during the summer, when families moved from place to place gathering berries, hunting reindeer, and catching fish to create stockpiles for the winter. Igloos, which are dome-shaped structures made of blocks of ice, were used during winter on extended hunting trips, particularly in the north of Greenland. (The word "iglu" actually means "house" in North Greenlandic.) The most common Inuit houses were turf houses, which were made of stones, turf, and driftwood, and resembled small hills. Turf houses were often located close to the sea so that the Inuit hunters could easily access their hunting kayaks. Turf houses were used well into the 1950s, and can still be seen in some towns today.

During the period of Danish colonization, which lasted from the early 18th century through World War II, clapboard A-frame houses made from imported European wood and painted in bright colors were popular. Today, these houses are considered distinctly Greenlandic. During the 1950s and 1960s, attempts by the Danish government to create a commercial fishing economy led to the resettlement of many coastal villagers into mass housing blocks, great grey cement structures capable of housing hundreds of people. Blok P, one of these structures, was the largest apartment in Greenland's capital, Nuuk, and held one percent of Greenland's population. It was carefully demolished in 2012. Many residents of the building now live in Qingorput, the newest suburb of Nuuk.

## Food

Greenland's cuisine is closely related to the country's harsh environment and the culinary traditions of its indigenous people. Fish is a staple, and game meat such as musk ox, reindeer, and seal are traditional Greenlandic foods. The meat of the musk ox and the reindeer, in particular, are popular in stews, which are easy to prepare over an open fire when hunting. Although the musk ox was formerly threatened with extinction due to over-hunting, today a lottery-based hunting system has helped the population thrive. Polar bear is also considered a rare delicacy as well, and the meat is reputedly delicious and tender, and tastes like chicken. However, only a minimal number are permitted to be hunted each year.

Seal hunting, on the other hand, is not regulated, and seal meat is a popular food of Greenlanders. It has a rich and dark color, and a texture akin to liver. The national dish of Greenland is seal stew, or suaasat, which includes boiled seal meat, onions, and rice. Traditional Inuit beliefs hold that seal meat keeps the body warm, and recent scientific research has suggested that consuming seal blubber improves blood circulation. In addition, fermented seal oil is used to preserve or flavor foods, from locally-caught dried cod to imported European grapes.

Another local dish is blubbery whale skin, called mattak. This dish is a key supplier of vitamin C in the Greenlandic diet, where fresh fruit and vegetables are rare. A tasty summer treat is fjeld kvana, a thin, green, celery-like herb that is rich in vitamin C and has a bitter flavor. Fjeld kvana is often sold at roadside stands as a snack. It is usually eaten dipped in sugar or stewed in a compote (fruit stewed in syrup) as an accompaniment to meat dishes. Blueberries and crowberries, the fruit of the dwarf evergreen shrub, are two of the rare fruits that grow during Arctic summers and are often used in desserts.

Although meat has long been the main component of a Greenlandic diet, and has played a vital role in keeping Greenlanders healthy, today the consumption of meat is actually having a negative effect on the island's population. Although Greenland itself produces very little pollution, currents sweep toxins from industrialized nations into Arctic waters, which contaminate fish and sea mammals. By consuming these animals, Greenlanders themselves imbibe the toxins. In 2003, a study from the Arctic Monitoring and Assessment Programme (AMAP) found that in some parts of East Greenland, most Greenlanders surveyed—nearly 100 percent, in fact—had unacceptable levels of toxins in their blood. Because of this health risk, Greenlanders face the necessity of changing their traditional diet and lifestyle to include less meat.

## Life's Milestones

Traditionally, Greenlanders would observe many important milestones such as weddings, confirmations, and even the first day of school by donning their traditional costume of sealskin boots and a beaded coat. Special events are usually celebrated with a kaffemik, where family and friends gather to socialize in the host's home.

The birth of a child is considered a communal event in Greenland; even during pregnancy, the unborn child is considered a part of the community. When the child is born, it is traditional to display a flag at the home of the grandparents, signaling neighbors and friends to bring gifts.

Children born in the summer are called "axigirn", or "ptarmigans" (an arctic bird), and those born in the winter are "aggirn", or ducks. Based on whether they are axigirn or aggirn, children are given different foods to eat and made to play different roles in traditional ceremonies. One particularly important traditional milestone in a child's upbringing is a child's first hunt or catch, whether it be ptarmigan, a reindeer, or a seal. This is often considered a coming-of-age event, and like other special events, this occasion is commonly celebrated with a kaffemik.

## CULTURAL HISTORY

### Art

In Greenlandic, the word for art is "erqumitsuliaq", which literally means "something odd that has been constructed." Many traditional Greenlandic art forms have their origins in mythology and magic. Materials used were mostly gathered from the natural environment, and include soapstone, fish skin, sealskin, bone, musk ox wool, and antlers. Though soapstone was originally used for practical everyday objects, such as fishing tackle, containers, utensils, and lamps, recent Inuit artists have begun to craft figurines and sculptures out of soapstone as well. Today it is widely used by Greenlandic artists for sculptures, reliefs, and etchings.

Tupilaks are small figures from Inuit mythology carved of tooth, bone, or stone. The word "tupilak" refers to the spirit or soul of an ancestor, and these spirits were thought to inhabit the tupilak to work their sinister magic. In Inuit tradition, these small figures were used to revenge oneself on one's enemies. Carved in secret, tupilaks were then thrown into the sea and sent to find the maker's enemy. (However, according to traditional beliefs, if the enemy's magic was stronger, it could potentially deflect the tupilak's power so that it would be used against its maker instead.) After contact with the Europeans in the 19th century, tupilaks began to be made and sold as collector's items, and they remain popular souvenirs.

Western-influenced art such as expressionism and landscape painting did not emerge until the 19th and the 20th centuries. A prominent early Greenlandic visual artist was Aron of Kangeq (1822–1869), whose wood block prints and watercolors depict scenes from Inuit mythology and daily life. The perspective and style Aron employed was influenced by illustrations from the Bible and other European sources brought over by Danish, German, and Norwegian missionaries.

Although not typically considered an art form by contemporary Western standards, hunting is a vital part of Greenlandic cultural history. Many elements of Greenlandic culture, from songs to houses, have their roots in traditional hunting practices. Over the years, the needs of hunting have led to the development of specific, detailed cultural tools such as the ulo, a curved knife used by women to carve up the carcasses of seals, and the qajaq (kayak), a means of individual sea transportation now used around the world. The qajaq was traditionally made from a driftwood frame over which were tightened sealskins from which the hair had been removed. Each qajaq was designed to fit the body of the man who used it, and so the production of a qajaq required great skill and cooperation among the builders. From a young age, children would practice balancing in their qajaqs, learning how to execute swift rolls and turns to keep themselves from capsizing on rough waves.

The work of many modern Greenlandic painters includes natural imagery from Greenland juxtaposed or overlaid with images of modernity, such as faces, manmade materials, or Greenlandic script. A well-known artist, Pia Arke (1958–2007), attached photographs of people to maps to explore the nature of colonialism. Aka Høegh (1947– ), one of the most famous of Greenland's female artists, creates sculptures of people in the faces of rocks. From 1993–1994, Høegh pioneered the sculpture project "Stone and Man," in which 18 Scandinavian artists carved boulders in the town of Qaqortoq into reliefs and sculptures. Anne-Birthe Hove (1954–2012) was a renowned graphic artist whose works contain clear political elements.

## Music

Drum songs and dances were a central part of traditional Inuit culture. They usually took place in a qaggi, a large igloo built for community events. The drum, called a "qilaat", was typically made from animal skin, such as a bear bladder or walrus stomach, stretched over a small wooden frame with a handle. The handle had to be perfectly smooth; knots in the wood were considered to be points of spiritual power from the ancestors, which would unduly aid the drummer in a drum fight.

Christian missionaries banned drum songs and dances, and encouraged hymn-singing in four part chorales instead. Today choral singing in Greenland has evolved into a cultural practice with its own distinctive sound. One of the most widely-known choral groups is MIK, which was formed in 1961 to represent Denmark at a cultural festival in Italy. Since then, MIK has achieved recognition throughout Europe. The group is best known for appearing in traditional costume during performances: high white sealskin boots (kamikker) and beaded blouses for the women, and black boots and white anoraks for the men.

In the 1970s, more native bands began to merge these new elements with traditional music to form a unique national sound. The first widely popular local band was the progressive rock band Sume, whose 1973 album *Sumut* was sung in Greenlandic, and incorporated sounds from traditional drum dances. Their music inspired later rock bands to explore traditional culture

and social problems. In the 1980s, funk and reggae became popular, and hip-hop has recently inspired bands such as Nuuk Posse, who rap in Greenlandic, Danish, and English. Nuuk Posse, whose music encourages Greenlandic youth to remember Inuit culture, was awarded a National Culture Prize from the government of Greenland in 1996, and performed at the 2004 Global Hip-Hop Summit and Concert in Barcelona, sponsored by the United Nations Human Settlements Programme (UN–HABITAT).

Many kinds of drum dances existed in the Inuit culture, serving different social functions: some were for entertainment, some for communicating with spirits, and some for settling disputes. The drum fight was part of the latter category. In this "song duel," participants would dance and sing their dispute with each other. The one who received the most laughs and applause was considered the winner of the dispute.

Drum dances were outlawed for many years, a result of influence from Christian missionaries. Today, they are performed primarily as entertainment for tourists. Nevertheless, the drum's symbolism is still revered in Greenland. In fact, a drum will hang in most courtrooms as a symbol of an ancient form of the law.

## Literature

Storytelling played a key role in traditional Inuit culture. With the introduction of writing in the 18th century and the establishment of the first Greenland printing press in 1857, written literature emerged. The first person to publish a novel in Greenlandic was Mathias Storch (1883–1957), whose novel *Singnagtugaq* (*A Greenlander's Dream*, 1915), deals with issues of Greenlandic identity. In the early 20th century, Storch spoke out for the rights of indigenous Greenlanders as part of a social movement known as peqatigiinniat ("those who would like to be together") that emphasized national communality.

Prior to the 1970s, the Greenlandic language was considered subordinate to Danish, but concerned Greenlandic poets, writers, and musicians have worked to bring it again into the sphere of popular culture. Today most literature of Greenland is written in Kalaallisut, or Danish. One of the seminal Greenlandic authors was Knud Rasmussen (1879–1933), whose father was Danish and mother Inuit. An adventurous explorer and anthropologist, Rasmussen was the first person to cross the Northwest Passage by dogsled. He compiled and translated many Inuit folk legends and wrote extensively on Inuit culture. One of his best-known books is *The People of the Polar North* (1934).

The connection between local identity, politics and literature can be seen in the work of such Greenlandic poets as Moses Olsen (1938–2008), who helped found Siumut, the social democratic party of Greenland, and is considered one of the founders of the Greenland Home Rule Government (GHRG). The work of poet, politician, and activist Aqqaluk Lynge (1947– ) is another example of how Greenlanders combine art and politics. In his poems, Lynge draws on traditional Inuit imagery to explore the conflict between ancient and modern and between native tradition and colonialism. His works, such as the poem "A Life of Respect," promote national and cultural pride and veneration while challenging foreign culture and modernity, which can be interpreted as promoting Greenland's increased independence from Denmark.

# CULTURE

## Arts & Entertainment

Since the 1960s, much of Greenlandic art has dealt with issues of identity. During the period of Danish colonization (1721–1953), Danish culture and language were dominant, and missionaries worked to subordinate local beliefs and traditions to Christianity and Western ideologies. After Greenland was granted greater autonomy in 1979, increased attention began to be paid to conceptions of Greenlandic identity, as well as to the conflict between modern and traditional culture. This shift in thinking, from acceptance of colonization to pride in native traditions, was reflected in Greenlandic literature, art, and music.

A central theme in Greenlandic art has been negotiating the double identity of Inuit and European heritage. For instance, one series of photographs by contemporary artist Julie Edel Hardenberg (1971– ) features two people: a woman of Inuit descent holding a Danish flag, and a woman of Danish descent wearing a traditional Inuit anorak (parka, or a heavy and hooded coat). Visual art such as painting, photography, and sculpture has become especially important for artists dealing with this hybrid cultural space. Visual art allows both cultures to be represented equally, whereas in literature, choosing which language to write in automatically implies a specific identity. Artists such as Hardenberg, Miki Jakobsen (1965– ), and Gukki Willsen Møller (1965– ) represent a group of young artists who are breaking away from what has normally been perceived as traditional Greenlandic art, but still maintain their connection with their cultural background.

Leisure activities in Greenland, among both tourists and natives, still center on hunting and fishing. The country's whaling history and rugged landscape tends to make these otherwise functional activities into ceremonial community events, complete with their own rituals and customs.

The abundance of snow has made snow sculpting a popular pastime for residents and visitors. This activity culminates each year in the Nuuk Snow Festival, an annual international competition that draws sculptors from around the world to the city.

Just about all of Greenland's small villages and towns make use of the milder weather and endless daylight of the summer months to host festivals, jubilees, and town meetings complete with sheep sheerings, dog-sled races, and cultural events.

## Cultural Sites & Landmarks

The Ilulissat Icefjord on the west coast of Greenland was named a United Nations Educational, Scientific and Cultural Organization (UNESCO) World Heritage Site in 2004 (listed under Denmark). The Icefjord covers an area of

40,240 hectares (99,435 acres) and is located 250 kilometers (155 miles) north of the Arctic Circle. It is one of the few glaciers that connect the Greenland ice cap with the ocean, serving as the sea mouth of the glacier Sermeq Kujalleq. As one of the fastest changing glaciers in the world, Sermeq Kujalleq moves an average of 19 meters (62 feet) a day. Every year, a substantial amount of ice breaks off the glacier and travels down the iceberg-laden fjord, creating a powerful spectacle accompanied by dramatic booming sounds. This area has been studied for two-and-a-half centuries, and has played a significant role in understanding the effects of global warming.

A valuable cultural site is the Viking farm ruins at Nipaatsoq. Called the "Viking Pompeii," this site was the ancient settlement of the legendary Erik the Red (c. 950–1003), and the first Nordic settlement in Greenland. The farm lay buried under sand for 600 years, until it was discovered by hunters in 1990. Other Viking archaeological sites have been found throughout the western and southern sides of the island, such as the home of Erik's son, the explorer Leif Erikson (c. 970–c. 1020). These old villages were inhabited beginning in 1000 CE, and eventually abandoned over the period from 1350–1450 CE for unknown reasons, possibly due to climate change. A wealth of Viking artifacts have been found at these sites, such as soapstone utensils, woven cloth, whalebone tools, and the largest medieval loom found in the North Atlantic.

The National Park in the Northeast of Greenland is the largest national park in the world and features starkly beautiful and isolated landscapes. Home to many species of wildlife such as polar bears and giant walruses, the only people with regular access to the park are sealers and whalers from the closest settlement, Ittoqqortoormiit, as well as scientists studying the flora, fauna, and archaeology of the region. Tourists must obtain a special permit from the Ministry of Nature, Environment, and Justice or participate in an organized group expedition in order to visit the park. The park is also a popular destination for adventurous travelers.

The aurora borealis (also known as the northern polar lights) are one of the most spectacular of Greenland's natural wonders. Although they take place all year round, these natural light displays are especially visible from September to April each year. Ancient Inuit folklore says that when these northern lights are seen, it means that the dead are playing ball with a walrus skull.

## Libraries & Museums

The Greenland National Museum in Nuuk is home to many of the country's archeological artifacts, including the 500-year-old Greenland Mummies, the mummified remains of six women and two children, including a six-month old baby, which were discovered in a cave in 1972. There are over twenty museums throughout Greenland. The National Library of Greenland (Nunatta Atuagaateqarfia) houses the largest collection of Inuit and Greenlandic material in the Arctic region.

## Holidays

Greenlanders celebrate Christmas, Good Friday, Easter, Ascension Day, Great Prayer Day (falling on the fourth Friday after Easter), Whit Monday, and Greenlandic National Day (June 21).

Greenland's largest celebration is undoubtedly the festivities that mark the end of the winter's long polar night. The date of this celebration varies according to where one is in the country, but always involves the entire town or village meeting at a high viewing spot in order to witness the return of the sun. The end of polar night generally comes in January and February, and in the capital city of Nuuk, it is marked with an international snow-sculpture festival. Residents of Uummannaq Fjord, on the other hand, host the world ice golfing championships during this time.

## Youth Culture

Hunting still plays a large role in Greenlandic society and learning to hunt with one's family members and friends has become an important part of growing up. In addition, outdoor athletics and recreations such as hiking, kayaking, dog-sledding, and soccer are popular among young Greenlanders. (Most Greenlandic youth root adamantly for Danish soccer teams.) The Arctic Circle Race, a 160 kilometer, three-day cross-country ski competition, provides an annual challenge for skiers from all over Greenland, Denmark, and Europe. The Miki Race, held in conjunction with it, has a shorter course and is intended primarily for young people and children. Greenland also participates in the Arctic Winter Games, which features performances and competitions of traditional Inuit skills such as throat-singing and dog-sledding.

Greenland is known for having a lively music scene and industry, and the genres of hip-hop, rock and pop music have become important aspects of Greenland's youth culture. The fusion of Inuit and hip-hop culture—of which Nuuk Posse is the most well-known export—has even resulted in a unique genre that has increasingly grown more popular among youth. In fact, it is estimated that between 10 and 15 albums by Greenlandic artists are released annually, with the most popular discs selling roughly 5,000 copies, a significant feat for a population of less than 60,000.

## SOCIETY

### Transportation

Traditional forms of transportation in Greenland were the kayak and the dogsled. Today, because there are no roads between the towns, the only way to travel around Greenland is by snow-mobile, dogsled, or personal boat for shorter distances. Boat and air travel, via plane and helicopter, is common for longer distances. Dogsleds are used primarily in the northern and eastern regions of Greenland. In Tasiilaq, on the eastern coast, it is even possible to obtain a dogsled driving license. For those driving within cities, cars drive on the right side of the road in Greenland. Drivers and passengers are required to wear seatbelts and cell phone usage is prohibited while driving.

Plane travel within Greenland is operated by Air Greenland, which uses helicopters as well as 50-passenger Dash-7 and Dash 8-200 planes. The Arctic Umiaq Line (AUL), the country's national shipping service, offers passenger service between Narsarsuaq in south Greenland and Ilulissat in north Greenland between April and December. In the summer season, Blue Ice Explorer sails four different boats. Internationally, there are tri-weekly flights from Copenhagen to Greenland's Kangerlussuaq International Airport, as well as seasonal flights from Reykjavík to East and South Greenland.

### Transportation Infrastructure

There is no established road system in Greenland, although roads exist in cities, but not between them (with the exception of a road between Ivittuut and Kangilinnguit). There are a total of 370 kilometers (230 miles) of paved road. There are also no rail systems or inland waterways.

### Media & Communications

Kalaallit Nunaata Radioa (KNR, or the Greenland Broadcasting Corporation) oversees radio and television services in Greenland. Broadcasting languages are Greenlandic and Danish. There are no daily newspapers on the island, but *Atuagagdliutit Gronlandsposten* is published twice a week, and *Sermitsiaq* is published weekly. Both are national, tabloid-style newspapers published in Greenlandic and Danish. *Sermitsiaq* also publishes an English edition online.

The only provider for telephone and post services in Greenland is the public company TELE-POST. An interesting fact is that, although the population of Greenland was 57,733 in 2015, in 2014 there were 62,005 mobile phones in service on the island. Internet use is also growing rapidly; the estimated number of Internet connections is 11,918 (2014) and 40,100 users in the country in 2014. Internet cafés and Wi-Fi hotspots are available in urban areas.

## SOCIAL DEVELOPMENT

### Standard of Living

The United Nations does not provide a separate human development ranking for Greenland.

## Water Consumption

Greenland has substantial water resources residing in its glaciers. In the early 21st century, the government has established standards for the bottling of this water to be sold in the world market.

## Education

Greenland has nine years of mandatory childhood education through elementary and junior high school. The nation's high schools arose out of the optional two-year "continuation schools" and "course schools," for students with advanced educational needs. Since obtaining home rule from Denmark in 1979, Greenland has been working on a substantial overhaul of its school systems. All classes are now taught in Greenlandic, and many include a component of traditional Inuit culture in the curriculum.

Municipal school boards and parents run their own local public schools in accordance with national standards and with financial support from Greenland's Legislative Assembly. Because of the country's sparse population, Greenland has a system of settlement schools, some of which are too small to have a principal. This system also permits home schooling in isolated areas of the country.

Although education is not free after the compulsory level, Greenland's government provides grants to those who proceed to vocational schools, secondary schools, or universities. The University of Greenland goes by its Inuit name, Ilisimatusarfik.

Greenland's literacy rate is 100 percent. The majority of the population speaks both Kalaallisut (Greenlandic) and Danish, and many also speak English.

## Women's Rights

The status of equal rights for women can be traced back to traditional Inuit culture, in which men hunted and fished while women assumed the domestic responsibilities; however, there was significant cooperation and respect between the sexes. In 1948, equal voting rights for women in Greenland were introduced and the legalization of abortion followed in 1975. During the mid- to late

20th century, however, autonomy from Denmark was the dominant issue with regard to equality in Greenland. As a result, women's rights received less attention than issues of ethnicity and self-determination.

After the granting of Home Rule in 1979, Greenlandic women's organizations worked with their counterparts in Denmark to promote awareness of women's rights and gender equality. Less than 20 years later, Greenland's Equal Status Council was established in 1998. The organization conducted surveys on women's participation in the home, the workplace, and public life. The results found that, although women were underrepresented in the workplace, their numbers were increasing. In 1999 and 2002, the ICC (Inuit Circumpolar Council) committed to gender equality in accordance with the goals of the United Nations Convention on the Elimination of All Forms of Discrimination against Women (CEDAW), and in 2003, the Home Rule government adopted legislation emphasizing equal treatment of women and men in public service areas and employment. The first minister responsible for gender equality was appointed in 2011.

In recent years, women have experienced increasing gains in Greenlandic politics. In fact, in 2013, Aleqa Hammond, former leader of the Siumut Party, became the first female Prime Minister (but stepped down in September of 2014). A short-lived Women's Party (Arnat Partiiat) promoted women politicians and feminism between 1999–2004, securing as much as 2.4 percent of the vote in the 2002 legislative election, but no seats. In 2014, twelve of the members of parliament were women.

Currently, an estimated 45 percent of the workforce in Greenland is made up of women. However, higher-paying jobs in the corporate sector are still most often held by men. In terms of education, the number of women at higher institutions of learning is significantly larger than that of men; in high school, advanced degree, and university programs, the ratio of women to men was 63 to 37 in 2006.

One downside of the improving situation of women in Greenland is that traditional skills performed by women, such as the technique of flensing (stripping the blubber from a whale carcass), are becoming less commonly practiced and may, in time, be lost. Additionally, Greenland offers a minimum of 21 weeks of paid maternity leave for parents, of which the father can take six weeks. The government also provides public day care facilities for the children of working parents.

Domestic abuse is a problem for women in Greenland. In 2005 and 2006, the Greenland Gender Equality Council began conducting awareness campaigns about physical and mental violence towards women through such methods as television ads. As of 2008, Greenland had six crisis shelters to aid women and children suffering from abuse.

## Health Care

The government provides health care through a network of health posts and small hospitals. The larger towns along what Greenlander's call "the Coast" are each provided with a small hospital, furnished with basic diagnostic equipment. Up to four general physicians provide patient care in each of these hospitals. Villages that have more than 300 residents are each appointed a nursing station, while smaller villages may only have a designated health aide.

Greenland's outlying villages, those with fewer than 70 residents, generally have a health worker who is certified only to dispense certain medications under the direction of a physician. A shortage of physicians and Greenland's chronically poor weather make the quality and reliability of health care poor in these areas.

Queen Ingrid's Hospital, in the capital city of Nuuk, is the central hospital for the country, and its specialists visit the larger towns along the coast. Patients with more serious illnesses and injuries are flown to Denmark for care.

---

## GOVERNMENT

---

## Structure

Greenland is a parliamentary democracy under the Danish constitutional monarchy. In 2008,

Greenland voted for self-autonomy when it passed the Greenland Self Government Act. Although Denmark still controls matters of international diplomacy and national security, Greenland's home government has assumed responsibility for the judiciary, the police, and the management of its natural resources. Greenland still elects two representatives to sit on the Parliament of Denmark and receives subsidies from the Danish government that amount to a sizeable portion of the nation's gross domestic product (approximately 56 percent of government revenues in 2012). It is anticipated that as the Greenland government takes increasing control of its natural resources, the relationship with the Danish government will shift in terms of dependency.

The Greenland government recognizes four municipalities: Qaasuitsup, Qeqqata, Sermersooq, and Kujalleq. The Northeast Greenland National Park is unincorporated, as is the Thule Air Base.

The executive branch consists of Denmark's Queen, who is represented in Greenland by a High Commissioner. The Greenland parliament, called the "Inatsisartut" (formerly known as Landsting), elects a prime minister based on the strength of participating political parties. The Inatsisartut has 31 members who are elected by popular vote to four-year terms.

## Political Parties

Parliamentary democracies often have a large number of political parties, which have a tendency to shift in terms of political platform and their alliance with other parties sharing common interests. Often, parliamentary systems are ruled by coalitions of two or more parties that unite to form a majority coalition. These coalitions differ in nature, with some coalitions having a lasting strength and others failing to govern at all. Additionally, it's not unusual for parties to dissolve because of personality conflicts within the organization.

In Greenland in 2014, there were about five political parties. The Inuit Ataqatigiit (IA, Community of the People) Party is a left of center party that strives for Greenland's independence. In the 2014 elections, their representation in the Inatsisartut was 11 seats (of 31).Given the momentum of the independence movement in Greenland, further steps towards independence are anticipated.

The center-right Siumut (Forward) Party (social democrats) is the second most powerful party in the nation, with 11 seats in the parliament. The liberal Demokraterne (Democrats) Party and the center-right, agrarian Atassut (Solidarity) Party each held four and two seats, respectively in the 2014 election. The newly formed Partii Naleraq held three seats in the parliament. Prime Minister Aleqa Hammond, who won the 2013 elections, stepped down from office and as leader of the Siumut Party in September of 2014, following a case of misuse of public funds. Kim Nielsen, a former minister in Hammond's government, assumed office in late 2014.

## Local Government

In 2009, Greenland shifted its local governmental structure from 18 municipalities to four principal municipalities with one administrative location in each.

## Judicial System

In 2009, the Greenland government assumed control of its judicial system, while still retaining Dutch law. The Danish Supreme Court, the Landsret, is still the highest court in the judicial system.

## Taxation

Income in Greenland is taxed at a flat rate of 37 percent of income nationally; taxes are also levied on pensions. Corporations pay a flat tax of 31.8 percent as of 2010.

## Armed Forces

Greenland relies on Denmark for its national security. A coast guard, under the control of the Danish government but staffed largely by Greenlanders, patrols Greenland's coast. As Greenland moves toward independence, it intends to gain increased control over the coast guard.

Thule Air Base, in the north, acts as the northernmost command of the United States Air Force. Greenland became a strategic point for the United States following World War II and during the Cold War, as it stands midway between New York City and Moscow, Russia. Today, it serves as a missile warning site for the North American Aerospace Defense Command (NORAD) and hosts the 23rd Space Operations Squadron (Detachment 1).

## Foreign Policy

As a former colony of the Kingdom of Denmark, Greenland was under Danish rule. After a public referendum voted for Home Rule in 1979, the Greenland Parliament and Cabinet became the institutions for domestic self-governance. However, Greenland's foreign policy is determined by the government of Denmark (which classifies Greenland as an autonomous constituent country). A referendum was approved in November 2008 that favored further autonomy. For the Inuit people, the vote for increased independence marks a step toward the creation of the world's first Inuit state. It changes the official language from Danish to Greenlandic (Kalaallisut), and also names Greenlanders as a separate people recognizable under international law. Under the referendum, which went into effect in 2009, the Danish government would continue to maintain its influence over Greenland's foreign policy and security.

Of particular concern in the vote—in which, of the 28,200 Greenlanders who voted, an estimated 75.5 percent favored increased autonomy—is the self-governance over natural resources. Under the referendum's plan, Greenland would receive revenue from future oil, gas, and mineral discoveries. This point is particularly appealing to Greenlanders, as the melting of Greenland's ice cap has made areas that are potentially rich in minerals or petroleum, but were previously unreachable, more open to exploration. In 2008, the U.S. Geological Survey (USGS) estimated that between 10 and 20 billion barrels of oil might be located off Greenland's coast, though it warned it could be several decades before the oil is found.

Greenland has established several formal ties with several organizations outside its relationship with Denmark. Greenland is a member of the Inuit Circumpolar Council (ICC), a UN-recognized non-governmental organization (NGO) representing the needs of the Inuit peoples in Canada, Russia, Greenland, and Alaska. Greenland is also an independent member of the Nordic Council, which also includes Sweden, Norway, Finland, Denmark, Iceland, the Åland Islands, and the Faroe Islands. It is also a member of the Arctic Council, which was founded in 1996 by nations bordering the Arctic (Russia, Canada, United States, Iceland, Denmark, Greenland, Sweden, Norway, and Finland) in order to cooperate on environmental issues. Additionally, two representatives from Greenland sit in the Danish parliament, the Folketing, and two seats in the UN delegation from Denmark are reserved for Greenlanders. Greenland withdrew from the European Union (EU) in 1985 due to a concern over fishing rights; Denmark maintains its membership in the EU.

Relations between the U.S. military and Greenlanders have been generally friendly, although occasionally subject to tension. During World War II, the United States established a military air base, the Thule Air Base (also called the Thule Defense Area), in northern Greenland. The establishment of the base was controversial in that it displaced a group of northern Inuit. Further exacerbating the issue was the 1968 crash of a U.S. B-52 plane carrying four nuclear bombs, which resulted in radioactive plutonium contaminating the surrounding environment, affecting local residents and wildlife. Today the air base functions as part of the missile defense shield of the North Atlantic Treaty Organization (NATO).

## Human Rights Profile

International human rights law insists that states respect civil and political rights, and also promote an individual's economic, social, and cultural rights. The United Nations Universal Declaration on Human Rights (UDHR) is recognized as the standard for international human rights. Its authors sought the counsel of the world's great thinkers, philosophers, and religious leaders, and were careful to create a document that reflects the core values shared by every world culture.

(To read this document or view the articles relating to cultural human rights, go to: http://www.un.org/en/documents/udhr/).

Perhaps the single most important human rights issue in Greenland is the status of the indigenous Inuit. Greenlanders of Inuit descent formerly experienced a degree of second-class citizenship under Danish rule. Native language and cultural practices were repressed while European and Christian beliefs encouraged. Under Home Rule—which, in 1979, granted Greenland greater self-government—this situation has improved. (However, the International Work Group for Indigenous Affairs [IWGIA] notes that, whereas Danish language ability is often a prerequisite for employment in Greenland, Greenlandic language ability is usually not.) Danish law protects the indigenous rights of Greenlanders, and the justice system in Greenland has been designed to incorporate elements of traditional Inuit legal practices with Western jurisprudence. Additionally, the ICC was established in 1977 in order to promote the rights of Inuit people in Greenland and Canada.

The Inuit have also been the victims of forced displacement. In 1953, the Inughuit people of northern Greenland, the northernmost Inuit group, were forcibly resettled by the Danish government in order to make way for the U.S. Thule Air Base. In 1999, a Danish court mandated that the government provide compensation to the Inughuit or their descendants. In 2004, the Inughuit filed an appeal with the European Court of Human Rights (ECtHR) for greater compensation and the right to return to their native lands, which is still pending.

Recently, the hunting practices of the Inuit people of the Arctic region, including Greenland, have come under pressure from animal rights groups such as Greenpeace. Hunting, particularly seal hunting, is considered an intrinsic part of Inuit culture. It is also an important part of the subsistence economy of Inuit families, who eat the meat and sell the furs of the animals they catch. According to indigenous peoples' rights organizations such as the IWGIA, anti-hunting campaigns have displayed a lack of tolerance and understanding of Inuit way of life and have made it more difficult for Inuit families to engage in traditional cultural practices. For instance, the campaign against hunting baby harp-seals launched by Greenpeace in the 1970s caused a drop in the demand for all sealskin products, even those made from the furs of mature animals. This, in turn, destroyed the market on which many Inuit hunters had depended. However, groups like Greenpeace and other wildlife protection organizations list the threat of species endangerment and extinction as viable reasons for altering traditional hunting practices. This conflict is still a point of tension today.

Greenland has a comprehensive welfare systems modeled after those of the Scandinavian countries. Hospitals and medical treatment is free, and child care benefits as well as pensions for the elderly are provided to those who demonstrate financial need. Despite its welfare system, Greenland's population suffers from alcohol abuse, domestic violence, and neglect, as well as high suicide rates. In 2006, there were 56 suicides in Greenland (in a population of roughly 57,000). Greenland's problem with alcoholism is usually attributed to cultural stress, seasonal affective disorder (SAD), and the genetic susceptibility of Inuit people to alcohol.

## ECONOMY

### Overview of the Economy

Since it obtained Home Rule, Greenland has instituted economic policies designed to keep inflation and budget deficits low. However, the country still relies on the Danish government for a substantial amount of aid. In 2011, Greenland's estimated gross domestic product (GDP) was $2.16 billion USD, with a per capita GDP of $38,400 USD (2008). In the 2012, Danish subsidies totaled about $651 USD million.

With home rule comes Greenland's increased control over exploitation of natural resources. The melting of the ice sheet due to global warming has presented possibilities for mineral mining and oil extraction. Both are potentially lucrative endeav-

ors for an increasingly independent Greenland, but it will require a substantial initial investment to establish these industries. Two state-owned companies have been formed in order to further this development: the National Oil Company of Greenland (NUNAOIL), focused on exploring hydrocarbon resources off of Greenland's coast, and NunaMineral, a mining company seeking mineral resources within Greenland.

### Industry

Greenland's largest industry is fishing. Traditional skills, including carving, tanning, and small ship construction and repair, still make up a significant portion of the country's industrial base. However, Greenland's efforts toward developing the mining and petroleum industries should make a marked difference in Greenland's economy.

### Labor

According to the US CIA Factbook, Greenland boasts a labor force numbering 26,990 (2012) people. Unemployment in 2010 was estimated at 4.2 percent, yet in 2013 it rose to 9.4 percent.

### Energy/Power/Natural Resources

Greenland's most apparent natural resources are the fish, seals, whales, and other marine life that have sustained human habitation on the island for the past 5,000 years. However, the island also has natural reserves of zinc, iron ore, coal, lead, platinum, uranium, cryolite, molybdenum, and gold. There is a possibility that Greenland's ice cap also hides supplies of oil and natural gas.

### Fishing

The fishing industry is Greenland's largest. Disko Bay, on the southwestern coast, is one of the world's richest sources of shrimp. Because of recent declines in the cod population, shrimp and halibut now dominate Greenland's fish processing industry.

### Forestry

Greenland has no measureable forests or expanse of trees due to its climate. All lumber is imported.

## Mining/Metals

Greenland has begun to step up mining and mineral extraction operations, which include uranium, niobium, tantalite, iron, gold, and diamonds. Difficult climate conditions have delayed growth in this sector, and specialists estimate that it may be several years before hydrocarbon and mineral explorations lead to further production.

## Agriculture

Greenland's arctic and sub-arctic climates prevent any significant agricultural industry. However, foraging is still practiced among Greenlanders, and a select few vegetables are grown in gardens and greenhouses.

## Animal Husbandry

Greenlanders raise herds of sheep and caribou.

## Tourism

Most of the people who travel to Greenland are scientists who flock to the icy north to look for early signs of the Earth's formation. Other tourists tend to be adventurers and big game hunters willing to brave the summer climate to see one of the world's most dramatic landscapes.

*Evelyn Atkinson, Amy Witherbee, Alex K. Rich*

---

### DO YOU KNOW?

- In some places, Greenland's ice sheet is up to 3,375 meters (11,070 feet) thick. Greenland's icy landscape is believed to hold about 10 percent of the world's fresh water, prompting efforts to start an ice-processing industry in the country. Greenland's favorite polar explorer was native Greenlander Knud Rasmussen (1879–1933), who between 1921 and 1924, decided to forego his North Pole expeditions to go on a "Great Sledge Journey" to collect traditional Inuit legends and songs.

- Nuuk is home to Greenland's only pedestrian crosswalk light, as well as the country's only roundabouts, or circular road junctions.

- Because Nuuk is the closest city to the North Pole, Santa Claus has a mailbox, post office, and address there.

---

### Bibliography

Erlich, Gretel. *This Cold Heaven: Seven Seasons in Greenland*. Pantheon Books. USA: 2001.

Koncnik, Damjan and Kevin Kato. *Greenland—The End of the World*. Blue Fuji Publishers. 2010.

Loukacheva, Natalia. *The Arctic Promise: Legal and Political Autonomy of Greenland and Nunavut*. University of Toronto Press. Canada: 2007.

Lynge, Aqqaluk (translated by Marianne Stenbaek and Ken Norris). *Taqqat uummammut aqqutaannut takorluukkat apuuffiannut/ The Veins of the Heart to the Pinnacle of the Mind*. International Polar Institute Press. Hanover and Montreal: 2008.

Nuttall, Mark. *Arctic Homeland: Kinship, Community and Development in Northwest Greenland*. University of Toronto Press. Canada: 1992.

O'Hara, Kevin and Peter Trueman. *South Greenland: An Arctic Paradise*. Kevin O'Hara.Greenland: 2003.

Rasmussen, Knud. *Across Arctic America: Narrative of the Fifth Thule Expedition*. G.P. Putnam's Sons. New York, London: 1927.

Vaughan, Richard. *Northwest Greenland: A History*. University of Maine Press. USA: 1991.

## Works Cited

Alley, Sam. "Knud Johan Victor Rasmussen." EMuseum at Minnesota State University, Mankato. 2007. http://www.mnsu.edu/emuseum/information/biography/pqrst/rasmussen_knud.html.

"Arctic Circle Race." Arctic Circle Race. www.acr.gl.

"Artic Temperatures." The Official Tourism and Business Site of Greenland. http://www.greenland.com/en/about-greenland/nature-climate/the-weather-in-greenland/ .

"Arts & Crafts." The Official Tourism and Business Site of Greenland. 2008. http://www.greenland.com/content/english/tourist/culture/arts_crafts.

*Atuagagdliutit/Grønlandsposten.* 2008. www.ag.gl.

Bevanger, Lars. "Toxin threat to Inuit food." BBC News. 1 April 2003. http://news.bbc.co.uk/2/hi/science/nature/2906357.stm.

Bilawka, Patrice. "Nobody Goes to Greenland." 19 September 2007. http://nobodygoestogreenland.blogspot.com.

Brooke, James. "Story of Viking Colonies' Icy 'Pompeii' Unfolds from Ancient Greenland Farm." *The New York Times.* 8 May 2001. http://www.nytimes.com/2001/05/08/science/08VIKI.html?ex=1226120400&en=63c325188ff5943c&ei=5070.

Brown, Dale Mackenzie. "The Fate of Greenland's Vikings." *Archaeology Magazine.* 28 February 2000. http://cat.he.net/~archaeol/online/features/greenland/index.html.

Brueggemann, Rudy. "Back to Basics in Wild Greenland." August 1998. http://www.rudyfoto.com/fjordstory.html.

Brueggemann, Rudy. "Greenland/Kalaallit Nunaat." October 1999. http://www.rudyfoto.com/grl/greenlandarchitecture.html.

"Communications." The Official Tourism and Business Site of Greenland. 2008. http://www.greenland.com/content/english/tourist/travel_info/communications.

Cowell, Alan. "Greenland Vote Favors Independence." *The New York Times.* 26 November 2008. http://www.nytimes.com/2008/11/27/world/europe/27greenland.html?_r=1&ref=europe.

"Culture of Greenland." NationMaster Encyclopedia. 2005. http://www.nationmaster.com/encyclopedia/Culture-of-Greenland#Traditional_skills_at_risk.

"Danish Doubts over Greenland Vote." BBC World News. 27 November 2008. http://news.bbc.co.uk/2/hi/europe/7752660.stm.

"Denmark." *Country Reports on Human Rights Practices—2007.* U.S. Department of State. 11 March 2008. http://www.state.gov/g/drl/rls/hrrpt/2007/100556.htm.

"Doing Business in Denmark." Kwintessential Cross Cultural Solutions. 2008. http://www.kwintessential.co.uk/etiquette/doing-business-denmark.html.

"Denmark—Language, Culture, Customs and Etiquette." Kwintessential Cross Cultural Solutions. 2008. http://www.kwintessential.co.uk/resources/global-etiquette/denmark-country-profile.html.

"Dwellings of the Inuit Culture." The Official Tourism and Business Site of Greenland. 2008. http://www.greenland.com/content/english/tourist/culture/hunting_culture_of_greenland/dwellings_of_the_inuit_culture.

Eltorp, Thomas Bojer. "Duplo's Blog." October 2008. http://my.opera.com/Duplo.

Ertel, Manfred. "Greenland Braces for Independence and Wealth." Spiegel Online International. 12 November 2008. http://www.spiegel.de/international/world/0,1518,590078,00.html.

"Facts about the Greenlandic Dog." Greenland Home Rule Government Department of Information. http://www.wavez.at/pages/d_999.php?u=15463&p=73304.

"Famous Sons of Ilulissat and Others with Local Connections." Illulissat Kommuneat. 2008. http://www.ilulissat.gl/En/Turisme/Beroemte/index.html.

"Fourth and Fifth Periodic Reports—Denmark." United Nations CEDAW Review, 27th Session. 2008. http://www2.ohchr.org/english/bodies/cedaw/docs/co/DenmarkCO27.pdf.

"Explore Greenland." The Official Tourism and Business Site of Greenland. www.greenland.com.

George, Jane. "Greenland Legislature Welcomes Youthful Politicians." Nunatsiaq News. 19 November 2004. http://www.nunatsiaq.com/archives/41119/news/nunavut/41119_09.html.

"Government." NANOQ. 2008. http://uk.nanoq.gl/Emner/Government.aspx.

"Greenland." CIA World Factbook. https://www.cia.gov/library/publications/the-world-factbook/geos/gl.html.

"Greenland." City Population. http://www.citypopulation.de/Greenland.html.

"Greenland." International Work Group for Indigenous Affairs. June 2006. http://www.iwgia.org/sw15466.asp.

"Greenland in Figures—2008." Statistics Greenland, Greenland Home Rule Government. 2008. http://www.stat.gl/LinkClick.aspx?link=Intranet%2FGFIF+2008+WEB.pdf&tabid=36&mid=371&language=en-US

"Greenland in Figures—2015." http://www.stat.gl/publ/en/GF/2015/pdf/Greenland%20in%20Figures%202015.pdf

"Greenlandic Cuisine." The Official Tourism and Business Site of Greenland. 2008. http://www.greenland.com/content/english/tourist/culture/greenlandic_cuisine.

"The Greenlandic Kayak." The Official Tourism and Business Site of Greenland. 2008. http://www.greenland.com/content/english/tourist/culture/hunting_culture_of_greenland/the_greenlandic_kayak.

"Greenland Sees Education as Key to Independence." Associated Press. 30 November 2008. http://

www.google.com/hostednews/afp/article/
ALeqM5jRKCrqCWLTUnZUjiRhY20Bk6gQjQ.

"Greenlandic Music." The Official Tourism and Business
Site of Greenland. 2008. http://www.greenland.com/
content/english/tourist/culture/greenlandic_music.

"Greenlandic Visual Artists." The Official Tourism
and Business Site of Greenland. 2008. http://www.
greenland.com/content/english/tourist/culture/visual_art/
greenlandic_visual_artists.

Hanke, Peter. "Choral Singing in Greenland."
Nordic Sounds. 2004. http://dvm.nu/hierarchy/
periodical/ns/1997/02/?show=data/periodical/
ns/1997/ns1997_2XML/periodical-ns1997_2_07.
tkl&type=periodical.

"Health and Welfare Services." NANOQ. 9 February 2000.
http://www.gh.gl/uk/facts/health.htm.

Herscovici, Alan. "Forgotten Story: The Impact of 'Animal-
Rights' Campaigns on the Inuit." Native Americans and
the Environment. 2000. http://ncseonline.org/nae/docs/
inuit_and_ban.html.

"History." TELE-POST. 2008. http://www.tele.gl/uk/
history/index.htm.

"Hunting Culture of Greenland: A Question of Survival."
The Official Tourism and Business Site of Greenland.
2008. http://www.greenland.com/content/english/tourist/
culture/hunting_culture_of_greenland

"ICC Executive Council Resolution 03–02." Inuit
Circumpolar Council. June 2003. http://www.inuit.org/
index.asp?lang=eng&num=245.

"Ilulissat Icefjord." World Heritage, UNESCO. http://whc.
unesco.org/en/list/1149.

"Ilulissat Icefjord: A UNESCO World Heritage Site." The
Official Tourism and Business Site of Greenland. 2008.
http://www.greenland.com/content/english/tourist/
towns_regions/north_greenland/ilulissat/ilulissat_
icefjord

"International Relations." NANOQ. 31 July 2008. http://
uk.nanoq.gl/Emner/International_relations.aspx.

"The Inuit." Arctic Voice. 22 June 2007. http://www.
arcticvoice.org/inuit.html#culture.

"Inuit Myths and Legends." Qikiqtani Inuit Association.
www.inuitmyths.com.

Jensen, Inge Mørch. "Greenland: Art and Culture." Royal
Danish Ministry of Foreign Affairs. 2008. http://www.
um.dk/publikationer/um/english/denmark/kap7/7-1-20.asp.

Jensen, Ole G. "The Heartbeat of Ammassalik."
Ammassalik Museum. East Greenland Database.
2008. http://www.eastgreenland.com/database.
asp?lang=eng&num=203.

"Kaffemik: A Look into a Greenlandic Home." The Official
Tourism and Business Site of Greenland. 2008. http://
www.greenland.com/content/english/tourist/culture/
kaffemik.

"Local Transport." The Official Tourism and Business Site
of Greenland. 2008. http://www.greenland.com/content/
english/tourist/travel_info/local_transport.

Klausen, Anne-Mette. "Inequality in the Kingdom of
Denmark." KVinfo – All About Gender in Denmark.
Danish National Council of Women. 2003. http://www.
kvinfo.dk/side/674/article/62/.

Laugrand, Frédéric and Jarich Oosten. "Quviasukvik.
The Celebration of an Inuit Winter Feast in the Central
Arctic." Journal de la Société des Américanistes. Vol.
88. 2002. http://jsa.revues.org/document2772.html.

MacPherson, Tamara. "Youth and Elders Game for Throat
Singing." Nunatsiaq News. 13 July 2001. http://www.
nunatsiaq.com/archives/nunavut010731/nvt10713_11.
html.

Mahr, Krista. "Greenland Wants to Rule Itself—And Its
Resources." TIME World. 26 November 2008. http://
www.time.com/time/world/article/0,8599,1862343,00.
html.

"Maniitsoq—Culture." Eurotravelling.net. 2004. http://
www.eurotravelling.net/greenland/maniitsoq/maniitsoq_
culture.htm.

Marquardt, Ole. "Greenland's Demography, 1700–2000:
The Interplay of Economic Activities and Religion."
Populations and Migrations. Vol. 26 No. 2. 2002.
p. 47–69. http://www.erudit.org/revue/etudinuit/2002/
v26/n2/007645ar.html.

"Mary's Gift to Children in Crisis." Denmark.dk: The
Official Website of Denmark. 2008. http://www.
denmark.dk/en/servicemenu/News/GeneralNews/
Archives2008/MarysGiftToChildrenInCrisis.htm.

"Milkycat Gives Mad Props to Nuuk Posse." 5 January
2000. http://www.milkycat.com/reviews/nuukrvw.html.

Minogue, Sara. "Women's Movement Skews Gender
Issues in the North." Nunatsiaq News. 7 October 2005.
http://www.nunatsiaq.com/archives/51007/news/
nunavut/51007_13.html.

Montgomery-Andersen, Ruth. "Referral in Pregnancy: A
Challenge for Greenlandic Women" (thesis). Nordic
School of Public Health. 2005. http://www.nhv.se/
upload/dokument/forskning/Publikationer/MPH/
MPH2005–37_R.Montgomery-Andersen.pdf.

"Naalakkersuisut: About Greenland." http://
naalakkersuisut.gl/en/About-government-of-greenland/
About-Greenland

"The National Park: An Arctic Natural Paradise." The
Official Tourism and Business Site of Greenland. 2008.
http://www.greenland.com/content/english/tourist/
nature_climate/the_national_park.

"News from Greenland." Sermitsiaq.gl. 2008. http://
sermitsiaq.gl/rss/en_newsletter.jsp.

"Northern Lights—Aurora Borealis: A Spectacular Sight."
The Official Tourism and Business Site of Greenland.
2008. http://www.greenland.com/content/english/tourist/
nature_climate/northern_lights.

Nuttal, Mark. "Greenland—Importance of Kinship."
Marriage and Family Encyclopedia. 2008. http://family.
jrank.org/pages/747/Greenland-Importance-Kinship.
html.

Olsen, Pernille Lind. "Bodil Begtrup—Blazing a Trail for Human Rights." KVinfo–All About Gender in Denmark. Danish National Council of Women. 2000. http://www.kvinfo.dk/side/674/article/9/hilight/greenland/.

Petersen, Robert. "Colonialism as Seen from a Former Colonized Area." *Arctic Anthropology.* Vol. 32, No. 2, pp. 118–26. 1995. http://arcticcircle.uconn.edu/HistoryCulture/petersen.html.

Rendal, Ole. "Leading Politician Dies at 70." September 2008. http://sermitsiaq.gl/indland/article56336.ece?service=print&lang=EN.

Scobey, Joan. "Extreme Eating in Greenland." Travel and Adventure Lifestyle Columns. 2008. http://www.creators.com/lifestylefeatures/travel-and-adventure/extreme-eating-in-greenland.html.

Sorenson, Bo Wagner. "'Men in Transition': The Representation of Men's Violence against Women in the Arctic." University of Copenhagen, Denmark. 1999. http://www.eurowrc.org/13.institutions/3.coe/en-violence-coe/18.en-coe-oct99.htm.

"Statement by Ms. Vibeke Abel, Deputy Permanent Secretary, Department for Gender Equality." 36th Session of the Committee on the Elimination of Discrimination Against Women. Ministry of Foreign Affairs of Denmark. 9 August 2006. http://www.missionfnnewyork.um.dk/en/menu/statements/UNGASessionCommitteeEliminationDiscrWomen.htm

"Previous Prize Winners and Nominations." Norden. (The Nordic Council). 11 December 2007. http://www.norden.org/nr/pris/lit_pris/uk/arkiv.asp.

"Regions and Territories: Greenland." BBC News. 23 July 2008. http://news.bbc.co.uk/1/hi/world/europe/country_profiles/1023393.stm.

*Sermitsiaq.* 2008. http://www.sermitsiaq.gl.

Stenbakken, Anders. "The Ammassalik Kitchen." Destination East Greenland. 2008. http://eastgreenland.com/database.asp?lang=eng&num=211.

Thisted, Kirsten. "Greenlandic art." Bryggen Art, North Atlantic House. 2008. http://www.bryggenart.com/en/art_greenlandic.php.

Thomsen, Marianne Lykke. "Ethnicity and Feminism: Inuit Women in Greenland and Canada." *Northern Perspectives.* Vol. 17, No. 3. August–October 1989. http://www.carc.org/pubs/v17no3/4.htm.

Thomsen, Marianne Lykke. "Indigenous Women." Third Session of the Permanent Forum on Indigenous Issues, Ministry of Foreign Affairs, Denmark. May 2004. http://www.missionfnnewyork.um.dk/CMS.Web/Templates/GenericWidePage.aspx?NRMODE=Published&NRNODEGUID={56B780F9-41EC-48D4-A5A1-62FE17A9D737}&NRORIGINALURL=/en/menu/statements/IndigenousWomen.htm&NRCACHEHINT=NoModifyGuest&printmode=True.

Thuesen, Soren T. "Coping with Crisis: Greenlandic Views on Crisis ca. 1860–1920." University of Copenhagen. 1991. http://webarkiv.hum.ku.dk/ipssas/publications/2005/18_Thuesen.pdf.

"Traditional Dress." The Official Tourism and Business Site of Greenland. 2008. http://www.greenland.com/content/english/tourist/culture/traditional_dress.

"Tupilak." The Official Tourism and Business Site of Greenland. 2008. http://www.greenland.com/content/english/tourist/culture/arts_crafts/tupilak.

"U.S. Expands Greenland Relations in Support of Missile Defense." Environment News Service. 9 August 2004. http://www.ens-newswire.com/ens/aug2004/2004-08-09-02.asp.

"The Veins of the Heart to the Pinnacle of the Mind" (Book Review). Siku News. 13 March 2008. http://www.sikunews.com/art.html?catid=21&artid=4668.

"Welcome to the Greenlander Troup 'MIK'." 2008. http://www.mik-koret.dk/eng.html.

"Women's Party (Greenland)." NationMaster. 2005. http://www.nationmaster.com/encyclopedia/Women%27s-Party-(Greenland).

You, Nicholas. "UN-HABITAT and Hip-Hop join forces to empower urban youth." UN-HABITAT. September 2004. ww2.unhabitat.org/cdrom/wuf/documents/Special%20events/Messengers%20of%20Truth/background/Hip-Hop.pdf.

*A traditional Mexican dance. iStock/Windzepher*

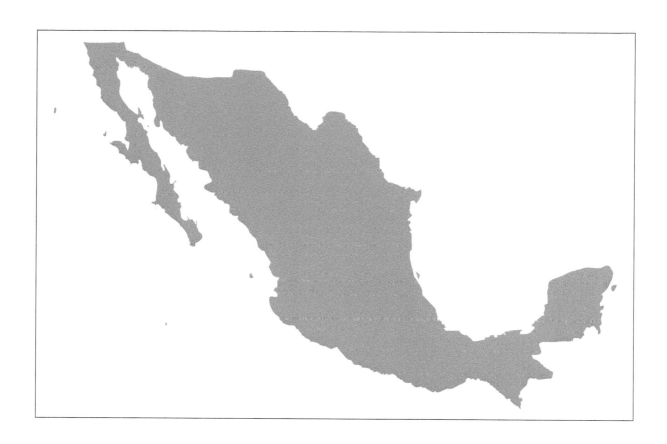

MEXICO

## Introduction

Mexico is formally known as the Estados Unidos Mexicanos, or the United Mexican States. It is the southernmost nation in North America, and one of the most populous countries in the Western Hemisphere. Mexico also has the highest population of Spanish-speakers in the world. Its modern culture embodies the influences of its ancient and Aztec and Mayan cultures, its Spanish colonial past, and its position in 21st-century North America.

## GENERAL INFORMATION

**Official Language(s):** Spanish
**Population:** 120,286,655 (2014 estimate)
**Currency:** Mexican Peso
**Coins:** Mexican coins come in both centavo and peso denominations. There are 100 centavos to one peso. Centavos come in denominations of 5, 10, 20, and 50, although those coins less than 50¢ are rarely used and most stores ask patrons to round up to the next 50¢ or one peso, with the difference going to charity. Pesos are also issued in the form of coins and banknotes; peso coins include $1, $2, $5, $10, $20, and $50 denominations.
**Land Area:** 1,943,945 square kilometers (750,561 square miles)
**Water Area:** 20,430 square kilometers (7,888 square miles)
**National Anthem:** "Himno Nacional Mexicano" (Spanish, "Mexican National Anthem")
**Capital:** Ciudad de Mexico (Mexico City)

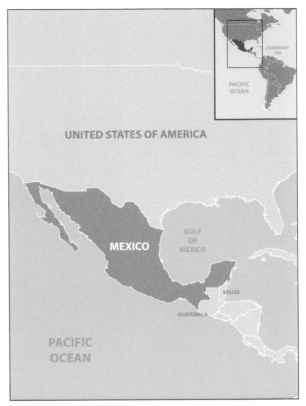

**Time Zone(s):** Mexico encompasses three times zones: Pacific Standard Time (GMT -8); Mountain Standard Time (GMT -7); and Central Standard Time (GMT -6).

**Flag Description:** The Mexican Flag presents three bold vertical and equal stripes of green, white, and red, with the Mexican coat of arms emblazoned in the center of the white stripe. The flags colors are those of Mexico's national liberation army. The coat of arms depicts an eagle, perched on a cactus, eating a snake. The cactus is situated on a rock above a lake. This seal recalls an Aztec legend in which the gods told the people to found their city in a place where an eagle ate a snake atop a nopal (cactus). This same emblem is the pictogram for Mexico City (formerly the Aztec city-state Tenochtitlan).

## Population

Mexico is one of the most ethnically and linguistically diverse nations in the world. The majority of Mexicans, referred to as Mestizos, are an ethnic mix of Mestizo Indian and European

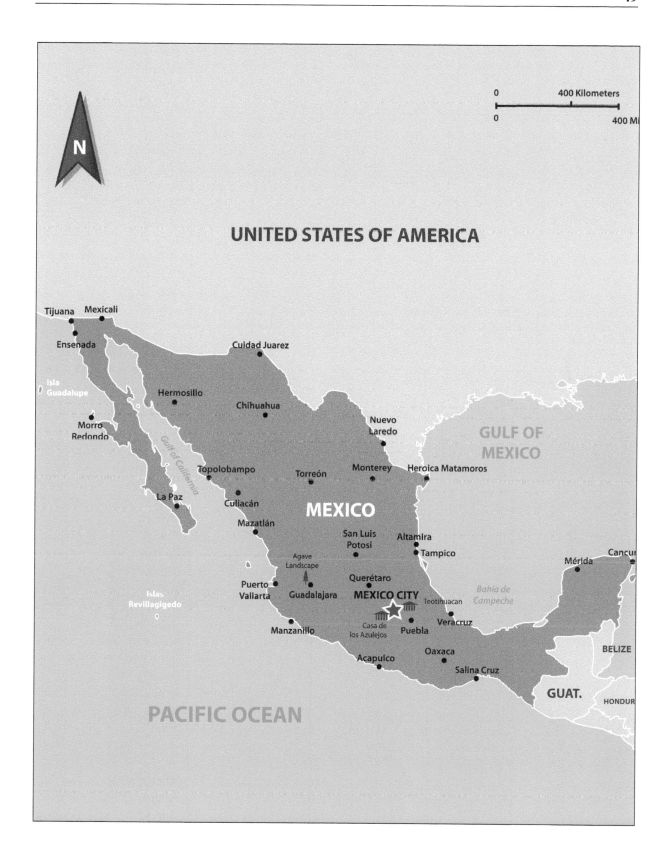

**Principal Cities by Population (2010):**

- Mexico City (8,851,080)
- Ecatepec (1,655,015)
- Guadalajara (1,495,182)
- Puebla (1,434,062)
- Ciudad Juarez (1,321,004)
- Tijuana (1,300,983)
- León (1,238,962)
- Zapopan (1,142,483)
- Monterrey (1,133,070)
- Nezahualcóyotl (1,104,585)

(mostly Spanish), a mix that occurred during the years following the settlement and population of Latin America by European powers. Mestizos number about 60 percent of the population.

The next largest ethnicity in Mexico is Amerindian, many of whom are descended from indigenous peoples such as the Olmecs, Maya, Aztec, and other historical Mexican Indian tribes. Sixty-two indigenous groups have been identified in Mexico and the Amerindian population numbers about 30 percent. There are also small populations of Mexicans of purely European descent (mostly Spanish, but also some Germans, Italians, and French), some of whom identify as White Mexicans, which number about nine percent of the population. Like the other nations of North America, Mexico has attracted immigrants from all over the world, including China, Lebanon, Germany, the Philippines, and several Latin American countries.

The majority (about 78 percent) of Mexicans live in urban areas. The highest density areas are along the east-to-west strip between the Gulf of Mexico and Pacific Ocean in the southern half of the country, near Guadalajara and Mexico City. The Sonoran Desert area of northern Mexico (which also includes parts of Arizona and California) contains some of the least populated areas in the world. In rural areas, there are large populations of campesinos (agrarian workers), many of whom migrate to the United States.

The largest urban centers in Mexico are Mexico City, with a metropolitan area population of 21 million people, Ecatepec, Guadalajara, Puebla, Juarez, and Tijuana.

## Languages

Spanish is the official language of Mexico, and about 93 percent of the population speaks Spanish only. Nearly 300 other languages are spoken in Mexico, including more than 60 indigenous languages. Among these are dialects of Nahuatl, Mixteco, and Mazateco. Nearly six percent of the population speaks Spanish in addition to an indigenous language. Because of the remoteness of some villages in Mexico, dialects often differ within a small geographic distance.

## Native People & Ethnic Groups

Prior to Spanish conquest of the land in the 16th century, most regions of what is now known as Mexico had already been settled at various times by indigenous tribes. These included the Mayas of the Yucatan region, the Olmecs of south central Mexico, and the Aztecs, whose capital city at the time of first European contact was the city of Tenochtitlan, which is now Mexico City.

After conquest, the indigenous populations and European settlers rapidly integrated to create the Mestizo ("mixed") race. There are still very large populations of indigenous peoples throughout Mexico. Among the many tribes are the Tarahumaras, Nahuas, Huicholes, Zapotecas, and Mayas.

The main issues affecting indigenous people of Mexico in the 21st century are the continuing struggles for civil rights, education, encroachment on native lands by farmers and ranchers, religious freedom, and racism.

## Religions

Like the United States, Mexico's constitution guarantees the freedom of religion for its people. However, in some areas, such as the state of Chiapas, many non-Catholic, indigenous people have been the victims of religious discrimination. According to the 2010 census, the majority of Mexicans (about 82.7 percent) are Roman Catholic and nearly seven percent self-identify as Protestant. The remaining population practices other native religions or claims no religious affiliation.

## Climate

In general, the Mexican climate ranges from arid to tropical, temperate to humid, and rainy to dry, depending on the region. Because of the considerable elevation differences in Mexico, which vary from the high, mountainous regions to the low coastal areas, there are many differences in climate.

The average temperature in the northern portion of Baja California and throughout the northwest coastal region of Mexico is about 20° Celsius (68° Fahrenheit). At the southern point of the peninsula and along the west coast of Mexico, the average temperature is 25° Celsius (77° Fahrenheit). The average annual temperature in the central plateau region is 18° Celsius (65° Fahrenheit), while in the Yucatan Peninsular region it is 27° Celsius (80° Fahrenheit).

The average temperature of Mexico City is around 22° Celsius (72° Fahrenheit), with an annual rainfall of 66 centimeters (26 inches). The Gulf Coast area also has an annual temperature of 22° Celsius (72° Fahrenheit). Annual rainfall varies as well, from 12.7 centimeters (5 inches) in the northwest to two meters (80 inches) in the Gulf Coast.

---

## ENVIRONMENT & GEOGRAPHY

## Topography

Lying directly south of the United States, Mexico's west coast sits on the Pacific Ocean, while its east coast is on the Gulf of Mexico. Guatemala and Belize lie along the southern border and the coastal border above Belize marks the northernmost point of the Caribbean Sea. Between the Baja California peninsula and the rest of Mexico lies the Gulf of California. The Yucatan Channel separates Mexico from Cuba.

The Mexican terrain varies from north to south: northern Mexico is mostly desert, while southern Mexico is situated in a tropical rain forest region. Mexico contains several mountain ranges, including the Sierra Madre Occidental and the Sierra Madre Oriental, both of which stretch between Mexico and the United States in the north; the Cordillera Neovolcanica in central Mexico; and the Sierra Madre del Sur in southern Mexico. The coastal areas and the Yucatan Peninsula in southern Mexico are characterized by lowlands. Mexico also has many volcanoes. The highest point in Mexico, at 5,700 meters (18,700 feet), is at Volcan Pico de Orizaba, in Veracruz.

Reaching through central Mexico from the U.S. border to the southern regions is a large central plateau. Mexico City lies in the Valley of Mexico, in the central Mexican plateau. The high altitude of the city requires that newcomers take time to become accustomed to the oxygen-thin air.

Several major rivers run through Mexico: the Rio Bravo (known as the Rio Grande in the United States) and the Lerma-Santiago River. The largest lake is Lake Chapala, near the city of Guadalajara. The Mexican coastline is 9,330 kilometers (5,797 miles) long.

## Plants & Animals

Because of the diverse geography of Mexico, it is home to flora that is typical of both North American deserts (cacti, mesquite trees, and scrub grass) and rainforests (fern and high canopy). Mexico, like Brazil, has a very large variety of rainforest plants, including thousands of species that are native to Mexico. The mountainous regions contain several varieties of tree, including oak and pine.

Like the plants, the animals of Mexico vary from region to region. Common desert animals include the mountain lion, javelina, deer, bears, and coyotes, while the southern region contains such rain forest animals as tapirs and jaguars (as well as their cousin, the much smaller but no less ferocious jaguarundi). Toucans, hawks, vultures, and many other types of bird are very common throughout Mexico. The Crested Carcara is the national bird of Mexico.

## CUSTOMS & COURTESIES

### Greetings
In a professional or formal setting, the handshake is always the most appropriate way to greet someone in Mexican culture. When meeting, Mexicans will usually exchange a handshake, and some may use the formal phrase "Para servirle," or "Here to serve you."

In more informal situations, two male friends may greet each other with a handshake, accompanied by a hug and pat on the back. Between women and men, or between two women, it is common to greet each other with a single, light kiss on the cheek. When greeting a group of people, Mexicans greet each person individually with a handshake, kiss, or other physical gesture. In Mexico, just saying "Hello" without making any physical contact would be perceived as indifferent or unfriendly.

Across Mexico, it is common to greet other diners as you enter a restaurant, especially if you make eye contact with them. In addition, before asking for directions or assistance in a store, it is also polite to greet the person helping you first and then ask your question. In some cases, Mexicans will repeat a long string of polite apologies and formal greetings before asking a question. While these formal expressions may sound excessively elaborate, they are quite natural in Mexican society.

### Gestures & Etiquette
Overall, Mexicans are typically very formal with each other. Using a professional title is an important way to confer respect in Mexico. For example, a college graduate is known as a licenciado, and therefore, in many business situations, Mexicans refer to their colleagues by this title. Similarly, Mexicans may use doctor, engineer, architect, or teacher to address a professional in that field. It is also considered polite to address an elder as "Señor," or "Sir," "Señnora" or "M a'am," and "Seññorita," or "Miss."

Before beginning a meal, it is common to say "Buen provecho" to other diners. The phrase is similar to the well-known saying "Bon appétit," French for "Enjoy your meal." If one must leave a meal before everyone has stood up from the table, it is also customary to say "Provecho" again. When dining out, Mexicans generally do not split the bill. In most situations, even informal ones, one party will invite the others to the meal. The treat can be reciprocated at the next meal. Tipping servers in a restaurant is also standard etiquette in Mexico.

Conversations between friends can be very animated, and Mexicans often use their hands to express a point when talking. Many Europeans and Americans also notice that Mexicans tend to stand close to each other when they have a conversation. In addition, Mexicans are physically friendly and outgoing, frequently patting friends on the back, placing a hand on the shoulder, or making other light physical contact while talking.

In Mexico, time is less structured than in the United States or Europe. Mexicans are often punctual, but it is not considered excessively rude to arrive a bit tardy for a date or appointment, unless it is a very important event like a wedding or baptism. Mexicans are generally polite, even in harried situations. When passing someone on a crowded bus or moving past someone on the sidewalk, it is common to say "Con permiso," meaning "With your permission."

### Eating/Meals
Typically, Mexicans eat three meals each day: breakfast, a mid-day meal called "la comida", and dinner. Breakfast is usually a light meal, eaten in the morning and accompanied by juice, coffee, or hot chocolate. A larger breakfast or brunch is called "almuerzo", typically eaten a bit later than a regular breakfast (from ten o'clock to twelve o'clock in the morning). Almuerzo is usually more substantial than a typical breakfast, consisting of hearty dishes like scrambled eggs, beans, or enchiladas (stuffed tortillas in chili sauce).

Traditionally, the largest and most important meal of the day is la comida, which is eaten at about two o'clock in the afternoon. It usually consists of several courses: soup, followed by a pasta or rice course, and a main dish. Most meals are accompanied by a basket of bread or, more traditionally, flatbreads called tortillas. Diners are expected to help themselves to tortillas throughout the meal.

Throughout Mexico, many small businesses close between two o'clock and four o'clock to accommodate the comida and a short siesta, or nap. In larger cities, however, work schedules have made it more difficult for professionals to take a long break in the middle of the day. Therefore, it is increasingly unusual for businesses to close for the comida in urban areas.

Dinner is usually much lighter than lunch and eaten late in the evening, between eight and ten o'clock. Traditionally popular dinner foods include sweet bread and coffee, or tamales (corn cakes) with atole (a sweetened corn drink). While these three meals are the most common, they are by no means the only time that Mexicans eat. At any time of the day, Mexicans may sit down in a restaurant for antojitos, or snacks, and a drink.

### Visiting

Family gatherings are common in Mexico, and being invited to someone's house is usually a warm and casual experience. Guests are not typically expected to bring a gift when invited to the home of a Mexican family. However, it's always appreciated when someone offers a small contribution to the meal, such as flowers, a bottle of wine or sweets. If the family has children, it is also polite to bring a gift for a child.

---

## LIFESTYLE

---

### Family

In Mexican culture, the family is extremely important. Throughout Mexico, it is not uncommon to be very close with first and second cousins, as well as aunts, uncles, nieces, nephews, and in-laws. Mexican families were traditionally very

large, and in the 1970s, the average mother had six children. In 2014, due to widespread family planning campaigns, the average had declined to just over two.

Mexican families tend to stay close throughout their lifetime. Even in larger cities, children rarely leave their parents' home until they get married. Later in life, a parent will often live with their children and grandchildren. As such, Mexican families are an important economic community, as well as a fundamental emotional support structure.

In the 1990s, there was a surge in Mexican immigration to the United States. Immigrants who enter the United States illegally are often unable to return to Mexico for many years. As a result, many families are separated for long periods of time, even decades. In small towns with a high rate of immigration (most notably, in the central states of Michoacan and Guanajuato), very few adult men remain, interrupting the traditional family structure. However, with the American financial downturn that began in 2008 and continued political pressure within the United States to stop undocumented immigration, the rate of migration to the United States has fallen sharply.

### Housing

Traditionally, many homes in Mexico were constructed using adobe, earthen bricks composed of sun-dried mud, straw, manure, and other natural ingredients. Today, adobe is used as an inexpensive building material in rural communities. It is also simultaneously employed by some of Mexico's wealthier residents to construct traditional colonial-style homes.

In contemporary Mexico, most homes are built of brick, concrete, or stone. In urban environments, families usually live in concrete houses, apartment buildings or modern highrises. In wealthier neighborhoods, families may also live in renovated colonial era homes, typified by their Spanish architecture, stone or adobe construction, and central courtyards. By contrast, homes in rural communities are more often constructed with natural materials and many have earthen floors. Along the coast, it is common to see palapas, a thatched roof made from dried palm leaves. Often, these are used as shade on the beach or as a roof to a rustic home.

There was a severe shortage of adequate housing in Mexico during the 1980s. Today, however, most homes have access to municipal services, such as piped water, gas, and electricity. Even so, poor families often live in makeshift dwellings.

## Food

Corn, squash, beans, and chili peppers have formed the basis of the Mexican diet since pre-Columbian times. In addition to these staples, traditional Mexican food uses a variety of products native to the Americas, including tomatoes, avocados, potatoes, peanuts, nopales (prickly pear cactus), tomatillos (green tomatoes), papaya, sweet potato, and turkey. When the Spanish arrived in Mexico, the traditional cuisine evolved to incorporate European culinary techniques with new ingredients such as wheat, cheese, onions, rice, chicken, pork, and beef.

Throughout Mexico, corn or wheat dough is rolled and grilled to create tortillas, a round flatbread that accompanies most meals. Tortillas may also be wrapped around seasoned meat or vegetables to form a taco, a mainstay in popular Mexican cuisine. In addition to tortillas and other corn-based flatbreads, maize is the principal ingredient in tamales, cornmeal cakes that are stuffed with savory or sweet fillings then steamed in a banana leaf or cornhusk.

Spicy food is popular in Mexico. Salsa, a sauce made from ground chili peppers and other condiments, accompanies most dishes. Fresh fruits and juices are consumed across the country, and seafood is abundant along the coasts. Beef is prepared throughout Mexico, but is particularly popular in the north, where grilled skirt steak called carne asada is among the most popular dishes. Coffee and chocolate are also cultivated in Mexico, and are both widely consumed as a hot beverage.

In addition to daily fare, Mexican cuisine includes many highly elaborate and distinctive dishes that require time-intensive preparation. To prepare chiles en nogada, a large poblano pepper is roasted and peeled, and then stuffed with almonds, raisins, apples, cinnamon, and shredded pork. The stuffed chili is then bathed in a sweetened cream sauce and decorated with pomegranate seeds. The resulting dish features the same colors (red, white, and green) as the Mexican flag.

## Life's Milestones

The majority of Mexico's population is baptized according to Catholic tradition. In addition to the religious significance, baptism is an important event because it is the day a child's godparents are named. In Mexico, godparents are not only responsible for the child's well-being, they are also regarded as a child's spiritual guides.

The fifteenth birthday, or quinceañera, is a celebrated milestone in the life of a Mexican woman. In the past, the fifteenth birthday was regarded as the age that a girl passes into womanhood, marking her official presentation to society. Today, the quinceañera is similar to a "sweet sixteen" celebration in the United States. The quinceañera is usually celebrated with a mass at church, followed by a party. The quinceañera can often be a lavish affair and an opportunity for friends, neighbors, and extended family to gather.

It should also be noted that death plays a very important role in Mexican culture. Every November, Mexicans celebrate Dia de los Muertos (Day of the Dead), a unique holiday in which the dead are honored with altars, gifts, and remembrance. Although many Mexicans mourn their lost loved ones on this day, it is not necessarily a serious or dark holiday. On the contrary, many families celebrate the Dia de los Muertos by bringing food and drink to the cemetery, and then throwing a little party at the grave of a lost relative.

## CULTURAL HISTORY

## Art & Architecture

The indigenous peoples of Mexico were accomplished artists and craftsmen. They were skilled at weaving, metalwork, basket making, carving, embroidery, painting, and ceramics. Many pre-Columbian cultures, such as the Aztecs and Maya, were also accomplished architects and city planners. While techniques and building materials varied by region, tall limestone pyramid-temples are characteristic of most large Mesoamerican cities. Many were also built around large central plazas, which functioned as each community's commercial and religious center.

Sculpture was a popular medium among the ancient Aztec and Maya cultures. The art of the Aztecs, in particular, was largely influenced by war, and included the decoration of helmets, shields, and knives. Mayan art is believed to have flourished during the civilization's classic period (200–900 BCE), and largely featured stucco, natural glass, and jade. The Maya and Aztecs were also both known for their creation of codices, books that are largely pictorial with some ornamental script, or hieroglyphs. Religious themes are evident in the paintings found on temple walls and the discovery of colorful masks used to honor gods or in religious rituals.

With the arrival of the Spanish in the 15th century, these indigenous cultures were introduced, even forced, to learn new techniques and disciplines, such as leatherwork, beading, and glass blowing. Over time, they integrated their traditional art and architecture with Spanish culture, and the blend of these two cultures gave way to a distinctive Mexican tradition in the popular arts.

Talavera, the oldest glazed ceramic technique in the Americas, dates back to the 16th century. Craftsmen from Talavera de la Reina in Spain came to the Spanish colony and taught the indigenous people to work the region's clay and create decorative tiles and religious sculptures. Talavera flourished in the city of Puebla.

To ensure the quality and distinctive style of the ceramics of this region, a guild was formed with strict regulations governing craftsmanship. For example, the hallmark of the finest Talavera ceramics was a distinctive blue color, a pigment difficult and expensive to procure. It was therefore reserved for only the most expensive pieces. Potters were required to sign their product to guarantee authenticity. Even today, the potter's signature indicates that the Talavera piece originated in Puebla, Mexico.

In the centuries following the Spanish conquest, the arts in Mexico were closely linked to European movements. After Mexico declared independence from Spain in 1821, national identity became more pronounced. During that era, the graphic artist José Guadalupe Posada (1852–1913) produced hundreds of satirical cartoons that would later become synonymous with Mexican popular culture. His work is considered to be well-known examples of folk art.

After the Mexican Revolution of 1910, Mexico's fine art scene flourished. The government established a department to protect folk arts, and commissioned well-known painters for a new public mural program. The era would bring international fame to artists, including the famous muralists Diego Rivera (1886–1957), credited with reintroducing fresco painting into modern art; José; Clemente Orozco (1883–1949), known for his murals depicting social realism; David Alfaro Siquieros (1896–974); and expressionistic painter Frida Kahlo (1907–1954).

Printmaking has a long history in Mexico, particularly in cities such as Oaxaca, Mexico City, Morelia, and Zacatecas. Of all art forms, printmaking has a particularly strong connection to politics, rooted in the work of the 19th century artist and satirist José; Guadalupe Posada. This tradition was continued in the early 20th century by El Taller de Grááfica Popular (The Popular Graphics Workshop), which used printmaking and graphic images to promote political causes and to criticize the government of President Láázaro Cáárdenas, who was president from 1934–1940. Today, the link between political activism and printmaking continues.

## Drama

Drama has a long history in Mesoamerica. Dramatic performances, often with comedic elements, acrobats, and music, were popular among the Aztecs. During the colonial era, Spanish monks staged plays and processions to inspire the native people to convert to Catholicism.

Traditional theater companies grew during the subsequent centuries, and Mexican-penned productions contributed to the nationalistic sentiment that fueled Mexico's independence. By the late 19th century, there were numerous Mexican dramatists.

Mexican cinema dates back to the early 20th century and flourished after the Revolution. The 1930s and 1940s are generally considered the "golden age" of Mexican cinema, spearheaded by directors like Fernando de la Fuentes (1894–1958) and cinematographers like Gabriel Figueroa (1907–1997). In particular, Mexican comedies were famous throughout Latin America and the world, bringing international stardom to film personalities such as Tin-Tan (Germán Valdés, 1915–1973), Cantiflas (Mario Moreno, 1911–1983), and Pedro Infante (1917–1957). During the 1950s, Spanish surrealist filmmaker Luis Buñuel (1900–1983) made many of his most important films in Mexico, eventually becoming a Mexican citizen.

At the beginning of the 21st century, Mexican cinema experienced an exciting resurgence. Claiming a new artistic direction, Mexican movies began to capture modern life from a more contemporary and urban perspective. This new approach was ushered in by the critically acclaimed *Amores Perros* (2000), directed by Alejandro González Iñárritu. The film offers a gritty depiction of life in contemporary Mexico City.

A few years later, director Alfonso Cuarón returned to Mexico from the United States to make *Y Tú Mamá Tambien* (2001), a road movie about two teenage boys from Mexico City. *Y Tú Mamá Tambien* broke box office records in Mexico and was widely distributed throughout the world. At the same time, Hollywood continues to exert an incredible influence over Mexico's cinema. American movies outnumber Mexican productions in Mexican movie theaters, and many of Mexico's talented actors, cinematographers and directors also work extensively in Hollywood.

### Music

Mexico's musical history is diverse and full of various cultural influences, beginning with the pre-Columbian cultures of the Aztecs and Maya. While not much is known about this ancient music, archaeological evidence suggests that Mayan music featured percussion and flutes. It is believed that Aztec music was strictly used for religious purposes, often accompanying Aztec dance in a prayer-like ritual.

During the colonial era, traditional Mesoamerican songs were combined with popular European compositions and instruments to create a unique regional music tradition in Mexico. During the 18th century, the central Mexican state of Jalisco gave birth to the mariachi band. Mariachi bands feature several violins, trumpets, a small five-string guitar, and a jarana, which is a larger five-string guitar common in Mexican folk music. The robust vocal style that accompanies mariachi music is also one of its trademarks. At the same time, music on the Gulf coast was heavily influenced by Caribbean sounds. Huapangos is a well-known style from the region, traditionally played by a three-piece band comprised of a guitar, a violin, and a jarana.

Inspired by the Spanish "romance" style, Mexican corridos are popular ballads that recount stories with a distinctly patriotic flavor. Corridos have their roots in the 19th century, and flourished during the Revolution of 1910, when they were used to pass stories and messages between insurgents and countrymen. European styles such as polka and waltz also began to influence Mexican music in the 19th century. This influence can be heard in musica norteña, a uniquely Mexican musical style that combines the bajo sexto (a twelve-string guitar) with the button accordion.

Dance, like drama, stems from the religious rituals of the pre-Columbian cultures. These traditions later blended with Spanish traditions to create diverse regional folk dances. Of the many dances that proliferated in the post-colonial era, one example is the Jarabe Tapatio from Jalisco. Considered Mexico's national dance, the Jarabe Tapatio is danced in pairs to a series of nine melodies, typically following an upbeat, heel-to-toe step.

In the early 19th century, the artistic rejuvenation of Mexico resulted in an increased interest in contemporary and classical dance. In the 1940s, the National Academy of Dance was formed. In the 1950s, Amalia Hernandez founded a unique dance troupe. Known today as the Ballet Folklórico de Mexico, the troupe performs folk dances from across the country in the Palacio de Bellas Artes (the Palace of Fine Arts) in Mexico City.

## Literature

Before the arrival of the Spanish, Mesoamericas's most celebrated poet was Nezahualcoyotl (1402–1472), an Alcolhua prince from the city-state of Texcoco. An accomplished philosopher, city-planner and ruler, Nezahualcoyotl's verse was recited widely and inspired many other indigenous poets, before and after the conquest. However, many argue that the birth of Mexican literature began with the great conquistador, Hernán Cortés (1485–1547), who wrote descriptive accounts of the conquest of Mexico. At the same time, other colorful chronicles of the conquest were produced by both Spanish and indigenous writers.

During the colonial era, Mexican literature followed European styles and trends. Among the most celebrated writers was a 17th-century nun named Sor Juana Inez de la Cruz (1651–1695), a poet and humanist. Her contemporary, Juan Ruiz de Alarcón (1581–1639), also earned a long-standing reputation as a Baroque dramatist. In addition, Mexican writer José Joaquín Fernández de Lizardi (1776–1827) is credited with having the first novel written and published in Latin America. The novel, *El Periquillo Sarniento* (The Mangy Parrot), is considered a definitive example of a picaresque novel, which employs the first-person narrative of a low-social class hero.

During the 19th century, Mexican literature was influenced by European romanticism. Mexico later became a center for modernism in Latin America. The 20th century introduced a wealth of contemporary novelists and thinkers to the literary scene, including poets José Gorostiza (1901–1973), Xavier Villaurrutia (1903–1950), and Mariano Azuela (1873–1952), who wrote fictionalized accounts of the 1910 Mexican Revolution. Many of these 20th century writers became well-known for exploring national themes and identity. In 1990, renowned poet and essayist Octavio Paz (1914–1998) was awarded the Nobel Prize in Literature.

# CULTURE

## Arts & Entertainment

Leading up to and after the Mexican Revolution of 1910, the arts took on a distinct Mexican character, exploring the mixture of indigenous and Spanish cultures that defines modern Mexican society. During this period, the Mexican government invested heavily in popular culture. Important intellectuals such as José Vasconcelos, a former minister of education, initiated many public arts programs that would have lasting effects. The work of Mexico's muralists and other politically minded artists brought worldwide renown to the country's modern art scene.

In contemporary Mexico, a closer relationship with the United States and the international art community has created more freedom of expression. As revolutionary fervor subsided, subsequent generations abandoned the strong political, patriotic and didactic, or instructive, themes that dominated Mexican art for the first half of the 20th century. Mexico's renowned Oaxacan painter, Rufino Tamayo (1899–1991), became internationally recognized for his abstract, expressive, and personal paintings, using a vibrant palette of colors. Moving away from overt nationalism but retaining a unique, Mexican character, Tamayo's work had a major impact on 20th-century painting in Mexico.

Today, Oaxacan artists such as Sergio Hernandez and Francisco Toledo have built on Tamayo's style to develop a unique Oaxacan school of art. This is characterized by whimsical, magical, or mythological symbols and saturated colors. Outside of Oaxaca, Mexican contemporary art has evolved to include genres such as digital photography and performance art to minimalist sculpture and representational painting. Some contemporary artists, such as the Castro Leñero brothers, have moved away from the use of distinctly Mexican imagery. Others, like Damien Flores Cortés, continue to use traditional Mexican symbols and concepts as the basis of their work. In addition, printmaking continues to be an important art for evoking political activism. For example, during the 2006 teacher's strike in Oaxaca, groups of politically minded artists made woodblock prints in support of the uprising.

While Mexico's rural population has experienced a drastic decline in recent decades, traditional arts and crafts continue to flourish in the 21st century, especially in smaller towns. Today, Mexico is famous for its production of textiles, woodworking, toys, embroidery, ceramics, baskets and tooled leather, among other crafts. To celebrate the rich heritage of Mexican craft, there are numerous popular art museums throughout the country which retain samples from the cultural traditions of the region. Although most craftwork relies on centuries-old techniques and design, it does respond to current events. After the indigenous insurrection in the state of Chiapas in 1994, local women began weaving small woolen dolls resembling the rebel leader, Subcomandante Marcos.

Throughout Mexico, music continues to be a uniting force. Street musicians are common in many cities. Most Mexicans, young and old, know the lyrics to dozens of corridos, rancheras (country songs), and other traditional tunes. Mariachi bands play at weddings and other special events, and often perform at the Plaza de los Mariachi in the city of Guadalajara. Throughout Mexico, there are annual festivals celebrating every style of folk song and folk dance. For example, Oaxaca's annual Guelaguetza festival unites the music and dance traditions from the state's eight regions.

Traditional songs, especially corridos, are still widely played by contemporary banda and norteña music groups. In the past decades, corridos have evolved to include modern tales of violence and betrayal by the drug cartels, in what is referred to as a narco-corrido. Sinaloa-born band

Los Tigres del Norte have incorporated Latin rhythms like cumbia into their norteña sound, often drawing huge crowds on both sides of the U.S.–Mexico border.

Contemporary Mexican music has also grown to embrace more international sounds. New music groups in Mexico range from rock, pop, and dance, to reggae and techno. Mexico is one of the biggest producers of rock en español (rock music in Spanish), as well as other modern genres like hip-hop and rap. Creative and popular, Mexican rock often does more than simply copy American and British styles. The premiere example is Café Tacuba, a Mexico City group whose catchy music combines a surprising number of musical styles and genres.

Many contemporary Mexican novelists and writers continue to address Mexican themes in their work. The 20th century's great poet and thinker, Octavio Paz, was the author of *The Labyrinth of Solitude* (1950), a controversial exploration of the Mexican psychology. Paz's contemporaries include novelists such as Juan Rulfo (1917–1986), José Revueltas (1914–1976), Vicente Leñero, Jorge Ibargüengoitia, and Carlos Fuentes.

## Cultural Sites & Landmarks

Mexico has been continuously inhabited for thousands of years. The ancient cultures of Mesoamerica were among the most elaborate and populous civilizations of their time. Because of its history, Mexico is home to numerous historic centers and pre-Hispanic archeological sites. In fact, Mexico boasts nearly 30 United Nations Educational, Scientific and Cultural Organization (UNESCO) World Heritage Sites.

As far back as 1200 BCE, the Olmec civilization inhabited the Gulf coast, building one its largest cities at La Venta in the Mexican state of Tabasco. Today, the ruins of La Venta are one of Mesoamerica's most important archeological sites. The anthropology museum in Jalapa, Veracruz, holds an extensive collection of Olmec art and artifacts. In the valley of Oaxaca, the Zapotec civilization built the picturesque mountaintop city of Monte Albán around 300 BCE. In modern Oaxaca's historic center, a corresponding museum in a former convent contains numerous artifacts from Monte Albán, as well as anthropological exhibits on Oaxaca's cultural history.

To the south, the Maya flourished between 250 and 900 CE. Today, the jungles of southern Mexico are dotted with the ruins of ancient Mayan cities. The ruins of Chichén Itzá, located on the Yucatan peninsula, and Palenque, located in eastern Chiapas, are the most sizable, well-known, and widely visited Mayan sites. The ancient city of Calakmul, in the Mexican state of Campeche, is also one of the largest Mayan sites discovered.

Located just outside Mexico City, construction began on the massive pre-Columbian city of Teotihuacan in the first century CE. At its height, Teotihuacan was one of the largest cities in the world, covering 20 square kilometers (7.7 square miles). Built by an unknown civilization, the most distinctive feature of this unique monument are two enormous pyramids—the Pyramid of the Sun and the Pyramid of the Moon—which tower over an elaborate grid of avenues. It became a World Heritage Site in 1987.

Mexico City's Centro Histórico, or Historic Center, has been designated a UNESCO World Heritage Site. The hub of this district is its main square, the Plaza de la Constitución, familiarly known as El Zócalo. This square covers the former ceremonial center of Tenochtitlan and contains buildings dating to the 16th century. While many similar pre-Columbian cities were abandoned by the 15th century, the Aztec capital of Tenochtitlan was a powerful metropolis when the Spanish landed in the New World. After overpowering the Aztecs, the Spanish built a new city upon the ruins of Tenochtitlan. Taking stones from the Aztec pyramids, the Spanish constructed the metropolitan cathedral, which still stands in modern Mexico City's central square.

Adjoining the cathedral are the ruins of Templo Mayor, the great Aztec pyramid that was destroyed in the conquest. Today, the Templo Mayor archeo-logical site and accompanying museum offer a deeper look into the ancient Aztec city.

Another World Heritage Site in Mexico City is the floating gardens of Xochimilco. Flower gardens on reed boats, or chinampas, provide fresh blooms such as gardenias, hibiscus, and roses. This spot, away from the noise and smog of the city, is popular with both tourists and locals.

Other famous sights in the capital include the Casa de los Azulejos (House of Tiles), a particularly beautiful example of 17th baroque architecture; the National Autonomous University of Mexico, whose walls are famously covered with murals, and the shrine of the Virgin of Guadalupe in the Villa Gustavo A. Madero. The Palacio de Bellas Artes (Palace of Fine Arts) is the home of the famed Ballet Folklorico de Mexico and the National Museum of Anthropology, which has artifacts from 5,000 years of Mexican history. The Bosque de Chapultepec (Chapultepec Park) boasts forests and gardens, Chapultepec Castle, museums, a lake, an amusement park, and the official residence of the president of Mexico.

Other magnificent Mexican colonial cities are architecturally unique and very beautiful. Many have also received the designation of World Heritage Site, including Puebla, Morelia, Guanajuato, and Zacatecas.

Finally, some of Mexico's natural landmarks include the protected islands in the Gulf of California, a whale sanctuary, and the Mariposa Monarca Biosphere Reserve, created to protect the Monarch butterfly. All three nature sites are protected as UNESCO World Heritage Sites.

## Libraries & Museums

During the 19th century, many French-style buildings were constructed in Mexico City's center. Among these, the Palacio de Belles Artes (the Palace of Fine Arts) is considered a fine example of neo-classical and art deco design. Designed by the 20th-century architect Pedro Ramírez Vázquez, the impressive National Anthropology Museum in Mexico City is another famous landmark, housing an extensive collection of art, ceramics, human remains and other artifacts from Mexico's pre-Hispanic cultures.

The late 20th-century artists and revolutionaries Frida Kahlo and Diego Rivera are Mexico City's most famous residents. Their home and studio has been preserved as a museum, and their work is exhibited throughout the city. Mexico City is home to over 60 museums.

The National Library of Mexico dates back to the early 19th century. Among its collection is a rare edition of Dante's *Divine Comedy* dating back to 1498.

### Holidays

Holidays in Mexico include Constitution Day (February 5), the Birthday of Benito Juarez (March 21), Cinco de Mayo (May 5), Independence Day (September 16), Day of the Dead (November 2), Revolution Day (November 20), and Christmas Day (December 25).

### Youth Culture

In contemporary Mexico, youth culture is greatly influenced by the United States—and American films, brands of clothing, and music are widespread. In addition, punk, goth, and hippie subcultures have also taken root across Mexico. In fact, the influence of American culture continues to grow as more Mexicans spend time north of the border. However, many young people embrace the traditional cultures of Mexico, especially in smaller or rural cities and towns. In northern Mexico, traditional musical genres such as ranchera and norteño are as popular with youth as they are with adult listeners. Throughout Mexico sonideros (deejays) that play cumbia and other Latin dance music are extraordinarily popular as well.

Many Mexican youth are focused on their future. Academics are taken seriously in middle class families, and many students also study art, traditional dance, or music. Football (soccer), a nationally popular pastime, is particularly popular with youth. Attending a match between two rival teams is the distinct dominion of rowdy youngsters. Nightlife is also popular, and discos, clubs, and bars are often packed during the weekend with revelers in most medium-sized and large cities.

## SOCIETY

### Transportation

Cars in Mexico travel on the right side of the road. According to the U.S. Department of State, those U.S. citizens who wish to travel using their own vehicles in Mexico may do so (a U.S. driver's license is accepted in Mexico), but are advised to purchase Mexican insurance and to obtain a temporary import permit. Additionally, driving at night can be dangerous, as driving lanes and road shoulders tend to be narrow. Mexico has an extensive system of toll roads that are fairly well maintained.

Despite the availability and affordability of public transportation, a third of the population in Mexico City uses a car for transportation. This creates daily traffic jams and gridlock. Excessive use of automobiles has created a persistent smog problem in Mexico City. The government has tried to improve the situation by banning certain groups of cars (based on registration numbers) one day a week. Strict industrial regulations have also considerably improved the air quality in the city.

The major airport is the Benito Juárez International Airport (also known as the Mexico City International Airport).

### Transportation Infrastructure

Mexico's highways are extensive, modern, and well maintained, serving every major region in the country. However, there are many rural communities, especially in the southern states, that are not serviced by paved roads. Overall, Mexico's public bus system is efficient, offering affordable transportation between major urban areas, as well as smaller towns. Often, rural communities are serviced by colectivos (taxis or small vans) that function as an alternative or replacement for bus services.

Mexico City's neighborhoods are linked by one of the world's most extensive and inexpensive subway systems. In 2007, the city also added a new rapid transit bus line.

## Media & Communications

Large media conglomerates control most of Mexico's communications channels. Historically, Televisa Group is the largest and most powerful media company, with deep political ties. The media corporation's holdings include numerous television stations, newspapers, radio stations, and museums. After the election of Vicente Fox in 2000, however, Televisa's political ties weakened slightly. This resulted in more competition in the market. In addition to privately owned stations, the government runs two public television stations, available on a limited basis throughout the republic.

There are many daily newspapers in Mexico, some distributed nationally and others strictly regional. Dailies in Mexico range from the intellectual and opinionated leftist paper *La Jornada* to sensationalistic tabloids that graphically cover violent crimes and murders, often related to Mexico's increasingly violent drug cartels and trade.

Internet use is widespread throughout the country, as is telephone and cell phone use. Previously state-owned, Telmex is now a private company that controls over 80 percent of the country's ground lines. The owner of Telmex, Carlos Slim Helú, also controls a majority of the country's Internet service and over 70 percent of the cellular market.

## SOCIAL DEVELOPMENT

## Standard of Living

The median age among Mexicans is approximately 26 years, while life expectancy is 73 years for men and 79 years for women. The infant mortality rate in Mexico is 12.58 deaths per 1,000

live births (2014 estimate). Mexico's Human Development Index (HDI) rank is 71.

## Water Consumption

According to the World Health Organization and UNICEF, as of 2012, 95 percent of the total population used improved drinking sources (but only 91 percent in rural areas). Eighty-five percent of the population used improved sanitation facilities, with that number dropping to 79 percent in rural areas. Water and sanitation in Mexico, as the statistics show, is improved in cities, but is a real concern in rural areas. Historically, Mexico City has suffered from water shortages that have forced the city to ration running water.

Reports indicate that most of the running water in Mexico is extracted from rivers and lakes, which suffer from over-exploitation and pollution. The Mexican government, through its agency the National Water Commission (CONAGUA) is increasing investment in improving water resources, and while Mexico leads Latin America, it still faces significant challenges.

As of February 2010, the Mexican government had established the National Infrastructure Fund, a national effort to invest in infrastructure spending targeted at highways, waterworks, and ports. The government hopes to expand access to clean water. As part of that effort, a 200-kilometer pipeline is planned from Falcon Lake to Matamoros.

## Education

The right to a free education is guaranteed by the Mexican constitution. Public education is compulsory for Mexicans through secondary school, but the education levels achieved by many in this poor nation are not, on average, very high. This is due in part to the inability of the government to keep pace with explosive population growth in the last few decades, as well as extreme poverty throughout the country.

According to a 2005 study conducted by the RAND Corporation, Mexico's educational system suffers from low achievement, insufficient enrollment, high drop out rates, and a lack of secondary institutions in rural areas. Additionally, the study points to an insufficient number of educational professionals to address the basic needs of schools.

Only 36 percent of Mexicans over the age of 15 have any primary education, while only two percent of the population has a college education. Despite this, most Mexican states have at least one university, and overall there are 240 post-secondary institutions. Among the most prominent colleges in Mexico are the National Autonomous University of Mexico, the University of Guadalajara, and the National Polytechnic University.

The literacy rate in Mexico is about 93.5 percent, a significant rise over previous years, thanks in part to a public literacy drive (2011 estimate). Men enjoy an advantage, averaging a literacy rate of 94.8 percent to the female literacy rate of 92.3. Although statistics show that the rate of school enrollment has risen rapidly, from 1970s totals of 9.7 million students to 2000 totals of 21.6 million, advances have not kept pace with enrollment. In 2005, Rand reported that the total enrollment in all levels, including university, stood at 31 million students.

### Women's Rights

Women have always played an important role in Mexican society and culture, though their legal protections and civil rights have not always been equal to those of their male counterparts. In 1947, women were given the right to vote, but could not stand for election. In 1975, an equal rights amendment was added to the Mexican constitution. As of 2012, 48 percent of women over the age of 15 are active in the workforce (as opposed to 83 percent of men) and women are now represented in a wide range of professional and managerial positions. It is not uncommon to see female journalists and academics, and women occupy about 20 percent of the country's government posts.

A predominantly Catholic country, Mexico was slow to adopt family planning into its public health agenda. However, education about family planning has become more far-reaching in recent decades. In 2000, Mexico's public office of reproductive health was honored with the United Nations Population Fund's (UNPFA) Population Award. UNPFA's commendation of Mexico's family planning work included praise for its youth education program, which includes age-appropriate sexual education resources through non-governmental organizations (NGOs) and governmental institutions. In 2007, Mexico City legalized abortion during the first 12 weeks of pregnancy.

Due to immigration and child abandonment, Mexico's percentage of single-mother households is over 20 percent. Female-headed households have a higher poverty rate than two-parent homes. This has been referred to as the "feminization of poverty." Despite advances, a lack of health and legal services for women persists in rural communities. Currently, only 84 percent of births are attended by a skilled practitioner. In addition, domestic violence continues to be widespread and underreported. In 2007, President Calderón signed a law that obligates federal and local authorities to prevent and punish domestic violence and violence against women. On the state level, however, several states do not criminalize intra-familiar violence, and other states only punish repeat offenders. Similarly, rape victims find little recourse through the legal system, and therefore, rarely file complaints against their attackers.

Many women have taken key roles as political organizers and community activists. When participating in protests, women are often arrested and imprisoned, where they are more vulnerable to rape and abuse than their male counterparts. In 2006, a protest in San Salvador Atenco, the municipal seat of Mexico State, lead to the arrest of at least 45 women, 26 of who reported physical and sexual assault from police officials while they were detained.

Mexico has also come under international scrutiny for the unsolved homicides of hundreds of young women in Ciudad Juarez, beginning in 1993. Amnesty International has publicly repudiated authorities for failing to apprehend the criminals or put a stop to the violence. In 2007,

Amnesty International reported that members of the pro-women organization Nuestras Hijas de Regreso a Casa (Our Daughters Return Home) had received death threats for their attempts to raise awareness about the crimes.

## Health Care

Health care in Mexico is subsidized by the government based on employment status. The Instituto Mexicano del Seguro Social (IMSS) or Mexico's social security system offers healthcare to those in the private sector, and those premiums are covered by employees, employers, and the federal government.

Government employees are covered by the Instituto de Seguridad y Servicios Sociales de los Trabajadores del Estado (ISSSTE). Those who fall outside of those two systems are covered under state insurance plans, which benefit from federal subsidies. Mexico's primary health care challenges are a direct result of poverty: in rural areas and on the fringes of large urban centers, health care is endangered by a lack of resources and little, if any, public health awareness. Other challenges include state health expenditures and a lack of quality in existing health centers.

Because of these and other problems, national health care has been an area of consideration, with the goal of achieving universal health care, greater health equality for all Mexicans and the institution of massive public health education reforms. In 2006 and in 2009, the government implemented health care insurance advances for children and pregnant women.

## GOVERNMENT

## Structure

Mexico is comprised of 31 states, each with its own capital city and state constitution, and one federal district, which contains the capital city, Mexico City. It is a federal republic with executive, legislative, and judicial branches of government.

The president, both head of state and head of government, is elected to a six-year term. The Mexican legislative body is the Congress, comprised of both a Chamber of Deputies and a Senate. Neither the president nor members of Congress may be elected for consecutive terms.

For many years, Mexico was ruled by the Partido Revolucionario Institucional (PRI), but has been ruled by the Partido Accion Nacional (PAN) between 2000–2012, with PRI's Enrique Peña Nieto winning the presidential election in 2012. The current Mexican constitution was adopted in 1917.

## Political Parties

In 2015, Mexican politics was characterized by three dominant parties: the National Action Party (PAN), the Institutional Revolutionary Party (PRI), and the Party of the Democratic Revolution (PRD). While other parties existed, such as the Labor Party (PT), Green Ecological Party of Mexico (PVEM), and Convergence, they are not considered major parties with significant influence.

Of the three major parties, the PRI has enjoyed the longest held control of the executive and legislative branches since the revolution. The PRI is a center-left party, often characterized as neoliberal. In 1997, as a result of an economic crisis and claims of corruption, the PRI lost its majority in the congress. In the presidential election of 2000, they also lost the presidency. In the early part of the 21st century, the PRI experienced internal struggles, but gained seats in the congress in the 2009 legislative elections, putting them in a plurality in the congress. It also took the presidency in 2012.

The PAN is a center-right party that held the presidency for over a decade beginning in 2000, when Vicente Fox's election thwarted the efforts of the PRI. His successor, Felipe Calderón, was elected in 2006, but the PAN lost to the PRI, headed by Enrique Pena Nieto, in 2012. The PAN party is more conservative in nature, favoring privatization, free-enterprise, and opposing abortion and gay marriage.

The PRD finds its history in the PRI. Established in 1989, the PRD was founded by left-wing members of the PRI. The PRI holds considerable influence in Mexico City or the federal district, where it has held power since 1997. It came close to winning the presidency in 2006, but was edged out by Calderón by .58 points. Another close call occurred in 2012.

## Local Government

Although Mexico's 31 states have their own constitutions, governors, legislatures, and judicial systems, as well as right to levy taxes, they are highly dependent on the federal government for revenue to support municipalities. Historically, and more so when the PRI held political power, the president had much influence in local politics and in determining the candidates for state governor.

State governments are led by a governor, who is elected for a six-year term (and no more), and a unicameral legislature. The legislature meets for two sessions each year; members are elected for three-year terms.

Municipalities within states, led by a mayor or regente and a council, serve three-year terms. Municipalities provide for public services, infrastructure, and public safety. Municipalities may levy local taxes, as well as tap into federal funding.

The federal district, Mexico City, was traditionally led by the president of Mexico and an appointed elected mayor. In the 1990s, this changed and the mayor and a Legislative Assembly are now elected by residents of the district to deal with local affairs. Unlike the states, the federal district does not have a constitution, but a Statute of Government. The legislature in Mexico City is known to be less conservative than the federal government and many Mexican states, as it has expanded access to abortion and legalized gay marriage.

## Judicial System

The Supreme Court of Justice is the nation's highest court, consisting of ten judges and one chief justice. In the federal court system, which largely handles civil cases and major felonies, there are three levels: the Collegiate Circuit Court deals with issues of individual rights; the Unitary Circuit Court deals with appeals; and District Courts address commercial, civil, criminal, and labor issues.

States have their own local courts that address more common civil, familial, and criminal matters with limited economic significance.

In Mexico, the constitution dictates that a trial and sentence must occur within 12 months of an arrest. The legal system in Mexico is based on civil law, which means that laws are codified, with the legislature the source of the law, and where courts are not bound by judicial precedent.

## Taxation

The bulk of taxation in Mexico takes place on the federal level and includes income tax, value-added tax (VAT), and payroll taxes (a one percent tax on salary, social security, and housing tax). The federal government also levies excise taxes and taxes on alcohol, cigarettes, fuel, telephone, and cars.

Corporations pay an income tax as well as taxes on the value of corporate assets.

Local taxes are levied on real property (buildings, land, homes, etc.), salaries, and the acquisition of real property.

## Armed Forces

The Mexican armed forces number about 280,000 service personnel (2013 estimate), with an army (that also encompasses the air force), and a navy. The Mexican government has adopted a non-interventionist policy when it comes to international affairs, but there have been recent discussions of a shift in the policy in recent years to allow forces to assist in United Nations— peacekeeping efforts.

In the first decade of the 21st century, armed forces in Mexico spent considerable time addressing issues surrounding drug trafficking and organized crime, particularly along the U.S. border. According to the U.S. Department of State, 400 officers out of an 8,000 total number of individuals were killed in 2009 due to drug-related violence.

## Foreign Policy

Officially, Mexico's foreign policy is based on several guiding principles. Most notably, Mexico promotes a policy of non-intervention, banishment of the use of force, respect for the self-determination of nations, and the legal equality of all states. Traditionally, the Mexican government has been more concerned with national issues than with world affairs, and Mexico has a history of maintaining neutrality throughout international conflicts.

Although Mexico's focus is largely internal, the country's foreign policy has been shaped by its powerful neighbor. The United States has considerable influence over the Mexican economy. Furthermore, it is estimated that 10 percent of Mexican nationals live in the United States. As such, it has always been in Mexico's national interest to maintain a positive relationship with its neighbor to the north. To that extent, Mexico, the United States, and Canada co-signed the North American Free Trade Agreement (NAFTA) in 1994. NAFTA opened up more foreign policy interaction between Mexico and Canada and fortified Mexico's link to the United States. Today, Canada is Mexico's second largest export market.

At the beginning of the 21st century, the relationship between the United States and Mexico warmed. The administrations of both President Vicente Fox and President George W. Bush discussed the possibility of granting amnesty for Mexicans living illegally in the United States. However, after the terrorist attacks of September 11, 2001, North American security became the chief concern of the U.S. government, putting immigration and free trade on a back burner. During the administration of U.S. President Barack Obama, amnesty—or any path to citizenship—became a polarizing political issue, as Republicans cooled on the idea. While Mexico had already become a lower priority for the United States, the relationship cooled further with the denial of President Fox's request for the extradition a Mexican national on death row in Texas (Mexico does not allow capital punishment).

In 2002, Mexico took a seat as a non-permanent member of the United Nations Security Council. This provided Mexico with an opportunity to cast an important vote on the American resolution for the forcible disarmament of Iraq. Fearing further strain with their northern ally, Mexico did not immediately cast a vote.

Eventually, due to the widespread anti-war sentiment among the Mexican people, Mexico voted against U.S. –led involvement in Iraq.

Mexico's relationship with Cuba has reflected its foreign policy of free determination and non-intervention. Mexico traditionally maintained a friendly relationship with Cuba. It was the first country on the American continent to open diplomatic relations with Fidel Castro's communist government. Through much of its history, Cuba depended on Mexico's support to integrate more fully into the Latin American and global community. During the Vicente Fox administration (2000–06), however, the historically warm relations between Mexico and Cuba began to cool. In one case, Mexico voted against Cuba in human rights condemnations in the United Nations , which lead to greater isolation of the island nation.

**Human Rights Profile**

International human rights law insists that states respect civil and political rights, and also promote an individual's economic, social, and cultural rights. The United Nations Universal Declaration on Human Rights (UDHR) is recognized as the standard for international human rights. Its authors sought the counsel of the world's great thinkers, philosophers, and religious leaders, and were careful to create a document that reflects the core values shared by every world culture. (To read this document or view the articles relating to cultural human rights, go to: http://www.udhr. org/UDHR/default.htm.)

Mexico has an inconsistent record in regards to human rights. While Mexico holds itself accountable to almost every international human rights treaty, reports of human rights violations are widespread. In addition, the Mexican government has provided few pathways for victims to report or prosecute human rights abuses.

Article 19 of the UDHR protects an individual's right to freedom of opinion and expression. In 2007, Mexican president Felipe Calderón officially decriminalized defamation, libel, and slander at the federal level. Only three of Mexico's 31 states have followed suit, leaving journalists and writers vulnerable to criminal suits for defamation.

Throughout Mexico, investigative journalists and commentators are often threatened or attacked after covering organized crime, drug cartels, government activity, or other sensitive topics. In 2007, for example, the office of a regional newspaper in Hermosillo, Sonora, was attacked with grenades. In 2008, two indigenous radio announcers were ambushed and murdered in San Juan Copala, Oaxaca. The crime was officially condemned by the director general of UNESCO. Due to these and other similar occurrences, the watchdog organization Reporters Without Borders has declared Mexico the most dangerous country in Latin America for journalists.

Although Article 20 protects the right to peaceful assembly, recent political gatherings have resulted in reports of unlawful suppression and related human rights violations in Mexico. For example, during the seven months of political protests in Oaxaca in 2006, there were widespread reports of arbitrary detention, a violation of Article 9. There were also reports of other human rights abuses, including excessive use of force, torture, and harassment of journalists. This is in direct violation of Article 5, which demands that no one be subjected to torture or to cruel, inhuman or degrading treatment. During the events in Oaxaca, an American photojournalist was shot and killed while covering the protests. Furthermore, there is little evidence that the state or federal government has conducted a thorough investigation in response to the reporter's death.

Mexico's National Human Rights Commission (Comision Nacional de los Derechos Humanos, or CNDH) has a disappointing history of inefficient prosecution of human rights violations. The commission's shortcomings were the focus of a 2008 Human Rights Watch report. Human Rights Watch lists numerous examples of the CNDH's inability to bring criminal actions to justice. For example, in 2006 anti-globalization protestors in Guadalajara were arrested and arbitrarily detained, many reporting that police abused them. In response to these claims, CNDH created a document stating that torture and other abuses took place, and called on the governor of Jalisco to prosecute. When the governor received the report, he denounced the findings, effectively ending the investigation.

Also troubling is the violence related to Mexico's drug cartels. With the election of President Felipe Calderón in 2006, increased activity from international drug cartels led to greater militarization of the country, blurring the lines between legal enforcement and excessive force. There were reports of the military using excessive force against civilian citizens in the Sinaloa, Oaxaca, Michoacan, and Mexico State during 2007, though none of these cases were officially investigated by the government. Under President Pena, militarization was scaled back somewhat, but gang violence against civilians, and the escape from prison of a few major drug kingpins, created a call for heightened response to crime by the government.

## Migration

The United States is the leading choice for Mexican immigrants seeking a higher standard of living. About nine percent of the Mexican-born population lives in the United States. According to the Pew Hispanic Center, the Mexican-born population in the United States numbered 11.4 million in 2012, the majority settling in California, Texas, and the South, and accounting for one-third of the illegal immigrant population in the United States. While traditionally an agricultural migration that was circular in nature (meaning that immigrants traveled back and forth between Mexico and the United States), the influx of immigrants from Mexico to the United States in the early 21st century has been attributed to jobs in the construction and service industries, with only a portion of the population returning to Mexico.

## ECONOMY

### Overview of the Economy

In its recent past, Mexico experienced periods of sustained economic troubles due to foreign debt, an overvaluation of the peso and ineffective economic policies. Beginning in the 1990s, however, there were signs of some economic growth and reform, and Mexico entered the 21st century in a better economic position than might have been expected.

Mexico is considered an upper-income country and is highly dependent on its export market. The North American Free Trade Agreement (NAFTA) is credited with tripling trade in Mexico and the country is engaged in 12 trade agreements with over 40 countries. With the onset of the global economic recession in 2008, trade figures for 2009 indicated a decrease in gross domestic product (GDP) of seven percent. However, the Mexican GDP recovered quickly and as of 2013 totaled $1.261 billion (USD).

Increasing privatization and modernization characterize the country's growth priorities. The service sector accounts for 61 percent of the economy, manufacturing more than 34 percent, and agriculture four percent. Unemployment in the country was estimated at 9.4 percent in 2012 according to the U.S. Central Intelligence Agency. The employment force, numbering 51 million people, is primarily employed in the service sector and 52.3 percent of the population lives below the food-based poverty line, while 47 lived below the asset-based poverty line (2012 estimate).

The major conservation issues facing Mexico include hazardous waste treatment; large urban migration; lack of potable water in some areas, most notably the north; industrial pollution and massive air pollution in major cities, including Mexico City; and deforestation in the rainforest region.

## Industry

Mexico's major manufacturing industries are food and beverage production, tobacco, chemicals and petrochemicals, iron and steel, petroleum, and tourism. Among its most important exports are manufactured goods, oil and oil products, silver, fruits, and coffee. Mexico is also one of the largest suppliers of crude oil to the United States. The major export partners for Mexico are the United States (which consumes 70 percent of its goods), Japan, and China. In 2013, Mexico's estimated per capita GDP was an estimated $15,600.

## Labor

Mexico's labor force consists of 51 million people. The unemployment rate was around nine percent in 2013, but nearly 25 percent of workers are considered underemployed, which translates into high rates of poverty even among those who are working.

## Energy/Power/Natural Resources

Because of its uneven, often harsh, terrain, Mexico has few natural agricultural resources. Major natural resources of Mexico include petroleum, silver, copper, fluorite, manganese, gold, lead, zinc, gypsum, natural gas, and timber.

## Fishing

With 11,500 kilometers of coastline, the Pacific coast accounts for the bulk of the nation's total catch; this includes lobster, shrimp, croaker, albacore, skipjack, and anchovies. The Gulf of Mexico is also a source for shrimp. The Mexican fishing industry, despite its access to fertile fishing grounds, lags behind that of the United States, Canada, and Japan. Again, infrastructure spending in processing and freezing plants would address some of these issues.

## Forestry

Of Mexico's forested area, which accounts for nine percent of its territory, about 65 percent consist of hardwoods, which are the backbone of its commercial market. Hardwoods include mahogany, cedar, primavera, sapote, oak, copa, and pine. Forestry only contributed one percent to the nation's GDP. The nation's forests are under threat of overexploitation.

## Mining/Metals

Mexico is considered one of the major producers of metals in the world. It is the second major producer of silver, bismuth, and fluorspar and sixth producer of zinc. Iron copper, silver, and zinc represented the bulk of mining exports and in 2006, the mining industry in Mexico was valued at $8.1 million (USD).

## Agriculture

The most important agricultural commodities in Mexico are corn, beans, wheat, soybeans, rice, cotton, coffee, and dairy products. Subsistence farming is a major part of Mexican agriculture, but does not produce many goods for sale.

## Animal Husbandry

Beef and chicken are the most important livestock in Mexico.

## Tourism

Each year, tourism generates around 13.2 percent of Mexico's GDP. More than 22 million international tourists, mostly from the United States, visited Mexico in 2008, earning Mexico $13.2 billion (USD) for the year.

Popular destinations in Mexico include coastal attractions on the Baja California Peninsula, and in Cancun, Puerto Vallarta, and Puerto Escondido. Cultural attractions abound in most cities and regions of Mexico, such as Acapulco, Guadalajara, Puebla, Guanajuato, and Mexico City. There are also many archaeological attractions in such places as Campeche and Calakmul. In addition, there are many natural features of Mexico that attract tourists, including the volcanoes Popocatetetl and Iztaccihuatl.

Many U.S. citizens enjoy trips to the northern border cities of Ciudad Juarez, Chihuahua (Texas at El Paso), Nogales, Sonora (Arizona at Nogales) and Tijuana, Baja California (California at San Diego), but these destinations are derided as tourist locales because they offer travelers an extremely limited view of Mexican culture.

*Julie Doherty, Ellen Bailey, Craig Belanger*

## DO YOU KNOW?

- Mexico declared its independence from Spain in 1821.
- "Chapultepec" means "hill of grasshoppers."
- Famous entertainers from Mexico include actors Salma Hayek, Diego Luna, and Gael Garcia Bernal.
- Chocolate is made from the beans of the cacao tree, a native plant in Mexico. Chocolate dates back to the Mayan and Aztec civilizations.

## Bibliography

Beezley, William H. and Michael C. Meyer. *The Oxford History of Mexico*. New York: Oxford University Press, 2010.

Coe, Michael D. and Rex Koontz. *Mexico: From the Olmecs to the Aztecs*. 5th ed. London: Thames & Hudson, 2002.

Coe, Michael D. *The Maya*. 5th ed. London: Thames & Hudson, 1999.

Coe, Sophie D. *America's First Cuisines*. Austin: University of Texas Press, 1994.

Fehrenbach, T. R. *Fire and Blood: A History of Mexico*. Cambridge: Da Capo Press, 1995.

Herrera, Hayden. *Frida Kahlo: The Paintings*. New York: HarperPerennial, 1993.

Krauze, Enrique. *Mexico: Biography of Power*. New York: HarperPerennial, 1998.

Posada, José Guadalupe. *Posada's Popular Mexican Prints*. Mineola: Dover Publications, 1972.

Riding, Alan. *Distant Neighbors*. New York: Vintage Books, 2000.

Rochfort, Desmond. *Mexican Muralists: Orozco, Rivera, Siqueiros*. San Francisco: Chronicle Books, 1998.

Sayer, Chloe and Sievert Lavender. *Arts and Crafts Mexico*. San Francisco: Chronicle Books, 1990.

Walt, Peter and Roberto Zepeda. *Drug War Mexico: Politics, Neoliberalism and Violence in the New Narcoeconomy*. London: Zed Books, 2012.

## Works Cited

Balletdeamalia.com. Ballet Folklórico de México de Amalia Hernández Website. Accessed online March 15, 2015. http://www.balletfolkloricodemexico.com.mx/

Chacón, Susana. "Mexican Foreign Policy: The Limits and Importance of the United States of America." Paper presented at the annual meeting of the ISA's 49th Annual Convention, San Francisco, CA. March 26, 2008. Accessed March 15, 2015. http://citation.allacademic.com/meta/p_mla_apa_research_citation/2/5/4/5/6/pages254562/p254562–1.php

Coe, Michael D. *The Maya*. 5th ed. London: Thames & Hudson, 1999.

"Country Profile: Mexico." September 4, 2012. BBC News. Accessed March 15, 2015. http://news.bbc.co.uk/2/hi/americas/country_profiles/1205074.stm

Curl, John. "Ancient Mesoamerican Poets." Foundation for the Advancement of Mesoamerica Studies Website. Accessed March 15, 2015. http://www.famsi.org/research/curl/nezahualcoyotl_intro.html

Dávila, Consuelo. "Mexico's Foreign Policy and Security in North America." Paper presented at 48th Annual ISA Convention, February 28—March 03, 2006, Chicago, Illinois. Accessed March 15, 2015. http://citation.allacademic.com/meta/p_mla_apa_research_citation/1/7/9/5/8/pages179587/p179587–1.php

De la Mora, Sergio. "Forging a National and Popular Art Cinema in Mexico." Academia.edu. Accessed March 15, 2015. https://www.academia.edu/8041353/Forging_a_National_and_a_Popular_Art_Cinema_in_Mexico_Mar%C3%ADa_Candelaria

"Egyptian Health Minister and Mexican Family Planning Foundation Win United Nations Population Award." March 20, 2000. United Nations Population Fund. Accessed March 15, 2015. http://www.unfpa.org/news/egyptian-health-minister-and-mexican-family-planning-foundation-win-united-nations-population

Gluek, Grace. "Graphic Evidence of Mexico's Ferment." 22 Dec. 2002. *The New York Times*. http://www.nytimes.com/2006/12/22/arts/design/22mexi.html?_r=2&fta=y&oref=slogin&oref=slogin

Gonzalez, David. "Castro Defies Fox of Mexico As Once-Warm Ties Sour." April 23, 2002. *New York Times*. Accessed March 15, 2015. http://www.nytimes.com/2002/04/23/world/castro-defies-fox-of-mexico-as-once-warm-ties-sour.html

Hearn, Kelly. "Who Built the Great City of Teotihuacan?" National Geographic. Accessed March 15, 2015. http://science.nationalgeographic.com/science/archaeology/teotihuacan-/

Human Rights Watch. "Mexico's National Human Rights Committee: A Critical Assessment." February 2008. Online. Accessed March 15, 2015. http://hrw.org/reports/2008/mexico0208/

Joseph, Gilbert M.; Rubenstein, Anne, and Zolov, Eric. *Fragments of a Golden Age: The Politics of Culture in Mexico Since 1940*. Durham, NC: Duke University Press. 2001.

Kandall, Jonathan. "Octavio Paz, Mexico's Man of Letters, Dies at 84." *New York Times*. April 21, 1998. http://www.nytimes.com/1998/04/21/books/octavio-paz-mexico-s-man-of-letters-dies-at-84.html

Mallan, Chicki, and Mallan, Oz. *Colonial Mexico: A Traveler's Guide to Historic Districts and Towns*. Emeryville, CA: Avalon Travel, 2001.

Mexico. Instituto Nacional de Esadística y Geografía (INEGI). "Delimitación de las zonas metropolitanas de México 2005." p.35. Accessed online, March 15, 2015. http://www.inegi.gob.mx/prod_serv/contenidos/espanol/biblioteca/Default.asp?accion=1&upc=702825001537&s=est&c=14103

"Mexico: Further Information on Fear for Safety/Death Threats." May 28, 2008. Amnesty International. Accessed March 15, 2015. https://www.amnesty.org/en/documents/AMR41/033/2007/en/

"Mexico's President Snubs Bush." CBS News Online. August 15, 2002. Accessed March 15, 2015. http://www.cbsnews.com/news/mexicos-president-snubs-bush/

Molina Ramírez, Tania. "Sonideros Mexicanos Crean Comunidad Transfronteriza Virtual en EU: Ragland." October 22, 2007. La Jornada. Accessed March 15, 2015. http://www.jornada.unam.mx/2007/10/22/index.php?section=espectaculos&article=a19n1esp

Nájar, Alberto and Vinicio González, Marco. "Una Navidad Binacional." December 29, 2002. La Jornada. Accessed March 15, 2015. http://www.jornada.unam.mx/2002/12/29/mas-vinicio.html

Noble, John, et al. *Mexico*. London: Lonely Planet, 2014.

Riding, Alan. *Distant Neighbors*. New York: Vintage Books, 2000.

Roura, Alma Lilia. "El Taller de Grafica Popular." Mexico Desconocido, No. 32 Septiembre / Octubre 1999. Accessed online March 15, 2015. http://www.mexicodesconocido.com.mx/notas/5328–El-taller-de-Gr%E1fica-Popular

Solis, Felipe. "Los Olmecas: Misterioso Pueblo Perhispánico." Mexico Desconocido. Accessed March 15, 2015. http://www.mexicodesconocido.com.mx/el-misterioso-pueblo-olmeca.html

"Telecoms in Mexico: Slim's Pickings." *The Economist*. July 10, 2008. Accessed March 15, 2015. http://www.economist.com/node/11707800

Toor, Frances. *A Treasury of Mexican Folkways*. New York: Bonanza Books, 1985.

Troshinsky, Lisa. "Mexican Migrantion Create 'Cities Without Men'." University of Maryland Philip Merrill College of Journalism. Accessed March 15, 2015. http://

d2oqb2vjj999su.cloudfront.net/users/000/094/006/381/
attachments/Datelinepdf.pdf

UNESCO. "Director General Condemns Murder of
Mexican Journalists Felicitas Martínez Sánchez
and Teresa Bautista Merino." April 4, 2008. Online.
Accessed March 15, 2015. http://www.unesco.org/new/
en/member-states/single-view/news/director_general_
condemns_murder_of_mexican_journalists_felicitas_
martinez_sanchez_and_teresa_bautista_merino-1/#.
VQuVkEa-3oA

"UNESCO World Heritage Center: Mexico." UNESCO.
Accessed March 15, 2015. http://whc.unesco.org/en/
statesparties/mx

UNICEF. "At a Glance: Mexico." Online. Accessed March
15, 2015. http://www.unicef.org/infobycountry/mexico_
statistics.html

United States. U.S. Department of State. "Country Reports
on Human Rights Practices—2013. Released by the
Bureau of Democracy, Human Rights, and Labor."
March 27, 2014. Accessed March 15, 2015. http://www.
state.gov/documents/organization/220667.pdf

Weiner, Tim. "Threats and Responses: The U.N. Debate;
Holding Swing Vote, Mexico Tells Bush It Won't
Support Iraq Resolution U.S. Favors." October 28, 2002.
*New York Times*. Accessed March 15, 2015. http://www.
nytimes.com/2002/10/28/world/threats-responses-un-
debate-holding-swing-vote-mexico-tells-bush-it-won-t.
html

"World Report 2015. Mexico." Human Rights Watch.
Accessed March 15, 2015. http://www.hrw.org/world-
report/2015/country-chapters/mexico

# UNITED STATES OF AMERICA

# Introduction

The United States of America, centrally located on the North American continent, is the world's third largest country in both geographic size and population (not including the European Union). It is bordered on the south by Mexico and by Canada to the north. The United States comprises 50 states, 48 of which are contiguous, and has a democratic government. It is among the world's richest countries in terms of gross domestic product, and is known for its impact on culture and entertainment around the globe.

Entertainment and the arts are an integral part of American life. The United States is well known for its motion picture, television, and music productions; and these industries are primarily concentrated in Hollywood, California, and New York City. New York City is also a major center for the performing arts, and most of the city's successful plays and musicals are concentrated on Broadway. Other major cities also have theater districts, and community theaters are often popular in smaller towns. Arts patronage remains a firmly rooted aspect of American society, and the United States has a plethora of museums and symphonies. Professional sports are a very popular source of entertainment for Americans, highlighted by the Super Bowl, annually among the most watched sporting event on television.

Washington, DC (District of Columbia) is the capital of the United States. The capital and its outlying areas are considered a federal district, and not part of any state; named for the first president of the United States, George Washington, it is located on the east coast of the United States by the Potomac River. The capital is home to many renowned national monuments and memorials, ranging from the temple-like Lincoln Memorial and the towering Washington Monument to Arlington National Cemetery, iconic structures and attractions that are often synonymous with American democracy and liberty. The nation's capital has become synonymous with the federal government, as all three branches of government are centered in the city.

## GENERAL INFORMATION

**Official Language(s):** While there is no official language, English is the de facto national language, and is predominantly spoken.
**Population:** 321,368,864 (2015)
**Currency:** United States dollar
**Coins:** The U.S. dollar is divided into 100 cents. Coins are available in denominations of 1, 5, 10, and 25 cents, with a 50 cent and 1 dollar coin both rarely used.

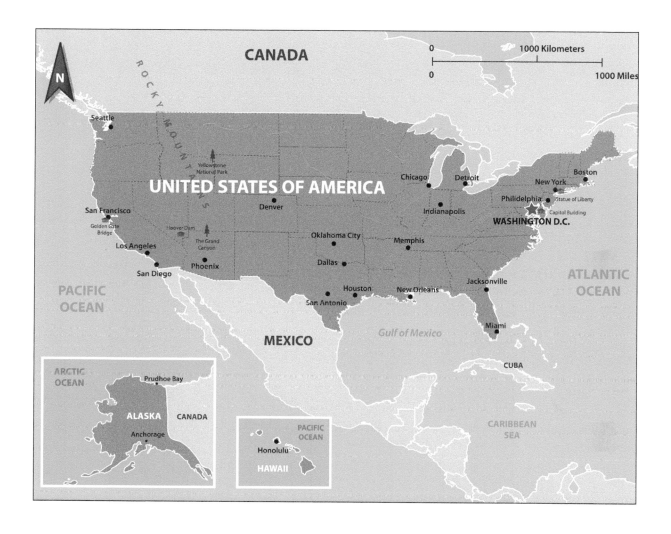

## Principal Cities by Population (2014 est.):

- New York, New York (8,491,079)
- Los Angeles, California (3,928,864)
- Chicago, Illinois (2,722,389)
- Houston, Texas (2,239,558)
- Philadelphia, Pennsylvania (1,560,297)
- Phoenix, Arizona (1,537,058)
- San Antonio, Texas (1,436,697)
- San Diego, California (1,381,069)
- Dallas, Texas (1,281,047)
- San Jose, California (1,015,785)

**Land Area:** 9,161,966 square kilometers (3,537,454 square miles)

**Water Area:** 664,709 square kilometers (256,645 square miles)

**National Motto:** "E Pluribus Unum" (Latin, "Out of Many, One")

**National Anthem:** "The Star-Spangled Banner"

**Capital:** Washington, DC (District of Columbia)

**Time Zone(s):** The United States has nine standard time zones across its states and territories, four of which—Eastern, Central, Mountain, and Pacific Standard Time—are used in the contiguous United States. (The states of Hawaii and Alaska have separate time zones.) In the "continental" United States, standard time ranges from GMT -5 to GMT -8.

**Flag Description:** The United States flag features a light blue rectangular field in the canton (upper hoist, or left, side), with 50-pointed white stars representing the 50 states arranged in rows. Thirteen equal horizontal stripes of red alternating with white fill out the rest of the flag, with the red occupying both the top and bottom stripes. The alternating stripes of red and white stand for the thirteen original colonies. Ideals represented by the flag's colors include courage, truth, justice, and purity.

## Population

In the United States, much of the population is of European descent. The largest minority group within the United States is Hispanic, a factor which also contributes to the increased use of the Spanish language throughout the country. Hispanics (which, according to the U.S. census, includes those persons of Spanish, Hispanic, or Latino origin) make up over 15 percent of the overall population, or nearly 50 million. African Americans make up the next largest minority group, accounting for 13 percent of the total population. The next largest minority groups are Asian Americans (5.4 percent of the population) and Native Americans (1.2 percent). About three percent of the population list "multiracial" as their primary category, but many researchers think that this figure is low.

The state of Alaska is the largest in area, at 656,424 square miles, while the state with the largest population is California, with 38.8 million residents, followed by Texas, Florida, and New York. Rhode Island is the smallest state in size at 1,545 square miles, but the state of Wyoming has the fewest residents at 493,782. Other states with small populations include Vermont, North and South Dakota, and Alaska. New Jersey has the highest population density, while Texas showed the largest growth (as of 2014).

The largest cities in the United States include New York City, Los Angeles, Houston, and Chicago. The city of Washington, DC, is home to about 660,000 people, though the metropolitan area of the District of Columbia has a population of six million (2014 estimate). Approximately 82 percent of the population resides in urban areas (2015 estimate).

In recent years, population increases have occurred primarily in the states of Florida, Georgia, Virginia, Arizona, Texas, California, and Colorado. West Virginia experienced the largest decrease in population. States that had a negative population growth rate between 2008 and 2009 were Rhode Island, Maine, and Michigan.

The United States is the third most populous country in the world. As of the 2015 census, the U.S. population was 321,368,864 (which includes illegal immigrants, many of which come from Mexico). The population growth rate was 0.7 percent in 2013.

## Languages

English is primarily spoken in the United States, though the country does not have an official language. (The state of Hawaii, however, lists Hawaiian as the official state language.) As of 2011, approximately 79 percent of the population listed English as their primary language, while almost 13 percent were Spanish speakers; Indo-European and Asian and Pacific island languages account for just over seven percent.

## Native People & Ethnic Groups

Native Americans, or American Indians, were the first to inhabit the lands of the United States. The culture is composed of a great number of tribes that continue to function as political groups. A few tribes include the Sioux of the Great Plains region, the Cherokee of the southeast, and the Iroquois of the northeast. Scientists speculate that the first Native Americans migrated from Siberia.

Upon the European colonization of America during the early 17th century, Native American tribes were displaced from their territories. Although the two groups often traded with each other, battles for land were also frequent. The Native American population was devastated by diseases brought by Europeans, against which the Indians had no immunity.

Many Native Americans now live on reservations and lands under their own jurisdiction. Eskimos and Aleuts, natives of Alaska, still live in the area in large populations.

## Religions

The majority of people in the United States adhere to the Christian religion. Protestants represent approximately half of the country's Christian population, while an estimated 24 percent are Roman Catholic and 1.7 percent Mormon. Approximately 1.7 percent of the population is Jewish. Buddhism, Islam, Hindu, and Unitarian Universalist faiths are also practiced, but each by less than one percent of the population. The remainder of the population practices no religion at all, with a small percentage of people who profess to be agnostic or atheist.

## Climate

There is an extensive range of climates within the United States to go along with the country's geographic diversity. Northern parts of the country are generally cooler, with the northernmost state of Alaska reaching sub-arctic temperatures. The Pacific Northwest has the wettest climate in the country, while the Southwest experiences desert conditions. Much of coastal California has a Mediterranean climate.

In general, most areas of the United States experience cooler temperatures in the winter and warmer temperatures in the summer.

## ENVIRONMENT & GEOGRAPHY

## Topography

The United States has two major coastlines. The East Coast borders the Atlantic Ocean, while the West Coast borders the Pacific Ocean. The country borders Canada to the north and Mexico to the south. The state of Hawaii is an island in the Pacific Ocean, while the state of Alaska borders Canada and has a Pacific coastline.

Because of the country's vast size, there are numerous rivers, mountain ranges, deserts, plains regions, and coastal areas within the United States. The major mountain ranges include the Rocky Mountains in the Midwest, the Adirondacks in the New York state region, and the Appalachian Mountains on the eastern coast. Active volcanoes include Mt. Saint Helen's in Washington state and Kilauea in Hawaii.

The highest point in the United States is Mt. McKinley (20,320 feet), located in Alaska. In the lower 48 states, California's Mt. Whitney is the highest point, at 14,495 feet. The lowest point in North America is Death Valley, which is located around 100 miles from Mt. Whitney. Death Valley lies 282 feet below sea level.

Notable rivers include the Mississippi River, the Missouri River, the Delaware River, the Potomac, and the Hudson River. The United States is also home to the Great Lakes, located near the Canadian border. These five lakes

(Lake Superior, Lake Erie, Lake Huron, Lake Michigan, and Lake Ontario) are the largest freshwater lakes in the world. Another noteworthy landmark within the United States is the Grand Canyon, located in northern Arizona. The canyon is one of the seven wonders of the natural world, and was carved out by the Colorado River.

Washington, DC (also known as DC or "the District") is situated at the geographic center of the east coast. The city is east of the Potomac River, with the state of Maryland to its north, and Virginia to its south. The District of Columbia is composed of the city of Washington, as well as seven counties of Maryland and five Virginian counties.

### Plants & Animals

A diverse range of plants and animals exist in the United States, due to the extremes in geography and climate throughout the country. Animals such as squirrels, birds, and small reptiles are indigenous to most areas.

The Northeast, including the areas of New England, New York, and Pennsylvania, is known for its deciduous forests, which display colorful autumn foliage. Coniferous trees are also common. Animals native to these areas include bears, deer, rabbits, raccoons, opossums, fox, and coyotes. Along the more coastal regions, aquatic creatures such as fish, clams, crabs, and lobsters are common.

The Southeast is known for its more tropical foliage, such as palm trees, Spanish moss, and fruit trees. Much of the fruit grown in the United States is grown in Florida, Georgia, South Carolina, and similarly warm regions. The Florida Everglades is a critical ecosphere that is protected by the National Park Service. Numerous endangered animals live in this area, including the manatee. Exotic birds, crocodiles, alligators, and many other species also make this area their home.

The Midwest is known for its plains regions. Tall grasses and small shrubbery are common, trees are scarce, and the area is the main center for the country's farming industry. Buffalo were once abundant in the area, but their population has dwindled immensely due to human development and hunting. Prairie dogs, bats, wolves, lynx, and other large cats are among the animals commonly found in the area.

The Southwest is primarily desert with evergreen trees and cactus among the prevalent plant life. Animals such as kangaroo rats, spiders, scorpions, vultures, and wolves inhabit the area.

The Northwest region of the United States is vastly different, with thick forests and vegetation. The area is known for its redwood trees, the largest trees in the world. Animals that inhabit this area include mountain lions, bears, owls, bobcats, and eagles.

The states of Alaska and Hawaii both differ greatly from the lower 48 states in terms of plant and animal life. Alaska's arctic climate nurtures large coniferous forests, and animals such as moose, bears, large cats, eagles, and wolves. Hawaii's tropical island climate allows lush rainforests to thrive, and tropical birds, insects, turtles, dolphins, and other sea life inhabit the state.

## CUSTOMS & COURTESIES

### Greetings

Americans tend to be casual and brief in greeting each other. Greetings are typically informal, with an equally brief and informal reply. Often, the greeting is followed by a general inquiry into a person's well-being, a question which, more often than not, is not to be answered literally or in great detail. While people are generally friendly, prolonged conversation is typically not expected. Among youth, greetings can even achieve a higher level of informality. However, young people are expected to show respect to their elders, and typically greet them formally using honorific titles and surnames. Additionally, it is quite normal for Americans to exchange greetings or nod while walking past another person, with neither person slowing down. If someone stops, then it signals that they are interested in a longer exchange.

Shaking hands is common when meeting for the first time, but after that, it is not usually employed. In shaking hands, Americans prefer a firm handshake in which both people will squeeze the other's hand slightly; a limp handshake is often considered a sign of weakness or insecurity. When family or close acquaintances have not seen each other in a while, it is common to embrace. However, this type of affection is generally more common among women than it is among men.

Americans are often friendly to strangers and will engage in conversation without any greeting at all. This occurs most often while waiting in line together, riding public transportation, or sitting next to each other at a large event. Typically, most topics, including religion and politics, are not generally taboo, and many Americans consider an argumentative conversation or friendly debate as a source of enjoyment.

## Gestures & Etiquette

Americans will often introduce each other by first name only, and it is considered customary and friendly to address someone by their first name, regardless of age or social status. Generally, one should refer to the person in the way they were introduced. While Americans generally prefer an arm's length of personal space, they also consider direct eye contact polite. Those who avoid eye contact may be considered suspicious or meek; staring, however, is considered rude.

Americans tend to be punctual and may judge people based on their timeliness, as well. For professional events, it is especially important to be on time, whereas for social events, it is acceptable to be late (sometimes known as "fashionably late"). However, business meetings or social engagements that require a reservation typically demand punctuality. Other events, such as evening parties or afternoon picnics, are generally more flexible.

Americans tend to refrain from gesturing when speaking. More succinctly, they tend to keep their elbows drawn in and usually raise their arms above their shoulders only when waving. There are a few gestures that are universally understood to be positive in American culture. One such gesture is the thumbs-up sign, in which

the thumb is extended upright with the other four fingers tucked into the palm. This usually signifies a positive result or the obtainment of something sought after. The V-sign, in which the index and middle fingers are extended upwards while tucking in the other fingers, originally symbolized victory, but is now more often used to mean "peace."

## Eating/Meals

Traditionally, Americans eat three meals per day, corresponding to breakfast in the morning, lunch at mid-day, and dinner in the evening. Because "American" is now representative of many different cultures, it is difficult to ascribe particular eating habits, except for the fact that most Americans eat in the "zigzag" or American style: knife in the right hand, fork in the left. One characteristic that most Americans do share, however, is their lack of free time.

Many Americans are self-described as "workaholics," and view this term as a positive characteristic in achieving a successful career. Add to this the fact that two-thirds of American mothers have entered the workforce, and the result is that meals are increasingly rushed and rarely made from scratch, and convenience has taken precedence over nutrition. Despite extensive health initiatives and education, fast food has become more popular than ever, with Americans spending more than $115 billion each year on fast food. This amounts to more than what is spent on cars, computers, or higher education. In recent years, a "slow food" movement has developed to buck this trend, but it is a luxury enjoyed by few. Fast casual restaurants, which typically offer no table service but serve food of higher quality, are also becoming more common.

With adequate time, traditional American meals adhere to certain characteristics. For example, traditional breakfasts are often hearty, and include foods such as pancakes and waffles, eggs with meat and potatoes, or freshly baked pastries. Cereal has become one of the most popular American breakfast foods, and simply involves pouring dried grains and milk together in a bowl. Sandwiches are the most common American lunch food, largely due to their convenience and portability. Chicken and beef are next most common foods after sandwiches, and a typical dinner is chicken or meat served with vegetables and a starch like rice, potatoes, or pasta.

## Visiting

When entering an American's home, the host will often take a guest's coat or outerwear (in cooler weather), but guests are not customarily expected to remove their shoes (unless they are particularly wet or dirty). When eating a meal in someone's home, it is common to pass dishes around, family-style, and for guests to take as much or as little of what is being offered. While a good host will want to ensure their guests have eaten enough, they will not push guests to eat more than they would like.

Meals are generally casual and guests are welcome to join in the conversation, though it is likely that the host will prompt the guests with questions. While most topics of conversation are welcome, subjects such as age, personal finances, or those of a very personal nature (such as why a couple has no children) are avoided. It should also be noted that many Americans have pets (often cats or dogs) that are often treated as members of the family. It is appropriate to tell the host if one is uncomfortable with their pet, but guests may be typically expected to be friendly with pets if they are able to. Americans do not generally bring gifts to each other on casual social visits, but a small token is typically welcome, especially when visiting for dinner.

## LIFESTYLE

## Family

The traditional nuclear family (two married parents and their children) has become increasingly less common in the United States. In its place are family units composed of a single parent, stepparents and same-sex parents, as well as multigenerational, cohabitating, or blended families. Additionally, as more and more women focus on their careers, they either have children later

or not at all. In 1940, 90 percent of American households considered themselves "family." In 2002, 51.9 percent of families defined themselves as a "married couple family," 16.1 percent were "other family," and 31.9 percent were "nonfamily."

It is common to have adopted children, stepchildren, and children out of wedlock in the United States. Although more traditionally conservative areas may still frown upon such family structure, it is becoming an obvious reality in most urban areas. More and more people are also choosing to live alone, and the number of non-family homes (dominated by individuals) increased from 10.6 percent in 1950 to one-third of all households in the United States in 2011. People living alone constituted 17.1 percent of the United States in 1970 and 27 percent in 2012.

## Housing

Houses in the United States are as diverse as the geography, and there is no one defining style. Many American architectural styles are determined by climate, with pointed roofs in areas with snowy winters and flat roofs in desert regions. Some styles, like the prairie house, known for their horizontal design and open interiors, are uniquely American. Other homes derive from European styles, such as colonial architecture in New England, French-inspired architecture in New Orleans and the Mississippi Valley, and Spanish-style architecture in Florida and the American southwest.

American homes are often associated with open interior floor plans, high ceilings, large doors and windows, exposed beams and decks or balconies. American single-family homes have grown larger over the years, up from an average of 983 square feet in 1950 to 2,600 square feet in 2014. The average American has more than 721 square feet of personal living space, which makes U.S. dwellings among the most spacious in the world. Early houses were often made with a timber frame, due to the abundance of wood during the 17th and 18th centuries. In the 20th century, wooden frames again became popular and remain so today.

Houses are common in rural areas and smaller towns, but in urban areas like New York City, most people live in apartments. As early as 1900, 75 percent of urban Americans lived in apartments.

## Food

American cuisine has a diverse range of influences and varies from region to region. Most dishes that are considered American are rooted in other cultures, but have evolved into what many consider as "all-American" food. In a 2007 survey on American cuisine, five dishes were voted as iconic American foods: hamburgers (grilled meat patties sandwiched between a sliced bun, traditionally served with lettuce, tomato, and onions, or with cheese and condiments); barbecue (meat, vegetables, and/or potatoes grilled on an open flame, often accompanied by tangy, sweet or smoky sauces); fried chicken (breaded chicken that is deep fried); macaroni and cheese (traditionally, elbow pasta with melted cheese); and apple pie (baked apples, usually spiced with cinnamon, in a pastry crust). Other foods that are largely associated as classic American fare include pizza, hot dogs, spaghetti dishes (such as pasta primavera), and buffalo wings.

Different regions of the United States are famous for different dishes and cuisines, as well. The south, for example, is known for its barbecue and fried chicken; New England in the northeast is known for its seafood, specifically clams; and Louisiana is known for both Creole and Cajun cuisine (featuring dishes such as jambalaya, a spiced rice stew with seafood, meat, and vegetables). Southwestern cuisine is typically influenced by Latin American and Mexican tastes and techniques (known as "Tex-Mex"), while contemporary American cuisine is often a fusion of Asian and European cooking. California cuisine is another trend that some interpret as fusion cuisine and others as simply using fresh, local ingredients. In addition, "fast food" originated in the United States and is one of the country's biggest industries. The first major fast food restaurant was McDonald's, known for its hamburgers and milkshakes.

## Life's Milestones

Outside of national holidays and the observance of birthdays, there are no fixed American rites of passage that every citizen shares. This is particularly so in the early 21st century as traditional roles become more flexible and family structures become more diverse. For example, marriage and birth were traditionally significant milestones (and still are for many), but more Americans are choosing other variations of family life, including cohabitation without marriage, marriage without children, and single parenthood.

"Sweet 16" parties and debutante balls, which used to be celebrations announcing a young woman's eligibility into the dating community, have fallen out of fashion, with the exception of Latina girls in the United States who may still celebrate their fifteenth birthdays with quinceañeras. Now, more significant milestones for American youth include receiving their driver's license, which many equate with freedom, and high school graduation.

A 2014 survey indicated that nearly 71 percent of Americans identify as Christian, and many American milestones are rooted in the Christian faith. This includes baptisms, marriage, and funerary practices. The United States is a secular nation, however, and other religious milestones unique to their faiths are commonly observed, particularly in childhood. For example, Jewish children celebrate their bar or bat mitzvah when they turn 13, signaling their new role with more responsibility within their faith community. Catholic children are confirmed between the ages of seven and 16 (usually around 12), in which they consciously choose to affirm their faith.

## CULTURAL HISTORY

### Native American Art

The indigenous peoples of the United States, though marginalized by European colonization, still constitute an important aspect of American culture. They are known for their unique way of life and spirituality and their traditional arts and crafts, which include beadwork, jewelry, clothing, basketry, pottery, and woodcarving, among others. Many traditional arts are specific to a certain tribe, such as sand painting by the Navajo and kat'sina dolls made by the Hopi. Native American Indians are also known for their strong oral and dance traditions, including the ghost dance, a circle dance incorporated by many Native American tribes. Native Americans also have their own distinct architecture, ranging from the traditional teepee (a conical tent made of animal skins) to the earthen pueblo architecture of the southwestern Pueblo peoples. Many traditional Native American art forms are still practiced today and include fine arts such as Western-style painting and sculpture.

## Fine Art

Early art produced in America was largely viewed as transatlantic, in that it was influenced by European styles and schools such as landscape painting and portraiture during the colonial and post-independence period. Painters, mostly of Dutch and British descent, tended to create images that were flat and imposing, similar to English prints popular at the time. American art fully emerged during a roughly 100-year span—between the mid-18th century and the mid-19th century. Prominent themes during this period included historical and marine subjects, and America's unspoiled wilderness and naturalism. Another major theme was the portrayal of rural America and American life, popularized by artists such as Winslow Homer (1836–1910), and later Norman Rockwell (1894–1978). The visual arts in America received a boost during the New Deal of the 1930s, a series of government programs and initiatives that followed the Great Depression.

By the middle of the 20th century, American art had become world-renowned. As the United States rose to prominence after World War II, New York surpassed Paris as the art capital of the world. Abstract expressionism (1940–1960) is considered the first American art movement to influence artists internationally. It emphasizes deeper meaning and the process of creating art. Jackson Pollock (1912–1956) became a controversial symbol of this emerging art form. He rejected traditional brushes, canvases and easels, and instead would spread his large canvases on the floor and drip, fling or smear paint on them. Other American artists to emerge in the 20th century include Andy Warhol (1928–1987) and Roy Lichtenstein (1923–1997), both known for their pop art, a movement that emerged in the 1960s.

## Architecture

In the 17th and 18th centuries, American art and architecture were often reproductions of established European styles and methods. Government buildings were often built in the federal or neoclassical styles, and churches tended to be Gothic. British colonists used wood or brick to build their colonial-style homes in New England and the mid-Atlantic, while Spanish settlers in the southwest used adobe (sun-dried mud bricks).

By the end of the 19th century, American architecture had carved out its own distinct identity. This was the era of the American Renaissance (1870s–1914), a period of architecture and art that extolled nationalism, neoclassicism, and new technology, such as the Brooklyn Bridge (the longest suspension bridge in the world upon its completion). During the 19th century, American architecture also created the skyscraper and the country house. The skyscraper was made possible by metal-frame construction, which supported taller buildings, and the invention of the passenger elevator in the 1850s. The country house was known for its more fluid design, which revolved around a common living room and embraced the connection between indoor and outdoor space.

Perhaps the greatest American architect is Frank Lloyd Wright (1867–1959). He advocated "organic architecture," in which a building resides seamlessly and harmoniously in its natural habitat. During his lifetime, 532 buildings of his design were completed. His Fallingwater house, built over a waterfall in Pennsylvania in 1939, was considered by the American Institute of Architects (AIA) to be the greatest work of American architecture.

## Film

In 1896, the American public viewed its first movie on a screen in New York City. By 1905, hundreds of nickelodeons, small movie theaters that charged a nickel per show, had opened. Three years later, there were an estimated 9,000 nickelodeons operating, and by 1910, specific actors had become recognizable to the public and the American film industry was born.

The popularity of Warner Brothers' *Don Juan* (1926) and *The Jazz Singer* (1927) made it clear that audiences preferred movies with sound over silent films. By 1929, with sound fully integrated into the movie-watching experience, the number of moviegoers doubled to 110 million per week. By 1930, Hollywood had become the fifth largest industry in the country, and 83 cents of every dollar spent on entertainment in the United States was spent on movies.

Films reflected the times as the United States entered into the Great Depression (1929–1939), World War II (1939–1945), the era of McCarthyism (late 1940s to the late 1950s) and the Cold War, which lasted until the early 1990s. Two seminal films of the 1950s were *The Wild One* (1953) and *Rebel without a Cause* (1955), starring Marlon Brando (1924–2004) and James Dean (1931–1955), respectively, as nonconformist rebels. The 1960s and 1970s were filled with anti-establishment ideals in popular films, such as *The Graduate* (1967), *Bonnie and Clyde* (1967) and *Easy Rider* (1969). The blockbuster film, which generally focuses on adventurous tales and features exciting special effects, was born in the late 1970s with such popular films as *Star Wars* (1977), *Superman* (1978), and *Indiana Jones and the Raiders of the Lost Ark* (1981). It remains one of the most popular genres of American film.

## Music

Early music, like the fine arts, stemmed from European influences and tradition. American musicians did not create their own distinct styles of music until the mid-19th century, with minstrel show songs such as "Oh, Susanna" (1854). After this breakthrough, American music teemed with creativity, with African Americans playing a large role, creating such genres such as ragtime, blues, rhythm and blues (also known as R&B), jazz, soul, and more recently, hip-hop. Today, Americans also listen to folk, country and western, rock and roll, or simply rock (post-1955), Motown, gospel, bluegrass, disco, punk, heavy metal, and rap.

Elvis Presley (1935–1977), known for his crooning voice, unique personal style and uninhibited performances, changed the music scene and is generally considered the first rock star. With 52 gold records and 33 movies, critics say that the success of the "King" was due to his tapping into his background in rockabilly, country, and R&B. This created a sound that appealed to both white and black listeners of that time. Some even argue that the rising popularity of rock music and both black and white musicians into mainstream culture contributed to America's progress toward racial integration.

As rock began to spread from the United States to the rest of the world, it also started to affect how young people danced, dressed, spoke, and thought. Other notable musicians who have had a profound impact on American music include composers Charles Ives (1874–1954) and Aaron Copeland (1900–1990), singers Frank Sinatra (1915–1998) and James Brown (1933–2006), soul artist Aretha Franklin (1942– ), singer-songwriter Bob Dylan (1941– ), rock band the Beach Boys, and Motown artist Marvin Gaye (1939–1984).

## Literature

Much of American literature has included themes of individuality and innovation. Early essays by the founding fathers detailed their visions of the ideal government and society. In 1836, Ralph Waldo Emerson (1803–1882) proposed what became known as transcendentalism, whereby one could find spiritual peace through nature rather than through organized religion. Henry David Thoreau (1817–1862) brought Emerson's theories to life in *Walden* (1854), an account of his decision to live alone in nature. Emerson's ideas of self-reliance and Thoreau's ideas on civil disobedience have been cited in later nonconformist counterculture movements. Walt

Whitman (1819–1892), known for his lyrical, free-flowing verse, is often considered the poetic counterpart to Emerson and Thoreau.

In contrast to the idealistic transcendentalists were the dark romantics, such as Edgar Allen Poe (1809–1849), who is credited with creating the detective genre; Nathaniel Hawthorne (1804–1864), known for his allegorical work; Herman Melville (1819–1891), whose novel *Moby-Dick* (1951) is considered an American masterpiece; and poet Emily Dickinson (1830–1886), whose work remains quite popular in contemporary times. Another important American writer is Harriet Beecher Stowe (1811–1896), who wrote *Uncle Tom's Cabin* (1852). This singular piece of literature bore such an immensely powerful and urgent anti-slavery message that many credit it with planting the seeds for the abolitionist movement of the mid-19th century.

Mark Twain (the pseudonym of Samuel Langhorne Clemens, 1835–1910) brought literature closer to the people by using vernacular speech in works such as *The Adventures of Huckleberry Finn* (1885), which is often called the prototypical "great American novel." During the 20th century, Ernest Hemingway (1899–1961) popularized narrative, understated writing, while F. Scott Fitzgerald's *The Great Gatsby* (1925) expressed the materialism of the "roaring twenties" or Jazz Age. Both writers belonged to the so-called "Lost Generation," a group of American writers that lived in Europe, most notably Paris, following World War I. Hemingway would win the Nobel Prize in Literature in 1954 for his influence on the contemporary style. William Faulkner (1897–1962), another Nobel Prize-winning American writer, helped to define Southern literature in the United States.

After World War II, the Beat writers, such as Jack Kerouac (1922–1969), Allen Ginsberg (1926–1997) and William S. Burroughs (1914–1997), emerged onto the literary scene. Considered precursors to the later hippie subculture, they were known for rejecting mainstream American expectations, pushing boundaries, and experimenting with religion, language and other facets of American life. J.D. Salinger (1919–2010)

pushed this disillusionment further in *Catcher in the Rye* (1951), which depicts adolescent alienation. Struggles against the constraints of modern life were explored by John Updike (1932–2009) in his *Rabbit* series of novels, while autobiographical material was used to good effect by Philip Roth (1933– ). "Postmodern" concerns inform the work of Thomas Pynchon (1937– ). In recent decades, minority literatures have flourished, as well.

## CULTURE

### Arts & Entertainment

American popular culture pervades the global scene, and it is rare to find a place that does not have American music, film, or cultural icons. Aside from the significant influence British culture had on American entertainment and culture in the 1960s (termed the British Invasion), there has not been a cultural presence like the current American one dominating the world today.

The popularity of American film and television overseas has come as a surprise even to industry experts. Domestic box office sales have remained steady from 2003 to 2008, at an average of $9.5 billion year, increasing to a high of $10.9 billion in 2013. Foreign box office sales, however, have skyrocketed, accounting for significantly more than 50 percent of worldwide sales in 2013. The market share of content on European television from the United States rose from 57.7 percent in 2009 to 66.4 per cent in 2013. Television networks such as MTV and Nickelodeon, which launched in the Middle East in 2007 and 2008, respectively, have also been very well received, despite negative views of the United States.

Though much of popular culture is superficial entertainment, it cannot help but reflect values of the time. This trend dates back to the minstrel shows of the 1830s, which were parodies of African Americans. Many artists have strived to have a more meaningful influence rather than simply entertaining their audiences. Often, art has served as a medium for protest, to examine the realization or destruction of the

"American dream," or to simply push boundaries and exercise free speech. Contemporary art, particularly in the form of film documentaries, has also helped to educate the American public, specifically about issues such as the tobacco industry, gun violence, corporate behavior, and the health effects of fast food. Historically, American art has also focused on patriotic solidarity, which was again evidenced in 2001 after the terrorist attacks the killed approximately 3,000 people. Art even served as a vehicle in schools to help children express their feelings in the aftermath of this tragedy.

## Cultural Sites & Landmarks

The capital of Washington, DC is home to many of the most recognizable American landmarks, including the Capitol Building. Construction of the famed neoclassical building started in 1793, and continued until the last 102 rooms were added in 1960. In 2014, a project to restore the dome began, slated to end in 2017. The United States Senate and the House of Representatives have met in the Capitol for over two centuries, and it also serves as a museum of American culture and history. The 580,000 square foot Capitol Visitor Center was opened in 2008, located underground at the east side of the Capitol. Alongside the Capitol Building are the White House, construction of which began in 1792; the Washington Monument, a white marble obelisk built to commemorate George Washington (1732–1799); and the Lincoln Memorial, which remains open at all times to the public and continues to be a popular site for speeches and protests. The American capital is also home to several war memorials and numerous museums.

Outside of Washington, DC, the Statue of Liberty is probably the most familiar American landmark. Located on Liberty Island outside of New York City, the Statue of Liberty (formerly called Liberty Enlightening the World) features a copper-clad robed woman holding a torch. It was given to the United States by France in 1886 and was declared a national monument in 1924. In 1984, the statue was designated as a World Heritage Site by the United Nations Educational,

Scientific and Cultural Organization (UNESCO). Other notable American landmarks include the red-orange 1.7-mile-long Golden Gate Bridge, which was the longest suspension bridge in the world when it was completed in 1937, in San Francisco, California; the 50-foot-high white letters of the Hollywood sign, built in the Hollywood Hills in 1923 for an advertisement in Los Angeles, California; the immense Grand Canyon in Arizona; and Mount Rushmore, into which the faces of U.S. Presidents George Washington, Thomas Jefferson (1743–1826), Abraham Lincoln (1809–1865) and Theodore Roosevelt (1858–1919) are carved, near Keystone, South Dakota.

In addition to the Statue of Liberty, America is also home to 22 other World Heritage Sites, most of which were recognized for their natural importance to humanity. They include the Everglades National Park, in Florida; Hawaii Volcanoes National Park; Yellowstone National Park, in Wyoming; Yosemite National Park, in California; and Mammoth Cave National Park, in Kentucky, the longest cave system in the world. American World Heritage Sites recognized for their cultural heritage include Independence Hall, in Philadelphia; San Antonio Missions, in Texas; Monticello (residence of Thomas Jefferson) and the University of Virginia, in Charlottesville, Virginia; and Pueblo de Taos, an ancient community in New Mexico dating back 1,000 years that continues to be occupied.

## Libraries & Museums

Museums remain an important part of the cultural landscape of the United States. In fact, according to the Institute of Museum and Library Services (IMLS), the United States is home to some 35,144 museums, which is double the estimate from the 1990s. Museum subject matter ranges from general topics such as the American Civil War, to peculiar focuses such as the history of the hammer. Many of the most prestigious cultural institutions are located in America's major cities.

Washington, DC is home to the Smithsonian Institute, a collection of 19 associated museums. Museums within the Smithsonian Institute include the Hirshhorn Museum and Sculpture

Garden, the National Air and Space Museum, the National Museum of American History, the National Museum of African American History and Culture (opening in 2016), and the National Museum of Natural History. (The only Leonardo da Vinci painting in the United States, in fact, is located in the National Gallery of Art in Washington, DC.) The Museum of Fine Arts is one of the premier museums of Boston, while New York City is home to renowned museums such as the Metropolitan Museum of Art and the Museum of Modern Art. Other major cities, such as Chicago and Philadelphia, are home to their own art, history, and science-based museums.

The United States is also home to several national libraries, including the Library of Congress, considered the largest library in the world; the National Library of Medicine; the National Agricultural Library; the National Library of Education; and the National Transportation Library. The Library of Congress, in fact, is America's oldest federal cultural institution, having been established in 1800. According to the International Federation of Library Associations and Institutions (IFLA), the United States was home to an estimated 16,540 public libraries and nearly 100,000 school libraries in 2010. The United States is also known for the strength and scope of its university-level libraries, as there are over 3,700 nationwide.

## Holidays

The United States celebrates ten major national holidays. Included in these are New Year's Day (January 1), Martin Luther King Day (third Monday in January), President's Day (third Monday in February), Memorial Day (last Monday in May), Independence Day (July 4), Labor Day (first Monday in September), Columbus Day (or Indigenous Peoples Day; second Monday in October), Veterans Day (November 11), Thanksgiving (fourth Thursday in November), and Christmas (December 25).

## Youth Culture

The first real generation gap appeared after World War II, when parents were struggling to support

their families in order to spare their children from their Great Depression and wartime experiences. This period brought about a significant counter-culture in which American youth began embracing different trends in music, fashion, and speech, as well as different and more accepting attitudes toward formerly taboo behaviors. Cultural and social movements that characterize this period include the emerging rock 'n' roll movement, the civil rights movement, and the Beat movement of the 1950s—a social and literary movement that heralded the rejection of mainstream values.

As this generation shifted into leadership roles in the 1960s and 1970s, America began reexamining and establishing rights for all groups of people, including students, women, African Americans, gays and lesbians, and Native Americans. In addition, social concerns such as environmental protection became prominent issues that continue to polarize youth in the early 21st century. This counterculture also spawned other countercultural movements. For example, after the 1950s, American youth began embracing mod culture, hippie culture, punk culture, etc. These evolved into current trends and subcultures such as hip-hop, goth, rave, and emo, to name a few.

Generally speaking, American youth culture continues to reject the preceding or dominant culture or values. While fashion and music continue to be prioritized in a largely consumer culture, the Internet has also had a profound impact on youth in the United States. American youth are increasingly viewing themselves more in a global context, and are learning to speak out in ways that embrace globalization. Young Americans are also becoming more technology-savvy, and use Internet-based communication technology such as texting and interacting on social networking sites.

## SOCIETY

## Transportation

Automobile use continues to be the dominant mode of transportation; Americans spend 46 minutes driving per day and drive, on average,

29 miles per day. In fact, the number of cars has surpassed the number of drivers, with the national average being 1.8 drivers and 2.8 cars per household. Traffic moves on the right-hand side of the road.

In densely populated cities such as New York, San Francisco, Boston, and Washington, DC, mass transit systems such as light rail or metro rail systems (subways) are common. Public transportation such as buses and taxis are also available in cities and large urban centers, and are less commonly seen in suburban or sparsely populated rural areas. Driving continues to be the main mode of transport in metropolitan cities. However, the American Public Transportation Association (APTA) reported that public transportation use in the United states rose to 10.7 billion trips in 2013—the highest number in 57 years. In addition, as of 2013, 86 percent of all working Americans commuted to work by private vehicle at an average of 25.5 minutes one-way daily commute.

### Transportation Infrastructure

The United States has a well-developed transportation system. The U.S. highway system is extensive and covers over four million miles; in fact, it has the largest road network in the world. However, a 2013 report by the American Society of Civil Engineers (ASCE) stated that one-third of America's roads are in poor to mediocre condition. The report issued a slightly better outlook for the efficiency of rail service and the condition of bridges. Trains exist in some areas of the United States, but are used more for freight than passengers.

There are over 13,500 airports with service to most destinations in the world. For longer distances within the continental United States, Americans will typically travel by airplane. Water transportation, much like rail transportation, is used largely for freight.

### Media & Communications

Americans pride themselves on their freedom of speech, and their abundance of media outlets (television, radio, film, magazine, newspaper, and Internet) allows a wealth of forums for any opinion. As of 2006, there were 2,218 television channels and almost 14,000 radio stations to choose from.

There is no national American newspaper, but many newspapers are sold across the United States, including the *New York Times*, *USA Today*, the *Washington Post*, the *Los Angeles Times*, *International Herald Tribune*, and the *Wall Street Journal*. Among the most popular newsmagazines are *Time*, *Newsweek*, and *U.S. News and World Report*.

Until the early 1990s, mobile phones were largely considered a luxury item, but as they became smaller and more affordable, they became the norm, especially among younger adults. This has caused landline use to decline in recent years. In 2014, there were 129 million landlines and 317 million cell phones in use. Internet is also widely available—there were an estimated 276.6 million Internet users in 2014.

## SOCIAL DEVELOPMENT

### Standard of Living

The United States ranked 5 out of 187 countries on the 2014 United Nations Human Development Index (HDI), which measures quality of life and standard of living indicators.

Despite a relatively high standard of living, the United States still has a high infant mortality rate when compared to other industrialized nations, as well as lower life expectancy. The United States also lags behind other Western nations in terms of health care as, in the United States, health insurance and health care tend to fall under the auspices of the private sector; however, there are several publicly funded health care initiatives in the United States, such as Medicaid, Medicare, the Veterans Administration, and the state-run Children's Health Insurance Program. Health care reform has been a hot button issue in the early 21st century political realm, with conservatives tending to favor private-sector health care and insurance and liberals advocating a government-run system.

As of 2010, an estimated 15 percent of the population lived below the poverty line.

## Water Consumption

In 2010, it was estimated that a daily 355 billion gallons were being used in the United States, whether for public use, industrial use, or agricultural. Significant sources of water include groundwater and surface water, which was the main source for the public water supply, as well as for the industrial, thermoelectric, and agricultural sectors. An estimated 98 percent of the rural population and approximately 99.5 percent of the urban population have access to an improved water source.

## Education

Most children in the United States attend a preschool or kindergarten before formal schooling begins. At the age of five or six, children begin elementary school. At grade six, children enter junior high school, and begin high school at grade nine. Students are required to attend high school until the age of 16, though the age of graduation is typically 17 or 18.

The United States has over 5,000 colleges and universities, both private and publicly funded. Among the most notable are Harvard University, Yale University, Williams College, Stanford University, Swarthmore College, the Massachusetts Institute of Technology (MIT), the University of Chicago, and Columbia University.

The U.S. gender gap in education favors female students in the early 21st century, particularly in the realm of higher education; in 2015, it was reported that female students accounted for as much as 60 percent of college enrollment.

## Women's Rights

The women's rights movement began in earnest in 1840 when women were excluded from the World Anti-Slavery Convention in London. This prompted Elizabeth Cady Stanton (1815–1902) and Lucretia Mott (1793–1880), noted social reformers, to formally establish the woman's rights movement. In 1848, Stanton and Mott held the first Women's Rights Convention, attended by 300 people, in Seneca Falls, New York. Sixty-eight women and 32 men signed the Declaration of Sentiments, modeled after the Declaration of Independence.

Individual states gradually permitted women to vote, and by 1920, the Nineteenth Amendment to the Constitution was ratified, granting all American women the right to vote. Following the Great Depression and the onset of World War II, more women began entering the workforce, assuming both labor and administrative roles formerly held by men. After World War II, more women elected to attend college and became frustrated by discrimination that prevented them from advancing in the workplace. It was during this period that author Betty Friedan (1921–2006) published *The Feminine Mystique* (1963), which voiced the growing frustration among women within a male-dominated society and helped renew feminism and women's rights activism.

In 1964, the Civil Rights Act was passed, which made sex discrimination in employment illegal. This was followed by the establishment of the National Organization for Women (NOW) in 1966 to ensure that the Civil Rights Act was enforced. (As of 2015, NOW had more than 500,000 members and is the largest feminist group in the nation.) In 1973, the United States Supreme Court ruled in a landmark case, *Roe v. Wade*, that women should have the right to terminate their pregnancy through an abortion. Beginning in the 1970s, as more women were elected to governmental office, more legislation that protected women was passed, including prohibiting discrimination against pregnant women in employment in 1978; protection of pension rights for widows and divorced women; stricter child support laws in 1984; and federally funded childcare in 1990.

Although American women have made significant strides in their fight for equality, there are still gender inequality issues. Despite women making up over half of the workforce, they still earn less than their male counterparts. They also hold fewer positions of leadership, despite being equally educated and qualified. Furthermore, women struggle to balance family and professional life, often sacrificing one for the sake of the other. A 2002 study found that 86 percent of corporate women had planned on having children, but 42 percent of them had no children by the age of 40.

## Health Care

Health care in the United States is provided primarily by health maintenance organizations, or HMOs. They consist of consortiums of physicians who follow standard care policies along with hospitals. The health care plans often limit certain benefits in order to avoid high rates and costs. For workers who have injured themselves on the job, worker's compensation is generally available and compensates workers for a percentage of the amount that they would have earned while working.

Medical care is also provided for the elderly and disabled through Social Security, a government program that provides a monthly stipend. In addition, the Medicaid and Medicare health care programs cover many medical costs for these patients. Residential housing for the elderly and disabled is often partially covered by these programs, but still remains very costly to the patient. Nursing homes and assisted living residences are common throughout the United States.

Health care reform has been a contentious issue in the United States for decades, and with the enactment of two bills, the Patient Protection and Affordable Care Act, amended by the Health Care and Education Reconciliation Act of 2010, the health care landscape of the United States is shifting. Reform, particularly in recent years, has been driven by a variety of factors, including the number of uninsured Americans—an estimated 50.7 million in 2009—as well as rising costs for health care. The bills were aimed at providing universal coverage for all American citizens. By 2013, the number of uninsured Americans had decreased by nearly 9 million.

## GOVERNMENT

### Structure

The United States government is a federal republic that is guided by the nation's Constitution. The government consists of a federal government, state governments, and local governments in cities and towns. The federal government is composed of three branches. The executive branch consists of the president, who is limited to two consecutive four-year terms. The president is elected by the Electoral College, based on the popular vote.

The legislative branch is made up of the Senate and House of Representatives, known collectively as Congress. Members of the Senate are elected to six-year terms, while members of the House of Representatives are elected to two-year terms. The judicial branch consists of the Supreme Court, whose judges serve unlimited terms. The nine Supreme Court justices are first appointed by the president of the United States, and are then approved by the Senate.

### Political Parties

National politics are dominated by two political parties: the generally conservative Republican Party, and the more liberal Democratic Party. Additional political parties include the Green Party, formed in 2001, which espouses environmental and social justice, as well as the Libertarian Party, formed in 1971, which advocates a free-market economy, civil liberties, and free trade.

In the wake of the November 2014 election, Democrats held 46 Senate seats and 184 House seats, while Republicans held 53 Senate seats and 244 House seats, gaining the Republicans a majority in the House of Representatives and the Senate.

### Local Government

State governments are relatively autonomous, though federal laws supersede state laws. State governors are elected by popular vote, and each state has its own Senate and House of

Representatives. Local governments are generally led by mayors or a board of selectmen, but can take on various forms.

## Judicial System

The U.S. judicial system is made up of two court systems: the federal and the state. This judicial structure is grounded in the ideals of federalism, which advocate the sharing of powers between the federal and state governments.

The federal court system of the United States includes the Supreme Court, which is the highest court in the country, as well as the Court of Appeals, District Courts, Bankruptcy Courts, and Courts of Special Jurisdiction.

State court systems vary by state; however, the most common court systems include Trial Courts of Limited Jurisdiction (such as probate courts, family courts, etc.); Trial Courts of General Jurisdiction (these are typically referred to as either circuit courts or superior courts); Intermediate Appellate Courts; and Highest State Courts, which are commonly referred to as State Supreme Courts.

## Taxation

As of 2015, the top income and corporate tax rate in the United States was 39 percent; other taxes include estate taxes, FICA taxes, and excise taxes. Tax systems vary by state. For example, some states (such as Alaska, Florida, South Dakota, and Texas) do not levy an income tax. Others, such as New Hampshire, Delaware, and Oregon, do not levy state or local sales taxes. Other taxes levied in the United States include gasoline taxes, gift taxes, property taxes, real estate taxes, sales taxes, school taxes, and luxury taxes. In 2014, tax revenue accounted for 17.4 percent of the U.S. gross domestic product (GDP).

## Armed Forces

The United States Armed Forces is made up of several service branches, including the U.S. Army, the U.S. Marine Corps, the U.S. Navy, the U.S. Air Force, and the U.S. Coast Guard. As of 2014, the United States ranked first in the world in active personnel, and was engaged in several international conflicts and wars, most notably in Afghanistan and Iraq. There is no conscription, and 18 is the minimum age for voluntary service (though age 17 is permissible with parental consent). As of 2012, military expenditures accounted for nearly 5 percent of the gross domestic product (GDP). The prohibition of female service members from serving in international combat forces and the "Don't Ask, Don't Tell" policy that restricts lesbian, gay, bisexual, and transgender members from openly serving remain contentious issues surrounding the U.S. armed forces. However, in late 2010, the United States Senate passed and President Barack Obama signed a bill to repeal "Don't Ask, Don't Tell."

## Foreign Policy

Supported by its victories in World War I (1914–1918) and World War II (1939–1945), the ascension to superpower status during the Cold War of the 1950s through the 1980s, and solid economic prosperity, the United States is the world's most powerful country. Although modern globalization has somewhat diminished the role of America as the only superpower nation left in the world, it still has the largest diplomatic presence and maintains positive relations with a great many countries. The only nations with whom it does not have official diplomatic ties are Bhutan, Iran, North Korea, and Taiwan. Although not officially recognized by the United States, informal relations with Bhutan and Taiwan are friendly. Diplomatic relations between United States and Cuba were restored in 2015 when embassies in each other's capital were reopened. At that time, though, Congress still held in place the economic embargo on Cuba. Economic sanctions against Iran were lifted in 2015 in connection with a deal regarding oversight of Iran's nuclear industry.

The United States has had a long history of isolationist policy (a focus on domestic issues and avoiding involvement in international disputes) dating back to George Washington in the 18th century. In the 1930s, after World War I and the Great Depression, isolationist sentiment soared in the United States. Once Japan bombed

Pearl Harbor in Hawaii in 1941, however, the United States had no choice but to become a part of World War II, signaling its entry into the international community.

In 1945, after World War II, the United States helped form the United Nations (UN), an international organization dedicated to worldwide cooperation through dialogue in order to protect human rights and the environment, promote free trade and social progress, and work toward world peace. As a founding member, the United States became one of the five permanent members—along with Great Britain, France, China, and the Soviet Union—of the United Nations Security Council (UNSC), a 15-member body that wields more decision-making power than the rest of the general assembly. By 2011, the United Nations had 193 member states and continued to wield significant international influence.

In the second half of the 20th century, U.S. foreign policy was focused on the Cold War against the Soviet Union and its communist allies. In 1949, the United States joined the North Atlantic Treaty Organization (NATO), a military alliance with 28 member states (as of 2014). In 1951, America signed the ANZUS treaty, a three-way defense pact, with Australia and New Zealand. In 1993, the United States signed the North American Free Trade Agreement (NAFTA), along with neighboring Canada and Mexico. Significant trading partners of the United States include Canada, Mexico, China, Japan, the United Kingdom (UK), and Germany. A Pacific trade pact was pending as of fall 2015.

Since 2001, U.S. foreign policy has been characterized by preemptive war and an aggressive stance on extremism, most notably the global "war on terrorism." This included the 2001 NATO invasion of Afghanistan that was largely a response to terrorist attacks on U.S. soil on September 11, 2001, and the 2003 U.S.-led Iraq War, in which the United States invaded Iraq under the premise of rooting out weapons of mass destruction and overthrowing Saddam Hussein (1937–2006). When no weapons of mass destruction were found, American popularity overseas waned. During this period, foreign relations between several countries, particularly Muslim nations and communist nations such as North Korea, deteriorated. Nonetheless, national security (in particular, nuclear proliferation), the worldwide sponsorship of democracy, the protection of American citizens and business abroad, and the promotion of foreign aid, investment and education remain fundamental priorities of American foreign policy.

## Dependencies

As of 2015, the United States had many dependencies, including American Samoa, Baker Island, Guam, Howland Island, Jarvis Island, Johnston Atoll, Kingman Reef, Midway Islands, Navassa Island, Northern Mariana Islands, Palmyra Atoll, Puerto Rico, Virgin Islands (United States), and Wake Island.

## Human Rights Profile

International human rights law insists that states respect civil and political rights, and also promote an individual's economic, social, and cultural rights. The United Nations Universal Declaration on Human Rights (UDHR) is recognized as the standard for international human rights. Its authors sought the counsel of the world's great thinkers, philosophers, and religious leaders, and were careful to create a document that reflects the core values shared by every world culture. (To read this document or view the articles relating to cultural human rights, go to: http://www.un.org/en/documents/udhr/.)

The United States is known for extolling democratic principles and freedoms, including freedom of speech, freedom to assemble, and freedom of religion. These freedoms and rights are guaranteed by the Bill of Rights, which has served as a foundation for numerous other nations and organizations, including the UDHR, which the United States played a pivotal role in drafting in 1948. The United States is led by a democratically elected government with separate branches designed to prevent an abuse of power; has sheltered refugees and those seeking political asylum; and believes itself to be a moral nation that upholds its promise to assist others.

Furthermore, Americans are legally protected against discrimination based on race, gender, age, and disability. Although far from perfect in reality, America continues to push for equality for all people in the early 21st century, particularly regarding issues surrounding sexuality, gender, and race.

In practice, however, the nation has found it difficult to live up to such lofty ideals. President Jimmy Carter (1924– ), who served from 1977 through 1981, made a bold move toward pushing human rights issues to the forefront of his foreign policy, but was thwarted by a lack of unity in his own administration. Later presidents also struggled with trying to balance human rights concerns with trade and other international issues and relationships, and they faced the daunting challenge of upholding their word in the face of unforgiving scrutiny. President George H. W. Bush (1924– ), who served from 1989 until 1993, was not in favor of ceding foreign policy in favor of human rights considerations. President Bill Clinton (1946– ), in office from 1993 until 2001, believed that opening trade would benefit the nation more than clamping down on human rights violations overseas.

More recently, President George W. Bush (1946– ), who served in office from 2001 until 2009, was especially criticized for his administration's anti-terror campaign, which many feel violated human rights laws. Of particular concern is how the United States has interpreted the rights of certain terrorists (categorized as "unlawful combatants"), its use of international detention centers and methods of interrogation to circumvent international human rights treaties such as the Geneva Conventions (known as extraordinary rendition). It has also been criticized for its non-participation in, or failure to ratify, other standard human rights treaties, such as those involving the rights of children and migrant workers. One of the most glaring examples of international human rights abuse involving the United States stems from the detention of prisoners during the Iraq War, specifically the abuse of prisoners at Abu Ghraib prison in Iraq in 2004, much of which was photographed. The United States has also come under criticism for the detention of suspected terrorists at the Guantánamo Bay military base. The use of drones in U.S. air strikes, targeting suspected terrorists in countries like Pakistan and Yemen, were increased by President Barack Obama (1961– ) starting in 2009. The legality and effectiveness of such strikes have also been contested.

On the national front, known problems include police brutality, high murder and crime rates, and one of largest prison populations in the world. The United States has also come under considerable scrutiny for its use of capital punishment—since 1977, over 1,400 people have been executed—and for its lack of universal health care. (The death penalty, which had been outlawed in 19 states as of 2015, was reexamined by the United States Supreme Court in 2008; the court ruled in April in *Baze v. Rees* that lethal injection did not constitute cruel and unusual punishment.) Additionally, since the start of the U.S.–led Iraq War in 2001, the United States government has come under attack for allegedly violating the privacy rights of citizens under the guise of national security, and for not providing universal health care to all its citizens, as covered by the UDHR.

## Migration

In 2015, the U.S. migration rate was estimated at 3.86 migrants per 1,000 population. Immigration has become a heated issue in the early 21st century, as increasing numbers of immigrants seek economic security in the United States. Immigration populations are dominated by peoples from Mexico, China, India, and the Philippines. The immigration debate in the United States has centered on how the United States can protect its borders, both to limit immigrants and to protect the country from terrorists who may slip through. To that end, the United States has beefed up security at its borders, and some have proposed a fence along the Mexican border. The immigration debate has also become tangled with other political issues such as unemployment, entitlements, gun violence and urban crime, housing, health care, and other social issues.

## ECONOMY

### Overview of the Economy

In 2009, the estimated gross domestic product (GDP, the total value of all goods and services produced by the country) of the United States was $17.42 trillion. The per capita GDP was $54,600.

### Industry

The United States has many strong industries, including manufacturing, tourism, and entertainment. The largest is the service industry, and at least three-quarters of Americans work in this sector. The farming industry is also extremely large, and the country is among the top producers of corn, wheat, and other agricultural products.

The United States manufactures a tremendous number of products contributing $2.09 trillion to the U.S. economy.

### Labor

The labor force was estimated at 156 million in 2014. The majority of the labor force—nearly 40 percent in 2009—was employed in managerial, professional, or technical occupations, while agriculture accounted for less than one percent of the workforce. The services sector was the largest contributor to the (GDP), accounting for more than 77 percent in 2014.

Following the global recession that began in 2008, unemployment became a hot-button issue in the United States. In February 2010, the unemployment rate in the United States was estimated at 10.4 percent, but by 2014 the unemployment rate was 6.2 percent.

### Energy/Power/Natural Resources

The United States is rich with natural resources. The fishing, forestry, and metal refining industries all take advantage of the country's resources. Minerals and metals mined in the United States include coal, copper, lead, uranium, phosphates, gold, iron silver, nickel, zinc, mercury, and tungsten. Oil is also found in some areas, such as Alaska and Texas, but the United States produces only three percent of the world's oil. Diamonds are mined in Arkansas, the only state to have a diamond mine.

### Fishing

According to the National Oceanic and Atmospheric Administration (NOAA), the commercial fishing industry (including processors and retailers) of the United States supported roughly one million jobs and generated over $70 billion in revenue in 2011. In 2010, commercial fishermen alone generated $4.5 billion in revenue from a collective catch of both fish and shellfish that was estimated at roughly 7.9 billion pounds. Overall, the top commercial species caught by American fishermen are shrimp, Pacific Salmon, sea scallop, Pollock, and lobster, followed by tuna, halibut, and blue crab.

Fishing also defines a way of life in certain states. For example, the fishing industry is the largest private employer in the state of Alaska, where salmon and king crab are the most commercialized species (along with Pollock and sablefish), whereas Maine is synonymous with lobster, and Maryland is famous for blue crab, and both are huge revenue earners in their respective states. The southern coastal and Gulf states rely heavily on the fishing industry, for both commercial and recreational purposes, with shrimp a valuable commercial commodity in that region.

Overfishing and illegal fishing continue to be pressing issues facing the U.S. fishing industry, and the United States government issued regulations as part of a national oceans policy in 2010—aimed at reducing overfishing, including a "catch shares" program in regions where overfishing was prominent, such as New England. Natural disasters have also had a significant effect on the health of the industry in recent years. In 2005, for example, it was reported that the effects of hurricanes, notably Katrina and Rita, cost the state of Louisiana alone $2.2 billion in sales within the fishing industry, while the 2010 Gulf oil spill devastated the local fishing industries of several states, both commercially and recreationally, including Louisiana and Florida. Damage caused by hurricane Sandy (Superstorm Sandy), that hit the northeast coast in 2012, amounted to about $75 billion.

## Forestry

The United States is one of the largest producers (and consumers) of forest products. The country has approximately 745 million acres of forest—approximately one-third of which is owned by the federal government, while the remaining two-thirds are owned by an assortment of entities, including state and local governments, companies, and citizens. In 2012, approximately 10,500 people were employed in the forestry sector, and an additional 44,000 were employed in the logging industry.

## Mining/Metals

The mining industry in the United States can be divided into four major sectors: coal mining, metal ore mining, oil and gas extraction, and nonmetallic mineral mining and quarrying. A fifth segment of the mining industry comprises support activities for mining (e.g., drilling, construction, and repair). In 2012, approximately 800,000 people were employed in the mining industry. An additional 180,000 worked in gas and oil extraction; 40,000 worked in metal mining; and 107,000 worked in nonmetallic mineral mining. Approximately 327,000 people worked in occupations to support the mining industry.

States such as Texas, Louisiana, Oklahoma, California, and Alaska have significant mining industries.

## Agriculture

The United States is one of the major agricultural producers in the world. The interests of farmers and exporters are regulated and protected by the United States Department of Agriculture. The country's biggest cash crops include corn, soybeans, wheat, alfalfa, cotton, hay, tobacco, rice, sorghum, and barley. Corn is the number one agricultural product in terms of both volume and value. As of the turn of the 21st century, American farms were producing $100 billion

worth of crops and livestock annually. In 2012, there was a 33 percent increase in agricultural sales for a total of $395 billion.

In 2012, an estimated 2.1 million people were employed in the agriculture, forestry, and fishing sector; an additional 800,000 people worked in this sector but were either self-employed or worked for no wage (e.g., family farms).

## Animal Husbandry

Livestock is a major division of agriculture, and U.S. ranchers raise dairy cattle, beef cattle, swine, poultry, and sheep. Horses, turkeys, goats, and bees are also raised on American farms. In fact, cattle meat, cow's milk, and chicken meat rank behind corn as the top agricultural products in the United States. Organic livestock farming has increased in recent years; as of 2010, the state of Colorado had the largest percentage of land set aside for organic livestock, with 76 percent, while Idaho had the most organic farms of any state. American farms produced $395 billion worth of crops and livestock in 2012.

## Tourism

Tourism is a major industry in the United States. States such as Florida, Hawaii, and California attract tourists with their warm climates, entertainment destinations, and resorts. Mountainous states such as Colorado and Vermont entice skiers and other winter sports enthusiasts. New York City is also a major tourist destination, due to its abundance of entertainment, theater, and cultural attractions. Tourism is also the second largest economic force in the capital, behind the federal government, as millions of people from around the world travel to Washington, DC each year to visit the government buildings, numerous monuments, museums, and other attractions.

According to the United States Department of Commerce, the tourism industry contributed 2.7 percent to the country's GDP and accounted for 7.9 million jobs in 2014. That same year, an estimated 75 million people visited the United States, with more than half of those tourists coming from either Canada or Mexico.

The nation's national parks and wildlife refuges are also popular among both domestic and foreign tourists. Included in these attractions are the Grand Canyon in Arizona, Yosemite National Park in the Northwest, the Everglades of Florida, and Niagara Falls in New York.

*Jennifer Kan Martinez, Erika Bruce,*
*Amanda Wilding*

## DO YOU KNOW?

- The first United States president to be inaugurated in Washington, DC was Thomas Jefferson. The first and second presidents were inaugurated in New York City.

- Among the many notable innovations invented in the United States are the telephone, automobile, desktop computer, steam locomotives, FM radio, air conditioner, sewing machine, helicopter, and pencil.

- The United States has hosted a total of seven Olympic Games. The cities that hosted the events include St. Louis, Missouri (1904); Los Angeles, California (1932 and 1984); Lake Placid, New York (1932 and 1980); Atlanta, Georgia (1996); and Salt Lake City, Utah (2002).

## Bibliography

Ashby, LeRoy. *With Amusement for All: A History of American Popular Culture since 1830.* Lexington, KY: University Press of Kentucky, 2012.

Boyer, Paul S. *American History: A Very Short Introduction.* New York: Oxford University Press, 2012.

Crawford, Richard. *America's Musical Life.* New York: W.W. Norton & Company, 2001.

Ellis, Richard J. *American Political Cultures.* New York: Oxford University Press, 1996.

Foster, Gerard L. *American Houses: A Field Guide to the Architecture of the Home.* New York: Houghton Mifflin Harcourt, 2004.

Josephy, Alvin M. *The Longest Trail: Writings on American Indian History, Culture, and Politics.* New York: Vintage, 2015.

Lewis, Jon. *American Film: A History.* New York: W.W. Norton, 2007.

Marcus, Greil and Werner Sollors, eds. *A New Literary History of America.* Cambridge, MA: Harvard University Press, 2012.

Nicholls, David. *The Cambridge History of American Music.* Cambridge: Cambridge University Press, 2004.

Peterson, James W. *American Foreign Policy: Alliance Politics in a Century of War, 1914–2014.* New York: Bloomsbury Academic, 2014.

Schlosser, Eric. *Fast Food Nation.* New York: Houghton Mifflin Company, 2002.

Smethurst, James. *The Black Arts Movement: Literary Nationalism in the 1960s and 1970s.* Chapel Hill, NC: University of North Carolina Press, 2005.

Susman, Warren. *Culture as History: The Transformation of American Society in the Twentieth Century.* Washington, DC: Smithsonian Books, 2003.

Woodard, Colin. *American Nations: A History of the Eleven Rival Regional Cultures of North America.* New York: Penguin Books, 2012.

## Works Cited

"2009 World Report: Obama Should Emphasize Human Rights." Human Rights Watch, 14 Jan. 2009. http://www.hrw.org/en/news/2009/01/14/2009–world-report-obama-should-emphasize-human-rights.

"About the United Nations." United Nations. http://www.un.org/en/about-un.

Adler, Margot. "Behind the Ever-Expanding American Dream House." National Public Radio, 4 July 2006. http://www.npr.org/templates/story/story.php?storyId=5525283.

Arango, Tim. "World Falls for American Media, Even as It Sours on America." *New York Times*, 30 Nov. 2008. http://www.nytimes.com/2008/12/01/business/media/01soft.html?ref=media.

"America's Families: Changing Family Structure." Library Index. http://www.libraryindex.com/pages/1315/America-s-Families-CHANGING-FAMILY-STRUCTURE.html.

"America's Families: Households." Library Index. http://www.libraryindex.com/pages/1314/America-s-Families-HOUSEHOLDS.html.

"American Popular Song: A Brief History." History Matters, American Social History Project, 2006. http://historymatters.gmu.edu/mse/songs/amsong.html.

"Background Note: Bhutan." U.S. Department of State. http://www.state.gov/r/pa/ei/bgn/35839.htm.

"Background Note: Taiwan." U.S. Department of State, September 2008. http://www.state.gov/r/pa/ei/bgn/35855.htm.

Bailey, Megan. "The Dark Romantics of Literature." Associated Content, 21 April http://www.associatedcontent.com/article/1603/the_dark_romantics_of_literature. html?cat=38.

Barber, E. Susan. "One Hundred Years towards Suffrage: An Overview." National American Woman Suffrage Association Collection, 1998. http://memory.loc.gov/ammem/naw/nawshome.html.

Bellis, Mary. "The Kinetoscope." About.com: Inventors. http://inventors.about.com/od/kstartinventions/a/Kinetoscope_2.htm.

Bigler, B. Philip. "Washington Monument." Encyclopedia Brittanica Profiles: The American Presidency, 2009. http://www.britannica.com/presidents/article-9076193.

Bogle, Lara Suziedelis. "Children and 9/11: Art Helping Kids Heal." National Geographic News, 10 Sept. 2002. http://news.nationalgeographic.com/news/2002/09/0910_kidsart.html

Brewster, Mike. "Elvis Presley: Birth of the Rock Star." *Business Week*, 24 Sept. 2004. http://www.businessweek.com/bwdaily/dnflash/sep2004/nf20040924_2301_db078.htm.

Brewster, Mike. "Frank Lloyd Wright: America's Architect." *Business Week*, 28 July 2004. http://www.businessweek.com/bwdaily/dnflash/jul2004/nf20040728_3153_db078.htm.

Brown, Richard. "William Kennedy-Laurie Dickson." Who's Who of Victorian Cinema, British Film Institute, 1996. http://www.victorian-cinema.net/dickson.htm.

"Census Bureau Announces Most Populous Cities." U.S. Census Bureau News, 28 June 2007. http://www.census.gov/Press-Release/www/releases/archives/population/010315.html.

Champoux, Paul. "Tips for Visiting the Home of an American Family." New Life

Church Resources for Conversation Partners: Tips for Internationals Visiting an American Home. http://www.newlifechurcha2.org/files/resources/conversation%20friends/AppendixC%20Tips%20for%20Internationals%20Visiting%20an%20American%20Home.doc.

Chilvers. Ian. "American Art and Architecture." Microsoft Encarta Online Encyclopedia, 2008. http://uk.encarta.msn.com/encyclopedia_761563773/american_art_and_architecture.html.

Danto, Arthur C. "The Art of 9/11." The Nation, 5 Sept. 2002. http://www.thenation.com/doc/20020923/danto.

Davis, Mitchell and McBride, Anne. "The State of American Cuisine." The James Beard Foundation, 2008. http://www.jamesbeard.org/files/jbf_state_of_american_cuisine.pdf.

"Eleanor Roosevelt. Universal Declaration of Human Rights, 2001". http://www.udhr.org/history/Biographies/bioer.htm.

"Elisha Otis."PBS: 'Who Made America?' series, 2004." http://www.pbs.org/wgbh/theymadeamerica/whomade/otis_hi.html.

"Facts about the Death Penalty." Death Penalty Information Center, 8 Dec. 2008. http://www.deathpenaltyinfo.org/FactSheet.pdf.

Fewins, Clive. "Get the Look—American Style." Homebuilding and Renovating, October 2006. http://www.homebuilding.co.uk/feature/get-look-american-style.

Freeman, Nancy. "Ethnic Cuisine: United States." Sally's Place. http://www.sallys-place.com/food/cuisines/us.htm.

Gibbs, Hope Katz. "America's Changing Rites of Passage." *Social Technologies*, 8 May 2006. http://socialtechnologies.com/FileView.aspx?fileName=PressRelease05082006.pdf.

Gjelten, Tom. "September 11 Attacks." Microsoft® Encarta® Online Encyclopedia, 2008. http://encarta.msn.com/encyclopedia_701509060/September_11_Attacks.html.

Glassman, Carl. "Born of Tragedy, 9/11 Art Finds a Home." *The Tribeca Trib.*, 5 Jan. http://www.tribecatrib.com/news/newsjan09/sept11art010936.html.

"Golden Gate Bridge: Bridge Design and Construction Statistics." Golden Gate Bridge, Highway and Transportation District, 2008. http://www.goldengatebridge.org/research/factsGGBDesign.php.

"Government Doubles Official Estimate: There Are 35,000 Active Museums in the United States." Institute of Museum and Library Services. 19 May 2014. https://www.imls.gov/news-events/news-releases/government-doubles-official-estimate-there-are-35000-active-museums-us

Hall, Elizabeth Armstrong. "Apartment Houses." *US History Encyclopedia*. http://www.answers.com/topic/apartment-building.

"Harriet Beecher Stowe's Life & Time." Harriet Beecher Stowe Center, 2005. http://www.harrietbeecherstowecenter.org/life/.

Holguin, Jaime. "Sept. 11 Sculpture Covered Up." CBS News, 19 Sept. 2002. http://www.cbsnews.com/stories/2002/09/19/national/main522528.shtml.

Ibach, Marilyn. "Timber-frame Houses in the Historic American Buildings Survey." The Library of Congress Prints and Photographs Division, May 2003. http://www.loc.gov/rr/print/list/100_tim.html.

"International Trade Administration Industry and Analysis—National Travel and Tourism Office: Fast

Facts_United States Travel and Tourism Industry 2014." http://travel.trade.gov/outreachpages/download_data_table/Fast_Facts_2014.pdf

Junod, Tom. "The Falling Man." *Esquire*, 11 Sept. 2008. http://www.esquire.com/features/ESQ0903–SEP_FALLINGMAN

Kahn, Richard and Kellner, Douglas. "Global Youth Culture." UCLA Graduate School of Education & Information Studies, 2003. http://www.gseis.ucla.edu/faculty/kellner/essays/globyouthcult.pdf.

Leung, Rebecca. "The Biological Clock." CBS News, 60 Minutes, 17 Aug. 2003. http://www.cbsnews.com/stories/2003/08/14/60minutes/main568259.shtml.

"Michael Moore (II)." The Internet Movie Database, 2009. http://www.imdb.com/name/nm0601619/.

Mintz, S. "Hollywood as History." Digital History, 2007. http://www.digitalhistory.uh.edu/historyonline/hollywood_history.cfm.

Moore, Barbara and Mann, Donna. "Jackson Pollock." National Gallery of Art. http://www.nga.gov/feature/pollock/index.htm.

Morse, Jane. "Women's Rights in the United States." America.gov, 26 Feb. 2007. http://www.america.gov/st/washfile-english/2007/February/20070226171718ajesrom0.6366846.html.

Murphy, Paula. "Ken Bruen's *American Skin* and Postmodern Media Culture." Americana: *The Journal of American Popular Culture*, Spring 2008. http://www.americanpopularculture.com/journal/articles/spring_2008/murphy.htm.

"National Household Travel Survey." Research and Innovative Technology Administration, Bureau of Transportation Statistics, 2002. http://www.bts.gov/programs/national_household_travel_survey/.

"National September 11th Memorial & Museum." National September 11th Memorial & Museum at the World Trade Center, 2008. http://www.national911memorial.org

O'Hagan, Sean. "Fifty Years of Pop." *The Observer*, 2 May 2004. http://www.guardian.co.uk/music/2004/may/02/popandrock.

O'Malley, Michael. "The Minstrel Show," History 404: A Jacksonian Democracy course information, George Mason University, 1999. http://chnm.gmu.edu/courses/jackson/minstrel/minstrel.html.

"October 2008 Web Server Survey." Netcraft News, 29 Oct. 2008. http://news.netcraft.com/archives/2008/10/29/october_2008_web_server_survey.html.

Paul, Stella. "Abstract Expressionism." *Heilbrunn Timeline of Art History*, The Metropolitan Museum of Art, 2000. http://www.metmuseum.org/toah/hd/abex/hd_abex.htm.

Rector, Robert E. and Johnson, Kirk A. "Understanding Poverty in America." The Heritage Foundation, 5 Jan. 2004. http://www.heritage.org/Research/Welfare/bg1713.cfm#pgfId-1070525.

Reuben, Paul P. *Perspectives in American Literature: A Research and Reference Guide*. California State University, Stanislaus, 2008. http://www.csustan.edu/english/reuben/pal/TABLE.html.

"Rites of Passage." *Encyclopedia of Childhood and Adolescence*, 1998. http://findarticles.com/p/articles/mi_g2602/is_0004/ai_2602000456.

Rosenberg, Matt. "Countries Without Diplomatic Relations with the United States." About.com: geography, 17 May 2006. http://geography.about.com/od/politicalgeography/a/nodiplomatic.htm.

Taylor, Pamela. "An American View of Human Rights." *Human Rights Tribune*, 16 Dec. 2008. http://www.humanrights-geneva.info/An-American-view-of-human-rights,3930.

"United States." *Central Intelligence Agency: The World Factbook*. https://www.cia.gov/library/publications/the-world-factbook/geos/us.html.

"United States Country Summary." *Human Rights Watch*, January 2009. http://www.hrw.org/sites/default/files/related_material/us.pdf.

"United States of America." Cyborlink: International Business Etiquette and Manners, 2008. http://www.cyborlink.com/besite/us.htm.

"United States of America Press." *The World Press*, 2008. http://www.theworldpress.com/press/unitedstatesofamericapress.htm.

"United States Isolationism." *NationMaster Encyclopedia*, 2005. http://www.nationmaster.com/encyclopedia/United-States-isolationism.

"United States People." *MSN Encarta Encyclopedia*, 2008. http://encarta.msn.com/encyclopedia_1741500824_10/United_States_People.html.

"USA: Language, Culture, Customs and Etiquette." Kwintessential: Cross Cultural Solutions. http://www.kwintessential.co.uk/resources/global-etiquette/usa.html.

"Washington, DC: A National Register of Historical Places Travel Itinerary." National Park Service, U.S. Department of the Interior. http://www.nps.gov/nr/travel/wash/index.htm.

"We Shall Overcome: Historic Places of the Civil Rights Movement." National Park Service, U.S. Department of the Interior. http://www.nps.gov/history/nr/travel/civilrights/dc1.htm.

Weakley, Sonya. "Religious Rites of Passage Are Steps towards Adulthood." America.gov: Telling America's Story, 26 Aug. 2008. http://www.america.gov/st/diversity-english/2008/August/20080826115353xlrennef0.1725733.html.

"World Trade Center Site Memorial Competition." Lower Manhattan Development Corporation, 2004. http://www.wtcsitememorial.org/index.html.

*A tropical white sand beach in the Caribbean. iStock/David Coleman*

*A map of the Caribbean from 1678.*

# THE CARIBBEAN

*St. John's waterfront on the island of Antigua. iStock/Andrew Gosling*

# ANTIGUA & BARBUDA

# Introduction

Known in colonial days as the "Gateway of the Caribbean," the island of Antigua was originally the home of the Arawak and Carib Indians. A former British colony, Antigua and Barbuda became an independent state in 1981.

The islands were once central to the slave, shipping, and sugar trades, but today the country of Antigua and Barbuda is a tourist paradise. Tourism is the mainstay of the economy, although international financial conditions have slowed tourist traffic in recent years. The islands are part of the Lesser Antilles archipelago, and are susceptible to tropical storms and hurricanes; Hurricane Hugo in 1989 and Hurricane Luis in 1995 were particularly devastating.

## GENERAL INFORMATION

**Official Language(s):** English
**Population:** 92,436 (2015 estimate)
**Currency:** East Caribbean dollar
**Coins:** The Eastern Caribbean dollar comes in coin denominations of 1, 2, 5, 10, and 25; there is also a one-dollar coin.
**Land Area:** 442 square kilometers (170 square miles)
**National Motto:** "Each Endeavoring, All Achieving"
**National Anthem:** "Fair Antigua, We Salute Thee"
**Capital:** St. John's
**Time Zone(s):** GMT -4

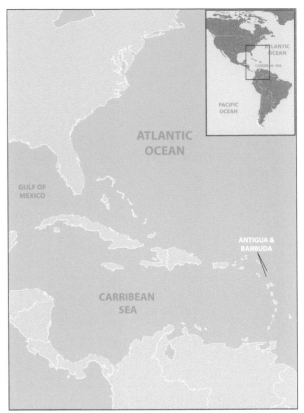

**Flag Description:** The flag features an isosceles triangle, the base of which runs the length of the top of the flag, and the point of which touches the base of the flag at its center. Flanked on either side of this large triangle are two red, right-angled triangles. The central triangle is broken up into three bands of color. The top band is black and features, at its center, a yellow sun. The central band is blue, and the bottom band is white.

## Population

The population of Antigua and Barbuda is mostly rural, with only 23.8 percent living in urban areas. Located on Antigua, the larger island, St. John's is the country's capital and only city; in 2011, about 22,000 people resided in St. John's, with an additional 30,000 living in St. John's parish.

## Languages

The official language is English. Almost all residents speak English, and most islanders also speak an English patois or Antiguan creole, a local variation of the language.

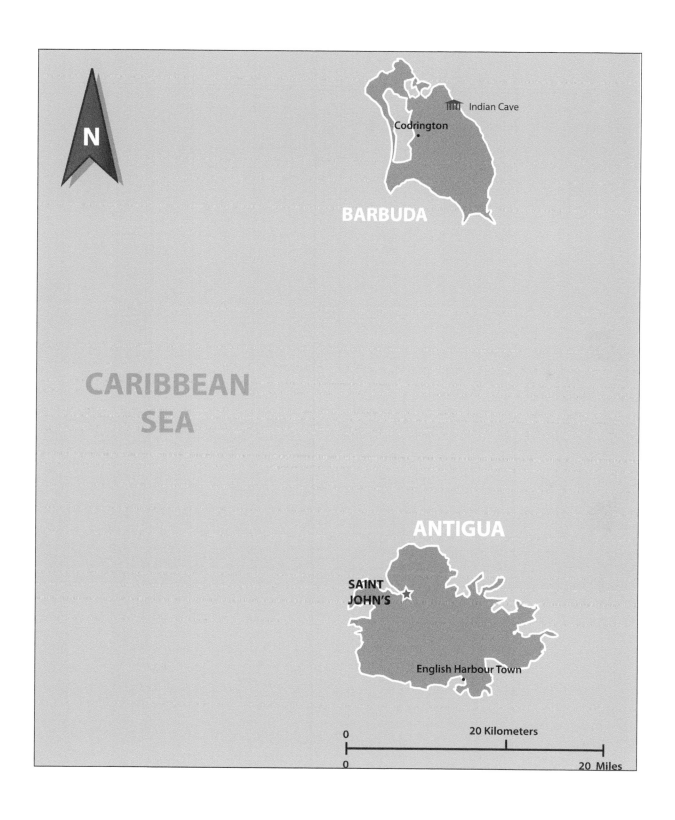

**Principal Cities & Settlements by Population (2011, except where noted):**

- St. John's (22,219)
- All Saints (3,900; 2001)
- Liberta (2,560; 2001)
- Potters Village (2,066; 2001)

## Native People & Ethnic Groups

The earliest known inhabitants of Antigua were the Siboney (Guanahuatebey), whose name means "Stone People" in Arawak. The Siboney arrived about 2400 BCE. They lived throughout the Caribbean, subsisting on conch (a shellfish) and fish. Little is known about them, but artifacts, including jewelry and tools of stone and shell, have been found at numerous sites on the islands.

The Siboney were succeeded by the Arawak (also called Taino and Lucayan), who arrived from South America during the early decades of the first century CE. The peaceful Arawak practiced slash-and-burn agriculture. They cultivated cotton, indigo, sweet potatoes, beans, corn, and pineapple.

In the 12th century, the more aggressive Caribs, for whom the Caribbean Sea is named, supplanted the Arawak. The Caribs, however, did not live on Antigua, evidently using it only as a supply base. Both the Arawaks and the Caribs were skilled boat-builders.

Christopher Columbus sighted and named Antigua in 1493, on his second voyage. He did not settle the island, however, because it lacked fresh water. Most of the indigenous peoples of the Caribbean soon succumbed to European and then African diseases, as well as warfare and poverty.

In 1632, British settlers established the colony of Antigua, including the uninhabited island of Redonda. They brought in African slaves to work the sugarcane plantations. Slavery was abolished in 1834, the earliest abolition of slavery in the Caribbean. However, black Antiguans found themselves still economically dependent on the Europeans.

The largest ethnic group is descended from black Africans, some of whom were slaves on the islands' sugar plantations. In 2011, it was estimated that 87.1 percent of the population was black. It was also estimated that approximately 4.7 percent of the population were of "mixed" ancestry, 1.6 percent were white, and 3.5 percent identified as being "other" or "unspecified." Minority groups include British, Portuguese, Lebanese, and Syrians.

## Religions

There is no established church on the islands, and freedom of religion is guaranteed by the constitution. The government works closely with the Antigua Christian Council; the Salvation Army and the Methodist, Moravian, Roman Catholic, and Anglican churches are all members of the council. Most of the people (68.3 percent) are Protestant Christians. Minority religions include Roman Catholic, Baha'i, and Islam.

## Climate

Antigua and Barbuda's tropical maritime climate is tempered by sea breezes and the trade winds. There is little variation in temperature. The average temperature is 27° Celsius (81° Fahrenheit), but it can get as hot as 33° Celsius (93° Fahrenheit) from May to October.

Rainfall is usually light, amounting to roughly 1,140 millimeters (45 inches) annually. However, long droughts frequently occur.

In addition to droughts, natural hazards include hurricanes and tropical storms, which often strike the island between July and October. Sometimes these storms also cause damaging floods.

In 1989, Hurricane Hugo caused two deaths and $80 million USD in damage. Hurricane Luis killed two people in 1995, and caused $300 million USD in damage. Other hurricanes since then have also caused extensive damage and flooding.

## ENVIRONMENT & GEOGRAPHY

### Topography

In the eastern arc of the Lesser Antilles, 692 kilometers (430 miles) north of Venezuela, lie the three islands that constitute the nation of Antigua and Barbuda.

The northernmost of the three islands is uninhabited Redonda, the smallest, with an area of only 1.6 square kilometers (0.6 square miles). About 40 kilometers (25 miles) southwest of Redonda lies Barbuda, with an area of 161 square kilometers (62 square miles). Forty kilometers (25 miles) south of Barbuda lies Antigua, the largest of the British Leeward Islands, with an area of 280 square kilometers (108 square miles).

Antigua's shoreline has many bays and harbors; the capital of St. John's is situated on Deep Water Harbor, a bay located on the northwest side of Antigua, where cool breezes help moderate the tropical temperatures. Barbuda has one very large harbor on the west side. The total coastline of Antigua and Barbuda is 153 kilometers (95 miles) long. The highest point in the nation is Boggy Peak, at 402 meters (1,319 feet).

The volcanic islands are composed of limestone and coral. They have been worn mostly flat by the wind and rain. The islands' white-sand beaches are famous.

## Plants & Animals

The island of Redonda, a small rock of an island that is a dependency of Antigua and Barbuda, is not only uninhabited, but has very little vegetation. The islands of Antigua and Barbuda were largely deforested when the trees were cut down to make room for sugarcane plantations. Dry scrub remains, and many varieties of hibiscus flourish.

The national plant is the West Indian dagger log. Fishing rafts were once made from the stem of this plant, and fishing bait was made from the white leaf pulp. The national tree is the whitewood.

The small, sweet Antiguan black pineapple, named for its dark green skin when ripe, is the national fruit. Introduced by the Arawak Indians, the pineapple was used in various rituals as well as for twine and cloth (made from the leaves). The plant is used today to treat sprains and the stings of sea urchin spines and wasps.

The widdy widdy is the national weed. This bush, along with cockles (a shellfish), supplemented the food supply of plantation workers during the long 1951 strike.

The national bird is the frigate, which grows as large as 1.4 kilograms (3 pounds), with a wingspan of up to 2.4 meters (8 feet).

The national animal is the fallow deer, which was introduced from Europe in the early 18th century. This deer, which now lives only in Antigua and Barbuda, is the eastern Caribbean's only large animal. The hawksbill turtle is the national sea creature.

The black horse spider, a highly poisonous tarantula, is also found in Antigua. The tropical bont tick is particularly troublesome to domestic animals. It causes heartwater, a fatal disease, as well as dermatophilosis, a skin infection that affects sheep.

## CUSTOMS & COURTESIES

### Greetings

English is the official language of Antigua and Barbuda, but most residents also speak an English, or Antiguan, Creole. Antiguan Creole blends elements of Hindi, African dialects and indigenous languages with British English, and is similar to other Caribbean creoles. Basic greetings consist of "Hello" (pronounced with a silent "h"), "Marning" ("Good morning") or "Hail up." ("Hi"). The propensity among Antiguans and Barbudans to use slang in everyday speech often makes their language difficult for outsiders. The phrase "Ow gwain," for instance, translates as "how are you doing?" The answer to this could be "I'm here," pronounced "Me yah," meaning that the person is still living and going about their life.

It is also customary to politely greet every person one encounters throughout the day. Failure to do so, even in passing, can be seen as rude. Men generally shake hands when greeting, while making eye contact. Close friends and family may embrace or kiss in greeting.

### Gestures & Etiquette

As in many Caribbean nations, though the culture is tied to an oceanic way of life, Antiguans and Barbudans dress conservatively when out in

*A woman wearing the traditional costume of Antigua.*

## Eating/Meals

Antiguans and Barbudans typically eat three meals a day that correspond to breakfast, lunch, and dinner. The morning meal is usually heavy in fruits and grain, but may also include light portions of seafood or meat, or simple dishes consisting of porridge or eggs. Many Antiguans and Barbudans take coffee or tea with their breakfast, while others prefer fruit juices. Some islanders may have mid-morning tea, with some light snacks, between their morning and afternoon meals.

The afternoon meal is typically more substantial than the morning meal and may contain a variety of roasted meat or seafood dishes, with fruit drinks, soft drinks, or beer. Some may consume rum, an island delicacy, along with their afternoon meal. The afternoon meal is commonly combined with business meetings and socializing. (Many Antiguans and Barbudans may also pause from work in the late afternoon for a "tea break," which may include pastries or other light snacks.)

The evening meal is traditionally the time for family socializing, romantic meals, and gathering with friends. The evening meal is often the most substantial of the day and is typically the only meal that may be served in courses, with appetizers, entrees, and desserts.

## Visiting

Antiguans and Barbudans are known for their hospitable nature and are often enthusiastic about inviting guests to their homes. It is considered polite, but not required, for guests to bring small gifts for their hosts. Pastries, candies, and flowers make good gifts; but white flowers, especially lilies, should be avoided as they are used for funerals. Likewise, roses should be avoided, as they symbolize romantic intentions.

Most Antiguans and Barbudans live in simple homes with few amenities, but guests should take care to compliment their hosts on their home and on any offerings, such as food, while they visit. Islanders generally appreciate good manners and guests are mainly expected to be polite and to show visible gratitude to their hosts.

public. Religion is important—the nation is predominantly Christian—on Antigua and Barbuda and most will dress for the occasion, wearing their best dresses and/or conservative clothing on Sundays. While the island nation, like most Caribbean countries, is a tourist destination that often depends on that revenue, foreigners are also generally expected to observe similar dress and etiquette.

The pace of life in Antigua and Barbuda is slow by comparison to the normal lifestyle in most Western cultures. When engaged in any activity, it is considered proper to take one's time, engaging in small talk and friendly conversation before launching into the activity at hand. When asking for assistance, for instance, an Antiguan or Barbudan will first offer a friendly greeting and perhaps inquire about the person's health and general well-being before settling into business. Nonetheless, punctuality is still emphasized, as tardiness can be perceived as a sign of disrespect.

## LIFESTYLE

### Family

The nuclear family, consisting of two parents and their children, is the basic unit of society in Antigua and Barbuda. Many families live in the same village or town as their extended families. It is common for extended family members to work together or to cooperate in child-rearing and other domestic activities. Most families are more strongly bonded to the maternal side of the family, a commonality between Antiguan and Barbudan culture and their African ancestors. As such, many families choose to live near the bride's family rather than the husbands.

Family planning has only begun to take hold on the islands in recent years, and many Antiguan and Barbudan couples have children out of wedlock, despite religious conventions discouraging unmarried child-rearing. It is customary for men and women to live together for a time before marriage, usually in the female's home. This tradition, which is also found in many other Caribbean communities, is known as a "visiting family."

The necessity to travel in order to find work has begun to erode the traditional structure of family life in Antigua and Barbuda. It is common in the 21st century for a woman to care for children on her own while the man works in another part of the island. Families may also be separated for part of the year, as many men and women find work in the tourist industry and may travel during certain parts of the year to capitalize on the increase in tourism.

### Housing

Most Antiguan and Barbudan families live in small and detached single-family homes or apartments in urban areas. The traditional "wattle" houses can still be found in some parts of the country. Wattle houses first became popular in the 1940s, when the population was suffering from an extreme rise in poverty. Many individuals and families constructed one- or two-room houses built from wattle and daub (plant fibers secured with mud). The roofs of wattle houses

are usually thatched from palm leaves or discard from the annual sugarcane crop.

In urban areas, many islanders live in small one- or two-bedroom apartments, usually constructed of brick or concrete. Single-family homes are also typically made from stone or concrete, though wooden houses can be found in some areas, especially in coastal communities. Some families living in coastal areas might construct their homes on stilts to avoid damage from flooding.

Most of the buildings that survived from the colonial period are sturdily constructed from stone, allowing them to withstand periodic windstorms and hurricanes. There are some colonial villas remaining in parts of the country that once housed wealthy landowners and members of the colonial aristocracy. Some of the old colonial homes have been repurposed as museums and commercial buildings, while others are owned by wealthy islanders and have been updated with modern amenities.

### Food

Antiguan and Barbudan cuisine is a blend of Caribbean, African, and European culinary traditions. Islanders often use tropical fruits in their cuisine both as side dishes and to make sauces and flavorings. The primary grain is rice, but corn is also available and cornmeal is the chief ingredient in one of the island's national dishes, fungie. This baked dish is made of cornmeal, water, and salt, sometimes with peppers and vegetables added for flavor. Fungie is used as a replacement for bread, and may be eaten in the morning with jam or butter or mixed in with savory dishes at lunch or dinner.

The Antiguans and Barbudans also make several varieties of pepperpot, a dish that is found, in modified versions, across the Caribbean. Most pepperpot varieties use pork products, usually the less desirable pieces like the snout, feet, and intestines, which are cooked in a stew with vegetables and greens, including spinach, onion, tomato, chives, okra, and eggplant. Pepperpot is usually seasoned with hot peppers, giving the dish its name. Traditionally served with pieces of fungie, which are either served on the side or mixed into the pot like dumplings, pepper-pot is eaten in the afternoon or evening. Other popular dishes include callaloo, a creamy spinach soup made with cloves or crab, and dukuna, a steamed sweet dumpling of grated sweet potatoes, flour, and spices. Local specialties include fried plantain, breadfruit, rice and beans, barbecued chicken, and roast suckling pig.

Seafood is an important component of Antiguan and Barbudan cuisine and culture. During the slavery period, salt cod, which was a cheap product, was often imported to feed slaves. Saltfish, as it is locally known, is still a popular component to the local diet. Saltfish may be served with rice and "peas," which can include any variety of legumes, or it may be served roasted with various vegetables. A popular saltfish presentation uses a piece of cod, or other salted fish, roasted in butter and served with eggplant, which is locally called "antrobe".

Other seafood dishes served on Antigua and Barbuda include oysters, clams, conch, and lobster. Most seafood is served with rice or vegetables and the ubiquitous fungie, which can act as a side dish or functions to soak up any leftover sauces. Antiguans and Barbudans use conch, a type of ocean mollusk, to make fritters with pieces of conch flesh fried in spicy batter. Conch fritters are commonly sold as street food by vendors across the island.

Dessert in Antigua and Barbuda may consist of simple fare, like fresh fruit sprinkled with powdered sugar, or more elaborate pastries and sweet dishes. One popular dessert in Antigua is tamarind stew, which uses the juice and flesh of the tamarind bean, known for its sweet flavor, mixed with sugar and other juices to create a sweet porridge. Tamarind is also used to prepare sauces that can be added to both sweet dishes, like cakes and pastries, or mixed with savory ingredients like garlic and onion to create unique sauces for seafood and meat dishes.

## Life's Milestones

As most Antiguans and Barbudans are Christian, many follow traditional Christian rights of passage including baptism, first communion, and marriage. The Caribbean baptism is considered an excellent time for celebration, and friends and family are usually invited to the family's home for dining and socializing. Some families may also celebrate a child's first communion with a similar ceremony.

Marriage is the transition to adulthood in Caribbean culture and islanders often accompany weddings with music, dancing, and a family or community meal. It is customary for guests to give small cash donations or other gifts to the new couple to help them start their life together. The family of the bride is usually more deeply involved in the marriage rituals and celebrations than the family of the groom; for example, the bride's family typically hosts and arranges the reception.

Funerary customs in Antigua and Barbuda follow British tradition, with guests wearing dark clothing and usually giving small gifts to the family of the deceased. White flowers, especially lilies, are given to express consolation and grief, as in British custom. It is also customary for friends and family members to gather after the church service for a reception at the family's home.

## CULTURAL HISTORY

### Arts & Crafts

The Antiguan and Barbudan people have a rich tradition of artistry that includes weaving, painting, and several styles of pottery making. The original inhabitants of the islands, the Arawak people, developed several characteristic styles of potting that are still practiced by natives, though they have been blended with West African and modern techniques. While the Arawak usually used maritime themes to decorate their pottery, modern Antiguan and Barbudan potters use a variety of decorative themes, including abstract designs and colorful glazing techniques. Today, the production of folk pottery is a cottage industry.

Like the native tribes that once inhabited the region, Antiguans and Barbudans became skilled canoe makers and maritime explorers. Many native canoes are designed and built in the same manner as canoes built by the Arawak Indians, while others are constructed with modern materials and techniques. The traditional technique involves using a single log, hollowed out by carving into the surface with a graded series of tools. In addition to fishing, Antiguans and Barbudans use boats for recreation and entertainment. An annual regatta, which is held in the spring, is a major celebration for the Antiguans and Barbudans.

The unique West Indian colonial furniture so prized by collectors was created and built by Antiguan slaves. Traditional motifs include fish, stylized snakes, and pineapples (a symbol of hospitality).

## Architecture

Architectural highlights in Antigua and Barbuda include the St. John's Anglican Church. The first church built on the site was constructed of wood—a basic structure characterized as lacking "beauty and comfort." Its successor, built in brick, was damaged in an 1843 earthquake. The third and latest iteration is baroque in style, built of freestone, and features two towers on the west end, which some have remarked resemble salt and pepper shakers. Others see the cathedral as an imposing and impressive edifice. As of 2015, it continues to be under renovation due to damage from a 1974 earthquake.

Another architectural gem is Clarence House, the historic home-away-from-home of Prince William Henry, who would go on to become King William IV of England. It now serves as the country residence of the governor general. It features a stone foundation with an open floor plan; verandas surround the structure, which boasts a tripartite hip roof.

In the wake of the failure of the sugar trade in the 19th century, many plantation homes were abandoned. Weatherhills, which was built in 1890, remains. The structure illustrates the blend of the home's Caribbean and English heritage. It, too, has a tripartite hip roof, extensive verandas, and shuttered windows.

## Drama

Theater came to the islands of Antigua and Barbuda in the late 18th century, when amateur dramatists and actors wrote and staged plays for the public. In the 1830s, a play titled *Harlequin Planter* (or *Age of Promise*) was widely performed in the country. The play, which deals with life on the islands and features aboriginals, slaves, and Europeans as characters, is considered to be one of the earliest examples of native Caribbean drama.

Native playwrights in the 20th century include Dobrene O'Marde, whose plays, such as *This World Spins Only One Way* (1998), address the various social and political issues of the islands. Other prominent playwrights include Glen Edwards, who wrote *Dreams…Faces…Reality*, and Rick James, known for his one-man play *Oulaudah Equiano*.

## Music

Historically, the music of Antigua and Barbuda is a blend of African, English, and Caribbean influences. As in most Caribbean nations, the West African slaves who worked in Antigua and Barbuda brought their traditional musical styles to the island. Over generations, these techniques were blended with European classical and folk music to create unique variations.

One of the nation's folk traditions is a style of music known as "benna" (or "bennah"). It is derived from the song-dance tradition brought over by West African slaves that also influenced various other musical folk traditions in the West Indies and Caribbean. (The word "benna" comes from a West African word meaning "song-dance.") Benna musicians use simple, rhythmic songs to convey stories and traditional legends. This Afro-Caribbean music is typically characterized by witty, improvised verses, usually telling stories from the singer's life or talking about relevant events in the community. Famous benna singer John "Quarkoo" Thomas, who was active in the 1940s and 1950s, used benna to deliver community bulletins as well as to tell amusing stories about life and native culture.

In more modern times, calypso and stee-plan (pitched percussive instrument) music have become the most popular forms of music. They are performed across the islands at clubs and public festivals. At the annual Carnival celebration there is a highly popular calypso competition in which local bands compete for prizes and the potential to have their music professionally recorded. In addition to entertainment, calypso is traditionally an informative type of music in which singers compose songs about relevant social issues and use their music to protest controversial policies.

## Literature

The first Antiguan writer to gain international fame was Jamaica Kincaid (1949– ), who was born Elaine Potter Richardson in St. John's. She later adopted a pen name out of fear that her writing would embarrass her family. Kincaid's talent for writing was discovered while she was living in the United States and working at the *New Yorker* magazine as a photographer. She began her writing career by penning short articles for the magazine and eventually transitioned from magazine writing to publishing novels about her life and Caribbean culture.

Though Kincaid remained in the United States, her success as a novelist remains a point of pride for Antiguans. Kincaid's novel *A Small Place* (1988) explores the issue of colonization and independence in the Caribbean told through the perspective of those in small, rural communities. Her subsequent works are more biographical in nature, but are still valuable as reflections of native culture and customs.

Other acclaimed authors include Joanne C. Hillhouse and Marie Elena-John (1963– ). Working primarily in fiction, Hillhouse's characters provide additional views of life in Antigua from a modern perspective as she investigates issues that concern families and women across the Caribbean. Elena-John's novel *Unburnable* (2006), while a work of fiction, is fueled by her unique knowledge of African and Caribbean history. It explores community and political themes that affect many Caribbean nations.

## CULTURE

### Arts & Entertainment

The contemporary arts play an important role in Antiguan and Barbudan culture. The local education system offers basic education in fine arts and music as part of the primary curriculum. Students of the university system also have the option to study the arts at the higher education level. On a cultural level, music, performance art, and dancing are part of every native celebration and ritual.

Antiguan calypso and other types of Caribbean music are a source of national pride. Government functions, national celebrations, and other festivities often include calypso performances, as well as examples of Amerindian dancing and singing. The mas band, short for "masked" band, is a tradition at Caribbean carnival celebrations. Members sing, play percussion, or accompany with horns while other members dance. Mas bands often wear elaborate costumes, fashioned from fabric and wire, which may depict animal figures and decorative patterns inspired by the natural environment.

Each year the government funds the local Carnival celebration and may also allow some limited funding for mas bands and other types of entertainers. Carnival began as a spontaneous expression of joy when slavery was abolished. Today, Carnival lasts for ten days each summer, and includes parades, dances, jump-ups, evening shows, and competitions for Carnival Queen and other titles. In addition to being a celebrated part of local culture, the annual carnival is also the height of the island's tourist season, making it an important economic focus across the islands.

The national sport is cricket. Official matches are usually held on the weekends throughout cricket season (January through July). A new stadium named for Antigua's most famous cricket player, Sir Isaac Vivian (Viv) Alexander Richards, opened outside of St. John's in time for the 2007 World Cup tournaments. Roads in St. John's were named for Viv Richards and Andy Roberts, another well-known cricket player. Antigua and Barbuda also hosts the annual Tennis Week and the Sailing Week regatta.

## Cultural Sites & Landmarks

One of the most prominent landmarks in St. John's is the Cathedral Church of St. John the Divine (St. John's Anglican Cathedral) with its 21-meter (70-foot) high twin towers. The original cathedral was destroyed in an earthquake and rebuilt in 1846. The capital of St. John's is also home to two forts, Fort James and Fort Bennington, which date back to the 18th century. (At one time, there were forty British forts on the island, built to defend against invaders and protect the sugarcane plantations.) On the outskirts of St. John's is Betty's Hope, a former sugar plantation founded around 1650. It includes the curing house, the boiling house, and the twin windmill towers that once used wind power to crush sugarcane. The grounds also contain authentic artifacts left by some of the roughly 390 slaves who once lived and worked at the plantation.

Victoria Park in St. John's offers an historic Botanical Garden and other green spaces for outdoor activities. Next to the Park are the National Archives, home to important government documents. Nearby is the site of the main public library.

Antigua is also home to the historic district of English Harbor, which was developed in the early 18th century as a British naval base for the Leeward Islands (the northern islands of the Lesser Antilles). The district is home to many historical landmarks, as well as a collection of authentic and replica sailing vessels and the Dockyard Museum, a small building with hundreds of artifacts and items left behind by the former British fleet. The district is also home to Nelson's Dockyard National Park (named after British admiral Lord Horatio Nelson). The park claims to be the only remaining working Georgian-era dockyard in the world.

The island of Barbuda, the northern smaller sister to Antigua, is known for its landscapes, as more of it has escaped development. The island is home to a number of natural attractions, including serving as a breeding ground for migrating flocks of frigate birds. The frigate bird, a relative of pelicans and boobies, is known for its long-distance flying ability and tendency to nest in large flocks. The colony on Barbuda, located on the island's northern end within a large stand of mangroves, is recognized as one of the largest ever identified, at times reaching a population of more than 2,000 birds.

Barbuda is also home to Indian Cave, a natural cavern that was expanded by miners when the island was the sight of a bustling phosphate mining community. The cave's chambers feature nesting bat colonies, remnants from the dormant phosphate-mining industry, and Amerindian petroglyphs (rock images) on the walls. Another natural landmark is Darby's Cave, which is actually a sinkhole that formed in prehistoric times. Within the chasm, geological forces combined to create stalactites and stalagmites, features usually associated with caves.

## Libraries & Museums

The Antigua Public Library was formed in 1830 and is located in St. John's, the country's capital. The library offers patrons access to computers, the Internet, and word processing software. In addition, it offers a summer reading program for children. The Museum of Antigua and Barbuda resides in the historic courthouse building of St. John's, which is the oldest building in the capital; dedicated in 1750, it required major renovations after two earthquakes. The museum features exhibits on the history of the islands from early Arawak culture to the present, including the bat of cricketer Vivian Richards. Artifacts of British colonial life are interspersed with tools and equipment used by the Carib and Arawak peoples in the museum's small exhibit hall.

## Holidays

Official holidays observed in Antigua and Barbuda include Sir Vere Cornwall Bird Sr. Day (December 9), honoring Antigua's first prime minister after independence; and Carnival, a celebration of African heritage and emancipation that features calypso and reggae music (August). Among the major celebrations in St. John's is Independence Day, which has been celebrated on November 1 of each year since 1981, when the islands gained their independence from Great Britain.

## Youth Culture

Because Antigua and Barbuda is a poor dual-island nation, children often begin working at a young age. Many teenagers and adolescent children find work in the tourism industry. Children from rural families are expected to begin helping with chores and/or agricultural work at a young age.

Children in Antigua and Barbuda play a variety of games, including cricket and football (soccer), two of the most popular games on the island. The country has amateur and junior leagues for cricket and softball, and both sports are usually included as part of the physical education program at most primary and secondary schools. Most towns and villages have grassy areas set aside for cricket and softball, and these are popular gathering places for children and teenagers. The national game of Antigua and Barbuda is "warri," a strategy game similar to chess and played on a carved wooden board. The Antiguans and Barbudans traditionally use "nickars," the seeds of the nickar tree, as game pieces. The progression of the game involves using strategy to capture the opponent's pieces while preventing one's own from being captured.

Music is an important factor in the recreational lives of Antiguan and Barbudan teenagers. Calypso music, a standard in the Caribbean, is the most popular genre in the nation and is considered to be the national musical style. Teenagers often meet at music clubs to dance and socialize and many also play music for recreation. In addition to calypso, other Caribbean styles have become popular in Antigua and Barbuda, including reggae and soca music from Jamaica. Antiguan and Barbudan teens also have access to imported music from the United States, such as hip-hop and rock.

## SOCIETY

## Transportation

Buses are the most popular mode of public transportation in Antigua and Barbuda. They connect the major cities to many of the more remote towns and villages. Antiguans may find it more efficient to hire taxis for short distance travel. Taxis are available in all the major cities, but most are not metered. The public bus system is more extensive in Antigua, with a hub in the capital of St. John's and routes to most towns and villages across the country. Because of inconsistent traffic and a relatively small fleet of public service vehicles, schedules are subject to change and many buses run behind schedule. Visitors can recognize public service vehicles by their license plates, which will include the letters HA for those in Antigua and HB for those running in Barbuda.

For those traveling between Antigua and Barbuda or from the islands to other nearby locations, there are also maritime transportation options including ferries, private chartered boats, and public transport craft. There are three airports on the island, but only two with paved runways.

Drivers in Antigua and Barbados travel on the left-hand side of the road.

## Transportation Infrastructure

As of 2011, only 386 kilometers (240 miles) of the country's estimated 1,170 kilometers (726 miles) of roadways were paved, and even paved roads tend to be in poor condition. In addition, many of the country's roadways are inaccessible at times of the year due to damage and weathering.

The nation's principal economic port is located in St. John's, but there are smaller ports around the islands and numerous watercraft travel between Antigua and Barbuda carrying both commercial and passenger traffic.

## Media & Communications

The Antiguan and Barbudan government places no censorship restrictions on media outlets. Television, print, and Internet media sources regularly produce programs with views critical of government policy. Members of the Bird family, a political dynasty that led the government from 1976 until the elections of 2004, and their political group the Antigua Labor Party (ALP), own most of the media outlets on both Antigua and Barbuda. The ALP allows its radio and television stations to broadcast views critical of ALP policy. However, there have been accusations that the ALP had delayed access to other independent groups wishing to obtain broadcasting licenses. The nation's first independent radio station, Observer Radio, began operation in 2001.

The nation has two primary daily newspapers, the *Antigua Sun* and the *Daily Observer*, both of which are published in English and available across the islands. The ALP also runs its own publications providing news and economic coverage. In addition, there are a variety of international publications available in Antigua and Barbuda imported from the United States, Jamaica, and elsewhere in the Caribbean.

Access to satellite television and the Internet has expanded in Antigua, particularly in the area surrounding the capital. However, coverage is still limited in Barbuda. As of 2014, there are an estimated 81,900 Internet users, representing nearly 90 percent of the population for both islands. The government-owned Antigua and Barbuda Broadcasting Service provides free television coverage, including both news and entertainment programming. Several popular programs are rebroadcast from other Caribbean nations to supplement the relatively small number of nationally produced programs.

## SOCIAL DEVELOPMENT

### Standard of Living
The country ranked 61 on the 2014 United Nations Human Development Index (HDI), which measures quality of life indicators.

### Water Consumption
Water management is a concern because natural freshwater sources are scarce. There are no underground water sources and no streams. Rainwater is collected in cisterns, but the amount of rainfall is inadequate. Tourist resorts have desalination plants, but the management still asks guests to limit water use. Clearing trees to increase agricultural production further limits the water supply. In 2015, 97.9 percent of the urban population had access to improved drinking water sources and 91.4 percent had access to improved sanitation facilities.

### Education
Antigua and Barbuda's well-developed primary- and secondary-school system is based on the British educational system. School is compulsory for students between the ages of five and sixteen.

Primary school begins at age five and usually lasts for seven years. Secondary school, beginning at age twelve, is provided in two cycles—with one lasting three years and the other lasting two years.

The average literacy rate is 99 percent (2012). Education expenditures account for 2.6 percent of the nation's gross domestic product (GDP).

The country also hosts a department of the University of the West Indies, which prepares students for advanced study at other branches of the university.

### Women's Rights
In traditional Caribbean society, males are considered superior to their spouses and other women in the community. Though the constitution guarantees equality and equal treatment, cultural norms contribute to an environment in which spousal abuse is tolerated and rarely punished.

The Domestic Violence Act of 1999 established the most recent classifications and penalties for domestic abuse and covered rape, spousal abuse and spousal molestation, with penalties including fines and prison sentences. However, cultural norms often discourage women from reporting abuse to authorities. In 2008, women's rights organizations and the government office of gender affairs engaged in outreach education programs to inform women of their rights to protection and prosecution.

The office of gender affairs trains police and judicial officials to appropriately address domestic cases. According to some reports, police are reluctant to arrest men accused of domestic abuse unless clear evidence of abuse is present. Antiguan and Barbudan women have a number of shelters available, including both state-run and privately operated organizations. Some of these offer psychological services and childcare in addition to legal aid.

Sexual harassment is commonly reported by women working in a number of industries, but was rarely investigated or prosecuted by authorities. Although women constitute more than half of the domestic work force, the relative number of women holding management positions suggests that women suffer from inequality in hiring and advancement. There are no laws guaranteeing equal pay for women, and numerous reports indicate that women receive less compensation, on average, than men in similar positions.

### Health Care

Average life expectancy in Antigua and Barbuda is seventy-six years; seventy-four years for men and seventy-eight years for women (2015 estimate). There is one doctor available for every 900 people, and the annual health expenditure is 4.9 percent of the GDP.

The country has only one hospital and two private medical clinics. Doctors often expect immediate payment for services. As there is no hyperbaric recompression chamber, divers suffering from compression sickness ("the bends") must be evacuated to the nearby islands of Saba or Guadeloupe.

Primary causes of death include circulatory diseases (including pulmonary and other heart diseases), cancer, and disorders of the endocrine and metabolic systems.

---

## GOVERNMENT

### Structure

Antigua and Barbuda is a constitutional monarchy with a bicameral parliament. Suffrage is universal at age eighteen. A member of the British Commonwealth of Nations, Antigua and Barbuda has a legal system based on British Common Law.

The British monarch is the nominal head of state, but appoints a governor-general to act as his or her representative in the country.

After elections, the governor-general appoints the leader of the majority party (or majority coali-

tion) in Parliament as prime minister. Together, the prime minister and the governor-general appoint the ministers of the cabinet. The cabinet is responsible to the House of Representatives.

Parliament consists of the House of Representatives and the Senate. The seventeen representatives are elected to terms of up to five years. The seventeen senators are appointed by the governor-general.

### Political Parties

The two main political parties are the Antigua Labour Party (ALP), led by Lester Bird, and the United Progressive Party (UPP), led by Baldwin Spencer. In the June 2014 election, the UPP won three seats in the House of Representatives, and the ALP won fourteen.

### Local Government

The island of Barbuda, as a result of the Barbuda Local Government Act, is governed by an island-wide local governing council known as the Barbuda Council. The island of Antigua, however, does not have a local government.

### Judicial System

The country falls under the Eastern Caribbean Supreme Court, which is based in St. Lucia. Other courts include magistrate's courts and an industrial court.

### Taxation

Taxes levied include a personal income tax, property transfer tax, and sales tax. There is no inheritance or capital gains tax. Taxes and other revenues make up 19.4 percent of the annual GDP.

### Armed Forces

The Royal Antigua and Barbuda Defence Force is made up of an infantry, a support force, a coast guard, and a cadet corps.

### Foreign Policy

As a small nation with no international disputes, Antigua and Barbuda has a positive record of friendly international relations. Antigua and Barbuda is a member of the United Nations (UN), the Organization of American States

(OAS), and the Eastern Caribbean's Regional Security System (RSS). Though the government of Antigua and Barbuda is active in international affairs, the country's primary concern is in forming profitable economic partnerships that will improve the nation's economic situation.

The United States maintains a permanent military presence on the island of Antigua and operates a satellite tracking station from the island. The Antiguan and Barbudan government has also cooperated with US–led anti-narcotics operations on the island and in surrounding maritime territory. The United States also cooperates with the Antiguan and Barbudan government to monitor international waters for illegal shipping and trafficking activity (as the country is a destination for sex trafficking and forced labor).

One of the government's primary concerns is environmental protection. Antigua and Barbuda has been active in creating and promoting environmental legislation and has participated in cooperative programs to protect natural resources. Deforestation is one of the islands' pressing issues. Some scientists believe that Antigua and Barbuda are at risk for "desertification," wherein the scarcity of vegetation leads to soil degradation, which can result in falling agricultural yields. In addition, as fishing is crucial to native culture and industry, the government takes an active interest in measures to monitor and protect populations of important oceanic fish species.

## Dependencies

The uninhabited island of Redonda is a dependency of Antigua and Barbuda. Essentially a large chunk of rock, the island has been a dependency of Antigua and Barbuda since 1967.

## Human Rights Profile

International human rights law insists that states respect civil and political rights, and also promote an individual's economic, social, and cultural rights. The United Nations (UN) Universal Declaration of Human Rights (UDHR) is recognized as the standard for international human rights. Its authors sought the counsel of the world's great thinkers, philosophers, and religious leaders, and were careful to create a document that reflects the core values shared by every world culture. (To read this document or view the articles relating to cultural human rights, go to: http://www.udhr.org/UDHR/default.htm.)

The parliamentary republic of Antigua and Barbuda has a positive record of protecting the rights and freedoms of its citizens. Government policy and the national constitution are generally in keeping with the spirit and principles established under the UDHR. The primary human rights concerns in the nation stem from lack of resources and training preventing the government from effectively addressing issues such as prison conditions, women's rights, and child welfare.

The national police force generally respects the rights of accused prisoners, in keeping with Article 9 of the UDHR. There have been isolated complaints of police using excessive force when detaining and/or interrogating suspects. Human rights monitoring groups have also claimed that there is insufficient supervision to prevent police abuse. Conditions in the nation's sole prison, Her Majesty's Prison, were a major cause for concern as prisoners had inadequate access to sanitation and medical facilities, constituting a violation of Article 5 of the UDHR. In addition, because of inadequate facilities, underage inmates were housed with the adult prison population, a violation of Article 25, guaranteeing that children receive special treatment under national law.

Some human rights agencies have alleged that child abuse and molestation are widespread in Antigua and Barbuda, though statistics are lacking. The government has no specialized facilities or police apparatus to investigate child abuse, and cultural customs are permissive on the issue of corporal punishment in the home, though it is prohibited by the penal code. Additionally, due to traditional beliefs against homosexuality, some openly homosexual couples and individuals suffer from discrimination and abuse. Although all creeds and lifestyles are protected under the penal code, it is alleged that police inadequately prevent the abuse and discrimination of homosexuals.

## ECONOMY

### Overview of the Economy

Tourism is the most important part of the economy of Antigua and Barbuda. Revenue generated by tourists accounts for 60 percent of the country's gross domestic product (GDP). In 2009, the GDP was estimated at $1.522 billion USD, with a per capita GDP of $17,800 USD. Because of the global economic crisis between 2009 and 2011, tourism steeply declined causing economic hardship for the country from which it has not entirely rebounded.

### Industry

After tourism-related service businesses, industry is the country's largest economic sector, employing nearly 11 percent of the labor force and accounting for 18.5 percent of the GDP. The government encourages small industries, which include the production of textiles, handicrafts, alcohol, paint, and household appliances.

Manufactured products include beer and malt, clothing, handicrafts, furniture, and electronic components. Most of the items manufactured in Antigua and Barbuda are exported. Exports earn approximately 52 percent of the GDP annually ($56.5 million USD according to 2014 estimates).

### Labor

The unemployment rate is approximately 11 percent of a workforce of 30,000.

### Fishing

Common species include lobster, conch, tuna, mackerel, and marlin. The fishing industry, as part of agriculture, represents approximately two percent of the country's GDP.

### Forestry

The forestry industry is virtually nonexistent as only around four percent of the country is forested.

### Agriculture

Sugar was the mainstay of agriculture in Antigua and Barbuda until the latter half of the 20th century. Today, primary crops include cotton, cucumbers, pumpkins, bananas, papayas, soursops, sweet potatoes, mangoes, oranges, guavas, coconuts, limes, melons, and pineapples. Shrimp, lobster, and crabs are also farmed. Most agricultural products are grown for domestic consumption.

The lack of fresh water on the islands limits Antigua and Barbuda's agricultural production. The shortage of labor is also a problem, as many people leave farms for better-paying jobs in construction and tourism.

### Animal Husbandry

In 2014, the livestock industry made up less than one percent of the country's GDP. In 2004, it was estimated that there were 14,300 head of cattle in the country, as well as 19,000 sheep.

### Tourism

Antigua and Barbuda's greatest natural resource is its climate, which attracts tourists to the islands. Most of the labor force works in tourism, which is the major sector of the economy. Antigua and Barbuda attracts nearly 200,000 visitors a year, many from the United States. Tourism receipts generally account for more than $270 million USD annually, although this has been reduced since 2009 with the global economic crisis. Only a small percentage of visitors choose to visit Barbuda and instead opt for the destination resorts that line the Antiguan coastline.

Tourist attractions include the numerous sugar mills left over from colonial days, excellent beaches, scenery, resorts, climate, regattas, shopping, restaurants, bars, casinos, and festivals, such as Carnival. Antiguans boast that with 365 beaches, there is "one for every day of the year."

*Micah Issitt, Ellen Bailey, Sally Driscoll*

## DO YOU KNOW?

- Wadadli, the brand of local beer, is the old Arawak name for Antigua.

- Early English settlers in Antigua and Barbuda often built relatively quick and easy houses using the "wattle-and-daub" type of construction. The "wattle" is comprised of the logs and twigs used to construct the frame, while the "daub" is a mud and grass mixture used to cover the frame and fill gaps.

- Before Antigua and Barbuda became one entity, Codrington used to be the capital of Barbuda. It is the largest village on the island.

## Bibliography

Ali, Arif. *Antigua and Barbuda*. 6th ed, Hertford, UK: Hansib Publishing, 2008.

Beale, Christopher. *Antigua and Barbuda: Island Guide*. Washington, DC: Other Places Publishing, 2008.

Blouet, Olwyn M. *The Contemporary Caribbean: Life, History, and Culture Since 1945*. New York: Reaktion Books, 2007.

Dyde, Brian. *Antigua and Barbuda: The Heart of the Caribbean*. New York: Macmillan Caribbean, 1999.

Dyde, Brian. *The History of Antigua: The Unsuspected Isle*. Northampton, MA: Interlink Publishing, 2003.

Epstein, Irving and Leslie Limage. *The Greenwood Encyclopedia of Children's Issues Worldwide*. Westport, CT: Greenwood Publishing Group, 2008.

Etherington, Melanie. *The Antigua and Barbuda Companion*. New York: Macmillan Education, 2002.

Philpott, Don and Ellen Anderson. *Landmark Visitors Guide Antigua & Barbuda*. 2nd ed. Walpole, MA: Hunter Publishing, 2004.

Permenter, Paris and John Bigley. *Adventure Guide to the Leeward Islands: Anguilla, St. Martin, St. Barts, St. Kitts and Nevis, Antigua and Barbuda*. Walpole, MA: Hunter Publishing, 1998.

Vaitilingam, Adam. *The Rough Guide to Antigua and Barbuda*. 2nd ed., London, UK: Rough Guides, 2002.

By Micah Issitt, Ellen Bailey, Sally Driscoll

## Works Cited

"Antigua and Barbuda: Country Report on Human Rights Practices." Bureau of Democracy, Human Rights and Labor. *United States Department of State*. http://www.state.gov/g/drl/rls/hrrpt/2006/78876.htm

"Antigua and Barbuda." *CIA World Factbook Online*. February 10, 2009. https://www.cia.gov/library/publications/the-world-factbook/geos/ac.html

"Antigua and Barbuda and the IMF." *International Monetary Fund Online*. http://www.imf.org/external/country/ATG/index.htm

"Antigua and Barbuda." National Geographic Travel Guide. *National Geographic Online*. http://travel.nationalgeographic.com/places/countries/country_antiguaandbarbuda.html

"Country Profile: Antigua and Barbuda." *BBC News Online*. November 20, 2008. http://news.bbc.co.uk/2/hi/americas/country_profiles/1191111.stm

"Human Rights in Antigua and Barbuda." *Amnesty International*. http://www.amnesty.org/en/region/antigua-barbuda

"Introducing Antigua and Barbuda." *Lonely Planet Online*. http://www.lonelyplanet.com/antigua-and-barbuda

Official Homepage of the Antigua & Barbuda Tourism Board. *Antigua and Barbuda Online*. http://www.antigua-barbuda.org/

"Parliament of Antigua and Barbuda." Official Site of the Government of Antigua Barbuda. http://www.ab.gov.ag/gov_v1/parliament/index.htm

*Pink façade on building in Aruba. iStock/Colonel1*

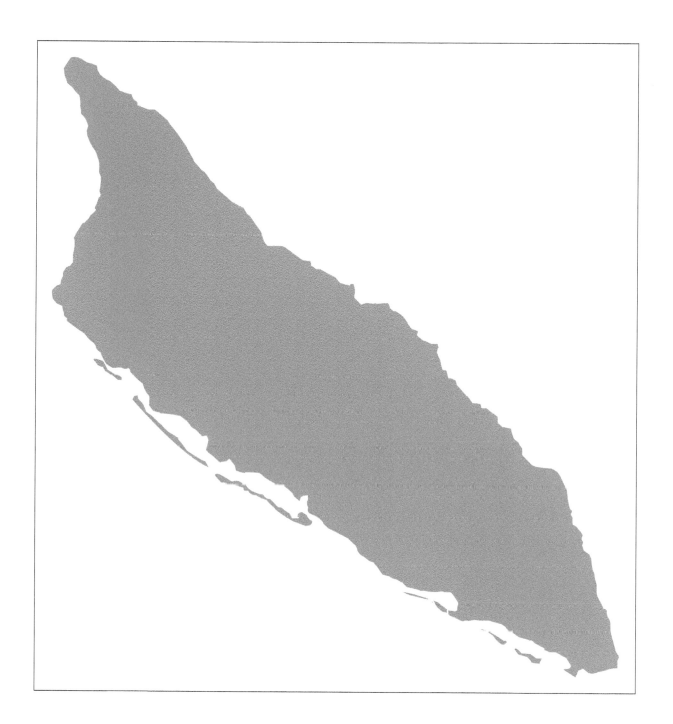

ARUBA

# Introduction

Originally Aruba was a possession of Spain, but came under Dutch rule in 1636. While gold and oil made up large parts of the economy early on, in the second half of the 20th century tourism became a major factor in the economy. Aruba still remains an autonomous member of the Kingdom of the Netherlands, gaining that position in 1986.

## GENERAL INFORMATION

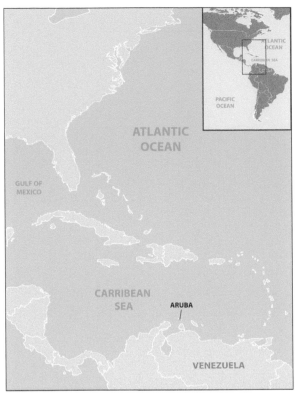

**Official Language(s):** Dutch and Papiamento
**Population:** 112,162 (2015 estimate)
**Currency:** Aruban florin
**Coins:** The Aruban florin is divided into 100 cents; coins are circulated in denominations of 5, 10, 25, and 50 cents, and 1, 2.5, and 5 florin.
**Land Area:** 180 square kilometers (69 square miles)
**National Motto:** "One Happy Island"
**National Anthem:** "Aruba Dushi Tera" (Papiamento, "Aruba, Precious Country")
**Capital:** Oranjestad
**Time Zone(s):** GMT -4
**Flag Description:** The Aruban flag consists of a four-pointed red star and two yellow stripes against a bright blue background. The four points on the star symbolize the island's diverse population. In addition, the star against the blue background symbolizes Aruba itself: a tiny island in the middle of the ocean.

## Population

Aruba is home to approximately 112,000 people, most of which are relatively young. The median age is just below 39 and12.7 percent of the population is 65 and older (2015 estimates). The vast majority of Arubans—about 80 percent in total—identify as being Dutch. Many Arubans have Dutch and/or Spanish roots, in combination with American Indian (Caquetio) ancestry. Some are also of partially African descent, as a result of the relatively small number of African slaves who were brought to the island during the period of Dutch colonization. In addition, Aruba has a sizable population of international immigrants who have settled there over the years from Europe, the Americas, various countries in Asia, and other Caribbean islands.

The average life expectancy, literacy rate, and total fertility rate in Aruba are comparable to those in developed countries. The two most densely populated cities in Aruba are Oranjestad, which houses about 28,294 residents, and San Nicolas, which houses an estimated 15,284 residents (2010 estimates).

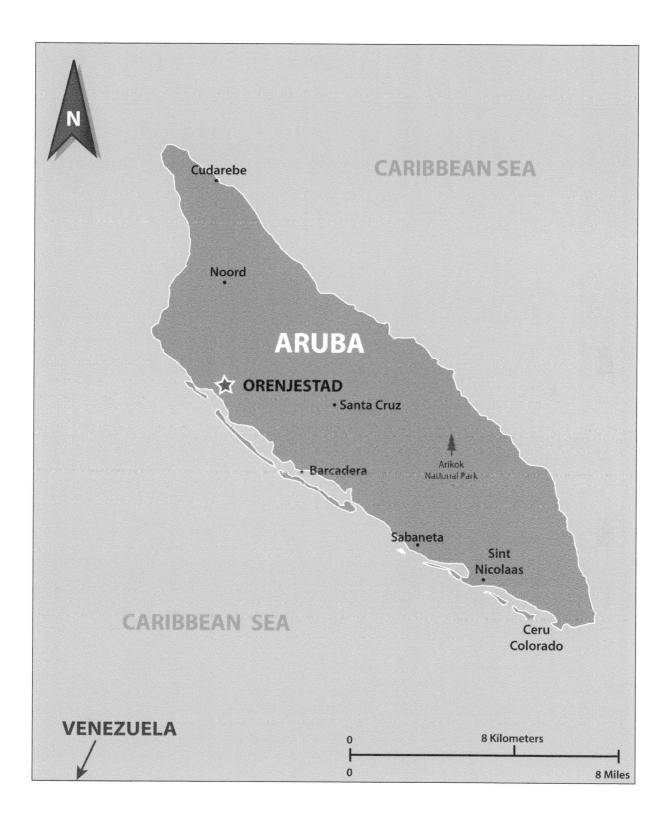

**Principle Cities by Population (2010 estimates):**

- Oranjestad (28,294)
- San Nicolas (15,284)

## Languages

Aruba's two official languages are Dutch and Papiamento, which is a complex and unique creole language whose grammar, vocabulary, and syntax are influenced by an eclectic combination of tongues. Papiamento is a mixture of Dutch, Portuguese, Spanish, and various West African languages, as well as the Arawak Indian language originally spoken by Aruba's native population. Papiamento is peppered with idioms that reflect aspects of the island's landscape and wildlife, such as the expression "Un macacu ta subi palu di sumpinja un biahe so" ("A monkey climbs a cactus only once"). Papiamento was not declared an official language in Aruba until 2003. English and Spanish are also commonly spoken.

## Native People & Ethnic Groups

Historically, Aruba's native population was made up of Caquetios Indians from the Arawak tribe. Originally from South America, the Caquetios are believed to have fled their home in the Paragon Peninsula of Venezuela after suffering repeated attacks from a neighboring tribe of Carib Indians. Artifacts they left behind—including cave paintings, fragments of pottery, and beads made of shells and stones—suggest that the Caquetios first settled in Aruba at about 1000 CE, and began organizing themselves into small farming villages.

When Spanish explorers, beginning with Alonso de Ojeda (c. 1465–1515), landed on the island in 1499, almost all the Caquetios were rounded up and sent to work in copper mines in what is now the Dominican Republic. Some years later, when the Spanish attempted to build a large horse and cattle ranch on Aruba, a small number of the Caquetios returned to the island. Since then, centuries of mixed marriages between the island's native people, Dutch settlers, Portuguese and Spanish missionaries, and African slaves have resulted in an almost total elimination of Aruba's pureblooded Amerindian population.

## Religions

Aruba is a predominantly Christian nation. Roman Catholics make up more than 75 percent of the population, while 4.9 percent of Arubans identify as Protestants and a small minority practice Hinduism, Islam, Judaism, or Buddhism.

## Climate

Aruba's climate remains fairly regular throughout the year, and there is very little change in temperature from season to season. The average daytime high is 28° Celsius (82° Fahrenheit), and Aruba's average annual rainfall is a relatively low 40.9 centimeters (16.1 inches). Trade winds constantly blow across the island's northeast coast, helping to keep temperatures comfortable and cool. Storms and hurricanes are rare on the island.

## ENVIRONMENT & GEOGRAPHY

## Topography

Aruba is a desert-like island whose terrain is generally flat and rocky. Only a few small hills can be seen dotting its landscape, and its native vegetation is both sparse and scrubby. Aruba's highest point is the peak of Mount Jamanota, which rises 188 meters (approximately 617 feet) above sea level.

The island's 68.5 kilometers (approximately 42.6 miles) of coastline boast pristine sand dunes on the southwestern side. In contrast, they are marked on the northeastern side by coral and limestone cliffs, as well as by deep natural caves carved out of rock. Until recently, a 100-foot-long arch known as the Natural Bridge, formed by the action of waves beating against coral limestone, extended over the sea on the northeast coast. The largest of eight similar formations on the island, the Natural Bridge was destroyed by waves in 2005. In addition, several imposing clusters of giant boulders can be seen further inland. Known as the Casibari Rocks, the precise origin of these mysterious rock formations is unknown. The Ayo Rock Formations, a similar site featuring stone boulders, was considered a sacred site to the native inhabitants.

## Plants & Animals

Aruba's dry climate is capable of sustaining a variety of hardy desert flora. Many species of cacti and aloe vera dot the island. Aruba is particularly famous for the gracefully curving trunks and branches of the watapana, or divi-divi trees. These trees have been shaped, over the course of many years, by the powerful trade winds that blow across the island. Their silhouettes have become a national symbol. By the shore, small green sea grape trees and flowering sea lavender plants can also be seen throughout the year.

Aruba's wildlife is equally varied and peculiar. The descendents of donkeys and goats that were introduced by the Spanish now roam wild in some areas of the island, while reptiles, such as lizards and iguanas, hide among the rocks. A small wetland ecosystem also exists at the Bubali Bird Sanctuary. There, seabirds, such as terns, cormorants, herons, gulls, and pelicans, hunt for fish among mangroves and buttonwood trees.

## CULTURAL HISTORY

### History

Archeological evidence indicates that the first people to inhabit Aruba were a tribe of Amerindians whose presence on the island predates the arrival of the Caquetios Indians. Traces of this tribe still remain, mostly in the form of primitive stone tools and bodies buried in what appear to be family groups. Ornaments and other artifacts from these early settlers can be seen in the Archaeological Museum of Aruba, located in the capital of Oranjestad.

Some 3,000 years after Aruba was first settled, a group of Caquetios Indians came to the island from Venezuela. They lived peacefully here as an agricultural people who grew mainly maize (corn). In 1499, Aruba was discovered by

Spanish explorers, who gave the island its name. There is no consensus on the precise origin of the name "Aruba," but some scholars suggest that it arose out of a Caquetios word meaning "guide." (Legend also has it that the name comes from the Spanish phrase meaning "it has gold," but the Spanish were never able to find gold on Aruba.) The Spanish were not particularly interested in the island itself, but they did remove most of its native population to nearby Santo Domingo (now the capital of the Dominican Republic) in order to make use of them as mine workers. Meanwhile, Aruba fell into a state of some disorder, with groups of pirates and smugglers seizing control of its surrounding waters.

In 1636, after more than a hundred years of neglect from its Spanish conquerors, Aruba (along with its neighbors Bonaire and Curaçao) was captured by the Dutch near the end of what had been a decades-long war between Spain and Holland. The Dutch West India Company took administrative control of Aruba, and established its capital. In fact, "Oranjestad" is a name derived from the surname of the Dutch royal family. During this time, the island's population steadily increased. Many European traders working in the Caribbean chose to settle in Aruba, and Venezuelans fleeing their country's internal conflicts added to its residents.

The Dutch retained uninterrupted sovereignty over the island for more than 200 years. The only exception to this was a period of about eleven years during the Napoleonic Wars (1805–1616), when Aruba was governed by the British. In 1824, gold was finally found near the base of Mount Jamanota, and the discovery sparked a small gold rush. By the time the island's supply of gold was exhausted approximately a hundred years later, Aruba's population, infrastructure, and trading ties had exponentially grown. When gold was no longer a viable export, Aruba's economy began to be driven by the production of aloe, a native plant that has a variety of medicinal uses.

The 20th century saw another important shift in the structure of Aruba's economy. In 1924, after a major oceanic oil deposit was found a few miles away, the Dutch built a large oil refinery in an area of Aruba called San Nicolas. The success of the oil refinery served as a significant boost to Aruba's material wealth, and the jobs it created caused a corresponding rise in immigrants arriving from the United States, Europe, and the Caribbean in search of employment. The importance of the oil refinery to the Allied Forces also made Aruba a strategic military target for the German army during World War II, but the island itself did not sustain any significant damage as a result.

When the war was over, American soldiers, who had been stationed in Aruba to protect it, began acting as informal tourism spokesmen, telling their friends and family what they had seen of the island's luxurious beaches and pleasant climate. Tourist arrivals increased, and Aruba started to actively market itself as an ideal tropical vacation destination. It built new hotels and casinos, while working hard to preserve the island's natural beauty. Aruba officially became a tourist-driven economy when the San Nicolas refinery was temporarily closed in the 1980s, thus shutting down the island's other major source of national income.

Until 1986, Aruba was a part of the Netherlands Antilles, a political and administrative unit consisting of six islands in the Caribbean under Dutch rule. The others were Curaçao, Bonaire, Saint Eustatius, Dutch St. Martin, and Saba. On January 1, 1986, Aruba seceded from the Netherlands Antilles and became recognized as a separate and autonomous entity. Technically, Aruba remains part of the Kingdom of the Netherlands, as it has not yet achieved the status of a fully independent nation. In 1990, Aruba requested to have complete independence deferred indefinitely. However, the island has its own governmental organization and essentially functions as an autonomous political entity.

## CULTURE

### Arts & Entertainment

As a whole, the character of the arts in Aruba reflects the diversity of the island's population and is strongly influenced by its natural surroundings. The country's music, dance, architecture, and creative arts all draw upon the complex interaction between Amerindian, European, African, and Caribbean cultures that has taken place over the centuries.

Music in particular occupies a central place in Aruban traditional life. Two unusual instruments have come to exemplify the national sound: the Aruban barrel organ and the wiri. The Aruban barrel organ is a large, stringed musical instrument with a crank that, when turned, causes hammers to thump against a series of piano keys. Borrowed from Italy in the 1800s, and enthusiastically adopted by Aruban musicians, the barrel organ is used to play folk songs, ballads, and lively Caribbean waltzes whose rhythms are influenced by both European and African musical traditions. The wiri is a distinctly Aruban percussion instrument made of a serrated metal tablet that is scraped to produce a rasping sound. As in the rest of the Caribbean, steel drums and copper timpanis (kettle drums) are also traditionally played.

Dance, in all its varied forms, is also very much a part of the Aruban identity. This is particularly evident during the month-long Carnival celebrations that take place every February. Four traditional folkloric dance forms that are especially identifiable with Aruba's history and culture are the mazurka, the waltz, the dansa, and the tumba. The mazurka, waltz, and dansa have Polish, Bavarian, and Spanish roots, respectively, but each was adopted by the people of various Caribbean islands centuries ago. The tumba is a unique Afro-Caribbean dance form that came to Aruba and its neighboring islands when African slaves were brought to the region between the 17th and 19th centuries.

One of the oldest folk art forms in Aruba is the crafting of sculptures, boxes, and other decorative items from the wood of the mopa-mopa tree. The tree's buds are boiled in water in order to produce a stiff, sticky resin that can then be dyed, stretched, molded, and cut into shapes that are carefully set into wood. Mopa-mopa art was brought to Aruba by its early Native American settlers, and is still created today by skilled artisans. Another natural material that Aruban artists have made use of is the djuco nut, which comes from a tree that grows in Venezuela and is carried on ocean currents to the island's shores. Djuco nuts are often made into jewelry on which a thin layer of gold filigree is painted. (Filigree consists of fine ornamental work made from twisted metal wires.)

In contrast to these traditional folk arts, the visual arts in Aruba have had a relatively short history. Its trailblazers were a small group of local painters who worked during the 1940s and 1950s, and who lacked any formal arts training. Having no way to support themselves through their work, these local painters spent their spare time creating relatively simple, realistic works that tended to depict the landscapes and scenes that surrounded them.

Over the next few decades, a number of international arts teachers arrived in Aruba, bringing with them modern and more Westernized tools and techniques. However, it was not until fairly recently that a new generation of Aruban artists began using painting in an overtly political way. Artists began to use their work to comment on social and cultural issues facing their country and its people. Prominent among these contemporary artists is Aruban painter Stan Kuiperi (1954– ), whose colorful, abstract works contemplate the complex, shifting relationship between man and nature.

## Cultural Sites & Landmarks

Aruba's most popular sites are its many attractive beaches, including Arashi Beach, Boca Catalina, Palm Beach, Eagle Beach, Rodgers Beach, and Baby Beach. All the beaches located along Aruba's southern coast boast calm, gentle, and warm waters that provide excellent conditions for swimming, snorkeling, diving, and other recreational activities. In contrast, the beaches on the island's northern coast, like Dos Playa and Boca Daimari, have rougher waters and more rugged shores. Nevertheless, their impressive sand dunes and rocky cliffs offer striking and picturesque vistas, and the stronger waves tend

to attract experienced surfers. In addition, two small private islands whose facilities are operated by resort owners—Renaissance Island and De Palm Island—are located in the harbor area near Oranjestad.

Aruba's natural beauty is itself an attraction. Arikok National Park is an expansive ecological preserve that is marked by unusual lava, quartz diorite, and limestone formations. The park contains several shelters left behind by early Native American settlers, as well as rock and cave paintings dating back to the same period. Aruba is also rich with fascinating natural geological sites. Among these are the Casibari Boulders, a mass of gigantic igneous rocks located north of Mount Hooiberg; the majestic and mysterious Ayo Rock Formations, which are covered in ancient petroglyphs (rock carvings); and the shallow, twisting hollows of the Guadirikiri, Fontein, and Huliba caves.

One of the most charming historical landmarks in Aruba is the Chapel of Alto Vista, a structure that is perched on a cliff overlooking the northern coast. This small chapel was built in 1750—it underwent major repairs in 1953—and is painted a sunny mustard-yellow color. It also has distinctive arch-shaped windows and doors. The Roman Catholic church of Santa Ana, located in Noord, is another notable building. Santa Ana dates back to 1776 and was constructed in a neo-Gothic style. The church's interior contains an impressive wooden altar that was donated by the Dutch.

Hudishibana, an area in the northernmost tip of the island, is home to another interesting piece of Aruban history: the California Lighthouse. Erected in 1910, the old stone lighthouse was named after an American passenger vessel that sank not far from the northern coast of Aruba. Two remnants of Aruba's gold rush period are also open to visitors: the Bushiribana and Balashi Gold Mill Ruins.

Aruba's most "well-traveled" historical landmark is perhaps its Old Dutch Windmill. The windmill, which is a peculiarity in the Caribbean, dates back to the early years of the 19th century, when it was used first as a means of water-draining, and then to power a grain mill. After it was damaged in a storm, the windmill was transported to Aruba in 1960. It has since housed a series of restaurants and bars.

## Libraries & Museums

Aruba's three major museums, the Historical Museum, the Archeological Museum, and the Numismatic Museum, are all located in Oranjestad. The Historical Museum is housed inside Fort Zoutman, a structure built by the Dutch in the late 18th century to help protect the island from raids by pirates.

## SOCIETY

### Transportation

Because of Aruba's small size, it does not take very much time to get around the island. Aruba is served by a somewhat limited, but efficient, public bus system. Used by both locals and visitors, the government-run bus service transports more than 2.5 million passengers per year. Buses leave the central bus station in Oranjestad for various destinations along the main beach and hotel area. Buses also travel between Oranjestad and other locations in Aruba, such as San Nicolas. Taxis are also readily available. In addition, motorcycles, mopeds, and scooters are popular modes of transportation in Aruba, as the island enjoys dry weather all year round. All the main roads in Aruba are paved, but many smaller roads leading to less well-traveled destinations are not, particularly towards the center of the island. For that reason, it is not uncommon to see jeeps and other rugged four-wheel drive vehicles on the roads.

### Media & Communications

The free press in Aruba, whose population has a literacy rate of more than 97 percent, consists of about a half dozen major newspapers. Each of these is published in either Papiamento or English. The paper with the largest circulation is the Papiamento daily *Diario Aruba*. Tele Aruba is the island's first national television and consists of 75 percent local programming.

As of 2014, approximately 80 percent of Aruba's residents had access to the Internet.

There is no government-initiated censorship of Internet sites in Aruba, although Internet access in public libraries is selectively filtered in order to safeguard children from potentially encountering obscene and other age-inappropriate online material. So far, only a relatively small amount of local content (content produced by Arubans themselves about issues relevant to their nation) is available on the Internet, especially in the Papiamento language.

## GOVERNMENT

### Structure

Aruba is a member country of the Kingdom of the Netherlands, but since 1986 it has had what is known as "status aparte," or "separate status." In effect, the island has been virtually self-governing. Although its government enjoys autonomy on all domestic issues, the Dutch government is ultimately responsible for administering Aruba's defense system and its foreign relations.

The Kingdom of the Netherlands is a constitutional monarchy with power passing along hereditary lines. The official head of state in Aruba is a governor appointed by the Dutch king; his or her term lasts six years. Aruba also has a cabinet, or Council of Ministers (the executive branch of government), consisting of eight members. The Council of Ministers is overseen by the prime minister and deputy prime minister, who are each elected by the twenty-one-member Aruban Staten (the legislative branch of government). The members of the Staten are elected by a popular vote to terms that last four years.

Aruba's legal and judicial system is based on Dutch law. Any legislation enacted in the Netherlands must be followed here, and vice versa. This occasionally causes some controversy, as Aruba is a much more socially conservative country than the Netherlands. For example, in 2005, two women were forced to battle for the right to marry in Aruba despite the fact that same-sex marriages are legal in the Netherlands.

Aruba has its own Common Court, but its rulings can be overturned by the Dutch Supreme Court.

## Foreign Policy

Aruba's foreign affairs are ultimately the responsibility of the Ministry of Foreign Affairs in the Netherlands. However, the Aruban prime minister is advised by a small governmental department of foreign affairs, which advises his office on matters of international relations. In particular, Aruba has important economic ties with many of its neighboring countries in the Caribbean, including Bonaire and Curaçao. It is also a member of the Association of Caribbean States (ACS), an intergovernmental organization dedicated to improving regional ties and strengthening the Caribbean economy while preserving the Caribbean Sea. In addition, Aruba is an observing, or non-voting, member of the Caribbean Community (CARICOM)—formerly known as the Caribbean Free Trade Association (CARIFTA). It is also an associate of the Economic Commission for Latin America and the Caribbean (ECLAC) and the World Trade Organization (WTO) through the Netherlands.

## Human Rights Profile

International human rights law insists that states respect civil and political rights, and also promote an individual's economic, social, and cultural rights. The United Nations (UN) Universal Declaration on Human Rights (UDHR) is recognized as the standard for international human rights. Its authors sought the counsel of the world's great thinkers, philosophers, and religious leaders, and were careful to create a document that reflects the core values shared by every world culture. (To read this document or view the articles relating to cultural human rights, go to: http://www.udhr.org/UDHR/default.htm.)

Aruba's constitution, like that of its parent nation, the Netherlands, guarantees full protection of human rights for all its citizens. According to the US Bureau of Democracy, Human Rights, and Labor, the human rights record in Aruba and its sister islands in the Netherlands Antilles is similar to that in the Netherlands. However,

some areas of concern exist with regard to human rights issues that are peculiar to Aruba itself.

One issue, pertaining to Article 2 of the UDHR (which upholds policies of non-discrimination) was resolved in 1998. At this time, Papiamento was officially made a second language of instruction in schools, in addition to Dutch. Prior to that, Dutch had been the only medium of instruction in schools. This situation persisted despite the fact that fewer than 6 percent of Aruban schoolchildren spoke Dutch at home and Papiamento was by far the dominant mother tongue.

In addition, according to the United Nations Human High Commissioner for Refugees (UNHCR), Aruba is one of several islands in the Caribbean that serves as a transit stop as well as a final destination for human trafficking, particularly for the purposes of forced labor, domestic servitude, and sexual exploitation—a violation of Article 4 of the declaration (which forbids slavery). In particular, some evidence suggests that women from Peru, Brazil, Colombia, and other Spanish-speaking countries are being brought to Aruba to serve in the local sex trade. In May 2006, new legislation was signed into effect in Aruba that strengthened the prohibitions on human trafficking and smuggling and increased the penalties for such acts.

# ECONOMY

## Overview of the Economy

Aruba enjoys a relatively strong economy that has shown a steady level of growth since the turn of the 21st century. As of 2009, its per capita gross domestic product (GDP) was $25,300 (USD) per person. During the period spanning 2003–2006, the average yearly growth in Aruba's nominal GDP was approximately 6 percent. This is largely due to an increase in the size of the country's tourist sector, which is the single largest industry in Aruba. In fact, approximately 35 percent of Arubans are employed in tourist-related enterprises and over 80 percent of the economy is tourist-based. The service industry as a whole, which includes hotels, restaurants, and other non-tourist-related businesses, is responsible for generating a little more than two-thirds of the country's GDP. The remaining 33 percent comes largely from industry, trade, and manufacturing, and a negligible amount arises from agriculture.

Unemployment is quite low, remaining at about seven percent.

## Industry

Industry, trade, and manufacturing in Aruba account for 33 percent of the gross domestic product (GDP). Aruba's major exports are livestock and animal products, art and collectibles, machinery and electrical equipment, transport equipment, and oil. The oil refinery that was opened in 1924 is still in operation. It was acquired by the Valero Energy Corporation in 2004 and is responsible for generating about 13 percent of Aruba's GDP.

## Energy/Power/Natural Resources

Apart from its white, sandy beaches and year-round warm climate—characteristics which, in combination, attract more than 1 million tourists to its shores each year—Aruba is not a country that is particularly rich in natural resources. However, the island does serve as the habitat for several species of flora and fauna that are not found anywhere else. These include the Aruba burrowing owl, the Aruban parakeet, the Aruban rattlesnake, and the Baker's cat-eyed snake. In addition, its waters contain a number of densely populated coral reefs.

In recent years, the Aruban government has put in place a variety of environmental initiatives designed to safeguard the plants, animals, and geological formations that make the island unique. Most significantly, approximately one-fifth of the island has been designated as protected land; most of this area is located within the sprawling Arikok National Park.

## Agriculture

Agriculture is not a significant contributor to the country's modern economy. This is due to the rise of the oil and tourism industries in Aruba, and partly because the island suffers from poor soil quality—barely a tenth of its total area is considered arable land—and relatively low levels of rainfall. However, the hot and arid conditions in Aruba create an ideal environment for the growth of aloe vera, which was introduced to the island in the 19th century. The plant was the first major source of income for Aruba, a fact that is reflected in the image of aloe on the country's coat of arms. Aruba harvests both wild and cultivated aloe vera plants in order to produce a wide variety of consumer products, including moisturizers, creams, and other skin-care items. It is currently the largest exporter of aloe in the world. A small amount of animal husbandry, including the raising of pigs, sheep, and goats for food and milk, is also performed on the island.

## Tourism

Two unexpected events precipitated a decline in the number of tourists Aruba received in the early years of the 21st century. The first was the attack on the United States on September 11, 2001, which resulted in a worldwide reduction in demand for tourism. However, Aruba recovered from this decline fairly quickly. More significant was the mysterious disappearance of Natalee Holloway, an American high school student from Alabama who vanished under suspect circumstances during a graduation trip to the island in 2005. Holloway was last seen leaving a downtown nightclub on May 30, 2005, and later missed her return flight to the United States. A massive investigation was launched into the case, which brought a great deal of negative attention to the island, particularly due to the American perception of the Aruban government's poor handling of the case. As visitors from the United States make up the largest proportion of Aruba's total visitors, the repercussions from the scandal, and the government's handling of the Holloway case, dealt a particularly hard blow to the tourism industry.

Official tourism figures for 2013 indicate that Aruba received more than 979,256 stay-over visitors and more than 688,000 cruise visitors.

Overall, these statistics represented a rise in total visitors of over eight percent compared to 2012. Tourism continues to be the biggest driving force behind the Aruban economy. It goes without saying that Aruba's most popular tourist attractions are its many spectacular beaches. The 7-mile stretch of sandy white shores along its southwestern coast includes Manchebo Beach, Eagle Beach, Palm Beach, and Arashi Beach. Most of Aruba's hotels, casinos, and resorts are located in this area.

*M. Lee*

## DO YOU KNOW?

- The annual celebration of Carnival did not begin taking place on Aruba until 1954. It was first initiated by a group of enthusiastic celebrants from the neighboring island of Curaçao, whose own festivities had been officially canceled in solemn recognition of the devastating floods that had struck The Netherlands that year. Disappointed, but resourceful, the Curaçaoans decided to coordinate an alternate celebration on Aruba. Carnival has been an essential holiday on the island ever since.

- The Aruban flag consists of a four-pointed red star and two yellow stripes against a bright blue background. The four points on the star symbolize the island's diverse population. In addition, the star against the blue background symbolizes Aruba itself a tiny island in the middle of the ocean.

## Bibliography

*Aruba.* 2009. Aruba Tourism Authority. 24 February 2009. http://www.aruba.com/

Henderson, James. *Caribbean and the Bahamas.* Guilford, CT: Globe Pequot, 2005.

Houston, Lynn Marie. *Food Culture in the Caribbean.* Westport, CT: Greenwood Press, 2005.

Lindley, Ken. *Aruba.* Hoboken, NJ: John Wiley, 2005.

Nalepa, Michael and Vernon O'Reilly-Ramesar. *Aruba.* New York: Fodor's, 2007.

Pons, Frank Moya. *History of the Caribbean: Plantations, Trade, and War in the Caribbean World.* Princeton, NJ: Markus Wiener, 2007.

## Works Cited

"Aruba." Encyclopædia Britannica. 2009. Encyclopædia Britannica Online. Online. http://www.britannica.com/EBchecked/topic/37333/Aruba

Aruba Numismatic Museum, various pages. Online. http://www.museumaruba.org/index.php?pg=home

Brushaber, Susan, et al. *Aruba, Bonaire, and Curacao Alive!* Edison, NJ: Hunter, 2002.

*CIA World Factbook.* "Aruba." Online. https://www.cia.gov/library/publications/the-world-factbook/geos/aa.html

International Federation of Library Associations and Institutions. "IFLA/FAIFE World Report 2007: Aruba."

Online. http://www.ifla.org/faife/report/18%20IFLA-FAIFE%202007%20CR%20-%20Aruba.pdf

InternationalReports.net. "Aruba 2002: The Mirror of the Times." *The Washington Times.* Online. http://www.internationalreports.net/theamericas/aruba/2002/themirror.html

Levinson, David. *Ethnic Groups Worldwide: A Ready Reference Handbook.* Phoenix, AZ: Oryx Press, 1998.

Official website of SETAR (the Aruban government's telecommunications company). "About SETAR: History." Online. http://www.setar.aw/index.php?option=com_content&task=view&id=198&Itemid=150

Official website of the Aruban Department of Foreign Affairs. "History." Online. http://www.arubaforeignaffairs.com/afa/getPage.do?page=BACKGROUND_CHARTER

Prengaman, Peter. "Aruba, Holland Miles Apart on Gay Marriages." The Associated Press, August 22, 2005. Online. http://seattletimes.nwsource.com/html/nationworld/2002447982_aruba22.html

The Official Tourism Website of Aruba, various pages. Online. http://www.aruba.com/

United States Department of State. "Trafficking in Persons Report 2008—The Netherlands, 4 June 2008." Online. http://www.unhcr.org/refworld/docid/484f9a2f3c.html

*Cottonwick fish are just some of the sea life in the Bahamas.  iStock/ NaluPhoto*

# BAHAMAS

# Introduction

The Commonwealth of the Bahamas consists of a string of islands in the Atlantic Ocean, southeast of Florida. The site of Christopher Columbus' first landfall in 1492 and a British colony for almost two centuries, the small nation remains a favorite of American and British tourists seeking year-round warm temperatures and miles of sandy beaches and clear waters.

## GENERAL INFORMATION

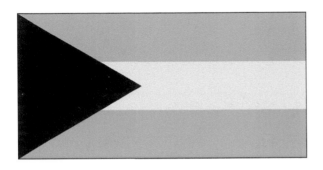

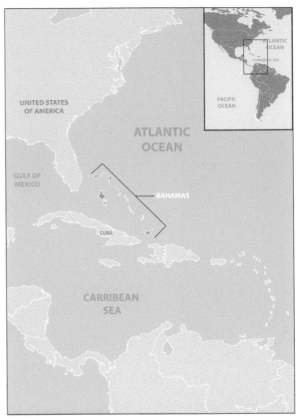

**Official Language(s):** English
**Population:** 324,597 (2015 estimate)
**Currency:** Bahamian Dollar
**Coins:** 100 cents equal one Bahamian dollar. Bahamian coins are available in denominations of 1, 5, 10, 15, 25 cents, although the 15 cent coin is rarely used.
**Land Area:** 3,864 square miles (10,010 square kilometers)
**Water Area:** 1,494 square miles (3,870 square kilometers)
**National Motto:** "Forward Upward Onward Together"
**National Anthem:** "March On, Bahamaland"
**Capital:** Nassau
**Time Zone(s):** Eastern Standard Time Zone (GMT -5)
**Flag Description:** The Bahamian flag is embodied with the colors of black, gold, and aquamarine, and features an equilateral black triangle in a chevron design, superimposed over a centered, horizontal gold stripe, with equal parts aquamarine on either side, forming three equal stripes.

## Population

Although the Spanish first colonized the Bahamas in 1495, British settlement beginning in the mid-17th century set the lasting character of the islands. The Bahamas officially became a British colony in 1783, after the American colonies gained their independence and British loyalists fled to the islands.

The British brought slaves from Western Africa to work cotton plantations in the Bahamas; the plantations eventually failed due to the islands' meager soil. Under British law, all slaves were emancipated by 1834. Today, the descendents of these freed slaves account for 85 percent of the population of the Bahamas. Likewise, most of the 12 percent of white full-year residents are of British descent.

More than 70 percent of the population live on New Providence, most in the capital, Nassau. About 15 percent of the population live on Grand Bahama, home of country's second largest city, Freeport/Lucaya. The island of Abaco is home

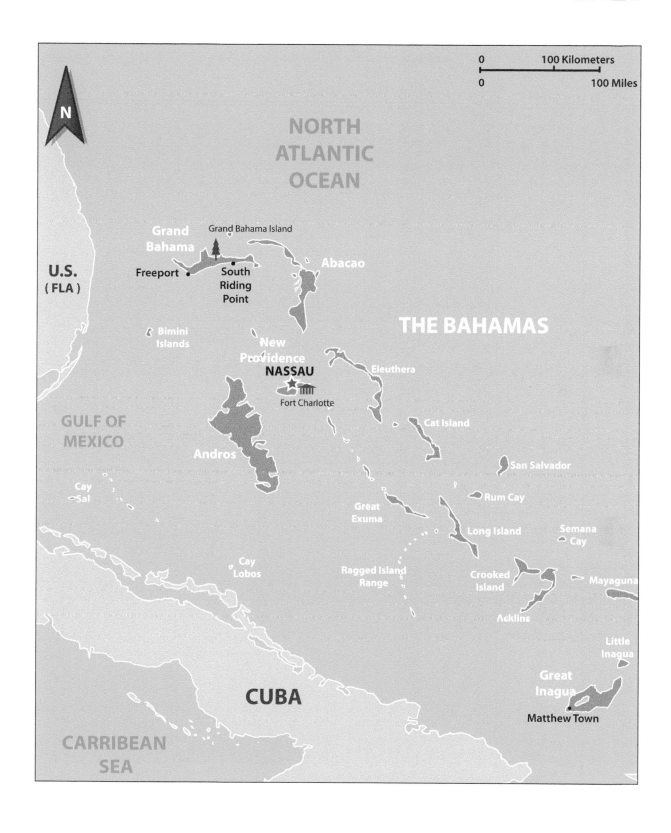

North Atlantic Ocean

Grand Bahama
Grand Bahama Island
U.S.
( FLA )
Freeport
South Riding Point
Abacao
THE BAHAMAS
Bimini Islands
New Providence
NASSAU
Fort Charlotte
Eleuthera
Cat Island
San Salvador
Gulf of Mexico
Andros
Rum Cay
Cay Sal
Great Exuma
Long Island
Semana Cay
Cay Lobos
Ragged Island Range
Crooked Island
Mayaguna
Acklins
Little Inagua
CUBA
Great Inagua
Matthew Town
Carribean Sea

0     100 Kilometers
0     100 Miles

**Principal Cities by Population (2010, except where noted):**

- Nassau (246,329)
- Lucaya (28,000)
- West End (12,724; 2005)
- Cooper's Town (8,413; 2005)
- Marsh Harbour (4,368)

to four percent of the total population. All other islands have populations of less than 8,000.

## Languages

English is the official language of the Bahamas, and there is no official second language; many citizens speak in a unique dialect known as Bahamian Creole (or Bahamas Creole English). Immigrant languages include Haitian and Greek.

## Native People & Ethnic Groups

At the time of the Spanish takeover of the Bahamas, the native people were the Lucayans, part of the Arawak, an Amerindian people that had migrated north from South America some 600 years earlier. Of the estimated 50,000 Arawaks on the islands at that time, all had disappeared within three decades. They either died, often due to the small pox virus carried by the Spanish, or sold into slavery and transported from the islands.

About 20 percent of today's black Bahamians are Haitians who fled poverty and political persecution in their native country. English is the prevailing language of the Bahamas, but many Haitians speak Creole. About half of the country's Haitians are legal residents, most due to a 1985 law granting legal status to undocumented Haitian immigrants who arrived prior to 1981.

Nassau includes descendents of black African slaves and European colonists. About 90 percent of the population is black, 4.7 percent is Caucasian, and three percent is Hispanic and Asian. The majority of Caucasian Bahamians are of English, Irish, and French descent. A socioeconomic class separation between Bahamians of African and European descent still exists.

Natives of Nassau are known as Nassuvians. Most Nassuvians are English-speaking. Those of African descent generally speak with a common West Indian dialect, while those of European descent speak with a slight British accent.

## Religions

There is a strong religious heritage among Bahamians. Of the more than 95 percent that listed themselves as Christians in 2000, 35 percent were Baptist, about 15 percent Anglican, 14 percent Roman Catholic, and eight percent Pentecostal. Other Protestant or evangelical denominations made up most of the remainder. There are more than 90 churches on the island of New Providence. Less than five percent of the population is non-religious or unidentified.

## Climate

The Bahamas have a moderate tropical climate in the heavily populated northern islands. Temperatures in both Nassau and Freeport seldom fall below 16° Celsius (60° Fahrenheit) in winter, although the temperature can fall as low as 4° Celsius (40° Fahrenheit).

Average annual rainfall is 1,140 millimeters (45 inches), most coming during brief intense showers during the May to October rainy season. During summer, the average temperature in Nassau is 32° Celsius (90° Fahrenheit), with a low of 23° Celsius (74° Fahrenheit).

Regular prevailing winds can on rare occasion make winter months uncomfortably cool, but they are a substantial relief during the summer months. Humidity is worst in September, coinciding with the peak of the August to October hurricane season. Damaging hurricanes hit the islands about once per decade. Hurricane Floyd, which struck in 1999, caused minimal damage in heavily populated areas, but did cause extensive property losses in Abaco and Elbow Cay. In 2012, however, much more extensive damage was done to the Caribbean and the Bahamas when Hurricane Sandy swept through the islands. Forty-three people were killed and extensive property and ecological damage was done to the islands.

## ENVIRONMENT & GEOGRAPHY

### Topography

The Commonwealth of The Bahamas consists of a string of islands in the Atlantic Ocean, southeast of Florida. The archipelago of the Bahamas includes some 700 islands and more than 2,000 small islets. About 660 of these are cays (pronounced "keys"), and approximately thirty islands are inhabited. The principal islands are most-populated Grand Bahama and New Providence. Other "family islands" include Abaco, Acklins, Andros, Bimini, Cat, Crooked, Eleuthera, Exuma, Great Inagua, Harbour, Long, Mayaguana, and San Salvador (Watling Island).

The capital city of Nassau stretches along the northern coast of New Providence Island. The island is 33.79 kilometers (21 miles) long and 11.26 kilometers (7 miles) wide. It is located in the center of the Bahamian archipelago.

The Bahamas' total area is slightly less than the total area of the small American state of Connecticut. The largest island is Andros, with an area of 5,957 square kilometers (2,300 square miles). The islands' 1,220-kilometer (760-mile) arc runs parallel to Florida, stretching southward to within about 80 kilometers (50 miles) of Cuba. The islands' total coastline is approximately 3,542 kilometers (2,200 miles) long.

The islands are formed from coral over a limestone base. It is believed that the Bahamas, along with the Florida Keys, were formed about 120,000 and 80,000 years ago, when the sea level in the area was at least 6 to 9 meters (20 to 30 feet) higher than it is today. Coral reefs were exposed as the sea level dropped. The name Bahamas is thought to be derived from the Spanish "baja mar" ("shallow waters").

The islands are all relatively flat and most are sand covered, although some are rocky or forested. The highest point is on Cat Island at the peak of Mount Alvernia, 63 meters (206 feet) above the surrounding forest and about 122 meters (400 feet) above sea level.

As there are no substantial rivers on the islands, there is no silt runoff into the surrounding waters, leaving them phenomenally clear in most areas. At a length of approximately 19 kilometers (12 miles), the country's largest lake is Lake Rosa on Inagua.

Caves are common due to the action of the water against the limestone. Usually flooded or lying entirely underwater, these caves are referred to as "blue holes" because of the distinctive water color seen at their mouths due to the change in depth and water temperature. Andros has 178 such caves. One freshwater cave in Lucayan National Park on Grand Bahama Island runs for about 10 kilometers (6 miles).

### Plants & Animals

While the land territory of the Bahamas is small, the islands encompass nearly 259,000 square kilometers (100,000 square miles) of marine territory. The most important feature of this expanse is the 2,330 square kilometers (900 square miles) of coral reef, representing nearly five percent of all such reefs worldwide. The coral attracts clownfish, eel, and grouper and helps shelter the islands' fragile beaches from ocean storms. Nearby waters are also known for dolphin and whale sightings.

The national bird is the flamingo. Lake Rosa at Inagua National Park is home to more than 50,000 of these famous pink birds. Other tropical birds in the park include egrets and parrots, along with turtles and rare, protected rock iguanas.

The few indigenous mammals prior to colonization included the raccoon and the hutia. Also known as the banana rat, the hutia is a guinea pig-like nocturnal animal naturally found only on East Plana Cay.

The most common mammal on the islands is the bat, along with occasional wild donkeys, pigs, and horses (most notably the wild horses of Abaco). Abaco is also home to the rare Bahama parrot, endangered in part because it nests on the ground, making it easy prey for feral cats. Cat Island is named after pirate Arthur Catt.

Tree systems on the islands include mangrove swamps (swashland), pine forests, and whiteland and blackland hardwood forests (coppices). Whiteland coppices are areas of meager soil that support shrubs, including brasiletto and acacia, some trees, such as balsam, and numerous cactus plants. They are the favored habitat of land crabs. Blackland coppices are more fertile, supporting cedar and mahogany trees, although few large specimens remain. Northern islands contain yellow (Caribbean) pine forests.

## CUSTOMS & COURTESIES

### Greetings
English is the official language of the Bahamas and is used in all administrative and educational contexts. Most Bahamians speak a creole that blends English with elements of African and Caribbean dialects. Some unique features of Bahamian Creole include the omission of plural forms in most cases and a tendency to omit the "h" sound in most words.

While Bahamians typically say "Hello" as a basic greeting, they may use the more formal derivatives of "Good morning," "Good afternoon," "Good evening," and "Goodnight." Visitors often note that Bahamians tend to adopt a friendly familiarity almost immediately. It is not uncommon for Bahamians to ask "How are you," to people they have just met.

Both men and women shake hands in greeting, though it is considered polite to wait for a woman to extend her hand before a man extends his. Only close friends and family embrace or kiss when greeting. Though Bahamians are not uncomfortable with familiarity, strangers are expected to behave in a more formal, polite manner upon first meeting. If seeking information, for instance, it is considered rude to make a request without taking a moment to engage in friendly small talk.

### Gestures & Etiquette
The Bahamians enjoy a friendly, relaxed culture but are socially modest in many situations. Punctuality is generally important, though Bahamian culture employs a different sense of time than that of other Western cultures. For example, Bahamians customarily rarely rush to get anything done, and will typically allow even

basic activities to take more time than necessary. While some might perceive this as a generalized version of the stereotypical Caribbean idea of laziness and relaxation, Bahamians believe that their view of time allows for a relaxed, healthy lifestyle.

Bahamians are expressive in conversation and may use a variety of hand gestures. Close contact with Americans and Europeans has taught the Bahamian people to recognize most Western hand gestures and facial expressions. One gesture to be careful of is the West African gesture of extending the hand with five fingers facing upward. This is considered an insult indicating that the person in question has five fathers.

### Eating/Meals
Most Bahamians eat three meals per day: a morning meal, a midday or afternoon meal, and an evening meal. Many Bahamian families serve meals family or buffet style, with guests serving themselves from communal dishes. In business and formal occasions, Bahamians may serve plated meals in courses, including appetizers, soups and salads, entrees and desserts.

The morning meal is generally light, consisting of eggs, fruit, and pastry served with coffee and fruit juice. The midday meal is more substantial than the morning meal, and consists of sandwiches, a variety of seafood and roasted vegetable dishes, and soups. Many meals are accompanied by potatoes or rice. As a former British colony, many Bahamians continue to indulge in the tradition of afternoon tea, which consists of tea and coffee accompanied by a light snack. The evening meal is usually the most substantial meal and is considered the prime time for entertaining and family gatherings.

### Visiting
It is considered polite, but not customary, to bring small gifts when visiting in Bahamian culture. This includes flowers and candies, or small gifts for the host's children. However, white flowers and lilies should be avoided, as these are associated with mourning and funerals. Likewise, red roses may be taken as a sign of affection,

as in Western tradition, and should therefore be avoided unless a romantic message is intended. If a visit includes dining, guests typically wait for their hosts before being seated or beginning to eat. As a general rule, table manners and dining etiquette are relaxed in Bahamian culture.

## LIFESTYLE

### Family

The nuclear family, consisting of a couple and their children, is the primary unit of Bahamian society. In recent years, the necessity to migrate for work has led to an increase in the number of single parent (usually single mother) households in the Bahamas. Males in rural villages may spend part of each week living in Bridgeport or one of the other cities, where there are greater opportunities for employment. Additionally, many men find seasonal employment working in the tourism and hospitality sector.

Bahamians expect women to behave in a conservative manner with regard to relationships, while Bahamian men are traditionally not held to the same standard. For example, there is no social stigma attached to men who have children out of wedlock with more than one woman. This tradition has begun to change in the early 21st century, however, as women have begun to achieve greater equality within Bahamian society.

Unlike many Caribbean and African cultures, the extended kin group does not play a major role in Bahamian culture. However, grandparents and older female relatives are sometimes enlisted to help care for children, especially those of a young couple. Divorce has become more common in the 20th and early 21st centuries, largely due to relaxed social customs regarding women leaving their husbands.

### Housing

Housing in the Bahamas ranges from detached single-family houses and simple apartment complexes to lavish colonial mansions. Most families live in small one- or two-bedroom houses, with clapboard exteriors, similar to oceanfront architecture found in parts of New England and other Caribbean isles. Few families have indoor air conditioning and houses are constructed with numerous windows to allow for airflow. Due to the instability and impermanency of wooden structures, many Bahamians have shifted to using concrete blocks for home construction.

Certain parts of the island are renowned for their colonial mansions and villas. Some wealthier Bahamian families live in former British estates, which more often resemble colonial villas. Colonial mansions may have three or more bedrooms and often have extensive, manicured green spaces surrounding the building. Typically, the estates also have separate quarters for servants, as well as stables or workhouses near the main building. Upper-class residents and expatriates sometimes construct new homes that resemble colonial housing, but have modern amenities.

### Food

As in most Caribbean nations, Bahamian cuisine is a blend of European and African influences, with seafood forming the backbone of the staple diet. Common African spices, such as spicy peppers, nutmeg, and ginger, have been integrated into Bahamian cuisine and are the most common flavoring for entrees. Most desserts and pastries have European characteristics and are based on cream, butter, sugar, and white flour.

The conch, a marine mollusk, forms an important part of Bahamian cuisine. The Bahamians began harvesting conch during the colonial period because of its overwhelming abundance. In fact, British slave owners would often feed conch to their slaves. Over the centuries, conch was integrated into the culinary traditions of the Bahamian people and became a delicacy for islanders. One of the most popular preparations for conch is to fry strips of spiced conch in oil served with potatoes, rice, and vegetables. Another popular preparation is to mix bits of conch flesh with dough before frying; known as conch fritters, these have become a popular snack and are often sold by street vendors.

Bahamian fish stew is another popular dish, consisting of fish cooked slowly in a hot liquid with celery, tomatoes, and spices. Fish stew may be made from any variety of fish, but cod and salted cod are popular choices. Salt cod was first brought to the island as a cheap food for the slave population, but has since become a delicacy. There are hundreds of Caribbean recipes utilizing cod and other white fish. It is also commonly served roasted or fried with tomatoes, ginger, and spices on a bed of rice and peas. Peas, in this case, can refer to chickpeas, black-eyed peas, or any variety of legumes. The rice and peas are usually served spicy, with peppers and salt. Though still considered a "peasant" dish, some Bahamian restaurants serve a gourmet version.

Another crucial ingredient in Bahamian cuisine is the crawfish. Locally referred to as a "lobster," crawfish may be served fried or steamed or mixed in a variety of other dishes using rice, potatoes, and other ingredients. Curried lobster is a dish made from spicy curry, onions, crawfish meat, and potatoes, sometimes served with rice. Johnnycakes are a typical dish made from fried sweet dough. Johnny cakes are served across the Caribbean and each country has developed a unique presentation.

Though many Bahamians enjoy fruit and cocktails for dessert, there are also a variety of native desserts made in the Bahamas. Rum coconut cake is a typical Caribbean dessert, featuring heavy, sweet sponge cake with shredded coconut and covered in rum infused icing. Other recipes include lime and other types of fruit. Because the Bahamas produce a variety of tropical fruits, these items tend to feature prominently in local cuisine.

### Life's Milestones

As a predominantly Christian people, Bahamians tend to follow the standard Christian rights of passage, including baptism, communion, and marriage. A child's baptism is accompanied by a family celebration with food and music; guests bring small gifts for the child's parents. Marriage traditionally marks the transition between adolescence and adulthood and continues to play an important role in Bahamian culture. Bahamian weddings are usually held in the church with a traditional service, followed by a celebration with friends and family. Wedding celebrations are often lavish affairs, and guests commonly give cash or small gifts to the young couple to aid with expenses.

Funerals in Bahamian culture are usually formal, and include a formal service followed by a gathering of friends and family. Mourners typically wear dark colored clothing and bring gifts for the family or flowers to commemorate the deceased. As in European tradition, white flowers, typically lilies, are given to the family of the deceased.

## CULTURAL HISTORY

### Art

Prior to the mid-20th century, there was little that could be considered a native or national artistic culture in the Bahamas. (The earliest inhabitants of the islands were the Lucayans whose culture, despite having several craft traditions, became virtually non-existent within thirty years of the arrival of the Spanish.) Early Bahamian artists usually concentrated on realistic or impressionist landscape painting, a tradition that continues to dominate the Bahamian visual arts. The most prominent artist to emerge from the Bahamas is sculptor Antonius Roberts (1958– ), who played a major role in the development of the local artistic community. In 2003, Roberts led the multidisciplinary effort to create the first national art gallery in the Bahamas. Roberts's installation sculptures have gained international fame and his work is featured prominently in the national gallery.

Another Bahamian artist, Brent Malone (1941–2004), became famous for the paintings and sculptures he completed in Nassau, where he owned a private gallery. Malone aided Roberts in outreach efforts for local artists in the 1990s. Many of Malone's paintings are realistic depictions of local culture, including landscapes and portraits of Bahamians in Nassau. Malone has painted several now-famous portraits of individuals performing in the Junkanoo festival, a street and music festival that has become a unique Bahamian tradition. Artists from the Bahamas were recognized in a documentary called "Artists of the Bahamas," produced in 2008 and directed by Karen Arthur and Tom Neuwirth.

Some of the oldest sculptural techniques used in the Bahamas make use of one of the nation's natural resources: coral. Rich coral reef systems surround the Bahamas (though global warming and habitat loss now threaten the stability of the reef system), and early Bahamian sculptors would often collect or harvest coral to use in making sculptures. Now considered more of a traditional craft than a form of fine art, many coral sculptures made by artisans on the archipelago are sold to tourists. One popular technique involves attaching pieces of coral together to resemble native flora.

## Music

The Junkanoo festival is a unique Bahamian tradition celebrated on New Year's Day, Boxing Day, and Independence Day. Hundreds of attendees gather to dance and parade through the streets in colorful costumes. According to local legend, the Junkanoo was the brainchild of John Canoe, a former African tribal chief who was brought to the islands as a slave and who promoted the African festival tradition among his fellow slaves. The festival has been celebrated continuously since the 16th century and is considered a symbol of the nation's cultural heritage. Prizes are awarded annually for the best Junkanoo performers and costumes, and the festival is accompanied by Junkanoo music.

The evolution of Junkanoo costumes provides another example of how African traditions evolved in the Caribbean. In the early days of Junkanoo, attendees painted their skin and decorated their bodies with feathers and fabric. Over the centuries, Junkanoo costumes became more elaborate. Attendees started using wire and fabric in the 1960s, and this led to the construction of larger costumes with extensions attached to the clothing. Today, the official Junkanoo parade has an elaborate system of rules governing the construction of costumes and the materials that can be used. Costumes also differ depending on the person's role in the parade.

*An example of an elaborate costume worn at a Junkanoo festival in the Bahamas.*

Junkanoo music is a type of celebratory marching music traditionally played with a variety of drums, bells, whistles, and horns. Junkanoo music takes some inspiration from goombay, which is an improvisational form of music that uses drums, whistles, and horns, and is usually performed in large groups. Goombay music is similar to the slave spirituals performed across the Caribbean. Though not nearly as popular as Junkanoo, traditional goombay performances still occur in villages across the archipelago.

On the streets of Bahamian cities, visitors might also encounter a type of musical performance known as "rake 'n' scrape," in which a small group of musicians use a variety of percussion instruments to accompany stories or simple songs. This traditional, improvised style is usually performed on the streets, but has also found a home in Bahamian clubs where performers entertain tourists and locals. The basic strategy in "rake 'n' scrape" music is to use any instrument or object at hand to keep rhythm or add to the improvised melody.

## Literature

As a relatively young nation, the Bahamas has only recently begun to develop a unique native literary movement. Early literature, written in the latter half of the 20th century, focused on universal themes such as natural identity, social change, and the beauty of the islands. There was no prevalent style, and poetry was perhaps the most popular medium.

A small number of Bahamian novelists, playwrights, and poets have been recognized in the international community, including poet Susan Wallace (1931– ), whose poems blend spiritual visions with realistic views of native life and culture. Modern author, educator, and poet Nicolette Bethel is another of the few Bahamian literary figures who has gained national attention. In addition to writing plays produced by Bahamian drama companies, Bethel publishes articles about Bahamian culture and is an expert on the local Junkanoo festival tradition. Furthermore, the wealth of plays that are now extant are oftentimes produced by the Bahama Drama Circle and can be seen around the world.

## CULTURE

## Arts & Entertainment

The contemporary arts occupy an important place in Bahamian culture, and the native artistic community has begun to gain international attention in recent years. The National Art Gallery of the Bahamas, founded in 2003, is the nation's only national art gallery, and provides a home for native Bahamian art. The gallery's collections are divided into historical exhibits, including a collection of photographs of Bahamian cities in the early 20th century and a variety of impressionist and realistic painters. Small, independent groups in Nassau and some other cities provide support and education for artists, musicians, and writers.

In addition to providing limited funding for visual arts programs, the Bahamian government funds the annual Junkaroo festivals in an effort to preserve this element of native heritage. One of the most popular Bahamian festivals, Junkanoo commemorates the traditional respite that was given to slaves between Christmas and New Year's Day. The festival includes two large parades, on December 26 (Boxing Day) and January 1. Parade participants perform dance steps while wearing huge, extravagant costumes that are judged in various contests. Musical groups include large drum and brass sections.

Junkanoo is also accompanied by goombay music, the traditional percussion-heavy music of the islands. Goombay mixes West African rhythms with colonial European influences. Traditional rake 'n' scrape bands use homemade instruments, including goatskin drums and saws raked with a file or screwdriver, along with maracas, cowbells, and noisemakers, such as whistles and bicycle horns. Calypso and reggae music are also common in resort areas, although they originated in Trinidad and Jamaica, respectively.

Bahamian hand crafts, which include basket weaving, wood sculpture, canoe building, and coral sculpture, are also considered a part of the nation's cultural heritage. Many are generally funded through tourist and commercial revenues rather than governmental assistance. Numerous Bahamian artisans travel to the cities on weekends to sell their crafts. The International Bazaar of Freeport and the adjacent Straw Market are both popular marketplaces where native foods and crafts are sold.

The arts in the Bahamas are largely overshadowed by the huge tourist trade, with its emphasis on shopping and entertainment. One notable local artist is Exuma-born Amos Ferguson, a former house painter who turned to producing original artworks in his forties. A devout Baptist, Ferguson portrays common sights in the Bahamas and religious motifs in a bright, simplistic style using house paint on cardboard.

## Cultural Sites & Landmarks

The capital of Nassau, on New Providence Island, is known for the charm of its old colonial buildings, the relaxing atmosphere of its many beaches, the business savvy of its commerce district, and the abundance of nightlife and sports options available to residents and visitors. It is also the gateway to the renowned resort center: Paradise Island. Nassau is the birthplace of the commonwealth's native culture, and offers the most extensive variety of historic attractions on the archipelago.

Once the military capital of the colonial government, the city is still home to many fortified structures and forts from the nation's colonial period. Fort Fincastle, located on Bennett's Hill, was one of three forts constructed to guard Nassau Harbor. Built in 1793, the fort still has its original architecture as the walls of the fort were carved from the limestone cliffs. The other forts atop the Queen's Staircase are Fort Montague, completed in 1741, and Fort Charlotte, completed in 1788. Fort Charlotte is the largest and is considered the best of the three. It contains a maze of rooms, including a dungeon and barracks. To access the forts, visitors climb the Queen's Staircase, one of the most visited attractions of Nassau. Carved from solid limestone by slaves in the 18th century, the staircase features sixty-five steps, one for each year in the reign of England's Queen Victoria (1837–1901).

New Providence Island also has its fair share of natural cultural sites and landmarks. One of the more popular sites is Ardastra Gardens, the island's zoological park. The gardens occupy 2 hectares (5 acres) of landscaped green space with winding paths leading to enclosures that feature more than 300 species. One of the most popular attractions at the gardens is the flamingo display, where keepers have trained flocks of pink flamingos to march to a trainer's commands. The zoological park is also active in promoting the conservation of local wildlife, including an important breeding program for the endangered Bahamian parrot, which is threatened by habitat loss.

The Bahamas are also a popular destination for recreation, including water sports and other beach activities. Grand Bahama Island, which contains the cities of Freeport and Lucaya, represents the best location for these activities. In addition, the International Bazaar of Freeport and the adjacent Straw Market are both popular marketplaces where native foods and crafts are sold. Grand Bahama Island is also home to Lucayan National Park, which contains prime dunes and a 500-acre pine forest. Though small by comparison to some national parks, Lucayan is home to a variety of native flora and fauna and is an important site for conservation research.

## Libraries & Museums

The Pompey Museum of Slavery and Emancipation in Nassau, known also as the Vendue House, was once a slave market. It features exhibits on the history of the islands' black population, as well as a large Amos Ferguson collection.

The Pirates of Nassau Museum, located in downtown Nassau, offers information and displays relating to the history of piracy in the Caribbean. A number of now-famous pirates, including Edward "Blackbeard" Teach (c. 1680–1718) and Samuel "Black Sam" Bellamy (c. 1689–1717) used the islands of the Bahamian archipelago as their base from which they raided French, British, and Spanish ships during the "golden age of piracy" (1650s to the 1720s). Among other exhibits, the museum contains a nearly life-size replica of the pirate ship *Revenge*, one of the most feared and famous vessels to sail the Caribbean.

The Nassau Public Library and Museum was built in 1797 as a jail. Today, it houses historical island documents along with Arawak artifacts. Balcony House Museum, a colonial era house that was restored in 1985, lays claim as the oldest residential structure in Nassau. In addition, the Bahamas Historical Society Museum features Arawak and British artifacts from centuries past.

## Holidays

Official holidays in the Bahamas include Boxing Day (December 26), Labor Day (first Friday in June), Independence Day (July 10), Emancipation Day (first Monday in August). Discovery Day, also known as Heroes Day or Columbus Day, is observed on October 12.

## Youth Culture

As in other countries, music, dancing, and socializing are important aspects of Bahamian youth culture. Club culture has become increasingly popular, and Bahamian youth often congregate to listen to music and dance. Because the Bahamas is a Caribbean nation, the most popular types of music include calypso, reggae, and soca. Imported music from the United States and Europe, particularly hip-hop, has become increasingly popular with Bahamian teens in the early 21st century.

The Ministry of Education, Youth, Sports and Culture is the government agency responsible for promoting youth recreational and educational opportunities. This includes cultural and athletic development, sports promotion, and vocational and technical training. Particular youth sports programs that the ministry sponsors include boxing, surfing, football (soccer), and track and field competition. As it is elsewhere in the Caribbean, cricket is popular in the Bahamas, but the Bahamian population is uniquely focused on softball and basketball. Bahamian youth teams also compete in the CARIFTA Games, a multi-sport, track and field event for children aged thirteen to nineteen. (CARIFTA, or the Caribbean Free Trade Association, was the predecessor to Caribbean Community and Common Market (CARICOM).

In recent years, rampant poverty has led to an alarming crime rate amongst Bahamian teens. In particular, urban street gangs have become an increasing problem, and combating gang crime has become one of the top priorities for the Bahamian authorities. Some estimates indicate that as many as 10,000 Bahamian youth in New Providence have been involved in youth gangs.

## SOCIETY

## Transportation

On popular tourist islands, such as New Providence and Grand Bahama Island, public bus service is generally available. While buses are generally inexpensive, schedules are subject to change on short notice, and buses often fail to arrive on time to their scheduled location. Travelers and residents looking for more expedient transportation within the islands may choose to hire a taxi, which are generally more expensive, but plentiful within popular tourist destinations, resort areas, and major cities. Vehicles are driven on the left side of the road, reflecting Britain's historical influence on the Bahamas.

Most of the islands offer ocean traffic, including commuter ferries. Travel by ferry is inexpensive and convenient, but many ferries operate on inconsistent schedules. Some of the smaller islands in the Bahamas are only accessible via ocean transport. There are 61 airports on the islands, as of 2013, but only 24 with paved runways.

## Transportation Infrastructure

There are two principal international airports serving the 700 islands that make up the Bahamas: Lynden Pindling International Airport (formerly the Nassau International Airport), which is located near the capital of Nassau on New Providence Island, and Grand Bahamas International Airport, which is located in the city of Freeport, on Grand Bahama Island. In all, the country has six major airports offering international and domestic service and flights to nearby Caribbean nations. The island nation also has 23 seaports.

As of 2011, the Bahamas had roughly 2,700 kilometers of roadways and highways.

## Media & Communications

The Bahamian government allows freedom of the press and imposes no censorship restrictions on radio, television, or Internet agencies. The government owns the archipelago's only domestic television station, ZNS Bahamas, which offers a blend of commercial broadcasting, news, and entertainment programming. The publicly-owned Broadcasting Corporation of the Bahamas (BCB) places no restrictions on content produced and broadcasted through ZNS Bahamas. The television network regularly broadcasts programs providing critical views of governmental policy.

The Bahamian government also owns a radio network, with four stations offering music, news, and public service information. There are two major commercial radio stations, Love 97 FM and 100 Jamz, both offering music programming and limited commercial and news programming. Cable and satellite television are available in most of the larger cities and provide a variety of international programming options.

There are four primary dailies published on the archipelago; *The Nassau Guardian, The Bahama Journal, The Tribune,* and *Freeport News.* Most domestic publications concentrate on local news and issues while some papers provide international news. Nassau and Freeport, the two largest cities in the nation, were the joint hubs for the islands' publication networks. In addition, a variety of international and foreign language publications are available in Bahamian cities.

Internet access in the Bahamas has expanded in the early 21st century. Though private Internet service is available in some cities, Internet cafés offer public access for a fee. High-speed Internet is available only in the larger urban areas and islands and its usage has expanded rapidly in the last decade. As of 2014, there were an estimated 247,200 Internet users—representing 76.8 percent of the population, 45 percent more than in 2007.

## SOCIAL DEVELOPMENT

### Standard of Living
The Bahamas is ranked 51 out of 187 on the 2014 United Nations (UN) Human Development Index (HDI).

### Water Consumption
In 2015, an estimated 98.4 percent of the population had access to clean drinking water, while an estimated 92 percent of the population had access to improved sanitation. That same year, the daily water consumption of tourists was estimated at 400 to 1,000 liters per head, per day, while residential consumption was estimated at 150 to 200 liters per head. The conservation and use of freshwater resources has become a growing

concern across communities of the island nation in recent years, prompting the development of desalination and water reuse projects.

### Education
Education in the Bahamas is free and compulsory for children between the ages of five and sixteen. There are more than 150 state-run schools on the islands, and another fifty that offer private, often religious alternatives. These include Queen's College, a Methodist school established in 1890, and the exclusive, non-denominational Lyford Cay School. Education is based on the British system.

Colleges on the islands include the College of the Bahamas, established in 1974, and Success Training College, founded in 1982 and offering two-year technical and vocational programs. Many students study abroad, typically in U.S. colleges or at the nearby University of the West Indies (UWI), founded in 1948 in Jamaica, with campuses in Barbados and Trinidad.

The literacy rate for those fifteen-years-old and older was 95.6 percent in 2009. According to 2009 reports, the net enrollment rate for boys in primary school was 87 percent, as compared to 89 percent for girls. The net enrollment rate for boys in secondary school is 83 percent, as compared to 85 percent for girls. Recent reports on the Bahamian educational system suggest that a lack of emphasis is being placed on educational achievement, and that many public high school graduates in the Bahamas are ill-prepared for the 21st-century workforce.

### Women's Rights
Though women are considered equal under the Bahamian constitution, women's rights organizations report that spousal abuse, sex crimes, and gender inequality remain major concerns in the Bahamas. While Bahamian law prohibits abuse and battery, there are no laws specifically prohibiting domestic violence. Women's rights organizations have reported that police are often reluctant to intervene in cases of domestic violence, and that the prevailing culture considers it acceptable for a man to abuse his spouse. While

police action is widely considered to be insufficient, the Royal Bahamas Police Force provides training in domestic abuse as part of its basic officer training.

Bahamian law prohibits sexual harassment and provides a system of penalties involving fines and incarceration, with a maximum of two years imprisonment. Harassment cases are rare, owing to societal norms that discourage women reporting harassment. While the constitution holds the women are equal citizens, there are no laws specifically addressing discrimination against women.

In the early 21st century, women constitute approximately 40 percent of the native workforce. They are chiefly involved in the domestic labor, agriculture, educational, and social assistance sectors. Bahamian law guarantees equal pay for equal work and, according to internal investigations, women are paid wages equal to male counterparts in similar positions. However, according to some women's rights organizations, women are less likely to be offered advancement opportunities. Women are also discriminated against through inheritance and citizenship laws. For example, without a will, the estate of a deceased individual will pass to the son or oldest living male relative.

## Health Care

Health care is accessible in large cities, such as Nassau and Freeport. Facilities include the government-run Princess Margaret Hospital in Nassau and Rand Memorial Hospital in Freeport. While there are medical clinics spread throughout the rest of the country, serious emergencies on the outlying islands usually require medflight evacuations to one of the larger hospitals. National social services programs were introduced in 1974 and offer limited coverage for health, disability, and retirement.

The HIV/AIDS virus is a serious threat in the Bahamas; as of 2013, more than three percent of the adult population is living with HIV and there were 500 HIV/AIDS related deaths in 2013. Haiti is the only other country in the region with a rate above two percent.

## GOVERNMENT

### Structure

The Commonwealth of The Bahamas is the second oldest parliamentary democracy in the British Commonwealth; its first meeting took place in 1729. Although functionally autonomous since 1964, full independence was granted on July 10, 1973, when the nation ratified a new constitution. Unlike Haiti and Jamaica, the Bahamas remained largely politically stable throughout it transition to independence.

Traditionally, the country's head of state is the British monarch, represented by the governor general. The acting head of government is the prime minister (PM), who leads a nine-member cabinet of parliament members. The PM must be from the House of Assembly and is usually the head of the elected majority party. At least four cabinet members must be from the minority party.

The bicameral parliament is composed of a forty member House of Assembly, elected to five-year terms, and a sixteen member Senate, appointed to five-year terms by the governor general.

The basis of Bahamian law is English Common Law. Since the 1990s, the government has moved aggressively to promote and diversify foreign investment and interest in the Bahamas.

### Political Parties

There are two dominant political parties in the Bahamas: the Free National Movement (FNM) and the Progressive Liberal Party (PLP). In the 2012 election, the FNM won 23 of 41 seats in the parliament, making it the ruling party; the PLP holds 18, and was ousted as the majority party during the 2007 elections. Other parties, such as the Bahamas Democratic Movement and the National Development Party (NDP), have no parliamentary representation.

### Local Government

Local government is divided into administrative divisions that include all of the family islands and a few of the larger cays. Subdivided by districts, local governance oversees building maintenance, traffic, business licensing, and town planning. Larger districts may have town councils with certain low administrative responsibilities.

## Judicial System

The independent Bahamian judicial system is based on the English common law tradition. At the top of the system are the Supreme Court and the Court of Appeal. Justices for both are appointed by the governor general—twelve to the Supreme Court and five to the Court of Appeal. There are seventeen courts of first instance throughout the island nation. The Court of Appeal is the highest court.

## Taxation

Property taxes are the only direct tax in the Bahamas; there are no sales, personal, or corporate income, capital gains, or inheritance taxes. Other taxes include a departure tax, levied at $15, and a casino tax. Import duties remain the primary source of government revenue, but taxes and other revenues make up 19.7 percent of the annual GDP.

## Armed Forces

The only active military branch in the Bahamas is the navy, known as the Royal Bahamas Defence Force (RBDF). It is comprised of roughly 1,000 personnel. The RBDF is based at Coral Harbour, an ex-hotel and marina facility located at New Providence.

## Foreign Policy

The Bahamian government has several key foreign policy objectives, including the promotion of Bahamian culture, national security, and the improvement of the quality of life of its citizens, particularly through economic regional stability. Many of the nation's foreign policy objectives are influenced by its relations with the United States and neighboring Caribbean nations. These include issues of immigration, drug trafficking, and economic integration. In addition, the Bahamas holds membership in numerous key international organizations, most notably the United Nations (UN), the Organization of American States (OAS), and the Non-Aligned Movement (NAM). Within the UN, the Bahamas is closely involved with the International Labor Organization (ILO), the International Monetary Fund (IMF) and the International Criminal Police Organization (INTERPOL).

Bahamian foreign policy is strongly focused on issues concerning the Caribbean Community (CARICOM), and Bahamian leaders meet regularly with representatives of other Caribbean nations to discuss issues involving immigration, trade, and cooperative policing of Caribbean maritime territory. One of the Bahamian government's primary concerns is to create agreements to cooperatively control fishing activities in an effort to preserve and maintain the island's natural resources. The Bahamas has taken an active role in forming international conservation agreements regarding Caribbean waters. However, the Bahamas has differed with CARICOM in regard to the situation in Haiti, particularly because the Bahamas is concerned about Haitian illegal immigration.

The Bahamian government maintains close ties with both the European Union (EU) and Australia, particularly through the island nation's membership in the Commonwealth of Nations (which is made up of former British colonies). Among its EU allies, Spain features prominently as a trading partner, purchasing rum, fruits, vegetables, and certain industrial commodities. Because of the close proximity of the United States to the Bahamas, the two nations have cooperated on a variety of maritime issues. The United States is the country's primary import and export trading partner, accounting for nearly a quarter of the country's export revenues. The United States also maintains a permanent military research facility on Andros Island and provides military support to Bahamian efforts to control drug trafficking.

## Human Rights Profile

International human rights law insists that states respect civil and political rights, and also promote an individual's economic, social, and cultural rights. The United Nations (UN) Universal

Declaration on Human Rights (UDHR) is recognized as the standard for international human rights. Its authors sought the counsel of the world's great thinkers, philosophers, and religious leaders, and were careful to create a document that reflects the core values shared by every world culture. (To read this document or view the articles relating to cultural human rights, go to: http://www.udhr.org/UDHR/default.htm.)

The Bahamian government operates as a functional democracy and generally respects the rights of its citizens. Nonetheless, human rights monitoring agencies have identified several areas of concern. These include the failure to adequately protect the rights of women and children, the use of excessive force and arbitrary detention, and recurring problems with the nation's penal and judicial systems. The protection of children remains a priority for the Bahamian government, but child welfare continues to be a concern. International monitoring agencies have identified child neglect as a major problem, as there are large numbers of children living without parental supervision or who are homeless. This societal issue is further exacerbated by the contention that government outreach, counseling, and child endangerment programs receive inadequate funding to ensure child welfare.

Human rights monitoring agencies such as Amnesty International (AI) have expressed concern that Bahamian authorities use excessive force when interrogating and detaining suspects. Police administrators acknowledge isolated incidents of abuse by officers, but claim such incidents are not indicative of a widespread problem within the justice system. In 2006 and 2007, there were several charges of arbitrary arrest and detention brought against the Royal Bahamas Police Force. There were also accusations of excessive incarceration, often more than one year, without trial. Independent investigations indicate that the judicial system is unable to expediently address all cases because of a shortage of staff and inefficient recordkeeping procedures. The Bahamas also has a large population of illegal immigrants from Haiti and Cuba. The country uses a specific facility, the Carmichael Road Immigrant

Detention Center, to detain immigrants until they are repatriated. Length of detention ranges from 24 hours to periods exceeding several months.

Discrimination pertaining to religion and sexual orientation also continues to occur. While the Bahamian constitution permits freedom of religion, the law prohibits the practice of certain sects of Vodou (or Vodun), including Obeah, an African-derived form of folk magic practiced throughout the Caribbean. In practice, police rarely enforce these prohibitive laws, but the practice of the religion carries a sentence of up to three months in prison. While homosexual relationships are legal under Bahamian law, there are no statutes specifically addressing abuse of and discrimination against homosexuals and transgender persons. According to internal investigations, discrimination against homosexuals is common. In addition, the government does not provide adequate protection for disabled persons, particularly against discriminatory hiring practices.

One of the most pressing human rights concerns in the Bahamas is the penal system and conditions at Fox Hill Prison, the nation's sole prison. Investigations have revealed that overcrowding is a major problem at Fox Hill, with more than 700 maximum-security prisoners occupying a facility designed to hold no more than 450 inmates. Human rights organizations also contend that inmates at Fox Hill suffer from inhumane treatment, including poor medical care, nutrition, and inadequate sanitation.

## Migration

As of 2008, there were between an estimated 30,000 and 40,000 Haitians living illegally in the country, and discrimination against Haitians remains a persistent concern. (Some estimates put the number of illegal Haitians between 20,000 and 50,000, or as high as 78,000.) Overall, immigrants comprise an estimated 9.7 percent of the population in 2010. A new regulation in 2015 was aimed at Haitians living illegally in the Bahamas, and requires every person to have a Bahamian passport. Furthermore, permits and residency stamps will be required for each student attending school in the Bahamas. This is part of a larger Caribbean-wide shift to stem illegal immigration, especially of Haitians.

## ECONOMY

### Overview of the Economy
The economy of the Bahamas relies on the tourist trade, encouraging growth in the services sector as well as in construction. Financial services are another significant business on the islands. In 2014, the gross domestic product (GDP) of the Bahamas was estimated at $9.022 billion USD. It remains one of the wealthiest nations in the Caribbean. Because of its dependence on tourism, the economic crisis of 2009 caused a slowing of economic growth, but in the years since, the Bahamas have remained economically stable.

Government spending contributes 20 percent to GDP; the financial sector 15 percent. Once tied to money laundering and tax evasion schemes, the sector is now compliant with regulations of the Financial Action Task Force (FATF) aimed at combating money laundering. The islands remain very tax-friendly to individuals and corporations, with no levy on capital gains and corporate or personal income.

### Industry
Second only to tourism, the primary industry of the Bahamian capital is banking. The industry focuses on offshore banking for businesses and investors from the United States. There are over 400 banks from thirty-six different countries represented in the Bahamas, including 184 with a physical presence in the islands. Banking in the Bahamas is governed by The Central Bank of the Bahamas, which operates out of Nassau.

One important industry in the Bahamas is salt production on Inagua. Each year, up to 1 million pounds of salt is evaporated from salt water holding ponds thanks to the island's hot, dry summers.

Industry accounted for about seven percent of GDP in 2014, and employed five percent of the workforce, while agriculture accounted for about two percent. Other significant industries included ocean shipping services, steel pipe production, chemicals, and pharmaceuticals.

The United States is the Bahamas' principal import and export partner.

### Labor
The total employed labor force of the Bahamas in 2013 was approximately 196,900; the unemployment rate was 15 percent. It is estimated that about 30 percent of the labor force is unionized.

### Energy/Power/Natural Resources
The Bahamas have very limited natural resources. New Providence even has to import fresh water by tanker barge from Andros Island. Matthew Town on Inagua is home to one of the island's only major industries, salt production. Minor exports include aragonite, fish, and chemicals.

Elimination of solid waste is a leading environmental problem for the Bahamas.

### Fishing
According to the Caribbean Regional Fisheries Mechanism, the Bahamian commercial fishing industry is based mostly on shallow water bank areas. Primary fisheries include crawfish, queen conch, and scalefish. In 2015, the total fish catch was estimated at about 16,000 tonnes.

### Forestry
Caribbean pine is the dominant species of Bahamian forests. Pine forests can be found on the northern islands of Grand Bahama, Andros, Abaco, and New Providence. Commercially, the Caribbean pine, also known as the Yellow pine, is a useful species, and the Bahamas have a history of logging and mill operations. Though logging ceased in the 1970s, mature trees have renewed the opportunity for future operations. Housing development also poses a threat to the forest ecosystems of the island nation.

### Mining/Metals
The primary, commercially useful mineral products from the Bahamas are salt and aragonite, a type of limestone that has many common industrial uses.

## Agriculture

Agriculture accounts for approximately two percent of GDP. Important agricultural products include citrus and vegetables, and animals including poultry. Most of the islands' food supply is imported from the United States. Bacardi rum is distilled on a 61-acre facility on New Providence, capable of producing 27 million liters per year.

## Tourism

Tourism is by far the most important industry in the Bahamas, accounting for roughly half of the country's yearly GDP, and employing about half of the islands' workers. Tourism declined in the Bahamas in 2009, an indicator of recent economic downturn following the financial crisis in the United States. Due to the falloff of tourism, one luxury hotel, the 500-acre Four Seasons Resort Great Exuma, closed its doors in May 2009. Overall, though, the economy of The Bahamas fared well during the world-wide economic crisis.

The Bahamas are within 80 kilometers (50 miles) of the United States, an overnight cruise for ships from Ft. Lauderdale, Port Canaveral, and Miami. About 85 percent of tourists come from the U.S. Cruise lines such as Disney, Holland America, and Norwegian have bought their own islands to accommodate guests.

The largest resort/casino is Atlantis, adjacent to Nassau on Paradise Island. This multi-million dollar property of Kerzner International boasts more than 2,300 rooms.

Favorite tourist activities include swimming, scuba diving, snorkeling, parasailing, and sport fishing. Resorts offer golf, gambling, and duty-free shopping (since 1992) for luxury goods including crystal, fragrances, watches, and jewelry.

*Micah Issitt, John Pearson, Lynn-nore Chittom*

## DO YOU KNOW?

- The etymology of the word "cannibal" can be traced to the Bahamas. It is a Spanish translation of the Lucayan term "galibi," changed to "caniba" by Christopher Columbus.

- Famous residents of the Bahamas have included Sean Connery, Richard Harris, and Ernest Hemingway, who wrote on and about Bimini in the 1930s.

- Nassau is home to the Graycliff Restaurant, a five-star restaurant situated in an 18th-century mansion. The restaurant includes one of the largest wine cellars in the Western Hemisphere, with over two hundred thousand bottles of vintage wine. Graycliff also boasts its own cigar factory.

## Bibliography

Craton, Michael and Gail Saunders. *A History of the Bahamian People: From the Ending of Slavery to the Twenty-First Century.* Athens, GA: University of Georgia Press, 2000.

Dold, Gaylord, Vaitilingam, Adam, and Natalie Folster. *The Bahamas: Includes Turks and Caicos.* New York: Rough Guides, 2003.

Johnson, Howard. *The Bahamas from Slavery to Servitude, 1783–1933.* Gainesville, FL: University Press of Florida, 1997.

Ludmer, Larry H. *Cruising the Western Caribbean: A Guide to the Ports of Call.* Walpole, MA: Hunter Publishing, Inc., 2003.

Matchar, Emily, et al. *Lonely Planet Bahamas.* Oakland, CA: Lonely Planet Press, 2012.

Saunders, Gail. *The Bahamas: A Family of Islands.* New York: Macmillan Education, 2000.

## Works Cited

"Artists of the Bahamas." Video, 2008. http://www.imdb.com/title/tt1549719/?ref_=fn_al_tt_1

"Bahamas: Country Reports on Human Rights Practices." *U.S. Department of State.* Bureau of Democracy, Human Rights and Labor, Western Hemisphere. March 11, 2008. http://www.state.gov/g/drl/rls/hrrpt/2007/100626.htm

"Bahamas: Human Rights in Commonwealth of the Bahamas." *Amnesty International Online.* http://www.amnesty.org/en/region/bahamas

"CARICOM Member State—the Bahamas." *Caribbean Community Secretariat.* February 2006 http://www.caricom.org/jsp/community/bahamas.jsp?menu=community

"Country Profile: Bahamas." *BBC News Online.* http://news.bbc.co.uk/2/hi/americas/country_profiles/1154642.stm

Epstein, Irving and Leslie Limage, eds. "The Greenwood Encyclopedia of Children's Issues Worldwide." Westport, CT: Greenwood Publishing Group, 2008.

"Hurricane Sandy Blows Out of Bahamas, after Killing 43 in Caribbean, en route to US Coast." *FOX News.* 26 October 2012. http://www.foxnews.com/world/2012/10/26/hurricane-sandy-rages-through-bahamas-after-killing-21-in-caribbean-en-route-to/

"Recreational Fishing Accounts for Half of All Fish Caught in the Bahamas." *The Pew Charitable Trusts: Environmental Science.* 2 June 2015. http://www.pewtrusts.org/en/about/news-room/news/2015/06/02/recreational-fishing-accounts-for-half-of-all-fish-caught-in-the-bahamas

Robles, Frances. "Immigration Rules in Bahamas Sweep Up Haitians." *The New York Times.* 30 January 2015. http://www.nytimes.com/2015/01/31/world/haitians-are-swept-up-as-bahamas-tightens-immigration-rules.html?_r=0

"The Bahamas." Background Notes. *United States Department of State Online.* http://www.state.gov/r/pa/ei/bgn/1857.htm

"The Bahamas." *CIA World Factbook Online.* https://www.cia.gov/library/publications/the-world-factbook/print/bf.html

"The Bahamas." Overview. *Lonely Planet Online.* http://www.lonelyplanet.com/the-bahamas

*Barbados is known for its beautiful tropical flowers. iStock/prwstd*

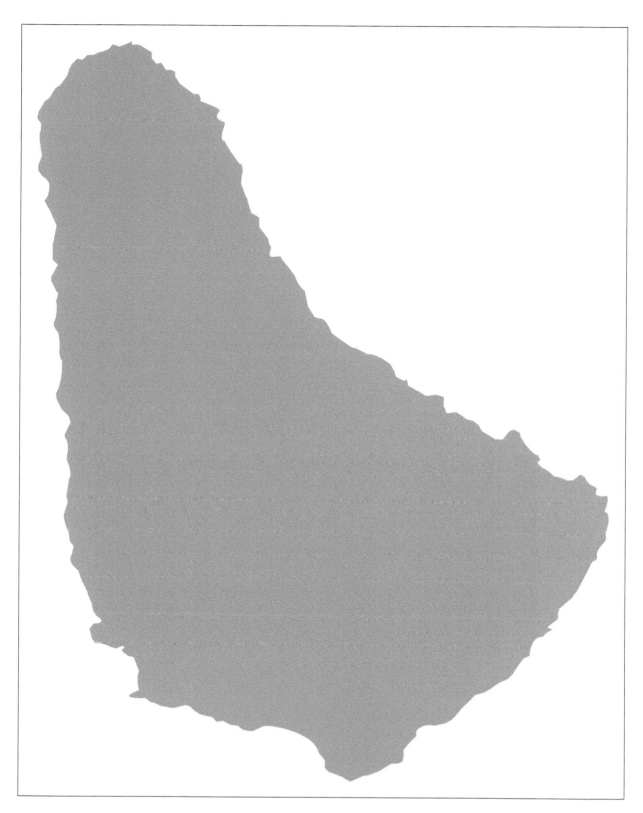

BARBADOS

## Introduction

Barbados is an independent nation located between the North Atlantic Ocean and the Caribbean Sea. The easternmost of the Caribbean islands, Barbados is part of the Windward (or eastern) Lesser Antilles island chain.

Throughout its history, several Amerindian tribes have settled in Barbados, including the Arawaks, who came from Venezuela, which lies to the southwest of the island. It is thought that the island was named Barbados (Spanish for "bearded") by Spanish explorers, in reference to the island's fig trees, whose long roots resemble hanging beards.

With influences from both England and Africa, Barbados has a very diverse blend of cultures. While music and art demonstrate the island's African heritage, the most popular sport in Barbados is cricket, a reminder of the prominent English presence in the island's history. Once dependent on the sugar trade, Barbados is now a popular tourist destination, and is one of the most developed countries in the Caribbean.

## GENERAL INFORMATION

**Official Language(s):** English
**Population:** 290,604 (2014 estimate)
**Currency:** Barbadian dollar
**Coins:** The Barbadian dollar is subdivided into 100 cents. Coins are available in denominations of 1, 5, 10, and 25 cents, and $1.

**Land Area:** 431 square kilometers (167 square miles)
**National Motto:** "Pride and Industry"
**National Anthem:** "In Plenty and In Time of Need"
**Capital:** Bridgetown
**Time Zone(s):** GMT -4
**Flag Description:** The flag of Barbados is comprised of three equal, vertical stripes of blue, gold, and blue. A broken trident adorns the golden center stripe and symbolizes the end of the country's colonial past. The blue of the flag represents the sea and the gold represents the color of the country's sand.

## Population

Barbados is a predominantly rural country with a surprisingly high population density (660 people per square kilometer or 1,704 people per square mile). The urbanization rate, as of 2015, is 31.5 percent. Barbados is, in fact, one of the world's most densely populated islands.

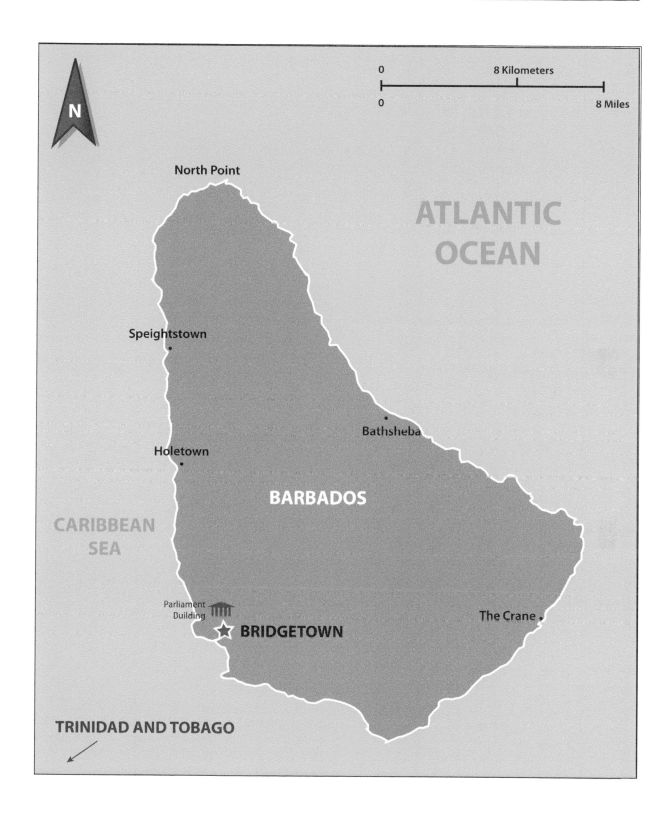

**Principal Cities by Population (2014, except where noted):**

- Bridgetown (90,000)
- Speightstown (3,634; 2005)
- Oistins (2,285; 2005)

Bridgetown, the capital, is located in the southwest corner of the island and is the largest population center. Other major cities include Speightstown in the northwest, Oistons in the southeast, and Holetown in the east.

The majority (nearly 93 percent) of Barbados' population is of African descent; most of the island's black population descends from West African slaves who were brought there to work on sugar plantations. Minority groups include Asians and whites. Colloquially, Barbadians may refer to themselves as "Bajan."

## Languages

English, the country's official language, has been widely adopted by the population with few exceptions. Bajan, or Barbadian Creole English, is generally spoken among the island's lower socioeconomic class, and in some remote fishing villages.

## Native People & Ethnic Groups

As early as the 4th century, Amerindians from Venezuela migrated to Barbados, navigating the strong currents of the Atlantic Ocean in dugout canoes on their way to North America. The Arawak people arrived in the early 9th century, and named the island "Ichirouganaim."

In the early 13th century, the Carib people arrived, displacing the earlier native population. The island was also visited, but not colonized, by the Portuguese.

The Caribs were conquered by the Spanish in the 15th century, and the combination of slavery and introduced European diseases wiped out the island's Amerindian population. The Spanish abandoned Barbados in search of larger Caribbean islands, paving the way for the British to begin colonizing the uninhabited island in 1627.

When the British colonized Barbados, they populated the island with wealthy families from England, as well as slaves and indentured servants. Today, ancestors of these colonists and laborers still call Barbados home.

## Religions

Barbados is overwhelmingly Christian. The majority of Barbadians (about 66 percent) identify as Protestant (including Anglicans, Pentecostals, Methodists, and others). Roman Catholics number just under four percent and others who identify as simply "Christian" measure 5.4 percent. Four percent of the population falls outside of Christianity, as "other," and about 20 percent of the population claims no religious affiliation.

## Climate

Barbados has a warm, tropical climate, with fairly consistent temperatures year-round. The average temperature ranges between 20° and 30° Celsius (70° and 90° Fahrenheit). Relief from the intense tropical sun is offered by the sea breezes that cross the island.

The dry season lasts from December until May. July typically sees the most rainfall, and the central plateau receives more precipitation than the coast. Average annual rainfall is between 1,270 and 1,900 millimeters (50 and 75 inches).

## ENVIRONMENT & GEOGRAPHY

## Topography

Unlike many Caribbean islands, Barbados has both a Caribbean and an Atlantic coast. The island is actually a large coral growth that was thrust up out of the water by a shifting of the earth's plates. For this reason, much of Barbados is characterized by flat terrain, particularly on the outer edges of the island, with hills and highlands in the center. The island's highest point is at the peak of Mount Hillaby, 336 meters (1,102 feet) above sea level.

At its widest point, Barbados measures 23 kilometers (14 miles) across. The island is

34 kilometers (21 miles) long. The coastline measures 97 kilometers (60 miles).

Because the island consists of layers of coral on top of sedimentary rock, many underground waterways have formed in the porous coral, the most famous of which is a popular tourist attraction known as Harrison's Cave.

Coral surrounds nearly the entire island, preventing Barbados from having a natural deepwater harbor. The east coast is not as inviting as the clear, tranquil waters found off the west coast; both have white sand beaches, however.

## Plants & Animals

Many species of birds can be seen on Barbados, though most species are migratory, and very few make their nests on the island. Barbados is a common stopping-off point for many North American species that fly to South America for the winter. Nearly 200 species of birds are commonly sighted, from herons and egrets to finches and hummingbirds.

Mammals introduced to the island by its many visitors range from the exotic green monkey and mongoose to the common mouse and rat. There are also a host of reptiles and amphibians, and eight species of bats.

Although the island is known for its lush gardens and beautiful flowers, there is not much native vegetation left. One native tree that visitors should be wary of is the Manchineel, which bears small, green poisonous apples. Warning signs advise people not to stand under these trees while it is raining, as water dripping from these apples can blister the skin.

## CUSTOMS & COURTESIES

## Greetings

English is the official and dominant language in Barbados. Most Barbadians also speak Bajan or Barbadian Creole, a language created by blending British English with several African dialects. Barbadians use Standard English for official functions, such as in school, governmental meetings, and when featured on television or radio broadcasts, while Bajan is typically used in informal situations.

Because English is the most widely spoken language, common English phrases of greeting are customary. Barbadians are more likely to be formal in their greetings, using phrases such as "Good day" and "Goodnight." It is also proper to ask "How are you?" as a basic greeting, rather than reserving the question for close friends and acquaintances. Similar phrases are used as greetings in the Bajan language, but with altered pronunciation. For example, the phrase, "How are you doing" may be pronounced, "How ya gain?" Among close friends and youth, Barbadians may use the slang expression "Way yuh sayin," meaning "What is happening?"

Both men and women shake hands when greeting one another. Barbadians appreciate formalities, including addressing business associates and others by appropriate honorific and professional titles. Embracing and kissing is reserved for spouses and close friends. Age is also an important factor in Barbadian relationships, and it is expected that younger persons address seniors by their title.

## Gestures & Etiquette

Barbadian culture is highly formal compared to other Caribbean nations. Barbadians appreciate appropriate manners and use formal expressions in a variety of situations. Dress codes are also generally adhered to, and both men and women tend to dress conservatively when visiting restaurants, meetings, social engagements, and any public place other than beaches. Punctuality is important to most Barbadians and schedules should be adhered to closely to avoid appearing rude. Barbadians usually exercise polite etiquette in public, including giving up seats on public transportation to elderly, pregnant or disabled passengers. When speaking in public, it is considered polite to keep one's voice at a low level.

## Eating/Meals

Barbadians typically eat three meals each day: one in the morning, one at midday or in the afternoon, and one in the evening. While Barbadian cuisine is heavily influenced by African culture, Barbados is rooted in British customs, including formal dining routines for social meals.

Barbadian breakfasts are typically light, consisting of pastry and fruit with coffee and/or juice. Some families substitute eggs and meat. Breakfast may be followed by mid-morning tea, where cookies and some small pastries are served with tea and/or coffee. The afternoon meal is more substantial than breakfast, but lighter than the evening meal. Some Barbadians will take afternoon tea, between the midday and evening meals, which sometimes replaces mid-morning tea. The evening meal is usually the largest meal of the day. The morning and midday meals are often served family style, with guests serving themselves from communal dishes. The evening meal is more likely to be served in courses, with appetizers, soup, and salad and a variety of entrees.

Rum is an important product in Barbados and is shipped around the world from local rum factories. Rum also occupies a unique place in the cultural and social life of the Barbadian people. Rum is ubiquitous with any meal, as well as at any festival, holiday, or social occasion. Rum was also integrated into native religious traditions and it is not uncommon for Barbadian Christians to drink small quantities of rum as part of their worship ceremonies.

### Visiting

Although many Barbadians live at or near the poverty line, they tend to take pride in their hospitality and the opportunity to invite visitors to their homes. If invited to a Barbados home, it is customary to bring small gifts for the hosts and toys or candies for the hosts' children. Flowers, liquor, and candies make acceptable gifts, though lilies are avoided as they are usually associated with mourning or funerary customs.

Even if invited to a casual gathering, guests dress for the occasion with a formal suit or dress. Barbadians are modest and guests are expected to refrain from asking personal questions or investigating the home without permission from the host.

## LIFESTYLE

### Family

Matrilineal relationships are important to family stability, a tradition common in some West African tribes. This tradition was furthered during the slavery period, when men were often separated from their wives and children. Women in modern Barbados still rely heavily on the aid of their mothers and other female relatives in child rearing.

Barbadian couples may cohabitate for long periods and have one or more children together before deciding to marry. According to some estimates, more than 70 percent of births occur out of wedlock. It is common for both men and women to have children with more than one partner. In many cases, children from previous relationships are left in the care of their grandparents if the mother makes the decision to remarry.

In addition to cultural traditions, the decision to postpone marriage is associated with poverty, which affects much of the population. Many of the people in Barbados work in "low skill" jobs (about 60 percent) and 13.9 percent of the population live in poverty. Poor families may also choose to live with their parents or other relatives for a period after marriage, as they are unable to afford a home of their own. Before marriage, men are sometimes said to have a "visiting" family, where the male visits his mate and children at her home. This may be a family home where the woman lives with her parents and/or other relatives. Overall, however poverty has decreased dramatically since the late 1990s.

Common law marriage is recognized by the Barbadian government, and pertains to couples living together for five or more years. In common law cases, women are entitled to half of the man's property in the case of separation. Women are less often expected to take part in work outside the home, but are typically expected to manage all domestic activities and child-rearing responsibilities.

### Housing

In modern Barbados, it has become more popular for individuals and small families to live in apartments or shared housing complexes in cities. Small houses are common in rural areas, with a couple and their children sharing a one- or two-bedroom home, with basic amenities. Barbados still has an obvious system of racial and social stratification that, while not supported by legal sanctions, is still respected by cultural norms. The traditional upper class, a small number of white families descended from the aristocracy of the colonial period, has given way to a system of social privilege based primarily on economic stability. The modern Barbadian upper class often lives near the cities, some in luxury colonial homes.

The chattel house, a simple, small one-bedroom structure that became popular in the period immediately following the end of slavery, is one of the more unique elements of Barbadian architecture. Because former slaves were often forced to move their homes, the chattel houses were constructed to be mobile, where the walls and roof could be deconstructed and transported with ease.

In modern Barbados, chattel houses are considered a part of the island's cultural heritage. The houses are usually constructed in a symmetrical design with a single, tall door in the center of the house and windows on either side. As a family gained prominence, additional shacks were added to the original chattel house, rather than expanding the structure. In this way, a family could acquire more territory while still remaining mobile. Most chattel houses are constructed of wood with simple tile or aluminum roofing. Chattel house owners are no longer forced to move their homes, and many are now attached to utilities, such as electricity and water, and have built attached gardens and porches onto the original structures.

## Food

The cuisine of Barbados was largely shaped by European influences, most notably British and French, as well as Afro-Caribbean and West Indian culinary traditions and tastes. Seafood is the central component to most Barbadian meals and the primary source of protein for the island's people. Rice and potatoes form an important part of the local cuisine as well, and are typically used as an accompaniment. Barbados has become world famous for its rum and other liquor production.

Flying fish is the national dish of Barbados and a major crop for local fishermen. A typical preparation is to use lime and season the fish with marjoram, salt, and pepper. Flying fish is also used to make fish cakes, which contain flour, herbs, and peppers mixed with chunks of fish. More than any other product, flying fish is deeply associated with Barbados culture. The annual fish crop, which has declined because of overfishing and global warming, is closely tied to the income of many rural Barbadians.

Barbadian natives have grown cassava since the colonial period, and use the flesh and juice of the cassava in a variety of dishes. Cassava flour is used to make bread and as a base for other baked ingredients and pastries. A typical cassava flour dish is cassava pone, which is fried bread made from cassava flour. Some cooks make cassava pone with onion and savory spices mixed into the dough before frying, while others use only salt to season the dough.

The pork industry is a major part of Barbadian society, and pork features prominently in local cuisine. A unique local dish is souse, or pickled pork, which is made by soaking pork in lime, salt, cucumber, and onion. Souse is sometimes served with black pudding, which is cow or pork intestine stuffed with ground, spiced meat. Souse and black pudding first became popular with British colonists, as black pudding is a popular dish in the United Kingdom, but remained popular with Barbadians after independence.

For dessert, Barbadians prepare a number of dishes that were established by the British colonists. A common Barbadian dessert is bread pudding, made with bread soaked in rum and milk with egg, sugar, vanilla, and other spices. Bread pudding is served heated, with a sauce made from rum or whiskey, sugar, egg, and flour. Barbadians also make several varieties of sweet bread, which are a popular breakfast, dessert, and snack item. One variety of sweet bread uses sugar, raisins, and shredded coconut baked into the loaf.

## Life's Milestones

A majority of Barbadians are Christian and follow standard Christian traditions in regard to rites of passage and cultural celebrations. The birth of a child is generally followed by a baptism ceremony, which may be attended by family, friends, and members of the extended community. It is traditional for guests to give small gifts at baptism celebrations. Marriage, a sign of adulthood in many cultures, has a reduced importance in Barbadian culture. If a couple decides to marry, it is common for the family to throw a modest party and for guests to bring cash or other gifts for the couple.

Funerals in Barbados are formal, with guests expected to display reverence and respect for the dead. Funerals are usually accompanied by traditional Christian services. As in European traditions, funeral guests generally give white flowers, most often lilies, as a gift to family of the deceased. Funerals call for conservative, dark colored clothing: men usually wear grey or black suits while women wear black dresses or suits.

---

## CULTURAL HISTORY

### Art

Prior to European discovery, the indigenous inhabitants of Barbados and the surrounding Caribbean were the Amerindians. Their contributions to art were mostly traditional crafts, and included ceramics, textile art, sculpture, and woodcarving, among others. With the advent of colonialism and the slave trade, traditional arts and crafts on the island began to reflect a West African influence. Traditional crafts that are still practiced today include basketry, wood sculpture, jewelry making, ceramics, and shell work and art. Artists from Barbados are slowly growing in prominence on an international stage, especially with the increasing presence of online access to Barbadian art and artists (such as the online profile of the National Art Gallery Committee).

### Architecture

During the island nation's colonial period, which lasted from 1627 until independence in 1966, the British exerted a dominant cultural influence over the island. This is particularly evident in the island's colonial architecture, which reflects a range of British styles. Many of the island's Victorian and Georgian mansions and colonial plantations were built with native coral, in addition to stone and wood. The country's architectural heritage also includes Gothic style churches and African influences such as chattel houses (small houses used for slaves), which were known for their vivid colors.

### Music

The African slaves who were brought to Barbados in the 17th century carried with them the indigenous music of their African homeland. Over the centuries, as the Barbadian slaves learned English and converted to Christianity, their indigenous African music became the basis for Christian spiritual songs and work songs. In the 20th century, immigrants from elsewhere in the Caribbean brought Afro-Spanish music to the island, transforming the local music scene in a short period of time. Modern Barbados now features a variety of native musical styles that represent the nation's African, Caribbean, and European heritages.

In particular, the Barbadians developed a unique musical form called "tuk," which draws heavily on the traditions of West African drumming. Tuk is performed by a group of musicians using several different types of drums, with flute and whistle players providing the melody. In addition to being a popular style of street music, tuk is played at celebrations that range from national holidays to family events.

Trinidadian calypso arrived in Barbados in the early 20th century, but did not become popular until the 1940s. While the music is still better known on Trinidad and other Caribbean islands, Barbadian calypso gave rise to spouge in the 1960s. Spouge blends the Afro-Spanish elements of calypso with elements of Jamaican reggae. Jackie Opel (1938–1970), a Barbadian calypso musician, is credited with introducing spouge when he returned from traveling in Jamaica. Spouge was the most popular type of Barbadian music for most of the 1970s. In the late 20th century, many Barbadians began listening to imported music from the United States and Europe. Spouge and Barbadian calypso remain two of the most popular musical genres on the island.

## Literature

Many African tribes have an oral tradition, in which history and culture are transmitted through storytelling rather than written form. For this reason, the first generation of Afro-Barbadians rarely transcribed their stories. Barbados did not produce a recognizable literary movement until the mid-20th century, when a small number of talented writers began gaining national and international attention. Many Barbadian novels, stories, and poems explore issues of nationalism and race relations, which have dominated Barbadian culture since the colonial period.

One of the key moments in the formation of Barbadian literary culture was the publication of the quarterly literary magazine *BIM*. The title is derived from a nickname for Barbados from when it was called "Bimshire" by the British colonial government. The magazine's publisher, Frank Collymore (1893–1980), became the nation's first internationally recognized literary figure. He was known for his poetry, novels, and stories that detailed life in Barbados. Collymore's legacy is evident across Barbados, where there are buildings, streets, and artistic awards named in his honor.

George Lamming (1927– ), a student of Collymore's who was first published in *BIM*, is one of the most prominent writers to emerge from the Caribbean. Lamming's novel *In the Castle of My Skin* (1953) gained widespread acclaim in the international literary community for its lyrical style and use of unusual narrative techniques. Lamming's novel also provides a detailed vision of traditional village life in Barbados and is considered an important historical account of Barbadian culture.

## CULTURE

### Arts & Entertainment

Although Barbados has a relatively small arts community, the island's people take pride in the accomplishments of local artists. Public art displays, most commonly mural painting, are common across the island, and the government offers programs to fund native art development and the establishment of public works programs. The Barbadian government also funds a system of arts education in the public school system.

The Barbados National Arts Council is responsible for artistic development. The National Art Gallery Committee was founded in 1998 to promote national arts and to work toward the establishment of a new gallery for showcasing native artists. Currently, the Barbados Gallery of Art in St. Michael and the Barbados Arts Council gallery in Bridgetown are the nation's most prominent visual arts galleries. They showcase painting, sculpture, and occasionally host literary readings and performance art. Bridgetown is the center of the nation's artistic community, and small venues throughout the city help to promote the arts by selling books and paintings of local artists or allowing performances.

The craft traditions of Barbados, which include a variety of basket-weaving techniques, cloth dying, and wood sculpture, are kept alive largely through the tourist trade. Barbadian woodcarving and basket-making techniques are believed to have been inherited from the first generation of slaves on the island, who learned the techniques in Africa. While Barbadians crafts have a distinct, Caribbean character, they are similar to baskets and carvings produced in West Africa.

The island's most popular event, the Crop Over Festival, originated as a celebration of the sugarcane harvest, an integral part of Barbados' history. Celebrated all over the island for three weeks beginning in July, the festival includes fairs and calypso music competitions, and ends with a costume parade on the first Monday in August. Other Barbadian festivals include February's Holetown Festival, a week-long celebration of the English settlement of the island. The Oistons Fish Festival is held during Easter, and features competitions and arts and crafts displays.

Another product of Barbados' colonial past is cricket, the national sport.

## Cultural Sites & Landmarks

As the nation's capital, Bridgetown offers a variety of landmarks and cultural sites. The city was founded in 1628 and contains one of the oldest administrative buildings in the Caribbean, the Parliament Building, which was built in 1871 in the neo-Gothic style. Another building of architectural importance is the Gothic-style St. Michael's Cathedral, which was rebuilt in 1789 after the original structure (built in 1665) was destroyed by fire in 1780. Heroes Square, located in front of the Parliament Building in Bridgetown, is a popular tourist spot for those interested in political history. Among statues of important Barbadians, visitors will find the Dolphin Fountain, which was built to commemorate the construction of a pipeline to bring fresh water into Bridgetown. It remains dry to symbolize the desire to preserve the nation's limited water supply.

Bridgetown's only urban park, called Queen's Park, was established in 1909 in honor of Britain's Queen Victoria. The park is a popular spot for both locals and tourists and contains a theater where local companies perform plays and dance productions. At the center of the park there is a single baobab tree, a species native to Africa that historians believe was imported by the British. The Queen's Park baobab tree has a trunk that is 18 meters (59 feet) in circumference, making it a relatively young specimen. Older baobabs in Africa and Madagascar have been found with circumferences of more than 40 meters (131 feet).

In the Farley Hill area of Speightstown, a trading town, is the Barbados Wildlife Reserve and the Farley Hill National Park. The wildlife reserve is popular among birdwatchers for the dozens of parrot and water bird species that make their homes there. In addition, the wildlife reserve is the best place to see the Barbados green monkey, also known as the vervet, which was imported from Africa in the 17th century. Today, scientists recognize the Barbados green monkey as a distinct regional variety.

Animal Flower Cave, a group of shallow cave pools located on the northern coast, was named for its assemblage of anemones, representing dozens of species that live in the cave' pools. The Barbadians have turned Animal Flower Cave into a tourist destination with an attached restaurant. The primary attraction is the view of the ocean from within the pools, some of which are deep enough for swimming. Other prominent landmarks on Barbados include the Mount Gay rum distillery, self-described as the oldest rum in the world; and the Gun Hill Signal Station, a military outpost dating back to the 17th century. Holetown, the earliest settlement on the island, hosts the annual Holetown Festival. This celebration of music, cuisine, and dancing commemorates the founding of Barbados.

## Libraries & Museums

One of the most popular landmarks in Bridgetown is the Barbados Museum. The museum contains over 250,000 well-preserved artifacts detailing the history of the island, including Amerindian artifacts and the furniture from an 18th-century plantation manor. The museum is housed in a former British military prison. The Sugar Museum, which focuses on the history of sugar cultivation on the island, is housed in an old sugar factory.

Barbados' national library system is headquartered in the capital of Bridgetown. The National Library Service was established in 1847.

## Holidays

Barbados celebrates its Independence Day on November 30. Other national holidays observed in Barbados include Errol Barrow Day (January 21), which commemorates the role of the country's first prime minister in gaining Barbadian independence. Kadooment Day (August) marks the end of the Crop Over Festival.

## Youth Culture

Education is free and compulsory to age sixteen, and reports indicate that approximately 90 percent of Barbadian students finish secondary school and 98 percent of Barbadians are literate. After graduation from secondary school, however, a relatively small number of Barbadian teens go on to achieve higher education. Widespread poverty also limits the recreational and social options of many Barbadian youth

Sports are the most popular form of recreation for Barbadian youth, with cricket ranking as the nation's top sport. Barbados is part of the West Indies Cricket Team, and many young Barbadians follow the progress of the annual cricket season via the radio or televised broadcasts. Many Barbadian communities have small, community-maintained fields where youth gather to play cricket or football (soccer).

From an early age, many Barbadian children are taught to view the ocean as a source of livelihood and enjoyment. As an island community, water sports such as parasailing and surfing are also popular with teenagers. Like tourists who visit Barbados, many young Barbadians enjoy spending a majority of their time near the ocean. In addition to swimming and water sports, some Barbadian teens begin working by taking tourist groups to ocean attractions, teaching surfing or scuba diving, or working with fishing companies.

Barbadian teens enjoy a variety of imported music and fashion items. Clothing trends from Europe and the United States can be found in Barbados, though economic concerns often prevent Barbadian youth from obtaining the most fashionable apparel. Reggae, hip-hop, and other forms of imported urban music are increasingly popular with Barbadian teens.

---

## SOCIETY

---

## Transportation

Domestic transportation options include a public bus system, rental cars, and private automobiles. The public bus system, called the Barbados Transport Board, is based in Bridgeport but services the entire island. Public buses run on regular schedules and generally offer service until midnight on most major routes. There are even special routes in place for tourists wishing to visit historic sites and/or museums. Public buses are often crowded and schedules vary according to traffic along specific routes.

Taxis and minibuses are also available for transport within the island. Minibuses are common in Barbados, and will take visitors to any location for a moderate fee. Taxis are available in the cities, but are usually cost prohibitive for travel to remote island locations. Traffic moves on the left-hand side of the road.

## Transportation Infrastructure

Barbados has roughly 1,600 kilometers (994 miles) of roads, of which an estimated 1,578 kilometers (981 miles) are paved. All of the island's major transportation systems begin in or near Bridgetown. This includes the seven primary highways of Barbados and the nation's public bus system.

Barbados has only one airport, Barbados Grantley Adams (BGA), located in Christchurch on the southern coast of the island. BGA offers international flights to the United States, Europe, Jamaica, and elsewhere in the Caribbean. The airport is approximately 13 kilometers (8 miles) southeast of Bridgeport and is accessible by both taxi and bus.

## Media & Communications

Barbados has a strong record of providing for and protecting the freedom of the press and open expression among the citizenry. The nation has two daily newspapers, *Barbados Advocate* and *The Nation*, both of which regularly publish views critical of government policy without fear of reprisal. There are no censorship restrictions and the nation's high literacy rate translates to significant readership for local publications.

Barbados has a single television station, CBC TV, produced by the government-owned Caribbean Broadcasting Corporation (CBC). Monitoring agencies have reported that television programming was also free from obstruction or censorship and programs on CBC TV present a wide variety of political and social views. Cable and satellite television are available in some areas and provide foreign broadcasts.

Barbados has both public and privately-owned radio stations providing news, talk, and music programs. A private company, Starcom Network, operates that nation's two most popular radio stations; Hott 95.3 and Love 104.1. The Hott 95.3 station provides a variety of native and Caribbean music, including calypso, soca, and reggae music programs. The government-owned radio stations generally provide news and informative content, but some also offer music and entertainment programs.

Internet coverage is mainly available in Bridgeport and the surrounding areas and has grown in the last decade. Internet usage measures about 78.5 percent of the population as of 2013. The government has no laws governing online content and allows for the free exchange of political opinions and information through Internet communication.

---

## SOCIAL DEVELOPMENT

### Standard of Living
Barbados ranked 59 out of 195 countries on the 2014 United Nations Human Development Index (HDI), which measures quality of life and standard of living indicators.

### Water Consumption
United Nations International Children's Emergency Fund (UNICEF) estimates that 99.7 percent of the population of Barbados has access to improved drinking water. In terms of improved sanitation, UNICEF estimates that 96.2 percent of the urban and rural populations have access to improved sanitation.

### Education
The people of Barbados enjoy a high literacy rate (99.7 percent) due in large part to the government's focus on education. Barbadians benefit

from free tuition and textbooks at all levels of education.

Education is compulsory for children between the ages of four and sixteen, and is modeled after the British system. There are more than 100 government-run and private primary schools on the island, and more than thirty secondary schools.

Beyond the secondary level, students may attend one of the islands community, technical, or teacher training colleges. The Cave Hill campus of the University of the West Indies opened on Barbados in 1963.

### Women's Rights
The Barbadian constitution and penal code guarantee equal rights for women. The law contains specific laws against rape, which include domestic sexual violence and rape, and provide a maximum penalty of life in prison. Domestic violence is considered a crime with a system of fines and prison sentences based on the severity of the crime and whether the abuse resulted in serious injury. Laws covering domestic abuse also pertain to persons involved in common-law relationships. The Royal Barbados Police Force (RBPF) maintains a civilian-based victim support unit, which offers counseling and other services to victims of domestic abuse. The Barbadian government also allows and supports the establishment of non-governmental outreach and counseling organizations to supplement government-sponsored programs.

The Bureau of Gender Affairs is the governmental branch responsible for evaluating and establishing programs aimed at protecting the rights of women and families. Among other programs, the Bureau of Gender Affairs helps to obtain and distribute funding to aid organizations, shelters, and women's rights programs. Women's rights groups have cited lack of adequate funding for aid organizations as one of the primary factors placing Barbadian women at risk. Although legal sanctions support women leaving abusive spouses, many women are faced with having few options after leaving home.

While there are fewer women than men involved in the national workforce, internal and external evaluations indicate that the number of women in professional positions is rising in the early 21st century. Women are allowed to hold public office and to serve in the armed forces and the RBPF. On average, women are less likely to obtain management positions than men employed in the same position.

## Health Care

Barbadians enjoy one of the highest standards of living in the region. The average infant mortality rate is 10.42 deaths per 1,000 live births, and the average life expectancy at birth is approximately seventy-five years—almost seventy-three years for women and seventy-seven years for men (2015 estimate).

The modern Queen Elizabeth Hospital in Bridgetown is the largest medical facility on the island. Government-run clinics throughout the island provide basic care at no charge. In the past, Barbados has struggled with shortages of medical staff and supplies, and with caring for people in remote areas. In recent years, however, the quality of care received by all Barbadians has improved.

## GOVERNMENT

### Structure

Barbados is a parliamentary democracy. Although the country gained its independence from Great Britain in 1966, the government retains many English influences.

The chief of state is the reigning English monarch, who appoints a governor-general to represent the British crown on the island. The head of the government is the prime minister, who advises the governor-general on the appointment of the cabinet. After legislative elections have been held, the governor-general usually appoints the leader of the majority party to be the prime minister. The prime minister in turn appoints the deputy prime minister.

The legislative branch of government consists of the Senate and House of Assembly. The twenty-one members of the Senate are appointed by the governor-general, while the thirty seats of the House of Assembly are elected by popular vote.

### Political Parties

There are three major political parties in Barbados. The Democratic Labour Party (DLP) is the more left-leaning of the country's two socially democratic parties. The second major party, the Barbados Labour Party (BLP), is the more moderate party. The last party is the People's Empowerment Party (PEP). In the 2013 general elections, the ruling DLP garnered 16 in the assembly. The BLP gained fourteen seats in the assembly. Smaller parties each earned less than one percent of the vote.

In addition to official parties, there are several political "pressure groups." These are the Barbados Secondary Teachers' Union, the Barbados Union of Teachers, the Barbados Workers Union, the Clement Payne Labor Union, the Congress of Trade Unions and Staff Association of Barbados, and the National Union of Public Workers.

### Local Government

Barbados is divided into eleven parishes and the City of Bridgeton. Local government no longer exists, and the administration of local services is performed by the central government and various administrative departments.

### Judicial System

The Supreme Court (comprised of the Court of Appeal and the High Court) is the country's highest court. Magistrate courts are the courts of first instance and hear criminal, civil, domestic, and juvenile matters.

### Taxation

The government of Barbados levies personal income, corporate, excise, and value-added taxes. There are no capital gains, estate, or inheritance taxes. Taxes are considered high, and the top personal income tax rate is 35 percent. Taxes and other revenue make up 25.7 percent of the annual GDP (2014 estimate).

## Armed Forces

The Barbados Defence Force (BDF) consists of a main land force, a maritime force (Coast Guard), and the Royal Barbados Police Force (RBPF). There is no conscription. The Eastern Caribbean Regional Security System is also regionally based in Barbados.

## Foreign Policy

Barbados is active in the international community and generally restricts its policy advocacy to issues directly affecting Caribbean nations. Barbados is a member of the United Nations (UN) and the Organization of American States (OAS), and also an active participant in the Caribbean Community and Common Market (CARICOM). In 1994, Barbados joined the newest Caribbean international organization, the Association of Caribbean States (ACS), and participates with other Caribbean countries in joint economic, peacekeeping, and anti-crime activities.

Barbados is also one of the Caribbean nations that opposed Venezuela's claim that the Aves Island can support human habitation. If determined that Aves Island can support habitation, Venezuela would be permitted, under UN statutes, to extend its territorial claims over portions of the Caribbean Sea.

Barbados has close diplomatic relations with the United States and cooperates in US–led operations to restrict and deter drug trafficking in the Caribbean. Barbados and the United States signed a mutual assistance agreement to this effect in 1996. There are an estimated 3,000 American expatriates living in Barbados. In addition, more than 30 percent of the nation's imports come from the United States, including machinery, electronics, and a variety of consumer goods.

The Barbadian government is also concerned with environmental degradation and participates with several UN groups and non-governmental organizations (NGOs) to address environmental issues. As a nation closely tied to the ocean, one of Barbados' chief concerns is maintaining fish populations in Caribbean waters. The flying fish, which once migrated into Barbadian waters in overwhelming numbers, now rarely migrates closer than 100 miles from the island because of population decline. Once known as "Land of the Flying Fish," Barbados considers the animal a national symbol and the fish's image appears in murals, emblems, and the national currency.

## Human Rights Profile

International human rights law insists that states respect civil and political rights, and also promote an individual's economic, social, and cultural rights. The United Nations (UN) Universal Declaration of Human Rights (UDHR) is recognized as the standard for international human rights. Its authors sought the counsel of the world's great thinkers, philosophers, and religious leaders, and were careful to create a document that reflects the core values shared by every world culture. (To read this document or view the articles relating to cultural human rights, go to: http://www.udhr.org/UDHR/default.htm.)

The Barbadian constitution adheres generally to the principles of the UDHR, though human rights monitoring organizations have identified several concerns, including domestic and child abuse and a deteriorating detention system.

The Barbadian government funded the construction of a new prison in 2007, after Glendairy Prison was destroyed during a riot in 2005. While the updated prison was designed to adequately house a prisoner population of up to 1,200 detainees and convicts, human rights and press inquiries indicated that prisoners do not have adequate sanitary facilities. This is a violation of Article 5 of the UDHR, guaranteeing freedom from inhumane treatment.

In 2006 and 2007, there were accusations that members of the Royal Barbados Police Force (RBPF) used excessive force when detaining or interrogating subjects, a violation of Article 5 of the UDHR. Internal investigations indicate that, while some Barbadian police officers were guilty of abusive behavior, incidents were isolated and did not constitute a failure of the overall system. NGOs have alleged that poor supervision of police behavior is the primary factor leading to incidences of abuse. Additionally, though the constitution guarantees impartial trial procedures for those accused of crimes, there have been cases where accused persons remain in detention for more than a year while awaiting trial. Internal investigations reveal that lengthy pre-trial periods are a result of an overburdened judicial system and not of institutional corruption.

The Barbadian government acknowledges that, while the government is committed to protecting the rights of children, as stated in Article 25 of the UDHR, child abuse is a continuing problem. This is due in large part to cultural conventions that permit corporal punishment of children by their parents. The state-sponsored welfare department is the governmental agency charged with providing counseling and outreach services for children suffering from abuse.

While the Barbadian constitution recognizes the right of privacy for its citizens, consensual same-sex relations are illegal under Barbadian law. Human rights organizations and the UN have criticized the Barbadian government for failing to protect gay men and lesbians from discrimination and abuse. There are also no laws protecting disabled persons from discrimination and/or abuse, and some reports indicate that disabled persons were unable to obtain satisfactory employment because of discriminatory hiring practices.

## ECONOMY

### Overview of the Economy

The economy of Barbados traditionally relied on sugarcane processing, but more recently has been turning toward light industry and tourism. Offshore banking is another growing economic sector. In 2014, the per capita gross domestic product was estimated at $16,200 USD (2014).

Bridgetown is the center of industry, services, education, and government for Barbados. Its major industries include banking, retail sales, tourism, natural resources, and the offshore market. Bridgetown is fully modern in its use of high-tech telecommunications, wireless services, and the Internet. The city also provides a regulated stock exchange for native and Caribbean industries.

### Industry

Barbados, having very few natural resources, is seeking to diversify its economy through the industrial sector. Industry employs 15 percent of the labor force and accounts for 12 percent of the GDP, representing a slight drop from the recent past (16 percent in 2008). The island's light industry focuses on the manufacture and assembly of electronics and plastics. Other industries include clothing and furniture.

Rum and molasses are produced for export from the island's sugarcane crop. Barbados' main trading partners are the United States and Trinidad.

### Labor

In 2014, the workforce totaled approximately 142,800, the majority of which—an estimated 75 percent—were employed in the services sector. Unemployment, estimated at 12.7 percent of the workforce in 2014, is a problem that continues to grow, but work is being done to try to alleviate it by privatizing government-run industry and diversifying the economy.

### Energy/Power/Natural Resources

Barbados has no mineral resources, and no deposits of oil or natural gas. Most of the land has been cleared for the cultivation of sugarcane. The island's chief natural resources are its tropical climate and natural beauty, which support the tourist trade, and the fish found offshore.

Heavy tourist traffic has come at an environmental price. Waste disposal from large cruise ships has caused water pollution, leading to the deterioration of the coral reef. The island is also experiencing erosion problems due to the clearing of land for agriculture. The government has taken steps to preserve the integrity of the coral reef by creating a marine reserve.

### Fishing

The fishing industry in Barbados employs a percentage of the population and is a large tourist industry. The catch relies heavily on four-winged flying fish (the stocks of which are reduced), dolphin fish, and kingfish.

Seafood is a large part of Barbadian food. The flying fish is such a large part of the local culture that it has become a symbol for the tourism industry. This widely popular fish is prepared in fancy restaurants, and may also be found in sandwiches at beachside fish shops.

### Forestry

Most of Barbados' natural rainforest has been cleared, but small sections do still exist.

### Agriculture

Once the mainstay of the Barbadian economy, agriculture now contributes only 3.1 percent to the GDP and employs 10 percent of the workforce. Sugarcane is the backbone of island agriculture; the island produces over 350 metric tons per year. Sugar products such as molasses and rum are major exports.

Other important agricultural products include cotton and vegetables, and livestock such as sheep, cattle, and goats. Much of the land formerly used for agriculture has been sold to tourism interests.

### Animal Husbandry

Sheep, cattle, pigs, and goats are the most common livestock breed on Barbados. In addition, there are approximately more than 400 farmers involved in the poultry industry.

### Tourism

After the sugar industry declined in the 19th century, tourism took over as the primary industry of Barbados. Bridgetown continues to serve the island as the central port for the tourism business. Located on Carlisle Bay, which offers catamaran tours, boat tours, snorkeling, and diving, Bridgetown offers a blend of modern and colonial architecture.

St. Lawrence, southeast of Bridgetown, is a popular tourist destination thanks to its luxurious scenery. Holetown is not only the island's oldest city, but is also popular among tourists interested in water sports. Sam Lord's Castle offers visitors a sampling of paintings, architecture, antiques, and folklore.

The services sector in Barbados accounts for an estimated 85 percent of the GDP, and employs three-quarters of the workforce. Tourism is a major contributor of capital, directly accounting for large percents of both of the GDP and the workforce. More than 1 million tourists visit Barbados each year, many from Great Britain or nearby Venezuela. Despite recent economic woes, which hurt the tourism revenues between 2008 and 2011, cruise ship passenger arrivals increased in 2009.

*Micah Issitt, Christopher Stetter,*
*Lynn-nore Chittom*

## DO YOU KNOW?

- When the British first settled Barbados, the island was a dense tropical rainforest that had a very large population of wild pigs.

- George Washington's only documented trip abroad was to visit Barbados with his ailing half-brother Lawrence, in the hope that the island climate would restore him to health. Washington and his brother stayed in a home in the historic Garrison district of Bridgetown. The home has been restored as a historic site.

### Bibliography

Beckles, Hilary McD. *A History of Barbados: From Amerindian Settlement to Caribbean Single Market.* New York: Cambridge University Press, 2007.

Best, Curwin. *The Popular Music and Entertainment Culture of Barbados.* Lanham, MD: Scarecrow Press, 2012.

Cameron, Sarah. *Footprint Barbados.* Bath, UK: Footprint Handbooks, 2013.

Carmichael, Trevor A. *Barbados: Thirty Years of Independence.* Miami, FL: Ian Randle Publishers, 1996.

Vaitilingham, Adam. *Barbados.* New York: Rough Guides, 2007.

## Works Cited

"About Barbados." *UNDP in Barbados & the OECS.* http://www.bb.undp.org/content/barbados/en/home/countryinfo/barbados.html.

"Artist Listings." *National Art Gallery Committee.* http://www.nagc.bb/section.asp?Sec=3

"Barbados: Country Reports on Human Rights Practices." *U.S. Department of State.* http://www.state.gov/g/drl/rls/hrrpt/2007/100627.htm

"Barbados: Human Rights in Barbados." *Amnesty International* http://www.amnesty.org/en/region/barbados

"Barbados." *CIA World Factbook Online.* https://www.cia.gov/library/publications/the-world-factbook/print/bb.html

"Barbados." *Lonely Planet Online.* http://www.lonelyplanet.com/barbados

"Barbados." Political Database of the Americas. *Georgetown University Online.* http://pdba.georgetown.edu/constitutions/Barbados/barbados.html

"Barbados." *U.S. Department of State.* Bureau of Western Hemisphere Affairs. http://www.state.gov/r/pa/ei/bgn/26507.htm

"Barbados." *World Health Organization Online.* http://www.who.int/countries/brb/en/

"Country Profile: Barbados." *BBC News Online.* http://news.bbc.co.uk/2/hi/americas/country_profiles/1154116.stm

"Government of Barbados Information Network." Barbados Government Online. http://www.barbados.gov.bb/

"On-Island Transportation." *Barbados Online.* http://www.visitbarbados.org/explore/transportation.aspx

"Transport Board." *Barbados Transport Board.* http://www.transportboard.com/schedule.php

*Buildings in Bermuda are often pink with white roofs. iStock/wwing*

BERMUDA

# Introduction

Originally settled by English colonists who shipwrecked on their way to Virginia in 1609, Bermuda has become a center of tourism and offshore banking for the international community. Bermuda also holds the title for the oldest British overseas territory, although it became self-governing in 1620. It is still a part of the United Kingdom as a referendum for independence was defeated in 1995.

## GENERAL INFORMATION

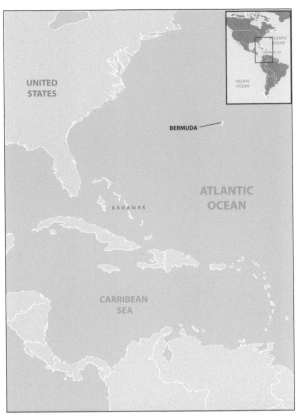

**Official Language(s):** English
**Population:** 70,196 (2015 estimate)
**Currency:** Bermudan dollar
**Coins:** The Bermudian dollar is subdivided into 100 cents; coins in circulation include 1, 5, 10, and 25 cents, and 1 dollar.
**Land Area:** 54 square kilometers (20 square miles)
**National Motto:** "Quo fata ferunt" (Latin, "Wither the Fates carry [us]")
**National Anthem:** "Hail to Bermuda" (unofficial); "God Save the Queen" (official)
**Capital:** Hamilton
**Time Zone(s):** GMT - 4
**Flag Description:** Bermuda's flag features the United Kingdom flag upper left. The green and white badge displays a red lion holding a shield that symbolizes the sinking of the Sea Venture about one mile off the coastline of Bermuda in the summer of 1609. The ship was caught in a hurricane, and subsequently struck a reef.

## Population

Bermuda is home to an estimated 70,196 people, of whom 53.8 percent are black and 31 percent are white, with the remaining population of mixed or other ethnicity. About three-fourths of Bermudians are natives of the islands, and immigrants from the United Kingdom, United States, Canada, British West Indies, and Portugal make up much of the remaining population. Although Bermuda has a relatively low population, its population density of nearly 2,800 people per square mile is the highest among all Atlantic island nations and one of the highest in the world.

The second largest city is St. George, with a population of about 1,010, followed by Bermuda's capital, Hamilton, home to about 1,743 people (2010 census estimate). Much of the population is concentrated in and around these two cities, with settlement patterns typically following major roadways. Bermuda's population growth is very low, and the average age of a Bermudian is about forty-one years of age. Men and women

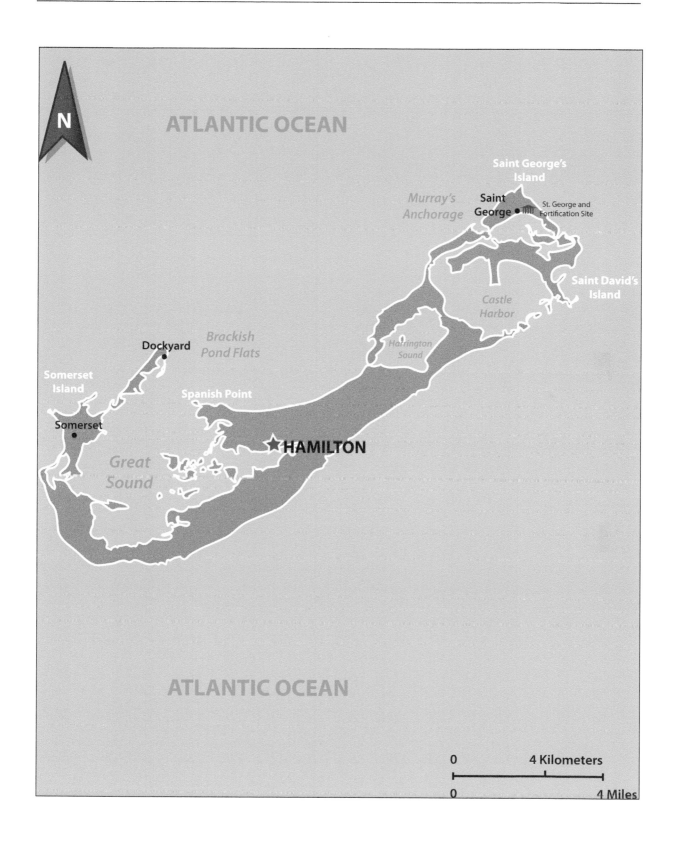

make up roughly equal portions of the resident population.

## Languages

The official language of Bermuda is English, although some people speak Portuguese. Bermudian English is closely related to British English, but distance and time have added some unique features to Bermuda's dialect. For example, Bermudans often say "horse" instead of motorcycle or motor scooter and may interchange the pronunciations of the letters "w" and "v."

## Native People & Ethnic Groups

Prior to British settlement in 1609, Bermuda was uninhabited. Today, about 60 percent of Bermudians are descendants of Africans who came to the islands as part of the British slave trade. After Great Britain outlawed slavery in 1834, many former slaves remained on the islands and adapted to the British culture. In the late 19th century, blacks from the West Indies immigrated to Bermuda. These Bermudians maintain some of their West Indian cultural practices and beliefs. Most white Bermudians have British or Portuguese heritage.

## Religions

Most Bermudans are Christians, with about 15 percent of the population belonging to the Anglican Church. Many people follow the Roman Catholic (about 15 percent) and African Methodist Episcopal faiths, and other Protestant denominations, while Judaism and Islam are also represented.

## Climate

The Atlantic Ocean is an important factor in Bermuda's climate. Because of the warming effects of the ocean and the Gulf Stream, Bermuda enjoys a mild climate; high temperatures in the summer months average about 29.4° Celsius (85° Fahrenheit) and low temperatures in the winter months average around 14° Celsius (57° Fahrenheit). Temperatures in Bermuda have never reached the freezing point, so the islands have never experienced snowfall. The islands average about 142 centimeters (56 inches) of rainfall each year.

The Atlantic Ocean also contributes to the humid conditions common on the islands. Occasionally, hurricanes and tropical storms directly strike Bermuda; more often, these strong storms pass through waters within hundreds of miles of the islands, causing heavy rainfall and strong winds.

## ENVIRONMENT & GEOGRAPHY

### Topography

Bermuda is an archipelago made up of about 138 islands and islets. The seven main islands form a fishhook shape, with Grand Bermuda—also called Main Island—as the largest land mass at about 19 kilometers (11 miles) in length. The total area of the islands is approximately 53 square kilometers (20 square miles).

The islands sit atop a 200-foot-thick limestone cap covering the remains of an extinct oceanic volcano. Because the islands' limestone-laden soil readily absorbs water, Bermuda has no lakes or rivers and only occasional freshwater streams and ponds. Rugged limestone cliffs and pink-tinged beaches line Bermuda's 102 kilometers (64 miles) of coastline. Bermuda's interior is mostly covered by gently rolling hills. The Peak, located on Main Island, is the nation's highest point at 78.9 meters (259 feet).

Rim Reef, a barrier reef located to the southeast of Bermuda, is the world's northernmost coral reef. A smaller coral reef lies along the southern coast of Main Island. These reefs protect Bermuda's lagoons from strong ocean waves. Bermuda's rock formations and limestone cave systems such as the Crystal Caves are well-known natural features.

### Plants & Animals

Bermuda is home to about 1,600 different types of plants and animals, of which less than one-quarter are native species. The invasive species brought to the islands over the past four centuries

*The cahow bird is a cliff-dwelling bird native to Bermuda.*

have increasingly threatened Bermuda's native species. Some of these—including the cedar tree, the palmetto bush, and the cahow (a cliff-dwelling bird)—exist only on the islands. All three of these species have experienced significant declines over the past few centuries, to the point that the cahow was thought to be extinct.

Many migratory birds visit Bermuda each year, including the longtail, Bermuda's national symbol. Bermuda's terrestrial wildlife includes a variety of reptiles such as the giant toad and the native skink, a lizard that was Bermuda's only land animal prior to the arrival of humans. Hundreds of varieties of sea dwellers, including angelfish, coral, sea horses, and sharks, live in the surrounding waters.

In addition to the cedar and palmetto, many subtropical plants, such as the hibiscus, poinsettia, and cassava, flourish on Bermuda. Pine trees were introduced in the 20th century as numbers of cedar trees dwindled, and flowering trees and evergreen bushes can be seen throughout the country. Many Bermudians have ornamental gardens inspired by those of Great Britain, with roses, geraniums, and birds-of-paradise.

## CULTURAL HISTORY

### History

Although Spanish explorer Juan de Bermúdez first sighted the Bermuda islands in 1503, the history of Bermuda did not begin until 1609. A group of English settlers heading for Virginia aboard the *Sea Venture* shipwrecked on the islands after being blown off course by a hurricane. Led by Admiral Sir George Somers (1554–1610), the group of about 150 colonists spent the next several months on Bermuda, where they built two new ships. In May 1610, nearly all of these colonists left Bermuda—which they had dubbed the Somers Islands—for Virginia aboard the completed ships *Patience* and *Deliverance*.

Bermuda soon came under the control of the Virginia Company, a private corporation undertaking the colonization of North America. In 1612, that organization dispatched sixty colonists to join the two remaining Bermudian settlers. These colonists founded the first capital of Bermuda, St. George. Soon, the Virginia Company turned over control of the islands to the purpose-founded Somers Islands Company. Under the Somers Islands Company's direction, settlers tried with little success to make Bermuda's poor soil yield crops such as sugarcane and tobacco.

In 1684, Bermuda reverted to crown rule and was appointed a British governor. Early Bermudians—including settlers from England, Ireland, Portugal, and Scotland, as well as enslaved Africans and Native Americans—turned to shipbuilding and the sea trade. Bermudians suffered when a number of North American colonies suspended trade with the British-controlled islands during the American Revolution, and again when America retaliated against a British attack launched from Bermuda during the War of 1812. Some Bermudians responded to these setbacks by becoming pirates and smugglers.

By the time that Hamilton became the colonial capital in 1815, Bermuda was rebuilding its sea trade and becoming an important center between the West Indies and North America.

Slavery was abolished throughout the British Empire in 1834, freeing the many enslaved residents of Bermuda. However, Bermuda aided the proslavery Confederacy during the American Civil War in the early 1860s. Bermudian ships smuggled food and goods from Great Britain past the federal blockade to southern ports. On the return voyage, they carried American cotton that was then sent on to Great Britain. This black market trade brought great profits to the islands, but the end of the war in 1865 brought this era of sea-faring dominance to an abrupt halt.

During the late 1800s, Bermudians again tried to coax their soil into producing crops, this time with greater financial success. With its mild climate, Bermuda was able to support the cultivation of vegetables such as potatoes, celery, and the popular Bermuda onion. These crops were exported to cooler regions, particularly New York City. Because Bermudians had little agricultural experience, they imported indentured, or contracted, workers from Portugal's Madeira and Azores islands. Bermuda returned to its seafaring roots in the early 20th century when it began operations to smuggle rum into the Prohibition-era United States (1920–1933). By the early 1930s, the end of Prohibition and the enactment of a stiff agricultural tariff ended these two industries. Bermudians were forced to find another basis for their economy.

As early as the 1880s, tourists from the United States and Great Britain traveled to Bermuda during the cold winter months. Early visitors included English Princess Louise (1848–1939)—for whom Bermuda's first resort, The Princess Hotel, was named—and writers such as Mark Twain (1835–1910). After the decline of agriculture and rum-running, tourism became Bermuda's dominant industry, with wealthy visitors arriving first via ocean liner and later by airplane. Although tourism temporarily stopped during World War II, tourists again flocked to Bermuda after the close of hostilities in 1945. The success of the tourism industry led to a great deal of population growth as new residents came to the islands to take jobs building and staffing tourist facilities.

Great Britain relinquished direct control over the islands in 1957, granting Bermuda self-government. During the 1960s, Bermudians faced the task of establishing an independent government while trying to manage increasingly tense race relations between black and white residents. Long-standing segregationist and discriminatory policies led to race riots in 1968. Although desegregation slowly spread, racial tensions were fueled by the 1973 assassination of white Bermudian governor Sir Richard Sharples (1916–1973) by a group of black political dissidents. In 1977, the government began actively working to end the segregation still socially common on the islands, and race relations have greatly improved since.

Since the 1970s, some Bermudians have considered complete independence from Great Britain. However, in 1995 a wide majority rejected a measure to separate entirely, though the separatist debate remains. The 1980s saw Bermuda reach its peak as a tourist destination, with well over a half million visitors coming to the islands each year. Although tourism began to decline slightly during the 1990s, the rise of international business entities has kept Bermuda strong. Today, the country faces continuing challenges, including environmental concerns, an aging population, and a high cost of living.

## CULTURE

### Arts & Entertainment

Because of a cultural fusion of British, North American, African, and Caribbean elements, Bermuda has a diverse and vibrant artistic heritage. Perhaps the best-known native art lies in Bermuda's architecture. The combination of limited available resources and environmental necessity led to the development of a distinctive Bermudian style, which has been historically reliant on the local limestone as the primary construction material. Because of the coral present in the limestone, Bermuda's homes and businesses often have a striking pink tint. Gleaming white roofs cap Bermudian buildings for practical as well as aesthetic purposes. The absence of lakes and ponds on Bermuda means that rain water is the principal source of fresh water. Most buildings contain tanks to store rain water drained from the roof. Regular whitewashing of roofs helps ensure a clean and safe water supply.

Folk dancing and music continues to be a popular form of entertainment throughout the western Atlantic and Caribbean. On Bermuda, this is illustrated through a popular dance style known as gombey. First performed by enslaved Africans in the mid-1700s, gombey traditionally is a medium for portraying biblical stories. Gombey dancers are always male, with fathers often training their sons in the art form. Sporting elaborate costumes with masks, capes, tomahawks, and feather-plumed hats, gombey dancers perform to music produced by African drums (the name "gombey" comes from the word for a specific drum) and other instruments. Their movements are rhythmic and strong, showing gombey's roots in West African tribal dancing. Although gombey dancing appears throughout the region, Bermudian gombey dancers incorporate unique elements such as the British fife to reflect the country's diverse heritage. Gombey dancers can be seen chanting and parading through the streets of Hamilton on certain holidays throughout the year, as well as at special gombey performances.

African cultural heritage has also appeared in Bermuda's music. Calypso and steel pan (drum) music have long been common musical styles on the islands. Derived from the musical traditions of enslaved Africans on Trinidad during the 1700s, calypso combined saucy lyrics and Afro-Caribbean beats by the early 20th century. The form developed international popularity during the 1940s and 1950s. Calypso reigned supreme over Bermuda's musical scene until the 1970s, when newer genres such as reggae and disco captured the interest of younger audiences. Today, calypso remains an influence on Bermudian music, although American- and British-style rock, along with reggae, have become more popular.

Musical forms also reflect the island culture's British roots. Stemming from the presence of

Scottish soldiers on Bermuda during the 1700s and 1800s, bagpipe musicians are active in the island's local culture. For nearly forty years, the Bermuda Police Pipe Band and the Bermuda Cadets Pipe Band performed throughout Bermuda. In 1992, these groups disbanded and reformed into the seventeen-member Bermuda Isles Pipe Band. This band has taken Bermudian bagpipe music to international locations, including Canada and Scotland, as well as appearing at Bermudian ceremonies and events.

Bermuda's beauty and atmosphere have served as inspiration to artists from around the world. One of the best known of these visitors was American author and humorist Mark Twain, who came to the country frequently beginning in the late 1800s. Twain included the islands and its residents in his popular travel book *The Innocents Abroad* (1869), and influenced diverse aspects of island life. Along with former US President Woodrow Wilson (1856–1924), Twain was instrumental in gathering support for Bermuda's long-standing ban on automobiles.

In 1997, Bermuda launched its own independent film festival. Each year, Bermudians and visitors gather to see features, short films, and documentaries from around the world. Since beginning in 1997, the Bermuda International Film Festival has expanded greatly, growing from twenty-two films shown at two theaters to eighty-five films spread over four screens shown for a week, including live talks and other events.. Short films shown at the Bermuda International Film Festival qualify for consideration at the renowned Academy Awards.

## Cultural Sites & Landmarks

Built in the early 1600s, the city of St. George— the oldest continuously inhabited English settlement in the Americas—is recognized for its historic and cultural value. In 2000, the historic town and its related fortifications were designated as a World Heritage Site by the United Nations Educational, Scientific and Cultural Organization (UNESCO). The town features architectural styles unique to Bermuda, with homes and businesses constructed from the islands' indigenous coral limestone and topped with brilliant white roofs. There are numerous historical buildings, including the Old State House and Bridge House, the former homes of Bermuda's Parliament and governors, respectively, and St. Peter's Church. First constructed in 1612, the original structure of the church is still visible despite the devastating effects of a hurricane in 1712. The city is also home to the Unfinished Church, a cathedral begun in 1874 to replace St. Peter's that was never finished due to financial problems.

Near the city of St. George, numerous fortifications display the evolving English military technology of the latter half of the second millennium. A reproduction of the first English settlers' ship, *Deliverance*, can be seen at Ordinance Island. Other historic forts on the islands include Fort Hamilton, located near the capital. The fort is now the site of summertime performances by the Bermuda Isles Pipe Band. Hamilton is also the site of the Bermuda Cathedral, the seat of Bermuda's Anglican diocese, and the Bermuda National Gallery, which displays both Bermudian and international art.

Despite having limited open space, Bermuda boasts many national parks, some on repurposed land. In 1931, Bermuda's government began a small national railroad. With the end of a long-standing ban on motorized vehicles, buses overtook the rail system and the railway closed in 1948. After decades of neglect, this track became the Railway Trail in 1984, providing a route across most of the country for hikers and bicyclists. Since 2001, the Railway Trail has been a government-protected national site.

One of Bermuda's most popular tourist attractions for many decades, the Crystal Caves are an underground world of lakes, rock formations, and limestone caves. First discovered in 1907 by two boys looking for a lost cricket ball, the caves are one of the islands' best-known natural features. Bermuda's pink-tinged beaches, including Horseshoe Bay and Elbow Beach, are renowned for both their natural beauty and unusual limestone arch rock formations.

At Bermuda's 8,500-seat National Stadium, located near Hamilton, spectators can enjoy soccer games, cricket matches, and even an international annual rugby classic. Cricket clubs, golf courses, and tennis courts are scattered throughout the islands. Each spring, visitors flock to Bermuda's harbors to watch sailing contests, including the popular yacht competitions that take place during International Race Week.

## SOCIETY

### Transportation

Because Bermudian law limits the number and size of automobiles that residents can own and prohibits tourists from renting cars, Bermudians often rely on other modes of transportation. In fact, automobiles were banned on the islands altogether from 1910 until 1946, when most people and goods traveled via horse. As of 2005, fewer than 27,000 cars, trucks, and buses were present on Bermuda.

But today, bicycles, mopeds, and motor scooters are popular modes of transport in the islands, as well as small buses, taxis, and water ferries. The small size of the country means that walking is also a cheap and efficient way of getting from place to place. Only about half of Bermuda's narrow, winding roads are publicly maintained (225km of 447 total kms), and the speed limit throughout the islands is a modest 20 miles per hour. There is only one airport on the island, as of 2013.

### Media & Communications

In 2007, Bermuda's government began operating an informational television station, CITV, bringing the country's total terrestrial stations to six. Cable and satellite television are popular, mostly offering American and British programming. Two radio stations offer a variety of music, and Internet and cell phone usage is widespread. As of 2014, there were an estimated 68,300 Internet users, representing approximately 98 percent of the population.

Bermuda's largest daily newspaper, the *Royal Gazette,* offers both print and online editions and has a circulation of just fewer than

15,000 and boasts that it reaches 97 percent of the population. Other newspapers, including the *Bermuda Sun* and *Worker's Voice,* are published less frequently. Because of the many tourists, newspapers from the United States, Canada, and Great Britain are also readily available.

## GOVERNMENT

### Structure

After Hong Kong reverted to China in 1997, Bermuda became the largest British colony in the world. A self-governed overseas territory, Bermuda elects many of its own leaders and makes its own laws, but legally remains a part of the United Kingdom. This relationship is generally acceptable, as citizens have voted down measures to officially separate from Great Britain.

The modern government of Bermuda is based on the 1968 constitution. This document establishes Bermuda as a parliamentary democracy containing three branches of government: executive, legislative, and judicial. The head of both Bermuda's executive branch and the state is the reigning British monarch, who is responsible for selecting Bermuda's governor. The governor oversees the islands' internal security and external affairs on behalf of the British crown, as well as appointing the judges who make up Bermuda's judicial branch and some of the legislative branch's senators. In 2001, Bermuda's constitution was amended to add an ombudsman to the islands' government. This person hears and objectively decides on public complaints about the government and its agencies.

Most government power rests with Bermuda's premier, the leader of the party that holds the majority in Bermuda's parliament. The parliament comprises the Senate, made up of eleven members chosen by the governor or by the head of the opposition party, and the House of Assembly, a forty-member elected body. The House creates Bermuda's laws, which are then reviewed by the Senate. Since the 1960s, Bermudian politics has been dominated by the

*A commemorative postage stamp features Grape Bay and an image of the British king, King George VI.*

prominent Progressive Labour Party (PLP) and the United Bermuda Party (UBP). From 1968 until 1998, the UBP controlled the parliament and, thus, the premiership, making it the leading force in Bermudian politics. Support for the PLP grew during the 1990s, and it won a majority of parliamentary seats for the first time in 1998.

### Foreign Policy

Under the second amendment of Bermuda's constitution, all diplomatic, security, and defense issues for the islands remain under the control of the British crown. Thus, Bermuda's foreign policy is directly linked to that of its parent nation. As the monarch's representative on the islands, Bermuda's governor holds direct responsibility for the country's foreign affairs. For most of its history, Bermuda has exercised no official autonomy in foreign affairs. It has taken small steps toward an independent foreign policy in the early 21st century, particularly under the leadership of the independence-leaning PLP.

In 2003, Bermuda joined the Caribbean Community (CARICOM), a regional organization aimed at supporting the economic interests and overall economic, social, and political development of Caribbean nations. That same year, Bermuda also signed a memorandum of cultural understanding with communist neighbor Cuba, despite objections by the United States. Increasingly, Bermuda is relying on its Caribbean allies for support rather than on its traditional friendships with Great Britain and the United States. For example, Bermuda chose to forego American and British aid following a destructive hurricane—Hurricane Fabian—in 2003; instead, the country strove to rebuild damaged areas independently. Bermuda also accepted the assistance of workers sent from various parts of the Caribbean to rebuild Bermuda's electrical, cable, and telephone systems.

For the first 350 years of its history, Bermuda was the site of British military installations, ranging from 17th-century forts to the naval and air bases of World War II. During World War II, the United States also established a naval base on reclaimed Bermudian land at St. David's Island, occupied through a ninety-nine-year lease from the British government. British and American intelligence personnel, particularly code breakers, stationed on these bases contributed greatly to the Allied efforts. However, after the war, military operations in Bermuda declined. The British army garrison closed in 1957 with the granting of political autonomy to Bermuda, and closures of the remaining American, Canadian, and British bases followed during the 1990s. In 2002, the United States formally returned its leased Bermudian land to the islands' government.

Today, Bermuda maintains no regular military forces. The islands are protected from external threats by the British military, and internal security is handled by the Bermuda Police Service, the Reserve Constabulary, and the Bermuda Regiment. The Bermuda Regiment gains members through a conscription lottery, for which all Bermudian men are required to register (women enter the military strictly on a voluntary basis). Bermuda Regiment members serve for thirty-nine months on a primarily part-time basis. The main duties of the Bermuda Regiment are supporting other internal forces and assisting in disaster relief efforts both at home and throughout the Caribbean region, as well as marching in ceremonial processions.

## Human Rights Profile

International human rights law insists that states respect civil and political rights, and also promote an individual's economic, social, and cultural rights. The United Nations (UN) Universal Declaration on Human Rights (UDHR) is recognized as the standard for international human rights. Its authors sought the counsel of the world's great thinkers, philosophers, and religious leaders, and were careful to create a document that reflects the core values shared by every world culture. (To read this document or view the articles relating to cultural human rights, go to: http://www.udhr.org/UDHR/default.htm.)

Bermuda has a strong human rights record, with rights protected both in theory and in practice. In 1981, Bermuda demonstrated its commitment to human rights with the passage of the Human Rights Act. This legislation, which specifically references the UDHR as an influence, established the Human Rights Commission (HRC) and formally barred any type of discrimination. The HRC specifically works to support equality among Bermudians and to mediate human rights disputes.

The Human Rights Act strongly mirrors the tenets of Article 2 of the UDHR, condemning discrimination on the basis of race, sex, marital status, disability, legitimacy of birth, status as an unwed parent, and political or religious beliefs. Both men and women enjoy freedom to marry and divorce as outlined under Article 16 of the declaration. Same-sex couples enjoy no such protections under Bermudian law and are not generally socially accepted. However, the Bermudian government stated in 2007 that the omission of homosexual couples from the Human Rights Act was an oversight, and that full legal rights for gay families were forthcoming. Legislation further protects the freedoms of religion and speech, although hate speech and discriminatory materials are banned. Bermuda has also been recognized by Amnesty International (AI) for its December 1999 abolition of the death penalty.

Perhaps the most controversial human rights issue in Bermuda pertains to the difficulties of obtaining Bermudian citizenship. Because of Bermuda's already dense population, the Bermudian government has enacted laws that strictly limit the naturalization of citizens to those who have remained married to a Bermudian citizen for a minimum of ten years. This period greatly exceeds the three years required by the British mainland and the three- to five-year span common to most Western nations. Further restrictions regarding duration of continuous physical residence on Bermuda, character, and conduct apply. However, regardless of length of residence, those who are not married to Bermudian citizens have no legal route to citizenship. In fact, some island residents have lived on Bermuda for decades without any possibility of obtaining full citizenship. This causes numerous legal obstacles in all aspects of daily life.

Bermudian companies are legally bound to employ any Bermudian citizen in need of work before seeking non-Bermudians. In addition, non-Bermudians are banned from purchasing or holding any but the most expensive Bermudian properties. Being born on Bermuda does not automatically grant citizenship as occurs under British, American, and Canadian law, unless at least one parent is already a Bermudian citizen.

## ECONOMY

### Overview of the Economy

Bermuda's per capita GDP of just over $85,000 (USD) is the highest in the world. The strength of Bermuda's economy and strict pro-Bermudian employment laws kept unemployment at a low 2.1 percent in 2004, but in 2015, Bermuda entered its seventh year of recession, causing unemployment to rise to nine percent. In addition, the high cost of living, particularly the steep cost of housing, forces many Bermudians to hold two jobs. However, only about 11 percent of Bermudians live below the poverty line, a one percent rise from pre-recession years.

### Industry

Aside from construction, Bermuda has little industry, largely due to the small size of the island. Limited fishing and rock quarrying, in addition to the production of pharmaceuticals, food and beverages, cosmetics, paints, and concrete and wood products, make up about 5.2 percent of the country's gross domestic product (GDP). Instead, Bermuda relies on a service-based economy, with finance and tourism making up the two largest segments of the islands' economy.

Bermuda is a hub for international banking and insurance, and its lack of both corporate and personal income taxes continue to attract multinational corporations. By 2015, over 18,000 international corporations—relatively few of which have physical locations on Bermuda—were registered in the country, providing over 4,500 jobs for Bermuda's residents and creating a tax haven for many companies. Between 1997 and 2014, the GDP of these businesses more than tripled, contributing to an overall GDP of $5,198 billion (USD) in 2013.

### Energy/Power/Natural Resources

As a collection of small, rocky islands, Bermuda has little arable land and fewer natural resources. In fact, other than a few crops and fish, the limestone that forms the islands' surface is Bermuda's only natural resource. Practically all of the limestone quarried on Bermuda is made into blocks or roofing tiles that are used as building material on the islands.

Bermudians struggle to keep their small, densely-populated home in balance with nature. Extensive human development means that less than 10 percent of the islands remain wild, and tourism and boat traffic have negatively impacted Bermuda's coral reefs. With so many residents and tourists occupying such a small space, waste management is a particular challenge. Runoff from Bermuda's garbage dump and sewage disposal facility can damage both land and water.

In 2007, the Bermudian government opened a new recycling center and launched TAG (Tin, Aluminum, and Glass), a recycling awareness program aimed at easing the country's waste problems. The government has also set aside about seventy-five protected parks and nature preserves throughout the islands in addition to enacting strict anti-littering and graffiti laws.

## Agriculture

Nearly all of Bermuda's food is imported, mostly from the United States and Canada, as the high population density and lack of arable land on the islands greatly limit the production of crops. Locally produced agricultural products include eggs, dairy, potatoes, and subtropical fruits, in addition to Bermuda's most famous crop: the large, mild Bermuda onion. Crop cultivation takes place in small quantities to supply the needs of Bermudians and tourists. Bermuda's only agricultural exports are the bulbs of Easter lilies—originally brought to the islands during the 1800s—and other flowers. Even the Bermuda onions consumed outside of the islands are grown primarily in the United States.

## Tourism

Tourism is big business in Bermuda, making up a significant portion of the nation's GDP and directly or indirectly employing the largest segment of Bermuda's workforce. Over three-quarters of Bermuda's tourism comes from the United States, so the decline in travel following the terrorist attacks of September 11, 2001, contributed to a steep drop in overall tourism for the islands. However, tourism grew again, with over 650,000 people arriving at the islands through the Bermuda International Airport on St. David's Island or from cruise ships visiting the ports of Hamilton and St. George in 2007. But with the world-wide recession beginning in 2008/09, Bermuda's economy suffered heavily and are still slow in regaining the economic power lost in the recession.

Bermuda's mild climate and famed pink sandy beaches are the two greatest draws for visitors from colder climes, and have made it a longtime popular destination for weddings and honeymoons. Tourists also enjoy the country's golf and tennis courses, restaurants, and water sports, including acting as spectators at Bermuda's many popular yacht races. Historic sites, churches, museums, and gardens in St. George and Hamilton attract many visitors, as do educational sites and traditional gombey dancing performances.

*Vanessa Vaughn*

## DO YOU KNOW?

- Bermuda is the birthplace of the knee-length Bermuda shorts. When accompanied by a dress shirt, suit jacket, necktie, and knee socks, these shorts are part of Bermudian conservative business attire.

- One point of the infamous Bermuda Triangle touches Bermuda. Numerous ships and airplanes are reported to have been mysteriously lost in this region, although little proof of these disappearances or their possible causes exists.

- Bermuda has only one fast food restaurant—a Kentucky Fried Chicken—because of planning laws banning the establishment of fast food restaurants on the islands.

## Bibliography

Jarvis, Michael J. *In the Eye of All Trade: Bermuda, Bermudans, and the Maritime Atlantic World, 1680–1783*. Charlotte, NC: University of North Carolina Press, 2012.

Orr, Tamra B. *Bermuda*. New York: Marshall Cavendish Benchmark, 2009.

Porter, Darwin and Danforth Prince. *Frommer's Bermuda 2009*. Hoboken, NJ: Wiley's Publishing, 2011.

Sterrer, Wolfgang and Christine Schoepfer-Sterrer, eds., *Marine Fauna and Flora of Bermuda*. New York: Wiley, 1986.

Swan, Quito. *Black Power in Bermuda: The Struggle for Decolonization*. New York: Palgrave Macmillan, 2012.

## Works Cited

"About Us: BIFF History." *Bermuda International Film Festival*. Bermuda International Film Festival Foundation. http://www.bermudafilmfest.com/about_us/biff_history.html.

"Bermuda." *World Data Analyst*. Encyclopedia Britannica. http://www.world.eb.com.ezproxy.libraries.wright.edu:2048/wdpdf/Bermuda.pdf.

"Bermuda." *The World Factbook*. Central Intelligence Agency. https://www.cia.gov/library/publications/the-world-factbook/geos/bd.html.

"Bermuda." *U.S. Department of State: Diplomacy in Action*. United States Department of States. http://www.state.gov/r/pa/ei/bgn/5375.htm.

"Bermuda Railway Trail." *Bermuda.com*. Bermuda.com Limited. http://www.bermuda.com/attractions/railway/.

"Bermuda Triangle." *Encyclopedia Britannica*. Online. http://search.eb.com.ezproxy.libraries.wright.edu:2048/eb/article-9078823.

Crooker, Richard A., *Bermuda*. Philadelphia: Chelsea House Publishers, 2002.

Forbes, Keith Archibald. "Bermuda Online in 125+ Comprehensive Websites." *Bermuda Online in 125+ Comprehensive Websites*. 2009. The Royal Gazette. http://www.bermuda-online.org/.

"Historic Town of St. George, and Related Fortifications, Bermuda." *World Heritage Center*. UNESCO. http://whc.unesco.org/en/list/983.

"HRC." *Human Rights Commission*. Government of Bermuda. http://www.gov.bm/portal/server.pt?open=512&objID=495&PageID=0&cached=true&mode=2&userID=2.

"New Legislation: Bermuda Shows the Way Forward." *Amnesty International* 7 Jan. 2000. http://www.amnesty.org/en/library/asset/AMR17/001/2000/en/dom-AMR170012000en.html.

"19th Bermuda International Film Festival, March 4-11, 2016." *Bermuda International Film Festival*. http://www.biff.bm/.

Orr, Tamra B., *Bermuda*. New York: Marshall Cavendish Benchmark, 2009.

"PLP: Moving Bermuda Forward." Bermuda Progressive Labour Party. *Bermuda Progressive Labour Party*. http://plp.bm/about/history.

Porter, Darwin, and Danforth Prince. *Frommer's Bermuda 2009*. Hoboken, NJ: Wiley's Publishing, 2008.

Raynor, Tauria. "Bermuda Troubadours Honoured with Stamp." *Royal Gazette* 20 Mar. 2008 http://www.royalgazette.com/siftology.royalgazette/Article/article.jsp?sectionId=60&articleId=7d83a3330030009.

Rutstein, Dan. "Premier Turns Down UK Offer of Help." *Royal Gazette* 8 Sept. 2003. http://www.royalgazette.com/siftology.royalgazette/Article/article.jsp?sectionId=60&articleId=7d3940e30030003.

Skinner, Robyn and Amanda Dale. "Perinchief Further Backs Protection for Gay Families." *Royal Gazette* 18 May 2007. http://www.royalgazette.com/siftology.royalgazette/Article/article.jsp?sectionId=60&articleId=7d7593b30030004.

Smith, Tim. "Soldiers Fly out to Turks and Caicos." *Royal Gazette* 17 Sept. 2008. http://www.royalgazette.com/siftology.royalgazette/Article/article.jsp?articleId=7d898af30030000&sectionId=60.

"Statistics." *Bermuda Government, Department of Statistics*. Government of Bermuda. http://www.statistics.gov.bm/portal/server.pt.

Warren, Marcus. "Bermuda Refuses Navy Aid." *Telegraph* 7 Sept. 2003. http://www.telegraph.co.uk/news/worldnews/centralamericaandthecaribbean/bermuda/1440887/Bermuda-refuses-Navy-aid.html.

"Waste Management." *Office of the Auditor General*. Government of Bermuda. http://www.oagbermuda.gov.bm/portal/server.pt?open=512&objID=516&&PageID=1079&mode=2&in_hi_userid=2&cached=true.

Zuill, Lilla. "Caribbean Relief Workers Ring All the Right Bells for BTC." *Royal Gazette* 28 Oct. 2003. http://www.royalgazette.com/siftology.royalgazette/Article/article.jsp?sectionId=65&articleId=7d3ae1230030008.

*A tobacco field in Cuba. iStock/Jekurantodistaja*

CUBA

# Introduction

The Republic of Cuba is an island nation in the Caribbean Sea. Geographically, it is a close neighbor of the United States, Mexico, Haiti, and Jamaica. It is governed by an authoritarian, communist regime.

Cuban culture is influenced by its African and European roots, as well as the neighboring cultures of North America and South America. Discovered by Christopher Columbus in late October 1492, the island, originally populated by Amerindians, quickly became a Spanish colony, to which African slaves were imported to work developing sugar and coffee plantations. By the 19th century, following a series of three independence wars led by Cuban-born planters and other rebels, the United States helped to overthrow Spanish rule in 1898, during the Spanish-American War. The Spanish subsequently turned the island over to the United States on December 10, 1898. By mid-1902, Cuba achieved independence from the United States through the Treaty of Paris, and thereafter, a series of junta governments and corrupt officials ruled the island for decades. The Cuban Revolution of 1959 is Cuba's most significant recent historical, political, economic, and social event. However, Fidel Castro, who led the revolution and ruled Cuba for nearly fifty years, stepped down in February 2008, ceding his power to his younger brother Raúl.

Cuban music, including mambo, Cuban son, habanera, salsa, and Cuban jazz, to name just a few, have all left lasting imprints on neighboring cultures.

## GENERAL INFORMATION

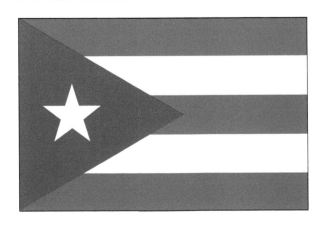

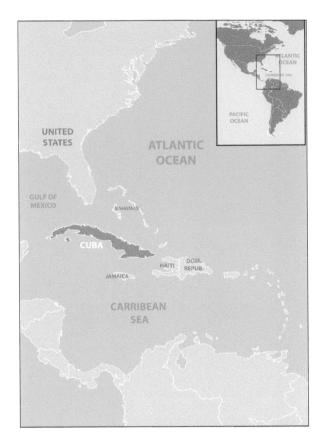

**Official Language(s):** Spanish
**Population:** 11,031,433 (2015 estimate)
**Currency:** Cuban peso
**Coins:** The peso is subdivided into 100 centavos. The most frequently used coins in circulation are the 20 centavos, 1 peso, and 3 pesos. Less frequently used are the 1 centavo and 5 centavos coins.
**Land Area:** 109,820 square kilometers (42,401 square miles)
**Water Area:** 1,040 square kilometers (401 square miles)
**National Motto:** "Patria y libertad" (Spanish, "Fatherland and Freedom")
**National Anthem:** "La Bayamesa" ("The Bayamo Song")
**Capital:** Havana
**Time Zone(s):** GMT -5
**Flag Description:** The Cuban flag consists of a red equilateral triangle on the hoist side (at left); centered in the red equilateral triangle is a five-pointed white star. Radiating from the triangle to

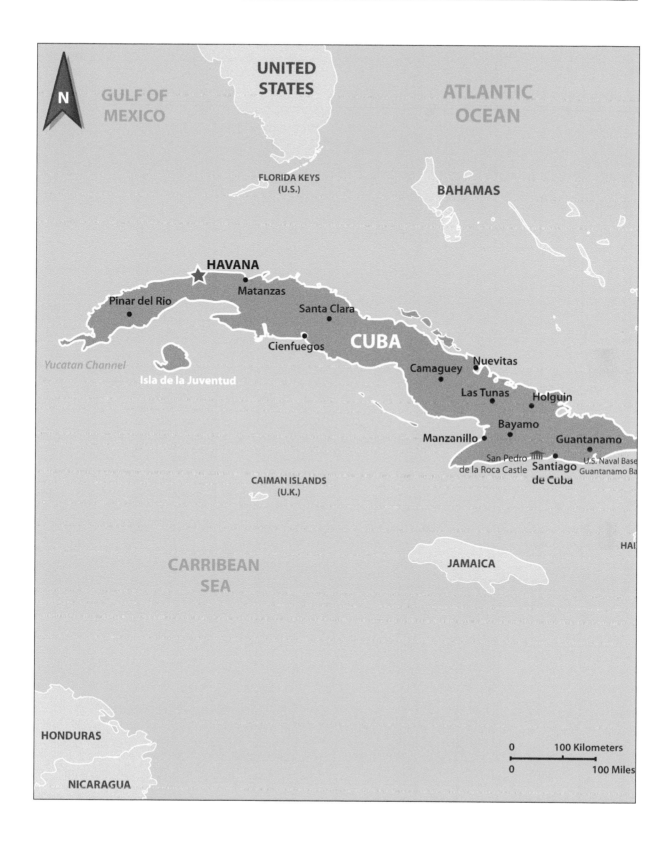

## Principal Cities by Population (2014):

- Havana (also, La Habana) (2,137,146)
- Santiago de Cuba (431,272)
- Camagüey (300,958)
- Holguín (287,881)
- Guantánamo (217,135)
- Santa Clara (211,925)
- Las Tunas (also, Victoria de las Tunas) (162,957)
- Bayamo (157,027)
- Ceinfuegos (147,110)
- Pinar del Río (140,230)

the right are five parallel, horizontal stripes alternating between blue, of which there are three, and white, of which there are two. Symbolically, the blue stripes represent the island's three old geographical divisions, including occidental, central, and oriental; white represents the virtue of independence. The triangle represents liberty, equality, and brotherhood, while the color red symbolizes the blood shed to attain these virtues. Finally, the white star, known as "La Estrella Solitaria" ("The Lone Star") symbolizes the light of freedom and was adapted from that on the Texas flag.

## Population

Like many Caribbean nations, as well as parts of South America, the ancestors of modern-day Cubans were European settlers and African slaves. The majority of Cubans (about 64.1 percent of the population) are white, while 26.6 percent are of mixed Afro-Spanish descent, or mestizo. Just over nine percent of Cubans are black. There is also a very small population of Chinese descent.

Most Cubans (around 77 percent) live in cities, with most living in Havana, the largest city, with a population of 2.137 million (2015 estimate). Government controls on population have helped contain Havana's growth. As a result, population in the capital has remained remarkably stable for the past fifty years. Overall, this is because of a national low birth rate (10

births per 1,000 people or 1.47 children per woman), a high rate of emigration abroad (–3.66 per 1,000 people), and a rigorous control on domestic migration.

Known on the island as Habaneros, Havana inhabitants are often of racially mixed backgrounds. Afro-Cubans, Chinese, and other ethnic groups are also represented in Havana. More than half of the city's population is female and government-provided health care helps sustain an above average proportion of elderly Habaneros.

## Languages

The predominant language in Cuba is Spanish.

## Native People & Ethnic Groups

Unlike many nations in Latin America, there are no indigenous people left in Cuba. The original inhabitants of Cuba were Taíno, Guanahatabey (also Guanajatabey), and Ciboney (also Siboney) Indians, but they were either killed off by Spanish explorers and settlers, or died of diseases brought to the New World by the Europeans. Both the Taíno and the Ciboney were related to the greater Arawak civilization of South America, had complex social structures, were agrarian, and maintained generally peaceable existences. The Europeans, however, viewed them as savages and had no tolerance for their natural rights.

None of these populations survived in any significant numbers past the 16th century. Despite this, there are some contemporary efforts—like those conducted in Puerto Rico via the 2003 Taíno genome project—to determine if these tribes have direct-line or intermixed descendents within modern Cuban society.

## Religions

Cuba is an atheist nation: under communism, religion is effectively banned, although there are still strong links between many Cubans and the Roman Catholic Church—an estimated 85 percent identified as Catholic prior to Castro's rule—as well as syncretistic religions, which are hybrids of traditional religions and folk beliefs.

One such syncretistic religion is Santeria, a combination of Christian and Yoruban beliefs. In Santeria, such elements as animal sacrifice and the worship of saints are not contradictory. A small Jewish community lives in Havana, along with a small population of Protestants and Jehovah's Witnesses.

## Climate

Cuba has a semitropical climate with alternating wet (late spring to mid-fall) and dry (mid-fall to mid-spring) seasons. The average annual temperature is 25° Celsius (77° Fahrenheit), but can range from 21° Celsius (70° Fahrenheit) to 27° Celsius (81° Fahrenheit). The country's average rainfall is 1,322 millimeters (52 inches). However, droughts are not uncommon, and the island is often buffeted by hurricanes and tropical storms. The hurricane season in Cuba runs from mid-summer to fall. Since 2010, Cuba has been experiencing the worst chronic drought in the country's modern history; crops and livestock have been impacted and potable water is now being trucked in, as reservoirs have reached critical levels. Emergency water rationing was enacted in 2014 and continues into 2015. El Niño weather system is being blamed for the dearth of precipitation and increasingly dry conditions.

## ENVIRONMENT & GEOGRAPHY

## Topography

Cuba is the largest island in the Cuban Archipelago, which is made up of over 3,000 islands and keys. It has 3,735 kilometers (2,321 miles) of coastline. It is also part of the Greater Antilles island chain.

Cuba is characterized by flat or rolling terrain throughout most of the country, with some mountainous and hilly areas in the southeast. In addition to the fertile valleys and plains, there are some marshy areas and several scenic coastal areas. It is part of a limestone platform that includes parts of Mexico, the United States, and the Bahamas. There are also many limestone caves throughout certain areas of Cuba, most notably near the city of Havana.

There are three mountain zones in Cuba: the Cordillera Guaniguanico, in which sit Sierra de los Organos and Sierra del Rosario; Sierra del Escambray, in the east; and the Sierra Maestra, Sierra del Cristal, and other ranges in southeast Cuba. The highest point in Cuba is at Pico Turquino (2,005 meters/6,578 feet) in the Sierra Maestra range.

The Isla de la Juventud is the second largest island in Cuba. The longest river in Cuba is the Cauto River, which stretches 343 kilometers (213 miles).

Located on Cuba's northern coast, Havana has a natural harbor that gives the capital an excellent port. The narrow entrance of the bay allows ships to easily pass through into the harbor, which is protected from strong winds and waves by nearby beaches. Altogether Havana has nearly 30 kilometers (18 miles) of coastline; the bay itself takes up over 5 square kilometers (3.1 square miles). However, Havana is mostly flat, lying at an elevation of only 59 meters (194 feet) above sea level. In total area, Havana is 721 square kilometers (278.4 square miles), but the government strictly regulates the city's population in order to prevent further urban growth.

## Plants & Animals

Common plants found in Cuba include over 2,000 species of palm tree, including the royal palm (the national tree) and the cork palm; forests of pine, ebony and mahogany; and a rich variety of tropical plants found throughout the region. The national flower is butterfly jasmine. Cuba also has several mangrove swamps.

Common animals found in Cuba include crocodiles, alligators, water turtles, iguanas, wild pigs, Cuban pygmy frogs, the torcoro (also the national bird), banana rats, greater bulldog bat, tarantulas, boa constrictors, and Cuban racers (a mildly venomous diurnal snake). There are also several species of hutia—a rodent resembling a North American groundhog—which are critically endangered. Other endangered species in

Cuba include the Cuban crocodile and the Cuban solenodon, a nocturnal insectivore that resembles a shrew, but has venomous saliva.

---

## CUSTOMS & COURTESIES

### Greetings

Cubans may commonly shake hands when greeting. Women may also kiss each other on the cheeks as a form of greeting. Men may also exchange cheek kisses with women of close acquaintance. Using the honorific titles "Señor," for a man, and "Señora," for a woman, is typical when meeting new people. In addition, Cubans may also use the term "Compañero" ("Comrade") when addressing each other.

Greetings in Cuba are similar to those in other Latin American countries. For example, the word "Bueno" ("Good") is generally said in conjunction with the time of day, as in "Buenos Días," ("Good day"), "Buenas Tardes," ("Good afternoon") and "Buenas Noches" ("Good night"). The informal greeting "Hola" ("Hello") is also commonly used among friends.

To understand Cuban greetings and other forms of conversation, it is necessary to understand the differences between Cuban and other types of Spanish. When the letter "s" appears at the end of a word, most Cubans will pronounce it with an aspirated sound, such as the English pronunciation of the letter "h." For example, the word "buenos" is pronounced "bwe′nō." Another difference is that Cuban speakers tend to affix the diminutive form "-ico" to the ends of words, whereas speakers in Mexico and other Spanish-speaking countries typically use the "-ito" suffix. Additionally, some native Cubans pronounce the personal pronounce "yo" ("I") as "joe," something that differs markedly from Spanish spoken in Spain, where the 'y' sound in 'yo' is generally maintained.

### Gestures & Etiquette

Cubans generally enjoy animated conversation and are not often offended by loud or boisterous behavior in social situations. Although Cubans typically tend to stand closer to one another than speakers do in other cultures, physical contact is mostly limited to friends and close acquaintances. Like many Latin American cultures, direct eye contact is important for communication; averting one's eyes is sometimes considered a sign of insincerity or hostility.

Cubans often make liberal use of hand gestures in conversation. While some gestures overlap with those of other cultures, the meanings behind certain gestures may be slightly different. For example, when beckoning for a person to approach, Cubans typically extend the arm with the palm facing down (extending the arm with the palm facing up can be considered a hostile gesture). In addition, extending the thumb and forefinger of the hand, generally about one inch apart, means "wait a minute" in Cuba, while in other countries it generally means "a small amount."

### Eating/Meals

Cubans generally eat three meals a day, with the largest meal served in the evening. Some Cubans also add a small snack served between the morning and afternoon meal, or between the afternoon and evening meal. The standard breakfast in Cuba generally consists of light fare and coffee. Fresh fruits, ham, chicken, eggs, and fruit juices are all common components of a standard Cuban breakfast. Fried breads, such as tostada, are also commonly served with the morning meal.

The mid-day meal may consist of sandwiches, soup or empanadas, which are fried turnovers typically filled with ground meat, cheese, and vegetables. The afternoon meal is generally more substantial than the morning meal, and many Cubans take more than an hour to eat their afternoon meal and relax before returning to work.

The evening meal, which is usually served between six and nine o'clock, is often the largest of the day. A variety of meat dishes, stews, rice, and bean dishes, as well as other entrees, are typically served at the evening meal. Unlike some cultures, Cubans generally serve all food at the same time, even in formal situations, rather than serving courses. Beer is the most common beverage with the evening meal.

Drinking alcohol is common in Cuban culture, and alcohol may be served at anytime during or following the mid-day meal. Liquor is commonly served with dinner, but there is no stigma attached to refusing liquor from the host. Beer is the most common alcoholic beverage served with both the mid-day and evening meals.

## Visiting

When visiting a Cuban home, it is considered customary and appropriate for guests to compliment their host on the appearance of the home. It is also common for a guest to give small gifts when visiting, such as candy, flowers, or liquor. As in many cultures, certain kinds of flowers have special significance and should be avoided as social gifts. Red roses generally signify romantic intentions, while lilies are used to express condolence. Alternatively, visitors may choose to give small household items, such as linens and wine glasses, when invited to someone's home.

While it is considered rude to be noticeably late, it is common for Cubans to assume a relaxed manner with regard to scheduling. It is, therefore, acceptable to arrive a few minutes late for a social engagement.

## LIFESTYLE

## Family

The nuclear family, typically consisting of two parents and their children, is the basic unit of Cuban society. Both women and men are involved in labor outside the home and, in most modern Cuban families, both parents work. While some Cuban families follow traditional roles—with men working outside the home and women concentrating on child rearing and domestic work—societal roles are changing, and women are now more likely to achieve specialized careers. In addition, young couples are finding it more difficult to afford their own houses and often live with in-laws. Some believe that this has contributed to Cuba's rising divorce

rates, which has been estimated at 56 percent in 2015. This is the highest rate in all Latin American countries. Other contributing factors may include a lower average age for marriage and Cuba's relaxed attitude towards divorce: it costs just $4 USD and less than half an hour to achieve.

Social status is tied to familial heritage in Cuba, and many prominent members of the Cuban government and major corporations are related to other high-ranking members of Cuban society. For this reason, it is common for families to form extended social networks in an effort to help their children achieve positions outside the family's social status. There are also a variety of racial groups in Cuba, including African, Asian, European, and indigenous groups, each of which is afforded different social status within society.

Though Cuba has an underdeveloped economy, the government has emphasized the care of children and mothers. Cuba's health statistics are similar to countries with greater access to resources, testifying to the government's focus on providing quality health care under the socialized system. Family planning has been a concern of the Cuban government since the 1970s. As part of its related policy, the government legalized abortion in the 1960s, making the procedure available through clinics and hospitals across the country.

## Housing

Housing in Cuba runs the gamut, from modern buildings to simple thatched huts. Many poor families live in combined housing, where several families share eating and hygienic facilities in a common building. In cities such as Havana and Santiago de Cuba, one- and two-bedroom apartments are common. In addition, most residential houses are constructed in "ranch" style, with one or two bedrooms. Cuba's hot and humid climate makes heating unnecessary, and only families in upper economic echelons can afford air conditioning. Tile roofing is commonly used because of frequent rain, and most houses are made of concrete and stone, which is excellent for resisting weather damage.

Before the Revolution of 1959, Cuba suffered from an extreme housing crisis. Government initiatives to provide housing began in the 1960s and continue into the 21st century. Public housing is also government-guaranteed and Havana residents live in homes and tenements rent-free. However, estimates in 2013 indicate that the country is some 600,000 houses short of what is required by its current population.

As of 2013, many buildings on the island are suffering from increasing deterioration, and Cuba's Instituto Nacional de la Vivienda (the National Housing Institute) reports that 8.5 out of 10 are in need of fundamental repairs or comprehensive restoration. Although the rules regarding construction licenses were relaxed in 2010, allowing the general public to purchase materials, make their own repairs, or build new homes, most Cubans do not have the income to support such activities, as supplies make basic projects cost prohibitive.

State authorities still build and own more than 80 percent of Cuban houses and buildings and obtaining a house requires a government permit. A 2008 *New York Times* article investigated an underground housing market called the "permuta," in which families pay extra money for access to new houses. Though it is illegal to sell property, it is not illegal for homeowners to exchange houses. In the permuta system, owners agree to "trade" houses and then charge an additional fee. Despite being illegal, reports indicate that it is still a common method for wealthy families to obtain better housing.

## Food

The cuisine of Cuba, while often classified as Latin American, is better defined as a "creole" cuisine, containing elements of African, Spanish, and other influences. There is considerable variation in cuisine across the country. In areas with larger populations of Afro-Cuban residents, certain dishes resembling African food are more common. Most Cuban cities also have restaurants serving a variety of international food.

Cubans frequently use beef as a main ingredient in their entrees. A common preparation con-

sists of shredded beef marinated in onions and spices and generally served with rice and beans. Slow cooking is a popular way of preparing many Cuban dishes, and slow-cooked beef is an essential component of many traditional dishes and stews. In addition, rice-based dishes are also common in Cuban cuisine, as are dishes that prominently feature sauces. Staple ingredients in Cuban cuisine include oregano, garlic, cumin, plantain, yucca, and pork, beef, or fish.

The empanada is a typical Cuban dish that has become well known outside the country. The dish typically consists of a variety of slow cooked and seasoned meats, such as chicken, pork, or shredded beef, served inside a fried pastry shell, creating a turnover. The empanada may also be filled with just vegetables or cheese. Some recipes also call for fruits, such as guava, to be mixed with the cheese and meat filling. Other traditional Cuban dishes include sofrito, a sauté of onions, green peppers, garlic, oregano, and bay leaves that is usually served with rice and beans; ropa vieja (literally, "old clothes"), shredded steak or meat in a tomato-based sauce, typically served with fried plantains and beans; and boliche, which is a roast stuffed with sausage and served with rice and plantains.

The Cuban sandwich has perhaps become the most famous example of Cuban cuisine served outside the country. The basic recipe is to combine smoked ham, Swiss cheese, and thin slices of pickle served on tostada. Some recipes call for seasoned, slow-cooked pork in addition to smoked ham. The ham may also be marinated in a pepper sauce before being served. Some prefer the sandwich toasted, while other vendors serve the sandwich at room temperature. Another popular Cuban sandwich is pan con bistec, which usually consists of a thin slice of steak on Cuban bread served with lettuce, tomatoes, and fried potato sticks.

Cuban bread, called tostada, is a white bread cooked with a small amount of fat in the dough. Similar to French baguette, toasted tostada is common at breakfast and often accompanied by fruits and coffee. Although standard brewed coffee is served in Cuba, some Cubans prefer a concentrated coffee served with milk, called café con leche.

## Life's Milestones

As a predominantly Catholic nation, many of Cuba's cultural traditions revolve around the nation's Catholic heritage. Birth, baptism, communion, marriage, and death are the major milestones of Cuban life and are generally accompanied by both a religious ceremony and a family gathering. The birth of a couple's first child is considered a major cause for celebration and is generally accompanied by a feast among family and friends.

Like many Latin American countries, Cubans celebrate a young girl's fifteenth birthday, often called a quinceañera or "quinces" for short. This celebration marks a girl's transition to young womanhood and, historically, served as the point at which a girl became eligible for marriage. In contemporary society, however, young women who have celebrated their fifteenth birthday are often permitted greater freedom in deciding how to dress, how late to stay out with friends, and whether or not to wear make-up and jewelry.

Marriage marks the transition to true adulthood in Cuban society. Until marriage, many Cubans remain in their parents' homes, although because of the long-standing housing shortage, couples are often forced to remain with parents or in-laws following the wedding. Many families celebrate marriage with an extended feast and party that often includes music and dancing. An old tradition that is still sometimes practiced is the "money dance," where every man in attendance takes a turn dancing with the bride and pins a small amount of money to the bride's gown. The money is typically and traditionally intended to help pay for wedding expenses.

## CULTURAL HISTORY

### Art

When Spanish settlers arrived in Cuba in the 16th century, they introduced many European artistic and architectural traditions to the indigenous population. Soon after their arrival, Spanish colonists also began importing African slaves to serve as agricultural laborers. This blend of European and African influences with native folk art traditions led to the creation of a unique and national style of art that used Cuban life and culture as its foundation and inspiration.

José Nicolás Escalera (1734–1804) was one of the first Cuban painters to gain popularity in Europe. His art drew heavily from the Old Masters of Europe, but depicted subjects unique to Cuba. Following Escalera's popularity, the first academy of art—the Academia Nacional de Bellas Artes—opened in Cuba in January 1818. This was only the second such art academy established in the Americas. After the academy's founding, European instructors and directors were brought to Cuba to lead the nation's art education. As a result, the influence of European art began to dominate the work of local artists.

A popular genre among early Cuban artists was landscape painting, which remained popular from the 18th century until the modern era. Painters such as José Joaquín Tejada Revilla (1867–1943), a native of Santiago de Cuba, typify the landscape genre, which often drew upon scenes of daily rural and urban life in Cuba as inspiration. In particular, many painters of this era began to also blend realism with impressionist elements.

In the 1920s, a new artistic movement called the "Vanguardia" movement spread across Cuba. Led by artists who had lived and studied abroad—and who had brought new and experimental genres such as cubism and impressionism to Cuba—the movement culminated in international recognition for Cuba's modern art community. In 1944, the Museum of Modern Art (MOMA) in New York City produced an exhibition of Cuba's Vanguardia painters. Famous Cuban painters associated with this movement include Wifredo Lam (1902–1982), Víctor Manuel García Valdés (1897–1969), and Amelia Peláez (1896–1968). The Vanguardia movement also influenced sculptors such as Agustín Cárdenas Alfonso (1927–2001), a descendant of African slaves whose sculptures serve as an example of early expressionist sculpture in Cuba.

After the Cuban Revolution of 1959, the Cuban artistic community found itself isolated from North American artistic culture. While exchange with Europe continued, many Cuban artists also suffered under an increasingly restrictive commercial and creative environment. In the 21st century, Cuban artists continue to produce a wide variety of work, from traditional landscape paintings to pop art and animation. Though trade restrictions continue to limit contact between the United States and the Cuban art culture, communities of Cuban artists living in exile have helped to carry the unique features of Cuban art around the world.

## Architecture

Cuba's architectural heritage displays a range of styles, from Spanish colonial architecture to the neoclassical style of France (such as the French tombs of Cienfuegos). Havana, in fact, is often referred to as the "city of columns," owing to its rich heritage of colonial-baroque architecture, evident in the centuries-old missions and cathedrals. Columnar arcades, opulent stained-glass windows, decorative grilles and balcony banisters, and high doors are just some of the characteristics of Cuba's transcendent colonial architecture, as are Havana's cobblestone avenues and numerous fountains and squares.

In the 1950s, Cuba experienced a sort-of "golden age" of Cuban architecture, and modernist styles predominated. Adapting the architecture to the tropical and sun-drenched environment, architects of the period adapted elements such as large eaves, large or double-wide doors to allow for air flow, and multi-level roofs to help deflect tropical rains. This period also saw the construction of Havana's modernist high-rise buildings. However, many of these homes and buildings have fallen into disrepair in the decades following the 1959 revolution, while the state took over many wealthy homes, converting them into government offices or public schools.

## Drama

Film first arrived in Havana in 1897, when the cinematographe, a film camera and projector invented by the Lumière brothers, Auguste Marie (1862–1954) and Louis Jean (1864–1948), began touring the Americas in the late 19th century. The cinematographe, which featured the screening of short films, was brought by Gabriel Veyre (1871–1936), an influential figure in the development of Mexican cinema. Veyre later played a hand in the production of Cuba's first native film, *Simulacro de Incendio* ("The Fake Fire"), a documentary about firefighting.

Between 1897 and 1959, there were fewer than 150 films produced in Cuba. Of these, many were documentaries on various aspects of Cuban culture. Documentarian Enrique Díaz Quesada (1883–1923), who was active between 1905 and 1920, is considered one of the pioneers of nonfiction Cuban film. In the fiction genre, films generally centered on imitation of European or American genres, including westerns and slapstick comedies.

After the Revolution of 1959, the film industry was placed under the control of the Instituto Cubano del Arte y la Industria Cinematográficos (ICAIC). This government organization was responsible for censoring and approving all films shown, imported and produced in Cuba. While the revolutionary government placed some censorship restrictions on Cuban directors, they also supported and fostered many young filmmakers who became leaders of modern Cuban cinema.

Director Humberto Solas (1942–2008), who directed the influential film *Lucia* in 1969, and some of his contemporaries are considered the fathers of modern fiction film in Cuba. Post-revolution directors, such as Tomás Gutiérrez Alea (1928–1996) and Mikhail Kalatozov (1903–1973, a Soviet), created unique works ("Death of a Bureaucrat" in 1966 and "I Am Cuba" in 1964, respectively), which are still considered to be among the most important Cuban films works of the 20th century.

A unique characteristic of the Cuban film history is the focus on documentaries and historical review films. Hundreds of short educational, scientific, and cultural films were produced immediately after control passed to the Cuban Institute of Cinematographic Art and Industry (ICAIC), and documentaries have remained a specialty for many Cuban directors. This focus was influenced by several factors, including an overall lack of funding to support a fiction film industry. In addition, a number of young directors were excited by the potential to capture elements of the revolution and Cuba's reconstruction. Director Santiago Álvarez Román (1919–1998) provides a prime example of the typical Cuban documentarian. His short film *Now* is one of the most famous Cuban films known outside the country.

By the late 20th century, Cuban filmmakers produced films in a variety of genres. Animated films, science fiction, and other big-budget productions also emerged from Cuba, though such films were rare because of economic constraints. The theme of emigration appears repeatedly in Cuban films produced and directed after the Cold War. Exploring the desire to leave Cuba and the work of Cubans living in exile has provided new political and social dimensions to Cuban cinema in the early 21st century.

## Music

Cuban music, traditionally rooted in African culture and heritage (and often referred to as Afro-Cuban music), as well as the country's Spanish influence, includes mambo, Cuban son, habanera, rumba, salsa, and Cuban jazz, to name just a few. All have left lasting imprints on neighboring cultures. Much of Cuban music is integrated with (or accompanied by) dance, such as mambo and conga, and thus Cuba's many musical styles are often percussion-based, and dominated by Latin rhythms.

Some consider Cuba's national music to be son (meaning "rhythm" in English)—or, at the least, its most important musical genre. Combining percussive rhythms with guitar, or tres (and thus, combining both Spanish and African elements), son vaulted in popularity in the early 20th century, ascending from the lower classes. Pioneered by musicians such as Ignacio Piñeiro (1888–1969), a Cuban rumba musician early on in his career, this style of music is believed to have had the biggest influence on all other Cubano musical styles and dances, such as salsa and mambo (which Cuban bandleader

Perez Prado (1916–1989), often called the "king of mambo," helped popularize stateside in the mid-20th century). In dance form, Cuban son is similar to ballroom dancing.

Danzón, like many other Cubano styles, is both a style of music and dance. It is described as an elegant style of music, and the ballroom-style dance that accompanies it was once referred to as Cuba's national dance. Danzón is rooted in the contradanza style that African slaves and Frenchmen carried to Cuba from Haiti from the Haitian revolution in the latter half of the 18th century.

Other styles of Cubano music that lend their namesake to their accompanying dances include conga, a marching style of dance prevalent at carnivals; the percussive rumba, which is based on a five-stroke clave (rhythm) pattern and which, as a dance, was suppressed early on due to its perceived lewdness; the cha-cha-chá, a style of dance music and a variant of danzón, the creation of which is attributed to Cuban composer Enrique Jorrín (1926–1987); the rapid-tempo and lyricized guaracha; and the creolized habanera, a simplistic and rhythmic dance music popular as early as the 18th century, and which is considered the first dance music imported from Cuban culture.

## Literature

The written recording of Cuban literature first began during the Spanish colonial period, which lasted nearly 400 years (circa 1515–1898). During the earliest stages of colonial Cuba, writers tended to focus on daily life as the subject of most fiction. Stories of plantation agriculture and the struggle between Cubans and colonial Spanish are common themes in early Cuban fiction. During the late 19th century, stories with abolitionist themes became more common.

Gertrudis Gómez de Avellaneda (1814–1873) is one of several writers whose fiction captured international attention during the late 19th century. The fiction of la Avellaneda provides a glimpse of 19th century Cuban life and helped establish her as an important figure in the history of feminist literature. Cirilo Villaverde

(1812–1894), a journalist, novelist and poet, is another writer whose work was important in portraying the struggle against the Spanish colonial power. In addition to writing several classics of Cuban literature, Villaverde was a freedom fighter during the independence war.

From 1900 to 1959, there were a number of novels published that explored the problems of Cuban society, including the dominance of the agricultural industries and exploitation of the workers. This pre-revolutionary literature provides a glimpse at the underlying social dissatisfaction that set the stage for the Cuban Revolution. Though the post-revolution government prohibited the publication of literature that was critical of the government or socialism, a number of Cuban classics describe elements of the revolution and the reconstruction in detail.

The body of Cuban literature became more diverse after the 1970s. In the modern era, Cuban writers began to publish works in a variety of genres. Modern masters such as Pedro Juan Gutiérrez (1950– ), whose work uses evocative imagery and profanity while exploring unusual aspects of Cuban society, have helped to establish Cuba as an important center for modern literature.

Other notable Cuban writers include journalist and poet José Martí (1853–1895); novelist, screenwriter, and critic Guillermo Cabrera Infante (1929–2005, in exile after 1965); novelist and musicologist Alejo Carpentier (1904–1980); and poet, novelist, and playwright Reinaldo Arenas (1943–1990). Arenas was a victim of state censorship and harassment because of his homosexuality. He fled Cuba in 1980 as part of the Mariel boatlift (a mass emigration from the island); the 2000 film *Before Night Falls* was adapted from his memoirs.

## CULTURE

### Arts & Entertainment

The Cuban arts scene is influenced by its African and European roots, as well as the neighboring cultures of North America and South America.

Until the 1990s, the Cuban government restricted the art market as part of a policy that art should be used primarily as a vehicle for spreading socialism. Gradually, the government eased restrictions during the late 20th century in an effort to prevent the nation's artists from leaving the country. As a result, art is now situated prominently at the center of Cuban culture, with the government providing funding and support for arts education at every level of the national education system.

The Casa de la Trova, located in Santiago de Cuba, is one of the most important artistic centers in the nation. Established through a government program for the preservation of native culture, music and dance, the Casa de la Trova attracts musicians from across Cuba and abroad. Generally, visitors are charged a small fee for entrance to the center. Performances begin early in the afternoon and may continue until the entire lineup of musicians has had an opportunity to perform. Since the inception of the Casa de la Trova, there has been an increase of interest in traditional Cuban music among young Cubans. While there are other, similar institutions known by the same name in other Cuban cities, the one in Santiago de Cuba is the most famous, and has attracted a host of musicians from around the world to experience the improvisational performances.

Baseball has huge national following in Cuba. Among the many renowned Cuban baseball players who emigrated to the United States are Hall of Fame infielder Tony Perez (1942– ) and Minnie Minoso (1925–2015 ), whose professional career spanned seven decades as well as more recent players, such as Rey Ordóñez (1971– ), a three-time Gold Glove Award winner; All-Star pitcher José Contreras (1971– ), a one-time Gold Glove and Silver Slugger Award winner; and four-time World Series champion Orlando Hernández (1965– ). Cuban teams have maintained a high profile internationally, including at the Summer Olympics and several international tournaments.

Cuban entertainers known to US audiences in recent decades include Desi Arnaz (1917–1986), singers Celia Cruz (1925–2003) and Gloria

Estefan (1957– ), actor Andy Garcia (1956– ), and television personality Daisy Fuentes (1966– ).

## Cultural Sites & Landmarks

Many of Cuba's most famous and significant cultural landmarks have their origins in the nation's colonial period. Portions of the capital, Havana, are lined by colonial architecture in the neoclassical and baroque style, popular during the 16th and 17th centuries. In fact, Havana is famous for its colonial district, known as Havana Vieja (Old Havana). The area was designated as a World Heritage Site in 1982 by the United Nations Educational, Scientific and Cultural Organization (UNESCO). Old Havana developed on an irregular grid of tight narrow streets and small city blocks. Squares and churches became the dominant features of the colonial city. A well-known example is the Plaza del las Armas (Arms Square) where two palaces, the Palacio del Segundo Cabo (the Executive Palace) and the Palacio de los Capitanes Generales (the General Captains' Palace, or governors' mansion), are well-preserved examples colonial Cuban architecture. The Catedral de Havana (Havana Cathedral) remains the center of Catholic worship in Havana.

As a port, Havana has a complex series of fortifications and castles to defend the city. By the end of the 18th century, four major fortifications defended Havana. On the eastern side are the Castillo de la Real Fuerza (Castle of Royal Force) and the San Salvador de la Punta (Fort of St. Salvador at the Point). Across the harbor are two other forts, Castillo de Los Tres Reyes Magos del Morro (the Castle of the Three Eastern Kings) and San Carlos de la Cabaña (Fort of St. Charles). The remains of La Muralla (The City Wall) encircles the interior of Old Havana and served as the last defense against attackers.

Havana also contains a number of cultural landmarks of more recent origin. El Floridita, a bar located at Plazuela de Albear in Old Havana, was often prominently featured in the novels of Ernest Hemingway (1899–1961). It was also known as one of Hemingway's favorite loca-

tions in Cuba. In addition, an estate owned by Hemingway outside of Havana is now a museum dedicated to the famous author. In the midst of modern Havana, visitors can also visit the Tropicana, a famous nightclub that was frequented by European and American socialites in the 1940s and 1950s, when Cuba was a popular vacation spot for Westerners.

In the city of Santiago de Cuba lies the fort of San Pedro de la Roca, also known as Castillo del Morro. The fort, largely built in the 17th century, was designed to protect the Cuban port city from ocean assault, particularly from pirates. The fort is considered one of Cuba's best-preserved examples of Spanish-American military architecture. Situated on a series of rocky cliffs, it also provides excellent views of Santiago de Cuba and the ocean. The fort was inscribed as a World Heritage Site in 1997.

In an effort to preserve the country's natural resources, the Cuban government has designated several ecological sites for protection and species preservation. Among the most popular natural areas in Cuba is Alejandro de Humboldt National Park, which spans more than 71,140 hectares (275 square miles) and contains thousands of unique plant and animal varieties. The biodiversity of the park is unique because toxic chemicals leached, or extracted, from the bedrock make it difficult for alien and introduced plant species to flourish. As a result, the native plant and animal communities display a high degree of endemism (exclusively belonging to a specific place) when compared to other ecological preserves of similar size. The park was listed as a World Heritage Site in 2001.

Cuba is home to six other UNESCO World Heritage Sites. They include the historic centers of the cities of Camagüey and Cienfuegos, inscribed for their colonial architecture and urban planning, respectively; the Viñales Valley, a major recreational and tourist attraction, inscribed for its cultural traditions and natural beauty; Desembarco del Granma National Park, designated in 1999; and Trinidad and the Valley de los Ingenios, a series of interconnected valleys famous for the production of sugar.

## Libraries & Museums

Capitolo (The Capitol), a replica of the US Capitol dome, is a major landmark in Havana, and is now home to the Cuban Academy of Sciences. There is also the former Presidential Palace, which was home to Cuban presidents for much of the 20th century and is now the Museo de la Revolución (Museum of the Revolution). Central Havana also contains many other museums, including the Museo Nacional de Bellas Artes de Cuba (National Museum of Fine Arts), the premier location for the exhibition of Cuban art. A large portion of the museum's 30,000-piece collection is of neoclassical European painting and Cuban works from the 17th century onward. However, the museum also boasts a significant collection of modern and contemporary art, including room-sized installations.

Cuba's national repository, National Library José Martí, dates back to 1901, and its collection consists of rare and valuable manuscripts from as early as the 15th century, nearly 9,000 magazine titles, and approximately 14,000 books in its Cuban Collection. It also offers digitized full-text versions of some of its rare books, whose age, value, and condition prevent them from circulating. Nationwide, there are over 400 libraries throughout the Cuban public library system.

## Holidays

Holidays in Cuba include Revolution Victory Day, also called Liberation Day (January 1); the Beginning of the War of Independence observance (October 10), and Christmas Day (December 25).

## Youth Culture

The public education system in Cuba is free up to the university level, and compulsory from ages six to sixteen. After age seventeen, youth can choose to remain in school or join the Youth Movement, an organization that teaches socialist theory and ideals. Children typically do no work in Cuba, though many are enlisted to help in family businesses.

Recently, hip-hop music and culture have become a prominent aspect of youth culture, particularly in Cuba's urban areas. In Havana and other cities, underground hip-hop groups have become popular among young Cubans, who have embraced the unique way in which hip-hop music expresses the realities of urban life. For this reason, Cuba's hip-hop culture is particularly centered in the poor regions of cities. However, some older Cubans perceive hip-hop culture as representative of the negative elements of American culture. Nonetheless, the government now considers hip-hop to be a legitimate form of musical expression and an important part of Cuba's musical landscape.

The promotion of sports remains a major focus in socialist Cuba. (In fact, Fidel Castro was an athlete before he became Cuba's leader.) Sports education is available everywhere, and there are numerous junior and young adult sports leagues in sports ranging from baseball to track and field. Cuba's athletics programs are world famous for producing a number of prominent Olympic athletes, including boxers Teófilo Stevenson (1952–2012) and Félix Savón (1967– ), volleyball player Regla Torres (1975– ), high jump champion Javier Sotomayor (1967– ), wrestler Mijaín López (1982– ), and pitcher Pedro Luis Lazo (1973– ). Volleyball is the most popular sport among young women, whereas baseball and soccer are the most popular sports for young men.

## SOCIETY

## Transportation

The major forms of public transportation in Cuba are buses, rail transport, and private taxi services. In urban areas such as Havana and Santiago de Cuba, buses typically travel all the major thoroughfares, and also have routes that take visitors to smaller towns and villages. There are two varieties of buses—express and local—which differ in the number of stops they make before reaching their final destination. Most buses in Cuba are repurposed vehicles imported from Europe and China. In Havana and other cities, visitors can pay extra for trips on specialized tourism buses that have additional amenities such as air conditioning and reclining seats.

Taxis are common in Cuban cities. Cuba also has a well-maintained highway system, extending from the Carretera Central (Central Highway), which is 1,435 kilometers (892 miles) long, was built in 1927, and is the oldest highway in the country.

Traffic moves on the right-hand side of the road in Cuba.

## Transportation Infrastructure

Although budget difficulties prevent extensive public investment, Havana has a modern infrastructure of highways, roads and public transportation. While in need of repair, a functional highway system encircles the city and public buses or collective taxis serve as the mainstays of public transportation.

Cuba built the first railway system in the entire Spanish Empire, and portions of Cuba's first railroad, built before 1848, are still used as part of the modern rail system. There are 11,968 km (7,436 miles) of rail that radiate in different directions throughout the island, and a good deal of it is used by sugar plantations for the transport of goods. However, the primary artery of the rail system stretches from Havana in the far south to Santiago de Cuba in the northwest. There are numerous small rail lines extending to other cities, towns and villages, some standard gauge and others narrow gauge. Some trains have air conditioning and reclining seats, while others offer no amenities at a reduced cost. Although trains along the central route are reliably spaced, those along shorter routes may not run on time or may go into hiatus for a week or more.

## Media & Communications

The Cuban government controls all media through one of several state offices. Though the government has the power to censor any content, government censors generally only restrict media that is seen as anti-socialist or anti-government.

There are four public television networks in Cuba: Tele Rebelde, established in 1968; Cubavisión; Cubavisión International, both founded in 1986; and Multivisión, established in 2008. Networks feature a variety of programming, including documentaries, sports, news, and situation comedies/dramas, some of which are imported from the United States. Cuba's television stations only broadcast during some hours of the day and there are few options for late-night programming. There are also local channels that broadcast only within the towns or cities of their origin. As Cuban television stations are state funded and do not rely on advertising revenues, there are no advertisements.

There are more than seventy radio stations in Cuba, broadcasting a range of subjects from news, weather, music, and other programs. Although most radio stations are oriented for regional audiences and broadcast only news and information pertinent to those areas, there are a few national stations, such as the popular Radio Habana Cuba, which is broadcasted across the country. Radio Granma, an offshoot of the newspaper *Granma*, has become a popular station in Cuba. It features bilingual news in Spanish and English. Radio Martí has been broadcast from the United States since 2007.

Though Cuba has more than 100 print publications, including newspapers and magazines, few are published on a reliable, regular schedule. Because of economic and resource shortages, other newspapers and magazines publish at irregular intervals or may be restricted to one monthly or bi-monthly edition. Recent debates between the government and Cuban journalist associations indicate that some media outlets may begin operating on advertising revenues in an effort to compensate for a lack of funding. In addition, the average Cuban citizen has limited or no access to the Internet, as owning a computer and visiting the web require special government authorization, and web filtering is in place, preventing users from freely accessing the Internet. In order to gain access, however, some Cubans go to large hotels, which offer terminals, or purchase access codes on the black market. As of 2014, it was estimated that approximately 27.5 percent of the population were Internet users.

## SOCIAL DEVELOPMENT

### Standard of Living

In 2014, Cuba ranked 44 out of 187 countries on the United Nations Human Development Index (HDI), which measures quality of life and standard of living indicators using 2012 data. Cuba has one of the highest life expectancy rates in the Caribbean region.

### Water Consumption

As of 2015, an estimated 94.9 percent of the Cuban population had access to potable water, with 96.4 percent of the urban population enjoying use and 89.8 percent of rural populations. In the same year, an estimated 93.2 percent of the population had access to improved sanitation facilities. The National Institute for Water Resources (Instituto Nacional de Recursos Hidraulicos, INRH), created in 1989, is responsible for providing water and wastewater services and often does so through individual, state-owned companies that are part of the INHR group. INHR is also responsible for 241 dams and 175 hydropower plants in Cuba.

A drought beginning in 2008 and extending through harsh conditions in the summer of 2010 severely depleted Cuba's water supply, with reservoirs at a 40 percent capacity in the summer of 2010. By August 2015, with continued drought, many Cuban residents were relying on trucked-in water, as reservoirs are well below capacity and underground sources continue to be depleted. Emergency water rationing is currently in place.

### Education

The education system is a source of pride among Cubans. Although the Cuban Revolution proved to be disastrous for many social and cultural systems, education has generally improved under the regime of President Fidel Castro. All Cuban education is free, and it is compulsory from age six to age sixteen. All students wear uniforms, whose color indicates grade level.

Cuban primary schools have a very high enrollment rate; secondary education is often augmented by occupational training. Less than 20 percent of Cubans attend college or university. The largest college in Cuba is Havana University, founded in 1728; other important institutions of higher learning are the University of Santiago de Cuba (also known as Universidad de Oriente) and the University of Camagüey, both established in the mid-20th century. There are also several technical and trade schools throughout the country; the number of years spent at these institutions lead to either a skilled worker or mid-level technician certification.

The literacy rate in Cuba is high, at 99.9 percent for men and 99.8 for women (2015). This is in part due to a national literacy campaign championed by Castro.

### Women's Rights

Women in Cuba have struggled to overcome the prejudices of Cuba's traditional, male-dominated society. In traditional Cuban culture, women were expected to take charge of domestic duties and child rearing while men engaged in work outside the home. Before the socialist revolution, women composed less than 20 percent of the national workforce. Following the revolution, Fidel Castro established a national literacy program designed to bring women into the education system and professional society. Many women joined the workforce after 1959, and women have continued to play a major role in the workplace. In 2000, women represented almost half of the national workforce, and also accounted for more than 45 percent of technical and scientific employees.

In terms of equality before the law, Cuba's penal code includes significant penalties for domestic abuse, rape, and other abuse towards women. However, monitoring agencies have reported that a vast majority of abuse and rape cases are unreported. According to statistics gathered by the US Department of State, police rarely investigate cases of alleged abuse unless clear signs of physical abuse are present. Women's groups have reported that domestic violence and abuse are major problems and that little is being done to protect victims of abuse.

Under Cuban law, women and men are equally empowered with the right to obtain a divorce. In modern Cuba there is little stigma surrounding divorce, and the divorce rate has risen to 56 percent in 2015. The law requires that spouses play alimony and child support to the parent caring for children out of marriage.

### Health Care

Another source of pride among Cubans is their universal and free health care system. Like education, it is a fundamental right of all Cubans and is very inexpensive. As of 2010, Cuba had 6.72 doctors per 1,000 people and spent 8.8 percent of the GDP on healthcare, according to Central Intelligence Agency (CIA) estimates. A considerable number of Cuban health care personnel also work abroad; in fact, at one point in 2008, an estimated 38,000 health workers from Cuba were working internationally, spanning seventy countries, and in 2010, that number jumped to 50,000. The life expectancy of Cubans is 78 years—76 for men and nearly 81 for women (2015 estimate).

The main problem in Cuban health care, however, appears to be a disparity between the very good levels of care offered to both tourists and government officials versus the lesser standard of care offered average Cubans. In addition, Cuban doctors are also paid very low wages—cited as $25 per month on average—and many choose to work abroad to receive the additional stipend paid for international work.

## GOVERNMENT

### Structure

As a communist state, Cuba is officially a republic governed by its only legally recognized political party, the Cuban Communist Party. In reality, it is a dictatorship controlled by one man with a few important party officials as assistants.

The chief of state and head of government is the president of the Council of State and the president of the Council of Ministers. The office of prime minister was abolished in 1976. The president appoints his own cabinet and effectively controls all other governmental entities.

The legislative branch of Cuban government is the National Assembly of People's Power, members of which are also elected for five-year terms. The judicial branch is the People's Supreme Court.

Cuba achieved its independence from Spain only when it was ceded to the United States by the Treaty of Paris in 1898. It gained independence from the United States in 1902; by this agreement, the United States was allowed to lease a portion of the island, the US Naval Base at Guantanamo, an area it still leases in the early 21st century.

In the mid-1950s, a revolutionary group led by the exiled insurrectionist Fidel Castro, a lawyer and leader of only a few dozen revolutionaries, began making plans to overthrow the government of Fulgencio Batista. Among the dozen or so men who survived early attacks by the Cuban army were Castro, his brother Raúl, and the Argentine revolutionary Che Guevara.

By late December 1958, Castro and his forces had succeeded in driving out most resistance to their ever-growing numbers and took control of the country in a very short time. By the following week, the Cuban Revolution was in full blossom and Castro was in absolute control of the government and the military.

The early days of the Revolution were marked by several important events. The first of these was the nationalization of foreign holdings, in particular several corporations belonging to the United States (including United Fruit and the International Telephone and Telegraph Company). This action resulted in an economic embargo that would change the ideological course of the country ever after.

After the failed Bay of Pigs operation was launched by the United States in 1961, Cuba announced that it would thereafter align itself with the Soviet Union and follow communist ideology, earning further ire from the United States. There followed a final economic embargo by the United States and, for the next several decades, Cuba and the United States would remain bitterly divided over the course of political history in the Western Hemisphere.

Following the end of the Soviet Union in the late 1980s and early 1990s, Cuba was faced with severe economic difficulties. Since then, Cuba has strengthened some sectors of its economy, but has not entirely rebounded from its pre-1990 financial situation.

To many Cubans, Fidel Castro, the dominant public figure in Cuba for six decades, is a beloved revolutionary leader. To the United States and other democracies worldwide, he is considered a tyrant. The truth about him may lay somewhere in between: he is responsible for violently suppressing dissents, but he is also responsible for risking his own life to free millions of people from what he and many other people around the world considered the shackles of economic and social disempowerment.

In 2006, Castro temporarily transferred the power of the Cuban presidency to his brother, Raúl Castro. Castro was suffering from an unknown illness of the digestive system that required he undergo surgery. Following surgery, his public appearances remained limited, although he appeared on television and in Cuban news continues to report his improved good health. Castro officially retired from the presidency on February 18, 2008, stating that he would not accept the position even if it was offered to him. Castro's brother, Raúl, assumed the presidency in February 2008. Raúl has proved to be, in some ways, more moderate than Fidel, and in April 2015, Raúl and US President Barack Obama met for the first time at the Summit of the Americas in Panama, just four months following their joint announcement that the two countries would reestablish diplomatic ties. While restrictions on remittances and travel to Cuba have been abolished, the US–Cuba trade embargo is likely to remain in place for now, as lifting it requires Congressional approval.

## Political Parties

The Cuban Communist Party is the only recognized political party in Cuba. However, a politically active dissident community, opposed to one-party rule in Cuba, exists in Havana. This dissident community had a tumultuous relationship with President Fidel Castro; periodic government crackdowns resulted in the imprisonment, exile, and even occasional dissident executions. Unauthorized political parties in the country include the 1959–established Christian Democratic Party of Cuba, the 1992–founded Democratic Social-Revolutionary Party of Cuba, and the Democratic Solidarity Party, also founded in 1992. This year is particularly important for opposition groups, as changes to the Cuban constitution decriminalized the formation of political parties. However, campaigning and political participation is still not permitted. Other important political groups include National Association of Small Farmers, Damas de Blanco (Ladies in White), the Cuban Commission for Human Rights and National Reconciliation, and the Patriotic Union of Cuba.

## Local Government

Cuba is divided into fifteen provinces and one special municipality, Isla de la Juventud (Isle of Youth), which is the second largest Cuban island and is not included within any province. Otherwise, the fifteen provinces are subdivided into 168 municipalities. Elections for municipal bodies occur every two-and-a-half-years. In April 2015, two dissident candidates made it through the first round of municipal elections, something that was previously unheard of. In the 2015 local elections, some 27,000 candidates ran for 12,589 in municipal assembly seats, indicating a shift from the single-party dominant politics of decades past.

## Judicial System

Cuba's legal system is based on Spanish civil law. The People's Supreme Court is the highest court, with provincial, regional, and municipal courts filling out the country's three-tiered judicial system. Supreme Court judges are elected by the National Assembly to serve two-and-a-half-year terms.

## Taxation

Cuba's income tax rate is high, at 50 percent. The corporate taxation rate is 30 percent. Other taxes levied in Cuba include sales tax and a property transfer tax. Sales tax stands at 20 percent, while value-added tax (VAT) is 2.5 percent.

## Armed Forces

Cuba's armed forces, the Revolutionary Armed Forces (Fuerzas Armadas Revolucionarias, FAR) of Cuba, consist of a navy, army, an air defense force, and several paramilitary forces, including a Youth Labor Army (Ejercito Juvenil del Trabajo, EJT). Following the loss of military assistance from the Soviet Union in 1989, the armed forces have seen their manpower cut in half; once estimated at over 200,000 men strong at its peak, the armed forces are now at 49,000 active personnel and 39,000 reserves as of 2015. There is mandatory conscription, which lasts two years, and both men and women, ages fifteen to forty-nine, are eligible.

## Foreign Policy

Cuba's economy began to deteriorate after the collapse of the Soviet Union, which was the nation's strongest economic ally. Recent cooperation with the People's Republic of China (PRC), Venezuela, and Bolivia has helped to restore the Cuban economy. For example, Cuba purchased new railroad cars from the PRC in 2006 to replace aging railcars and expand the rail system. Cuba also relies on South American trade, especially with Venezuela. In fact, Venezuela has become one of Cuba's strongest economic and political allies, largely owing to the close relationship that developed between Venezuelan President Hugo Chávez and Fidel Castro during the late 1990s. The close partnership between the two countries continued under the leadership of Raúl Castro, who assumed the presidency in 2008 after serving as acting president when Fidel Castro became ill in 2006. In return for medical personnel and teachers Cuba sends to aid Chávez's programs, Venezuela often provides Cuba with discounted petroleum. Cuba has also strengthened its ties with Brazil, including the signing of an oil pact in 2008, allowing the South American nation to explore Cuba's oil-rich waters, and the investment of $1 billion into Cuban projects, including

spurring small businesses and port reconstruction.

Since 1959, the United States has maintained an embargo against Cuba that makes it illegal for US corporations to conduct business with Cuban corporations. In 1996, the United States passed a new law with more significant penalties for companies that illegally conduct business with Cuba. In 2001, despite protests from the Cuban government, the United States listed Cuba as one of a group of nations with the potential to harbor or support terrorism. In, 2009, signaling a foreign policy shift, the United States eased travel and remittance restrictions for Cuban-Americans. And in late 2014, US President Barack Obama indicated that the United States would begin greater economic and diplomatic engagement with Cuba. Obama and Raúl Castro met for the first time in April 2015, indicating a genuine softening of relations.

Cuba is a member of the UN and part of the Non-Aligned Movement (NAM), a group of nations that do not formally ally themselves with any sphere of influence or power bloc. Cuba is also a lead member of the UN Human Rights Council, a member of Caribbean Community (CARICOM), and has embassies in many Caribbean countries, including Dominica and Jamaica. Cuba has limited relations with the European Union (EU) because the EU accuses Cuba of blatant human rights violations, although Cuban ambassadors have been negotiating with EU representatives since 1996 to improve relations and economic integration between Cuba and the EU. As of 2015, Cuba has diplomatic relations with 160 nations and provided civilian aid workers to over twenty countries.

## Human Rights Profile

International human rights law insists that states respect civil and political rights and also promote an individual's economic, social, and cultural rights. The United Nations (UN) Universal Declaration on Human Rights (UDHR) is recognized as the standard for international human rights. Its authors sought the counsel of the world's great thinkers, philosophers, and religious leaders and were careful to create a document that reflects the core values shared by every world culture. (To read this document or view the articles relating to cultural human rights, go to: http://www.ohchr.org/EN/UDHR/Pages/Introduction.aspx.)

Cuba is a totalitarian regime controlled by President Raúl Castro and the Communist Party of Cuba. Though human rights conditions have improved since the 1990s, monitoring agencies such as Amnesty International (AI) and Human Rights Watch (HRW) maintain that the Cuban government is guilty of numerous human rights violations. These include unlawful detainment, execution of political rivals and political persecution.

In particular, the Cuban legal system is consistently accused by international monitoring agencies as failing to comply with articles 10 and 11 of the UDHR, which guarantee the assumption of innocence and free, public trial procedures. Reports of arbitrary detention and detainment, which are in violation of Article 9 of the UDHR, are also reportedly common, especially toward political dissidents and opponents of the government. In addition, reports from former prisoners indicate that the conditions within Cuban detention centers and prisons violate Article 5, guaranteeing freedom from inhuman and cruel punishment.

Under Cuban law, individuals are prohibited from any speech or expression that may be seen as critical of the government or socialism in general, and the government maintains strict control of all media outlets. Cuban laws controlling speech and expression violate Article 19 of the UDHR, which guarantees freedom of speech and expression. Although reports that police abuse of political dissidents remains common, instances have declined since the late 1990s.

Cuban law allows police to arrest any individuals engaged in an unauthorized assembly of more than three persons. And even though the formation of political parties was decriminalized by the 1992 constitution, the law also prohibits both gatherings of and collective action by such political and social groups,

particularly those not formally recognized by the government. For example, the Cuban government does not currently recognize human rights agencies such as Amnesty International (AI) and, therefore, does not protect the activities of such groups. Though Cuban law allows freedom of religion, all religious organizations must be licensed by the state before they can hold public or private meetings. The government also places restrictions on the import of religious material.

Reports indicate that the Cuban education system is geared toward extolling the virtues of the Cuban socialist system and is reportedly biased against alternative political and social systems, a violation of Article 26. According to some reports, the government continues to call for the dismissal of teachers whose political views differ from the state-approved curriculum.

While Cuban law allows citizens to freely leave the country, restrictive policies and illegal persecution of those seeking to leave the country are in violation of Article 13 of the UDHR. There have also been reports that officials denied travel permits to individuals for political reasons, and that police and other government officials routinely harass and abuse those seeking legal permission to emigrate.

Discrimination in the distribution of goods, services and employment is prohibited under Cuban law. However, numerous reports indicate that Afro-Cubans and members of foreign ethnic groups experience prejudice in hiring and public service. Furthermore, members of minority groups represent a higher proportion of the penal population, while composing a lower proportion of high-ranking government and executive positions overall.

As of December 2014, since US President Barack Obama announced a reestablishment of diplomatic relations, a softening of economic restrictions, and authorization for travel between the two nations, Cuba has made some of the required concessions, including the January 2015 release of fifty-three political prisoners the country had been holding. Cuba has also agreed to allow human rights monitors into the country for periodic visits. Still, in 2014, there were 8,899 short-term detentions, up from 6,424 in 2013. Arbitrary arrests also increased, from 2,900 in 2013 to 7,188 between January and August of 2014. Human Rights Watch indicates that arbitrary arrests and detentions are still used to intimidate and harass dissidents as well as those who assert ideas contrary to the government system.

## Migration

In 2010, Cuba's migration rate was estimated at −3.66 per 1,000 people. Immigration talks between the United States and Cuba have been renewed recently, with a third round of talks taking place in the summer of 2010. US policy on Cuban migration is dictated by the US–Cuba Migration Accords of 1995, and is informally known as the "wet foot, dry foot" policy, meaning those Cuban immigrants who reach US soil are permitted to stay, while those intercepted at sea are turned back. The CIA notes that, as of 2015, illicit migration continues to be a significant problem, with many émigrés leaving Cuba on homemade rafts, using counterfeit visas, or paying smugglers to bring them into the United States.

## ECONOMY

## Overview of the Economy

The two most important facts of economic life in Cuba are the economic embargo placed on it in 1962 by the US government and the enormous economic losses it faced after the breakup of the Soviet Union in 1989 and 1990. It was to the Soviet Union that Cuba primarily turned for aid after the US blockade went into effect. When the Soviet Union abruptly collapsed, 85 percent of Cuba's foreign trade was wiped out, and Cuba suffered widespread economic hardship.

In the years following the Soviet collapse, Cuban officials took drastic steps to improve the economy. Foreign tourism became a major source of income for the government, earning more than $2 billion in 2002. In addition, Cuba's vibrant black market is an unofficial yet stable aspect of the national economy.

Despite the embargo, the Cuban government allows the American dollar as an accepted currency. Although the embargo limits trade with Cuba, Cubans living in the United States are allowed to send money to relatives in Cuba. These cash remittances give needed income to Cuban residents who can convert the dollars to pesos in government shops. In turn, the government sells these dollars to foreign tourists.

With a workforce highly dependent on the government, in 2010 the Cuban officials announced a reduction in the workforce totaling approximately 20 percent, or 1 million state workers. To ease the layoffs, Cuba has reduced economic restrictions on private businesses, which has spurred hiring, the creation of new jobs, and a growing number of self-employed workers, who in turn hire others. However, Cuba's economy was also hampered by a series of damaging hurricanes in 2008 and a subsequent drought, which has persisted for several years, impacting crops, livestock, irrigation and water distribution, and other segments of the economy.

## Industry

Cuba's major industries include sugar, petroleum, cobalt, pharmaceuticals, tobacco, construction, steel, cement, and agricultural machinery. Its main exports include sugar, nickel, petroleum, medical products, tobacco, fish, citrus, and coffee. As of 2014, Cuba's industrial production growth rate was a modest, but steady, 4.6 percent.

Venezuela is Cuba's main export partner (33.5 percent), followed by Canada (15.9 percent), China (9.5 percent), and the Netherlands (4.5 percent). It is widely believed that improved relations with the United States, its largest and most important economic neighbor, would dramatically improve Cuba's economic strength. To that end, in 2010, the Cuban government took on a more conciliatory tone with the administration of US President Barack Obama and has cited steps that the US government can take to soften the embargo, although as of 2015, it has not yet been lifted.

## Labor

In 2014, the Cuban labor force consisted of 5.092 million people, with an estimated 72.3 percent working in state-run industries and 27.7 percent working in the non-state sector. In 2014, the country had an unemployment rate of 3.6 percent. Signaling a new economic revolution, in 2010, the Cuban government announced a reduction of almost 20 percent of the workforce, or 1 million jobs, and by 2014, 600,000 had indeed been removed from state payrolls. Since then, the private sector has grown, with 500,000 people moving into self-employed positions, cooperative farming, and other commercial cooperative enterprises. An estimated 85,000 people were also working in the newly expanded private sector as of 2014.

## Energy/Power/Natural Resources

The major natural resources of Cuba include cobalt, nickel, iron ore, chromite, manganese, copper, limestone, salt and timber, such as pine and mahogany. Among important conservation issues facing the country are deforestation, which the country is actively combatting; conservation of its arable lands (which are considerable); biodiversity; and air and water pollution.

In 2006, Cuba implemented a state initiative to conserve its energy resources. The initiative consisted of the distribution of 10 million energy-saving bulbs, the installation of efficient power generators, as well as the free distribution of electric-powered pressure cookers and rice cookers.

In 2013, the country produced an estimated 19.14 billion kWh, which exceeded the country's demands of 16.2 billion kWh. However, while it is self-sufficient in electric production, the country is not yet exporting any of its generated production.

## Fishing

Commercial fishing in Cuba is characterized as highly selective, due to the phasing out of prac-

tices such as trawling. However, longline fishing, a controversial fishing technique due to its incidental catches, is practiced to a limited extent by commercial fishing vessels. The large percentage of Cuba's commercial fishing fleet is harbored at the port city of Manzanillo, on Cuba's southeastern coast. The Cuban fishing industry has focused on increasing their lobster and spiny lobster catches in recent years.

## Forestry

As of 2011, 27.3 percent of Cuba was covered in forest and efforts are focused on increasing that level to 29 percent by the end of 2015. Reforestation has been a significant focus in Cuba in recent years. For example, during a nine-month period in 2008, approximately 2.1 million trees were planted in the city of Havana, totaling nearly three percent of all trees in Cuba. A year earlier, in 2007, a United Nations Environmental Programme (UNEP) supported global campaign was responsible for the planting of almost 137 million trees throughout Cuba. Cuba is one of few countries to show yearly forestry growth, and the forestry division employs 40,000 people, of which 1,200 have earned a specialized degree in the field.

## Mining/Metals

Nickel remains one of Cuba's top exports, along with cobalt. Other mineral commodities include iron ore, chromium, salt, silica, and petroleum.

## Agriculture

Approximately 60 percent of Cuba is devoted to agricultural land, nearly 34 percent of which is arable. Another 3.6 percent is devoted to permanent crops, and 23 percent is permanent pasture. The most important and largest sector of Cuban agriculture is the sugar industry, which makes up about 75 percent of the Cuban export market and employs about 20 percent of the work force. The decline of the sugar market since the late 1990s became a source of economic trouble. Tobacco, coffee, beans, and citrus have traditionally been, and continue to be, very important crops. As of 2012, 84 percent or more of food in Cuba was imported, and a tightening of the US embargo in the 1990s gave rise to organic farming in the country, although in the second decade of the 21st century, this embargo has loosened.

## Tourism

Before the late 1990s, the Communist government imposed a tourism embargo, banning all contact between native Cubans and outsiders. However, with the collapse of the country's biggest trading partner, the Soviet Union, Cuba recognized that economic expansion would be necessary for survival. Therefore, beginning in 1997, the government spent a great deal of money improving its resorts and hotels to accommodate an expected visitor increase following the end of the tourism ban. Cuba's tourism industry is now the greatest single source of revenue to the nation, bringing in around $2 billion USD per year, with approximately 3 million tourist arrivals annually. Visiting the island nation each year are tens of thousands of US citizens and Western Europeans, as well as Canadians, a group that alone made up one-third of all tourists in 2014. Since the United States reestablished diplomatic relations with Cuba in 2015, US visitors are similarly expected to increase.

Popular destinations in Cuba include Old Havana, a UNESCO World Heritage Site; tobacco plantations in Pinar del Rio and elsewhere; Revolution-related attractions, including the historical hiding places of revolutionary heroes Fidel Castro and Ernesto "Che" Guevara; the Vinales Valley; and the many miles of coastline beaches and resorts around the island.

*Micah Issitt, Craig Belanger, Jeffrey Bowman,*
*& Savannah Schroll Guz*

## DO YOU KNOW?

- No American-made automobiles have been exported to Cuba since the days of the Revolution. As a result, many of the vehicles in operation on Cuban roads are models that were imported prior to 1959.

- One of the most popular Cuban musical combos in recent history is the Buena Vista Social Club, comprised of many elderly musicians such as Ibrahim Ferrer (1927–2005) and Compay Segundo (1907–2003). These musicians had been nearly forgotten by the international music community before being recorded by American musician Ry Cooder (1947– ). The Buena Vista Social Club's self-titled album won a Grammy Award after its release in 1997.

- The American novelist Ernest Hemingway kept a home in Havana that has been re-made into a museum dedicated to his life and work.

- World-famous cocktails such as the mojito, the Cuba Libre, and the daquiri were credited as having been invented in Havana during the first tourism boom in the early 20th century.

## Bibliography

Boobbyer, Claire. *Frommer's Cuba*. Hoboken, NJ: Frommer's Publishing, 2011.

Chanan, Michael. *Cuban Cinema*. Minneapolis, MN: University of Minnesota Press, 2004. Cultural Studies of the Americas Ser.

Corbett, Ben. *This is Cuba: An Outlaw Culture Survives*. New York: Basic Books, 2007.

Foster, David William. *Cuban Literature: A Research Guide*. New York: Garland, 1985.

García, Enrique. *Cuban Cinema After the Cold War: A Critical Analysis of Selected Films*. New York: McFarland, 2015.

Henken, Ted. *Cuba: A Global Studies Handbook*. Oxford, UK: ABC-CLIO Publishers, 2008.

Kapcia, Antoni. *Havana: The Making of Cuban Culture*. Gordonsville, VA: Berg Publishers, 2005.

Marcos, Rafael and Rosemary Fox. *Old Havana Cookbook: Cuban Recipes in Spanish and English*. New York, Hippocrene Books, 1999.

Pelaez, Ana Sofia. *The Cuban Table: A Celebration of Food, Flavors, and History*. New York: St. Martin's Press, 2014.

Sainsbury, Brendan, and Luke Waterson. *Lonely Planet Cuba*. 8th ed. Oakland, CA: Lonely Planet Press, 2015.

Sweig, Julia E. Cuba: *What Everyone Needs to Know*. Oxford, UK: Oxford University Press, 2013.

Tompkins, Cynthia and Kristen Sternberg. *Teen Life in Latin America and the Caribbean*. Westport, CT: Greenwood Publishing Group, 2004.

Walter, Lynn. *Women's Rights: A Global View*. Westport, CT: Greenwood Publishing Group, 2000.

Zebich-Knos, Michele and Heather Nora Nicol. *Foreign Policy Toward Cuba: Isolation Or Engagement?* Lanham, MD: Lexington Books, 2005.

## Works Cited

Altieri, Miguel A. and Fernando R. Funes-Monzote. "The Paradox of Cuban Agriculture." *Monthly Review* 63.8 (January 2012). Web. http://monthlyreview.org/2012/01/01/the-paradox-of-cuban-agriculture/.

Associated Press. "Divorce is Easy in Cuba but a Housing Shortage Makes Breaking Up Hard to Do." *New York Times*. The New York Times Company, 31 Dec. 2007. Web. http://www.nytimes.com/2007/12/31/world/americas/31cuba.html?_r=2&oref=slogin&oref=slogin.

BBC. "Country Profiles: Cuba." *BBC News*. BBC, 14 Aug. 2012. Web. http://news.bbc.co.uk/2/hi/americas/country_profiles/1203299.stm.

Bureau of Western Hemisphere Affairs. "U.S. Relations with Cuba." *US Department of State*. US Department of State, 21 Jul. 2015. Web. http://www.state.gov/r/pa/ei/bgn/2886.htm.

CIA. "Cuba." *The World Factbook*. Central Intelligence Agency, 2015. Web. https://www.cia.gov/library/publications/the-world-factbook/geos/cu.html.

Darias, Idolidia. "Home Construction Prices in Cuba Make for Tough Market." *Marti News*. MartiNews, 4 Nov. 2013. Web. http://www.martinews.com/content/home-construction-prices-in-cuba/27129.html.

Elmahdi, Rahma. "Cuban Healthcare Revolution: The Future of International Healthcare?" *A Global Village* 2.2 (May 2010). Web. http://www.aglobalvillage.org/journal/issue2/elmahdi/

Ford, Dana and Juan Carlos Lopez. "Cuba Releases 53 Political Prisoners." *CNN*. Cable News Network/Turner Broadcasting System, Inc., 12 Jan. 2015. Web. http://www.cnn.com/2015/01/12/americas/cuba-prisoners-release/.

Frank, Marc. "Cuba on Edge as Drought Worsens." *Reuters*. Thomson Reuters, 17 Aug. 2015. Web. http://www.reuters.com/article/2015/08/17/us-cuba-drought-idUSKCN0QM1P220150817.

_____ . "Trade with China Primes Cuba's Engine for Change." *The Financial Times*. The Financial Times Ltd, 7 Mar. 2006. http://www.ft.com/cms/s/0/de4f405c-ae0a-11da-8ffb-0000779e2340.html#axzz3pAPaFyR1.

Human Rights Watch. "World Report 2015: Cuba." *Human Rights Watch*. HRW, 2015. Web. https://www.hrw.org/world-report/2015/country-chapters/cuba.

"Introducing Cuba." *Lonely Planet Online*. Lonely Planet, 2015. Web. http://www.lonelyplanet.com/worldguide/cuba/.

Legon, Elio Delgado. "Reforestation in Cuba." *Havana Times.org*. Havana Times.org, 26 Nov. 2012. Web. http://www.havanatimes.org/?p=82743.

Renwick, Danielle and Brianna Lee. "Backgrounders: U.S.–Cuba Relations." *Council on Foreign Relations*. Council on Foreign Relations, 4 Aug. 2015. Web. http://www.cfr.org/cuba/us-cuba-relations/p11113.

"Taxes in Cuba: Get Used to It." *The Economist*. The Economist Newspaper Limited, 17 Sept. 2011. Web. http://www.economist.com/node/21529043.

UN Development Programme. "Table 1: Human Development Index and its components." *Human Development Reports*. UNDP, 2015. Web. http://hdr.undp.org/en/content/table-1-human-development-index-and-its-components.

WOLA. "Factsheet: Reforms in 21st Century Cuba." *WOLA Online*. Washington Office on Latin America, 10 Aug. 2015. Web. http://www.wola.org/commentary/factsheet_reforms_in_21st_century_cuba.

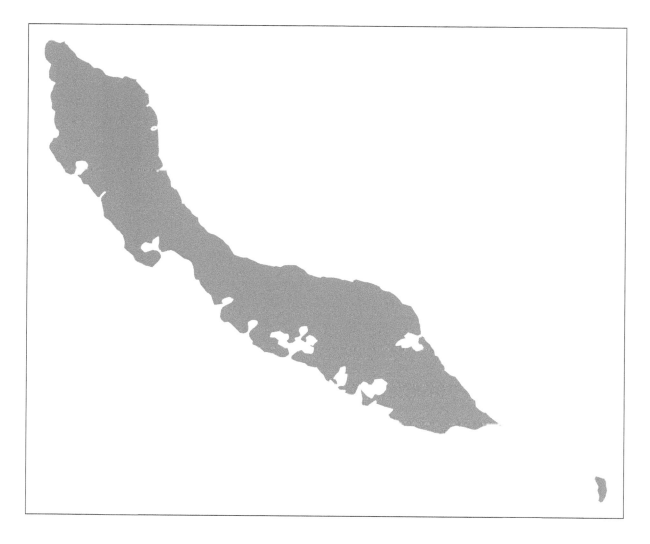

# CURAÇAO, SINT MAARTEN & THE CARIBBEAN NETHERLANDS

# Introduction

Curaçao, Sint Maarten, and the Caribbean Netherlands (made up of the islands of Bonaire, Sint Eustatius, and Saba), formerly known as the last remaining members of the Netherlands Antilles, changed their government structures in a series of referendum efforts beginning in 2000. (Aruba, formerly a member of the Netherlands Antilles, seceded in 1986.) Beginning in 2000, each remaining island in the Netherlands Antilles held a referendum on its future, choosing among four options: developing an even closer relationship with the Netherlands; remaining a member of the Netherlands Antilles; becoming an autonomous country within the Netherlands (like Aruba); or becoming completely independent. In the referendum votes, Curaçao and Sint Maarten voted for autonomy, while Saba and Bonaire voted for closer ties to the Netherlands. Sint Eustatius chose to remain a member of the Netherlands Antilles. A series of negotiations between the islands and the Netherlands resulted in the dissolution of the Netherlands Antilles on October 10, 2010. In its place, Curaçao and Sint Maarten became constituent countries of the Netherlands, while the islands of Bonaire, Sint Eustatius, and Saba—known as the Caribbean Netherlands or BES (Bonaire, Sint Eustatius, and Saba)—became special municipalities of the Netherlands.

Geographically situated at either end of a semicircle of Caribbean islands, Curaçao and Bonaire lie off the coast of Venezuela in the southern Caribbean Sea. These islands are culturally mixed, exhibiting a blend of the Spanish, Dutch, and Caribbean cultures that travelled and traded there. The islands of Sint Maarten, Sint Eustatius, and Saba are located at the upper half of the Caribbean island chain and are former Dutch colonies important to that nation's system of trade, which was at its height between the 17th and 19th centuries. It is important to note that since 1648 the Dutch-affiliated Sint Maarten has peacefully shared a landmass with Saint Martin, owned by the French. The cultural blend of the BES islands is more akin to that of its geographi-

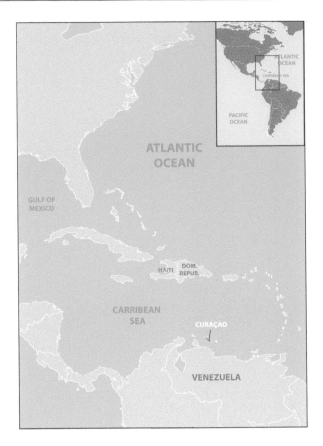

cal neighbors, reflecting African, French, Dutch, and English influences.

## GENERAL INFORMATION

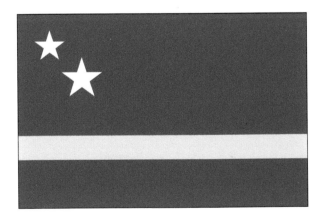

**Official Language(s): Curaçao & Sint Maarten:** Dutch, Papiamentu, English; **Bonaire, Saba, Sint Eustatius:** Dutch

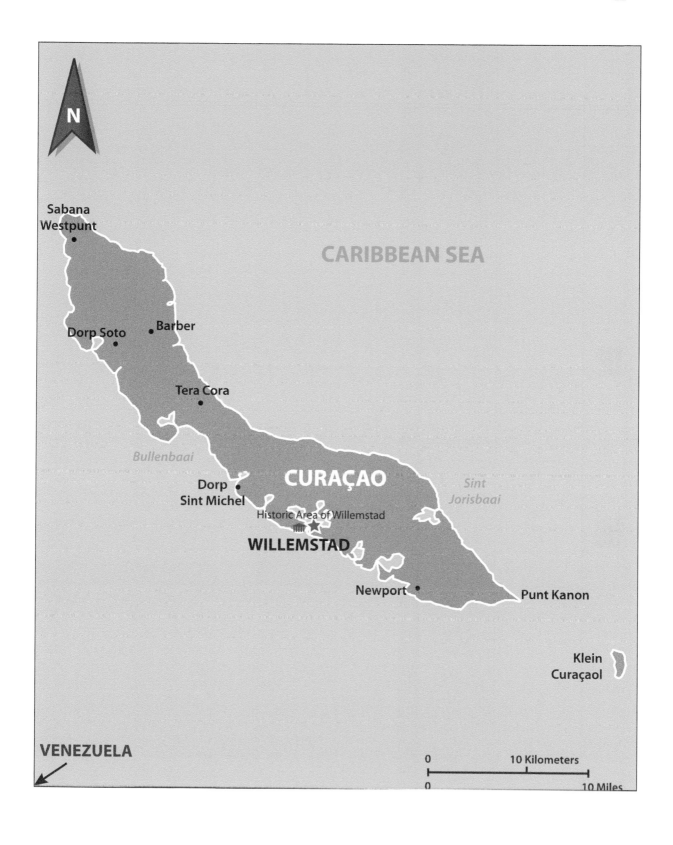

**Principal Cities by Population (2014):**

- Willemstad (135,000)
- Tera Cora (also, Tera Korá) (4,388)
- Labadera (2,627)
- Barber (2,411)
- Soto (2,233)
- Westpunt (738)
- Sint Willibrordus (588)
- Lagun (321)

**Population: Curaçao:** 146,836; **Sint Maarten:** 31,754; **Caribbean Netherlands:** 21,133 (2015 estimates)

**Currency: Curaçao & Sint Maarten:** Netherlands Antillean guilder; **Caribbean Netherlands:** US dollar.

**Coins:** In Curaçao and Sint Maarten, the guilder is divided into 100 cents. Coins are issued in denominations of 1, 5, 10, 25, and 50 cents, as well as 1, 2-1/2, and 5 guilders. In the Caribbean Netherlands, the US dollar is divided into 100 cents as well. Coins are available in denominations of 1, 5, 10, and 25 cents, with a 50 cent and 1 dollar coin both rarely used.

**Land Area: Curaçao:** 444 square kilometers (171.4 square miles); **Sint Maarten:** 34 square kilometers (13.1 square miles); **Caribbean Netherlands:** 328 square kilometers (126.6 square miles)

**National Anthem: Curaçao:** "Himno di Kòrsou" (Anthem of Curaçao); **Sint Maarten:** "O Sweet Saint Martin's Land" **Bonaire:** "Tera di Solo y suave biento"(Country of Sun and Gentle Breeze); **Saba:** "Saba you rise from the ocean"

**Capitals: Curaçao:** Willemstad; **Sint Maarten:** Philipsburg; **Saba:** The Bottom; **Sint Eustatius:** Oranjestad; **Bonaire:** Kralendijk

**Time Zone(s):** GMT - 4

**Flag Description:** The flag of Curacao is blue, with a yellow horizontal stripe slightly below the midline, and two white stars in the upper left corner. The blue symbolizes the sea and sky, and the yellow represents the sun. The two stars are for Curacao and Klein Curacao, but also stand for 'Love and Happiness.' Their five points symbolize the five continents that the people of Curacao come from.

## Population

Among the islands of Curaçao, Sint Maarten, and the Caribbean Netherlands, the population totals approximately 199,723 people (2015 estimate). A large proportion of the population is descended from African slaves who were brought to the islands between the 17th and 19th centuries. (Slavery was abolished on the islands in 1863.) The rest of the population is made up of descendants of European colonists, Carib Amerindians, and people from other Caribbean islands, East Asia, South Asia, and Latin America. There is also a Jewish minority.

The city of Willemstad, on the island of Curaçao, is the capital and largest city of these islands. The islands of Bonaire and Curaçao are part of the so-called "ABC" island chain (with Aruba) and are known also as the Leeward Islands of the former Netherlands Antilles. These islands are off the Venezuelan coast. Saba, Sint Eustatius, and the southern half of Sint Maarten (the northern half is a French territory) are known as the Windward Islands and are located east of Puerto Rico and the Virgin Islands.

## Languages

While the official languages of each of these islands vary slightly, Dutch, English, Spanish, and Papiamentu (in Bonaire and Curaçao) are widely spoken. Papiamento is a creole language predominant on Curaçao and Bonaire and the neighboring island of Aruba. It descends from Portuguese, West African, and Arawak native languages, with a strong Dutch influence. More recently, word substitutions from both Spanish and English have been adopted into the Papiamentu language.

## Native People & Ethnic Groups

Curaçao's original inhabitants have left few traces of their existence. Archaeologists conducting excavations around the island have found tools and human burial sites of two different ancient

Amerindian groups. It is believed that the first inhabitants of Curaçao probably migrated from Venezuela around 3000 BCE. The Caiquetíos Indians, an Arawak-speaking group, also came from Venezuela, particularly from the states of Lara and Falcon, around 500 CE in fishing canoes made from hollowed-out logs. A civilization of around 2,000 Caiquetíos is thought to have been living on Aruba, Bonaire, and Curaçao when the Spaniards arrived around 1500 CE. Legend has it that the Spaniards, reportedly impressed by the height of the Caiquetíos Indians, first called Curaçao "la isla de los gigantes" or "island of the giants."

The Spaniards virtually wiped out these early inhabitants, sending many of the Caiquetíos to the island of Hispaniola (what is now the Dominican Republic and Haiti) to work in the mines. When the Dutch took the island in 1634, they deported most of the remaining Caiquetíos, fearing they would act as spies for their former Spanish masters. By the beginning of the 19th century, none of the original inhabitants of the islands remained, although Dutch records indicate that the last full-blooded Arawak descendant died in 1862. Today, the Caribbean Netherlands have a mixed culture due to both the proximity of the islands to nearby countries such as Venezuela, and to the origins of the people who travelled from Europe or were brought from Africa as slaves. More recently, an American influence has been significant due to the islands' popularity as a tourist destination and the strong American media presence.

## Religions

The majority religion of Curaçao, Sint Maarten, and the Caribbean Netherlands is Christianity, dominated by Roman Catholicism (72.8 percent in Curaçao and 39 percent in Sint Maarten). A small Jewish population also formed on Curaçao, established by Portuguese Sephardic Jews who came from Brazil and Amsterdam and first settled in the islands around 1654. Similarly, on Sint Maarten, 3.4 percent of the population identifies as Jewish.

## Climate

Curaçao, Sint Maarten, and the islands comprising the Caribbean Netherlands generally share a tropical climate, with warm weather year round. Average annual rainfall is 60 centimeters (23 inches) on the Leeward Islands and 99 centimeters (39 inches) on the Windward Islands.

Sint Maarten has a warm and humid tropical climate; generally, the rainy season lasts from June to October. Hurricanes are also a possibility during this period. The driest months are those between February and April. Sint Eustatius is generally dry and sunny and cooled by trade winds; the rainy season generally runs from June through September. The island is located along the routes of hurricanes that can blow through from August and October, as is the island of Saba, which is often covered in clouds due to the presence of Mount Scenery, the Netherlands' highest peak and also a volcano, whose last eruption was in 1640. Curaçao and Bonaire are situated just outside the hurricane corridor and enjoy a warm, tropical climate tempered by north-to-east trade winds.

## ENVIRONMENT & GEOGRAPHY

### Topography

The five islands of Curaçao, Sint Maarten, and the Caribbean Netherlands are divided geographically into the Leeward Islands (northern) group, and the Windward Islands (southern) group. The hilly Windward Islands are all of volcanic origin, leaving little ground among the rocky, arid soil that is suitable for agriculture. In fact, just 10 percent of Curaçao is arable. The Leeward Islands have a mixed coral and volcanic origin. The highest point is Mount Scenery on the island of Saba; it reaches 887 meters (2,910 feet) and is also the highest point in the entire Kingdom of the Netherlands. Another point of prominence is on the Windward island of Curaçao, where Mount Christoffel rises to 372 meters (1,220 feet).

Also on the island of Curaçao, unique features include a series of limestone terraces and caves along the north coast, believed to be as much as 1.5 million years old. The island is also surrounded by a coral reef.

**Plants & Animals**
The volcanic soil and low rainfall make Curaçao, Sint Maarten, and the Caribbean Netherlands home to many species of cacti and other succulents, like aloe, some of which are used locally in foods, medicines, and shampoos. Most of the plant life found in these islands can thrive on very little water. Native trees such as the tamarind, acacia, mesquite, and divi divi (Curaçao's national tree, which is also known as the watapana tree) have a collection of small leaves, rather than broad flat ones. These small leaves help the native trees better catch droplets of rain and dew and reduce the evaporation of precious water.

Wild donkeys and goats that still populate Curaçao and some of the other islands were originally introduced by the Spaniards, though the rare white-tailed deer has been present since pre-Columbian times. Donkeys and goats are considered a nuisance, and people erect fences and plant thickets of cactus to keep the animals out of their gardens. Animals native to the islands include reptiles, such as geckos and iguanas. There are also many bat species native to Curaçao that live in limestone caves along the northern coast. Bonaire is known for its large populations of flamingoes, while Saba boasts a significant population of sea turtles, barracudas, and sharks.

## CULTURAL HISTORY

**History**
The islands now known as Curaçao, Sint Maarten, and the Caribbean Netherlands originally were inhabited by Arawak and Carib Indians (Caiquetíos). The island of Saint Maarten was sighted by Christopher Columbus (1451–1506) during his second voyage on November 11, 1493 (on Saint Martin's Day, hence its name). After the famous navigator Amerigo Vespucci (1451–1512) landed on Curaçao in September 1499, the

Spaniards established a small colony in the early 1500s. However, their disappointment at finding no gold or silver on the islands of Curaçao, Bonaire, or Aruba quickly led them to nickname them "the useless islands" and use them mostly as a place to raise their sheep, goats, and cattle.

The few Caiquetíos or Arawak Indians who were not deported by the Spanish were put to work raising the animals the Spaniards had introduced to the islands, chopping wood, and working the salt flats. The islands exported hides, salt, and dyewood back to Europe. The Spanish remained in power for 125 years in Curaçao, Bonaire, and Aruba. During and even after their reign, the Spaniards actively promoted the Catholic religion among the enslaved. As a result, Curaçao is one of the few places outside of Africa with a majority black Catholic population (72.8 percent in 2012).

In the early 17th century, Dutch privateers organized themselves into the West India Company and set their sights on the islands. They were attracted by the salt pans on Curaçao and Bonaire for economic reasons (salt was used as a preservative for fish), and to Curaçao for its protected harbor, ideal for a naval base. In July 1634, Johan van Walbeeck (1602–1649) arrived with a Dutch force of only a few hundred men. The Dutch won easily, deporting the Spaniards and most of their Indian slaves to the mainland, while keeping the rest as laborers.

During the Eighty Years' War between Spain and Holland (1568–1648), Curaçao served as a Dutch naval base. The Dutch eventually built Fort Amsterdam on Sint Maarten, with quarters for the director of the West India Company, representing the first local political leadership in the islands. Once the war ended with the signing of the Peace of Münster in 1648, Curaçao was free to blossom into a trade center. Less than fifty years after the Dutch took Curaçao, they declared the island a free port and began promoting trade throughout the region.

By the mid-17th century, the port of Willemstad on Curaçao was the hub of the Dutch trade empire in the Western Hemisphere. Prosperous Dutch and Jewish merchants, who had emigrated from Portugal, conducted a booming business trading with neighboring South America. The Dutch also took possession of the Windward Islands of Sint Eustatius, Sint Maarten, and Saba in the 1630s, but they never achieved the commercial status of Curaçao; Bonaire; and, to a lesser extent, Aruba. Sint Eustatius and Saba had no suitable harbors for large ships, and Sint Maarten was partitioned and shared with the French.

Because of its dry climate, Curaçao never developed large-scale plantations. Instead of producing cash crops for export, the Dutch islands relied on the shipment of goods produced or acquired elsewhere—including slaves. It wasn't long, in fact, before the Dutch became leaders in the international slave trade, with Curaçao becoming a major trading hub for slavery in the Caribbean. Using Portuguese trading posts along Africa's west coast, which became known as the "Slave Coast," the West India Company purchased African slaves for transport to Curaçao and South America (mostly Brazil). Most slaves were sold to plantation owners throughout North and South America, and remained on Curaçao for only a few short months. By the time slavery was abolished in the 1860s, the Dutch had transported some 500,000 Africans to slavery.

Curaçao's largest slave uprising began with the revolt of fifty slaves from the highly prosperous Kenepa Plantation on August 17, 1795. They were soon joined by over a thousand more from other plantations. While the revolt was eventually quelled and its leaders executed, it lasted several weeks and marked the beginning of the end of slavery and the slave trade in the islands. The 1848 abolition of slavery in France's Saint Martin resulted in the abolition of slavery in the island's Dutch side of Sint Maarten and a slave rebellion on Sint Eustatius. On Saba and Sint Eustatius slaves were emancipated in 1863.

During the height of piracy in the Caribbean region throughout the 17th and 18th centuries, the islands that are now the Caribbean Netherlands remained relatively unaffected. However, there were several attempts by both French and British adventurers to wrest the prosperous and stra-

tegically attractive island of Curaçao from the Dutch. French attempts were mostly failures, but in 1713, the French buccaneer Jacques Cassard (1672–1740) temporarily conquered the island. He left after being paid a ransom in money, goods, and slaves.

Another French attempt at invasion in 1800 was foiled by an English warship that happened to be in the harbor at the time. After defeating the French, the British ruled the island for three years. The island reverted back to the Dutch, but the British returned in 1807, this time ruling for eight years. Curaçao was returned to the Netherlands by the Treaty of Paris in 1815. Still, France has left its mark on the Caribbean Netherlands. Half of the island of Sint Maarten still belongs to France and is called Saint Martin. It is part of the French overseas territory that includes Guadeloupe.

In 1845, the six islands (then including Aruba) officially formed the Netherlands Antilles.

After the lucrative slave trade ended, the islands fell into an economic slump. This ended abruptly starting in 1914, when the discovery of oil deposits in neighboring Venezuela triggered the establishment of industrialization and oil refineries on Curaçao and Aruba. The lack of domestic labor resulted in the influx of thousands of industrial laborers from the surrounding Caribbean region and Latin America, as well as from Asia, along with teachers and government workers from the Netherlands. This multicultural wave, along with the descendants of former slaves, formed the current population of the islands.

In 1986, Aruba seceded from the Netherlands Antilles, becoming a country of the Kingdom of the Netherlands. After a series of referendum votes, the Netherlands Antilles was dissolved in October 2010 and Curaçao and Sint Maarten followed Aruba in becoming countries of the Kingdom of the Netherlands. The islands of Bonaire, Sint Eustatius, and Saba had elected to retain closer ties to the Netherlands—they were designated special municipalities and are now called the Caribbean Netherlands or the BES (Bonaire, Sint Eustatius, and Saba) islands.

## CULTURE

### Arts & Entertainment

The island of Curaçao boasts a majority of the islands' artistic culture. In particular, music and dance have a long and colorful history on the island. Curaçao's musical heritage blends African, European, Latin American, and Caribbean influences, and traditional musical styles from these and other places—jazz rhythms from the United States, for example—have been mixed together and modified over the years, creating several new music styles unique to the island's culture. In addition, since the 1960s, the Catholic Church began encouraging the use of local music and Papiamentu in church services.

Born in the tight-knit slave communities before the abolition of slavery, the local music known as tambú became one of the most vibrant cultural expressions and emotional outlet of an oppressed people. The music offered slaves some respite from their backbreaking labor in the fields. Tambú's basic instruments are the drum (also known as tambú) and the chapi (the flat metal portion of a garden hoe), which are both beaten in complicated rhythmic patterns. The instruments are accompanied by singing, which follows a set call-and-response pattern. Originally, the singing of tambú was done mostly by women.

A distinctive dance accompanies tambú music. The African-influenced dance style of tambú combines isolation of various body parts with elaborate and distinct hip movements. The dance's suggestive look, along with lyrics that sometimes call attention to social ills or complaints, led to tambú's suppression by both the Catholic Church and the government. Today, tambú is having a revival, thanks to the efforts of cultural groups. Due to a government ordinance, public tambú parties are often held at roadside stands or bars in December and January.

The island's most popular dance tune is perhaps the tumba, heard in the streets during the weeks preceding the annual Carnival. It is best known as Curaçao's official Carnival Road March. While Curaçao's annual Carnival is a fairly recent phenomenon, having developed in the 20th century, tumba predates Carnival and was played as far back as 200 years ago. Modern tumba has taken on a rhythm all its own, with influences of merengue and other Afro-Caribbean beats, as well as jazz harmonies.

In addition to Carnival, the island of Curaçao also hosts a traditional harvest festival called the seú (creole, "heaven"). Held annually, it involves a folklore parade held in the city of Willemstad the day after Easter. In the days before the discovery of oil in Venezuela and the subsequent refinery boom in Curaçao, the seú was a festive march in which farm workers carried their harvest to the warehouses. The women carried baskets on their heads, while the men accompanying them played a variety of instruments, including drums and the hollowed-out horns of a cow. The music was played to announce the celebration. Movements were graceful, and the participants mimed the actions of harvesting and planting. The rituals and dancing are intended as an expression of thanks to God—whom former slaves referred to as "Shon Grandi"—for help in overcoming challenges, particularly in relation to the growing season.

The traditional seú began to disappear in the mid-1900s, when the oil refinery opened and agriculture decreased. In an effort to preserve this rich cultural tradition to future generations, the Curaçao Department of Culture now organizes the folklore parade. More than 2,000 people, men, women, and children of all ages, many of whom are members of well-established folklore groups, participate in the march. The women's colorful costumes include elaborately tied head scarves and ruffled skirts, while the men's traditional attire consists simply of muslin clothes that were made out of old flour sacks.

### Cultural Sites & Landmarks

The island of Curaçao is home to one World Heritage Site, as designated by the United Nations Educational, Scientific, and Cultural Organization (UNESCO): the Historic Area of Willemstad, including the inner city and harbor. A traditional port city on the island of Curaçao, Willemstad boasts distinctive, multi-colored colonial architecture with a significant Dutch influence. The architecture reflects the port city's multicultural history and early European urban planning. According to a government monument bureau, there are 750 historic buildings in Willemstad.

Curaçao is also home to many other important cultural sites and landmarks, including a number of extant plantations. One such plantation, Landhuis Kenepa, was the site of a slave revolt on August 17, 1795. The Mikvé Israel-Emanuel Synagogue is one of Curaçao's most important sites and the oldest synagogue still in continuous use in the Western Hemisphere. The temple was dedicated in 1732 by the Jewish community, which had grown from the original twelve families who came from Amsterdam between 1651 and 1654. These families were later joined by Jews fleeing persecution from the Inquisition movements in Spain and Portugal. A drawbridge connects the historic quarter of Punda, where the synagogue is located, with the neighborhood of Scharloo, where the early Jewish merchants built stately homes. The colonial mansions along the main street of Scharlooweg, much of it from the 17th century, have been meticulously restored.

The capital of Sint Maarten is Philipsburg, one of the original old port cities of the Caribbean Netherlands. The city spans a mile along the shore and has five parallel streets, the main one being Front Street. Directly across from Wathey Square in the heart of the town are the historic town hall and the courthouse, built in 1793. The building has served a variety of functions, including as a jail, post office, and fire station. Front Street is also home to the Sint Maarten Museum, with a permanent historical display including ancient Arawak pottery shards and objects salvaged from shipwrecks throughout the island's history. On the island of Bonaire, salt flats and the tiny huts that once housed slaves can still be visited. Bonaire is also home to Onima, an ancient limestone site where native Arawak inscriptions and pictographs dating from the 15th century can still be seen.

Another important landmark is Fort Oranj, built in the city of Oranjestad on the island of Sint Eustatius in 1636. The fort played a historic role in the American Revolution when it became the first foreign entity to recognize the upstart new nation in 1776. Oranjestad also served as the former headquarters of Lord George Brydges Rodney (1718–1792), a British admiral who stripped the island of wine, gunpowder, and other goods in retaliation for Sint Eustatius's support of America. The restored house is considered Sint Eustatius's most important 18th-century dwelling, and now houses the St. Eustatius Historical Foundation Museum. Oranjestad is also home to the partially restored Dutch Reformed Church built in 1775, and to Honen Dalim, another of the Caribbean's oldest synagogues, dating from 1739.

## SOCIETY

### Transportation

The islands of Curaçao, Sint Maarten, and the Caribbean Netherlands are served by five airports and three major ports at Kralendijk, Philipsburg, and Willemstad. Inexpensive minibuses are common, though they often operate on an informal schedule. Ferry service is also available to and around Curaçao's main shopping areas. Taxis are readily available on most islands.

### Media & Communications

Curaçao, Sint Maarten, and the Caribbean Netherlands enjoy freedom of the press and speech as guaranteed under Dutch law. Most of the newspapers are printed on the island of Curaçao, even though they may be destined exclusively for another island. *Amigoe* and *Antilliaans Dagblad* print in Dutch, while *Extra*, *La Prensa*, and *Ultima Noticia*, publish in the Papiamento language. Bonaire has the *Bonaire Reporter*, an independent, English-language publication, while *Today* and *The Daily Herald*, both printed on Sint Maarten, serve the populations of the Leeward Islands, Sint Maarten, Sint Eustatius, and Saba.

There are three local television channels, as well as cable service that supply programs received from various American satellite networks and four channels from Venezuela. TeleCuraçao is the government-run TV station. Numerous AM and FM radio stations broadcast in English and Dutch.

## GOVERNMENT

### Structure

The Netherlands Antilles was officially formed in 1845. While still part of the Kingdom of the Netherlands, the Netherlands Antilles was granted full autonomy over its own internal affairs in 1954. Aruba, once part of the Netherlands Antilles, has had separate status within the kingdom since 1986. Between June 2000 and April 2005, each island of the former Netherlands Antilles had a referendum on its future status. The four options that could be voted on were closer ties with the Netherlands, remaining within the Netherlands Antilles, autonomy as a country within the Kingdom of the Netherlands (status aparte), or independence. Of the five islands, Sint Maarten and Curaçao voted for status aparte ("special status"), Saba and Bonaire voted for closer ties to the Netherlands, and Sint Eustatius voted to stay within the Netherlands Antilles. Through a series of negotiations between island governments and Dutch officials, a resolution was negotiated whereby the islands of Curaçao and Sint Maarten would be granted status aparte and the islands of Bonaire, Sint Eustatius, and Saba would be designated special municipalities under the Dutch government. On October 10, 2010, these changes in status were implemented.

As constituent countries within the Kingdom of the Netherlands, Curaçao and Sint Maarten imitate the government structure of Aruba in that they are directly responsible for internal affairs, but they defer to the Kingdom of the Netherlands in matters of national security, foreign policy, and human rights. The countries each have a governor general, who both represents and is appointed by the hereditary Dutch monarch. In addition, each country has a prime minister who acts as the head of government; the prime minister is usually the head of the majority party, elected by the popularly-elected Staten (parliament). The unicameral Staten van Curaçao has 21 members and 15 in Sint Maarten. Members are elected by proportional representation vote to four-year terms. A council of ministers works with the prime minister to develop and implement policy.

As special municipalities, the islands of Bonaire, Sint Eustatius, and Saba (the BES islands) are led by a lieutenant governor and the governing council. Local government is lead by an island council. Although the BES islands may vote in Dutch and European elections, the BES islands are not considered part of the European Union.

### Foreign Policy

Because Curaçao, Sint Maarten, and the Caribbean Netherlands are part of the Kingdom of the Netherlands, the Dutch government is responsible for the defense and foreign affairs of the islands.

Historically, the Netherlands has been a neutral state and has become a member of a large number of international organizations since World War II. The Netherlands prioritizes the integration of European states and participates in peacekeeping missions in other countries. A member of the United Nations (UN), the Netherlands is also active in the Organization for Security and Cooperation in Europe (OSCE), the Organization for Economic Co-operation and Development (OECD), the World Trade Organization (WTO), the International Monetary Fund (IMF), the Group of Ten (G10), the Inter-American Development Bank (IADB), the Organization for Security and Cooperation in Europe (OSCE), and was a founding member of the European Union (EU).

### Human Rights Profile

International human rights law insists that states respect civil and political rights and also promote an individual's economic, social, and cultural rights. The United Nations Universal Declaration on Human Rights (UDHR) is recognized as the standard for international human rights. Its authors sought the counsel of the world's great thinkers, philosophers, and religious leaders and were careful to create a document that reflects the core values shared by every world culture. To read this document or view the articles relating to cultural human rights, click here: http://www.ohchr.org/EN/UDHR/Pages/Introduction.aspx.

The Kingdom of the Netherlands generally respects and protects the rights of its citizens. These constitutional rights and protections extend to the islands of Curaçao, Sint Maarten, and the Caribbean Netherlands. However, some concerns remain, including prison conditions and the rights of workers and laborers. Prison conditions such as overcrowding and the detention of juvenile offenders with adults have been reported, though the government has recently allocated funds to address these situations. There were also allegations of labor law violations in 2005 and 2006, and a foreign court ruled in favor of three Cuban workers who worked under dangerous conditions for little pay.

While prostitution is legal in Curaçao, regulated by the government, and monitored by medical officials—with at least two well-known, open-air brothels in continuous operation since the mid-20th century—human trafficking remains a significant, unaddressed concern. Foreign women, especially those from Brazil, Colombia, the Dominican Republic, Haiti, and Peru, have been particularly vulnerable to sexually exploitative circumstances or domestic servitude, according to the US State Department, which indicates the Curaçao and Sint Maarten are both transit and destination countries for the sex trade as well as forced agricultural labor and domestic servitude. The State Department also reports that trafficked children are subjected into similar exploitative conditions and that the island governments have, thus far, done little to halt these activities.

Overall, however, women's productive participation in the labor market has increased since the mid-20th century; since the 1980s, the islands have had two female prime ministers and several female ministers. Women from the Caribbean and Latin America largely work in the tourism sector and as domestic servants.

## ECONOMY

### Overview of the Economy

In 1918, a booming workforce suddenly developed around the first Curaçao oil refinery when major oil fields were discovered in nearby Venezuela. The Venezuelan state oil company, known as PdVSA, now leases Curaçao's only refinery, which is under contract until 2019 and employs approximately 1,000 people. Venezuelan petroleum is refined here for export to the United States and Asia. The natural harbor, dry dock, and free-trade zone at the Port of Willemstad make Curaçao perfect as an export hub. Today, petroleum refining and shipping, along with tourism and offshore finance, are the mainstays of Curaçao's small economy. Although the gross domestic product (GDP) has remained somewhat stagnant in recent years, standing at $3.128 billion (USD) in 2012, Curaçao enjoys a high per capita income—estimated at $22,619 (USD)—and a well-developed infrastructure compared with other countries in the region.

Sint Maarten's economy centers on tourism and more than 83.7 percent of its people work in the services sector. Like Curaçao, it has a high per capita GDP, measured at $66,800 in 2014, the highest among the islands that used to comprise the Netherlands Antilles.

### Industry

Almost all consumer and capital goods are imported into the islands of Curaçao, Sint Maarten, and the Caribbean Netherlands, with the United States and Mexico being the major suppliers. The salt industry in Bonaire remains a small but significant industry, and dates back to 1633. The workforce of these islands is comprised of around 80,000. The most important industries by island are tourism (Curaçao, Sint Maarten, and Bonaire), petroleum refining and manufacturing (Curaçao), and salt production (Bonaire).

### Energy/Power/Natural Resources

Curaçao, Sint Maarten, and the Caribbean Netherlands have limited natural resources. Curaçao is a source of calcium phosphates, ingredients used in certain detergents and shampoos, and both Sint Maarten and Bonaire is a source of salt due to their salt flats. Conservation efforts are in place to preserve the coral reef and sea life around the island of Saba. The Saba Marine Park was established in 1987 to preserve and manage Saba's marine resources. The project was funded by World Wildlife Fund (WWF)-Netherlands, the Prince Bernard Fund, and the Dutch and Saban governments. Conservation groups also protect the limestone caves that serve as habitat for bats on Curaçao.

## Agriculture

Agriculture on the islands is difficult to sustain due to poor soil and inadequate water supplies. Only about 10 percent of all the land on the islands is suitable for agriculture, and the industry on all the islands together accounts for just over one percent of the economy (0.7 percent on Curaçao and 0.4 percent on Sint Maarten in 2012). Still, some agricultural products such as peanuts, vegetables, sorghum, and tropical fruit are grown, mostly for use by the people on the islands rather than for export. Aloe plants, which are more easily cultivated in the arid conditions of the islands, do provide some of the ingredients used in shampoos, sunburn remedies, and other products.

## Tourism

Tourism has been a main industry of the islands since the 17th century, when merchants conducting business were drawn to the tropical climate. Neighboring Venezuela provided many of the islands' tourists for many years. In the early 20th century, cruise lines began to make Willemstad a port of call.

Curaçao, Bonaire, and Sint Maarten have thriving tourist industries, with around 800,000 people visiting Curaçao alone each year. Tourism continues to spur hotel development, and the Dutch government invested in a new airport terminal in Curaçao in 2006. Hato International Airport, also known as Curaçao International Airport, can now accommodate 1.6 million passengers annually and boasts regular traffic from,

among others, American Airlines, Air Berlin, JetBlue, Air Canada, and Insel Air (Curaçao's national airline). In addition, the opening of new, larger piers boosted cruise-ship passengers to record numbers, while the architectural heritage of the islands has seen substantial investment in restoration in recent years. Today, the islands of Curaçao, Sint Maarten, and the Caribbean Netherlands boast five airports, one of which is Sint Maarten's Princess Juliana International, which saw the arrival of 500,000 people in 2013.

Bonaire's natural beauty is carefully protected. Established in 1969, the Washington Slagbaai National Park is the island's first nature sanctuary and is comprised of 5.643 hectares (14 acres). Additionally, all of Bonaire's coastal waters were turned into a national park in 1979, and Bonaire purchased the privately-owned outlying island of Klein Bonaire in 1999 to prevent unwanted development. Anyone diving around the island must purchase a one-year permit, and removing or damaging coral is strictly prohibited. Even with the restrictions, Bonaire draws divers and people interested in eco-tourism from all over the world to its premier location.

Many tourists are drawn to Carnival, right before the Christian season of Lent in late winter. The holiday is prominent in the islands, as it is in many other Caribbean and Latin American countries. Festivities include "jump-up" parades featuring ornate costumes, floats, and performers. Carnival on the islands of Curaçao, Sint Maarten, and the Caribbean Netherlands also includes a middle-of-the-night parade called J'ouvert (a contraction of "jour ouvert," which translates to "dawn" or "day break"), which lasts throughout the night and into early morning. The following morning, revelers burn a straw effigy of King Momo, a traditional ceremony thought to cleanse the island of sins and bad luck. King Momo is a feature of many Carnival celebrations in other countries, notably Brazil, and this tradition is believed to have come to the Caribbean islands via the Portuguese.

*Lisa Rothstein, Savannah Schroll Guz*

## DO YOU KNOW?

- Local legend has it that in the 1800s, the governor of Curaçao complained of migraine headaches and blamed the glare from the sun's reflection off the then-white structures of Willemstad. To alleviate the problem, he ordered the facades painted in the bright colors that are a major feature of the city today.

- The bricks used in the Dutch colonial buildings of Willemstad, which give the architecture its distinctive Dutch look, were brought from the Netherlands as ballast in the Dutch ships. Once the bricks were unloaded, the weight was made up with goods for trade with other countries, mostly rum and slaves.

- The island of Sint Maarten is the smallest land mass in the world shared by two independent states: the French territory of Saint Martin and the Dutch constituent country of Sint Maarten.

### Bibliography

Blakely, Allison. *Blacks in the Dutch World: The Evolution of Racial Imagery in a Modern Society.* Indiana University Press, 2001.

Colón, Christina Paulette. *Frommer's Portable Aruba, Bonaire and Curaçao.* 6th ed. New York: Frommers, 2011.

Gastmann, Albert L. *Historical Dictionary of the French and Netherlands Antilles.* Lanham, MD: Scarecrow Press, 1978.

Jong, Nanette de. *Tambú: Curaçao's African-Caribbean Ritual and the Politics of Memory.* Bloomington, IN: Indiana UP, 2012.

Page, Melvin E, ed. *Colonialism: An International, Social, Cultural, and Political Encyclopedia.* 3 vols. Santa Barbara, CA: ABC-CLIO, 2003.

Richardson, Bonham C. *The Caribbean in the Wider World, 1492–1992: A Regional Geography.* Cambridge, UK: Cambridge University Press, 1992. Geography of the World Economy Ser.

### Works Cited

Bureau of Western Hemisphere Affairs. "Background Note: Netherlands Antilles." *US Department of State.* US Department of State, 10 Oct. 2010. Web. http://www.state.gov/r/pa/ei/bgn/22528.htm.

———. "U.S. Relations with Curacao." *US Department of State.* US Department of State, 14 Feb. 2014. Web. http://www.state.gov/r/pa/ei/bgn/161154.htm.

CIA. "Curaçao." *The World Factbook.* Central Intelligence Agency, 2015. Web. https://www.cia.gov/library/publications/the-world-factbook/geos/cc.html.

———. "Sint Maarten." *The World Factbook.* Central Intelligence Agency, 2015. Web. https://www.cia.gov/library/publications/the-world-factbook/geos/sk.html.

"The Founding." *Welcome to Mikvé Israel-Emanuel.* Mikvé Israel-Emanuel Synogogue/CuraNow, 2003. http://www.snoa.com/snoa.html.

"Honen Dalim Synagogue Restoration Project." *Saint Eustatius Historical Foundation.* Saint Eustatius Historical Foundation, 2006. Web. http://www.steustatiushistory.org/HonenDalimSynagogue.htm.

Office to Monitor and Combat Trafficking in Persons. "Trafficking in Persons Report." US Department of State. *US Department of State,* 4 June 2008. Web. http://www.state.gov/j/tip/rls/tiprpt/2008/105388.htm.

*Saba Conservation Foundation.* Dutch Ministry of the Interior, 2015. Web. http://www.sabapark.org/.

Schoop, Shardinoushka. "Seú, the Swinging Harvest Festival of Curaçao." *Amigoe.* Uitgeverij Amigoe N.V., 20 Apr. 2014. Web. http://www.amigoe.com/amigoe-express/interviews/181338–seu-the-swinging-harvest-festival-of-curacao.

STINAPA Bonaire. "Washington Slagbaai National Park." *STINAPA Bonaire National Parks.* STINAPA Bonaire/WWF-Netherlands, 2012. Web. http://www.washingtonparkbonaire.org/.

*The rain forests of Dominica. iStock/wanderluster*

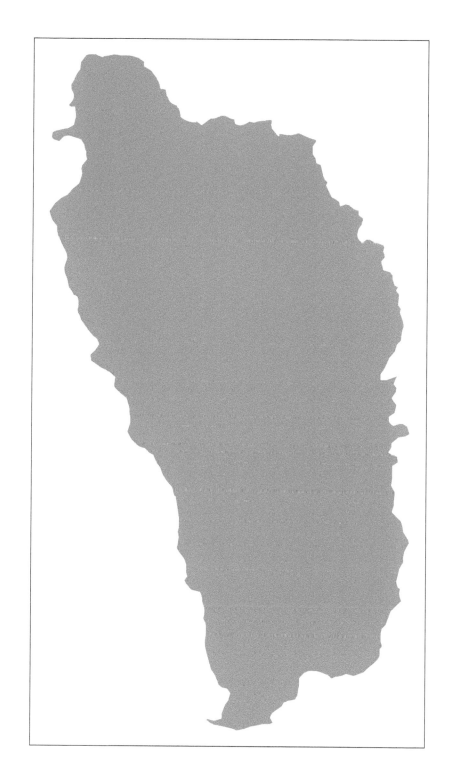

DOMINICA

# Introduction

Dominica is a small island nation in the West Indies. It is officially known as the Commonwealth of Dominica and is a member of the Commonwealth of Nations. The country is one of the largest of the Windward Islands; it lies to the north of Martinique and south of Guadeloupe. Because of its expansive national park system, thermal lake, volcanic peaks, and lush vegetation, it is often referred to as the "Nature Island of the Caribbean."

Formed by volcanic activity, the island is extremely rugged. It has extensive tropical rainforests and hot springs. Tropical fruits such as bananas, coconuts, mangoes, breadfruit, limes, and grapefruits are grown there; however, because only eight percent of the land is suitable for agriculture, most of the nation's food must be imported.

Tropical Storm Erika, which struck the island in August 2015, effected widespread destruction, including flooding and landslides, and a humanitarian crisis from which the country is still recovering. As of October 2015, reconstruction is estimated to cost $228 million. The country has been seeking aid in order to rebuild, as it does not have the resources to recover on its own. As of October 2015, Venezuela and Cuba have lent manpower and nurses, while Britain has organized engineers to assist in rebuilding distribution sources for potable water.

Dominica is one of the islands documented by 15th-century explorer Christopher Columbus and has a long history of colonialism. Nearly 87 percent of Dominica's native population is descended from the African slaves brought to the island to work the plantations during the 17th and 18th centuries. Today, Dominica is a popular destination for tourists interested in its tropical environment and beautiful scenery.

Dominican culture blends elements of French, British, and Amerindian culture with elements of nearby Caribbean cultures. The most popular sport on the island is cricket, though football (soccer) is also popular. Dominican cuisine utilizes seafood and spices, and a variety

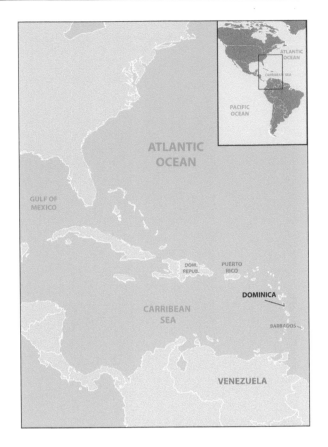

of native fruits and vegetables. Music and theatre borrow extensively from traditional French styles, but have developed into unique traditions that are similar to those found across the Caribbean.

## GENERAL INFORMATION

**Official Language(s):** English
**Population:** 73,607 (2015 estimate)
**Currency:** East Caribbean dollar (symbol: XCD)

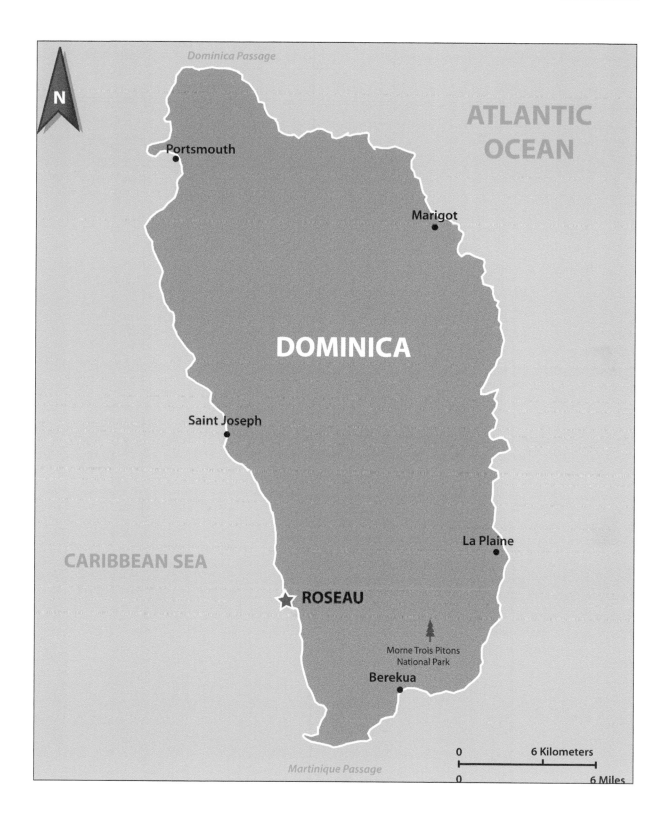

## Principal Cities by Population (2012):

- Roseau (15,000) (2014 estimate)
- Portsmouth (4,167)
- Marigot (2,411)
- Salisbury (2,147)
- Berekua (also Berricoa) (2,143)

**Coins:** The Eastern Caribbean dollar comes in coin denominations of 1, 2, 5, 10, and 25 cents; there are also one-dollar and two-dollar coins.

**Land Area:** 751 square kilometers (290 square miles)

**National Motto:** "Aprés le Bondie, C'est le Ter" (Kwéyò for "After God is the earth")

**National Anthem:** "Isle of Beauty, Isle of Splendor"

**Capital:** Roseau

**Time Zone(s):** GMT -4

**Flag Description:** The flag of Dominica uses a tri-colored cross design superimposed across a green field, a color symbolizing the island's vegetation. The cross consists of three vertical and horizontal bands of yellow (top and left), black (center), and white (bottom and right). Yellow represents the sun, the country's citrus fruits, and its native Carib Indians; black symbolizes the soil and the citizens' African heritage; while white signifies the purity of the rivers and waterfalls. A red circle, or disk, is centered in the flag's field; within the circle is the indigenous Sisserou parrot, Dominica's national bird, which is encircled by ten green, five-pointed stars edged by yellow; these stars represent the island nation's ten parishes. The red color of the central disc represents social justice.

## Population

Most Dominicans are descendents of African slaves, with 86.6 percent identifying as black. Approximately 9.1 percent of the population is composed of mixed African-Indian or African-European descent. There is a small population (2.9 percent) of native Carib Indians, who controlled the island through the 14th century. "Carib" is a term that was assigned to these peo-

ple by European colonists; there is some dispute over what the people actually called themselves. Today the Carib people live primarily on a reservation on the eastern coast of the island. Many Carib Indians have a mixed African heritage.

Roseau is the largest population center on the island. As of 2014, the Central Intelligence Agency (CIA) estimated that the capital city had a population of roughly 15,000 people, although the United Nations (UN) estimates the number as being closer to 16,500. Overall, the population is growing at a slow rate of 0.21 percent annually; this is primarily due to modest birth rates (15.41 births per 1,000 people), a nearly even infant mortality rate (11.25 deaths per 1,000 live births), and emigration away from the island. In 2015, for every 1,000 people, just over five residents were lost to migration. An estimated 69.5 percent of the total population is urban.

## Languages

English is the official language of Dominica and is used for governmental and educational purposes. Many Dominican residents also speak Kwéyòl (Dominican Creole), a form of French Creole that blends French, English, and native Amerindian linguistic elements.

## Native People & Ethnic Groups

The Carib Indians were living on Dominica when the Spanish arrived in the 15th century. Christopher Columbus named the island in 1493, after catching sight of it from his ship. This began a colonization process in which the Spanish, French, and British fought over control of the island, while the Carib people fiercely resisted colonization. The French eventually won control of part of Dominica in 1633.

Throughout the early 17th century, the Carib Indians plagued the French colonists by raiding their settlements. While the 1748 Treaty of Aix-la-Chapelle granted control of Dominica to the Caribs, the French slowly began an economic incursion into the island. They became involved with trade and also created plantations that were worked by African slaves. Although at first the Caribs tolerated the colonists, they began warring with the French once again in the mid-18th century.

The British intervened in the fighting on the pretext of protecting the Caribs, and eventually gained control of the island in 1764 after the Treaty of Paris was signed. Soon the Caribs were relegated to a small reservation on land that was poor in natural resources, and the rest of the island was divided up for private British investment. The Caribs continued to fight the British in the island's interior, with the help of escaped plantation slaves. However, they were ultimately defeated by the British in 1795.

## Religions

The religious composition of Dominica is largely a product of the island's colonial history. Over 61 percent of Dominicans practice Catholicism, while 21 percent identify with various Protestant denominations. Rastafarianism, brought to the island from surrounding Caribbean territories, accounts for 1.3 percent of the population. There is also a small population of Jehovah's Witnesses, amounting to 1.2 percent.

## Climate

Dominica has a tropical climate, and receives large amounts of precipitation each year. Elevation, air masses, and the topography of the island play a role in weather and temperature patterns, which can vary a great deal throughout the country.

The rainy season lasts from June to October, with the dry season occurring between February and May. On average, Dominica receives around 2,500 millimeters (98 inches) of rainfall per year. The capital of Roseau sees around 1,980 millimeters (78 inches) of rain, while higher altitudes can receive around 4,700 millimeters (185 inches). The most precipitation is generally recorded between July and October, when the country experiences a borderline monsoon climate.

During the day, the temperature averages between 25° and 32° Celsius (78° and 90° Fahrenheit), with September being the hottest month. In the higher mountain elevations,

temperatures can dip to 13° Celsius (55.4° Fahrenheit) and experience more extreme temperature changes than low-lying areas.

Because of its location, the island is prone to hurricanes and tropical storms. On August 27, 2015, Tropical Storm Erika struck the island. Ten inches of rain fell within one hour, causing landslides, flash flooding, widespread destruction, and subsequent loss of life.

## ENVIRONMENT & GEOGRAPHY

### Topography

Although it is a small country, Dominica is one of the largest of the Windward Islands. Its total land area amounts to 751 square kilometers (290 square miles) and has a coastline of 148 kilometers (92 miles). The island itself is 47 kilometers (29 miles) long and reaches a maximum width of 25 kilometers (16 miles).

Dominica has a steep and rugged coastline with few beaches or natural harbors. The interior of the island is mountainous and is covered with tropical rainforest. On the western side of the island, the interior mountains slope gradually down to the sea, while steep cliffs characterize the eastern coast.

The island of Dominica is volcanic; its highest peak, Morne Diablotins, has an altitude of 1,447 meters (4,747 feet). Volcanic features that can be found on the island include solfataras or volcanic vents, and a number of hot springs. The largest active sulfur geyser in the country is known as Boiling Lake, which is located just outside the capital in the Morne Trois Pitons National Park. Occasionally, this lake empties and emits dangerous sulfuric fumes.

Roseau is located in western Dominica. The city is bordered by the Caribbean Sea in the west and the Roseau (Queens) River in the north and northeast. Mountains surround Roseau and cover most of the island. Dominica has a history of volcanic activity; five active volcanoes—Morne Diablotin, Morne aux Diables, Morne Plat Pays, Morne Trois Pitons, and Morne Watt, the only one of the five to recently erupt, which occurred in 1997—are located within 10 kilometers (6.2 miles) of Roseau. Most of the city sits roughly at sea level, with a maximum elevation of 6 meters (20 feet) in the urban area.

## Plants & Animals

Because of its large expanse of rainforest, Dominica has a wide variety of tropical birds, plants, and animals. There are over 160 species of bird found there. Two native species are the Sisserou (or imperial) parrot (Amazona imperialis), which is the national bird of Dominica, and the red-necked or Jaco/Jacquot parrot (Amazona arausiaca). The blue-headed hummingbird (Cyanophaia bicolor) is also native to the island. Other birds found there include the brown pelican (Pelecanus occidentalis), the grey kingbird (tyrannus dominicensis), and the smooth-billed ani (Crotophaga ani).

Tropical flowering plants are common in Dominica. Orchids are plentiful there; the Bwa Carib orchid (Sabinea carinalis) is the country's national flower. There are over 100 species of fern on the island.

Large marine mammals, including whales, can be seen off the coast of the country, and Dominica is a sea turtle nesting destination. On land, the largest mammals are the agouti and the manacou, which is similar to the opossum. There are no poisonous snakes in Dominica; common snake species include the boa constrictor and the kouwes. Land crabs live in the tropical forests and are used in creole cooking, but are protected for part of the year in order to ensure their reproduction. The nation also boasts 55 species of butterflies.

## CUSTOMS & COURTESIES

### Greetings

English is the official language of Dominica, but many residents also speak a unique form of creole (kwéyòl), or blend of French, English, and the indigenous Carib language. French-speaking Dominicans use the word "Bon" ("Good") and the corresponding time of day as a common expression of greeting or farewell. For example, a morning greeting would be "Bon jou" ("Good day") and a common farewell would be "Bon swé" ("Good night"). The phrase "Eskize" ("Pardon me") is commonly used to get someone's attention. In some parts of the country, Dominican islanders speak a form of English creole known as Cocoy.

Dominicans shake hands in greeting, which is appropriate for both friends and acquaintances. Close friends and relatives may embrace or trade kisses upon the cheek when greeting. Men are expected to use proper etiquette when greeting unfamiliar women, and visitors are advised to allow women to determine the appropriate etiquette after greeting.

### Gestures & Etiquette

Dominicans, like many other Caribbean cultures, have an animated conversational style. They use a variety of facial gestures and hand movements to supplement verbal communication. Unlike some other cultures, smiling in the Caribbean is a default facial expression rather than an emotional expression. It is seen as a basic part of establishing a friendly, pleasant social atmosphere. In fact, people in the Caribbean in general are known for having developed a sense of humor that finds the lighter side in any situation.

While Dominicans value punctuality, social engagements such as meetings are generally scheduled within a range of time, rather than at a specific hour. Additionally, any activity, from meals to meetings, may take longer than is generally needed due to the relaxed pace in which many Dominicans (and other Caribbean people) live.

### Eating/Meals

Dominicans eat three meals a day, corresponding roughly to breakfast, lunch, and dinner in North America. Seafood is a staple of local cuisine because of the native fishing industry. Rich volcanic soil makes the island ideal for agriculture, and a variety of fruits and vegetables are grown in rural areas and sold in street markets and small retail shops.

The morning meal is typically light, consisting of coffee, fruit, and "bakes," which is dough fried in oil and sprinkled with sugar. Also popular is finely-ground cornmeal porridge that has been sweetened with sugar and served with condensed milk. Some Dominicans serve a more British-style of breakfast, involving eggs and fried meat. The mid-day meal is typically the largest meal of the day. Common dishes include seafood and fried or roasted meat dishes. The evening meal, served after dark, is generally a repeat of the midday meal, but in smaller portions. Many families simply reheat portions from the mid-day meal in the evening. Dining is usually casual in Dominica, with individuals serving themselves from communal dishes. On formal occasions, Dominicans may serve their meals in courses, consisting of plated appetizers, main courses, and desserts.

## Visiting

Dominica is an impoverished country and locals usually live modestly. Despite relative poverty, Dominicans tend to be proud of their hospitality and will often go to great lengths to make guests feel welcome. It is considered polite, but not expected, for visitors to bring small gifts, such as candies or pastries, for their hosts. Toys and candy for a host's children are also appreciated. When invited to dinner, guests are typically served first.

## LIFESTYLE

## Family

The primary domestic unit in Dominica is the nuclear family, consisting of a married or cohabiting couple and their children. Each family is also part of an extended kin group, which may include uncles, aunts, cousins, and grandparents. It is common for related families to settle close to one another, often within the same village. Some families choose to share a single household, with several generations living together for mutual benefit.

Families living in urban environments tend to more closely resemble the nuclear family units common in North America. Rural families tend to be larger with family and friends living in close proximity and cooperating in daily activities. Dominican society is built on strong community integration, where members of a single village know each other by name and often support one another. Strong community ties are bolstered by the fact that members of a single, extended family tend to settle within the same community. This factor of Dominican society has begun to change and deteriorate as individuals are forced to migrate to other parts of the country or abroad to find work.

Social stratification in Dominica is based on economic status, with the wealthiest residents forming an upper class, while most Dominicans live in, or near, established poverty levels. Approximately 29 percent of Dominicans live below the poverty line. Government workers and skilled artisans are sometimes considered members of the upper class, even if born into relative poverty.

## Housing

In Roseau and Portsmouth, the two largest cities in Dominica, families usually live in modest wooden or cement block houses, with corrugated tin roofs. Occasionally, the facades are covered with brightly painted stucco. However, by and large, houses are comprised of painted wooden siding. Few families live with more than two bedrooms, and it is common for a couple and their children to share a single-bedroom house. Wealthy families may choose to occupy buildings remaining from the French colonial period, which usually have several bedrooms and extensive green space. Wealthy families may construct homes with additional space for servants and security personnel. In comparison to Jamaica or other larger Caribbean islands, apartments are uncommon in Dominica.

Rural Dominicans typically live in small huts or houses, usually constructed with thatched or corrugated tin roofing, sheet metal, and earth or straw flooring. It is also common for Dominicans to construct their houses on stilts to avoid flooding. While urban homes usually have modern conveniences, such as electricity and on-site sanitation, rural villages may use gas or oil for light and heat and may share communal bathing and sanitation facilities. Both within villages and urban centers, housing is arranged around communal gardens and recreational facilities where residents gather to socialize and conduct business.

## Food

The Caribbean-influenced cuisine of Dominica borrows from the culinary traditions of Europe (notably Spain, France, and Britain) and has distinct African and East Indian influences. Fish and seafood are ubiquitous in Dominican cuisine, as are root vegetables such as yams and cassava, and tropical fruits such as mangoes and plantains. Cassava is also used to make bread, which is a common component of many meals. The national dish is the crapaud, involving the legs of a type of tropical frog also known as the giant ditch frog or the mountain chicken. The mountain chicken can grow as large as 167 millimeters (6.5 inches) and its legs are generally prepared roasted with sides of vegetables and rice. Crapaud is most often eaten in traditional Carib communities and is rarely served in restaurants. Moreover, crapaud is a protected species and can only be caught between October and February, making the dish seasonal.

A common entrée in Dominica is breadfruit served with salt cod, a product made by drying and preserving cod fillets in salt. Salt cod was brought to the Caribbean islands during European colonization and is still an important dietary component in many Island communities. In the Caribbean, salt cod is considered a delicacy. Breadfruit is a member of the melon family, with a pale, starchy flesh. Breadfruit was originally brought to the islands to feed African slaves but has been integrated into the local cuisine. The "johnny cake" is a pastry made from fried cornmeal flour, which has become popular in many types of Caribbean cuisine. With the morning meal, johnny cakes may be dusted in sugar or sweetened with honey. They may also be served as a savory item, with salt

and other herbs or spices mixed into the dough before frying.

Dominicans make a spicy stew known as pepper pot, which contains slow-cooked meat, like lamb, chicken or beef, cooked with onions, peppers, and spices. Traditionally, pepper pot is made with tripe (beef or pork intestine), which is a byproduct of the local meat industry. Over the centuries, pepper pot has been generalized with the inclusion of different meats and vegetables. Each Caribbean island produces a slightly different variety of pepper pot. Though originally a peasant dish, pepper pot has become a common Caribbean dish and is served in restaurants across the islands. Finally, fish broths and stewed chicken soups filled with dumplings, carrots, and other root vegetables are also widely enjoyed.

## Life's Milestones

Most Dominicans are Catholic and follow the standard Catholic traditions of baptism, communion, and marriage, each marking a transition to a new stage of life. A child's baptism is usually accompanied by a large family celebration. Those attending a baptism usually give cash gifts to the new parents and may also bring food for the celebratory feast.

Marriage is traditionally viewed as the point of transition between childhood and adulthood. In modern Dominica, cohabitation has become common, and many young Dominicans live together for years before marrying. Still, most Dominicans follow Catholic marriage traditions, including a church wedding. During the wedding ceremony, it is common for the bride's parents to escort her down the aisle. Traditionally, neither the bride nor groom designates a "maid of honor" or "best man." To celebrate the occasion, it is common for visitors to give small amounts of money or gifts to the couple. At Carib weddings, "black cake" is generally served; its name comes from the dark color imparted by the burnt sugar syrup, spices, and rum-soaked fruit incorporated into the batter. This traditional recipe, which may involve some specific family variations, is usually passed down from mother to daughter.

Dominicans usually celebrate death with a community feast and a viewing of the body, commonly followed by a church service. In contrast to the somber funerary traditions of Europeans, Caribbean funerals borrow elements from African tradition, and often include festive celebrations with music, dancing, and food accompanying funeral services.

## CULTURAL HISTORY

### Art

The native Carib tribes of Dominica are known for their traditional arts and crafts, particularly woodcarving. The art of canoe carving is considered an essential element of Caribbean cultural heritage The Caribs once carved canoes for ocean and river exploration, and many still use canoes carved by hand in the traditional manner. Canoes are usually designed in a utilitarian manner and some Caribs decorate their canoes with carved patterns or traditional designs.

Carib artisans also have a tradition of decorating gourds, which are used in both utilitarian and ceremonial fashion. Gourds may be hollowed and dried for use as storage containers, or they may be filled with dried beans and used as percussion instruments. Caribs also decorate dried gourds by carving into their surfaces. Once used for decoration and ceremonial purposes, many Carib artisans still carve dried gourds as souvenirs for tourists.

Basket weaving is another traditional art practiced by Dominica's indigenous population. Carib weaving has become important for its decorative nature in addition to functional uses. Caribs made baskets from reeds and grass and used them for utilitarian purposes such as storage. Over the centuries, weavers learned to create decorative patterns by weaving dyed leaves and different types of materials into their baskets.

### Architecture

Because Dominica was the last of the Caribbean islands to be colonized, much of its architecture is of precolonial origin. The Carib Indians (or Kalinago people) and Amerindians, who settled Dominica in the 14th century, favored wood for construction. Many of the island's houses and administrative buildings are built from native wood. This traditional architectural design involves using heavy wooden planks for the foundation. These planks were then attached to wooden pegs with mortise and tenon joints, a simple woodworking process used for centuries to join pieces of wood. Many of the island's original wooden buildings have survived, though some have been partially reclaimed by vegetation.

As Dominica entered into a period of colonization, the architecture of the island began to reflect European styles. French colonists, many from the island of Martinique, settled the Dominican towns of Bois Cotlette and Soufrière in the 18th century. (French missionaries, arriving in the 17th century, were the earliest Europeans to inhabit the island.) Most of the French colonists were employed in the sugar industry and built large, stone estate houses attached to the cane fields. Though the stone estates were built to individual specifications, many share a few basic features, including verandas, or pillared galleries, and manicured green spaces. Many estate homes were built near flowing streams with stone or wooden watermills to power the machinery used to crush sugarcane. In modern Dominica, the government protects the remaining watermills as remnants of the nation's cultural heritage.

The architecture of Roseau blends elements of colonial French and British design with modern structures. The Bay Street area along the Caribbean Sea contains a majority of the city's largest administrative and commercial buildings and is bordered by the French District, which is dominated by colonial-style, French architecture. The more distant portions of the city are zoned for residential use and are punctuated with commercial zones, which include small businesses and markets.

There are also numerous military buildings in Dominica that remain from British and French military encampments. One of the best-preserved examples of military construction is Fort Shirley, a defunct British fort located at Cabrits National Park in the northern part of the country and constructed mainly from native stone. Though usually simple in design, these military forts are of interest to architectural enthusiasts for their functional elegance.

### Drama

Theater in Dominica has its roots in the European traditions of performance art, and occurred mostly in educational settings such as schools in the mid-20th century. In 1967, the Little Theater (which became the People's Action Theatre, or PAT) was founded. As the group progressed in the 1970s and 1980s, they staged local, original productions as well as treatments of Broadways shows such as *Jesus Christ Superstar*. In 1978, the government established a cultural division to further support the arts, and the theater scene expanded. In the early 21st century, modern theater in Dominica is driven by the New Dimension Theatre, which was recognized in 2010 by the government and national culture council for theater development on the island.

### Music

Dominican culture is a blend of indigenous, European, and West African cultural and social traditions. West African culture, imported by the slave trade, is particularly evident in Dominican music and dance. Drums are an important traditional instrument and represent connections with the African heritage of Dominica; they are frequently made from wood and animal skins or metal. Flutes in Dominica are traditionally crafted from bamboo. Other folk instruments include a drum called the tambou bele; a long hollow bamboo flute known as the boom-boom; a gwaj, which is a grater and rubbed with a thin steel stick; a shak-shak, the equivalent of maracas; and the accordion. This type of music is called "jing ping" in Dominica and is said to have originated among the slave populations on the plantations of Dominica.

Zouk music, which is considered native to the French West Indies, is a blend of Haitian compas, West African dance, and Latin American music. Zouk became popular in the 1980s, when a number of prominent Caribbean bands began to gain national attention. Dominica is also a major hub for cadence-lypso, which is a blend of calypso and Haitian compas, and was popularized in the 1970s by Dominican musician Gordon Henderson. Since the 1970s, cadence-lypso has evolved by absorbing elements of American funk music.

In 1988, the Dominican band Windward Caribbean Kulture (WCK) emerged from Roseau, bringing a new type of music to the local and global scene. WCK's new style, which came to be known as bouyon, is a mixture of African and Caribbean elements. Bouyon uses modern instruments with traditional African rhythms. WCK was the first Dominican band to gain international fame with their 1993 release, *Forever*.

At Carnival, which is the most popular holiday in Dominica, West African dancing and music are a major part of the festivities. Many dancers at the Carnival wear "sensay costume," a type of clothing developed for African fertility ceremonies. Sensay costumes are covered with hundreds of strips of colorful cloth that accentuate the movements of the dancers. In 1997, Dominica hosted the first World Creole Music Festival, which has since become an annual tradition. In 2008, the Creole Music Festival attracted hundreds of bands from Dominica and many of its Caribbean neighbors. Now known as the World Creole Music Festival, the event was cancelled in 2015 because of damages and deaths following Tropical Storm Erika. However, relief concerts to assist in the country's recovery are being held in the festival's stead.

### Literature

Natives of Dominica have made important contributions to Western culture in the arts and literature. Jean Rhys (1890–1979)—also known as Ella Gwendolen Rees Williams—authored the 1939 novel *Good Morning, Midnight* and the 1966 postcolonial novel *Wide Sargasso Sea*, which is intended as a prequel to Charlotte Brontë's *Jane Eyre*. Phyllis Shand Allfrey (1908–1986) was a Dominican writer who also helped start the Dominican Labor Party. Other writers associated with Dominica include Elma Napier (1892–1973), a Scottish-born author who became the first woman elected to a Caribbean parliament, and Dominica-born Phyllis Shand Allfrey (1908–1986), whose 1953 novel *The Orchid House*, a progressive look at class in the colonial Caribbean, is considered a major work of the West Indian (or Caribbean) canon of literature.

## CULTURE

### Arts & Entertainment

The artistic community in Dominica is small and public arts projects are uncommon. Funding for the arts is limited, and artists often rely on commercial sales to maintain their businesses. The government has paid to erect several statues dedicated to important historic events in Dominican history, like the transition to independence. The government also honors local individuals and groups who contribute to art and culture through the annual Golden Drum Awards. Started in 1984, fields recognized through the awards range from herbal medicine and traditional dance to modern theater and the graphic arts.

In Roseau and Portsmouth, independent art galleries sell locally produced arts and crafts to collectors and tourists. Festivals include the annual Carnival celebration, which includes music, dance, performance art, and an exhibition of local art, as well as the World Creole Music Festival and Dive Fest (a scuba diving festival).

The most popular sport in Dominica is cricket. (It is said that every village in the West Indies has a cricket team.) International cricket is played at Dominica's Windsor Park stadium in Roseau. Other sports enjoyed by the Dominicans include football (soccer), tennis, basketball, and volleyball. Visitors to Dominica often participate in hiking trips, snorkeling, and scuba diving.

### Cultural Sites & Landmarks

Dominica is known as the "Nature Isle of the Caribbean," and has wealth of sites protected for their ecological or biological importance. Morne

Trois Pitons National Park, one of Dominica's premier ecological preserves, was designated by the United Nations Educational Scientific and Cultural Organization (UNESCO) as a World Heritage Site in 1997. The park occupies nearly 7,000 hectares (20.4 square miles), including lush tropical forest and an active volcano known as Morne Trois Pitons. It is the island nation's only entry on the World Heritage List, and the first UNESCO World Heritage Site in the Eastern Caribbean.

Visitors to Morne Trois Pitons can also visit Boiling Lake, a 63-meter (200-foot) boiling pool of mud and water heated by subterranean steam from the volcanic activity deep below the park. There are miles of hiking trails throughout the park, leading to numerous waterfalls and mountain pools. Among the hiking paths visitors can also find Ti Tou Gorge, a deep passage within the forest containing a pool where hot and cool water mix.

Within the capital of Roseau, visitors will find French and British battlements left from the nation's colonial period. Fort Young, located on the coast a short distance from the public library, is a major tourist attraction for its architectural beauty and oceanic landscape. Tours of Fort Young are available to tourists and many locals visit the fort for recreation. Portions of the fort have been reconstructed over the years to repair damage from weathering. Many visitors come to Roseau to enjoy the city's markets. Open-air markets open in the city several times each week and sell fruits, vegetables, and a variety of native crafts. The Old Market Place, which was once part of the city's slave market, now contains an iron memorial to commemorate the history of the island's slave trade. The market now has a variety of shops and serves as an urban park for the city's residents.

The Government House is the current headquarters for the Dominican government, though the building was originally constructed to house the nation's colonial governors. Built in the late 18th century, the Government House is of interest because of its colonial architecture; it also serves as the official residence for the president of Dominica. The Government House is surrounded by extensive gardens, which were reconstructed after suffering extensive hurricane damage in the 1970s.

The area on top of Morne Bruce Hill is a popular destination for visitors to Roseau, as its hilltop provides panoramic views of the city. Below the hill is the Dominica Botanic Gardens, the largest area of green space in Roseau. The Botanic Gardens are located on a former sugarcane plantation. The Botanic Gardens cover approximately 16 hectares (40 acres) and is divided into two sections, one for ornamental and exotic plants and one for the cultivation of scientifically and economically important species. In addition to showcasing native and imported plant species, the Botanic Gardens host cricket matches and national ceremonies.

Recreational scuba divers and maritime explorers have been coming to Dominica for decades to explore the island's rich marine reserves. Dominica has three major marine reserves, including the Soufriere Scotts Head Bay off the southern coast and the Cabrits Marine Reserve in the north. Diving is only permitted within established marine reserves in an effort to protect the integrity of the nation's marine habitats. Dominica's marine environments are home to a wide variety of marine life, including lush coral forests with a vast array of indigenous creatures.

## Libraries & Museums

The Dominica Museum, which is located near the old market area in Roseau, provides a visual tour of the nation's history. The museum contains Amerindian relics and artifacts, as well as photographs related to the slavery era and colonial period.

Main libraries in the country include the National Documentation Centre, the Roseau Public Library, and the Portsmouth Library. Along with the public libraries in Roseau and Portsmouth, the Grand Bay Branch Library, and the Marigot Branch Library make up the country's National Library Service (which, along with the National Archives and the National Documentation Centre, constitutes the Dominica Library and Information Service). The library system also operates a mobile library.

## Holidays

Carnival is a month-long celebration in Dominica that traditionally begins before the Catholic season of Lent. Two days of Carnival are devoted to street festivals, parades, and musical performances. Traditional Carnival performers include stilt walkers, who are known as "moko jumbies." Calypso music is frequently played throughout the holiday.

Carib Week is celebrated in Dominica each September to commemorate a violent conflict that occurred between the government and the Carib population in 1930. It involves youth rallies, debates, and events that celebrate the Carib culture and people.

## Youth Culture

Education is free and compulsory between the ages of five and sixteen, though poverty, agricultural responsibilities, and poor school conditions, including overcrowding, continue to deter participation. Severe poverty levels, particularly in the early 21st century, have also forced many Dominican teens and adolescents to find work at a young age. Tourism has been a primary source of income for many youth, and Dominicans often work as tour guides or in the service industry. However, jobs remain scarce, leading to a life in the streets for some youth. The National Youth Council of Dominica (NYCD), along with the Caribbean Federation of Youth (CFY), has helped create educational, vocational, and outreach programs for Dominican children and teens.

The youth culture of Dominica is a mixture of Caribbean elements coupled with imported culture, notably music and fashion. For example, calypso, reggae, Jamaican dancehall, and other styles of Caribbean music are popular among youth, as is hip-hop, rap, and rock. Dominica has particularly strong ties to France, and French literature and foreign films also have a strong following. American culture has also become increasingly popular, as most Dominicans also speak English. Cricket is the most popular sport in Dominica, and many youth organizations revolve around amateur sports, such as football (soccer).

## SOCIETY

### Transportation

There is no state-sponsored public transportation in Dominica, but privately-owned minibuses are common and provide transport within the cities and to surrounding rural areas. Minibuses can be recognized by their bright paint schemes and license plates beginning with the capital letter "H." Traffic moves on the left-hand side of the road.

### Transportation Infrastructure

There are approximately 780 kilometers (485 miles) of roads in Dominica, of which only a little over half—393 kilometers (244 miles)—are paved. The island's largest road is a circular stretch of highway called the Transinsular Road, which links Roseau with Portsmouth, Belles with Marigot, and connects to smaller roads radiating out to the rest of the country.

The Douglas-Charles Airport (formerly the Melville Hall Airport) near Marigot and an hour outside Portsmouth is the country's only international airport and one of only two paved airports in the nation, with the other being Canefield Airport, three miles northeast of Roseau. Most flights into or out of Dominica connect through one of the larger Caribbean islands, including Antigua and Barbados. From Canefield, the airlines Hummingbird Air and Coastal Air makes flights to St. Thomas and St. Croix. In August 2015, Douglas-Charles was temporarily closed due to damages wrought by Tropical Storm Erika. According to airport officials, much of the airport's equipment was damaged beyond use.

Dominica has two major oceanic ports at Portsmouth and Roseau, both of which offer limited passenger services. Most maritime traffic in Dominica is commercial, carrying crops and industrial products to nearby ports.

## Media & Communications

Dominican media are produced in two languages French and English. There are no daily newspapers or magazines published in Dominica, but the country has several weekly publications. The nation's largest newspaper—*The Sun*—is still published in print form weekly in English. However, most news media have moved to an online format. These include *Dominica News Online*, *Dominica Vibes*, and *The Dominican*.

The Dominica Broadcasting Company (DBC) is the nation's sole broadcasting company, providing both music and news programs. The DBC is owned by the government and funded through tax revenues. Radio Antilles, which broadcasts from nearby Montserrat, has become the second most popular radio station in the country. Dominica has no local television programs, but there is limited cable television coverage in Roseau, Portsmouth, and surrounding areas.

Dominica has no censorship restrictions on publications, television, or Internet coverage, and journalists regularly publish and broadcast views critical of the government. The government has only begun to shift information and services to the Internet. Dominica's Internet usage was estimated at nearly 59.1 percent of the population in 2014, with 43,400 Internet users.

## SOCIAL DEVELOPMENT

### Standard of Living

Dominica ranked 93 out of 187 countries on the 2014 United Nations Human Development Index (HDI), which measures quality of life and standard of living indicators using 2012 data.

Dominica has been one of the poorest Caribbean nations since the 19th century. As of 2014, 29 percent of the population lives in poverty and the unemployment rate stands at 23 percent. Roseau is underdeveloped in comparison to other Caribbean capitals. Less than a third of the island has adequate plumbing and waste is often released directly into the ocean. Public transportation consists largely of private taxi services and boats that carry passengers along the sea or through the Roseau River.

## Water Consumption

Dominica has an abundant supply of freshwater, and water and sanitation services in urban areas are relatively high. As a broad definition, as of 2015, approximately 95.7 percent of the population has access to improved drinking water sources and nearly 81.1 percent has access to improved sanitation.

## Education

Education in Dominica is directed by the Ministry of Education, and is based on the school systems in Great Britain and the United States. Schooling is compulsory for children between the ages of five and sixteen.

The government provides free education for all in state-run schools and has been focusing on providing its teachers with necessary training and preparation. The Catholic Church also has a large number of schools in the country; approximately 22 percent of primary students and 46 percent of secondary students attend Catholic schools.

There are four levels of education: pre-primary, primary, secondary, and tertiary. Basic education stresses reading, writing, and mathematics. Students must pass examinations to continue on to the secondary level of education.

The University of the West Indies has a campus in Dominica, as does the Dominica State University (formerly Clifton Dupigny Community College) in Roseau. Other tertiary institutions include Ross University School of Medicine in Portsmouth and All Saints University of Medicine in Roseau. Tertiary education also includes technical education and certification. The country has an average literacy rate of about 94 percent (2015).

## Women's Rights

One of the most prevalent issues facing women in Dominica is domestic violence. This is due to cultural norms that favor male dominance and discourage women from reporting to authorities. Furthermore, there are no laws specifically prohibiting spousal abuse in Dominica, and cases are prosecuted under general laws covering battery. The penal code, however, allows women to request protection from an abusive spouse without legal representation. Spousal rape is covered under the same provisions as other forms of rape, with prison sentences of up to 25 years, depending on the circumstances of the violation.

Few non-governmental organizations (NGOs) serve the island nation's female population. Instead, church outreach remains an option for abused women. The Dominican National Council of Women (DNCW), which operates a shelter in Roseau, provides counseling and outreach services for victims and their dependants. The Ministry of Community Development and the Women's Bureau were responsible for counseling rape victims and often coordinate with other organizations, including the DNCW.

The availability of gainful employment for women also remains an issue. In 2008, more than 50 percent of women were unemployed, and those who found employment tended to work in low-level positions or worked in the health, educational, and service sectors. These circumstances have continued into 2015. Additionally, few women obtain management positions and women, on average, earn less than their male counterparts in similar positions do. There are also no laws prohibiting sexual harassment in the workplace and NGO investigations have found that a large number of women suffered from some form of harassment. The Bureau of Gender Affairs, the governmental agency under the Ministry of Social Services, Community Development, and Gender Affairs responsible for lobbying for women's rights, has used marches, protests, and paid advertisements in recent years to raise awareness about these collective issues.

## Health Care

Health care in Dominica is administered by the Ministry of Health, and the government is working toward a national health insurance plan. The island has seven health centers and forty-four clinics. The largest hospital and major trauma center is the Princess Margaret Hospital, located in Roseau.

Some common medical problems in Dominica include a variety of intestinal, bacterial, and parasitic diseases; tuberculosis; and various sexually transmitted diseases. Diabetes is also a major health problem there, and in 2014, nearly 26 percent of the population was obese. The most problematic endemic disease is dengue fever, which is spread by mosquitoes and causes internal hemorrhaging.

Pregnant women have access to government-funded prenatal care. Child immunization rates are at or near 100 percent, although there have been outbreaks of measles in the country.

## GOVERNMENT

### Structure

After resolving conflicting territorial claims with Great Britain and Spain, France successfully established a colony on Dominica in 1635 and claimed the island for its own. France lost the island to Britain in the Treaty of Paris, which was signed in 1783 following the Seven Years' War.

Dominica remained a British colony until late 1978. Slavery was abolished on the island in 1833, and the black population began to gain political power and civil rights. Unhappy with the rising legislative power of the free black population, white plantation owners lobbied for more control. As a result, civil and political rights of free blacks were scaled back in 1865 following political reforms.

In the latter half of the 20th century, Britain began to prepare Dominica for independence. In 1967, the country gained more control over its internal administration and was known as an associated state of Great Britain. Dominica was granted full independence from Britain on November 3, 1978.

Today, Dominica is a parliamentary democracy and is a republic within the Commonwealth of Nations. Its government and legal system are modeled on those of Great Britain. The president and a prime minister make up the executive branch. The president serves for five years and is nominated by both the prime minister and the opposition party leader and ultimately elected by the House of Assembly. The president is eligible only for a second term.

Parliament, which forms the unicameral legislative branch of government, consists of the House of Assembly. The house is made up of thirty-two seats: twenty-one are directly elected representatives; nine are senators appointed by the existing House of Assembly; and two are ex-officio members. House members serve renewable, five-year terms.

### Political Parties

The country's main political parties are the Dominica Labour Party (DLP), the Dominica Freedom Party, the People's Democratic Union, and United Workers' Party (UWP). Essentially, the country has a two-party system, with the United Workers' Party and the Dominica Labour Party being the two dominant parties. The Dominica Labour Party won fifteen seats in the 2014 general elections, and the United Workers' Party, again the only other party represented besides independent candidates, won six seats.

### Local Government

Local government consists of town and village councils, which manage local affairs such as road maintenance. The island is also separated into ten administrative parishes; each is named after a saint, reflecting the long-standing influence of Roman Catholicism: Saint Andrew, Saint David, Saint George, Saint John, Saint Joseph, Saint Luke, Saint Mark, Saint Patrick, Saint Paul, and Saint Peter. The town council of Portsmouth and city council of Roseau are each headed by mayors. A Carib Council separately manages the affairs of the island's Carib Reserve. Local elections are held every three years, with the exception of the Carib Reserve Council, the elections of which occur every five years.

## Judicial System

The judicial system is modeled after English common law, and, since 2001, Dominica has been a member of the Caribbean Court of Justice (CCJ), based in Trinidad and Tobago. CCJ has jurisdiction over first instance and appellate cases. As of July 2014, Dominica's parliament has passed a bill making CCJ the final court of appeal. Lower courts include the Court of Summary Jurisdiction and local magistrate courts.

## Taxation

As of January 2015, taxes are levied at a graduated rate and apply to regular income, rents, dividends, pensions, and overseas proceeds. No taxes are imposed on earnings below XCD$25,000. However, there is tax of 15 percent on incomes between XCD$25,001 and XCD$45,000; 30 percent on income XCD$45,001 and XCD$75,000; and 35 percent on every dollar in excess of XCD$75,000. Other taxes include an environmental tax, value-added tax (or VAT, a consumption-like tax), and excise taxes.

## Armed Forces

Dominica does not maintain military forces. The Commonwealth of Dominica Police Force, which includes a Coast Guard, numbered about 400 in 2008 and nearly 450 in 2011. It handles matters of security. The minimum recruitment age is 18.

## Foreign Policy

Dominica is an active member of the international community and focuses primarily on Caribbean issues. One of the primary goals of its foreign policy, if not the main objective, is to create economic expansion and foreign investment within the country. It holds membership in various regional organizations, including the Organization of Eastern Caribbean States (OECS), the Caribbean Development Bank (CDB), the Caribbean Community (CARICOM), and the Organization of American States (OAS). Internationally, Dominica maintains membership in organizations such as the International Monetary Fund (IMF); the Commonwealth of Nations, which is largely comprised of former British colonies; the International Criminal Court; and the World Bank. Dominica is also a founding member of the United Nations (UN).

Dominica has established close ties with the United States, which has donated to Dominica's internal growth programs through the CDB and the US Agency for International Development (USAID). Dominica has also been supportive of US-led policies and initiatives in the UN, and the United States remains an important trading partner. Dominica also has trade agreements with Europe and the People's Republic of China. China is the country's primary trading partner, accounting for almost a quarter of Dominica's exports. Dominica also maintains a territorial dispute with Venezuela over Isla de Aves (or Aves Island, "Island of Birds"), a small islet west of Dominica. Many believe the uninhabited island is located near natural oil or gas deposits.

Despite not having a serious drug trafficking problem itself, Dominica is also a hub of the multinational effort to control drug trafficking in the Caribbean. Working with the United States and other Caribbean states, Dominica is attempting to prevent the oceanic shipment of illicit drugs. Dominica maintains extradition treaties with the United States to prevent drug traffickers from taking refuge in the country. While Dominica participates actively in the international anti-drug effort, estimates indicate that there are few drugs grown or manufactured on the island itself.

Tropical Storm Erika of August 2015 and the devastation it wrought have made Dominica entirely reliant upon foreign aid and manpower. To date, Venezuela, Cuba, Britain, Brazil, China, Trinidad, and Tobago, and the United States have provided emergency aid in the form of medical professionals, manpower, equipment, and emergency money to assist in humanitarian efforts, clearing landslides, reopening the international airport, and rebuilding bridges and roadways washed away by floods and landslides.

## Human Rights Profile

International human rights law insists that states respect civil and political rights and also promote an individual's economic, social, and cultural rights. The United Nations Universal Declaration on Human Rights (UDHR) is recognized as the standard for international human rights. Its authors sought the counsel of the world's great thinkers, philosophers, and religious leaders and were careful to create a document that reflects the core values shared by every world culture. (To read this document or view the articles relating to cultural human rights, go to: http://www.ohchr.org/EN/UDHR/Pages/Introduction.aspx).

Dominica is a constitutional republic with a positive record of upholding human rights to the standards set by the UDHR. Though plagued by insufficient funding and training, the Dominican police force is generally effective and has a positive record of punishing officers for the use of excessive force in making arrests or detaining suspects. Prison conditions, however, remain an area of concern for human rights monitoring agencies. Investigations have revealed that the nation's sole prison, known as Stock Farm, is overcrowded and in need of repair. Inmates also suffer from poor sanitation and a lack of adequate medical facilities. In 2008, Stock Farm's inmate population exceeded safety levels by more than 100 inmates, and in 2010, that inmate number was still estimated to be 289, still exceptionally high. However, the Dominica Prison Service has begun a training program whereby inmates are educated in agricultural and animal husbandry, as well as construction trades like masonry, in order to improve their prospects upon release.

One pressing problem in Dominica is the prevalence of violence against women and children. Although monitoring agencies reported that the government's commitment to child welfare was legitimate, child abuse remained common at home and in the school system. According to international investigations, police inefficiency is the primary factor affecting the continuing child abuse problem. In addition, the government welfare department, which is responsible for protecting at-risk children and providing outreach services, is critically underfunded. The Dominican government established a new program in 2007 to increase funding for child abuse.

However, while awareness of the problem is high in the country in 2015, UNICEF and the Government of the Commonwealth of Dominica still find the rates are too high and estimate that many incidents go unreported.

The indigenous Kalinago population, estimated at approximately 4,000 individuals in the early 21st century, suffers from widespread discrimination. The government recognizes the rights of the Kalinago and provides for their welfare through programs offered by the Ministry of Education. Although discrimination against the Kalinago is not related to governmental or institutional discrimination, some international human rights agencies working with the Kalinago community believe that the government does not effectively ensure that they are protected from abuse from the general population.

## ECONOMY

### Overview of the Economy

For the most part, Dominica relies on the agricultural sector to support its economy. The banana industry is the most important agricultural sector, employing 40 percent of the country's workers. Like other agricultural products, the banana crop is susceptible to weather-induced problems and price fluctuations on the world market. For this reason, hurricanes have had a devastating effect on the country's economy.

The services industry, including banking and financial services, restaurants, hotels, and tourism services, accounts for more than 71.1 percent of the GDP and employs 28 percent of the island's residents

The capital of Roseau and the town of Portsmouth are the country's two major international ports. Dominica belongs to the Eastern Caribbean Currency Union (ECCU), the Caribbean Community and Common Market (CARICOM), and the Organization of Eastern Caribbean States (OECS).

In 2014, its estimated gross domestic product (GDP) was $764 million USD; its per capita GDP was around $10,800 USD.

## Industry

More than one-third of the island's residents are involved in industrial employment, including timber processing. Export of furniture and textiles has become an important industry in the 20th and 21st centuries, though the government is attempting to regulate the industry in hopes of preserving natural resources. Soap, coconut oil, cement products, and rubber footwear are among the island's chief products; factories that produce these products can be found in the areas surrounding Roseau. In 2013, soap exports totaled about $11.4 million (USD). In addition to soap, Dominica's manufactured exports also include coconut byproducts and clothing. Industrial exports brought in $60.5 million (USD) in 2013. The country's five largest importers of Dominican goods are Jamaica ($10.4 million), Saudi Arabia ($8.12 million), Guatemala ($5.38 million), Guyana ($5.25 million), and France ($3.49 million).

## Labor

The unemployment rate in the country has remained at 23 percent since the first decade of the 21st century. Many Dominican workers continue to emigrate in the effort to find better employment opportunities. Approximately 28 percent of the workforce is employed in the service industries, while 32 percent are employed in industry and manufacturing.

## Energy/Power/Natural Resources

From colonial times, timber has been an important natural resource for Dominica. Water is plentiful and is used to create hydropower.

Pumice, a type of stone created by volcanic activity, is important to the island's construction industry. Other useful mineral deposits and soil resources include copper, limestone, and clay.

## Fishing

Dominica's artisanal fishing industry mostly meets domestic demand. Though many of the island's residents engage in fishing, the export of fish products has not significantly contributed to economic growth. Commercial species include blue marlin, big-eye and yellowfin tuna, skipjack, mackerel, ballyhoo, sailfish, wahoo, dorado, and prawn (inland). Unlawful fishing by foreign vessels in territorial waters has been a concern. The fishing sector was severely affected by Hurricane Dean in 2007, but has since recovered.

## Forestry

It was estimated that, at the turn of the 21st century, forested land accounted for 61 percent of the total land area. By 2011, this number dropped, with just 59.2 percent of the island covered in forests. Dominica's Forestry, Wildlife and Parks Division, established in 1949 and part of the country's Department of Agriculture, oversees forestry management, but has, to date, emphasized the development of National Parks and ecotourism over regulating commercial logging. The most sought-after species include mahogany, teak, and blue mahoe.

## Mining/Metals

Commonly mined materials include sand, gravel, clay, limestone, and volcanic ash. After an international mining company applied for a prospector's license in the late 1990s to mine copper in the island's northeastern quadrant, the government formally investigated the possibility of copper mining as a potential source of revenue and explored its potential economic value in relation to environmental risks in 2008. To date, however, copper mining has not been pursued.

## Agriculture

Because of its steep terrain and its heavy rainforest, there are few large farms in Dominica. Most of these are located in valleys throughout the island, although these are few in number. Small farmers often plant banana trees and other crops in steeper areas, where they have cut away the rainforest. In spite of the country's sparse farmland, 40 percent of the population is engaged in agriculture.

Bananas, which bring in about half of the country's GDP, are the most important crop in Dominica; however, citrus fruits like exotic fruits, flowers, limes, coconuts, copra, and the coconut oil that is pressed from it have become viable exports. Fruit and flower byproducts, such as essential oils and extracts, have also become more important to trade. Most staple foods in Dominica must be imported, generally from Japan, Trinidad and Tobago, and the United States.

## Animal Husbandry

Cattle, sheep, and goats are the primary livestock, with hogs, rabbits, and poultry raised to a lesser extent. Livestock production is generally modest; as of 2008, the largest cattle farm had eighty heads of cattle. Livestock is largely raised for domestic or family consumption. In 2014, the Dominica Prison Service began small-scale livestock breeding not only to provide meat for the prison population, but to provide inmates with future self-sufficiency skills.

## Tourism

In 2014, according to the Caribbean Tourism Organization (CTO), Dominica was the fourth least-visited island in the Caribbean and had just 78,277 stay-over visitors, 0.4 percent of the Caribbean's total arrival numbers for 2014. Only St. Vincent & The Grenadines, Anguilla, and Monterrat had fewer stay-over visitors. Cruise ships account for much of the country's tourist traffic. Some of Dominica's tourist attractions include rainforest hikes, swimming, scenic waterfalls, hot springs, and scuba diving. Snorkeling just off Champagne Beach and near the city of Portsmouth is also a popular activity. Dominica's beaches are unusual, with black or gray volcanic sands and a fairly rocky terrain, making sunbathing less popular than on other islands.

Ecotourism (tourist activities that have little or no negative impact on the environment) is the fastest growing economic industry. Moreover, the fact that two of the *Pirates of Caribbean* movies, *Dead Man's Chest* (2006) and *At World's End* (2007), were shot in Dominica has similarly helped to increase interest in the island. However, the Ministry of Tourism is implementing a long-range plan to improve stay-over tourist numbers between 2012 and 2022, including making improvements to Roseau and Portsmouth as well as upgrading buildings, beachfronts, and restaurants, of which there are still relatively few. However, the 2015 devastation caused by Tropical Storm Erika, which entombed some ecotourism resorts in landslide mud and washed away some bridges and roads, will likely have a negative impact on tourist arrival numbers for several years to come.

*Micah Issitt, Christina Healey, & Savannah Schroll Guz*

---

## DO YOU KNOW?

- The name "Roseau" was taken from the French term, "Roseaux," which refers to the reeds that grow along the Roseau River. Roseau was originally called 'Sairi' by the Kalinago people who settled in the area before the French arrived.

- Dominica has a mountainous terrain with only 10 percent of the land having a gradient of less than ten degrees. Because of the mountainous terrain, agriculture is sometimes challenging. According to 2011 estimates, less than 35 percent of Dominica is designated agricultural land, with eight percent of it arable.

- Christopher Columbus named Dominica after the Latin term for "Sunday," the day on which the island was first spied by the explorer.

## Bibliography

Aceto, Michael and Jeffrey Payne Williams. *Contact Englishes of the Eastern Caribbean*. Philadelphia, PA: John Benjamins Publishing Company, 2003. Varieties of English Around the World Ser.

Atwood, Thomas. *The History of the Island of Dominica*. Digital ed. Charlottesville, VA: University of Virginia Press, 2015.

Crask, Paul. *Dominica*. 2nd ed. Bucks, UK: Bradt Travel Guides, 2014.

Dominica National Development Corporation Division of Tourism. *Discover Dominica: The Nature Island of the Caribbean*. Oregon, Warren Associates Publishing, 1997.

Honychurch, Lennox. *Dominica: Isle of Adventure*. New York: McMillan Publishers Ltd., 1995.

_____. *The Dominica Story: A History of the Island*. New York: McMillan Publishing Ltd., 1995.

Pattullo, Polly. *Your Time Is Done Now: Slavery, Resistance, and Defeat: The Maroon Trials of Dominica (1813–1814)*. New York: Monthly Review Press, 2015. Web.

Rogonzinsky, Jan. A *Brief History of the Caribbean: From the Arawak and Carib to the Present*. 2nd ed. New York: Plume, 2000.

Saunders, Nicholas J. *The Peoples of the Caribbean: An Encyclopedia of Archeology and Traditional Culture*. Santa Barbara, CA: ABC-Clio Publishing, 2005.

Sullivan, Lynne M. *Adventure Guide to Dominica and St. Lucia*. Walpole, MA: Hunter Publishing, 2004.

Williams, Eric. *From Columbus to Castro: The History of the Caribbean 1492–1969*. New York: Vintage Books, 1984.

## Works Cited

Central Intelligence Agency. "Dominica." *The World Factbook*. Central Intelligence Agency, 2015. Web. https://www.cia.gov/library/publications/the-world-factbook/geos/do.html.

"Country Profile: Dominica." *BBC NEWS*. BBC, 16 Aug. 2012. Web. http://news.bbc.co.uk/2/hi/americas/country_profiles/1166435.stm.

Crask, Paul. "Dominica Asks for Aid after Tropical Storm Erika Devastates Island." *The Guardian*. Guardian News and Media Limited 4 Sept. 2015. http://www.theguardian.com/world/2015/sep/04/dominica-asks-for-aid-tropical-storm-erika-damage.

"Dominica among 10 Least Visited Caribbean Countries." *Dominica News Online*. Dominica News Online/Duravision Inc., 17 Sept. 2014. Web. http://dominicanewsonline.com/news/homepage/news/tourism-publicity/dominica-among10-least-visited-caribbean-countries/.

*Dominica's Wildlife and Forestry Division*. Delphis Ltd., 2006. Web. http://www.avirtualdominica.com/forestry/.

Government of the Commonwealth of Dominica. "Bureau of Gender Affairs." *Ministry of Social Services, Family, & Gender Affairs*. Ministry of Social Services, Family and Gender Affairs, 2015. Web. http://socialservices.gov.dm/index.php/divisions/bureau-of-gender-affairs.

_____. "Farming and Animal Husbandry." *Dominica Prison Service*. Government of the Commonwealth of Dominica, 2015. Web. http://prisons.gov.dm/programmes/farming-and-animal-husbandry.

_____. "Poll Says Child Abuse Rate Concerning for Dominica." *Government Information Service Dominica*. Government of the Commonwealth of Dominica, 5 Mar. 2015. Web. http://news.gov.dm/index.php/news/2287–poll-says-child-abuse-rate-concerning-for-dominica.

_____. "Tax Rates." *IRD & You*. Inland Revenue Division, 2015. Web. http://ird.gov.dm/index.php?option=com_content&view=article&id=127&Itemid=106.

Harris-Charles, Emaline L. and Carlisle A. Pemberton. "Copper Mining and Environmental Costs in Dominica." *Farm & Business: The Journal of the Caribbean Agro-Economic Society (CAES)* 7.1 (2007): 103–121. PDF file.

"Introducing Dominica." *Lonely Planet Online*. Lonely Planet, 2015. Web. http://www.lonelyplanet.com/dominica.

Marsteller, Amanda. "Caribbean Black Cake." *Honest Cooking Gastronomy & Travel*. Honest Cooking, 4 Jan. 2013. Web. http://honestcooking.com/caribbean-black-cake/.

Simoes, Alex. "Dominica." *The Observatory of Economic Complexity*. Massachusetts Institute of Technology, 2015. Web. http://atlas.media.mit.edu/en/profile/country/dma/.

"Travel & Tourism in Dominica." *Euromonitor International*. Euromonitor, July 2014. Web. http://www.euromonitor.com/travel-and-tourism-in-dominica/report.

UN Development Programme. "Table 1: Human Development Index and Its Components." *Human Development Reports*. UNDP, 2015. Web. http://hdr.undp.org/en/content/table-1-human-development-index-and-its-components.

UNICEF. "Dominica: Statistics." *UNICEF Online*. UNICEF, 2015. Web. http://www.unicef.org/infobycountry/dominica_statistics.html.

World Health Organization. "Dominica." *World Health Organization Online*. WHO, 2015. Web. http://www.who.int/countries/dma/en/.

# DOMINICAN REPUBLIC

# Introduction

Located on an island discovered by Christopher Columbus during his 1492 voyage, the Dominican Republic is located between the Caribbean Sea and the Atlantic Ocean. The national capital is Santo Domingo, the oldest city in the Americas. The country occupies the eastern two-thirds of the island of Hispaniola, which it shares with Haiti. The Dominican Republic's culture has been shaped by European, African, and indigenous Caribbean influences. Starting out as a Spanish colony, the country eventually gained independence in 1844 from the Haitians, who ruled them for twenty-two years following their first rebellion against the Spanish in 1821. After voluntarily returning to the Spanish Empire in 1861, they again launched an independence war in 1863 that won back their autonomy by 1865.

The Dominican Republic is host to two Masterpieces of the Oral and Intangible Heritage of Humanity as designated by the United Nations Educational, Scientific and Cultural Organization (UNESCO). One, proclaimed by UNESCO in 2001, is the Cultural Space of the Brotherhood of the Holy Spirit of the Congos of Villa Mella, a musical group that plays at festivals and funerals and retains the traditions of the 16th-century group. The second, proclaimed in 2005, is the Cocolo dancing drama tradition, a custom that survives from mid-19th century Caribbean slaves.

The worlds of music and dance also owe thanks to the Dominican Republic for giving them the merengue. The merengue is a uniquely Dominican style of music and dance that is largely recognized as the country's national dance.

Baseball maintains its important status in both the popular and youth cultures in the Dominican Republic. Numerous Major League Baseball (MLB) organizations continue to employ scouts based in the country, and Dominicans who can make a living as a professional baseball player in the United States are seen as role models and celebrities on the island.

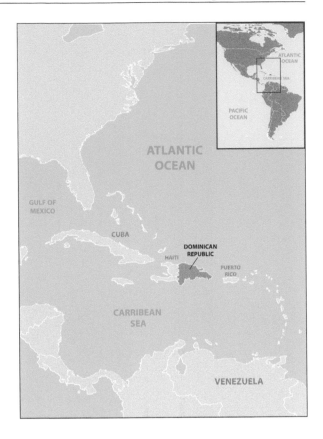

## GENERAL INFORMATION

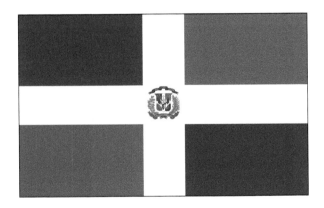

**Official Language(s):** Spanish
**Population:** 10,478,756 (2015)
**Currency:** Dominican Peso
**Coins:** One hundred centavos equal one Dominican peso. Coins are issued in denominations of 1, 5, 10, and 25.
**Land Area:** 48,320 square kilometers (18,656 square miles)

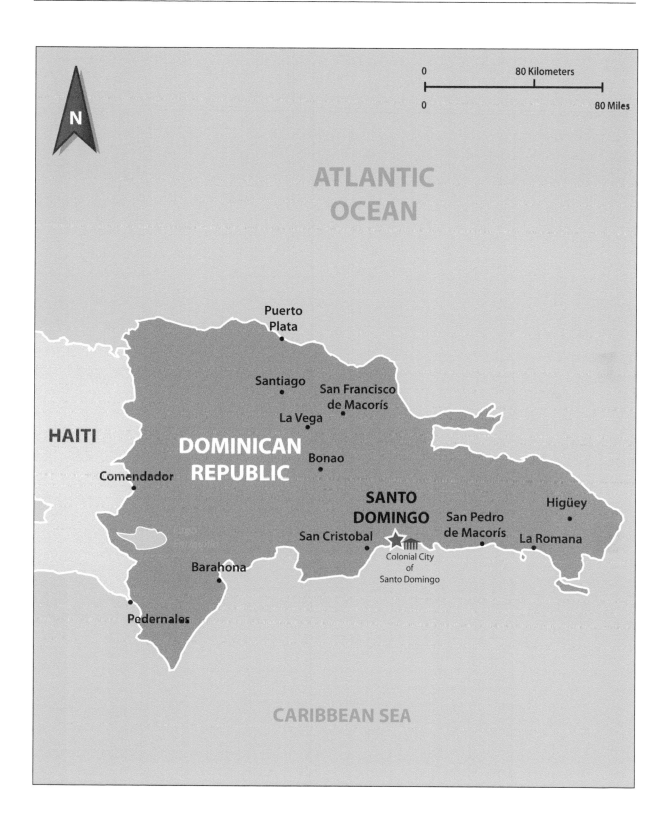

## Principal Cities by Population (2015):

- Santo Domingo (2,945,000)
- Santiago (also, Santiago de los Caballeros) (550,753)
- La Romana (224,882)
- Los Alcarrizos (245,269)
- San Pedro de Macorís (185,255)
- Higüey (also, Salvaleón de Higüey) (147,978)
- San Cristóbal (138,455)
- San Francisco de Macorís (132,725)
- Puerto Plata (also, San Felipe de Puerto Plata) (118,282)
- La Vega (also, Concepción de la Vega) (104,536)

**Water Area:** 350 square kilometers (217 square miles)

**National Motto:** "Dios, Patria, Libertad" (Spanish, "God, Fatherland, Liberty")

**National Anthem:** "Quisqueyanos valientes" (Spanish, "Valiant Quisqueyans")

**Capital:** Santo Domingo

**Time Zone(s):** GMT -4

**Flag Description:** The flag of the Dominican Republic is dominated by a large white cross, with blue filling the upper hoist (left) corner and lower right corners, and red in the upper right corner and the lower hoist corners. The white of the cross is said to symbolize salvation, the red stands for the blood of heroes, and the blue represents liberty. The country's coat of arms is centered in the cross.

## Population

The Dominican Republic's population is young and ethnically diverse. Nearly three-quarters (73 percent) of the population are of mixed African and European descent. Another 11 percent are of African ethnicity, and 16 percent are white.

Santo Domingo, the capital, is the country's largest city, with a population of 2.945 million. Santiago de los Caballeros is the second largest city, with almost 550,753 inhabitants. About 79 percent of the Dominican Republic's population lives in urban areas as of 2015.

Poverty is widespread, with 41.1 percent of the population living below the poverty line. Because of poverty and high unemployment, many Dominicans attempt to enter Puerto Rico and the United States illegally. Similarly, many Haitians cross the border into the Dominican Republic illegally, as the country's economy is more stable than that of its neighbor.

The average Dominican woman gives birth to, on average, 2.33 children; this number is small when compared with other countries in Central America, and due in part to government-sponsored family planning initiatives begun in 1967.

## Languages

Spanish is the official language of the Dominican Republic. English is the most common second language.

## Native People & Ethnic Groups

The Taíno—a subgroup of the South American-based Arawakan Indians—were the native people of Hispaniola and the first indigenous groups in the Western Hemisphere to have encountered Christopher Columbus and other explorers representing Spain. They numbered close to one million before the Spanish arrived in the late 1400s. It is estimated that conquest and disease decimated the island's population so entirely that the Taíno died out around 1550.

The name "Taíno" meant "noble," or "good" in the native language. As a people, the Taíno were organized and governed by chiefdoms. Their chief was not only the leader, but also a kind of facilitator of communication between the physical and spiritual realms.

Taíno society was divided into two classes: the nobles and commoners. The nobles, or nitaínos, were artists and craftsmen, whereas the commoners, or "naborias," were the providers—growing and harvesting crops, hunting, and fishing. There is also anthropological evidence that the Taíno played a ceremonial ball game called batey, which is similar to soccer. Remains of ball courts have been found on the island.

## Religions

The official religion of the Dominican Republic is Roman Catholicism, practiced by 95 percent of the population. Catholicism was brought to the island by Spanish conquerors. When North Americans arrived in the country in the 19th century, they brought Protestant denominations with them.

## Climate

The Dominican Republic is mainly tropical, with a distinct rainy and dry season. Annual rainfall totals vary by region, from 350 millimeters (14 inches) in the western desert to 2,740 millimeters (108 inches) annually. The rainy season lasts from May to November.

The Dominican Republic lies right in the middle of hurricane territory, so hurricanes are a way of life from June to September. In general, major storms occur about once every two years, and hit the southern coast the hardest.

The average temperature is 25° Celsius (77° Fahrenheit), though this also varies by region and altitude. The valleys and coastal regions tend to be warmer than the mountainous areas. On the beaches and coastal areas, highs register around 31° Celsius (87° Fahrenheit) and lows around 20°Celsius (68° Fahrenheit).

---

## ENVIRONMENT & GEOGRAPHY

## Topography

The terrain of the Dominican Republic is mountainous. The country's largest mountain range is the Cordillera Central, which extends across Hispaniola from Haiti to the southern end of the Dominican Republic. This range includes the country's highest point, Pico Duarte. At 3,175 meters (10,417 feet) above sea level, the peak is also the highest point in the Caribbean.

Two smaller mountain ranges, the Cordillera Septentrional and the Cordillera Oriental, run parallel to and extend the Cordillera Central. The fertile Vega Real ("Royal Valley"), also known as the Yuna Valley, lies between the Septentrional and Central ranges. The valley is part of the Cibao lowlands, which support most of the country's agriculture.

Yaque del Norte River is the country's most important river, and Lago (Lake) Enriquillo is the largest body of water and also the country's lowest point, at 46 meters (151 feet) below sea level.

In the country's numerous national parks, visitors can explore the wide variety of habitats that exist in the Dominican Republic, including cave formations, mangrove swamps, pine forests, cloud forests, rainforests, and sand dunes.

Santo Domingo is situated on the southern coast. The metropolitan area is divided by the Rio Ozama as it flows from the mountains north of the city into the Caribbean Sea. The Province of Santo Domingo, one of 31 provinces that comprise the Dominican Republic, is located on the eastern side of the river.

The island, Hispaniola, is seismically active; in January 2010, a magnitude 7.0 earthquake hit neighboring Haiti, causing widespread damage and a death toll of 230,000. The Dominican Republic experienced a magnitude 8.1 earthquake on August 4, 1946, with a death toll of about 100 people, but a 7.6-magnitude aftershock on August 8 and a subsequent tsunami exacted a higher toll, with between 1,600 and 1,800 reported fatalities. The Septentrional-Orient fault zone (SOFZ), which falls in the Cibao Valley, as well as the Puerto Rico and Hispaniola trenches combine to make the region's susceptibility to earthquakes that much more likely, as the area lies between the North American and Caribbean tectonic plates.

## Plants & Animals

Like the terrain, the vegetation found in the Dominican Republic is varied. Scrub brush predominates in the dry western areas, while rainforest vegetation and stands of pine and mahogany trees thrive elsewhere. Orchids are especially cultivated; the country has over 67 types and 300 species of the flower.

More than 200 species of birds are found in the Dominican, including the giant hummingbird, the flamingo, the cotica parrot, and the palmchat, which is the national bird. Small

*The palmchat is the national bird of the Domincan Republic.*

mammals and reptiles are also commonly found throughout the country.

In the ocean surrounding Hispaniola, there are many species of marine life, including sea turtles, pilot whales, humpback whales, and manatees. Manatees are one of the endangered animals of the area, along with a large rodent called the hutia, of which one-third of the animal's twenty different species are extinct.

Two museums dedicated to Dominican flora and fauna are located in Santo Domingo; the Jardín Botánico Nacional and the Museo de Historia Natural.

## CUSTOMS & COURTESIES

### Greetings

Common expressions of greeting in the Dominican Republic include "Buenos días" ("Good morning"), "Buenas tardes" ("Good afternoon"), and "Buenas noches" ("Good night"). All of these are also typically used when ending a conversation or entering public space. Generally, Dominicans try to be sociable and outgoing and will often greet each other as "amigo" ("friend") or possibly "mi amor" ("my love"). When addressing or introducing someone, it is polite to use the honorific, or formal, titles of "señor" ("mister"), "señora" ("misses"), and "señorita" ("miss" or "young lady"), depending on age and marital status. When addressing elders or strangers in high positions, Dominicans use the formal Spanish pronoun "usted" ("you")—as opposed to "tu," which is the informal form of "you," generally used with intimates, close friends, children, and familiar relatives—as well as the respectful forms of address, "don" for men and "doña" for women.

Kisses may be exchanged upon greeting and saying goodbye between women, and sometimes between women and men by touching cheek to cheek and making a kissing sound. Strangers might kiss if they're being introduced by a mutual friend; however, in large groups, an extended hand will suffice as a greeting. Dominican men usually greet with a hug or a handshake. The handshake is accompanied with a salutation such as "¿Cómo está?" ("How are you?") or an informal "¿Qué paso?" ("What's up?").

### Gestures & Etiquette

Dominicans typically stand close while conversing, and hand gestures and other forms of body language are often made to give signals or add emphasis to words. For example, Dominicans may signal for a person to come by placing a palm face down and waving their fingers inward toward the wrist. Puckered lips and an upward head nod indicate direction or a person to whom they are referring. If a Dominican scrunches up their nose, it usually means that they do not understand something that has been said or done, and if they touch the tip of their tongue with an index finger, it signals a lie has been told.

Additionally, Dominicans are not usually reserved about asking personal questions. For instance, inquiring about how many children someone has, how old they are, or how much money they make is considered quite common. Direct eye contact while conversing also demonstrates interest and respect in personal and business affairs.

## Eating/Meals

Breakfast is eaten early and informally in the Dominican Republic and usually consists of some type of bread and coffee. The afternoon meal is usually the main meal of the day and can traditionally last up to two hours. A mix of white rice and red beans, known as habichuelas, and plantains are typical staples of this meal. In addition, chicken, beef, pork, fish, or goat are eaten in small quantities and may be accompanied by sweet potatoes, yams, cassava, or potatoes. After this hearty meal, a light snack, such as a sandwich or cereal, is more common in the evening. On special occasions, such as Christmas or Easter, families will sit down together for feasts of roasted pig or dried and salted cod, which is known as bacalhau. Dominican food is usually not spicy.

For many rural Dominicans, food is almost always eaten in the home or at roadside food stands or diners. Many of these establishments offer a few select plates—usually a soup, meat, freshly squeezed fruit drink, and dessert—for one fixed price.

## Visiting

Punctuality is not vital in Dominican culture, and guests are generally not expected to arrive on time. In fact, arriving between thirty to forty minutes later than scheduled time is typical. However, it is important for guests to dress stylishly and have a well-groomed appearance. Dominicans try to always look their best, especially at social functions, and may sometimes judge others harshly if they are dressed unsuitably. Conversations around a dining table, formal or informal, can last long into the night and topics are generally light. Alcohol, such as rum or beer, is typically served along with music and dance.

## LIFESTYLE

## Family

Families in the Dominican Republic have had limited access to healthcare, education, and housing since the economic crisis of the early 1980s. Thus, family support has become increasingly necessary, and it is common for grandparents, cousins, and other relatives to live together in the same house. Wealthy relatives often give financial support to poorer relatives by offering land loans, wage-paying jobs, or food. Adoption, by which disadvantaged families give a child to wealthier relatives to raise, is also common. Many children are forced to join the work force to contribute to the family income and often never finish school.

When a couple marries, it is common for them to remain with one set of parents or live in a house nearby. Civil and religious weddings, as well as consensual unions—whereby a couple cohabits as if married, but the union is not legally recognized—are acceptable forms of matrimony. Civil marriage remains the most common; however, middle-class and upper-class groups will often have a formal engagement and a church ceremony.

Traditionally, men assume the dominant role within the family, while women are expected to be good housewives and devoted mothers. When a man is absent from the home, the oldest woman will typically assume the role as head of the family.

## Housing

The various types of residences found on the island include detached houses and apartments. Native materials, such as wood, palm, and concrete are commonly used construction materials. Generally, modest city apartments can accommodate a double bed and small table (but sometimes no kitchen), and more luxurious and expensive apartments are similar to those common in the United States.

On average, rural housing lacks many amenities, including electricity or indoor plumbing. Piso de tierra (dirt floors), outdoor cooking pits, and outdoor bathrooms are also common. In fact, the inability of people to pay for their electricity has resulted in government-mandated daily blackouts (*apagones*), which negatively affect businesses and the everyday routines of most citizens. The practice was established by the government in 2001 and remains in effect in 2015, largely because the country's current generating capacity and outmoded grid can only provide 85 percent of the current demand. Oil is required to generate 49 percent of the country's electricity, making the country dependent upon petroleum imports.

For much of its recent history, the Dominican Republic has experienced a housing shortage. This has been due to a variety of factors, including mass migration to urban areas and devastating hurricanes. In response, various government administrations have tried to build low-cost housing. Additionally, the US Agency for International Development (USAID) and other foreign assistance programs have worked with the Dominican Republic to complete, upgrade, or repair homes.

### Food

Dominican cuisine has largely been influenced by the culinary traditions of its Spanish, African, and Taíno inhabitants. It is similar to the cuisines of other Latin American and Caribbean nations, most notably Cuba and Puerto Rico. Meats such as fish, chicken or pork, native fruits, potatoes and plantains, and rice and beans are common ingredients, and dishes such as pasta reveal the influence of the Dominican Republic's cultural history.

In general, Dominicans eat plantains regularly because the fruit is plentiful, versatile, and low cost. Mangú, a typical breakfast dish, is a mix of plantains, butter, and fried onions, similar to mashed potatoes. La bandera Dominicana (literally, "the Dominican flag") is largely considered the national dish, and is typically eaten at lunch time, the principal meal of the day. Traditionally, it consists of rice, habichuelas (beans), stewed meat (goat), vegetables or salad, and fried plantains. Another unique dish is sancocho, which is

a Taíno-Creole influenced stew of rice; various starchy roots, such as cassava, yucca, or potatoes; green plantains; avocado; and chicken or beef. Goat meat, a staple of the Dominican diet, may also be used.

African colonists introduced sugarcane to the island. When the molasses fermented in the hot Caribbean sun, the results were mixed with water to create rum. Cuba libre, or rum and coke with lime, is perhaps the most popular way to drink rum among the locals. Dominican organic coffee beans present a bold taste and rich smell. To drink it "Dominican style" is to do so with a lot of sugar and a small amount of coffee.

With its abundance of sugarcane, desserts are popular in the Dominican Republic. Some common examples include arroz con leche (rice pudding), flan, dulce de coco (sweet coconut paste), shaved ice with fruit syrup, and aqua de coco (sliced coconuts mixed with sugar). The African and Haitian-influenced majarete is a corn pudding that is commonly sold by women carrying baskets of the treats balanced on their head. Papaya, passion fruit, bitter orange, guava, coconut, mango, and mamey (or mamey sapote, a fruit with a creamy, pink-to-orange-colored flesh and a thin, fuzzy shell) are tropical fruits found fresh and in abundance on the island.

As in other Central American countries, corn is also a large part of Dominican cuisine. A traditional Dominican corn dish is chacá, a boiled cracked-corn pudding, which is sweetened with cane sugar and flavored with cloves and cinnamon.

### Life's Milestones

The Dominican Republic is mostly Roman Catholic—an estimated 95 percent—and milestones and social traditions are largely rooted in the Catholic faith. As such, baptism remains an important milestone. An important bond, known as compadres or co-parents, is traditionally formed between parents and godparents when a baby is baptized. The compadres ensure their child is raised in the Catholic faith and aid in the child's success throughout their life. Compadres also may be responsible for financially supporting first communions, confirmations, and marriage celebrations.

Originating in Spain, and celebrated throughout Latin America, quinceañera occurs when a girl in the Dominican community turns fifteen years old. This celebration symbolizes the girl's entrance into womanhood. Being a Christian ritual, the event includes a religious ceremony typically held at a church to honor the girl, followed by a celebration with food and drink, live music, and friends and family. In some cases, the female celebrant will be able to wear makeup, nail polish, high heel shoes, and pluck her eyebrows or straighten her hair. She will also wear an elaborate dress similar to a bridal gown (though dresses may be changed for the reception). After the quinceañera, she is able to attend social functions, have boyfriends, and must accept the responsibilities of being a woman in Dominican society.

A funeral in the Dominican Republic is an event that traditionally gathers people together for nine consecutive days of Catholic masses. The nine days of mourning usually consist of three days of tears and reminiscences, three days of silent prayer, and three days for final farewells.

## CULTURAL HISTORY

### Art

At least five productive Taíno Indian kingdoms inhabited the island of Hispaniola (now the Dominican Republic and Haiti) before it was claimed by Christopher Columbus for Spain in 1492. Considered the most developed Caribbean culture at the time, the Taíno were highly proficient in traditional crafts such as sculpture, ceramics, jewelry making, and weaving. However, from the 16th to the 19th centuries, the pre-Columbian Taíno culture was assimilated, along with the culture of African slave workers, into Spanish culture. During Spanish colonization, European art movements influenced the Dominican culture. African tradition, Taíno mythology, and Creole culture (people of European descent who were born in the colonies) combined to create a unique style of Dominican art.

After March 3, 1865, when the Dominican Republic officially won its independence from Spain, a national style of Dominican art became more pronounced. One of the first national Dominican artists was cartoonist and painter Domingo Echavarría (1786–1849). During the 1920s and 1930s, realist artists were prolific, with Celeste Woss y Gil (1890–1985) one of the best-known painters. In addition to painting portraits and post-impressionist-inspired nudes of black and mulatto Dominican women, she is often credited with bringing the modernist movement to the Dominican Republic. Other well-known artists included Yoryi Morel (1906–1979), known primarily for his landscape and peasant paintings, but also for his incisive portraits.

From 1930 to 1961, freedom of expression stagnated as a result of the dictatorship of Rafael Trujillo (1891–1961). In spite of horrific human rights violations, Trujillo set aside large amounts of government money for the arts. Trujillo also granted many Spanish artists political asylum in the Dominican Republic during the Spanish Civil War. Expatriates such as José Vela Zanetti (1913–1999), Josep Gausachs (1889–1959), and Eugenio Fernández Granell (1912–2001) affected Dominican art in important ways. All played a significant role in founding the Escuela Nacional de Bellas Artes, or National Fine Arts School, in 1942. After the assassination of Trujillo in 1961, contemporary Dominican artists took up themes of social and political unrest in their work. Child prostitution, migration, and poverty are issues addressed in the work of contemporary Dominican artists.

### Architecture

Dominican architecture stylistically resembles that of Spain. During Spanish rule, major architectural projects had to be approved by the Spanish monarch before construction could begin in the colonies. Santo Domingo—the capital of the Dominican Republic—was the site of the first cathedral, hospital, and university in the Americas. The city's street grid became the model for all city streets in the New World. (Santo Domingo also remains the oldest European settlement in the Americas that has continuously been inhabited.)

Differences in geography and weather forced colonists to devise new architectural solutions for their growing cities. In the larger towns, the architecture resembles European cities of the past, while in the more rural areas building styles are a mix of Indian or African culture with Spanish influences. Bohíos (the Taíno word for dwelling) are pre-Columbian-influenced houses made from timber or cane, with a thatched roof and, traditionally, pattern-woven palm-leaf siding. Bohíos are often circular in shape, breathable, and built to withstand water, wind, and hurricanes. They can last up to twenty years in a tropical climate.

Creole architecture expanded and embellished upon Spanish styles. One example of this can be seen in Churrigueresque architecture. Named for the Churriguera family of Spanish architects, Creole-constructed Churrigueresque architecture consists of generously decorated, highly sculptural columns and façades—so filled with intricate ornamentation as to manifest a cultural propensity for *horror vacui* (fear of empty space). It is more aesthetically-pleasing than structurally practical. This Spanish baroque style of architecture adorns many churches and important government or university buildings on the island and is the signature style of Spanish colonial architecture.

## Music

Music and dance are important artistic traditions that are rooted in the pre-Columbian Taíno culture. It is believed that the Taíno used music as a motivational tool when working. Music was also used to record and remember history and to celebrate special occasions. Alongside music, the Taíno performed dance ceremonies for a variety of practical reasons, including healing purposes, for protection against hurricanes, or to ask for rain, abundant crops, and an available fish supply. The Taíno would also choreograph dance

and song ensembles to offer as tokens of love and respect to family and friends.

Following colonization, traditional Spanish music and dance became increasingly influential, and styles such as bolero, a slow tempo dance which originated in Spain in the late 18th century, and fandango, a folk dance associated with courtship that is also native to Spain, became popular. Additionally, an 18th-century Creole dance style known as barcarola criolla is considered the first distinctively Dominican style of music and dance to emerge on the island. Africans, brought to the island as labor, also introduced their own cultural influences and folk traditions, particularly through their work songs.

The most popular musical genres in Dominican Republic are merengue and bachata. Merengue is a uniquely Dominican style of music and dance that is largely recognized as the national dance of the Dominican Republic (it was made the official music and dance of the island by Trujillo). It is a mixture of African and European sounds blended together. It uses traditional instruments such as the melodeon (button accordion); güira (metal cylinder played either with a brush or scraped and used as a percussion instrument in merengue); and tambora (small, two-sided drum); along with more modern sounds, such as the saxophone. Merengue is also characterized by a two-step beat, dominating rhythms, and lyrics that often reference politics.

Bachata is a genre of music and dance that originated in Dominican shantytowns (informal settlements) and rural areas, when untrained street musicians attempted to imitate Cuban sounds. Largely a guitar-based music, it also evokes the bolero and is often characterized by melancholy lyrics about life in the fields and estranged relationships. Bachata first became recognized as a musical genre in the 1960s. In the 1970s, with the downturn of the Dominican economy, the music became associated with prostitution and poverty, and themes of violence and drinking became more prominent in the lyrics. It wasn't until the late 1980s, with the introduction of the electric guitar and less romanticized lyrics, that bachata became acceptable in the mainstream again.

The Dominican Republic also possesses two of what the United Nations Educational, Scientific and Cultural Organization (UNESCO) refers to as intangible cultural heritage. One is the Cultural Space of the Brotherhood of the Holy Spirit of the Congos of Villa Mella, a fraternity of conga drummers dating back to the 16th century. The second is the Cocolo dancing drama tradition. Cocolo culture is a migrant culture that blends traditions from Africa and Britain. Both of these cultural hallmarks are included among UNESCO's list of Masterpieces of the Oral and Intangible Heritage of Humanity.

## Literature

Historically, the canon of Dominican literature originated among the clergy and the non-native and university-educated upper class. Haitian occupation during the 19th century brought about nationalistic themes in Dominican literature. Poet Félix Maria del Monte (1819–1899), often regarded as the father of Dominican poetry, encouraged Dominicans to fight against the invading Haitians in his writings. Dominican literature began to significantly develop during the 20th century. Early literary figures included Américo Lugo (1870–1952) and Gastón Fernando Deligne (1861–1913), who were both influenced by modernism. More political themes began to emerge during the US occupation of the Dominican Republic in the 1920s. Social protest would become a major theme in the latter half of the 20th century as a result of Trujillo's dictatorial regime.

In terms of national literature, author Julia Álvarez (1950–) is a Dominican American writer who spent the first 10 years of her childhood in the Dominican Republic before her family took political refuge in the United States. Her historical novel, *In the Time of the Butterflies* (1994), is based on the death of the Mirabal sisters who were murdered during the Trujillo dictatorship. These women, referred to as "Las Mariposas" or "The Butterflies," were found at the bottom of a cliff in 1960, assassinated by the womanizing

dictator. She is consistently regarded as one of the most significant Latina voices of her time.

Junot Díaz (1968–) is a Dominican American writer and professor. Díaz's work involves analyzing the Dominican diaspora of the United States. *Drown* (1996), his first collection of short stories, focuses on the narrator's impoverished youth in the Dominican Republic and his struggle adapting to immigrant life in New Jersey. In 2008, Díaz won the Pulitzer Prize for Fiction for his novel *The Brief Wondrous Life of Oscar Wao* (2007). *The New Yorker*, which had previously published the author's short stories, listed him as one of the top twenty writers of the 21st century.

## CULTURE

### Arts & Entertainment

Entering the early 21st century, a variety of government and non-governmental organizations (NGOs) support a range of arts in the Dominican Republic. The Fine Arts Council, the National Conservatory of Music, the Fine Arts School, and the Institute of Dominican Culture are some of the institutions that promote cultural practice and support artistic expression. Additionally, traditional crafts have persevered, largely as a money-making necessity in the small towns and neighborhoods throughout the island. In response to a lagging economy, men and women sell colorful, oil-painted canvases depicting daily Dominican island life to tourists. Masks and musical instruments are made from cow leather and dried gourds and sold at Carnival. Women in rural areas weave hammocks and mold jewelry out of amber or shells to peddle at cruise ship stops.

Dividing his time between Santo Domingo and New York City, painter Freddy Rodriguez (1945–) paints about Dominican oppression under Rafael Trujillo. He works in colorful, geometric images of yucca plants, flowers, and wildlife as metaphors for the optimistic growth and evolution of his country. Artist José García Cordero (1951–), considered a surrealist and social realist, comments on the dangerous voyage many Dominicans undergo in illegal transnational migration. Raúl Recio (1965–) merges African-Christian myth with the thorny realities of Dominican life in semi-abstract images of poverty, crime, AIDS, and migration in his work. Artist Tony Capellán (1955–) evokes magic realism and fantasy through his art installations that often speak of the social ills associated with a lack of education, youth degradation, and the island nation's defective prison and justice system.

Contemporary merengue artists such as composer and singer Johnny Ventura (1940–), Wilfrido Vargas (1949–), and the Grammy Award-winning Juan Luis Guerra (1957–) incorporate different musical genres such as salsa, rock, and reggae into their sounds. This new style has become increasingly popular among Dominicans, and dancing the partnered merengue, with its hip sways and turns, is still considered a birthright. In fact, a common saying among Dominicans is that if a child does not learn to dance merengue by the age of five, he or she will live a dull, passionless adulthood. In recent years, reggaetón, a form of electronic dance music that fuses rap, reggae, and Jamaican dancehall sounds, has become popular on the island.

Each February, Dominican towns host Carnival prior to the start of the Christian season of Lent. Groups of people dress in bright, revealing costumes and dance down city streets to thunderous merengue music. Masks made of discarded materials and pieces of scrap cardboard or recycled plastic, from ancient African and Taíno traditions, are worn for protection against evil spirits during this time of music and dance indulgence.

Baseball is the national pastime, and major league games are played at Quisqueya Stadium. Many players from the Dominican Republic, including Sammy Sosa (1968–), Manny Ramirez (1972–), and Pedro Martinez (1971–), have been renowned and acclaimed professional baseball players in the United States. Many Dominican players also travel to Japan to play.

In other sports, the annual Encuentro Classic Eco-Surf Competition is held each December near Cabarete and tests windsurfers' skills against the elements. Horse racing is held at Las Americas International Speed Racing Course. Santo Domingo hosted the Pan-American Games in 2003.

**Cultural Sites & Landmarks**
Set on the northern Silver Coast, Puerta Plata is known for its historic architecture and colonial past. Old City Puerta Plata has preserved much of its Victorian history that originated during a brief British occupancy of the island. In the shady, tree-lined Parque Central (Central Park), pedestrians wander past colonial-era cathedrals and mansions. The Amber Museum, set in a renovated colonial era mansion, displays amber extracted from mines just south of Puerto Plata dating back several million years. On the outskirts of the Old City, San Felipe Fort and Prison was constructed by the Spaniards in 1540 as a defense against pirates and invading countries. In Puerta Plata's New City, a suspended cable car runs up to the top of Mount Isabela.

The Cordillera Central mountain range, often referred to as the Cibao Valley (its Taíno name), pierces through the central Dominican Republic. It contains the tallest peak in the Caribbean, Pico Duarte, standing at 3,175 meters (10,417 feet). Jarabacoa, a cool mountain village, is known for its coffee plantations. Deep pine forests protect three large waterfalls, trails are commonly used for hiking and horseback riding, and its deep canyons and rivers attract whitewater rafters. The village is also a good base location for renting donkeys and equipment, or obtaining food, supplies, and a guide for the three-day trek up Pico Duarte.

The Península de Samaná, or Samaná Peninsula, extending off the Dominican Republic's northeast coast, is a place to observe the migratory pattern of the humpback whale each winter. Santa Barbara de Samaná, a town significantly influenced by its European expatriate community, offers ferry rides to Cayo Levantado, a mangrove-entangled Bacardi Island photographed in the 1970s rum campaign.

Santo Domingo is the old Spanish colonial capital and it abounds with culture and history.

The city's Zona Colonial, or Colonial Zone, dates to the early 16th century and is still surrounded in part by its original wall. Some of the first structures built in the New World grace the narrow cobblestone streets there.

The Alcázar de Colón sits atop a bluff overlooking the Ozáma River. It was completed in 1517 for Diego Columbus (Colón in Spanish), Christopher's son, and his wife, Maria de Toledo, King Ferdinand's niece. Other explorers, including Ponce de Leon and Vasco Núñez de Balboa, found respite there as well. Parque Colón, or Columbus Park, houses the oldest churches and streets in the Americas alongside surviving European fortresses. It was designated as a World Heritage Site by UNESCO, which endeavors to protect cultural and natural sites worldwide through inclusion on the World Heritage List.

El Faro a Colón, (the Columbus Lighthouse) is a 210 meters (689 feet) tall landmark inaugurated in 1992 to mark the 500th anniversary of the arrival of Columbus in the New World. It houses a museum as well as the reputed remains of Columbus—both Spain and Italy also claim the remains.

## Libraries & Museums

Santo Domingo boasts several museums of interest to those students of early American history. The Museum of the Royal Houses is an example of a 16th-century palace, and sits next to the Alcázar de Colón, the former house of Diego Columbus and Maria de Toledo. Within the Plaza de la Cultura are several museums, including El Museo del Hombre Dominicano (Museum of Dominican Man), which houses one of the region's most comprehensive collection of Taíno artifacts; El Museo de Arte Moderno (Museum of Modern Art); the Museo Nacional de la historia y de la Geografía (National Museum of History and Geography); and the Museo Nacional de Historia Natural (National Museum of Natural History).

The Dominican Republic's national library, the Biblioteca Nacional Pedro Henríquez Ureña, serves as the national repository for content created and published in the country.

## Holidays

Dominicans celebrate the major Christian holidays, including Christmas and Easter (Semana Santa, or Holy Week). Catholic saints also receive special note; January 21 is a public holiday celebrating Our Lady of Altagracia (Día de la Altagracia), which celebrates the Virgin Mary, patron saint of the Dominican Republic. September 24 is set aside for Our Lady of las Mercedes, a feast day established in 1615, to celebrate the Virgin Mary, who is said to have appeared during a 1495 battle between the Spanish and Taíno Indians, who scattered in fear on her manifestation. Independence Day is observed on February 27 to mark the country's independence from Haiti in 1844; November 6 celebrates the establishment of the Dominican constitution.

## Youth Culture

It is common in the Dominican Republic for young people from upper class families to attend private schools and wear designer fashions as a sign of their social status. Additionally, it is more common for these privileged youth to complete all levels of schooling (over eight years of mandatory education is imposed by the Dominican government), including higher education. Youth born to lower-class families often work at an early age, and many never finish their mandatory education. This is further exacerbated by the fact that the majority of schools in the Dominican Republic are underdeveloped and overcrowded, with low teacher retention.

Furthermore, youth in urban areas, especially those of a lower socioeconomic status, are more susceptible to gang activity. In fact, some of Santo Domingo's most impoverished neighborhoods are said to be almost entirely controlled by youth gangs. Nonetheless, youth from all classes and ethnic backgrounds generally intermingle freely. Dominican parents are generally liberal when it comes to dating, and there is no traditional or common practice of arranged marriages in the Dominican Republic.

The urban hip-hop style of dress—including wearing baggy clothes and cornrow hairstyles—

has been one of the preferred styles among Dominican teens in the early 21st century. For older youth, nightclubs and bars are popular places to socialize. Popular music genres include merengue, bachata, salsa, rock, rap, and reggaetón (which combines Jamaican dancehall music with reggae, rap, and electronica).

Other popular pastimes of Dominican youth include dominos, watching rooster fights, or playing baseball. In fact, baseball continues to maintain its important status in popular and youth culture in the Dominican Republic. Numerous Major League Baseball (MLB) organizations continue to employ scouts based in the country, and Dominicans who can make a living as a professional baseball player in the United States are seen as role models and celebrities on the island.

## SOCIETY

### Transportation
Buses and shared taxis, or privately-owned cars called carro público, are two popular modes of public transportation in the Dominican Republic. Both buses and taxis are air-conditioned and considered relatively safe, and buses are generally inexpensive. Popular for shorter trips within towns, villages, and resort areas, motoconchos are unauthorized, independently-owned motorbikes whose drivers will give passengers a ride for a predetermined price. Guaguas are minivans designed to hold twelve passengers, but conditions may be overcrowded and poor.

The capital of Santo Domingo has a metro system known as the Santo Domingo Metro (Metro de Santo Domingo), the first line of which was inaugurated in 2008. A second line opened in 2012, and four more lines are yet planned. As of 2015, there were 30 stations along the current Metro lines. As of November 2014, daily ridership amounted to 173,070, while the annual ridership count stands at 61,270,054.

Traffic in the Dominican Republic drives on the right side of the road.

### Transportation Infrastructure
There are several railways in the Dominican Republic, mainly commercial, with none connecting to neighboring Haiti. The island is serviced by five major airports and five major highways (DR-1 through DR-5). The country boasts 19,705 km (12,244 mi) of roadway. However, only 9,872 kilometers (6,134 miles) are paved.

### Media & Communications
Media ownership, including television, radio, and newspapers, is largely concentrated, with little political censorship. Newspapers, once privately owned, are now run by banks and corporations. The *Listín Diario* (which has the largest circulation), *El Caribe*, and *El Hoy* have all been owned by large banks. However, some fear private control of the media will have negative effects on the politics and economics of the country. There are numerous independent radio stations, and Mexican and American TV broadcasts can be received.

The Dominican Republic has an advanced telecommunications infrastructure for a Latin American country, with over 9 million cell phones in use in 2012. As of 2013, an estimated 46 percent of the population were Internet users.

## SOCIAL DEVELOPMENT

### Standard of Living
The Dominican Republic ranked 102 on the 2014 United Nations Human Development Index (HDI), which measures quality of life and standard of living indicators using 2012 data.

### Water Consumption
According to the United Nations International Children's Emergency Fund (UNICEF), 84.7 percent of residents in the Dominican Republic have access to clean water (85.4 percent in urban areas and 81.9 percent in rural areas). Access to improved sanitation is measured at 84 percent overall, with urban populations

measuring 86.2 percent access to a rural population measurement of 75.7 percent.

In November 2010, plans to expand water and sanitation services to rural areas, with funding by the Inter-American Development Bank (IDB) and the Spanish government, were announced. Coverage will be expanded in seven poverty-stricken provinces, helping the Dominican Republic to meets its Millennium Development Goals in the areas of sanitation and water coverage. In 2012, IDB loaned the country $25 million (USD) to improve drinking water distribution in Santiago de los Caballeros and bolster the efforts of CORAASAN (Water and Sewerage Corporation of Santiago).

## Education

Schooling is mandatory in the Dominican Republic from preschool through eighth grade. Public school tuition is free, though students must pay for their own uniforms and school supplies. Private schools are mostly Catholic and are considered to be superior to public schools. In general, only middle and upper class families are able to afford private school tuition.

The Dominican Republic's average literacy rate is close to 92 percent, with men at 91.2 percent and women at 92.3 percent. A 2010 report from the United Nations Development Program reported that the Dominican Republic was failing to make strides in terms of education. Education was one indicator, but was tied to other issues such as health care and the reduction of poverty. Failure to progress was attributed to weak social policy and slow economic growth.

The Universidad Autónoma de Santo Domingo is the most respected university in the Dominican Republic. As the government provides funding, the university is able to offer free tuition to many students.

## Women's Rights

In general, middle- and upper-class families maintain patriarchal structures, with dominant father figures a regular presence in the home. Among the lower class, absentee fathers are more common, resulting in matriarchal family units. In such cases, the oldest married woman is the head of the household. Overall, Dominican women are traditionally seen as secondary income earners. However, the women's labor force has been increasing, primarily in the tropical agricultural industries. Dominican women also have higher educational levels than their male counterparts, as many more women than men complete high school.

Nonetheless, the Dominican labor market is segregated by gender, and women are often subjected to discriminatory company regulations. Human rights research has also established that pregnancy-based discrimination is widespread in the Dominican Republic. Women are also routinely subjected to involuntary HIV testing. Furthermore, women earn lower wages than Dominican men, with female wages averaging only 57 percent of male wages. In terms of political representation, by law, parties must reserve positions for women on their ballots. However, women candidates are usually poorly represented and funded, making it difficult for them to win an elected seat. Still, in 2012, former first lady Margarita Cedeño de Fernández became the 39th vice president of the Dominican Republic, the second female vice president after Milagros Ortiz Bosch, who served from 2000–2004.

The Dominican Republic has the world's fourth highest number of women working overseas in the sex trade. Often, women use the sex trade as a stepping stone to international migration. The Dominican Republic also has one of the highest rates of reported HIV/AIDS cases. As of 2014, there were an estimated 69,300 people living with HIV or AIDS in the Dominican Republic, and the number of Dominican sex workers was estimated to be more than 60,000 women, ranging in age from 14 to 35. Additionally, domestic violence and rape continue to be serious and often underreported problems.

In recent years, NGOs, the United Nations (UN), and government agencies have been working to improve the lives of Dominican women through advocacy, policy, and program development. In particular, they have targeted securing the rights of children and women, countering intra-family violence and abuse, and preventing the trafficking of women and girls for the commercial sex industry.

### Health Care

The Dominican Republic has a national health plan, administered by the Secretariat for Public Health and Social Welfare. The agency places special emphasis on services for disadvantaged and rural populations. However, common diseases such as dengue fever, typhoid, and hepatitis A still affect large portions of the population. Bacterial diarrhea is also a continuing problem.

The National Health Commission was formed in 1995 to determine how best to serve the basic health needs of all Dominicans. A National Food and Nutrition Plan, National Drinking Water Plan for Scattered Rural and Marginal Urban Areas, and the National Social Development Plan were all developed in an attempt to improve living conditions.

Average life expectancy is nearly 76 years for men and more than 80 years for women, though just over seven percent of the population is over the age of 65.

---

## GOVERNMENT

---

### Structure

The Dominican Republic is made up of 31 provinces, which is, as its name implies, a democratic republic. The voting age is 18, although legally married couples can vote regardless of age. Important to note is that, by law, members of the armed forces and the national police cannot vote. The executive branch consists of a president elected by popular vote. The office brings with it an enormous amount of executive power. The position serves as both chief of state and head of government, and while there is no prime minister, there is a vice president, who, like the president, is directly elected by popular vote. Each may serve four-year, renewable terms. The president nominates cabinet members who advise him

and participates in appointing members of the supreme and constitutional judiciary.

The legislative branch consists of a bicameral Congress (Congreso Nacional) made up of a Senate (Senado), with 32 members, and a Chamber of Deputies (Cámara de Diputados), with 195 seats, all directly elected by proportional-representation vote to four-year terms.

The country gained its independence from Haiti on February 27, 1844. However, its governments have frequently shifted between democracy and authoritarian leadership, depending on the constitution in use. Every time an amendment is ratified, a whole new constitution is drafted, the most recent of which was promulgated on January 26, 2010. As of 2015, there have been 38 versions of the country's constitution in a little more than 170 years. The 2009 iteration, which of course preceded the most recent, 2010 version, contained 40 articles, some of which were highly controversial, including a blanket ban on abortions, and an insertion of private property rights language on a public beach, river, and water access article.

### Political Parties

On the 2012 presidential election ballot, 24 parties were represented. However, the three most powerful political parties in the Dominican Republic include the Dominican Liberation Party (PLD), a center-left party; the Dominican Revolutionary Party (PRD), a social democratic party; and the Social Christian Reformist Party (PRSC), a conservative party. In the 2012 presidential elections, the PLD garnered 51.21 percent of the vote and the PRD took 46.95 percent of the vote.

Under the new constitution, promulgated in January 2010, the next general elections will be held in 2016, in order to synchronize congressional and presidential elections; this means that those congressional members elected in 2010 will serve for six years, rather than the usual four-year terms. In the 2010 parliamentary election, the PLD dominated again, getting more than 54 percent of the vote and gaining 105 seats in the chamber and 31 seats in the senate. The

PRD reached 41 percent of the vote and earned 75 seats in the chamber and no senate seats. The PRSC took only one percent of the vote, but gained three chamber and one senate seats.

## Local Government
Governors of the country's 31 provinces are appointed by the president. As of June 2014, elected mayors and councils govern the country's 159 municipalities (*municipios*) and the National District (Santo Domingo). In rural areas, municipalities are subdivided into districts, which are overseen by municipal councils. Because local governments do not have the power to levy taxes, few if any services or maintenance are possible at the municipal level.

## Judicial System
The judicial branch consists of a 16-member Supreme Court of Justice (Suprema Corte de Justicia) and a 13-member Constitutional Court (Tribunal Constitucional), which was established by a 2010 constitutional amendment. Supreme Court judges serve seven-year terms, while Constitutional Court judges serve nine-year terms. Lesser courts include the courts of appeal, courts of first instance, as well as special courts for land and labor disputes and juvenile cases. Judges are appointed by the National Council of the Judiciary, a group that includes the president. Dominican law is based on the French system, which is a code-based legal system. This is in contrast to the common law system of the United States, in which the law may be interpreted based on the outcomes of prior cases. The Criminal Procedures Code was modified in 2004 to allow for an accusatory system.

## Taxation
The government of the Dominican Republic levies taxes on income, corporate income (29 percent), capital gains, consumption, assets, property, property sale, mortgages, motor vehicles (a fixed rate of RD$2,500), fuel tax (a fixed rate of RD$6.30 per gallon), and inheritances and gifts. A value-added tax (VAT) of 18 percent is also collected on goods and services.

## Armed Forces
The Dominican Republic's voluntary military force is comprised of an army (Ejercito Nacional), navy (Marina de Guerra), and air force (Fuerza Aerea Dominicana). It is considered to be the second largest armed forces in the Caribbean region (behind Cuba). There is no conscription, and enlistees must have completed primary school and be citizens of the Dominican Republic to be eligible for service. Women may also volunteer.

## Foreign Policy
The foreign policy of the Dominican Republic is largely influenced by the country's relationship with the United States and other Caribbean and American states. American military intervention occurred as recently as the mid-20th century, and an estimated 200,000 Americans reside in the Dominican Republic as of 2013. In particular, the Dominican Republic's proximity to the United States and its status as the largest Caribbean economy have played a significant role in shaping its foreign relations. The country is a founding UN member and holds membership in regional organizations such as the Organization of American States (OAS) and the Caribbean Community and Common Market (CARICOM).

The United States remains one of the Dominican Republic's most important trading partners, with the United States receiving of over one-half the country's exports. In 2004, the Dominican Republic joined the Central America Free Trade Agreement (CAFTA, now commonly known as DR CAFTA), a free trade agreement with the United States and other Central American nations. As of the turn of the 21st century, the United States constitutes the majority of foreign private investment in the island nation, and both countries have partnered on issues such as drug trafficking and illegal immigration. Dominicans often cross the Mona Passage in small boats to reach Puerto Rico, with many continuing on to the US mainland.

Although the Dominican Republic shares the island of Hispaniola with Haiti, relations between the two countries have been strained throughout the 20th and early 21st centuries. (The country endured a 22 year period of Haitian occupation in the early 19th century, and in 1937, the regime of Trujillo oversaw the massacre of thousands of Haitians.) The border that divides them has been closed on several occasions, but there has been a significant increase in Haitian immigration in recent years, particularly following the earthquake of 2010. This influx of illegal immigrants and refugees has led to an increase of human rights abuses. In fact, the country depends on the cheap labor offered by Haitians during the sugarcane cutting season and for other low-wage and low-skill jobs. As of 2010, no extradition treaty exists between the neighboring countries.

The Dominican Republic is involved in the politics and economics of neighboring islands, and maintains trade relations with Venezuela and other Latin American states. However, the Dominican Republic has a troubled relationship with nearby Cuba, largely due to past military uprisings, opposing diplomatic alliances, and the fact that both nations compete in the world sugar market. Western European nations with ties to Dominican Republic include Germany, France, and Spain. In addition to migration from the Dominican Republic to the United States, there is significant authorized and unauthorized Dominican migration to Spain. A migration agreement to formalize Dominican-Spain migration has recently been signed and put into practice.

## Human Rights Profile

International human rights law insists that states respect civil and political rights and also promote an individual's economic, social, and cultural rights. The United Nations Universal Declaration on Human Rights (UDHR) is recognized as the standard for international human rights. Its authors sought the counsel of the world's great thinkers, philosophers, and religious leaders and were careful to create a document that reflects the core values shared by every world culture. (To read this document or view the articles relating to cultural human rights, go to: http://www.ohchr.org/EN/UDHR/Pages/Introduction.aspx.)

The Dominican Republic has historically been governed under political chaos and dictatorship that has largely denied and suppressed basic human rights to its citizens. The constitution adopted in 1966, after Trujillo's devastating reign—and one that provides the basis for the most recent constitution of 2010—stresses civil rights and liberties for the Dominican people. Nonetheless, Dominican politicians have maintained a reputation for endorsing corruption. Corrupt practices, such as illegal contracts, racketeering, and political favors are often overlooked in exchange for money and political power. This high level of corruption has had a trickle-down effect that continues to compromise the issue of human rights.

The judicial system in the Dominican Republic empowers judges—rather than juries—to decide all verdicts. The constitution grants an accused person the right to a trial, the right to a lawyer, and the right not to serve as a witness against him or herself. However, international rights agencies contend that the authorities commonly violate these rights. Arbitrary arrest and detainment by police also remains a prevalent issue. Prison conditions are characterized as overcrowded, unsanitary, and poor.

Additionally, detainees often report having suffered torture and sexual abuse while in custody. In response, lawyers are sometimes placed in high volume police stations to monitor investigations and ensure detainee rights, and some NGOs offer legal services free of charge.

Dominican law grants freedom of speech and press. However, even under the new constitution, media outlets are often prevented from airing critical commentary on government policies and politicians. Journalists and editors often practice self-censorship for fear of losing their jobs. The constitution also allows freedom of assembly. However, outdoor public marches and meetings require government permits (which are usually granted).

Discrimination laws protect Dominican citizens on grounds of race, sex, and disability. However, Haitian immigrants have been denied legal, educational, and citizenship rights in the

Dominican Republic. In addition, homosexual men and women are barred from becoming foster or surrogate parents. Laws also prohibit sexual harassment in the work place, though female workers frequently report sexual harassment by supervisors or coworkers. People with disabilities, HIV/AIDS, and women who are pregnant also very often encounter discrimination in the workplace.

Education law declares a requirement of eight years of formal education for children, but no laws enforce student education after primary schooling. Poor children are frequently forced to abandon education and work. These vulnerable children are often objects of human trafficking and sexual exploitation, issues of grave concern in the Dominican Republic. The government states its commitment to protecting children's rights, and is trying to eliminate child labor and prostitution. However, the CIA estimates that 180,423 school-age children are engaged in street vending, domestic servitude, and agricultural tasks, although this is widely considered a light estimate by human rights groups.

Lastly, the issue of Haitian immigration has raised concerns of human rights abuses in recent years. Haitian immigrants have been denied legal rights in deportation proceedings and Dominican-born Haitians are not eligible for citizenship in the Dominican Republic. Anti-Haitian discrimination has increased, as more Haitians have entered the Dominican Republic since the January 2010 earthquake that devastated that country. It is estimated that, after the 2010 earthquake, about one million Haitian nationals live within the Dominican Republic and, as of 2015, few have returned to Haiti or left the Dominican Republic since the disaster.

## Migration

Many nationals from the Dominican Republic migrate to the United States, where they send remittances back to their home country. In fact, in 2013, remittances amounted to 7.3 percent of the country's GDP, according to the World Bank. After the January 2010 earthquake, the number of illegal Haitian nationals in the Dominican

Republic was estimated to have reached one million people. And since then, many of these migrants have remained. The social cost of this large number of refugees has had a severe impact on the government of the Dominican Republic.

## ECONOMY

### Overview of the Economy

The Dominican Republic has experienced periods of recession followed by years of strong growth during the past few decades, but continues to be saddled with debt and a high poverty rate, which in 2013, was just over 41 percent. Some growth can be attributed to the free-trade zones, which were established in the 1980s under the Caribbean Basin Initiative and employ hundreds of thousands of Dominicans. The Central America-Dominican Republic Free Trade Agreement (CAFTA-DR) of March 2007, which has boosted both exports and foreign investment, has also helped to stimulate the economy.

Traditionally, the Dominican economy has relied on agricultural products (particularly coffee, tobacco, and sugar). In recent years, however, the economic emphasis has shifted to the service industry sector, as telecommunications and tourism have significantly increased. In 2014, the services sector represented 61.6 percent of the nation's GDP. Mining has also become a lucrative industry, thanks in large part to the Pueblo Viejo Gold and Silver mine. Still, the country is considered poor, and it relies heavily on the United States, which is its largest trade partner, as well as loans from organizations such as the International Monetary Fund (IMF).

In 2014, the per capita gross domestic product (GDP) was estimated at $13,000 USD. In 2013, 15 percent of the population was unemployed; however, in 2014, that number dropped to 6.4 percent.

### Industry

Santo Domingo is the center of Dominican industry. Industries represent about 32.1 percent of the country's gross domestic product (GDP).

Nearly 21 percent of Dominicans work in industries such as metallurgy, petrochemicals and plastics, food processing, pharmaceuticals, cement, and construction.

The major industries include tourism, sugar processing, ferronickel and gold mining, textile production, cement, and tobacco. More than 500 native companies manufacture goods for the US market, and such assembly-line manufacturing employs more than eight percent of the population. Mining has been similarly profitable for foreign companies as well as local ones, particularly since the Pueblo Viejo Gold and Silver Mine reached its extraction phase in 2012.

Construction is also an important industry, partly because almost all of the necessary materials can be found locally. Most construction jobs in the Dominican Republic are the result of private contracts.

### Labor

Clothing and other items manufactured in the country's free-trade zones are exported tax-free to the United States. However, for most workers in these industries, the wages do little more than provide food for a family. During the last few decades, some factories have been accused of sweatshop practices, and the government has done little to reform the problem.

### Energy/Power/Natural Resources

In addition to its fertile farmland and beautiful beaches, the Dominican Republic has significant mineral and metal resources, including deposits of gold, ferronickel, bauxite, nickel, and silver. Larimar is a semi-precious stone that is found only on Hispaniola. The country has no oil deposits, and petroleum must be imported, which has proven an expensive requirement for running the country's electricity generators. Each year, Dominican Republic's State-owned Electric Utility loses some RD$50 million (Dominican pesos) to supply its plants with petroleum products and, in some cases, diesel. Currently, there are 19 hydropower plants in the Dominican Republic, the most recent of which, Monción, was built on the Mao River in 2001.

The country's extensive mountains contain valuable pine and mahogany trees; however, much of the Dominican's untamed wilderness has now been converted into protected national parks. Some deforestation has occurred due to overpopulation.

### Fishing

The fishing industry is reputed to be underdeveloped in the Dominican Republic. Media reports have documented instances of illegal seine fishing in Samaná Bay, which involves dragging the ocean floor and damaging ocean habitats and catching eggs and young fish in their nets. Other reports document lobster poaching, which is banned in the Dominican Republic. The Christian-ecumenical NGO Food for the Poor (FFP), working in conjunction with Taiwan International Cooperation and Development Fund, has begun to develop the Dominican Republic's aquaculture and, since 2000, has built 54 tilapia ponds to promote self-sufficiency and eventually develop export prospects.

### Forestry

Nearly 41 percent of the Dominican Republic is covered by forests. USAID has made funds available for a Sustainable Agriculture Center (CEPAS) in order to allow farmers in the Dominican Republic to add value to their forest products. Artisan furnaces and wood-curing tubs will improve forestry products and make them more marketable. The deforestation of pine groves has been reported in the areas of Jarabacoa, Santiago, and Moca.

### Mining/Metals

Mining is the country's largest export market and consists of gold, ferronickel, bauxite, nickel, silver, and Larimar (a rare mineral found only in the Dominican Republic). In 2012, the Pueblo Viejo Gold and Silver mine reached its extraction phase, and by 2013, it was yielding more than 1.11 million ounces of gold and 3.85 million ounces of silver. Companies like the Canadian-based mining concern Barrick Gold and US–based Royal Gold, Inc. are just two of the many foreign companies now present in the Dominican Republic who are investing in extraction processes.

## Agriculture

Agriculture represents about 6.3 percent of the Dominican GDP and takes up just over 51 percent of the country's land area. Just over 10 percent is occupied by permanent crops, 24.8 percent is permanent pasture, and 16.6 percent is tillable land, planted with new crops annually. Exports include sugar, coffee, rum, cocoa, tobacco, bananas, and plantains. Open markets overflow with lush produce. Most Dominican agricultural products and other exports ship from Santo Domingo, which is one of the busiest ports in Latin America.

Dominican agriculture is subject to fluctuations on the world market, which can have a damaging effect on the economy. The main cash crop is sugarcane, which is a seasonal, labor-intensive product. Coffee is the second largest export. The two other chief exports are cocoa and tobacco.

Rice is the most common food crop, followed closely by beans. The country is generally self-sufficient with these two staple food crops. Other crops include cotton, potatoes, corn, bananas, and citrus fruits.

## Animal Husbandry

Dominican livestock include beef and dairy cattle, swine, poultry, and goats. Livestock products, particularly eggs and dairy products, are produced both for domestic use and export. Since 2000, the Christian nonprofit aid organization Food For the Poor (FFP) has invested in community development projects to enhance animal husbandry practices and combat malnutrition. Such work as FFP's "DR Chickens for Life" and "DR Goats for Life," projects designed to teach basic animal husbandry skills and thereby promote self-sufficiency, will continue until December 31, 2015.

## Tourism

Tourism is one of the chief industries in the Dominican Republic, representing 61.6 percent of the GDP, and employing 64.7 percent of the work force. The largest growth occurs in Santo Domingo. The country's prime location in the center of the Caribbean and its many beaches draw tourists, as do the nature reserves and natural parks.

According to the World Bank, just over 18 percent of the country is protected land, which has become national parks. Some of the major national parks include Los Haitises National Park, which contains both a wet forest and a subtropical rainforest, and Jaragua National Park, the largest park, which includes a lagoon and a desert-like area.

In recent years, the country's tourist infrastructure has expanded to include new hotels, restaurants, and other amenities. This, combined with relatively inexpensive prices, has begun to lure more tourists to the country.

*Jennifer O'Donnell, Rebekah Painter, Sally Driscoll, & Savannah Schroll Guz*

## DO YOU KNOW?

- The United States Marines introduced baseball and volleyball to the Dominican Republic when the United States occupied the country from 1916 to 1924.
- Santo Domingo is the oldest city in the Americas.
- La Guácara Taína is a multi-level Santo Domingo nightclub built in a cave.
- Called Ceiba by the Taíno, the silk cotton tree found in the Dominican Republic takes 70 to 80 years to mature and can live for over 300 years. Growing to over 80 feet high, Ceiba trees were used by the Taíno to build canoes; one nine-foot-wide, hollowed-out trunk was capable of carrying 100 men.

## Bibliography

Brennan, Denise. *What's Love Got to Do with It?:*
*Transnational Desires and Sex Tourism in the*
*Dominican Republic.* Durham, NC: Duke UP, 2004.
Latin America Otherwise Ser.

CIA and US State Department. *Dominican Republic:*
*Country Studies, A Brief, Comprehensive Study of*
*Dominican Republic.* Covington, WA: Zay's Place, 2012.

Clammer, Paul, Michael Grosberg, and Kevin Raub. *Lonely*
*Planet Dominican Republic and Haiti*, 5th ed. London,
UK: Lonely Planet Publications. 2011.

Derby, Lauren H. *The Dictator's Seduction: Politics and*
*the Popular Imagination in the Era of Trujillo.* Durham,
NC: Duke UP, 2009. American Encounters/Global
Interactions Ser.

Garrison, Vivian and Carol I. Weiss. "Dominican Family
Networks and United States Immigration Policy: A Case
Study." *International Migration Review: Special Issue:*
*International Migration in Latin America* 13.2 (1979).

Keegan, William F. *The People Who Discovered Columbus:*
*The Prehistory of the Bahamas.* Gainesville: University
Press of Florida, 1992. Florida Museum of Natural
History: Ripley P. Bullen Ser.

Martinez, Samuel. "Not a Cockfight: Rethinking Haitian-
Dominican Relations." *Latin American Perspectives*
30.3 (May 2003): 80–101.

Roorda, Eric Paul, Lauren H. Derby, and Raymundo
González, ed. *The Dominican Republic Reader: History,*
*Culture, Politics.* Durham, NC: Duke UP, 2014. Latin
American Readers Ser.

Rough Guides, ed. *The Rough Guide to Dominican*
*Republic.* 6th ed. London: Rough Guides, 2014.

Santiago, Richard. *1965 Revolution in the Dominican*
*Republic.* Free People's Movement Archive, 2013.

Wucker, Michele. *Why the Cocks Fight: Dominicans,*
*Haitians, and the Struggle for Hispaniola.* New York:
Hill & Wang, 2000.

## Works Cited

Brennan, Denise. "Women Work, Men Sponge, and
Everyone Gossips: Macho Men and Stigmatized/
ing Women in a Sex Tourist Town." *Anthropological*
*Quarterly* 77.4. (Fall 2004): 705–773.

Bureau of Western Hemisphere Affairs. "US Relations with
the Dominican Republic: Fact Sheet." *US Department*
*of State.* US Department of State, 18 Nov. 2013. Web.
http://www.state.gov/r/pa/ei/bgn/35639.htm.

Central Intelligence Agency. "Dominican Republic." *The*
*World Factbook.* Central Intelligence Agency, 2015.
Web. https://www.cia.gov/library/publications/the-
world-factbook/geos/dr.html.

"Dominican Republic." *Encyclopedia Britannica.*
Encyclopædia Britannica, Inc., 2015. Web. http://www.
britannica.com/EBchecked/topic/168728/Dominican-
Republic/54448/Literature.

"The Food of the Dominican Republic: Freshly Cooked and
Plenty for Everyone." *Visiting-The-Dominican-Republic.*
*com.* Al G. Smith, 2015. Web. http://www.visiting-
the-dominican-republic.com/food-of-the-dominican-
republic.html.

Food for the Poor. "Housing, Animal Husbandry,
Agriculture, Aquaculture, Medical, Orphanages, and
Water Projects—Dominican Republic." *NGO Aid Map.*
InterAction, 2014. Web. http://foodsecurity.ngoaidmap.
org/projects/5811.

Gonzalez, Clara. "Maiz Caquiao or Chaca (Cracked Corn
Pudding)." *Aunt Clara's Kitchen.* DominicanCooking.
com/Clara Gonzalez, 2003. Web. http://www.
dominicancooking.com/941-maiz-caquiao-or-chaca-
creamy-corn.html.

Human Rights Watch. "Dominican Republic: Women
with HIV Doubly Abused." Human Rights Watch.
HRW, 12 Jul. 2004. Web. http://www.hrw.org/english/
docs/2004/07/13/domini9054.htm.

_____. "Failure to Protect Women Workers against
Discrimination in Law or Practice." *Human Rights*
*Watch.* HRW, 2004. http://hrw.org/backgrounder/arms/
hearing0405/3.htm#_Toc101701604.

Inter-American Development Bank. "Dominican Republic
to Improve Access to Drinking Water for 329,000
People with IDB Support." *News/News Releases.* Inter-
American Development Bank, 21 Nov. 2012. Web.
http://www.iadb.org/en/news/news-releases/2012–11-21/
clean-water-and-sanitation-in-dominican-republic,10229.
html.

Martin, Philip, Elizabeth Midgley, and Michael S.
Teitelbaum. "Migration and Development: Whither
the Dominican Republic and Haiti?" *International*
*Migration Review* 36.2 (2002): 570–592.

National Museum of Natural History. "A New Collection
of Taíno Artifacts from the Dominican Republic."
*Smithsonian National Museum of Natural History.*
Smithsonian Institution, 2015. Web. http://anthropology.
si.edu/cm/taino.htm.

"No End in Sight to Dominican Republic's Blackouts."
*Dominican Today.* The Dominican Republic News
Source, 2 Dec. 2013. Web. http://www.dominicantoday.
com/dr/economy/2013/12/2/49818/No-end-in-sight-to-
Dominican-Republics-blackouts.

Reuters. "Busting Sex Tourists in the Dominican
Republic." *Newsweek.* Newsweek LLC, 1 Apr. 2015.
Web. http://www.newsweek.com/busting-sex-tourists-
dominican-republic-318735.

Royal Gold, Inc. "Royal Gold Announces Agreement to
Acquire Gold and Silver Stream on Barrick's Interest in
the Pueblo Viejo Mine." *Royal Gold, Inc. News.* Royal
Gold, Inc., 5 Aug. 2015. Web. http://www.royalgold.
com/investors/news/news-details/2015/Royal-Gold-
Announces-Agreement-to-Acquire-Gold-and-Silver-
Stream-on-Barricks-Interest-in-the-Pueblo-Viejo-Mine/
default.aspx

"Silk Cotton Tree: Home to the Spirits of the Forest."
  *Caribbean Archeology at the Florida Museum of Natural
  History*. Florida Museum of Natural History, n.d. Web.
  http://www.flmnh.ufl.edu/caribarch/ceiba.htm.

Tolentino, Marianne de. "Tony Capellan, Dominican
  Contemporary Art." *Latin Art Museum*. Fundacion Ureña
  Rib, 18 May 2013. Web. http://www.latinartmuseum.
  com/capellan.htm.

"Traditional Jatibonicu Taino Tribal Cultural Games."
  *Taino Culture*. The Jatibonicu Taino Tribe of Borikén,
  2015. Web. http://www.taino-tribe.org/tribal-culture.
  html.

UN Development Programme. "Table 1: Human
  Development Index and Its Components." *Human
  Development Reports*. UNDP, 2015. Web. http://hdr.
  undp.org/en/content/table-1-human-development-index-
  and-its-components

UNESCO. "Dominican Republic: Permanent Delegation
  to UNESCO." *UNESCO Worldwide Latin America
  and Caribbean*. UNESCO, 2015. Web/ http://portal.
  unesco.org/geography/en/ev.php-URL_ID=2497&URL_
  DO=DO_TOPIC&URL_SECTION=201.html.

_____. "The Cultural Space of the Brotherhood
  of the Holy Spirit of the Congos of Villa Mella."
  *Proclamation of Masterpieces of Oral and Intangible
  Heritage of Humanity*. UNESCO, 18 May 2001.
  Web. http://www.unesco.org/bpi/intangible_heritage/
  dominican.htm.

World Bank. "Paying Taxes in Dominican Republic."
  *Doing Business*. The World Bank Group, 2015. Web.
  http://www.doingbusiness.org/data/exploreeconomies/
  dominican-republic/paying-taxes/

_____. "Personal Remittances, Received." *Data:
  World Bank*. The World Bank Group, 2015. Web. http://
  data.worldbank.org/indicator/BX.TRF.PWKR.DT.GD.
  ZS

_____. "Terrestrial Protected Areas." *The World
  Bank Data*. The World Bank Group, 2012. Web. http://
  data.worldbank.org/indicator/ER.LND.PTLD.ZS.

*A view of the harbor and surrounding buildings in St. Georges, Grenada. iStock/wwing*

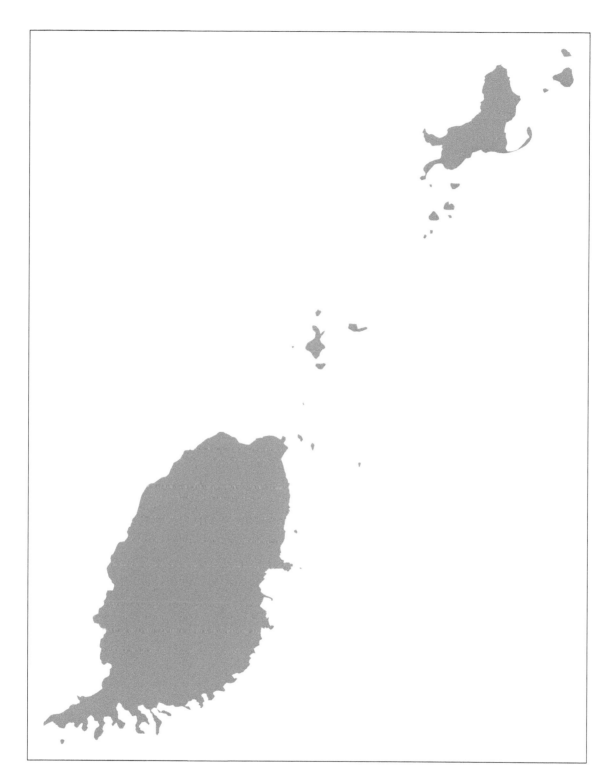

# GRENADA

## Introduction

Belonging to the Windward Islands in the southern Caribbean, Grenada reflects the powerful European empires that shaped its people and culture. The country is composed of three islands: Carriacou, Petite Martinique, and the largest island, Grenada.

After Christopher Columbus of Spain landed on the islands in 1498, French and British colonists descended on Grenada. Beginning in 1650, the islands have been under French colonial and then British rule, and have been repopulated by the descendants of European colonists, African slaves, and West Indian immigrants. The Grenada islands are in part famous for the 1983 US–led invasion. Grenada was devastated in September 2004, when Hurricane Ivan destroyed 90 percent of the country.

Grenada has a rich tradition of music, literature, theatre, and art. One of the birthplaces of calypso and reggae music, Grenada today boasts internationally renowned musicians. Grenada's African drumming and dance troupes, and particularly those of Carriacou, are known throughout the world for their sophistication and originality, though many Grenadian dancers also perform traditional European folk dances.

---

## GENERAL INFORMATION

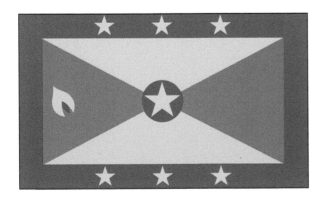

**Official Language(s):** English
**Population:** 106,000 (2013 estimate)
**Currency:** East Caribbean dollar

**Coins:** The Eastern Caribbean dollar comes in coin denominations of 1, 2, 5, 10, and 25; there is also a one-dollar coin.

**Land Area:** 344 square kilometers (132.8 square miles)

**National Motto:** "The Land, the People, the Light"

**National Anthem:** "Hail Grenada"

**Capital:** Saint George's

**Time Zone(s):** GMT -4

**Flag Description:** The flag of Grenada depicts a rectangle divided into four triangles: two yellow triangles in the top and bottom fields and two green triangles in the left and right fields. The four triangles are bordered on the outside by a red rectangle that includes six yellow stars—three on top and three on the bottom (representing the country's six parishes). In the center of the triangles is a red circle with a yellow star in the center (representing the capital Saint George). Finally, a clove of nutmeg (depicted using yellow,

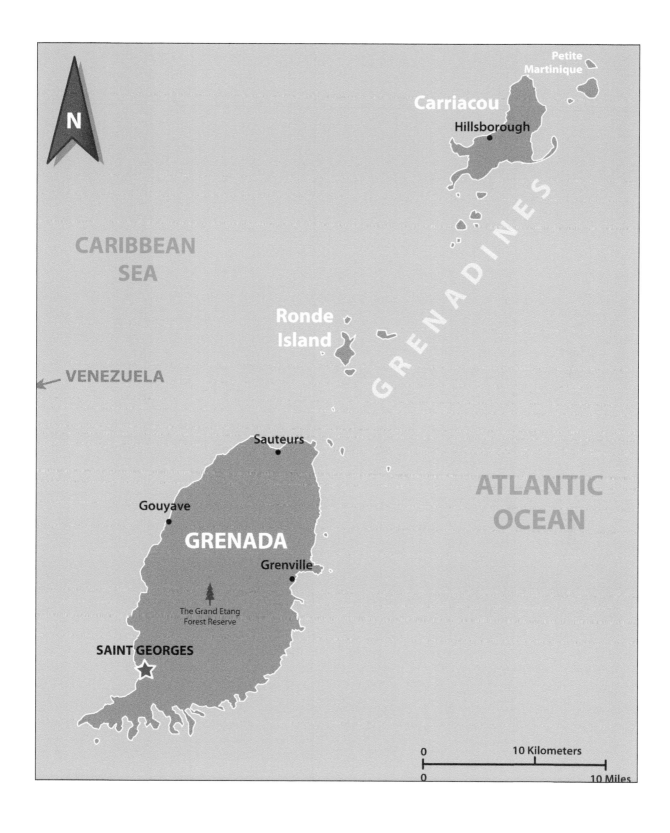

**Principal Cities by Population (2012):**

- St. George's (5,731)
- Gouyave (2,995)
- Grenville (2,403)
- Victoria (2,317)

red, and green) is featured in the flag's left green triangle. The nutmeg represents Grenada's history as a spice exporter. The flag uses yellow, green, and red to reflect Grenada's pan-African heritage.

## Population

Grenada's population reflects its eventful history. About 82 percent of Grenadians consider themselves to be black, 13 percent are said to be of mixed European descent, five percent European and East Indian, and a small number are Arawak mixed with Carib Amerindian. On the islands of Petite Martinique and Carriacou, people claim a unique heritage of mixed African, West Indies, French, and Scottish ancestry.

Grenada's high birth rate (19 births per 1,000 people) is largely offset by a high rate of emigration from the island (13 people per 1,000). Average life expectancy is fairly high by Caribbean standards, at 71 years for men and 76 years for women (2014 estimate). Grenada's infant mortality rate is an average of 11 deaths for every 1,000 live births (2013 estimate). Most people live in large extended families, with several generations living under one roof.

Grenada has a total area of only 344 square kilometers (132.8 square miles), which makes it possible for many people to work in St. George's, the capital and largest city, but live outside the town proper. The majority of Grenadians reside in rural villages scattered throughout the island with only around 4500 living in the capital; approximately 39 percent of the population lives in urban areas (2013 estimate).

## Languages

English is the official language of Grenada. A small and declining number of elderly residents still speak a French-based creole dialect. The youthfulness of Granada's society—nearly 27 percent of the population is under the age of fifteen—has accelerated the fading of traditional local ways in favor of Western popular culture. This shift has sparked a recent movement to preserve the island's traditional heritage by teaching French patois to schoolchildren.

## Native People & Ethnic Groups

When Christopher Columbus landed on the island of Grenada in 1498, he found it inhabited by the Carib Indians, a group of expert navigators and raiders who had made their way from the South American mainland and conquered the island's early Arawak and Ciboney peoples ("Carib" comes from the Arawak term for "cannibal").

Although the Carib forced the evacuation of England's first Grenadine colony in the early 17th century, French colonists supported by their military forced out the Carib and Arawak only 40 years later. Faced with capture by the French troops, the remaining Carib men, women, and children jumped to their deaths from the island cliffs at Sauteurs (now known as Carib's Leap or Leaper's Hill). Only scattered descendants and faint traces of these earlier inhabitants remain in modern Grenada.

The largest ethnic group in Grenada is Afro-Grenadian, which represent an estimated 82 percent of the population. Minority ethnic groups include Mulatto, Indian, and Arawak.

## Religions

Almost all of Grenada's citizens practice some form of Christianity: 45 percent are Roman Catholic, 14 percent are Anglican, and 33 percent adhere to other forms of Protestantism. There are, however, small numbers of Rastafarians, Muslims, Hindus, and Ba'hai.

## Climate

Grenada is positioned between the Caribbean Sea and Atlantic Ocean, about 100 kilometers (60 miles) north of Venezuela. Its tropical climate means warm temperatures, ranging from 24° to 30° Celsius (75.2° to 86° Fahrenheit), except in the slightly cooler mountains in Grenada's interior.

Grenada's dry season, lasting from February to May, is more than made up for by the rainy season between June and December. On the coast, annual rainfall averages about 152 centimeters (60 inches), but the rainfall over Grenada's lush interior forests averages far more, about 419 centimeters (165 inches) per year.

Grenada is also vulnerable to hurricanes that sweep across the Atlantic during the rainy season. Although no major hurricane had hit the islands since 1955, Hurricane Ivan ravaged Grenada in September 2004, devastating most of the country.

## ENVIRONMENT & GEOGRAPHY

### Topography

Grenada's three islands are volcanic in origin. The largest, Grenada, rises dramatically from the Atlantic Ocean with steep, rocky cliffs and white sand beaches. The mountainous interior of Grenada rises to its highest point on Mount Saint Catherine at 840 meters (2,756 feet) above sea level, and drops down in the form of dramatic waterfalls and steep hills. The island is well irrigated with streams and crater lakes, including the island's largest lake, Grand Etang. Petite Martinique and Carriacou, the nation's smaller islands, are flatter, with considerably less elevation above sea level.

St. George's is situated on the western side of the island of Grenada, the largest of the three islands that make up the nation of Grenada, which lies in the eastern Caribbean Sea. The capital is located in a parish of the same name. Grenada is a part of a Caribbean island group called the Windward Islands, which also includes Martinique, Saint Lucia, Saint Vincent, Barbados, Dominica, and the Grenadines island chain.

The capital is situated on the island's southwestern coast on a small peninsula with a shallow exterior bay. Its deep, natural harbor is considered one of the finest in the Caribbean and has historically played a key role in the area's

economy. The town's residential and commercial areas line the hillsides that follow the curve of the bay.

### Plants & Animals

The dry, sandy climate of the smaller islands limits animal and plant species to those capable of living amid sparse soil and scant water. Dry weather plants, lizards, iguanas, and a wealth of seabirds populate the islands of Petite Martinique and Carriacou.

The island of Grenada provides a far more lush range of habitats, from the mountains of the interior, to the crater lakes, to mangrove swamps. The tropical rainforest in the inland includes rare reserves of teak, native monkeys, opossums, iguana, mongooses, orchids, and other rare tropical flowers.

## CUSTOMS & COURTESIES

### Greetings

English is the island nation's official language, but Grenadian Creole, which is English-based, is also widespread. (A blend of Caribbean and French may be spoken in rural areas.) Informal greetings typically consist of "Hello" and may include a nod of acknowledgment or the tapping of clenched fists between friends. In rural areas, it is common to hear patois greetings such as "Hows tings?" ("How are things?") or "W'happen dey?" ("What's happening?"). Handshakes are the norm in formal situations, whether it is between men or women, or both. Honorific titles are customarily used, and friends normally address one another by a "call name" (nickname).

When women greet each other casually, they might embrace or kiss each other on the cheek, if they share a certain level of familiarity. Men greeting each other, on the other hand, will usually stick to simple nods of acknowledgment. In any case, courtesy is valued in all settings. Simple, polite salutations are expected at any time of day, whether greeting friends or strangers. It is not uncommon for people to call out the name of their friend or relative as they pass by the house, stopping to chat if the friend is home.

### Gestures & Etiquette

Contact while conversing is not uncommon, and Grenadians may stand close to each other during conversation. However, speakers with less familiarity will often stand an arm's length apart. In business settings, the distance between speakers may be even longer. Direct eye contact is expected, but considered rude if excessive. Children freely show their affection for each other, and it is normal to see boys walking with arms over each other's shoulders or girls walking hand in hand.

Public transportation is often crowded, meaning that passengers will be sitting extremely close to each other. Women, especially elderly women and women with children, are given priority seating on public transportation. Casual social meetings with friends might rarely be punctual, and it is expected that most people will arrive later than planned. (The planned time for business meetings and appointments, however, is generally adhered to.)

### Eating/Meals

There are typically three meals per day. Breakfast, normally eaten in the early morning, is generally accompanied by coffee and lighter fare. Families usually sit together for the main meal of the day, eaten around noon. Meals are usually eaten with a spoon and served in a bowl, though wealthier families may choose to eat with other utensils. The main meal is accompanied by fruit juice, soft drinks, or water. Supper is usually a light meal, such as bread and cheese. Dining out options in Grenada range from upscale European restaurants to inexpensive roadside eateries. Markets and food stalls along the beach commonly serve up freshly cooked local food, such as oildown (a breadfruit stew) or roti (a popular snack or appetizer made from meat and vegetables cooked in a flaky crust).

Meals are considered social gatherings, so holiday meals are given particular significance. On Christmas, for example, families and friends will visit each other's homes, stopping for meals at each house. These light meals may include spice cakes, ham, guava cheese, boudin (blood sausage), sweet ground cornmeal cake, or other traditional fare.

### Visiting

Grenadians are known for their warmth and hospitality. Unannounced visits are commonplace, particularly during the afternoon or early evening. Around this time, it is common to see Grenadians chatting in the road or on their front porches. When making an impromptu visit, people will usually call to their friend or relative from outside the house, and wait to be invited inside.

When offered refreshments at someone's home, it is considered rude to refuse all offers; one should at least accept a beverage. If one does not wish to eat at a fête (gathering or party), it is acceptable to take home food for later.

## LIFESTYLE

### Family

The extended family is a core element of Grenadian society. Relatives take care of each other domestically and financially, and it is common for several generations (and extended members such as cousins) to reside as one household. Men often provide a family's income, and the women normally take charge of the household duties. Parents will sometimes go abroad to earn more money, leaving their extended family to raise a child. In recent years, with more women joining the workforce, urban and wealthy families are more likely to be small and less traditional in their roles.

Due to embedded cultural traditions, children born out of wedlock are generally raised by their female family members, as the fathers do not bear the responsibility for child rearing. However, community support is strong, and resources are often pooled. Cohabitation before marriage is a common practice for couples, and children often continue to live with their families in adulthood.

Land is the main form of inheritance and is usually passed on to the next generation through the father's line.

## Housing

Only roughly one-third of Grenada's population lives in urban areas, while the majority live in the countryside. Many rural areas are far removed from the towns and cities, whether they are in the coastal regions or the forested highlands. Traditional housing in the highlands consists of mud-walled houses with thatched roofs. Contemporary housing varies widely, ranging from informal construction such as a wooden shack with a tin roof to the modern bungalow. Many Grenadians in rural areas own land on which they can practice subsistence farming.

Housing in urban areas shows more of a colonial influence, with 18th-century French colonial architecture alongside English Georgian architecture. Houses from this era often have iron balconies, large windows, and sedan porches (small, covered porches). Bright colors are a staple of housing design in Grenada, and many colonial styles are modified to include this Caribbean accent.

In 2004, Hurricane Ivan destroyed at least 85 percent of housing on Grenada, with more damage incurred the following year after Hurricane Emily. Grenada recovered from much of the damage relatively quickly through efficient domestic labor and international aid money.

## Food

Grenada is known as the Spice Island of the Caribbean and is home to a variety of locally-grown spices, including nutmeg, cinnamon, clove, and vanilla. This distinction, combined with the culinary influences of West Africa, Europe, Asia, and the local creole culture, has resulted in the unique and flavorful Grenadian cuisine. Staple foods are rice, bread, fruits, and vegetables. Chicken, fish, goat, and lamb are commonly eaten, while beef and pork are not readily available. Common vegetables include plantains, cassava, shallots, pumpkins, tomatoes, and sweet potatoes, while local fruits available include coconuts, mangoes, bananas, watermelon, papaya, guava, and soursop.

The national dish of Grenada is oildown, a stew normally cooked in large batches from local vegetables, salted meats, and seasonings. The vegetables used normally include breadfruit, callaloo, dasheen (a root vegetable), and plantains. Possible meat ingredients include pig tail, pig snout, chicken "back and neck," salt mackerel, or crab. The broth also has coconut milk, water, saffron, and various spices. Other popular dishes are grilled fish, fish broth, roti with curry chicken or vegetables, breadfruit and saltfish, and conch. "Callaloo" is used as the name for both a local vegetable and a popular soup made from that vegetable. A "bake" is fried bread used as a bun, often served with salted cod inside. Fried fish is also popular, and widely available.

Breakfast usually includes coffee or cocoa tea, which is made with spices and local cocoa. Other typical drinks include fresh fruit juices, soft drinks, and locally brewed beer and rum.

## Life's Milestones

Life milestones in Grenada reflect the dominance of Christianity. An estimated 45 percent of Grenadians in the early 21st century identify as Roman Catholic, while Protestants make up about 33 percent of the population. The deceased are traditionally honored, and funerals normally call for a banquet in honor of the dead. The Day of the Dead is another commemoration for the departed in which music, food, and drink are brought to the graveyard for a nighttime celebration. "Obeah", a term for folk magic in the West Indies, is also a prevailing belief among many Grenadian Christians.

## CULTURAL HISTORY

## Art

There is no strong tradition of fine arts education in Grenada and the majority of Grenadian artists are self-taught. The Grenadian visual arts reveal a strong West African influence—African slaves were brought to Grenada soon after the advent of

French colonialism—as well as a range of indigenous and European styles. One particular style, the naïve style of painting, became popular with North American and European art. This movement was characterized by a deliberate rejection of more complex techniques and the embrace of a bold, "childlike" style.

Canute Caliste (1914–2005) was the best-known Grenadian naïve painter. He lived on Carriacou, one of Grenada's two island dependencies, and painted scenes of traditional Grenadian life. His paintings showed the Carnival and other festivals, fishing boats, cricket matches, and other typical Grenadian scenes. Although his paintings were internationally renowned, he was famous in Grenada and Carriacou more as a talented fiddle player than a painter. Grenadian sculptors traditionally take advantage of the cedar, teak, and other types of wood available on the island, or they make innovative use of other natural items such as coconut shells or crab shells.

## Architecture

French and British colonialism had a significant impact on Grenadian architecture, particularly in the older towns and cities. Grenada's capital, St. George's, established by the French in 1650, is still home to 18th-century French colonial architecture, including distinct features such as elaborate iron balconies, pastel colors, and red tile roofs. There is a strong presence of English Georgian architecture as well, from when the capital became a British city in 1793, but these styles have usually been modified with a strong Caribbean accent. These modifications may include the use of bright colors and window design that takes full advantage of the cooling breeze and shelter from the sun.

In fact, Grenada's climate has been very influential in the development of the country's architecture. For example, it is common for school buildings to have big, open frames instead of windows. During storms, these frames can be sealed up with wooden boards. Houses from the 17th and 18th century may have a sedan porch, a small covered porch open on either side, built to take advantage of the outdoors and to shelter

residents from the sun. Unique decorations on houses include hollow eggshells balanced on the tips of cactus branches.

## Music

Traditional African music has had a strong influence on Grenadian music styles. Calypso is often regarded as Grenada's national music, though reggae, soca (dance music derived from calypso), and jazz are also widely popular. The old style of calypso, called "kaiso", has evolved over time to include more experimental modern styles. Grenadian calypso in the 1970s was strongly patriotic, as the music style was viewed as a significant part of the national identity in the time of independence. Modern calypso sometimes includes poetry, political commentary, and sounds influenced by Indian music.

Carriacou has a strong tradition of the Afro-Caribbean "Big Drum," a unique style of music that is often accompanied by dance. Big Drum originates from the 18th century, and is a style of music dedicated to honoring the ancestors of Carriacou's Afro-Caribbean "nations" (Afro-Caribbeans living in Carriacou define themselves in groups called "nations," which include the Cromanti, Manding, Chamba, Temne, Moko, Igbo, Arada, Kongo, and Banda.) The biggest nation, the Cromanti, traditionally begin Big Drum ceremonies, and their song is followed by other nations' songs. All songs are performed with boula drums and the high-pitched cut drum. These drums are traditionally made from rum barrels.

Contemporary music has been influenced by zouk, a French Caribbean musical style, and the steel band music from neighboring Trinidad and Tobago. Grenadian jazz has also gained recognition. The French and British colonization also left a musical legacy, in the form of lullabies, quadrilles, and sea shanties (shipboard working songs). Music festivals continue to be an important part of Grenadian cultural life, including Carnival, Carriacou Maroon Music Festival, and the Grenada Drum Festival. Carnival highlights calypso music, while the other two festivals focus on drumming.

Grenadian dances derive from both African dance and European styles such as quadrilles. Popular contemporary dances include the Carriacou Big Drum style and the heel-and-toe.

## Literature

Storytelling represents a significant form of Grenadian culture, one that holds more importance than written literature. These stories are usually passed down orally, though they are recorded in writing as well. Grenadian folktales derive from African and French traditions, and incorporate characters from both. These stories are sometimes called "crick-crack stories" because of a call and response tradition in which the storyteller begins by saying "crick" and the audience replies "crack." Like the folk tales of the African and French cultures, these stories typically feature the trickster character Anancy (or Anansi), a trickster spider god originating from West African storytelling traditions and now present in several Caribbean cultures. The she-devil La Diablesse and the werewolf Ligaroo are both derived from French traditions ("Ligaroo" is derived from "Loup Garoux").

A national literature did not emerge until the early 20th century. There is a noteworthy presence of Grenadian authors writing resistance literature, though their work is often not well known. Author Merle Collins (1950– ) uses the Caribbean dialect in her writing, which can be defined as resistance literature. Collins, along with other contemporary Grenadian writers, uses fiction, experimental techniques, and local myths and legends to address the often-untold perspectives on Grenada's history. After the coup and invasion of 1983, revolutionary writers and artists seemed more prone to self-censorship.

---

## CULTURE

---

## Arts & Entertainment

The performing arts are highly valued in Grenada, particularly dance, drumming, music, and drama. Performances happen regularly at festivals and in small theaters. The visual arts, on the other hand, have not yet gained a strong foothold in the mainstream. The visual arts are largely supported by tourists and expatriates, and many Grenadians make little distinction between art and craft. This view is further cemented by the lack of arts educational resources and the expenses of necessary materials that must be imported. The artists who do practice in Grenada use oil, acrylic, and watercolors, but they often use unconventional surfaces to paint on. Various local woods, cloth, calabash (gourd), and bamboo have all been used by different Grenadian artists.

Grenada, like many Caribbean islands, is known for its celebration of Carnival. Rooted in pre-Lenten and pagan traditions, Carnival annually occurs on the second weekend of August to promote tourism, and before Ash Wednesday—which is the traditional time—on the Grenadine islands of Carriacou and Petite Martinique. Music is at the center of the festivities, and includes Caribbean staples such as calypso, reggae, and steel pan (as well as more modern or emerging styles of music). Masquerading is a unique aspect of Carnival, and the celebrations feature numerous traditional and costumed characters. On Carriacou, a masquerade tradition known as Shakespeare Mas occurs during the Carnival festivities, and includes Shakespearean speeches diffused with original tales of boasting. Carnival celebrations also happen at the same time as Rainbow City, a tribute to Emancipation Day, celebrated in the parish of Saint Andrew's.

Traditional calypso maintains its important place in contemporary Grenadian music, but it has been modified and experimented with over the years. Modern calypso artists often incorporate sounds from both nearby and faraway cultures, and lyrics are sometimes used to convey a political or poetic message. Grenada's most famous calypso artist is Might Sparrow (1935– ), who is known as the "calypso king of the world." Sparrow's music is also known for its political and social commentary. Reggae and zouk also continue to be popular styles of Grenadian music.

Grenada has a fledgling cinema, and the country's first feature-length film, *Blinded*, was released in 2006 to highly positive reactions from the public. It is considered Grenada's first local film as it was entirely filmed and produced on the island, and featured a local cast. The movie, directed by Anderson Quarless, tells a story of domestic violence with the intent to educate Grenadian youth on how to avoid this type of violence and speak out against it.

Grenadians have a passion for sports. The most popular sports are cricket, football (soccer), and netball, although basketball, golf, and tennis are becoming increasingly popular. Visitors will also find children playing rounders, a baseball-style game that uses a cricket bat and tennis ball.

Every June, children between the ages of four and twelve participate in the Preparatory Games, a festival of athletic competitions. For the older children, Intercol provides an annual forum for athletic competitions of all sorts. Top athletes appear every year in the Grenada International Triathlon and the National Athletic Championship.

The Carriacou Regatta in August is only one of Grenada's boating events, combining competition with festivals, dancing, and street parties. The Spice Island Billfish Tournament draws fishermen from around the world to the plentiful waters of Grenada's coasts.

## Cultural Sites & Landmarks

St. George's, the capital of Grenada, was established by the French in the early 18th century. The city is home to the island's central natural harbor, Carenage, which attracts vessels ranging from modest fishing boats to enormous cruise ships. The French influence remains clear in the traditional architecture of houses topped with the red tile roofs and pastel colors associated with French towns. Buildings designed in the style of Georgian architecture reveal the later influence of English colonization. The York House, which is home to the country's Senate, House of Representatives, and Supreme Court, is an elegant example of early Georgian architecture.

The vibrant Market Square has remained a steady center of St. Georgian life for the past two centuries, offering not only markets of fresh produce, but also a venue for religious ceremonies, parades, and political speeches. The Roman Catholic Cathedral of St. George's adds another decidedly European accent to the city with its Gothic tower built in 1818. At the same time, its painted interior celebrates the local culture found throughout the Diocese of St. George's-in-Grenada. St. George's is also home to two colonial-era stone forts. Fort George was built by the French at the beginning of the 18th century and houses the police head-quarters. Located on an elevated position at the harbor's entrance, it offers a sweeping view of the capital. The fort still has working cannons, which are fired to mark ceremonial occasions. A smaller fort, the British-built Fort Fredrick, sits atop a hill located in the town center and dates back to 1791.

Grenada's second largest city, Grenville, houses the island's biggest nutmeg processing factory. Tourists can tour the facilities and learn about all the steps involved in preparing nutmeg for sale. Grenville is also known for its Saturday market, where local merchants, farmers, and fishermen sell various types of fresh produce and local crafts. Another main producer of spices is the Dougaldston Spice Estate, located outside Gouyave. This estate offers visitors a view into the growing and preparation processes of various spices.

Grenada is known for its beautiful beaches, but it offers a range of other natural attractions as well. The Grand Etang Forest Reserve is home to a wide range of native wildlife, and visitors can walk or hike along several different paths. The park is named for the nearby Grand Etang, a lake inside an ancient crater basin of the Central Range volcanic mountains.

## Libraries & Museums

Grenada's National Museum, located in the capital, documents Grenadian cultural and political history from ancient times through the present day. Its collections include artifacts from the Caribs, who were some of the earliest inhabitants of Grenada and surrounding Caribbean islands. Other museums of note include the Mabuya Fishermen Museum and the regional but small Carriacou Museum, whose collection includes pre-Columbian pottery.

The Grenada Public Library functions as the country's national library and archives. The National Documentation Centre serves as Grenada's legal depository, and the island country has a network of community libraries.

## Holidays

Grenadians celebrate national holidays with food, dance, and drink in homes in the rural areas, and at balls and hotel-hosted parties in the cities. Holidays include New Year's Day, Labor Day, Emancipation Day, Thanksgiving, and Boxing Day. Of all of these holidays, the most important is Independence Day (February 7), when a military parade takes place in St. George's and locals gather for beach parties.

Grenada's many Christians also celebrate Christmas with church services and caroling, Easter with kite-flying competitions, and Corpus Christi (in June) with the season's first plantings.

Grenada highlights it music, arts, and food during the Spice Jazz Festival during the last week in May. The end of June ushers in Fisherman's Birthday, when the feasts of Saints Peter and Paul are marked with the blessing of fishing nets and boats, boat races, and still more street festivals. In the second week of August (Spring in Carriacou), Grenadians celebrate Carnival with music, musical competitions, food, dancing, and street festivals.

## Youth Culture

In January 2009, the World Bank approved a $3 million (USD) credit toward offering private sector-driven skilled training to youth as part of an initiative to increase youth employment. Grenada's rate of unemployment is especially high in the youth population—as of 2005, the youth unemployment rate was reported as 31.5 percent. Skill training is important because many Grenadian youth do not make it past a primary level of education, and therefore would benefit from vocational and business training. Rural migrants are at an even greater disadvantage than urban youth, as they normally lack the social and workplace skills expected by employers. In addition, with more Grenadians forgoing educational and employment opportunities abroad, the government has recognized the importance of youth empowerment with entrepreneurial skills, particularly in the face of high unemployment. The project is also aimed at reducing youth-related crime by increasing the number of employed youth.

In 2000, it was reported that 51 percent of the population that was classified as impoverished were less than 20 years of age. The high unemployment rate is one significant reason for this, but teenage pregnancy is another noteworthy factor. Teenage pregnancy is very common in Grenada, and teen mothers are often single parents who end up having different children by different men. Studies have indicated that traditional Caribbean stereotypes perceive a man with many partners and children differently and with more esteem than in Western culture, which makes it more difficult to break the cycle. HIV/AIDS education for teenagers is also crucial, as a high number of teenagers are sexually active. Though there was initial unwillingness to discuss condom use, educational initiatives now offer comprehensive information.

## SOCIETY

## Transportation

Minibuses are a common means of public transportation, particularly in St. George's and other urban areas. Minibuses tend to be filled past capacity. Private cars, taxis, and water taxis are also available for local transportation. Buses and minibuses normally wait in the center of town until they are completely full. Taxis and private cars can normally be found at the airport, at major hotels, and along the harbor. Traffic moves on the left-hand side of the road.

## Transportation Infrastructure

The major road network in Grenada is in decent condition in most areas, having been largely rebuilt since 1984. Secondary roads, on the other hand, are poorly maintained. Grenada's only airport, Point Salines International, is located outside of St. George's. International flights are offered, as well as daily flights to Carriacou through Leeward Islands Air Transport. Ferry service to Carriacou is also available.

## Media & Communications

Grenada has a free media both in law and in practice. There are no government-owned newspapers, and no daily newspapers. Privately-owned weekly publications liberally exercise their freedom to criticize the government. Weekly publications include *The Grenada Informer*, *The Grenada Guardian*, *The Grenadian Voice*, and *Grenada Today*.

The principal radio and television stations, on the other hand, are owned by the Grenada Broadcasting Network (GBN), which is jointly owned by the government and the Caribbean Communications Network (CCN). GBN TV is the main television station, though the private station MTV Grenada is also available. Gayelle TV provides private cable service. As of 2014, there were four television broadcast stations. Public radio stations include Klassic Radio and HOTT FM, while Spice Capital Radio and Vibes are among the private FM stations. Harbour Light of the Windwards is a private Christian station.

As with most Caribbean islands, the mobile market has fueled Grenada's telecommunications sector since the turn of the 21st century. Broadband access is increasingly becoming the primary form of Internet access. As of 2010, there were an estimated 48,000 Internet users, representing roughly 45 percent of the population.

---

## SOCIAL DEVELOPMENT

## Standard of Living

Grenada ranked 79 out of 187 countries on the 2013 United Nations Human Development Index (HDI), which measures quality of life and standard of living indicators.

## Water Consumption

According to 2014 World Health Organization (WHO) statistics, approximately 98 percent of the population had access to improved sanitation. As of 2014, an estimated 97 percent of the urban population had access to improved drinking water. However, Grenada faces challenges related to waste water and the sustainability of its marine and costal environment.

## Education

Grenada follows a British model for its educational system. The first six years of primary education, from ages 6 to 14, are free and compulsory, giving the country its high rate of literacy. An estimated 96 percent of the adult population of Grenada is literate despite the fact that 32 percent of Grenadians live below the poverty line.

Grenada has 57 primary schools and 19 public secondary schools. All education is in English, although students must also take French and Spanish classes.

The country is home to a branch of the University of West Indies. TA Marryshow Community College has a school of agriculture and a teacher's training college. Run by American administrators, St. George's University on Grenada is well known internationally for its medical school.

## Women's Rights

Although women traditionally worked at home taking care of family and household duties, financial necessities in contemporary times often require women to hold a job outside the home in addition to performing household duties. Although men continue to dominate the workforce, women hold jobs in politics, banking, farming, and nutmeg processing stations. Unlike men, however, women are expected to return home from their day jobs to complete household duties, such as cooking and cleaning. Although men are expected to marry and have children, it is also common practice for a man to have a girl-friend on the side. Acceptance of this practice is gradually declining, particularly now that women are achieving more freedom through opportunities for education.

Although there are laws criminalizing rape and spousal rape, violence against women remains a significant problem. Domestic violence cases are normally addressed with prompt action, and sentences are specified according to the severity of the assault. A shelter for abused women and their children has been established, as well as an anonymous hot line to report abuse and get help. Although sexual harassment is prohibited by law, the lack of criminal penalties means that the harassed must address the case as a civil suit.

Lesbians, Gays, Bisexual, and Transsexual (LGBT) persons in general, often face a greater risk of rape and violence, in addition to abuse and discrimination. Statistics on discrimination against lesbians are unavailable, but advocates point out that their status as both women and homosexuals requires them a higher level of protection against discrimination.

## Health Care

Grenada has a strong health-care system, particularly by Caribbean standards. Based on World Health Organizations (WHO) models, Grenada's health network emphasizes widespread access to basic health care, attention to the prevention of disease, and specialized programs for prenatal and early childhood medical care. Free basic care is provided to those in need.

The country has three major hospitals: St. George's on Grenada in the town of St. George's, Princess Alice Hospital in the parish of St. Andrew, and Princess Royal Hospital on Carriacou. The country also has facilities for senior citizens and for mentally or developmentally disabled children. Free dental care is provided through the hospitals.

Grenada has a network of six health centers and thirty district medical clinics. St. George's medical school, part of St. George's University on Grenada, is a training center for medical providers throughout the Caribbean and beyond.

## GOVERNMENT

### Structure

French and British colonists struggled to subdue the Carib Indians who inhabited the islands in the 15th century. The French finally took control of the islands through the slaughter of these earlier inhabitants. Bringing in slaves from Africa, the French repopulated the islands and set up a colonial government primarily interested in exporting spices, indigo dyes, sugar, and cotton from the islands.

Fierce struggles between the French and British during the late 17th century and early 18th century finally resulted in British colonial control in 1763. The British continued to bring in indentured laborers to work the plantations into the 19th century. By the time slavery was abolished on the island in 1834, there were over 24,000 African slaves living in Grenada.

It was not until 1967 that Grenada was granted semi-autonomy by the British government, though still within the framework of the British Commonwealth. Joining with the Grenadine Islands of Petite Martinique and Carriacou in 1973, Grenada adopted a constitution in 1973 and became a fully independent nation in 1974.

Grenada's first independent government proved ineffectual and corrupt, but in 1979 a socialist-influenced group under the leadership of a London-educated lawyer name Maurice Bishop seized power in a bloodless coup. Calling itself the New Jewel Movement, the government instituted widespread economic reforms, restructured and improved education and health care, began construction of new infrastructure on the islands, and re-instituted human-rights protections. Though overwhelmingly popular, the government fell victim to a violent military coup in 1983, which resulted in the arrest and eventual execution of several leaders.

The new government dealt harshly with the popular protests that followed, shooting and killing or arresting protestors. Immediately afterward, the United States invaded the island, supported by a US–Caribbean pact, and ousted the leaders with military and civilian casualties. The

United States removed troops soon afterward, though Caribbean troops remained for several years afterward. Democratic elections have been in place since 1983.

Grenada is still a constitutional monarchy and a member of the British Commonwealth of Nations. Its monarch is drawn from Britain's line of royal succession and is represented within Grenada by a governor.

Grenada's Parliament is made up of a 13-member Senate and a 15-member House of Representatives. Senate members are appointed: 10 by the government and three by the opposition party. House members are elected by popular vote to five-year terms.

## Political Parties

Grenada's two major political parties are the liberal National Democratic Congress (NDC) and the conservative New National Party (NNP). Politics in the country operate in what is essentially a two-party system. The Grenada United Labour Party is the only major challenger to the two dominant parties.

## Local Government

Grenada is divided into six administrative subdivisions known as parishes. Local government is limited in each parish, as politics and government in the country remain centralized. In November 2010, the territories Carriacou and Petite Martinique announced that they would establish local government councils.

## Judicial System

Grenada's Supreme Court has two sections, the High Court of Justice and the Court of Appeals. The country's system of law is based on British common law. Unlike most countries in the Eastern Caribbean, Grenada has a legal aid system for civil and criminal defendants. In 2000, the country had seven presiding judges and 50 practicing attorneys.

In addition, the East Caribbean Supreme Court of Justice, the judicial branch of the Organisation of Eastern Caribbean States, is also based in Grenada.

## Taxation

Citizens and corporations in Grenada pay a flat income tax of 30 percent. The government of Grenada introduced a National Reconstruction Levy on those earning over 12,000 ECD annually in 2005, following Hurricanes Ivan and Emily. This tax was abolished in January 2009. Property taxes are also collected in Grenada.

## Armed Forces

Armed forces in Grenada consist of only the Royal Grenada Police Force and the Coast Guard. For matters of national defense, the police force maintains a paramilitary force.

## Foreign Policy

The Grenadian government has prioritized the promotion of Grenada's economic interests and image as the main objectives of its foreign policy. In doing so, the government has sectioned its foreign relations into bilateral relations with other nations and multilateral relations with international organizations and the promotion of world peace and development. This includes trade relations with the European Union (EU), focus on maritime law and anti-terrorism, and Grenada's association with the Non-Aligned Movement (NAM). Grenada's foreign relations are also responsible for the foreign aid the country has received in areas such as education, teacher training, childcare, health, and human rights.

Grenada has been a member of the United Nations (UN) since 1974, and holds membership in the International Monetary Fund (IMF), the World Bank, and the Organization of American States (OAS). Grenada also maintains leadership in regional affairs, and was one of 14 Caribbean countries in 1997 to attend the first US–regional summit for cooperation on trade, counter-narcotics, justice, finance, and development. Grenada is also a member state of the Commonwealth of Nations, the Caribbean Development Bank (CDB), the Organization of Eastern Caribbean States (OECS), and the Caribbean Community (CARICOM).

Grenada's relations with the United States have been far from consistently strong. When

Maurice Bishop (1944–1983) and the New Jewel Movement (NJM) political party gained power in the 1979 revolution, the United States immediately became hostile to the new regime, refusing to give aid for military defense. When Maurice Bishop then asked Cuba for assistance, the United States refused to recognize Grenada's ambassador, forbade emergency relief aid, and discouraged US tourism to Grenada. Hostilities intensified, including blocking aid through the World Bank and CDB, as well as restricting aid from the IMF.

The United States invaded Grenada in 1983 after Bishop was overthrown and subsequently executed by a military coup led by the more extreme NJM. One of the principal justifications for American intervention was to protect Americans in Grenada based on claims of endangerment. There was strong international opposition to the US invasion, and many believe that the true reason for invasion was to "punish" Grenada for not ceding enough control to the US government as other Caribbean states had done. The American forces did not ease control for several years, until finally allowing popular elections to take place. Since that time, the Grenadian government has been more in line with US foreign policy aims.

## Human Rights Profile

International human rights law insists that states respect civil and political rights, and also promote an individual's economic, social, and cultural rights. The United Nations (UN) Universal Declaration of Human Rights (UDHR) is recognized as the standard for international human rights. Its authors sought the counsel of the world's great thinkers, philosophers, and religious leaders, and were careful to create a document that reflects the core values shared by every world culture. (To read this document or view the articles relating to cultural human rights, visit: http://www.udhr.org/UDHR/default.htm.)

On December 10, 2008, the 16 anniversary of the UDHR, Grenada's Prime Minister Tillman Thomas (1945– ) restated his government's support of the document and signed a copy of the declaration to display his continued support. He particularly underlined efforts to protect women's rights. Nevertheless, Grenada has been accused of human rights violations in certain areas, particularly the treatment of homosexuals and transgender persons (LGBT).

Grenada has been criticized for legislation that effectively discriminates against members of the LGBT community. The discrimination apparent in this legislation is not only harmful in its enforcement, but also in the social stigma against homosexuality that it enforces. This social stigma can make it difficult for homosexuals to find employment, acquire suitable medical treatment, or find acceptable housing. Violence against LGBT persons reportedly occurs in the justice system as well as outside, with instances of torture cited.

Grenada has also come under criticism for its upholding of the right to a fair and public trial. This right has been particularly questioned in the case against the so-called "Grenada 17," convicted for the murder of Maurice Bishop in 1983. Amnesty International (AI) has called for investigations into this trial of the 17 political prisoners convicted of murdering the former prime minister and members of his cabinet. AI maintains that the trial was conducted in violation of international standards of fair trials. Violations include extraction of confessions under torture, denying defense lawyers access to the materials used by judges to uphold the convictions, and unfair irregularities in the selection process for the jury. On February 7, 2007, after 23 years in prison, 13 had their sentences converted from the death penalty to life imprisonment. There is hope that Grenada will conduct an independent judicial review of the trial convictions to assess possible violations.

Freedom of thought and religion is generally seen to be upheld by the government of Grenada. The Grenadian constitution provides for freedom of religion, and laws uphold that right. Freedom of opinion and expression is also seen to be upheld by the Grenadian government. There is an independent press and a democratic political system that maintain the right to freedom of speech and of the press. There were also no observed restrictions on Internet or e-mail use.

## Migration

Large numbers of Grenadians live as expatriates throughout the world, including in the United States, United Kingdom, and Canada. In addition, many live in other Caribbean countries, including Barbados and Trinidad. Grenada faces significant challenges related to youth migration as an increasing number of young people born in Grenada continue to seek opportunities elsewhere.

## ECONOMY

### Overview of the Economy

Although Grenada's economic base has broadened in recent years, it still revolves primarily around agricultural products such as nutmeg, mace, bananas, and cocoa. St. George's port is the critical facility through which the island's exports and imports pass. The bulk of trade is exchanged with the United States and the European Union (EU), as well as nearby Trinidad and Tobago. A small but growing manufacturing base also produces clothing and textiles.

The services sector, specifically tourism and higher education, represents a key and growing sector of the economy. The Grenadian government's transition from socialism to a privatized economy, which began in the 1980s, has stimulated foreign investment, which in turn spurred the growth of the services sector. For example, St. George's University, an American-owned medical and veterinary school, is an important source of revenue.

The 1984 completion of Point Salines International Airport provided a major boost to the tourism industry, as it made direct flights to the island possible; tourism represents the island's main source of foreign exchange in the early 21st century. However, government authorities in St. George's are still struggling to meet several economic challenges, despite

measures undertaken to liberalize and diversify the economy. Tourism and other service revenues, while a significant and growing source of income, have not been able to offset a significant trade deficit.

The recent shift to a more modern, services-oriented economy from the agrarian-dominated economy of the past has also created a growing demand for more food imports, a demand fueled by the burgeoning tourism sector. The government has continued, nonetheless, to invest significant resources into the development of the tourism industry, which it views as the best potential vehicle for reducing high rates of poverty and unemployment.

### Industry

Grenada's industrial sector represents approximately 15 percent of the country's GDP. Grenada produces food and beverages and textiles. The country has some light assembly operations and a small but significant construction industry. The impact of 2004's Hurricane Ivan on the islands cannot be overstated. Over 90 percent of Grenada's superstructure was damaged and up to 10,000 people were left homeless. The country's industries were devastated. With the help of foreign aid, Grenada began to rebuild and repair the destruction caused by the storm. Rebuilding occurred fast enough for Grenada to take part as a host of the 2007 Cricket World Cup.

### Labor

In 2013 unemployment in Grenada was 33.5 percent nationally and 55.6 percent among workers aged 16–25. The majority of Grenadians are employed in the country's service sector, which includes the tourist industry. Agricultural production is the country's second largest employer.

### Energy/Power/Natural Resources

Some of Grenada's most important resources are tropical fruit and timber. The country's coastlines also provide deepwater harbors. Most significantly, Grenada has a wealth of spices, earning it the reputation during the colonial 15th through

19th centuries as an "Isle of Spice." Of the many spices exported from Grenada, the most important is nutmeg, though cloves and cinnamon are also significant.

## Fishing

Fishing represents an estimated 30 percent of total agricultural production in Grenada. The country's fishing industry generated approximately $29 million in 2009. Local freshwater fish species include tilapia, tarpon, mojarra, and snook. Grenada is also an increasingly popular saltwater sport fishing destination. Tuna and marlin can be caught in the ocean waters surrounding the islands.

## Forestry

An estimated 15 percent of Grenada's total land area is forested. Hurricanes Ivan and Emily did significant damage to Grenada's forests. In addition, soil erosion caused by deforestation has negatively impacted the country's forest reserves. The Forestry and National Parks Department (FNPD), a division of Grenada's Ministry of Agriculture, introduced a 10-year strategic plan to improve forest resource management, watershed management, and wildlife conservation.

## Agriculture

Agriculture represents an estimated 10 percent of Grenada's gross domestic product (GDP). The country's farmers grow bananas, cocoa, citrus, avocados, root crops, sugarcane, corn, and other vegetables in the islands' fertile soil. The island nation is particularly well known for its spice crops, which include cinnamon and nutmeg.

## Animal Husbandry

Livestock in Grenada include poultry and chickens, which make up the primary livestock population, followed by goats, pig, and cattle. Livestock and animal products are produced for domestic consumption. The country imports the majority of its meat products.

## Tourism

Grenada has established a tourist industry based on the islands' picturesque coastlines and natural beauty. As with the agricultural and industrial sectors, tourism was hard hit by Hurricanes Ivan and Emily, which destroyed or damaged hotels, roads, telephone lines, and other key infrastructure. In October 2010, the government of Grenada announced a new marketing program for its tourism industry that focuses on the country's diving and sports tourism destinations and promotes Grenada as an ideal setting for weddings and honeymoons. In addition, the government announced initiates to increase domestic training and education in tourism. Tourism constituted 20.3 percent of GDP in 2013 when there were 120,000 visitors to the island. In 2014 American Airlines agreed to start daily flights to the United States.

*Zoë Westhof, Amy Witherbee, Beverly Ballaro*

## DO YOU KNOW?

- The wide use of stone building materials and low-lying architecture in St. George's reflects the capital's response to three separate fires that scorched large areas of the capital during the 18th century. It has also been stated that Grenadian law prohibits the construction of any building that reaches above the height of a coconut palm, a measure designed to prevent noise pollution.

- Grenada produces more nutmeg than any other country in the world except Indonesia. Nutmeg, in fact, is found as a national emblem on the flag, and the island's former name was the "Island of Spice."

## Bibliography

Brathwaite, Roger. *Grenada Spice Paradise*. Caribbean, 2002.

Brizan, George I. *Grenada Island of Conflict*. New York: Macmillan Caribbean, 1998.

Crandall, Russell. *U.S. Interventions in the Dominican Republic, Grenada, and Panama*. Lanham, MD: Rowman & Littlefield, 2006.

Martin, John Angus. *A–Z of Grenada Heritage (Macmillian Caribbean a–Z)*. New York: MacMillan Caribbean, 2007.

Phillips, Winston, J. *The Grenada Boys Secondary School Hostel: Reminiscing on a Boarding School Life in Grenada*. Denver, CO: Outskirts Press 2009.

Ross, Jacob. *Pynter Bender*. London: Fourth Estate, 2008.

Sinclair, Norma. *Grenada Isle of Spice (Macmillan Caribbean Guides)*. New York: Interlink Group, 2003.

Steele, Beverley A. *Grenada A History of Its People (Island Histories)*. New York: MacMillan Caribbean, 2003.

## Works Cited

Amnesty International—Grenada: Privy Council Orders Resentencing of 13 of the "Grenada 17": http://www.amnesty.org/en/library/asset/AMR32/001/2007/en/dom-AMR320012007en.html

Amnesty International—Grenada: 20 Years On, Time to Remedy Unfair Trial of Grenada 17: http://www.amnesty.org/en/library/asset/AMR32/002/2003/en/dom-AMR320022003en.html

Art in Grenada: http://www.grenadaexplorer.com/tip/art/

The Best of What Caribbean Art Has to Offer: http://www.clico-caribbean-art.com/arttalk_grenada.jsp

BBC News Country Profile: Grenada: http://news.bbc.co.uk/2/hi/americas/country_profiles/1209605.stm

Culture of Grenada—History and Ethnic Relations, Urbanism, Architecture and the Use of Space: http://www.everyculture.com/Ge-It/Grenada.html

Customs of Grenada: http://encarta.msn.com/sidebar_631524674/customs_of_grenada.html

Data: Improved Sanitation Facilities (% of population with access to improved water source). http://www.data.worldbank.org/indicator/SH.STA.ACSN

Decolonizing the Mind: Recent Grenadian Fiction: http://smallaxe.dukejournals.org/cgi/reprint/11/1/83

Eating Local and Cheap in the Caribbean—Grenada: http://www.bootsnall.com/articles/07-08/eating-local-and-cheap-in-the-caribbean-grenada.html

The Ethics of Housing the Poor: http://72.14.235.132/search?q=cache:xOCpTCYDv24J:www.informedesign.umn.edu/_news/jan_v04r-p.pdf+grenada%2Bhousing%2Bpoor&hl=en&ct=clnk&cd=1&client=firefox-a

Foreign Relations of Grenada: http://en.wikipedia.org/wiki/Foreign_relations_of_Grenada

Global Health Facts: Population under Age 15(percent) http://kff.org/global-indicator/population-under-age-15/

Grenada: http://www.state.gov/g/drl/rls/hrrpt/2007/100640.htm

Grenada Airport Information: http://grenada.caribbeanway.com/airport.asp

Grenada: Basic Data http://pressreference.com/Fa-Gu/Grenand.html

Grenada Broadcast—Bringing Back Fond Memories: http://www.grenadabroadcast.com/content/view/4277/1/

Grenada Broadcast: Thomas Signs Declaration on Human Rights: http://www.grenadabroadcast.com/content/view/3895/1/

Grenada—City Population: http://www.citypopulation.de/Grenada.html

Grenada—Culture, Customs, and Etiquette: http://www.culturecrossing.net/basics_business_student.php?id=84

Grenada—eDiplomat: http://www.ediplomat.com/np/post_reports/pr_gd.htm

Grenada—Explorations: http://www.geographia.com/grenada/gdpnt01.htm

Grenada—Income-Earning Opportunities for Rural Youth: http://www.ifad.org/gender/learning/challenges/youth/gr_6_3.htm

Grenada—The Impact of Gender Stereotypes on Youth: http://www.ifad.org/gender/learning/challenges/youth/g_6_3.htm

Grenada. *Nations of the World: A Political, Economic, and Business Handbook*. 14th ed. Amenia, NY: Grey House Publishing, 2015.

Grenada Radio Stations http://tunein.com/radio/Grenada-r101245/

Grenada—Wikipedia: http://en.wikipedia.org/wiki/Grenada

Grenada: World Bank Approves US$3 Million to Reduce Youth Unemployment: http://www.caribbeanpressreleases.com/articles/4504/1/Grenada-World-Bank-Approves-US3-Million-to-Reduce-Youth-Unemployment/Page1.html

Guardian—Canute Caliste: http://www.guardian.co.uk/print/0,3858,5341260-103684,00.html

*Historic Architecture in the Caribbean Islands*, by Edward E. Crain: http://books.google.com/books?id=H07DwOfAGn8C&pg=RA1-PA80&lpg=RA1-PA80&dq=grenada%2Bwindows%2Barchitecture&source=bl&ots=_Izb_U_KTB&sig=bfGIngj9SPxWiwGN3Lii7WsxAlM&hl=en&ei=KzOrSbyFKYT06QPCg4i0Bg&sa=X&oi=book_result&resnum=4&ct=result#PRA1-PA81,M1

Igniting the Caribbean's Past: http://books.google.com/books?id=Mji_8gVmrQYC&pg=PA36&dq=grenada%2Brural%2Bhousing&lr=&ei=PAqySf6AJY_AlQTS1Yy3Dg

Internet Users by Country (2014) http://www.internetlivestats/internet-users-by-country/

Music of Grenada: Encyclopedia II—Music of Grenada—Carriacou: http://www.experiencefestival.com/a/Music_of_Grenada_-_Carriacou/id/1784109

Oliver Benoit: http://www.oliverbenoit.com/index.html

Premiere of Grenada's First Movie: http://www.caribbeannetnews.com/cgi-script/csArticles/articles/000002/000272.htm

Reports: Human Development Grenada http://hdr.undp.org/en/countries/profiles/GRDUniversities and colleges in Grenada

School-Based HIV/AIDS Education in Grenada: http://cat.inist.fr/?aModele=afficheN&cpsidt=13457230

Sea Shanty – Wikipedia: http://en.wikipedia.org/wiki/Chantey

Sexuality, Gender, HIV Vulnerability & Human Rights in Grenada www2.ohchr.org/english/bodies/hrc/docs/ngos/LGBTShadow_Grenada.pdf

The U.S. Invasion of Grenada: A Twenty Year Retrospective: http://www.fpif.org/papers/grenada2003.html

Universities and Colleges in Grenada http://commonwealthofnations.org/sectors-grenada/education/universities_and_colleges/

West Indian Culture: http://www.westindianculture.com/index.php?option=com_content&task=view&id=129&Itemid=32

Youth Challenge International—Grenada: http://www.yci.org/html/programs/countries/grenada.asp

*A woman selling carrots in Jacmel, Haiti. iStock/MaestroBooks.*

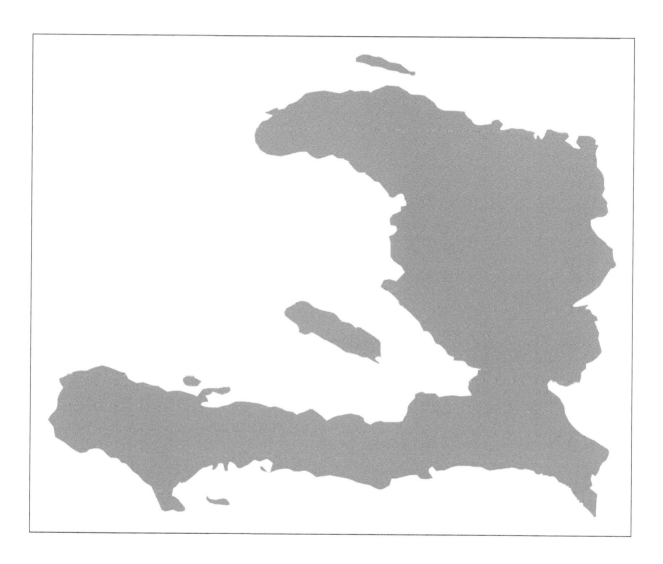

HAITI

# Introduction

The Republic of Haiti is located on the western third of the Caribbean island of Hispaniola. It shares the island with the Dominican Republic. Haiti is bordered on the south by the Caribbean Sea, on the north by the Atlantic Ocean, and on the west by the Windward Passage, a strait between Haiti and Cuba.

Haitians express themselves creatively through art, music, dance, and storytelling. Two distinctive Haitian art forms are cut-metal sculpture and "primitive" art (characterized by the use of bright colors, broad brush strokes, and skewed visual perspective to portray daily and religious life). Haitian art in the primitive style is world-renowned. Music and dancing are integral parts of Vodou ceremonies, a faith interweaved with beliefs and rituals of traditional West African religious practices and Roman Catholicism. Drummers play rada drums made of cowhide and petwo drums made from goatskin, while singers interact with attendees.

Haiti suffers from a myriad of social and environmental problems, including poverty, overpopulation, substandard health care, deforestation, and soil erosion, and an inadequate educational system. It is considered the poorest country in the Western hemisphere. In January 2010, the country suffered a devastating earthquake. Over 230,000 people were killed in the quake, which leveled the capital, Port-au-Prince, and most of its infrastructure. The country is still recovering from the devastation.

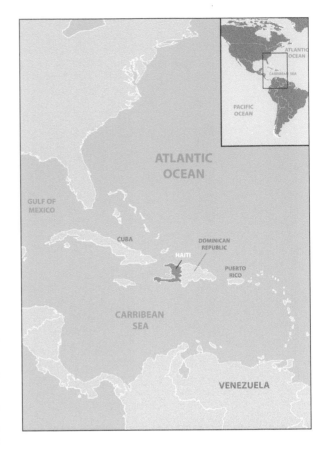

## GENERAL INFORMATION

**Official Language(s):** Kreyòl (Haitian Creole) and French
**Population:** 10,320,000(2013 estimate)
**Currency:** Haitian gourde
**Coins:** The Haitian gourde is divided into 100 centimes. Coins are available in denominations of 5, 10, 20, and 50 centimes, and 1 and 5 gourdes.
**Land Area:** 27,751 square kilometers (10,714 square miles)
**Water Area:** 190 square kilometers (73 square miles)
**National Motto:** "L'Union Fait La Force" (French, "Union Makes Strength")
**National Anthem:** "La Dessalinienne" ("The Dessalines Song")
**Capital:** Port-au-Prince
**Time Zone(s):** GMT -5
**Flag Description:** Haiti's national flag features a bicolor design, with two equal horizontal bands or rectangles of dark blue (top) and red. Centered in the flag is Haiti's coat of arms, boxed by a small white square. The coat of arms is highlighted by a

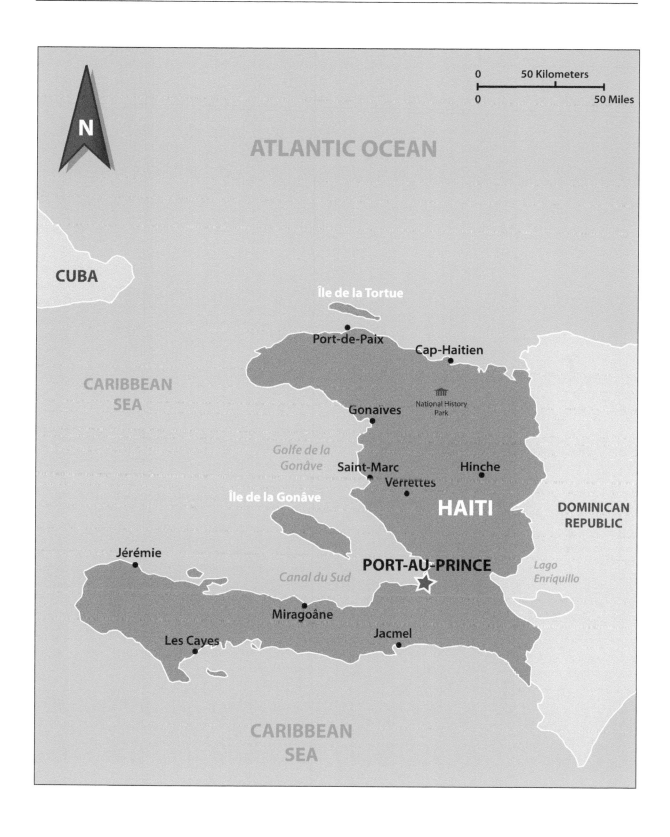

palm tree with a conical cap representing liberty perched atop it, and two cannons pointing outwards at its base.

## Population

Haiti is one of the most densely populated countries in the Western Hemisphere. It is divided into nine administrative regions, or departments, which are further divided into arrondissements and communes. Nearly half of Haitians live in urban areas. Port-au-Prince, Haiti's capital and largest city, located on the coast of the Gulf of Gonâve, was home, unofficially, to 1.1 million people—or substantially more, including outlying areas such as Citie Soleil, Port-au-Prince's most infamous slum, where residents live in cardboard houses and tin huts alongside open sewers—prior to the 2010 earthquake that devastated the city. (The capital's population was more than twice the next largest city, Carrefour.)

As of 2010, the country had a negative population growth rate and a net migration rate of –9.75 per 1,000. Life expectancy for the country is 63.18 years of age (2015 estimate).

## Languages

Language divides the affluent and the poor in Haiti. Although French and Krèyol are both official languages, only about 10 percent of the population, namely the wealthy mulatto elite, speaks French. French is the language of instruction in Haitian schools, and it is used in business and government. Nearly all Haitians speak Krèyol, a mixture of French and African dialects that originated in the Caribbean in the 17th century.

## Native People & Ethnic Groups

Approximately one million members of the Taíno Arawak tribe inhabited the island of Hispaniola when Christopher Columbus landed there in 1492. Peaceful hunter-gatherers, the Taíno were enslaved by the Spanish. Because of the terrible treatment they endured and the European diseases introduced to the island, the number of Taíno on Hispaniola dwindled to 500 within 50 years of Columbus' arrival.

There is a deep rift between people of African descent, who constitute 95 percent of the population, and mulattos (of mixed ancestry), who along with a small number of whites make up the remaining five percent of the population. Haiti's African population is descended from slaves brought to Hispaniola by the French in the 17th and 18th centuries, while mulattos are people of mixed race who descend from liaisons between French plantation owners and slaves. Haiti's mulattos are typically much wealthier and of higher social class than blacks.

## Religions

Approximately 80 percent of Haitians are members of the Roman Catholic Church. However, more than half the population practices Vodou, a religion of Caribbean origin that is similar to African pantheistic religions. Followers of Vodou believe in a hierarchy of gods who have the power to possess people and objects. They practice it in conjunction with Catholicism, incorporating elements of Catholic liturgy and rites into Vodou rituals and celebrations. Practitioners of Vodou in Haiti tend to be poor and uneducated. Haitians continue to embrace a deep belief in the powers, both good and malicious, of spirits to shape the destinies of living people.

## Climate

Haiti has a tropical climate characterized by high temperatures, heavy rainfall, and humidity. The trade winds that bring these conditions, however, are partially blocked by mountains, resulting in arid conditions in the northwest.

There are only two seasons in Haiti. The hot season lasts from March to November, with an average temperature of 34° Celsius (95° Fahrenheit). The cool season, from December to February, has an average temperature of 30° Celsius (85° Fahrenheit).

In Port-au-Prince, located at sea level, the average winter temperature is 23° Celsius (73° Fahrenheit), while the average summer temperature is 31° Celsius (88° Fahrenheit) in July. The city receives approximately 137 centimeters (54 inches) of rain annually, mainly during the two rainy seasons between April and November. High elevations experience lower-than-average temperatures and larger amounts of rain.

The southern coast of Haiti is regularly bombarded by hurricanes that cause severe destruction.

## ENVIRONMENT & GEOGRAPHY

### Topography

Haiti is crescent-shaped, with two peninsulas that extend east and west forming the Gulf of Gonâve. Haiti's territory includes five other small islands, the largest of which, Île de la Gonâve in the Gulf of Gonâve, is roughly 872 square kilometers (350 square miles).

Highland areas of hills and mountains, situated at an elevation greater than 180 meters (600 feet), dominate most of Haiti. On average, the southern part of the country has a higher elevation than the northern part.

Five mountain ranges and four lowland areas stretch across the country from west to east. The mountain ranges are the Massif du Nord in the north, the centrally located Montagnes Noires and the Chaîne de Matheux, the Massif du Sud in the south, and the Massif de la Selle in the east. The Massif de la Selle contains the Morne La Selle, Haiti's highest peak at 2,638 meters (8,793 feet) above sea level.

Lowlands lie between the mountain ranges, including the Plaine Centrale, the Plaine de l'Artibonite, and the Plaine du Nord. The lowland Cul-de-Sac lies between Port-au-Prince and the Dominican Republic. The lowland areas contain deserts, marshes, and grasslands.

Many of Haiti's rivers and streams flow from east to west. The longest and widest river, the Artibonite River, is 280 kilometers (174 miles) long and extends from the Montagnes Noires to the Gulf of Gonâve. The second longest, the Trois Rivières, runs from the Massif du Nord to the northern coast of the north peninsula.

Haiti has a few notable lakes, the largest of which is the Étang Saumâtre near Port-au-Prince, with an area of 182 square kilometers (70 square miles).

Port-au-Prince is located in the southwestern part of Haiti, on a sheltered bay of the Gulf of Gonâve, which opens out onto the Caribbean Sea. The city's 18th-century French colonial founders hoped to take strategic advantage of the inlet, which provided an ideal setting for a trading port. It also made the city somewhat less vulnerable to the hurricanes that frequently batter the Haitian coast. The city was devastated in 2010 by a massive earthquake. Most of the city was destroyed by the event, which killed hundreds of thousands of Haitians.

### Plants & Animals

Despite extreme deforestation, Haiti still has approximately 5,000 species of plants, many of which are tropical. In the mountains, where rainfall is high, there are small remnant rainforests as well as giant ferns and wild orchids (Haiti boasts approximately 600 species of ferns and 300 species of orchids).

Along the coast are mangrove trees and swampland, and in the arid regions of the northwest and lowland plains are desert grasses and brush, and several species of cacti. Indigenous coffee, cacao, coconut, avocado, orange, lime, and mango trees grow in the lowlands.

A few species of rodents are Haiti's only indigenous mammals that have not been hunted to extinction. Indigenous reptiles and amphibians include non-poisonous snakes, three species of crocodiles, small and large lizards, turtles, frogs, and salamanders.

Over 25 species of birds nest permanently in Haiti. Flamingoes, heron, ibises, and ducks are found near coastal waters and inland marshes and lakes. Egrets, parrots, guinea hens, pigeons, pheasant, Hispaniolan parakeets, golden swallows, and siskins are found in the lowlands and highlands. Many other species of birds migrate through Haiti.

Nearly 300 species of fish inhabit Haiti's rivers and coastal reefs and waters. Insects such as the mosquito are abundant and contribute to the transmission of diseases.

## CUSTOMS & COURTESIES

### Greetings

Haitians typically greet one another in either French or Creole (the two national languages) depending on their social class and education. Educated and wealthy Haitians tend to speak French while poor Haitians tend to speak Haitian Creole (or Krèyol). Common Haitian greetings include "Bonjou" ("Good morning"), "Bonswa" ("Good afternoon"), "Mesi" ("Thanks"), and "Komon ou ye?" ("How are you?"). English is also becoming more common due to the influx of American aid in the early 21st century.

In Haiti, strangers, acquaintances, or business contacts greet one another with a handshake. Friends and family may greet one another with an embrace and a kiss on each cheek. In rural areas, female friends may kiss one another quickly on the lips in greeting.

In Haiti, greetings are ritualized. Rural Haitians, in particular, greet one another in formal and predictable ways. When meting strangers, friends or family on a road or path, Haitians will say hello to each other numerous times prior to engaging in further conversation or passing by one another. When arriving at a house, visitors shout "Onè" ("Honor") and hosts respond by shouting "Respè" ("Respect"). People announce when they must leave and depart groups or meetings with a handshake or embrace to each person. Haitians consider it rude to leave a group or event without making a formal announcement or exit.

### Gestures & Etiquette

Haitians enthusiastically use their hands and arms when they speak, and people engaged in conversation often bump, hold, and poke one another to make their point. This physicality is considered normal and accepted by most Haitians. Despite the physicality and close quarters of conversation, Haitian men and women tend to be quite physically polite, modest, and respectful. It is considered polite to say "Eskize-m" ("Excuse me") when entering another's physical space. Friends of the same gender often hold hands when walking, but people of the opposite sex limit public displays of affection. Haitians share common hand gestures (such as thumbs up for approval) with other Western cultures. Haitians also make a "pssst" or "tssss" sound to get a waiter or friend's attention.

Young Haitian women generally do not smoke or drink in public. It is socially acceptable for older women, particularly those who work at markets, to drink rum or smoke tobacco. Haitian men drink alcohol and smoke tobacco at funerals, festivals, and cockfights. Personal hygiene and cleanliness are prized. Haitians haggle over money and prices of market goods. This negotiation is not considered rude, and discussions over money tend to be lengthy, loud, and animated. Discussions of government corruption are considered taboo and dangerous.

Haitians of the same economic and social classes tend to be very polite to one another and to visitors to the country. Haitians of different economic and social classes tend to have inequitable relationships. The tension between the poor majority and the small elite class creates tension. For instance, wealthy Haitians often display impatience with poor Haitians, as well as remark on their limitations, characteristics, or appearance.

### Eating/Meals

Food, refrigeration, and potable water are scarce in Haiti, and the majority of Haitians are malnourished. Due to a lack of refrigeration, Haitians primarily eat fresh, pickled, or salt-preserved foods. Restaurants and prepared foods are usually only enjoyed by tourists or very wealthy Haitians. Most Haitians procure food by growing it themselves or working for others as agricultural or field labor. Haitian households, when they are able to own or rent land, cultivate beans, sweet potatoes, maize (corn), bananas, and coffee. Wealthier Haitians buy food (such as salted codfish and manioc flour) at the market.

Meal times for most Haitians are dictated by the agricultural workday. The majority of Haitians eat an early (5 am) morning breakfast of coffee and manioc (a native root, also known as cassava) bread. A mid-day snack of porridge and fruit, eaten in the fields or at work, is common. The main meal of the day is eaten in the late afternoon. When employment and circumstance allow, Haitians prefer to leave their work and return home to eat with their families. The main meals, which are usually made of relatively bland staple ingredients, are typically spiced with a paste made of onion, garlic, and pepper. Beans and rice, corn porridge, or pumpkin soup are examples of common main meals.

## Visiting

In Haiti, visiting is particularly important and ritualized during religious events and holidays. Due to a relaxed sense of time, visitors are not required to be punctual. Hosts customarily offer their visitors coffee and, when possible, send visitors away with a small gift of food. Religious celebrations, both Roman Catholic and Vodou, are an opportunity for Haitian families and friends to join together to share food. During ceremonial occasions, hosts will offer visitors and guests the finest food that the household can afford. Popular festive drinks include colas, kleren (spiced rum), kremass (an alcoholic drink made with condensed milk), and Prestige (the national brand of beer).

Important Roman Catholic holidays for visiting friends and family include Good Friday, Easter Sunday, and Christmas. Important Vodou holidays for visiting friends and family include the November harvest festival and Manger-Yam

day. Manger-Yam Day is a celebration of yams as a source of food for poor Haitians. Important secular national holidays for visiting friends and family include All Souls' Day (also known as the Day of the Dead) and New Year's Day. On All Souls' Day, families come together to eat, drink, and tell stories about dead ancestors. On New Year's Day, families will offer all visitors bouyon (pumpkin soup) to celebrate abundance, harvest, and fertility.

## LIFESTYLE

### Family

A Haitian family typically includes the basic unit of parents and their children plus widowed or elderly relatives. Haitians also consider ancestors and godparents to be part of their families. Family ancestors, who are believed to affect the lives of the living, are ritually honored, fed, and remembered. Godparent relationships unite families and entail ritual and material responsibilities. For instance, godparents host their godchild's baptismal celebration.

Common law marriages are typical among Haiti's poor whereas wealthier Haitians generally marry in legal and religious ceremonies. Men generally build houses on their parents' land for their female partner as a symbol of future commitment and a means of establishing a separate family household. Approximately 10 percent of Haitian men have more than one wife, and this practice is socially accepted. Men and women share in the upkeep and duties of the household. Men are generally responsible for livestock and fields, while women are generally responsible for child rearing and household decisions.

### Housing

The housing in Haiti is reflective of the country's poor economic state. In rural areas, single-story wood huts, wattle and daub (a construction technique using soil, clay, sand, animal manure and straw) houses, and palm frond huts are common. Rural Haitians who can afford it often choose to paint the exterior of their homes in pastel colors. In urban areas, historical architecture, including foreign-inspired Victorian gingerbread houses, is quickly disappearing due to neglect, fires, and urban growth. New urban homes are usually constructed of block and cement. In some cases, wealthy Haitians adorn new cement construction with historical details such as cut stones, cement relief, shaped balusters, turrets, decorative cement roofing, balconies, and wrought-iron trim. Due to migration from rural to urban areas, Haiti has a shortage of affordable housing in its urban areas, and urban apartments and houses are often crowded and lack sanitary facilities.

## Food

The culinary flavors and traditions of Spanish, French, indigenous Indian, and African foods have greatly influenced Haiti's national cuisine. Historically in Haiti, the Arawaks (one of the first Indigenous Haitian Indians) cultivated guavas, pineapples, cassava, papayas, sweet potatoes, and corn. Europeans introduced and grew oranges, limes, mangoes, rice, and sugarcane. Africans introduced okra, taro root, and numerous spices. The French colonists cultivated sugarcane, coffee, cotton, and cocoa.

Contemporary staple foods and ingredients in Haiti include rice, corn, millet, yams, and beans. Popular locally grown fruits include avocados, mangoes, pineapples, coconuts, and guava. Wealthy Haitians eat meat such as pork and goat. Haiti's poorest people who cannot afford to buy or grow food will eat mud or clay cakes as a staple of their diet. The clay cakes, which are said to stop the hunger, are made of baked clay, salt, and butter or shortening.

Haitian food tends to be very peppery or spicy in flavor and fried in oil when one can afford to do so. Common dishes include riz et pois (rice and beans), mayi moulen (cornmeal mush), pikliz (spicy pickled carrots and cabbage), and corn porridge or pudding. Haitian rice and beans is cooked with onion, garlic, green pepper, vegetable oil, rice, beans, ham (if available), cumin, salt, red peppers flakes, and water. Haitian cornmeal mush is cooked with cornmeal,

water, salt, herbs, and spices such as cloves, garlic, pepper, cilantro, and parsley. Haitian corn pudding is cooked with cornstarch, flour, sugar, corn kernels, salt, egg, milk, vanilla, and butter.

## Life's Milestones

In Haiti, life's milestones largely correspond to Roman Catholic traditions and sacraments. (Haiti's population is estimated at 80 percent Roman Catholic and 20 percent Protestant.) Common Haitian milestones include baptism, confirmation, first communion, and marriage. Haitians often incorporate Vodou elements into Roman Catholic ceremonies through the use of Vodou flags or Vodou dances.

In the Roman Catholic tradition, baptism is a sacrament performed to admit someone, usually an infant, into the Catholic Church. The ritual involves a formal pronouncement by a priest, the verbal support of godparents, the sign of the cross made on the forehead of the baptized person, and the pouring of holy water on the head. In Haiti, godparents are expected to host and pay for the baptismal celebration. Confirmation and First Communion are initiation rituals in the Catholic Church that mark the growing importance of faith and church in the young person's life.

The marriages of poor Haitians are often unofficial or common-law. Haitians with the financial resources tend to have lavish weddings held in a Catholic church. The wedding includes a religious mass and a celebratory party with abundant food and music. Marriage, both common law and legal, is associated with maturity and adulthood. Husbands are expected to build their wives a home as a sign of commitment and means of establishing a new marital household.

## CULTURAL HISTORY

## Art

Art in Haiti dates back to the pre-Columbian culture of the Taíno, and includes traditions such as sculpture, textiles, wood carving, and ceramics. The Taíno often depicted their deities (gods) in their art, and this theme of religiosity and

*Drapo vodou flags like this one feature religious themes and are often embellished with sequins.*

spirituality is prevalent in another unique Haitian art form: the Haitian Vodou flag. These flags (called "drapo vodou" in Haitian Creole) blend the Haitian aesthetic and the religious symbols of Vodou, a hybrid religion combining African, Amerindian, and European religious traditions. Usually made of square cloths adorned with colorful sequins, Vodou flags often depict Haitian myths, legends, and personal stories. They date back to France's colonization of Haiti and were originally modeled on French banners.

While painting has a long history in Haiti, Haitian art gained international recognition in the 20th century. Important painting movements in 20th-century Haitian art include the indigenous movement and the naive or intuitive art movement. Indigenism, popular in the early 19th century, was rooted in a desire to reclaim Haiti's African history and develop a distinct and native cultural identity. Important artists in Haiti's indigenist art movement include Petion Savain (1906–1975), Luce Turnier (1924–1994), and Lucien Price (1915–1963).

Haiti's naive or intuitive art movement, championed by instinctual rather than formally trained artists, began in the 1940s. Strong colors and spontaneous or primitive lines that break with classical traditions and aesthetics characterize naive or intuitive painting. Important painters in Haiti's naive art movement include Hector Hippolyte (1894–1948), Castera Bazile (1923–1965), Wilson Bigaud (1931–2010), and Rigaud Benoit (1911–1986). The celebrated mural wall in Port-au Prince's Cathedral of Sainte Trinité is painted in the naive style. The cathedral, however, was heavily damaged from the 2010 Haiti earthquake.

### Dance & Drama

Haitian dance is deeply dramatic and theatrical. It is based on Afro-Caribbean, French colonial, Haitian Indian, and Vodou traditions. For example, French dances common during the colonial era, such as the quadrille, influenced Haitian dance movements. African dance and rhythm also influenced dance movements prevalent in Haitian dance.

Vodou traditions, such as spirit possession and trances, have had perhaps the greatest influence on Haitian dance. Haitian dance has numerous dances associated with specific Vodou gods and goddesses, and these dances are typically performed to drum music. Often, the drum rhythm and type of percussions used varies between dances. Haitian dancers also perform specific dances as a means of calling out to the Vodou gods and goddesses, referred to as L'wa, Lwa or Loa, for specific needs such as protection, healing, or insight.

The dances of Vodou gods and goddesses are divided into different groups based on the strength and characteristics of the spirit gods and goddesses. Popular dances of Vodou gods and goddesses include the djouba, kongo, nago, and ibo. The djouba is performed to ask for agricultural help, while the kongo, a popular couple dance with red and white costumes, is performed simply because the music is thought to please spirits. The nago, a fierce masculine dance, is performed to ask spirits for fatherly council and advice, and the ibo is performed in hopes of satisfying arrogant and difficult to please spirits.

## Music

Haitian musical styles, such as rara, mizik rasin (roots music), and compas, are closely tied to Vodou rituals, as well as American and European musical traditions. Haitian vocals are performed in Haitian Creole or French. Rara music is sung in Haitian Creole and performed during religious festivals, often while marching. Instruments include vaksen (bamboo or metal trumpet), drums, maracas, guiros (a percussion instrument made from a hollowed-out gourd), and bells. Rara has spread from Haiti to the Dominican Republic, which constitutes the other side of the island of Hispaniola.

Mizik rasin ("roots music") is a hybrid form of music that combines Vodou traditions, folk music, and contemporary rock and roll music. Called musique racine in French, mizik rasin is also known as a form of reggae-rock and is associated with global or world music. Rasin groups, such as Boukman Eksperyans, perform with electric guitars, trap drums, keyboard, Vodou drums, and a chorus of vocalists. Rasin groups often use call and response style between performers and the audience.

Compas is a distinctly Haitian musical style developed in the 1950s by Haitian band-leader Nemours Jean Baptiste (1918–1985). Considered the sound of Haiti's contemporary pop music, Compas incorporates swing, jazz, and Dominican meringue, and features Haitian rhythms and brass instruments.

## Literature

Haitian literature in large part chronicles the country's complicated cultural and political history. The growing international interest in Haitian literature and Caribbean literature, in general, has spread the stories about Haiti's historical slave revolts, devastating poverty, Vodou rituals and society, and Haitian military coups. The classics of Haitian literature were originally written in French, and translations into English have expanded its audience. Influential Haitian writers include Jean Price-Mars (1876–1969), Jacques Roumain (1907–1944), Marie Chauvet (1916–1975), Frankétienne (1936– ), Lionel Trouillot (1956– ), and Edwidge Danticat (b. 1969– ).

Jean Price-Mars wrote *Ainsi Parla L'oncle* (*Thus Spoke the Uncle*), an essay-collection, to record Haiti's sociological and intellectual development. The book, originally written in French in 1928, was first published in English in 1997. Jacques Roumain's book *Gouverneurs de la Rosée* (*Masters of the Dew*) is celebrated as one of Haiti's most beloved novels. The book, originally written in French in 1944, was first published in English in 1978.

Although male writers dominate Haitian literature, two women writers, Marie Chauvet and Edwidge Danticat, have gained acclaim, in part, by writing about the lives of Haitian women. Marie Chauvet's novel *Fille d'Haiti* (*Woman of Haiti*, 1953) describes the life of the biracial daughter of a Haitian prostitute. Haitian dictator François Duvalier (1907–1971) banned Chauvet's second novel, *Amour, Colère et Folie* (*Love, Anger and Madness*, 1968). Chauvet lived in exile in the United States until her death in 1975. Edwidge Danticat is a popular contemporary Haitian writer known for her works *Breath Eyes Memory* (1994) and *The Farming of Bones* (1998).

## CULTURE

### Arts & Entertainment

The country of Haiti (which means "land of many mountains" in Arawak) struggles socially, environmentally, economically, and politically. Haiti's arts help the country overcome its almost insurmountable challenges. The arts perform numerous functions and provide cultural continuity and solace during times of political and economic instability. Contemporary Haitian arts have also raised Haiti's collective social consciousness and lead to the formation of human rights and education campaigns.

Historically, the arts, particularly music and dance, helped keep 18th-century African slaves sufficiently united to stage a successful slave revolt and found the first free Black republic. Today, Haitians use the arts, particularly their sacred arts of Vodou music, dance, and visual media, to stay connected to one another and their shared cultural heritage. Vodou inspires many Haitian artists to create in multiple different media such as dolls, flags, paintings, dances, rhythms, and song. In the 21st century, the arts, particularly festivals such as Carnival, unite all Haitians including the very elite and the very poor. The Carnival's festival season marks the beginning of the holiest time of year in Haiti. Carnival season begins with periods of repentance and abstinence, and ends with the nation's largest celebration. Carnival festivities include floats, musical bands, pageants, and feasting.

The arts have also helped spread Haitian culture abroad. International recognition of Haitian arts has helped, in part, to increase understanding about Haiti's culture, as well as Haiti's vast political and economic need. For instance, Rara, a Haitian street festival that is both political and musical, has spread to cities worldwide. During a Rara festival, Vodou followers take to the streets to march, dance, and sing. Rara participants unite ancestors and contemporary Haitians. In large cities around the world, such as New York, Rara festivals are held as a means of publicizing the political corruption, racism, and human rights abuses. Exhibits of sacred Vodou art worldwide, such as the New York Museum of Natural History's Sacred Arts of Haitian Vodou exhibit in 1998 through 1999, has shown the world that Haiti has a rich and beautiful culture.

The arts in Haiti are also playing an integral part in creating self-awareness and self-expression for young Haitians. The Art Creation Foundation for Children, a non-profit arts organization, was founded in 2003 for education and personal growth of children in need in Jacmel. The organization has an integrated agenda to provide young Haitians with arts education, school, food, and health care. The Art Creation Foundation for Children meets the educational needs of 60 students. The artwork of Haitian students is used, in part, in international publicity

and fundraising campaigns. Dwa Fanm (which means "Women's Rights" in Haitian Creole) is an organization dedicated to eradicating all forms of discrimination, injustice, and violence against Haitian women and girls. Dwa Fanm promotes films directed by Haitian women as a means of sharing the experiences of Haitian women with a domestic and international audience.

## Cultural Sites & Landmarks

Haiti's cultural sites and landmarks are spread throughout the island of Hispaniola. The United Nations Educational, Scientific and Cultural Organization (UNESCO) recognizes one site in Haiti as requiring international recognition and preservation efforts: the National History Park. The park includes the Haitian monuments of the Citadel, the Palace of Sans Souci, and the buildings at Ramiers. These three Haitian monuments date to the 18th century when Haiti was first achieving independence. Freed black slaves built the monuments as symbols of personal and national liberty. Other important cultural sites and landmarks are found in the cities of Cap Haitian, Jacmel, and the capital of Port-au-Prince.

The French established Cap Haitian, along Haiti's northern coast, in 1670. The city is home to the first New World landing of explorer Christopher Columbus and numerous historically important slave revolts. In particular, visitors to Cap Haitian usually visit Bois Caiman, believed to be the location of the 18th-century Vodou ceremony that began the Haitian Revolution. Jacmel, along Haiti's southern coast, was founded in 1698. Today Jacmel is Haiti's cultural center and home to an annual film festival. Jacmel is particularly known for its indigenous arts and crafts. Visitors also come to Jacmel to tour the remaining French colonial buildings.

Port-au-Prince, Haiti's capital, is home to many cultural institutions, including the Presidential Palace and the Iron Market (Marché de Fer). The Iron Market is a large outdoor market with hundreds of street vendors selling clothing, art, food, and electronics. (The Iron Market is also the unofficial depot for Port-au-Prince's "tap-taps." These brightly decorated trucks provide a popular, although often hazardous, means of transport for both people and cargo.) Other key landmarks in Port-au-Prince include two churches, the Catholic Cathédrale Notre-Dame de l'Assomption, noted for its colonial-era architectural style, and the Episcopal Cathedral of the Holy Trinity. The Holy Trinity Cathedral is celebrated for its imposing murals depicting Christian subject matter in a distinctly Haitian style. However, much of Port-au-Prince, including the Presidential Palace, was heavily damaged following a major earthquake in January 2010.

Important ecological sites in Haiti include La Visite National Park and Pic Macaya National Park. La Visite National Park is located in the Massif de la Selle mountain range and protects limestone caves, endangered species of birds and plants, and rare occidental pines. Pic Macaya National Park is one of only a few remaining natural forests in Haiti. The park is located in the Massif de la Hotte mountain range and is home to Haiti's last area of virgin forest.

## Libraries & Museums

The National Museum of History, located near the National Palace, features artifacts tracing Haiti's development from the time of its original inhabitants to the 20th century. One of the museum's most popular attractions is a rusty anchor said to have been salvaged from the Santa Maria, one of the trio of ships Christopher Columbus sailed to the New World. Many of the museum's important collections survived the 2010 earthquake. The Haitian National Museum of Art, also located in the capital, contains a sizable pre-Columbian collection of art. It suffered extensive damage in the earthquake, however. In addition, the Musee d'Art Nader, which housed roughly 15,000 art pieces, was destroyed, while the Centre d'Art, an important art gallery and exhibit, also crumbled.

The National Library of Haiti is located in Port-au-Prince, and was established in 1939. It oversees roughly twenty municipal libraries throughout the country. Both the National Library and the National Archives suffered minor damage in the 2010 earthquake.

## Holidays

Haitians celebrate Independence Day on January 1, commemorating the hard-won freedom of Haitian slaves and the birth of the republic on January 1, 1804. Part of the celebration involves eating soup, a food that was forbidden by French slave owners. January 2 is Ancestry Day, or Hero's Day, and honors Haitain ancestors.

April 7 commemorates the death of Toussaint L'Ouverture (1743–1804), the man who helped orchestrate the slave revolt in 1791 and led the slave army in the ensuing battles. Dessalines Day (October 17) honors the death of Jean-Jacques Dessalines (1758–1806), who took over the slave revolt after L'Ouverture died and who declared Haiti a republic.

Vertières Day (November 18) celebrates the Battle of Vertières, the decisive battle of the Haitian revolution on November 18, 1803 that led to victory for the slaves. Discovery Day (December 5) commemorates Christopher Columbus' arrival in Haiti in 1492.

## Youth Culture

Haiti's general population is overall very young. As of 2008, the median age is estimated to be 19 years of age. Youth culture is largely shaped by Haiti's economic hardship and political instability. The majority of Haitians are poor and illiterate, and fewer than 70 percent of Haitian youth attend primary school. The government funds about 10 percent of Haiti's schools and families are expected to pay tuition as well as for uniforms and supplies. The cost of school is prohibitively expensive for many Haitian families. Additionally, children who attend generally walk long distances to and from school.

Unemployment or underemployment rates are also high. As a result, subsistence agriculture is the norm for most households. Family members, including children and teens, participate in the planting and harvesting of the fields. Farming is very difficult work and provides low yields due to the lack of nutrient-rich top soil. (Deforestation throughout Haiti has created poor soil conditions for farming.) Hunger and homelessness are common and Haitian youth—and poor Haitians in general—tend to own very few items of clothing. Despite extreme economic hardship, Haitian youth enjoy dancing, singing, and football (soccer).

## SOCIETY

### Transportation

Transportation in Haiti is limited by poor road conditions, typically caused by flooding, and limited transportation infrastructure. The majority of Haitians travel by foot, burro, or bus. Buses, which are often retired school buses or vans from the United States, connect the cities of Port-au-Prince, Cap-Haitien, Les Cayes, Jacmel, Jérémie, Hinche, Pétionville, and Port-de-Paix. Buses do not leave on a regularly set schedule so much as when they are full of passengers. Another common mode of transportation are pick-up trucks, known as "tap-taps," that operate as shared taxis, and are painted in bright colors. Regular taxi service is also available in larger cities. Traffic moves on the right-hand side of the road.

### Transportation Infrastructure

Haiti's transportation infrastructure is limited and haphazard and less than 20 percent of its roadways are paved. A majority of roads are in poor condition, and two significant highways link the southern and northern parts of the country. The country's operating rail line was limited to freight, particularly the transportation of sugarcane. The Toussaint Louverture International Airport (PAP) is the main international hub. The country's poor infrastructure has particularly hampered relief efforts following the devastating 2010 earthquake.

### Media & Communications

Haiti's low literacy rate—estimated at 52 percent of the population—is reflected in the small distribution numbers of the country's newspapers. Haiti's most popular daily newspapers are *Le Matin* and *Le Nouvelliste*. Haiti *Progrès* is a French weekly with online editions in Creole and English; the *Haitian Times* is an English weekly. Television and radio are available to those few in Port-au-Prince, Haiti's largest city, who can afford the technology and the cost of electricity. Radio remains the most widespread medium with over 250 stations in both private and public service. Télé-Haiti is a cable station relaying captured satellite signals on four channels. The Haitian constitution protects free speech and, as a result, the government does not generally censor the media.

Communication infrastructure and access in Haiti is also extremely limited. For instance, the US Central Intelligence Agency (CIA) considers Haiti's telephone system—which had 41,000 main telephone lines and 6.8 million cellular lines in use in 2014—to be inadequate for the local or domestic population and barely sufficient for international visitors and businesses. In fact, Haiti has the lowest telephone density (a measure comparing the number of telephones to the population at large) in the Caribbean. The Internet is equally limited, and in 2014 there were an estimated 1.2 million Internet users, representing roughly 11 percent of the population.

## SOCIAL DEVELOPMENT

### Standard of Living

Haiti ranked 168 out of 187 countries on the 2013 United Nations Human Development Index (HDI), which measures quality of life and standard of living indicators.

The index is based on factors such as life expectancy and infant mortality rate. In 2012, the average life expectancy was reported as 63 years, and the infant mortality rate was 55 deaths per 1,000 live births in 2013.

### Water Consumption

Prior to the 2010 earthquake that devastated parts of the country, water and sanitation coverage in Haiti was widely lacking and a dire concern for foreign aid and humanitarian organizations, with only approximately 58 percent of the population having access to clean or improved sources of drinking water, and an estimated 19 percent of the population having access to improved sanitation. Further, sanitation coverage in rural areas was only at 14 percent, with many lacking any health care services whatsoever. Poor water and sanitation conditions following the earthquake continue to pose threats to the recovering and displaced population, including a 2010 cholera outbreak in the capital that hospitalized nearly 10,000 people, and claimed more than 1,300 lives nationwide.

## Education

Haitian children receive 10 years of primary education and 3 years of secondary education. Children between the ages of 6 and 15 are required to attend school; however, in 1999, only 64 percent of eligible students were enrolled in school. Of those, only 30 percent finished primary school and 15 percent enrolled in secondary school.

Upper-class families often send their children to private schools. Private primary schools outnumber public primary schools, and have a higher attendance level as well. Public schools are free, while private schools charge tuition. However, the quality of education in public schools is poor, classes are taught primarily in French, and few students can afford to purchase textbooks. These factors contribute to Haiti's overall literacy rate of 60.7 percent (2015) Many students forego Haitian universities such as the Université d'État d'Haïti (State University of Haiti) in Port-au-Prince to attend universities in the United States and Europe. Following the 2010 earthquake, damages to the capital's three main universities—the state university, Quisqueya University, and Université des Caraïbes (University of the Caribbean)—were extensive. Many displaced students were accepted by American colleges and universities following the quake.

## Women's Rights

In Haitian society, women are not equal to men. In general, women are socially and economically subservient to their male counterparts. While women are often the heads of households, particularly in rural areas, women's work options are generally limited to the informal economic sector, and include farming, marketing, domestic labor, and sales. Although Haitian law, particularly the Labor Code, states that men and women are guaranteed equal rights, sexual harassment and economic discrimination against women are common occurrences.

Domestic violence, in the form of spousal abuse and rape, is common and significantly underreported. While Haiti's criminal law has established penalties for rape—10 to 15 years imprisonment—rapes are usually unreported. In addition, Haitian law tends to protect husbands who abuse their wives. For example, husbands are legally permitted to kill their wives if the wives are found committing adultery in the family home. Wives, on the other hand, are not legally excused from killing their husbands under any circumstances. Further complicating the issue of domestic violence is Haiti's lack of government-sponsored support and programs for women suffering abuse.

The social problem of violence against Haitian women is internationally recognized. In addition to the United Nations Commission on Human Rights (UNCHR), which identified interpersonal violence and rape against Haitian women as a growing area of concern, nations from around the world held the International Tribunal Against Violence Against Haitian Women in 1997. Haitian non-governmental organizations (NGOs), along with representatives from the Dominican Republic, St. Lucia, Dominica, Barbados, Rwanda, Uganda, Republic of Congo, Canada, and the United States, met to discuss strategies for eradicating violence against Haitian women. Issues that were discussed included the need for changes in the Haitian justice system and police procedures to support victims of crime, the need for increased services and education for women as well as victims of crime, and the need to educate all Haitians about the principles of equal rights.

Since the turn of the 20th century, women's rights groups, which are growing in number and influence in Haiti, have become increasingly involved in health education, rights education, and voter education initiatives. Women's rights groups are also tackling the problems for women caused by legalized prostitution. Prostitution is associated with the high number of HIV/AIDS deaths among Haitian women. Influential women's rights organizations operating in Haiti include the Organisation de Défense des Droits des Femmes (ENFOFANM), Fanm Viktim Leve Kanpe or Women Victims Stand Up (FAVILEK), the National and International Center for Documentation and Information on Women in Haiti, and Soladirite Fanm Ayisien, or Haitian Women in Solidarity (SOFA).

## Health Care

Health care in Haiti is almost completely privatized, meaning that the government does not fund any free health-care services except for the immunization of children up to one year of age. The majority of Haitians lives in poverty and must rely on international humanitarian organizations to fund life-saving medical and preventative care. These organizations, however, cannot tend to the needs of the entire country.

The overall health of the population is poor. Health-care infrastructure is insufficient and under-funded, and trained professionals are few and far between. Diseases (particularly malaria, tuberculosis, dysentery, and AIDS) are widespread due to malnutrition, contaminated drinking water, and lack of adequate and accessible medical facilities.

Already ranking as one of the worst in the Western Hemisphere, the country's health system was further ravaged by the 2010 earthquake. While hospital services were provided for free in the months following the disaster, the country, not set up to withstand a disaster of such magnitude, is struggling to provide health care going forward. A severe and deadly cholera outbreak in late 2010 continued to stress the lack of basic health-care services and infrastructure in the impoverished nation following the earthquake.

## GOVERNMENT

### Structure

Haiti is considered a semi-presidential republic and is in the process of transitioning to a democracy. The central government is comprised of an executive branch, a legislative branch, and a judicial branch. Its constitution, written in 1987 and based on that of the United States, divides power between the three branches.

The executive branch includes the president (the chief of state), the cabinet, and the prime minister (the head of government). The president is elected every five years by popular vote, and the prime minister is selected from the bicameral legislature. The cabinet is appointed by the prime minister.

The legislative branch consists of the bicameral National Assembly, a legislative body made up of the Chamber of Deputies and the Senate. The Chamber of Deputies has 99 members, each elected by popular vote to four-year terms. The Senate has 30 members, two-thirds elected by popular vote to six-year terms, and one-third elected to two-year terms. The National Assembly has been defunct since February 2004.

Following the 2010 earthquake, all but one government building was destroyed, and an estimated 20 percent of government workers were killed.

### Political Parties

As a country still transitioning to democracy, political parties are not strongly established in terms of a voting base in Haiti's multiparty political system. Parliamentary elections were held in Haiti on August 9, 2015, with a second round planned on October 25. Two-thirds of the Senate and all members of the Chamber of Deputies were up for election. Among the parties competing are Truth, Fanmi Lavalas, the Fusion of Haitian Social Democrats, the Struggling People's Organization, and Haiti in Action.

## Local Government

Haiti's system of local governance is often characterized as weak, and the ineffectiveness of centralization was apparent following the 2010 earthquake. The country is divided into nine departments, and further divided into districts and municipalities and communal sections. Representatives or councils or assemblies are elected to represent the varying levels of local governance. Following the 2010 earthquake, the UNDP will work with Haiti to implement decentralization and to strengthen democratic local governance in the country.

## Judicial System

The judicial branch consists of the Supreme Court, the Courts of Appeal, and the Courts of First Instance. Lower courts include various civil and local courts. The Supreme Court must accept rulings from the International Court of Justice.

## Taxation

Haiti's tax rates are relatively modest, and consist of top corporate and personal income rates of 30 percent. Taxes levied include a value-added tax (VAT, similar to a consumption tax) and a capital gains tax.

## Armed Forces

Haiti does not maintain a standing army, having disbanded their military in 1995. Limited military forces consist of the Haitian National Police (consisting of a paramilitary unit) and a coast guard. Since 2004, the United Nations Stabilisation Mission in Haiti has maintained a significant troop presence in the country. The peacekeeping mission has planned on strengthening the country's national police force, with plans to increase personnel to 15,000 by 2016.

## Foreign Policy

Haiti, a founding member of the UN, is a country in economic and social need. The government has trouble maintaining civil order, suppressing

human rights abuses such as narcotics smuggling and human trafficking, stopping corruption, and providing sufficient food for its population. As a result, Haiti's foreign policy is largely shaped by this political instability and extreme economic need. The country relies on international agencies and foreign aid, with that aid constituting nearly double the money earned through exports. The United States and the UN also believe that Haiti's political, social, and economic instability constitutes a threat to international peace and security in the region. The UN Stabilization Mission in Haiti (MINUSTAH)—which consists of 38 nations—has maintained 8,000 uniformed peacekeepers in Haiti since 2004.

Despite Haiti's economic hardships and the presence of a multinational force, the country has maintained an active profile in the Caribbean and surrounding regions. Haiti is a member of the Organization of American States (OAS), and joined the Caribbean Community (CARICOM) in 1997 in hopes of promoting trade and economic stability. However, Haiti's trade relations are few, and its agricultural industry is challenged by natural disasters, widespread deforestation, and a lack of topsoil on which to farm. The country's main trading partners include the United States, the Dominican Republic, and Canada; and imported food, manufactured goods, fuel and other needs are largely exported from North America, Brazil, the Netherlands, and China.

In 2005, Haiti paid its debt to the World Bank. This payment made Haiti eligible to received international economic aid from the World Bank and other aid organizations, including the Inter-American Development Bank (IDB), the European Union (EU), and the International Monetary Fund (IMF). In 2006, Haiti and the United States negotiated the Haitian Hemispheric Opportunity through Partnership Encouragement (HOPE) Act, which provided tariff-free access to the United States for Haiti's garment and automotive parts exports. The United States remains the largest donor country in terms of economic aid to the Caribbean state. American companies and NGOs continue to receive the lion's share of US aid funding for projects in Haiti after the earthquake. Critics argue that donors' practice of spending aid money through organizations located in their own countries has hampered efforts to build self-sufficiency in Haiti.

Despite strong and continued international social, political, and economic aid, Haiti remains one of the poorest countries in the world; 58.6 percent of Haitians live in poverty and unemployment and unequal resource distribution hinders economic growth.

The country's growth and foreign relations rely heavily on the fostering and strengthening of democracy. In 2006, Haiti instituted a democratic parliament and democratically elected its president. This democratic leadership and government followed over a century of political instability and rule by dictators, often characterized by large-scale suppression and extreme political violence. The United States will continue to play a primary role in establishing and promoting democracy and economic stability and growth in Haiti.

## Human Rights Profile

International human rights law insists that states respect civil and political rights, and also promote an individual's economic, social, and cultural rights. The United Nations Universal Declaration on Human Rights (UDHR) is recognized as the standard for international human rights. Its authors sought the counsel of the world's great thinkers, philosophers, and religious leaders, and were careful to create a document that reflects the core values shared by every world culture. (To read this document or view the articles relating to cultural go to, click here: http://www.udhr.org/UDHR/default.htm.)

Article 2 of the UDHR, which states that everyone is entitled to legal rights and freedoms without discrimination, is not specifically supported by Haiti's constitution. Haitian law also does not specifically prohibits discrimination on the grounds of race, gender, disability, language, or social status. Discrimination against persons with HIV/AIDS, women, children, dark-skinned people and poor people is common. The only exceptions are the laws governing working conditions and the split between urban and rural Haitians. Haitian law, which often goes un-enforced, does guarantee equal working conditions regardless of gender, beliefs, or marital status. In addition, the Haitian constitution forbids discrimination between the urban and rural populations. The right to progress, information, education, health, employment, and leisure for all citizens is generally protected by Haiti's constitution.

Many articles of the UDHR are protected by Haitian law. In practice, common-law marriage (plaçage or plasaj) is common in Haiti, particularly among the rural poor. Haitian women, in both official and common law marriages, have won new and expanded rights to own property. Divorce, once prohibited by the law, is allowed. Haitians enjoy the freedom to practice religion as they see fit, so long as the religious acts do not violate the law. For example, Voodoo is practiced simultaneously along with other established religions. Haiti's constitution also protects freedom of speech and freedom of the press. Haiti has an independent press that is generally respected by the government. The Haitian government does not restrict Internet access or content, nor does the government restrict academic freedom or cultural events.

Articles 27-29 of the UDHR, which invoke the need for national and international social, moral, economic, and cultural support for the rights and freedoms set forth in the declaration, are supported by Haitian law. Although Haitians have the legal freedom to participate in the cultural life of their country, retain ownership of their creative and scientific endeavors, and participate in their communities, economic and political instability prevent most Haitians from exercising their freedoms. Ultimately, Haiti's constitutional protections cannot, in many instances, overcome the political and economic instability that result in numerous human rights abuses. Examples of human rights violations include unreported killings by the Haitian National Police (HNP), overcrowded prisons, arbitrary arrests and detentions, government corruption, violence and discrimination against women, and child abuse and trafficking.

## ECONOMY

### Overview of the Economy

Haiti does not have any major industries, and agriculture is the foundation of the economy. In 2014, Haiti's GDP was estimated at $18.31 billion USD, with a per capita GDP of $1,800. Approximately 58 percent of Haitians live below the poverty line, and by some estimates more than two-thirds of the workforce is unemployed. Large numbers of the capital's residents, for example, remain unemployed or underemployed. The average annual income per family in Port-au-Prince is the equivalent of less than $400, and it tends to be even lower for families dwelling in the city's slum districts. Many people struggle to support themselves by peddling various wares and services on the streets.

### Industry

Industrial activity in Haiti is light, consisting mainly of flour milling, sugar refining, and some manufacturing. Taken together, these activities employ 11.5 percent of the workforce and account for 19.9 percent of the GDP. Haiti exports baseballs, electronic components and other assembled products, as well as coffee, cotton, sugar, sisal, bauxite, and essential oils. It imports food, petroleum, manufactured goods, machinery, and raw materials.

Port-au-Prince's modest industrial sector also includes sugar refineries, flour mills, food processing plants, and factories for the manufacture of cement, textiles, soap, and matches. Labor-intensive light industry accounts for a quarter of export profits. Many products—such as shoes, clothing, baseballs, toys, and electronics—are turned out by foreign-owned companies, eager to do business in a city with an abundance of cheap, unregulated labor and generous tax incentives put into place to attract outside investment.

### Labor

Haiti's labor market is characterized by under-employment and unemployment, and a large majority works in the informal sector or survives through subsistence farming. Exacerbating the situation is the lack of skilled or trained workers, as many skilled laborers leave the country to find work. The unemployment rate for Haiti is difficult to pin down, with estimates ranging from 41 to 70 percent.

### Energy/Power/Natural Resources

Haiti has small deposits of a few resources, including bauxite, manganese, limestone, coal, and marble. Because of the economic situation in the country, the most valuable deposits of gold, copper, and silver are largely unexploited. Haiti's bauxite mine was closed in the early 1980s.

### Fishing

Haiti's fishing industry is small and underdeveloped, and yields are affected by the use of poor technology. In the wake of the 2010 earthquake, many international observers feel that a revamped fishing industry—neglected, despite extensive resources and costal zones—would provide necessary food security to Haiti. The Food and Agriculture Organization (FAO), in particular, has helped rural communities to organize and support local fishing associations, including the purchasing of bigger boats and newer equipment. Potential commercial species include marlin, bonitos, sardines, and tuna. Annual catches are estimated at roughly 5,000 tons.

### Forestry

Haiti was once blanketed by tropical and semitropical rainforests. Before Christopher Columbus arrived in Haiti in 1492, there were over 2.7 million hectares (6.7 million acres) of rainforests of mahogany, rosewood, cedar, taverneaux, and tropical oak and pine trees. In 2000, only 88,000 hectares (217,000 acres) remained. Between 1990 and 2000, Haiti had the highest deforestation rate in the world. An estimated 99 percent of the country is now deforested.

### Mining/Metals

Mining activity in Haiti is underdeveloped and hampered by instability and lack of foreign investment. Known deposits in the country include copper, gold, iron ore, manganese, lead, tin, and zinc, among other minerals. Historically, the country has produced mineral commodities such as cement, limestone, marble salt, and construction materials such as sand and gravel. No significant mineral products were exported in 2009.

## Agriculture

Haiti's major cash crops are coffee, sugarcane, plantains, corn, rice, sorghum, beans, cacao, mangoes, and sisal. Subsistence farmers grow sweet potatoes, rice, peas, beans, cassava, mangoes, corn, okra, peanuts, and sugarcane for personal consumption. Prior to the earthquake that ravaged the island nation in 2010, an estimated 66 percent of the country's labor force worked in the agricultural sector, and approximately 28 percent of the country's entire economy relied on agriculture. Deforestation and hurricanes—four in 2008, alone—have also contributed greatly to Haiti's declining agricultural industries; in particular, deforestation, often to create cooking fuel, has ruined significant soil amounts.

## Animal Husbandry

Livestock raised for both sale and personal consumption includes cattle, pigs, goats, and chicken. Goats represented an estimated 40–50 percent of all livestock in the country. The vaccination and care of livestock became a primary priority following the 2010 earthquake, particularly as dairy products such as milk and eggs were needed for food.

## Tourism

The tourism industry is depressed due to Haiti's legacy of political turmoil, poor infrastructure, poverty, and disease. Political instability has had a particularly devastating impact on the capital's tourism industry, which has all but dried up in the aftermath of global travel advisories warning potential visitors of serious personal safety risks. The government in Port-au-Prince relies on international donors, chiefly the United States, to supply two-thirds of its budgetary needs. In 2005, the government paid off its debt to the World Bank and in 2006, the economy grew by almost two percent, thanks to a program of economic reforms developed with International Monetary Fund (IMF) assistance. However, the impact of the 2010 earthquake severely impacted economic gains made by Haiti in prior years.

*Simone Flynn, Jamie Aronson, Beverly Ballaro*

---

## DO YOU KNOW?

- In 2003, President Jean-Bertrand Aristide issued an executive decree sanctioning voodoo as an officially recognized religion in Haiti.

- Musician Wyclef Jean was born in Haiti. His extensive charitable works in the country and his success in music have made him a national hero to all Haitians.

- The most common form of public transportation in Port-au-Prince, the brightly decorated trucks that serve as communal taxis, are called "tap-taps" because passengers generally tap coins on the side of the vehicle as a means of signaling the driver to make a stop.

- President Michel Martelly, in office since 2011, is a former popular music performer who earned the nickname "Sweet Micky."

## Bibliography

Clammer, Paul, et al. *Dominican Republic and Haiti.* Oakland, CA: Lonely Planet, 2011.

Danticat, Edwidge. *The Dew Breaker.* New York: Knopf, 2004.

Dubois, Laurent. *Haiti: The Aftershocks of History.* London: Picador, 2013.

Girard, Philippe. *Haiti: The Tumultuous History.* New York: St. Martin's, 2010.

Wilentz, Amy. *Farewell, Fred Voodoo: A Letter from Haiti.* New York: Simon and Schuster, 2013.


## Works Cited

Cosentino, Donald J. Vodou Things: The Art of Pierre Barra and Marie Cassaise. Folk Art and Artist Series. Jackson: University Press of Mississippi, 1998.

"A Country Study: Haiti." U.S. Library of Congress Country Studies, 2005. http://lcweb2.loc.gov/frd/cs/httoc.html.

"Culture of HAITI." Countries of the World (n.d.). http://www.everyculture.com/Ge-It/Haiti.html.

"Food in Haiti." Food in Every Country (n.d.). http://www.foodbycountry.com/Germany-to-Japan/Haiti.html.

"Gender in Haiti". Haiti Net. http://northeastern.edu/haitinet/gender-in-haiti/

Haggerty, Richard A., ed. Haiti: A Country Study. Washington: GPO for the Library of Congress, 1989.

"Haiti". *Nations of the World: A Political, Economic, and Business Handbook.* 14th ed. Amenia, NY: Grey House Publishing, 2015.

"Haiti". UNESCO World Heritage List. http://whc.unesco.org/en/statesparties/ht.

"Haiti". World Vision. http://www.worldvision.org/our-impact/country-profiles/haiti.

"Haiti: Country Reports on Human Rights Practices." US Bureau of Democracy, Human Rights, and Labor. http://www.state.gov/g/drl/rls/hrrpt/2006/78895.htm.

"Haiti: The World Fact Book." U.S. Central Intelligence Agency. https://www.cia.gov/library/publications/the-world-factbook/print/ha.html.

"Haiti Earthquake: Where Is US Aid Money Going? Get the Data". *The Guardian* (10 Jan. 2014). Retrieved 8 Oct. 2015 http://www.theguardian.com/global-development/datablog/2014/jan/10/haiti-earthquake-us-aid-funding-data

"Haiti Human Rights." Amnesty International USA. http://www.amnestyusa.org/all-countries/haiti/page.do?id=1011166.

"Haiti Statistics: Haiti by the Numbers". Haiti Partners. http://haitipartners.org/about-us/haiti-statistics/

"Haitian." Culture Grid (n.d.). http://gasi-ves.org/diversity/greetings/haitian.htm.

"International Interests." Dwa Fanm, 2002. http://www.dwafanm.org/international.htm.

Kolbe, Athena R. and Royce A. Hutson. "Human Rights Abuse and Other Criminal Violations in Port-au-Prince, Haiti: A Random Survey of Households." Lancet (n.d.). SocINDEX with Full Text. EBSCO. http://search.ebscohost.com/login.aspx?direct=true&db=sih&AN=22209101&site=ehost-live.

Polk, Patrick Arthur. Haitian Vodou Flags. Folk Art and Artist Series. Jackson: University Press of Mississippi, 1997.

"Sacred Art of Haitian Vodou." The New York Museum of Natural History, 1998. http://www.amnh.org/exhibitions/vodou/.

Tompkins, Cynthia, ed. Teen Life in Latin America and the Caribbean. Westport, CT: Greenwood Publishing Group, 2004.

"The UN Stabilization Mission in Haiti". Better World Campaign. http://Betterworldcampaign.org/un-peacekeeping/missions/haiti.html/

"Universal Declaration of Human Rights." United Nations, 1948. http://www.udhr.org/UDHR/default.htm.

Valbrun, Marjorie. "Recovering Haiti's Lost Literary Legacy: Newer Books Help Readers Understand a Complex Cultural and Political Heritage, and Renew Interest in the Island Nation's Remarkable Homegrown Classics." Black Issues Book Review 7.1 (Jan. 2005): 60–61. Academic Search Premier. EBSCO. 2 Dec. 2008 http://search.ebscohost.com/login.aspx?direct=true&db=aph&AN=15420587&site=ehost-live.

Wilcken, Lois. "Vodou Music in Neo-traditional Contexts: Folklore and Roots Music." Vodou Music, 2005. http://svr1.cg971.fr/lameca/dossiers/vodou_music/eng/p6.htm.

JAMAICA

# Introduction

Jamaica is a small island nation located about 572 miles (920 kilometers) south of Miami, Florida. Once a central market for sugarcane and the slave trade, Jamaica is now an important tourist destination in the Caribbean. It is a member of the British Commonwealth of Nations and maintains strong ties to the United States. However, Jamaica continues to struggle with widespread poverty and economic weakness, an inheritance of its colonial past.

## GENERAL INFORMATION

**Official Language(s):** English
**Population:** 2,780,000 (2012 estimate)
**Currency:** Jamaican Dollar
**Coins:** The Jamaican dollar is equal to 100 cents. Cent coins come in 1, 10, and 25 cent denominations. Dollar coins are issued in 1, 5, 10, and 20 Jamaican dollar denominations.
**Land Area:** 10,831 square kilometers (4,181 square miles)
**Water Area:** 160 square kilometers (61 square miles)
**National Motto:** "Out of Many, One People"
**National Anthem:** "Jamaica, Land We Love"
**Capital:** Kingston
**Time Zone(s):** GMT -5
**Flag Description:** The colors of the Jamaican flag (gold, green, and black) are considered Pan-African colors. A gold diagonal cross (saltire) divides the flag into four triangles. The equilateral triangles on each side are black (sable), and the equilateral triangles on the top and bottom are green.

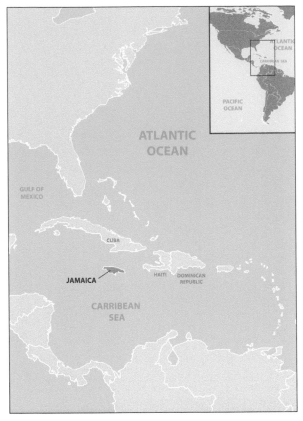

## Population

Approximately 1.3 percent of Jamaica's population is East Indian. Just over seven percent of residents consider themselves to be ethnically or racially "mixed," although the ancestry of the island's more than 90 percent population of "blacks" is well-blended. Jamaica also has small, but significant communities of Syrians, Lebanese, and Europeans.

Government-sponsored family planning programs and a high rate of emigration have slowed Jamaica's population growth to less than one percent, though Jamaica continues to be one of the world's most densely populated countries. Life expectancy has risen over the past few decades to an average 74 years—72 years for men and 75 years for women (2014 estimate).

The United States government estimates that approximately 1.5 percent of Jamaicans are infected with HIV/AIDS, but improvements in health care and urban planning have decreased the presence of contagious and air- or water-borne

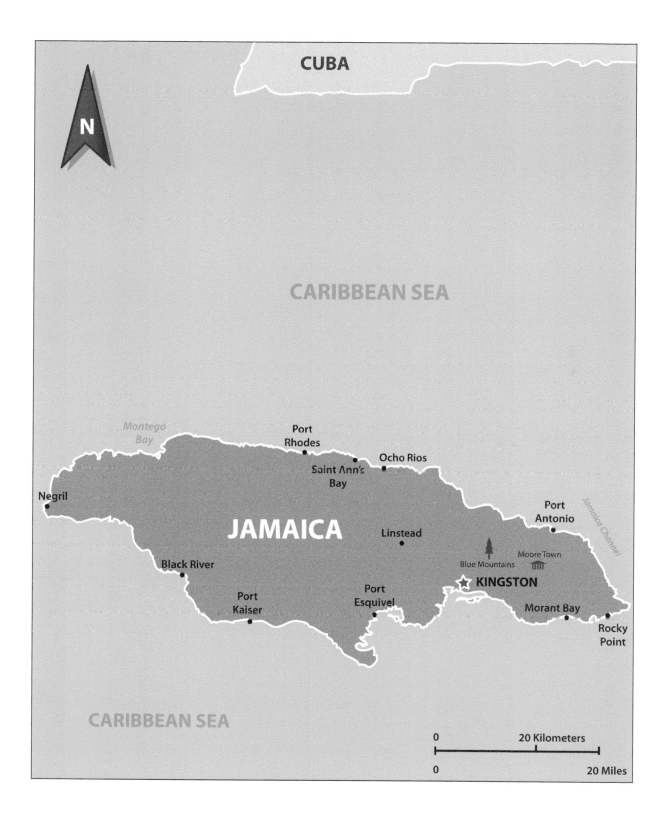

> **Principal Cities by Population (2012 estimate):**
>
> - Kingston (575,946)
> - Spanish Town (170,325)
> - Portmore (132,777)
> - Montego Bay (78,998)
> - May Pen (49,471)
> - Mandeville (48,849)

diseases. Most of Jamaica's health-care services are devoted to the treatment of chronic diseases, like heart disease or diabetes.

About 55 percent of Jamaica's population lives in urban areas, with Kingston & St. Andrews seeing the greatest concentration of people.

## Languages

English is the official language of Jamaica. The spoken languages of Jamaica also include Jamaican creole or patois formed by combining English with other languages—patois is the most widely spoken language in Jamaica and is associated with reggae—as well as Taino (mixed with Spanish) and Arawak in certain areas.

## Native People & Ethnic Groups

Jamaica's earliest recorded population consisted of Arawak Amerindians, probably originating in the South American Andes, who settled the island sometime around 700. Their word for the island, "Xaymaca" (meaning "land of wood and water"), became "Jamaica" after Spanish colonists settled the island in the 16th century.

When Christopher Columbus landed in Jamaica in 1494, approximately 10,000 Arawak were living on the island. However, the Spanish settlers who followed subjected the native population to slavery, introduced European diseases, and violently repressed any efforts at rebellion. As a result, the Arawak population appears to have disappeared completely by the beginning of the 17th century, leaving traces only in cave drawings, artifacts, and residual cultural practices.

The blending of cultures and histories that characterizes Jamaica makes standard ethnic designations impossible in the small, island nation. In fact, slaves, slave owners, slave traders, adventurers, colonists, and migrants repopulated Jamaica during the 16th through the 20th centuries after the first Spanish colonists eradicated the island's native population. Largely because of the impact of slavery on the island's history, most of Jamaica's populace claims West African ancestry, often without reference to a specific nation or tribe in Africa.

Jamaica's largest minority group (1.3 percent) consists of Chinese and Indian Jamaicans (descendants of Chinese and Indian indentured laborers who came to Jamaica in the mid 19th and early 20th centuries). Jamaica also experienced a migration of Germans to the country in the early to mid 19th century—those German peasants also served as indentured servants. In the late 19th century, a Syrian and Lebanese migration occurred as a result of Turkish oppression.

## Religions

Some of Jamaica's African-based genealogy is evident in the religious practices of the islanders. Rastafarianism is a blend of religious and social beliefs that include a devotion to Haile Selassie (born Ras Tafari), the late emperor of Ethiopia, himself a Christian. Many Jamaicans incorporate some form of African-derived spirituality into their religious beliefs. However, the overwhelming majority of Jamaicans who adhere to a religious faith are Christian (62.5 percent Protestant; 2.6 percent Roman Catholic). Islam, Buddhism, and Hindu are also represented amongst the country's religious faiths, and about one-fifth of the population claims no religious faith at all.

## Climate

Jamaica's high central mountain ranges break the island's climate into two zones. On the windward side of the mountains, to the northeast, trade winds deposit plentiful rainfall, giving this half of Jamaica an upland tropical climate. To the southwest, however, the mountains shield the island from rain, resulting in a warm, semiarid climate.

Average rainfall across the island is 1,960 millimeters (77 inches) annually, although this number rises to 5,080 millimeters (200 inches) per year in the highest elevations of the mountains, and drops to only 762 millimeters (30 inches) per year in the semiarid southwestern plateaus and coastline. Rainfall is heaviest from May to October.

Because of Jamaica's location near the equator, temperatures are fairly constant throughout the year. Average temperatures range from 25° to 30° Celsius (77° to 86° Fahrenheit) in the lowlands and 15° to 20° Celsius (59° to 68° Fahrenheit) in the mountains. Temperatures can drop below 10° Celsius (50° Fahrenheit) at night on Blue Mountain. Temperatures are moderated by northeast trade winds, an onshore breeze known as "the Doctor's Breeze," and an offshore breeze known as "the Undertaker's Breeze."

The island is prone to hurricanes, particularly between the months of July and November.

## ENVIRONMENT & GEOGRAPHY

### Topography

Jamaica is located about 572 miles (920 kilometers) south of Miami, Florida, just 90 miles (145 kilometers) south of Cuba, and 99 miles (160 kilometers) west of Haiti. The island nation is 235 kilometers (146 miles) long, and ranges from 35 to 82 kilometers (22 to 51 miles) in width.

In the eastern portion of the island, the Blue Mountains cover the central interior, forming a long ridge that reaches above 1,800 meters (5,900 feet) for a 3-kilometer stretch. The country's highest point is 2,256 meters (7,402 feet), atop Blue Mountain Peak.

West of the Blue Mountains, the John Crow Mountains and Dry Harbour Mountains are actually elevated limestone plateaus, created when the island's volcanic base was submerged in the sea billions of years ago. The Manchester Plateau lies to the south of the Dry Harbour Mountains. With their caves, sinkholes, disappearing streams, hummocks, and red soil valleys, these limestone plateaus are known as karst landscapes. On the western side of Jamaica, the karst landscape becomes particularly dramatic in the Cockpit Country, where deep basins, conical hills and ridges once provided ample hiding places for escaped slaves.

Jamaica's northeast coast is rugged, rocky, and steep, with small inlets providing the only safe harbors. To the west, however, narrow coastal plains create calm waters and white sand beaches that rise slightly on a plateau created by uplifted coral reefs. Jamaica's western coastline has the long, flat stretches of beach for which the country is famous.

The southern coastline beaches are smaller plains of black sand backed by limestone cliffs. Between these stretches, cliffs drop up to 300 meters (984 feet) into the sea. Only on the southwest shoreline do the coastal plains stretch significantly inland. In this area, the Black River runs through the widest of these plains into the sea. Swampland known as the Great Morass and Upper Morass dominates these plains.

### Plants & Animals

Many of Jamaica's indigenous plants and wildlife can still be found in the Blue Mountains, the central part of Cockpit Country, and along the coast from Discovery Bay to Rio Bueno.

Like its plant life, Jamaica's indigenous animal species are now difficult to find on the island, if they have not disappeared altogether. Although an array of bird, insect, and lizard species are still common even in populated areas, animals like the Jamaican flower bat, Jamaican fig eating bat, Macleay's moustached bat, and offshore, the American manatee, are all becoming scarce.

## CUSTOMS & COURTESIES

### Greetings

English, inherited from the former British colonial empire, is Jamaica's official language. However, a number of dialects are spoken in both urban and rural areas on the island. Jamaican Patois or Creole is a diverse combination of English and

African dialects, as well as other languages, that most Jamaicans can speak and understand. When spoken slowly, it is often understood by non-speakers and foreigners.

The most common greeting between men is a handshake. This may be accompanied by a pat on the opposite shoulder or arm. Jamaicans sometimes emphasize greetings by holding onto an initial handshake for a few seconds. Women may embrace and kiss on the cheek. The use of honorific titles and a person's surname are the customary and respectful way to greet others with whom one is not well acquainted. Jamaicans will then often invite strangers to call them by their first names, while between friends, nicknames are used.

Overall, politeness and respect, whether in greeting or casual conversation, signify a person's upbringing, and it is rude to ignore or not answer somebody. Additionally, those of the Rastafarian faith may express spiritual greetings of wellness, many of which have evolved into common expressions. These greetings, along with a head nod, are typical ways of affirming recognition and extending good will between strangers.

## Gestures & Etiquette

Jamaica's customs and etiquette are influenced both by the population's profound religious faith and by one's socioeconomic status. As such, even though proper etiquette and manners are expected, there is some variation. Blessings and prayers are commonly extended among family, friends and strangers. Jamaicans can also be quite conservative in their behavior and dress. Revealing clothing is considered to be inappropriate for women when in public, and formal dresses, hats, and suits are typically worn in church. Overall, Jamaicans are an outgoing and friendly people whose fundamental religious beliefs and hospitality yield a warm demeanor.

## Eating/Meals

Influenced by the British, a traditional breakfast in Jamaica might include hot tea or coffee. Boiled plantains with sautéed callaloo (a green leaf vegetable), ackee fruit, and salted codfish are also popular breakfast meals. Afternoon lunch is the main meal of the day and may consist of stewed, roasted, or jerked meat; boiled yams or plantains; rice and peas; or fried fish. In the evening, a light snack of plantains, jerked meat, fried stuffed patties or meat-filled pastries are enjoyed with hot coffee or fresh juice. Prayers may also be customarily said before each meal. Dining etiquette is mostly informal, and Jamaicans typically eat in the continental style, with the fork in the left hand and the knife in the right.

Many native Jamaican foods are associated with religious worship and festivals. For example, sweet potatoes, yams, plantains, and rice are sacred foods used in African and indigenous ceremonies and rituals. Certain animals, often not commonly eaten, are prepared during festive occasions such as Christmas and Easter. These include turkey, chicken, ox, and goat. The Rastafarian diet, which is based on vegetarianism, is rich in fruits and vegetables without synthetic additives, which complies with the belief that the body is maintained as a sacred temple. Rastafarians also refrain from alcohol and smoke cannabis (called ganja) as a spiritual act to cleanse the body, mind, and soul.

Because of Jamaica's tropical climate, eating outdoors is a customary practice. Take-away hot foods as well as pineapples, melons, and coconut water are sold by roadside vendors. Additionally, except for those who live in Kingston and other central urban areas, most Jamaicans prefer dining at home over visiting restaurants or food stands.

## Visiting

In the rural areas of the island, where modern technology is not prevalent, visiting is still a popular tradition. Talking with neighbors, family members, or strangers remains a typical way for many rural Jamaicans to pass the time. Visits are usually unannounced and informal, and are held at the house gate unless guests are invited inside. Conversations may be loud, animated, and infused with laughter. Guests customarily bring fruits or vegetables from their gardens or a bottle of rum or wine, depending on the occasion.

Jamaicans take pride in their religious institutions and will often invite guests to visit their church on Sunday. During the service they will go to great lengths to make introductions and help their guests feel like part of the community. Sermons are typically long affairs, often filled with song, dance, and physical contact between worshippers. After the preacher has finished, members of the community often enjoy an afternoon lunch for dignitaries of the church and invited guests.

Buffet-style meals are popular when having guests, and Jamaicans take pride in their hearty portions. If food is left on the plate, a Jamaican cook will assume it was not prepared well; it is considered polite to finish everything that is offered to eat.

## LIFESTYLE

### Family

The idea of family is particularly strong in Jamaican culture. Extended family members often live together for financial support and to help with child rearing. Additionally, the selection of a spouse is made by individual choice, but parents and relatives wield a great deal of influence over the selection. Child shifting—the rearrangement of children between family and friends—is sometimes paramount to the survival of poorer families. Traditionally, the family structure is patriarchal, and Jamaican fathers typically work outside of the home while female family members act as homemakers and caregivers.

The importance of family is particularly evident in the trusting partnerships extended between family and close friends, often in the form of financial arrangements. Joint family or community funds are used to make down payments for buying a house, a business, or land, rather than relying on banks or financial institutions. Years of corruption and crime at the state level have resulted in a deep Jamaican distrust of institutional authority.

Jamaicans raise children with a great amount of discipline, including physical punishment.

Children are customarily responsible for various household chores and typically attend church each Sunday as a way to develop socially. Education is important to many parents; for many poor families, proper schooling is perhaps the best path for their offspring to rise from poverty.

### Housing

During the colonial period, Jamaican cities were constructed around sugar, coffee, and tobacco plantations. These estates traditionally featured homes built with stone and wood on cement foundations, with separate living quarters for servants. These structures usually consisted of two rooms with a thatched roof and walls covered with mud or wood.

When the plantations declined and the urban population increased, Jamaican cities expanded through the addition of shantytowns, or informal settlements, to accommodate the growing urban poor. These outer city slums still exist and are characterized by dwellings made of scrap plywood, flimsy metal, and sheets of plastic. Shantytowns often do not have proper sanitation, electricity, or other modern amenities.

Traditional detached Jamaican homes are a mix of African, Spanish, and British influences. To complement the green seas and blue skies, houses in Jamaica are often painted in vibrant pastel pinks and blues. Victorian-style mansions and Spanish-influenced villas and other homes of the wealthy elite are often characterized by Spanish balconies, wrought iron and brick construction and ornamentation, and arched windows and doorways. In impoverished rural areas, houses built from Taíno-influenced palm fronds and mud walls are common

### Food

Jamaican cuisine is a combination of indigenous, African and European culinary traditions. Subsequent immigration of Americans, Chinese, and Indians has added new culinary elements to the local cuisine. Despite the many techniques and flavors used in Jamaican cooking, it is often characterized as spicy. This is due in large part to the fact that Scotch bonnet peppers figure prominently in many main dishes. The traditional staples found in Jamaican cuisine include rice, beans, yams, tomatoes, and peppers; fruits like mangos, bananas, papayas, pineapples, and grapefruits; jerked meats and seafood.

Jerked meat is often considered a Jamaican specialty. Rooted in indigenous culinary traditions, pork, goat, chicken, fish, beef, or sausage is rubbed with a very hot spice mixture and Scotch bonnet peppers. Cloves, cinnamon, onions, nutmeg, thyme, and garlic may also be added to give it a unique flavor. Jerk is best when barbecued over wood and charcoal; old oil barrel halves are also used as grills in some poorer communities. Street-side jerk stands are common on many central streets. Other common dishes included ackee and saltfish (made with ackee fruit, callaloo, and salted cod fish), the national dish; curried goat, a popular East Indian dish; and bammy or cassava bread, a standard food of the Arawak Indian. Soursop, grapenut, rum raisin, and mango ice cream are popular desserts made with coconut milk. Potato pudding, coconut cake, fried banana, and shaved coconut cookies are other popular desserts.

Boiled root, tea leaf and dried fruit elixirs serve as medicinal cures for many Jamaican families. Jamaican Blue Mountain Coffee, noted for its mild flavor, has a reputation as one of the most expensive and preferred coffees in the world. Beer and rum are among the most popular alcoholic drinks. Sugarcane cultivation and distillation was introduced to Jamaica in the 15th century. The slaves that cut the sugar discovered that an alcoholic beverage, now called rum, could be made by fermenting, then distilling, the sticky brown substance that remained after the sugar was extracted from the cane juice.

### Life's Milestones

Jamaica has a predominantly Christian population, and most milestones are rooted in the Christian faith. However, there are some distinct Afro-Caribbean influences. For example, in Afro-Caribbean Christian baptisms, an adult is submerged in a sacred river or lake by a minister of the church. Rastafarianism also has its own unique baptismal ritual, and Rastafarian elders in their community bless a newborn baby during a drumming ritual.

In Jamaica, a wedding ceremony customarily involves a large gathering of family and friends who have witnessed the maturation of the bride or groom. If the ceremony is held in a church, the groom will wear a suit and the bride a traditional white dress and veil. The reception includes toasting, eating, and dancing. In the Rastafarian faith, there is no formal marriage structure; a couple who lives together is generally regarded as husband and wife.

After death, family and friends gather at the home of the deceased to assist in funeral preparations such as washing and preparing the body for burial. Nine night services are ceremonies for the deceased occurring on the nine nights after death. On the ninth night, a celebration with dancing, singing and feasting is undertaken to usher the dead peacefully to the other side. If the nine night services do not take place, it is believed that the dead will haunt the earth. Rastafarians believe reincarnation follows death.

## CULTURAL HISTORY

### Art

The earliest art in Jamaica dates back to the island's indigenous inhabitants, the Arawak and Taíno, who settled the island between 4000 and 1000 BCE. Though these indigenous peoples were known for traditional crafts such as woodcarving, pottery and jewelry making, they are chiefly remembered for their ancient cave drawings. With the arrival of the Spanish in the 16th century, art in Jamaica underwent a long period of European influence and sensibility. During this time, any form of indigenous or African expression was considered primitive and insignificant.

A distinct and native Jamaican art did not emerge until the 20th century, and was largely a blend of African, European, and indigenous influences. Early themes included the island's natural beauty and the desire for independence, which is reflected in the island's art of the 1940s and 1950s. Edna Manley (1900–1987), an Englishwoman referred to as the "mother of Jamaican art," helped establish a national artistic movement. A prominent sculptor, she helped found the Jamaica School of Art in 1950 (now a part of the Edna Manley College of Visual and Performing Arts) to formally train artists to develop an interest in their homeland. Prior to Manley, art in Jamaica consisted mostly of watercolors and landscapes.

## Music

The traditions of West Africa, carried over by slaves, were kept alive in Jamaica's sugar plantations and fields through music, dance, and song. These traditions, combined with a fusion of sounds from neighboring Caribbean islands, the United States, and other immigrant populations, formed the many popular genres that define Jamaican music in the early 21st century.

Mento is a union of African and European musical styles that originated in Jamaica in the 19th century. The sound has an acoustic resonance and is typically referred to as Jamaican country music. Traditional instruments include the banjo, acoustic guitar, saxophone, clarinet, bamboo flute, and hand percussions. An urban jazz style developed from this sound in the 1920s with danceable, big band sounds. Lyrically, the songs are about Jamaica—its cuisine, nature, religion, and lifestyle. Aspects of mento can still be heard in newer genres such as reggae, dancehall, and ska. The latter, a combination of mento and American rhythm & blues, developed in the 1950s and 60s, and has a fast, rhythmic sound.

When Jamaica achieved independence in 1962, the island underwent dramatic change. Many young people began migrating to Kingston, the capital, to expand their economic and social prospects. During this period, certain musicians became famous for a slower and relaxed style of music called "rocksteady". From independence through the present day, music has evolved and changed with Jamaica. Though short-lived, the rocksteady style of music became the predecessor to reggae, a music that would define

Jamaica in the 20th century. Reggae was born out of the music and beliefs of disadvantaged Jamaicans, and the grassroots efforts to fight political corruption and racism. It also embraced pan-Africanism and the Rastafari movement. (Rastafarianism, which rejects Western ideals, first emerged in Jamaica as a way for displaced Africans to escape the colonial attitudes embedded in island society.) Ultimately, reggae would achieve world prominence through the music of Bob Marley (1945–1981). Other reggae artists that also received international acclaim and helped define the genre include Peter Tosh (1944–1987) and Jimmy Cliff (1948–).

In the early 1970s, studios began remixing songs, without their lyrics, leaving only instrumentals. These Jamaican remixes are known as the "dub" version of the original song. Dubbing allows musicians to "toast," or talk over the music, sharing stories of life on the Kingston streets, as well as other issues and daily problems. At the heart of this popular form of music and poetry is traditional African-Caribbean storytelling. Many consider this form of rap music as a significant influence on American hip-hop.

There are over 40 distinct traditional dances in Jamaica, most of which derive from imported African and European culture and traditions. There is also a distinct creole tradition that integrates both these influences. Many of these dances were associated with religious worship and celebrations. Some of the more vibrant and processional dances are still performed throughout the country's various street festivals.

Jamaica's contemporary dance traditions have their roots in music such as ska and dancehall and many of these dances are characterized by fast movement, typically of the hip and legs, and the flailing of the arms, with the beat of the music emphasized in the body's movement.

## Literature

Jamaican literature is rooted in the oral traditions of its slave-dependent colonial past. It specifically draws on the storytelling traditions of West Africa's griots, wandering poets and praise singers that carried the history and folklore of their culture. Because there was no written language in Africa, these storytellers kept track of important events through the spoken word. Each village usually had its own griot, who was highly respected and typically exempt from labor-oriented tasks. This folk tradition was first brought to the slave colonies of the Caribbean through the Atlantic slave trade during the 16th through the 18th centuries.

Early tales often involved sentient animals and god-like characters, as well as hidden meanings, similar to Aesop's fables. Anansi the spider is one of the most important characters in Caribbean oral tradition, gifted with quick wit and eloquent speech. He is a trickster, and often fools the other folkloric animals, like Tiger and Donkey, in these tales.

Another distinct aspect of Jamaica's early storytelling roots and subsequent literature is the local patois, or language, in which it is spoken and written. The Jamaican Patois (also known as Jamaican Creole or "broken" English) combines the native languages of West African, English, Portuguese, and Amerindian cultures. As Jamaican literature evolved from the oral traditions of storytelling, it incorporated this distinct dialect.

Jamaica has been home to a multitude of notable writers. One of the most famous Jamaican writers is poet Claude McKay (1889–1948). He is credited with inspiring the Negritude (or "Blackness") movement in France, which emphasized a shared black African heritage, as well as the Harlem Renaissance in the United States. As Jamaican literature continued to develop in modern times, it became a reaction against colonialism and the island's violent political past. With the rising popularity of reggae music in the latter half of the 20th century, both Jamaican literature and music became more multinational.

## CULTURE

### Arts & Entertainment

Contemporary Jamaican art is a fruit of the diverse cultures that have created the island's unique history. More significantly, it explores themes of nationalism, identity, colonialism, slavery, emancipation, and the corruption that have played a role in building present-day Jamaica.

Since the 1960s, two distinct genres of contemporary Jamaican art have developed: mainstream and intuitive. Mainstream art is created by artists that have undergone formal training. Intuitive art, often practiced by self-taught artists, utilizes African forms of expression such as storytelling, dance and song rituals to convey island life, magical imagery, and social issues. With many artists operating beyond the cultural mainstream, Jamaica has become known for raw talent in visual arts, dance, music, and literature.

One such artist, Mallica Kapo Reynolds (1911–1989), began developing his own unique style of island art through vibrant paintings and sculptures of the Jamaican landscape. Many of Kapo's pieces also confront racial hierarchies. In one of his most famous pieces, a black Christ figure sits reading biblical scripture by the Sea of Galilee (a biblical lake in Israel). Another piece, entitled *Two Angels*, depicts black and a white angels sitting face to face in a gesture of friendship.

Though more famous for its ties to the Caribbean island of Trinidad, calypso music is well established in Jamaica. Derived from a singing form of communication between slaves who were forbidden to talk with one another, calypso was popularized outside the islands by international musicians like Harry Belafonte during the first half of the 20th century.

More recently, soca music, a form of calypso with a faster beat, has spread around the Caribbean. Along with traditional reggae and calypso styles, fast-moving soca music has become an integral part of Jamaica's many festivals. Today, the most popular scene in Jamaican is called dancehall, a controversial style of dance music that fuses Caribbean and Jamaican roots music with hip-hop culture and sounds.

As the early 21st century unfolds, a new generation of Jamaican writers and poets are creating avant-garde dub poetry and performance art in the distinct Jamaican Patois. Oku Onoura

(1952–), Mutabaruka (1952–), and Michael Smith (1954–1983) have had much success in mainstream literary circles. Unlike toasting, the dub poet's performance is normally rehearsed, rather than performed freestyle or improvised. Dub poetry is mostly of a political and social nature, and less controversial than dancehall expression.

## Cultural Sites & Landmarks

As Jamaica's capital, Kingston is the island's commercial and cultural hub. Founded in 1692, the city's history is a large part of its cultural heritage. Numerous churches date back to the 17th century, and the city's architectural heritage blends colonial styles with Caribbean elements.

Behind Kingston, the Blue Mountains offer miles of woodlands and hiking trails. The most popular hike is also Jamaica's highest point, Blue Mountain Peak, at 2,256 meters (7,402 feet). Over 200 species of birds, as well as other exotic tropical fauna and flora, call the Blue Mountains home. The mountainous area is also famous for the cultivation of Jamaican Blue Mountain Coffee, an expensive and highly sought product on the international market. Blue Mountain coffee plantations are available to tour at the estates where coffee berries (which contain the coffee bean) are grown, harvested, and dried.

Moore Town, located in Jamaica's Blue Mountains, is home to the descendants of former runaway slaves, known as Maroons. These former slaves fled plantations in the early 1600s and were able to establish their own settlements in the mountains of eastern Jamaica. After warring with the British for over 80 years, they were granted autonomy in 1739. The Maroons thus became the first group of blacks to succeed in officially gaining recognized freedom. A distinct feature of Moore Town is the language, Kromanti, which is used in ritual ceremonies that involve African dancing, singing, and drumming. In 2003, the United Nations Educational, Scientific and Cultural Organization (UNESCO) named the Maroon Heritage of Moore Town as one of the Masterpieces of the Oral and Intangible Heritage of Humanity.

Other sites of cultural importance include Port Antonio, a northeastern port town that boasts Victorian era mansions and other historic architecture; the reefs and sandy beaches of Montego Bay and, further west, the still, translucent waters of the Negril coastline; and Appleton Estate, a 250-year-old sugar plantation and distillery and the oldest rum producing estate in the English-speaking Caribbean.

## Libraries & Museums

Downtown Kingston, Jamaica, is home to the National Gallery, with collections that range from ancient woodcarvings and sculpture to religious paintings. The Bob Marley Museum, also in Kingston, was the singer's home from 1975 until his death from cancer in 1981. The museum displays his silver, gold, and platinum records, as well as concert memorabilia. Other museums include the Military Museum, the Taino Museum of the First Jamaicans, and the People's Museum of Craft and Technology.

The National Library of Jamaica, established in 1979, houses over 47,000 titles. Some of its rare items include descriptions and surveys of the island dating back to the 1600s. The Jamaica Library Service oversees 124 public libraries and over 900 school libraries throughout the island nation.

## Holidays

Official holidays in Jamaica include Labour Day (May 23), Emancipation Day (August 1), Independence Day (August 6), and National Heroes Day (October 17). A number of Christian holidays are also officially recognized, including Christmas Day, Ash Wednesday, Good Friday, Easter Monday, and Boxing Day on December 27.

Jamaica does have its own set of unofficial holiday celebrations, as well. Jonkanoo, a Christmas celebration, involves street parades of people dressed in masquerade, and comes from African slave traditions. Jamaica's version of Carnival (celebrated the week after Easter) is a lively mix of Jamaica's unique and influential music: calypso, reggae, and dancehall soca.

## Youth Culture

As of 2013, 28 percent of Jamaica's population is made up of youth between the ages of 10 and 24. Many teenagers are from single parent homes where mothers are earning the minimum wage of $23 (USD) per week. A small number of adolescents are also living on city streets. Popular activities for Jamaican youth include games such as street dominos, watching rooster fights, or playing basketball, cricket, and other sports. Unfortunately, many youth live in an environment where drug use and violence is pervasive. In fact, many youth are arrested, jailed, and murdered at twice the rate of the general population.

In Jamaica, schools are very strict. Students in public schools wear uniforms; boys must have regular haircuts, and girls can not add extensions or color their hair. Devices such as cell phones and iPods, and casual clothing such as sneakers, are not permitted. It is also not uncommon for corporal discipline to be administered when students misbehave. Nonetheless, problems such as illiteracy, student and teacher absenteeism, and low pass rates on mandatory examinations plague Jamaican schools.

Skin bleaching is popular with many young Jamaican women. This is done with topical corticosteroids—in spite of research that has linked this drug with skin cancer—bleaching pills, or homemade mixtures of peroxide, baking soda, and curry powder. The majority of skin bleachers are females in their twenties and early thirties. Low self-esteem, Eurocentric ideals of beauty, and lack of African pride are contributing factors in why women choose to alter their appearance in such drastic and unhealthy ways.

## SOCIETY

## Transportation

Jamaica's public bus system is a popular mode of transportation, and fares are typically inexpensive. However, infrequent schedules, laid-back attitudes about picking up and dropping off passengers, and lack of amenities such as air conditioning, can make bus travel problematic. Private taxi service is also common, but most cabs in Jamaica are older vehicles that do not run on a registered meter. Special route taxis and minibuses, somewhat more comfortable and costly, are operated by the Jamaica Union of Travelers Association. These are marked by the union's emblem on the side of the vehicle—a red Public Passenger Vehicle or PPV plate.

Driving is done on the left side of the road, and steering wheels are placed on the right. Seatbelt use is required by law.

## Transportation Infrastructure

Jamaica passenger rail service was suspended in 1992, revived in 2011, closed again in 2012. There are three international airports in Jamaica—Donald Sangster in Montego Bay, Ian Fleming in Ocho Rios, and Norman Manley in Kingston. Air Jamaica is the national airline.

## Media & Communications

Jamaica employs freedom of press laws allowing its newspapers to criticize the country's political, religious, and cultural establishments. *The Jamaica Gleaner*, *The Jamaican Star* and *The Jamaica Observer* are the most widely circulated newspapers. *The Gleaner* claims the highest circulation and is the oldest operating newspaper in the Caribbean. In addition, foreign media from the United States and the United Kingdom are widely available.

Radio is a popular means of transmitting news and information to all parts of the island. The Public Broadcasting Corporation of Jamaica (PBCJ)—which replaced the defunct Jamaica Broadcasting Corporation—covers the island's rural, suburban, and urban parishes with music, news, and commentary. BBC Caribbean and other world broadcast programs are available on some FM networks, and several commercial stations play contemporary music, with Radio Jamaica Communications group hosting several contemporary music stations and a news website. Additionally, Jamaica's telecommunications and Internet infrastructure is improving, and in 2014 Internet usage was estimated at 49.8 percent of the population.

## SOCIAL DEVELOPMENT

### Standard of Living

The Human Development Index (HDI), published by the UN Development Program (UNDP) in 2014, ranked Jamaica 96 out of 187 countries. Jamaica is considered in the medium range of human development in comparison to the rest of the world, but it ranks on the lower end in the Caribbean.

### Water Consumption

Water use is overseen by Jamaica's Water Resources Authority (WRA). In a 2007 presentation on water accounting, several water-related issues were identified, including competing interests for water resources; water resource protection from pollution; groundwater contamination; dry season shortages; poor water quality; high cost of water treatment; rural challenges in potable water access; poor populations using untreated water from groundwater resources; and resistance to increased water prices.

According to the National Water Commission, only 30 percent of the water extracted from Jamaica is for domestic use, while the remaining 70 percent is used for agriculture. Approximately 95 percent of the urban population has access to water while only about 75 percent of the rural population does. Remaining citizens extract water from stand pipes, water trucks, or other community access sources.

Wastewater treatment is monitored by the National Water Commission. Sewer is available to 30 percent of the Jamaica's population. On-site systems handle the remainder of wastewater needs.

### Education

Since the introduction of radical education reforms in the 1970s, Jamaica has developed a system of education that includes primary, secondary, and college level study. Education is compulsory from primary school through age 16.

Primary and secondary schools were designed according to a British system that requires students to pass a series of exams working toward specialization in a single subject by the end of secondary school. This system was streamlined and to a large degree, centralized, in the 1980s.

The last two years of high school are still preparatory for university study for many students. Since the 1980s, however, the government has funded educational programs for vocational training at several Human Employment and Resources Training institutions under the HEART program. The Jamaican government has also created 14 community colleges, a Vocational Training Development Institute, and a comprehensive literacy initiative over the past two decades.

As a result of educational reforms since independence, Jamaica's literacy rate has increased from less than 68 percent during pre-independence to a 2015 estimate of 87 percent (82 percent among men and 92 percent among women).

Jamaica's local regional colleges include the University of the West Indies, the University of Technology; the Edna Manley College for the Visual and Performing Arts; College of Agriculture, Science, and Education; G.C. Foster College of Physical Education and Sports; Northern Caribbean University (formerly West Indies College), a dozen teacher training colleges and fourteen community colleges.

### Women's Rights

Due to a long-established attitude regarding a woman's societal role, women are traditionally expected to bear children in Jamaican culture. A childless woman is an object of sympathy, disapproval, or mockery. A woman who cannot have children for medical reasons may be blamed unjustly by the community for her condition. In addition, absentee fathers are typical in Jamaica, leaving women as the heads of many households.

Women work primarily in the service, retail, basic education, and social assistance sectors. Sexual harassment is also a problem, and though some reports of sexual harassment are filed with the police, many women do not report incidents. Although the law grants women equal pay for equal work, in practice women often earn less than their male counterparts. However, this is slowly changing. Jamaica has one of the highest rates of women in the labor force in the world. In 2006, Portia Simpson Miller (1945–) became the first female prime minister in Jamaica's history. Her term, while only lasting one year, signified a new era of political representation for Jamaican women.

Violence against women is prevalent in Jamaica, and many women fear being beaten, raped, or killed. More than 70 percent of all reported rape victims in Jamaica each year are under the age of 18. Rape is illegal and carries a penalty of up to 25 years of imprisonment. However a majority of rapes go unreported due to a lack of confidence in the police and fear of testifying in court.

Although it is illegal, prostitution and trafficking in women and girls is prevalent, especially in tourist areas. Due to Jamaica's deteriorating economic conditions, sex work is an easy way for many young women to make a living. Jamaican girls are at risk for unintended pregnancies, sexually transmitted infections, and other health risks. More women than men are HIV positive in Jamaica, at a rate of three to one.

## Health Care

Jamaica's health care system is run by the Ministry of Health. The island has twenty-four hospitals and more than 330 health care centers and specialized clinics. In recent years, the system has been completely restructured to provide for four regions: the Northeastern, Southeastern, Western, and Southern Health Authorities.

Under the current program, the government provides a limited set of services free to the public, including immunization, family planning, pre- and postnatal care clinics, and child health clinics, as well as certain targeted basic care programs. The government subsidizes other health services provided through health centers and hospitals, but Jamaicans must also pay a user fee for services, based on the service and the status of the patient. User fees may also be paid by health insurance plans.

The government also provides large subsidies to the island's only teaching hospital, the University Hospital of the West Indies. The island has a National Family Planning Board and a national Mental Health Service, which includes outpatient clinics and Bellevue residential hospital.

## GOVERNMENT

### Structure

Jamaica is a constitutional parliamentary democracy. As a member state of the British Commonwealth of Nations, Jamaica recognizes Britain's Queen Elizabeth II as the nation's monarch and the governor general as her representative on the island. However, a bicameral parliament and a prime minister wield all political power under the constitution.

The prime minister is chosen by the ruling party in the House. The prime minister, in turn, chooses a deputy prime minister and advises the governor general on appointments to the Cabinet.

The Senate's 21 members are formally appointed by the governor general, on the recommendation of the prime minister and the leader of the opposition party in the House of Representatives. The 60 members of the House of Representatives are elected by direct, popular vote to five-year terms.

### Political Parties

Parliamentary democracies often have a large number of political parties, which have a tendency to shift in terms of political platform and their alliance with other parties sharing common interests. Often, parliamentary systems are ruled by coalitions of two or more parties that unite to form a majority coalition. These coalitions differ in nature, with some coalitions having a lasting strength and others failing to govern at all. Additionally, it's not unusual for parties to dissolve because of personality conflicts within the organization.

Major parties in Jamaica include the Jamaica Labour Party (JLP, center-right) and the People's National Party (PNP, center-left, social democrats), which are the country's two strongest parties. The United People's Party (progressive liberals) and National Democratic Movement (NDM, conservative) are considered minor parties.

## Local Government

Jamaica's local government consists of a parish system, with 14 parishes. The Kingston and St. Andrew parishes are jointly run by the Kingston and St Andrew Corporation. Each parish has a mayor and council elected every three years. Local governments are responsible for public safety, public health, infrastructure planning and repair.

## Judicial System

The Jamaican judiciary is based on the British system and laws are based on British common law. The Court of Appeals is the highest court in the country, but Jamaicans may appeal to the Privy Council of the United Kingdom in certain instances. At a local level, a Resident's Magistrate hears criminal and civil cases at the local level; Petty Session Courts may hear minor criminal matters. The Supreme Court (lower than the Court of Appeals) hears a variety of matters and is specialized into Circuit, Gun, Commercial, Revenue, and Family courts.

## Taxation

The Jamaican government levies an income tax, a general consumption tax (GCT), payroll taxes, customs duty, property tax, a stamp duty and transfer taxes, and other indirect taxes. Corporations are taxed on income.

## Armed Forces

The Jamaican Defence Force has a ground force, coast guard, and an air division. There is no conscription in Jamaica.

## Foreign Policy

Jamaica ranks as a mid–level developing country and is known internationally for its dedication to the concerns of emerging economies. Jamaica is a member of the G15 and G77 organizations of developing countries, whose goals are to increase and support the economic progress of their members. A UN member, Jamaica holds various regional memberships, through the Organization of American States (OAS), the Caribbean Community (CARICOM), and the Association of Caribbean States (ACS), as well as international membership in organizations such as the Commonwealth of Nations, mostly made up of former British colonies. Jamaica has benefited from the Lome Convention, through which the European Union has granted the island special trade status. In recent years, Jamaica has also strengthened its foreign relations with Latin America and the United States.

The United States is Jamaica's most important trading partner. Jamaica is a popular tourist destination for Americans, receiving more than one million visitors annually. In addition, more than 10,000 American citizens permanently reside in Jamaica. As a major transit point for cocaine and marijuana to the United States and Europe, Jamaica is also working closely with the United States to curb drug trafficking. Operation Kingfish is a multinational task force consisting of Jamaicans, Americans, British, and Canadians working together to intercept vehicles, boats, aircrafts, firearms, and containers carrying large quantities of cocaine and marijuana bound for various ports in the world.

## Human Rights Profile

International human rights law insists that states respect civil and political rights, and also promote an individual's economic, social, and cultural rights. The United Nations Universal Declaration on Human Rights(UDHR) is recognized as the standard for international human rights. Its authors sought the counsel of the world's great thinkers, philosophers, and religious leaders, and were careful to create a document that reflects the core values shared by every world culture. (To read this document or view the articles relating to cultural human rights, go to: http://www.udhr.org/UDHR/default.htm.)

Crime and violence occur at alarming rates in Jamaica; Jamaica's police reported 1,193 murders in 2013. Inner city Kingston communities are at the highest risk, and are often troubled by gangs, delinquency, international drug trade, and random acts of violence.

Most human rights abuses that occur in Jamaica are concentrated in the country's judicial and prison systems. Due to insufficient staff and organization, trials can be delayed for years and are often dismissed due to inadequate filing systems. Although a defendant has the right to a lawyer, the courts only appoint counsel for serious offenses, and many defendants are not provided counsel. Jamaica's prison conditions are dire; they are overcrowded and provide inadequate dietary standards, poor sanitary conditions, and insufficient medical care. Juveniles are detained improperly and often victimized by adult prisoners. Additionally, many prisoners have complained of police brutality.

Under freedom of the press laws, newspapers in Jamaica regularly report on human rights abuses, particularly those involving the police. Foreign publications and television broadcasts are also unregulated and easily available. The constitution provides freedom of religion and assembly. However, members of the Rastafarian movement continue to allege that they are discriminated against. While Jamaican law provides rights for workers to form or join a union and to protest should they feel their rights are not being maintained, the minimum wage is widely considered inadequate.

Teenage involvement in the sex trade industry is increasing as a result of deteriorating economic conditions. Early sexual activity and lack of sexual education place Jamaican youth at risk for unintended pregnancies, disease, and other health threats.

Sexuality-based oppression in Jamaica is institutionalized throughout the legal system, welfare institutions, media, and popular culture. Sex acts between men are punishable by imprisonment, and gays and lesbians continue to be subjected to discrimination. The Jamaica Forum for Lesbians, All-Sexuals, and Gays (JFLAG) was founded in 1998 as the first human rights organization working toward a society in which the human rights of homosexuals are upheld.

Other social welfare systems that support Jamaican communities consist of local government and international programs. The social security and welfare system includes the National Insurance Scheme; employment, widow and widower, orphan, and special child benefits; and funeral grants. Over 150 local and international organizations support Jamaica in areas such as environmental protection, socioeconomic development, and education.

## Migration

Motivated by rising unemployment and a high crime rate, many Jamaicans have chosen to immigrate to other parts of the world to enhance their economic and personal prospects. The recent major exodus has been to the United States and Canada. It is estimated that roughly 20,000 Jamaicans arrive to the United States each year for work, enroll their children in public or private schools, and purchase property. Remittances, or money sent from expatriated Jamaicans to their families back on the island, contribute not only to the financial stability of Jamaican families, but to the overall Jamaican economy as well.

## ECONOMY

### Overview of the Economy

Jamaica's economy relies on services industries, most of which are part of the tourist trade. These industries account for more than half the country's gross domestic product (GDP). In 2013, Jamaica's GDP was estimated at just over $25 billion USD; per capita GDP was $9,000 USD.

Problems facing the economy include inflation, large debt, and high unemployment. As of 2010, 17.6 percent of Jamaica's population was living below the poverty line, a number that increasingly includes a population of working poor in the island's urban centers. Jamaica's poverty rates are also reflected in high crime rates, particularly in the Kingston area.

Remittances (funds sent back to Jamaican citizens from citizens working out of country) make up 15 percent of Jamaica's GDP.

## Industry

Tourism has become Jamaica's largest industry, replacing much of the earlier bauxite/alumina-based industry. Jamaica also produces or processes textiles, agricultural products, clothing, rum, cement, metal, paper, chemical products, and telecommunications equipment. Jamaica's largest trading partners are the United States and Canada.

## Labor

In 2015, Jamaica's labor force was made up of 1.1 million people. Unemployment was measured at 13.2 percent. The bulk of the workforce is employed in the service sector (60 percent), 19 percent of the workforce is engaged in the industrial sector, and the remaining 21 percent works in agriculture.

## Energy/Power/Natural Resources

In 2009, the Jamaican government began work toward the implementation of Vision 2030—National Development Plan, Jamaica's roadmap toward achieving developed country status by 2030. Within that plan, the government has set a goal to develop a "modern, efficient, diversified, and environmentally sustainable energy sector." Among the issues the government faces are securing diverse fuel sources, modernizing the energy infrastructure, developing renewable energy sources, and implementing both conservation measures and governance structures in the energy sector. Jamaica remains highly dependent on imported petroleum.

Today, the island's most important resources are its beaches, warm weather, and its position between Cayman Trench and Jamaica Channel, providing access to the Panama Canal.

## Fishing

Fishermen harvest a variety of fish species, but catch a larger supply of crustaceans and mollusks from Jamaica's coastal waters. Because of Jamaica's deep sea fishing in northern waters, the area has become a destination for those fishing for mahi mahi, marlin, sailfish, and barracuda. Shallow waters also hold bonefish and wahoo.

Inland fisheries have been developed and have seen steady growth.

## Forestry

Jamaica's forests have been significantly depleted, with the only remaining forests in the mountains. The Forestry Department is actively engaged in a reforesting plan.

## Mining/Metals

Jamaica has reserves of bauxite, gypsum, and limestone. Bauxite (used in the manufacture of aluminum products) was discovered on the island in the 1940s, and helped ease the Jamaican economy's reliance on bananas and sugarcane.

## Agriculture

Jamaica's arable land produces a wealth of sugarcane, bananas, citrus, yams, and vegetables, mostly for export. Coffee beans grown in the Blue Mountains are renowned and exported internationally. Rum is also produced domestically from sugarcane, and is an important export commodity.

## Animal Husbandry

Jamaicans also raise poultry, goats, and milk cows, almost entirely for use on the island.

## Tourism

Tourism is the backbone of the Jamaican economy. The country's political stability, transportation infrastructure, plentiful accommodation, English speakers, lively culture, and close ties to Britain and the United States have created a massive tourist industry on the island. More than one million tourists visit Jamaica each year.

Jamaica's tourist trade revolves around several large resorts, concentrated on the north coast of the island. Ocho Rios, Montego Bay, and Port Antonio, as well as Negril on the west coast, are among the country's most popular resort areas.

*Jennifer O'Donnell, Amy Witherbee*

## DO YOU KNOW?

- Though relatively small by international standards, Jamaica is the third largest island in the Caribbean.

- Every February, yacht owners from all over the World set out from Miami toward Jamaica's Montego Bay for the World famous Pineapple Cup Yacht Race.

- A British-run Jamaican Assembly abolished slavery on the island on August 1, 1834, after 400 slaves were killed in retribution for 1831 Christmas Rebellion, inspired by the passive resistance of Jamaican hero "Daddy" Sam Sharpe.

### Bibliography

Banks, Russell. *The Book of Jamaica.* Boston, MA: Houghton Mifflin, 1980.

Black, Clinton Vane de Brosse. *The History of Jamaica.* Harlow,UK: Longman, 1988

Coates, Robert, et al. *Rough Guide to Jamaica.* London: Rough Guides, 2015.

Manly, Rachel. *Drumblair: Memories of a Jamaican Childhood.* Westland, MI: Dzanc Books, 1996.

Monteith, Kathleen E.A. and Glen Richards. *Jamaica in Slavery and Freedom: History, Heritage, and Culture.* Kingston, Jamaica: University of West Indies Press, 2002.

Taylor, Frank Fonda. *To Hell with Paradise: A History of the Jamaican Tourist Industry.* Pittsburgh, PA: University of Pittsburgh Press, 1993.

Thomson, Ian. *The Dead Yard: A Story of Modern Jamaica.* New York: Nation Books, 2011.

### Works Cited

Advocates for Youth. "Youth Reproductive and Sexual Health in Jamaica." Online. http://www.advocatesforyouth.org/publications/factsheet/fsjamaica.htm.

Appleton Rum. "The History of Rum in Jamaica." Online. http://www.appletonrum.com/rum_jam_hist.php.

BBC. "Growing Up Gay in Jamaica." September 2004. Online. http://news.bbc.co.uk/1/hi/magazine/3653140.stm.

BBC. "Religion and Ethics—Rastafari." Online. http://www.bbc.co.uk/religion/religions/rastafari/ritesrituals/ritesrituals.shtml.

Blue Mountain Media. "Jamaica Tonics, Aphrodisiac Foods, and Herb Culture." Online. http://www.bluemountainmedia.com/Jamaican%20Tonics/Jamaica%20Tonics.html.

Brinkhoff, Thomas. "Jamaica." City Population. Online. http://www.citypopulation.de/Jamaica.html.

Bureau of Diplomatic Security. "Jamaica 2014 Crime and Safety Report. OSAC US Dept. of State". Online. http:osac.gov/pages/ContentReportDetails.aspx?cid=15864.

Charles, Christopher A. D. "Skin Bleaching, Self-Hate, and Black Identity in Jamaica." *Journal of Black Studies,* Vol. 33, No. 6. July 2003.

Commonwealth Health Online. "Jamaica". Online. http://commonwealthhealth.org/americas/jamaica.

Encyclopedia of the Nations. "Jamaica Foreign Policy." Online. http://www.nationsencyclopedia.com/World-Leaders-2003/Jamaica-FOREIGN-POLICY.html.

Encyclopedia of the Nations. "Jamaica Transportation." Online. http://www.nationsencyclopedia.com/Americas/Jamaica-TRANSPORTATION.html..

Every Culture. "Culture of Jamaica." Online. http://www.everyculture.com/Ja-Ma/Jamaica.html.

Get Jamaica. "Jamaican Food." Online. http://www.getjamaica.com/Jamaican%20Food.asp.

Global Destinations. "Jamaica, Eating Out." Online. http://www.globalgourmet.com/destinations/jamaica/jameatout.html.

Global exchange. "Jamaica: Economy". http://globalexchange.org/country/jamaica/economy. Online.

Go-Jamaica. "JA Police Release 2008 Murder Stats." January 2008. Online. http://www.go-jamaica.com/news/read_article.php?id=5678.

Human Rights Watch. "Open AIDS Meeting to All." June 2008. Online. http://www.hrw.org/en/news/2008/06/04/un-open-aids-meeting-all.

Index mundi. "Jamaica Life Expectancy at Birth". Online. http://indexmundi.com/jamaica/life_expectancy_at_birth.html.

Internet World Stats. "Jamaica Telecommunications Reports." Online. http://www.internetworldstats.com/car/jm.htm.

Jamaica Guide. "Slow Ride to Anywhere." Online. http://jamaica-guide.info/getting.around/buses/.

Jamaica Insider. "Jamaica Music: From Ska to Dance Hall." Online. http://jamaica-insider.com/jamaica_music.shtml.

Jamaican Culture. "The Typical Jamaican Family." Online. http://www.jamaicans.com/culture/intro/typical_family.shtml.

Jamaican Culture. "Jamaican Marriage Customs." Online. http://www.jamaicans.com/culture/articles_culture/JamaicanMarriageCustoms.shtml.

Jamaica Information Service. "Jamaica Library Service". Online. http://jis.gov.jm/agencies/jamaica_libraryservice.

Jamaica National Bank. "Remittances: A Lifeline for Poverty Alleviation". Online. http://jnbs.com/remittanceslifeline_Poverty_alleviation.

JFLAG. "Jamaican Forum for Lesbians, All Sexuals, and Gays." Online. http://www.jflag.org/.

Johnson, Neville. "Poverty Driving Boys into the Sex Trade." InterPress Third World News Agency (IPS). Online. http://www.hartford-hwp.com/archives/43/162.html.

Kwintessential Cross Cultural Solutions. "Jamaica—Language, Culture , Customs and Etiquette." Online. http://www.kwintessential.co.uk/resources/global-etiquette/jamaica.html

MSN Encarta. "Customs of Jamaica." Online. http://encarta.msn.com/sidebar_631522217/customs_of_jamaica.html.

Nations of the World: *A Political, Economic, and Business Handbook*. 14th ed. "Jamaica". Amenia, NY: Grey House Publishing, 2014.

O'Brien, Derek and Vaughan Carter. "Chant Down Babylon. Freedom of Religion and the Rastafarian Challenge to Majoritarianism." *Journal of Law and Religion*, Vol. 18, No. 1. 2002—2003.

Population Reference Bureau. "Population of Youth, Ages 10–24". Online. http://prb.org/DataFinder/Topic/Rankings.aspx?ind=19.

Press Reference. "Jamaica Press, Media, TV, Radio, Newspapers." Online. http://www.pressreference.com/Gu-Ku/Jamaica.html.

Red Stripe. "About Red Stripe." Online. http://www.redstripebeer.com/about.html.

Scaruffi, Piero. "The History of Popular Music before Rock." Online. http://www.scaruffi.com/history/reggae.html.

Statistical Institute of Jamaica. "Labour Force." Online. http://statinja.gov.jm/Default.aspx.

Travel Etiquette. "Etiquette in Jamaica." Online. http://www.traveletiquette.co.uk/EtiquetteJamaica.html.

UNESCO. "The Maroon Heritage of Moore Town." Online.l http://www.unesco.org/culture/ich/index.php?RL=44.

US Department of State. "Jamaica Country Reports on Human Rights Practices." http://www.state.gov/g/drl/rls/hrrpt/1999/393.htm. Online.

US Department of State. "Jamaica International Religious Freedom Report 2006." Online. http://www.state.gov/g/drl/rls/irf/2006/71466.htm.

Wardle, Huon. "Ambiguation, Disjuncture, Commitment: A Social Analysis of Caribbean Cultural Creativity." *The Journal of the Royal Anthropological Institute*, Vol. 8, No. 3. September 2002.

White, Ruth C. and Robert Carr. "Homosexuality and HIV/AIDS Stigma in Jamaica." *Culture, Health & Sexuality*, Vol. 7, No. 4. July—August 2005.

World Culture Encyclopedia. "Religion and Expressive Culture." Online. http://www.everyculture.com/Middle-America-Caribbean/Jamaicans-Religion-and-Expressive-Culture.html.

*El Morro in Old San Juan, Puerto Rico, is a UNESCO World Heritage Site. iStock/gregobagel*

# PUERTO RICO

# Introduction

Puerto Rico is an island territory in the Caribbean Ocean. Once a colony of Spain, it is now a commonwealth of the United States, and its culture is replete with Caribbean and Spanish influences. Citizens of the island were granted United States citizenship in 1917, and democratically elected governors have served since 1948. Puerto Rico's capital, San Juan, has one of the biggest and best natural harbors in the Caribbean, located on a key shipping channel to the Panama Canal. The island's name is Spanish, and translates to "Rich Port" in English.

---

## GENERAL INFORMATION

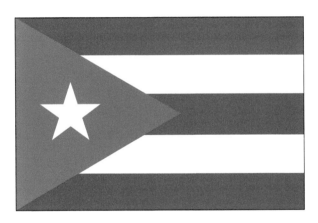

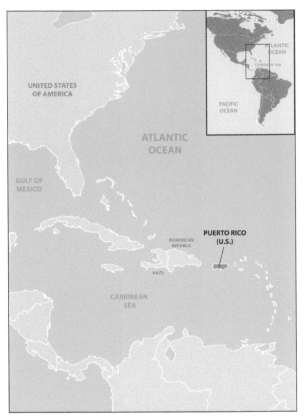

**Official Language(s):** Spanish and English
**Population:** 3,710,000 (2011 estimate)
**Currency:** US dollar, often referred to as "peso"
**Coins:** The dollar is divided into 100 cents, and coins come in denominations of 1, 5, 25, and 50 cents.
**Land Area:** 8,870 square kilometers (3,424 square miles)
**Water Area:** 4,921 square kilometers (1,900 square miles)
**National Anthem:** "La Borinqueña" ("The Land of the Puerto Ricans")
**Capital:** San Juan
**Time Zone(s):** GMT -4
**Flag Description:** The flag of Puerto Rico features five equally sized horizontal bands—the top, center, and bottom bands are red, and the remaining two are white. The base of a blue isosceles triangle rests on the hoist (left) side of the flag. In the center of the triangle is a white, five-pointed star.

## Population

The population of Puerto Rico was estimated to be 3,700,000 in 2013. Approximately one-third of the island's population lives in or near the capital of San Juan, and an estimated 99 percent of the population lives in urban areas. Puerto Rico features a high population density, with around 403 people per square kilometer (2014).

## Languages

Spanish and English are Puerto Rico's joint official languages.

## Native People & Ethnic Groups

Before Spain assumed control of Puerto Rico in 1493, the island was home to aboriginal peoples known as the Taíno. By the turn of the 20th century, the vast majority of these people had been

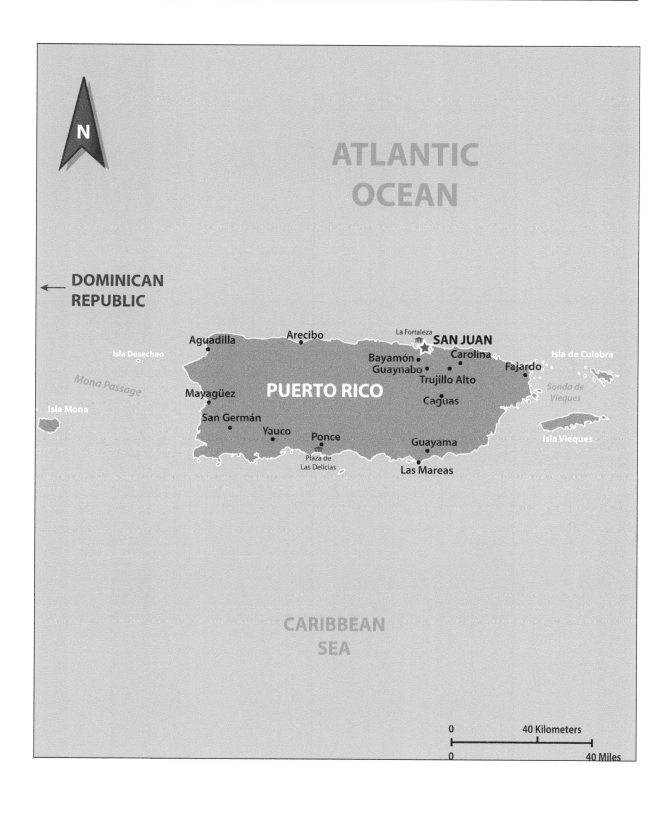

ATLANTIC OCEAN

DOMINICAN REPUBLIC

Aguadilla

Arecibo

La Fortaleza SAN JUAN

Isla Desecheo

Bayamón Carolina

Guaynabo Fajardo

Mona Passage

PUERTO RICO Trujillo Alto

Isla de Culebra

Mayagüez

Caguas

Sonda de Vieques

Isla Mona

San Germán

Yauco Guayama

Isla Vieques

Ponce

Plaza de Las Delicias

Las Mareas

CARIBBEAN SEA

0 40 Kilometers

0 40 Miles

**Principal Cities by Population (2012 estimates):**

- San Juan (402,141)
- Bayamón (194,115)
- Carolina (166,579)
- Ponce (142,317)
- Guaynabo (81,400)
- Caguas (79,550)

exterminated via warfare or European diseases, and the islands had a sizeable African slave population. After the Spanish American War, Puerto Rico fell under control of the United States.

Approximately 76 percent of the population is of European (largely Spanish) descent (2010), and almost12.4 percent identifies as black. Smaller ethnic groups include Asians and Amerindians, who each make up less than one percent of the population. Some four percent identifies as being of mixed race, and eight percent identifies as being "other."

### Religions

Approximately 85 percent of the Puerto Rico's population is Roman Catholic, while Protestantism, Islam, and Judaism are practiced by the remaining 15 percent (2010).

### Climate

Puerto Rico has a tropical marine climate and experiences little variation in seasonal temperatures; the average temperature is about 80°F (26°C). The rainy season falls between April and November, and the rainfall is dispersed unevenly, with some areas, such as those in the central mountainous regions, getting as much as 4,340 millimeters (170 inches) of rain, and others getting as few as 745 millimeters (29 inches) of rain.

## ENVIRONMENT & GEOGRAPHY

### Topography

Puerto Rico lies between the Atlantic Ocean and the Caribbean. It is the easternmost island of the West Indies group called the Greater Antilles, which also includes the larger islands of Cuba, Hispaniola, and Jamaica.

The island is mostly mountainous, and is surrounded by a broken coastal plain. Its climate is mild. Spanish and English are the joint official languages for the predominantly Hispanic and Roman Catholic population of nearly 4 million.

San Juan, Puerto Rico's capital city, has one of the biggest and best natural harbors in the Caribbean, located on a key shipping channel to the Panama Canal.

### Plants & Animals

Approximately 62.2 percent of Puerto Rico is covered in forest, and the Commonwealth of Puerto Rico is home to 547 native tree species, such as the ceiba, or the silk cotton tree. Shrubs and other low-lying plants include jasmine, gardenia, and the sea grape, while cacti such as the pipe organ and the prickly pear flourish in drier areas. There are over 200 bird species on the islands; common species include the grackle and the kingbird, while the Puerto Rican parrot and the Puerto Rican nightjar are both endangered.

## CUSTOMS & COURTESIES

### Greetings

The greetings used in Puerto Rico are typically traditional Spanish greetings. Handshakes are common and are accompanied by the appropriate verbal greeting in formal situations. Men customarily wait until the woman extends her hand before offering their own. When greeting friends, family, or close acquaintances, kissing is also common and consists of two air kisses, first on the left and then the right. A touch on the elbow or the abrazo, an embrace, are also common forms of greeting between friends and family. Informally, a nod of the head is often sufficient.

When introductions take place, they are typically offered depending on gender and then seniority; women are introduced first, followed by elders. It is also customary to shake hands with each person in a group when introduced, and also when departing. Eye contact is considered important during greetings and introductions, and should be maintained for the entire duration of a conversation. In formal situations, it is customary for a third party to introduce the newcomer.

In addition, honorific titles, coupled with last names, are customary when addressing someone. For example, men are addressed as "señor," married women as "señora," and unmarried women as "señorita." In more casual settings, however, only the first names are used. It should be noted that many people take both the names of their father and mother as their family names, and it is not uncommon for a person to have two first names.

The Latin American tradition of referring to people by their physical descriptions is observed in Puerto Rico as well. For example, a person may be referred to as "trigueño" ("wheat-colored") or "jabao" ("not quite white"). While these references may appear to be derogatory, they typically are not intended as such. The tradition of paying sexual compliments, called "piropos," to women in passing is also common. These compliments are usually paid to every woman, regardless of age or attraction.

## Gestures & Etiquette

Body language and gestures form an important part of Puerto Rican culture and communication. Conversations are routinely punctuated by hand gestures and body movements. Interruptions during conversation are also common and not perceived as rude, to the extent that sentences may be finished by others. Puerto Ricans also tend to stand very close to each other when conversing, and the concept of personal space is often nonexistent. In fact, moving away from a person during a conversation may be perceived as offensive. In addition, it is common to see women, and even men, walking hand in hand, as this does not signify anything more than close friendship.

There is a strong concept of dignity, known as dignitad, and respect among Puerto Ricans. All men, regardless of their social status, are thought to be worthy of respect. Thus, people treat each other with sincere formality, as lack of respect violates a man's dignitad. For this reason, there is hardly any self-deprecating humor and people refrain from making belittling remarks. In addition, because of the values of dignity and respect, Puerto Ricans may also tend to avoid direct confrontation and favor passive non-cooperation. There is also a strict social hierarchy, where obedience is demanded from inferiors. Thus, children, employees, and servants are expected to obey their superiors, and children are taught to extend every respect to their elders. This carries over to all facets of life, and includes the seating and serving of elders and women first during meals.

## Eating/Meals

Puerto Ricans follow a dining schedule similar to that observed in North America and Western culture. There are three main meals per day. Breakfast is generally the lightest and simplest meal of the day, and may consist of toast, cereal, and coffee. On the weekends, it may be more elaborate. Lunch is usually the main meal of the day, particularly on Sunday. This traditional meal is called cena, and is usually elaborate and lasts several hours. If the lunch is heavy, then dinner is usually light.

As more women begin to be employed outside the house, elaborate meals that take time to prepare are becoming less common and are replaced by quick, usually store-bought, dinners. In addition, American-style grocery products are becoming more readily available at large supermarket chains.

## Visiting

Socializing is a popular activity in Puerto Rico. Puerto Ricans are generally characterized as relaxed and socialize informally. Thus, it is common for friends and family to visit unannounced for a casual chat or a drink and a common greeting is "Esta es su casa" ("This is your house."). In fact, the tradition of hospitality is an old one in Puerto Rico, dating back to when unrealistic but extravagant promises were offered to make guests feel welcome. Additionally, if a guest happens to arrive at or near a mealtime, they may be urged to stay and partake of the family meal.

On formal visits, such as dinner parties, guests tend to bring gifts for the host and hostess, although this is not strictly expected. Gifts typically include chocolates, dessert pastries or wine, or gifts for the children, if applicable. In addition, all social events are expected to start late, as punctuality is not always a strict formality. Guests are in fact expected to be about an hour late. If they are punctual, they run the risk of disturbing their hosts as they prepare for the evening.

## LIFESTYLE

### Family
Puerto Rican family structures have been strongly influenced by the Spanish and the Catholic Church. Although little is known about Taíno culture, it is believed to have been matriarchal. After Spanish colonization, however, the family became a patriarchal institution. The father, as the head of the family, had complete authority reinforced by the Spanish Civil Code, a set of laws about marriage and inheritance. A wife served as a silent and trusted partner, and was at times revered as a second mother to her husband. Traditionally, there were also different moral standards for men and women. For example, a husband was not stigmatized if he carried on discreet affairs, and boys were encouraged to be aggressive. Girls, however, were trained to be obedient daughters, faithful wives and devoted mothers, and their chastity was fiercely protected. These family patterns, although changing, still persist.

Until the 20th century, many men and women, especially from the lower classes, lived together in consensual unions, without a religious or civil ceremony. The children resulting from these unions were officially recognized by the father. However, these are now less common and marriage has become the norm. Divorce has become more common in recent years.

In modern times, the traditional extended family system is fading. Because of urbanization and geographical constraints, families now tend to be nuclear (comprising of parents and their children only). However, the extended family is still important, and relatives meet as often as possible and offer assistance in times of need. Elderly parents are often taken in by their married children. An old tradition that is still practiced is that of compadrazgo, a system of co-parentage that is similar to the concept of godparents. During the child's baptism, the godparents take pledges about the child's upbringing and spiritual care, thus forming a sacred bond with the family.

### Housing
The rural countryside was historically the base of Puerto Rican society before urban migration. The traditional house of the jibaro (rural peasant) is called a bohio, which was a small, single-room hut that dated back to pre-Columbian times. This rustic hut had a wooden floor and shuttered doors and windows. The walls were framed by tree trunks, which were covered with commercial-grade wood on the exterior. The roof was also formed with tree trunks, which then supported a thatched roof. The bohios traditionally had a veranda and balcony and were furnished sparsely. Built with traditional methods, the hut retained a close connection with its environment.

During the three centuries of colonial rule, populations were concentrated in town and on haciendas (farmsteads). The town was home to the merchants, and their casas (homes) were elaborately made of wood and masonry following European architectural styles. The town itself consisted of an open plaza, which was surrounded by the church and the cabildo (religious and civic buildings). The plaza was the location of the informal market and social and religious gatherings. The haciendas were mostly isolated in the mountainous regions and formed small, self-contained communities.

Due to pressures of urbanization, the government began a program of building tract suburban housing in the urban centers beginning in the 1950s. Multi-family apartment buildings, single-family homes, and luxury suburban dwellings for the wealthy were created in modern styles using concrete construction. These urban centers are similar to North American towns. However, there are many shantytowns, or informal settlements, on city outskirts. These communities, often containing thousands of residents, comprise shacks and makeshift housing and typically have no sanitation facilities and electricity.

## Food

Puerto Rican cuisine has distinct Spanish, African, and American influences and uses indigenous seasonings such as coriander, papaya, cacao, nispero (loquat), plantains, and yampee (edible tubers). Meals generally begin with appetizers, and include bacalaitos (fried cod fritters), surtillitos (sweet cornmeal fingers), and empanadillas (turnovers filled with lobster, crab, conch, or beef). Frijoles negros (black-bean soup) is also a popular appetizer as are the sopon de garbanzos con patas de cerdo (chickpea soup with pig's feet) and sopon de pescado (fish soup). The fish soup is prepared with the head and tail added to garlic, spices, onions, tomatoes, vinegar, and sherry. The most traditional appetizer is perhaps the asopao, which is a gumbo made with chicken or shellfish and a variety of spices.

Many traditional dishes are flavored with adobo and sofrito, which are blends of herbs and spices. Adobo is made of peppercorns, oregano, garlic, salt, olive oil, and vinegar and is used to marinate meats. Sofrito is made of onions, garlic, coriander, and peppers browned in olive oil or colored with achiote (annatto seeds) and are used in soups. All meals are accompanied by rice, beans, or bread. Tostones, fried green plantain slices, are served with many meat dishes.

Stews, cooked in a heavy kettle, form an important part of entrees. A popular stew is carne guisada puertorriqueña (Puerto Rican beef stew), and is made of seasoned beef. The assortment of spices may include green peppers, sweet chili peppers, onions, garlic, cilantro, potatoes, olives, and seeded raisins. Meat may be eaten roasted, fried, or in the form of meat pies. Carne frita con cebolla (fried beefsteak with onions) and veal a la parmesana are also popular dishes. Puerto Rican cuisine also includes exotic meat dishes, such as

sesos empanados (breaded calf's brains), rinones guisados (calf's kidneys) and lengua rellena (stuffed beef tongue). A Puerto Rican specialty is lechon asado (barbequed pig). Usually roasted for parties and fiestas, the pig is traditionally basted with sour orange juice and achiote coloring, and served with a sour garlic sauce. It is often accompanied by roasted plantains. Even though Puerto Ricans do not eat a lot of fish, they have a number of seafood delicacies, such as camarones en cerveza (shrimp in beer) and jueyes hervidos (boiled crab).

Puerto Rican cuisine features a variety of desserts, which include flan (custard), nisperos de batata (sweet-potato balls with coconut, cloves, and cinnamon) and guava jelly with white cheese. Coconut is a common ingredient in desserts, and its milk, leche de coco, is used to make desserts such as coconut flan, coconut squares, coconut with meringue, and candied coconut rice. Coconut bread pudding is a traditional dessert as is palvo de amor (love powder), which is made with grated coconut, mixed with sugar and boiled and served when crisp and brown.

The leche de coco is also a key ingredient in the piña colada, a drink the islanders claim to have developed. The piña colada is the national drink of the islands. Black Puerto Rican coffee, locally produced, commonly follows meals. Puerto Rico is the world's leading rum producer, and this is another common drink among the islanders.

## Life's Milestones

The quinceañera is an old Latin American tradition that is still practiced in Puerto Rico. It was historically a rite of passage that marked a young girl's transition into womanhood. Traditionally, when a girl turned 15, she was taken from her family and prepared for womanhood by being taught the customs and traditions of her culture. Her return was celebrated as it signified her newfound knowledge of womanhood. In modern-day Puerto Rico, this is celebrated with a religious service at church, followed by a party of friends and relatives. The girl traditionally dresses in an elaborate white or pastel-colored gown. During the party, men take turns dancing with the girl; her first dance, a waltz, is reserved for her father.

As the majority of Puerto Ricans are Catholic, their weddings are conducted in the Catholic tradition. A uniquely Puerto Rican wedding tradition, however, is that of the bridal doll. This doll is dressed in a gown identical to that of the bride. It is then placed at the center of the table where souvenirs are attached to its dress. During the wedding reception, the bride and groom personally thank each person for their attendance, and present them with these souvenirs. In return, the guests pin money on the doll's dress.

Death has traditionally been an important social event, especially in the countryside where veladas (pre-funeral wakes) were held. Traditionally, neighbors gathered to help the family of the dying person in their time of grief. The family and friends pray for nine days after the death, and only after this period is the deceased believed to be truly dead. Some rituals have now become obsolete, such as the florons or maquines, which were special wakes held at the occasion of the death of a child and during which ritualistic games were played.

## CULTURAL HISTORY

### Art

Puerto Rico boasts a long artistic tradition that predates the Spanish colonial period. The visual arts and folkloric crafts developed early. Traditional crafts have been made on the island for centuries, dating to the indigenous Taíno, who made statues of their gods, called cemies. After the arrival of the Spanish in the 15th century, the islanders began making small religious statues called "santos", which depicted Christian saints. Believed to bring spiritual blessings, these small statues were made of clay, wood, stone, or even gold, and materials such as vegetable dyes and human hair were sometimes used as decorations.

Puerto Rico is also famous for handmade lace called "mundillo", a type of bobbin lace-making found only in Puerto Rico and Spain. The tradition was brought to the island by Spanish

nuns, who sold these laces to fund orphanages and schools. The earliest laces were known as torchon, or beggar's lace. Puerto Rico is also famous for its hand-woven hammocks, which date back to the island's pre-Columbian period.

The most famous Puerto Rican crafts are perhaps the máscaras or caretas, or papier-mâché masks. These frightening and elaborately decorated headpieces often feature long horns, bulging eyes, and teeth. Traditionally worn at island fiestas, they are also an important decorative art. The tradition of mask-making goes back to tribal Africa and a 17th-century Spanish tradition where masked vejigantes, carrying balloon-like objects made of cow bladders called "vejigas", pretended to be devils and frightened sinners. These masks are still worn in the annual festivals held in the towns of Ponce, Loiza, and Hatillo.

Puerto Rico's first 18th-century artist of note was José Campeche (1752–1809). A self-taught artist, Campeche developed the genres of portraiture, landscape, and religious painting in the Puerto Rican fine arts. Another prominent artist was Francisco Oller y Cestero (1833–1917), whose paintings portrayed everyday island life. He studied in France and was strongly influenced by the post-impressionist works of Paul Cézanne (1839–1906) and Pablo Picasso (1881–1973). Both Oller and Campeche were inspired by Puerto Rican life and culture, and formulated a distinctly Puerto Rican aesthetic. Other important artists include Ramon Fradé (1875–1954), whose works paid homage to the country peasant, and Miguel Pou (1880–1968), who contributed significantly to the island's artistic tradition.

After the United States acquired Puerto Rico as a territory in 1898, local artists began to incorporate political declarations of national and cultural identity into their art. In the 1940s, the government funded an extensive project of printmaking and literary illustrations. Famous poems, prose, memorable quotations, and political statements all gave rise to a tradition of poster art, which lasted into the 1960s. There was also renewed interest in international art movements by young Puerto Rican artists in the 1950s, many of whom were trained abroad. They also began experimenting with new media such as woodcuts, linoleum blocks, installation art, watercolors, and murals. Influenced by expressionism, their art was characterized by the search for an authentic Puerto Rican experience.

Modern Puerto Rican artists of note include graphic artist Lorenzo Homar (1913–2004); abstract expressionist Julio Rosado de Valle (1922–2008); Francisco Rodón (1934–), known for his portraitures, still life, and landscapes; and sculptor Tómas Batista (1935–), known for his three-dimensional woodcuts. Contemporary artists include Rafael Turiño, who is considered a "Nuyorican," the term for a Puerto Rican who has migrated to New York City. Turiño's large canvases are invariably painted in vivid colors. He usually paints scenes of poverty, as in *La Perla*, which is named for a picturesque slum in San Juan.

## Architecture

The architecture of Puerto Rico was heavily influenced by its Spanish colonizer. Old San Juan, the historic colonial section of the city of San Juan, features buildings and structures that date back to the 16th century, such as the military fortresses of El Morro and San Cristobal, which are made from sandstone and are a designated UNESCO World Heritage Site. Other historic structures in Old San Juan include the Dominican Convent, which was constructed by friars in the 16th century, as well as the Cathedral of San Juan, built in the same time period. Although the exterior of the cathedral was renovated in the 20th century, its interior structure remains one of the few examples of European medieval architecture in the Americas.

In the southern city of Ponce are many 19th-century buildings in a form of neoclassical architecture known as Ponce criollo; buildings in this style generally feature patios and columned balconies. In the southwestern town of San German, the second-oldest town in Puerto Rico, is the gothic-inspired Iglesia de Porta Coeli, or Heaven's Gate cathedral, considered one of the oldest churches in the Western Hemisphere.

## Drama

Theatre was slow to develop in Puerto Rico, emerging only in the second half of the 19th century. Early theatre practitioners aimed to promote Puerto Rican culture, strengthen national identity and address social problems. These included playwrights Luis Llorens Torres (1878–1944) and Nemesio Canales (1878–1923).

In the 1930s, Emilio Belaval (1903–1972) formed a theatre group called El Areyto, and the Ateneo Puertorriqueño began holding contests to encourage playwriting. (Belaval is often considered the founding father of Puerto Rican theater.) These endeavors produced a promising response and led to the emergence of prominent playwrights such as René Marqués (1919–1979), who explored new themes and modes of expression. A national theatre developed in the 1950s and the 1960s. In 1954, the Ballets de San Juan was founded, which fostered a fusion of dance and theatre.

Puerto Rican theatre loosely followed international trends. Thus, the plays of the 1940s were realistic, the plays of the 1950s were poetic, and those of the 1960s were absurdist. However, certain themes are unique to Puerto Rican plays, particularly the islands' history, culture, and folklore, as well as an insistence on placing Puerto Rican performing arts within an international context. Today, the Tapia Theatre in Old San Juan holds two theatre seasons a year, one of which is reserved for Puerto Rican plays and the other for international classics.

## Music

Puerto Rican music has distinct Taíno, Spanish and African influences reflected in its native musical instruments. The güicharo, or güiro, is a notched, hollowed-out gourd that is adapted from a pre-Columbian Taíno instrument. From the classical six-string Spanish guitar, the islanders derived at least four instruments; namely, the requinto, the bordonua, the triple, and the cuatro. The most common of these instruments is the cuatro, a guitar-like instrument with five pairs of strings. It is made from blocks of laurel wood and produces a variety of pitches and resonances.

Other instruments suggest an African influence, and include percussion instruments such as tambours, which are hollowed tree-trunks covered with stretched animal skin, and maracas, which are gourds filled with pebbles and mounted on handles.

The traditional folk songs played to these instruments are mostly the plenas, decimas, or aguinaldos. These ballads are usually performed impromptu and tell stories about the everyday lives of the islanders. Traditional musical dramas called zarzuelas, although less common today, were once an important part of the island culture.

Puerto Rico has a long history of classical music. Composers such as Manuel Tavares (1843–1983), operatic tenors such as Antonio Paoli (1872–1946), and pianists such as Jesús Maria Sanromá (1902–1984) were trained in Europe and adapted European styles to Puerto Rican rhythms. An example of the union of these two forms is the danza, a romantic musical form that evolved out of a Puerto Rican adaptation of the minuet. It lends the classical score a distinctly Caribbean refrain. Popularized by composer Juan Morel Campos (1857–1896), it evolved into a popular form of dance music. The danza is danced in two parts, involving a walk around the dance floor followed by a rhythmic meringue dance.

Other styles of Puerto Rican dance music include the bomba and plena. The bomba has distinct African rhythms and is danced to drums, sticks, and maracas. It is described as a dialogue between the dancer and the musician, each challenging the other to greater speed. The songs sung are those of joy and sorrow. The bomba developed along coastal regions like Loiza Aldea, where African slaves were first brought in the 16th century. The plena is a traditional folk music, emerging in the 19th century in Ponce. The songs, sung to the güiro, cuatro, and the tambourine, tell stories of everyday life. The dancers are traditionally costumed in brilliant colors.

The salsa is another popular dance. Quintessentially Latin American, it has a fast rhythm produced by a variety of musical instruments, including güiros, maracas, and drums.

Another recent musical styling is reggaeton. An aggressive combination of reggae, salsa, merengue, and hip-hop, it is danced to fast drumbeats.

**Literature**

The literary tradition of Puerto Rico dates back to Spanish colonization, when conquistadors and friars described life on the newly discovered world in their letters and memoirs. The first governor of Puerto Rico, Ponce de León (1460–1521), the poet Francisco Ayerra y Santa Maria (1630–1708), and bishops Fray Damián Lopez de Haro (1581–1648) and Diego Torres Vargas (1590–1649) all wrote detailed accounts of Puerto Rican life. Santa Maria is believed to be the islands' first native-born poet.

With the arrival of the printing press in 1807, Puerto Rican literature began to change dramatically. Although the restrictive policies of the Spanish kept literacy levels low during colonial rule, an indigenous literary tradition with a focus on drama and poetry developed nonetheless. Alejandro Tapia y Rivera (1826–1882) is considered the father of Puerto Rican literature. He wrote numerous short stories, essays, novels, plays, and poems—the most renowned of which is the allegorical poem "Sataniada: A Grandiose Epic Dedicated to the Prince of Darkness." Along with José Gautier Benitez (1848–1880), he pioneered the romantic literary movement. The poet José Gualberto Padilla (1829–1896), on the other hand, began a neo-classical trend.

Manuel Alonso Pacheco (1822–1889) was another significant literary figure of Puerto Rican literature. His collection of prose and poetry vignettes, *El Gibaro* (1845), provides an extensive insight into Puerto Rican life. The most renowned writer to emerge from the islands, however, is Eugenio Maria de Hostos (1839–1903), a prolific multi-genre writer, educator and critic. Salvador Brau's (1842–1912) numerous writings, including the *History of Puerto Rico* (1904), were also very influential. The novel was late to develop in Puerto Rico, and the first important novelist was Enrique Laguerre (1905–2005), who wrote *La llamarada* (*Blaze of Fire*, 1955).

When the United States acquired Puerto Rico, the island's writers, such as José de Diego (1867–1918) and Julia de Burgos (1914–1953), responded with protest literature. In the 1950s, a large number of islanders migrated to New York, which became a popular topic with fiction writers. For example, Pedro Juan Soto (1928–2002) wrote a short-story collection titled *Spiks* (1956) which depicts life in New York with a brutal realism. Contemporary Puerto Rican writers and poets write in a distinctly Caribbean context, and are very aware of their national and cultural identity.

## CULTURE

### Arts & Entertainment
The formal arts developed slowly in Puerto Rico, and it was only in the latter half of the 20th century that they began to receive local appreciation. Contemporary art now forms an important part of Puerto Rican culture. The two institutions that play a vital role in the promotion of local art are the Institute of Puerto Rican Culture, established in 1955 by a government decree, and the Ateneo Puertorriqueño, founded in 1876. The Ateneo Puertorriqueño has been a strong cultural influence in all areas of the formal arts. It offers annual monetary awards and medals for literary works, compositions of vocal and instrumental music, and for art works in all genres and media. Its Teatro Experimental and Accion Musical have provided many burgeoning dramatists and composers a chance to present their work before critics and audiences.

The Institute of Puerto Rican Culture also promotes all genres of art, both locally and abroad. It sends exhibits of promising local artists to prestigious international centers of art, such as the Museum of Modern Art in New York City, and arranges for art exhibitions all over the islands. It also presents local musicians to local and continental audiences and supports ballet and theatre groups experimenting with Puerto Rican folkloric themes. In addition, the institute arranges contests and provides scholarships for

advanced studies in the arts. The Institute of Culture founded the annual Puerto Rican Theatre Festival in 1958 and the International Theatre Festival in 1966, both of which fueled the local theatre. The Institute of Culture also sponsors the annual three-day Festival de la Calle de San Sebastían, which takes place in January. Held in San Juan, the festival celebrates local culture with parades, concerts, folkloric dance, and traditional crafts.

Puerto Rico boasts a number of art galleries and museums, which house art treasures from all periods of its history. Old San Juan is perhaps the greatest repository of these arts and crafts, being home to galleries whose collections range from pre-Columbian artifacts to paintings by contemporary artists. The Museum of the University of Puerto Rico in Rio Piedras has one of the largest collections of Puerto Rican art, while the Museo de Arte de Ponce (Ponce Museum of Art) is one of Puerto Rico's most famous museums. The building was designed by renowned architect Edward Durrell Stone (1902–1978), who also designed the Museum of Modern Art in New York. The museum consists of a honeycomb network of sky-lit hexagonal rooms and is itself a work of art.

Although the scenic islands of Puerto Rico have been a popular location for movie shoots, a local film industry has developed only in the 1980s. The government encouraged documentary filmmaking in the 1970s. The contemporary film industry, however, took flight largely through the work of directors like Jacobo Morales (1934–) and Marcos Zurinaga (1952–), as well as critically acclaimed films such as *La Guagua aérea* (The Airbus, 1993), directed by Luis Molina Casanova (1951–). The cinema has always had a large viewership, with the majority of the films shown being American, Spanish, and to a lesser extent, Mexican.

### Cultural Sites & Landmarks
Puerto Rico has a wealth of cultural and historical landmarks, many of which derive from its Spanish colonial heritage. Perhaps the finest example of Puerto Rico's preserved colonial past

is seen in Old San Juan, the historical colonial section of the capital of San Juan. The old town dates back to the early 16th century and is considered the oldest settlement in the territories of the United States. It is famous for its cobblestone streets and pastel-colored tile-roof buildings with ornate balconies and indoor courtyards. The San Juan Cathedral is another rare example of medieval Spanish colonial architecture. It encompasses a vaulted tower and four rooms, which date from 1540. The Dominican Convent, also in San Juan, dates back to the 16th century and houses the Institute of Puerto Rican Culture.

San Juan is also home to two World Heritage Sites, as designated by the United Nations Educational, Scientific and Cultural Organizations (UNESCO). La Fortaleza, which is the residence of Puerto Rico's governor, and the San Juan National Historic Site, featuring numerous fortresses and fortifications.

La Fortaleza, also called Santa Catalina Palace, is considered the New World's oldest mansion. It was also the first fortification constructed to defend colonial San Juan. A medieval-style fortress with two round towers, it eventually became the official residence of Puerto Rico's governors. Between the 15th and the 19th century, however, a series of fortifications and forts were constructed that would constitute one of the best displays of Spanish military architecture. Collectively designated as the San Juan National Historic Site, these fortifications include three forts, bastions, and the old city's wall. Fort San Felipe del Morro, better known as El Morro Fortress, stands guard over the San Juan Bay. San Cristobál fortress, which was begun in 1634, is the largest fortress built by the Spanish in the Americas. Fortín San Juan de la Cruz (Fort Saint John of the Cross), better known as El Cañuelo, guards the Bayamón River.

Like Old San Juan, the city of Ponce has a rich historical heritage. Its buildings and streets radiate outward from an open main square, the stately and elegant Plaza de Las Delicias (Plaza of Delights). The Plaza del Mercado was an old marketplace converted to an artisan's marketplace that sells traditional food, fruit, and flow-

ers. At one time it was an old art deco movie theatre. Also in Ponce is the Parque de Bombas (the Firehouse). This is a boldly-painted turn-of-the-century building that once housed the town's fire station and mobile, hand-pumped firefighting units. It has now been converted into a museum. There are also a number of restored homes in the city of Ponce that are architecturally and historically valuable, including the Castillo Serralles, home of the Serralles family, the oldest producers of rum on the islands. Situated on El Vigia Hill, it is a multi-storied Spanish-style hacienda with an open courtyard with elegant fountains.

## Libraries & Museums

Built as the family home of Ponce de Leon in 1523, Casa Blanca houses two museums: the Taíno Indian Ethno-Historic Museum, which focuses on the history of Puerto Rico's aboriginal inhabitants, and the Juan Ponce De Leon Museum, which focuses on the life of the island's first governor and his family. The Museum of Puerto Rican Music, located in Ponce, features collections on the development of Puerto Rican music and dance, as well as memorabilia from famous composers, musicians, and dancers. The Museum of the History of Ponce features exhibits on the history of the city, from pre-colonial times to the present day.

The General Archive and National Library of Puerto Rico, located in Puerta de Tierra, which is near Old San Juan, was established in 1973 and holds the largest collection of Puerto Rico's historic documents.

## Holidays

Holidays celebrated in Puerto Rico include the birthday of writer Eugenio María de Hostos, celebrated on January 11; the birthday of Puerto Rico's first elected governor, Luis Muñoz Marín, celebrated on February 18; Emancipation Day, which marks the abolishment of slavery in Puerto Rico, celebrated on March 22; the birthday of José de Diego, a writer and politician, celebrated on April 16; and the Discovery of Puerto Rico Day, celebrated on November 19. Christian holidays (and, more specifically, Roman Catholic holidays) are widely celebrated, including Christmas, the Feast of the Epiphany, Palm Sunday, and Ash Wednesday, which is preceded by a Carnival celebration.

## Youth Culture

The youth culture of Puerto Rico largely centers on music, particularly native music styles such as reggaeton. Based on Jamaican reggae, reggaeton is infused with native Puerto Rican musical styles such as salsa and is also influenced by hip-hop and rap from the United States. Its popularity with youth culture stems in part from its lyrical content, which deals largely with social issues such as social injustice, crime, and racism. Although the music—and accompanying dances such as "perreo"—can be raunchy, reggaeton culture has maintained its popularity through the first decade of the 21st century, gaining more international appeal, though critics have pointed to the explicit lyrics as a reason for the subculture's lack of definitive mainstream success.

Youth culture in Puerto Rico can be highly segmented, with young people choosing, through their dress and preferred style of music, which social group to belong to. In the early 21st century, young people have more freedom to choose their social groups, whereas in the past, a person's socioeconomic status was a strong determinant of their social life and standing.

## SOCIETY

## Transportation

Puerto Rico's transportation system is geared toward meeting the needs of its expanding economy. There is an extensive public transportation system in San Juan. Buses run all day at frequent intervals. There are also mini-buses, or "publicos," which carry about 12 people. However, these don't depart until the mini-bus is filled up, which may take a few minutes or a few hours. Metered taxis are also quite common. The majority of cars are imported from the United States.

Being an island nation, maritime transportation is particularly developed. San Juan is the main passenger port, and its harbor is the fourth busiest in the Western hemisphere. Other important ports include Aguadilla, Arecibo, Playa de Ponce, and Guayama. Puerto Rico handles daily flights to the United States, as well as international flights to a number of destinations. There are 12 commercial and two major private airports in Puerto Rico.

Traffic moves on the right-hand side of the road in Puerto Rico.

## Transportation Infrastructure

The road system is the most extensive form of transportation, with over 25,000 kilometers (about 15,500 miles) of paved roadways. The Las Americas Expressway connects San Juan in the north with Ponce in the south.

Due to the topography, the railway system is not extensive, with only about 100 kilometers (62 miles) of track. This is primarily used in the transportation of sugar cane. A 10-kilometer (6-mile) urban rapid-transit system, the Tren Urbano, connects the central financial center to the residential districts in San Juan, Bayamon and Guaynabo.

## Media & Communications

The press was introduced in 1807, and since then, the print media has played an important role in Puerto Rico. In the 19th century, the press was strictly censored. After the United States acquired Puerto Rico, there was a dramatic laxity in censorship. However, during the turbulent political periods, the national press, sensitive to government interests, chose to remain silent. On the other hand, opposition press was censored and its journalists incarcerated. Some covert suppression and self-censorship continues to occur, especially on sensitive issues. There are currently three main newspapers, namely the *El Nuevo Dia* (The New Day), *El Vocero de Puerto Rico* (The Voice of Puerto Rico), and *Primera Hora* (First Hour), as well as a number of other regional and business publications.

Television came to the islands in 1952, and as of 2009, over 99 percent of Puerto Rican households have TVs. Around 115 national commercial radio stations and nine television stations broadcast. The first radio broadcast from the islands was in 1923, and today, it broadcasts on many frequencies. News shows and popular music are the most listened to programs on the radio. All broadcasting in Puerto Rico is controlled by the United States Federal Communications Commission (FCC).

Puerto Rico has a reliable, American-style telephone service. In 2005, there were over one million telephones lines in use and over three million cellular connections. Internet services are also readily available through a number of service providers. In 2014, there were over two million Internet users; about 55 percent of the population.

## SOCIAL DEVELOPMENT

### Standard of Living

The average life expectancy is 79 years old, and the infant mortality rate is 7.73 deaths per thousand live births. Some quality of life indicators are bleaker; for example, according to the Annie E. Casey Foundation, a private charity, reports that 83 percent of children live in "high poverty areas" as of 2012. The Community Report of the U.S. Census (2010) reports that 56 percent of Puerto Rico's children live in poverty.

### Water Consumption

An estimated 100 percent of the total population has access to drinking water either through a public source or through household connections to a water supply, as well as access to sanitation services.

### Education

Education is compulsory in Puerto Rico for students between the ages of five and 18. The compulsory education track comprises primary school, which covers first through seventh grade, and high school, which covers eighth through twelfth grade. In 2013, there were 1,460 public schools in Puerto Rico and 764 private

educational institutions. Although study of the English language is compulsory and involved in all levels of primary and secondary education, the first language of the education system is Spanish. In 2000, approximately 60 percent of the population had earned a high school diploma or its equivalent, and 18 percent held post-secondary degrees. The literacy rate was around 92 percent for both men and women in 2010.

### Women's Rights

Women have historically played an important role in Puerto Rican society. The Taínos were a matriarchal people, and indigenous women had access to the highest political role in society, that of the tribal leader. Women contributed equally to the production of food, shelter and clothing, and were even known to handle weapons. Women also played a significant role during the colonial period and contributed significantly to the settlement of the islands as homemakers and educators.

In the 18th century, gender equality and empowerment gained momentum, and educators and activists such as Celestina Cordero (c. 1790–1860) founded schools for women. However, women remained largely illiterate. In the latter half of the 19th century, women began to play a more active role in politics, taking part in separatist movements against the Spanish. However, what greatly changed the social status of women in Puerto Rico were the economic changes that took place at the end of the 19th century. Because of capitalism, women were incorporated into the labor force, and this caused a dramatic shift in traditional values and gender perceptions, a trend which has continued into modern times. In the 20th century, feminist movements, including women's suffrage, began, and literate women were granted the right to vote in 1929, followed by universal suffrage in 1936.

In 1976, family and labor laws were revised in favor of women. Women entered all areas of the work force, but formed a majority in those professions that were thought to be closer to the traditional role of a woman, such as nursing, education, and secretarial positions. They also began to play a prominent role in politics. San Juan elected a female mayor years before a woman was elected to a comparable office in the United States. In 2000, Puerto Rico elected its first female governor, Sila Maria Calderon (1942–).

Despite legal equality, old perceptions, which see women as being inferior to men, still persist to some extent. These perceptions are reinforced by social institutions like the church, mass media, and schools, where textbooks still portray men and women as stereotypes. Thus, female subordination is reinforced. It is also reinforced by the fact that women still form the center of the domestic household and are still the primary caregivers and educators. As a result, women's liberation is often downplayed, as it is perceived to be a threat to the institution of the family.

Women also now bear the double burden of working for pay as well as performing the duties of a homemaker. Domestic abuse continues to be a major concern as well; for instance, in their latest study, issued in 2007, the Puerto Rico Department of Health's Center for Assistance to Rape Victims estimated that 18,000 people in Puerto Rico, mostly women and girls, are victims of sexual violence each year. Puerto Rico also has the highest per capita rate in the world of women over the age of 14 killed by their partners. In the early 21st century, Puerto Ricans still face inequality at the workplace, as well as sexual discrimination.

## Health Care

In 2015, already struggling with crippling debt and recession, Puerto Rico faced the possible collapse of its health-care system. More than two million patients—roughly 60 percent of the population—rely on Medicare, Medicare Advantage, or Medicaid. Reimbursement rates to physicians are much smaller than on the mainland. Experts say nearly 400 of the island's estimated 11,000 doctors leave the island each year.

## GOVERNMENT

### Structure

Puerto Rico is a commonwealth territory of the United States. Puerto Ricans were granted United States citizenship in 1917, and popularly elected governors have served since 1948.

In 1952, the people of Puerto Rico voted in favor of commonwealth status, and a constitution was enacted that provided for internal self-government. The island was declared the Commonwealth of Puerto Rico by the United States Congress on July 25, 1952. In subsequent votes, Puerto Ricans continued to choose commonwealth status over independence or statehood, although opposing political and nationalist sentiments run high over these issues.

Puerto Rico's citizens can vote in United States national primary elections, but not in general elections, and the Puerto Rican delegate to the United States House of Representatives can only vote in committees. Residents of the island do not pay federal income tax on money earned in Puerto Rico.

### Political Parties

The Popular Democratic Party (PPD) was established in 1938 and advocates Puerto Rico's status as an enhanced commonwealth under the United States. The New Progressive Party (PNP) was founded in 1967 and supports Puerto Rico attaining United States statehood. During the 2008 elections, the PNP gained a majority in both the House of Representatives and Senate of the Commonwealth of Puerto Rico. The Puerto Rican Independence Party (PIP) was established in 1946 and advocates Puerto Rico's independence and sovereignty from the United States.

### Local Government

Puerto Rico comprises 78 municipalities, each of which is governed by an elected mayor and municipal assembly.

### Judicial System

The Supreme Court of Puerto Rico, headquartered in San Juan, is the commonwealth's highest court and is presided over by a chief justice, who is usually appointed by the commonwealth's governor. As of 2010, there were seven justices on the Supreme Court. The United States District Court for the District of Puerto Rico, also based in San Juan, consists of seven judges. Appeals from the District Court are heard by the United States Court of Appeals for the First Circuit. Other courts include Appellate Courts and Courts of First Instance.

## Taxation

The tax system of the commonwealth of Puerto Rico is similar to that of the United States; however, rates and tax law do differ. Federal taxes levied in Puerto Rico include customs taxes; import and export taxes; and payroll taxes. The commonwealth also levies an income tax.

## Armed Forces

Puerto Rico falls under the military defense system of the United States. The United States National Guard is present in the commonwealth and is referred to as the Puerto Rican National Guard. It comprises air and infantry units.

## Foreign Policy

The United States acquired Puerto Rico, Guam, and the Philippines from Spain in 1898 and designated them as commonwealth territories. Under international pressure, the United States Congress authorized Puerto Rico to organize its own constitutional government (including executive, legislative, and judiciary authority) in a series of reforms lasting from 1947 to 1952. However, Puerto Rico is a dependent territory, and the question of its political status remains the subject of debate.

As a commonwealth, Puerto Rico has limited power over its own affairs, especially regarding other nations. It is subject to United States sovereign authority, and as such, its foreign relations ultimately support American foreign policy. Nevertheless, Puerto Rican governors have made attempts to carve out a limited foreign policy of their own. For example Governor Rafael Hernández Colón (1936–), who served from 1973–1977 and 1985–1993, pursued a policy to foster economic relations with other nations. This policy operated in three concentric circles: the first circle included Puerto Rico's traditional friends, such as Venezuela

and Costa Rica. The second circle extended to other Commonwealth Caribbean countries. The third extended to advanced capitalist states that were potential sources of investment and capital. Notwithstanding a lack of experience and full political authority, Colón also signed a number of treaties with its neighbors and made Puerto Rico an economic stronghold.

Puerto Rico's strategic geographical location in the Caribbean, combined with its historical and cultural ties to Latin America, make it an important territory for the United States. It is one of the most technologically and economically advanced nations of the region, enabling the United States to further its regional trade and commercial links. In addition, the United States has established several important military bases as vital to strategic defense and of high national security value. Moreover, the United States uses its presence in Puerto Rico to curb drug trafficking in the region. American economic interests in the Caribbean are also evident in a series of trade policies, known as the Caribbean Basin Initiative (CBI).

## Human Rights Profile

International human rights law insists that states respect civil and political rights, and also promote an individual's economic, social, and cultural rights. The United Nations Universal Declaration on Human Rights (UDHR) is recognized as the standard for international human rights. Its authors sought the counsel of the world's great thinkers, philosophers, and religious leaders, and were careful to create a document that reflects the core values shared by every world culture. (To read this document or view the articles relating to cultural human rights, go to: http://www.udhr.org/UDHR/default.htm.)

In its 400-year history, Puerto Rico has witnessed gross violations of human rights, beginning with the colonization of the indigenous Taíno and the continuation of slavery into the 19th century. In addition, the United States government was accused of carrying out a regime of oppression and persecution targeted at suppressing all movements that advocated the territory's independence. In 1937, twenty activists were killed by paramilitary forces, an incident which has come to be known as the Ponce Massacre. In the 1950s, a gag law known as "la mordaza" was established that imprisoned activists for written or verbal statements against the government. The human rights record of Puerto Rico has significantly improved in the last century, though some persistent issues remain.

The United States has been accused of ignoring the right to self-determination of Puerto Ricans, a violation of internationally recognized collective rights. For example, in 1996, the United States imposed capital punishment for approximately 60 different crimes in Puerto Rico, even though this explicitly contradicted the constitution and was opposed by a vast majority of Puerto Ricans. In the 1990s, on the pretext of combating high crime rates, police began to assault buildings and searching individuals and their residences illegally. Telephone calls were illegally intercepted, and the right to bail was eliminated at the discretion of the officer. Racism and high levels of intolerance toward homosexuals also continue to be serious issues in Puerto Rico, as are, to a lesser degree, job discrimination and police authoritarianism. It has been alleged that victims of racism are given differential judicial treatment and have limited access to judicial redress.

### Migration

There is a large population of Puerto Ricans living in the United States. In 2012, an estimated five million Puerto Ricans were living "stateside," and the states with the highest populations of Puerto Rican residents were Massachusetts, Florida, Pennsylvania, New York, and New Jersey.

---

## ECONOMY

### Overview of the Economy

In 2009, the gross domestic product (GDP) of Puerto Rico was $64.5 billion (USD). Puerto Rico's per capita income is low, at $17,687 (USD), compared to that of the United States,

but the island has one of the strongest economies in the region. Although economic emphasis has shifted to diverse industries including tourism, pharmaceuticals, electronics and manufacturing, agricultural products such as coffee, plantains, pineapples, tomatoes, sugarcane, bananas and mangoes are still important. Most of Puerto Rico's exports go to the United States.

### Industry

The industrial sector accounts for roughly 48.8 percent of the gross domestic product (GDP) and for 14 percent of the labor force (2012). Important industries include pharmaceuticals and electronics.

### Labor

In 2007, the labor force of Puerto Rico was estimated to be about 1.5 million. The unemployment rate hovered around 16 percent in 2012.

### Energy/Power/Natural Resources

Puerto Rico is primarily urban, and only four percent of the island is protected by local and federal governments, well below the internationally recommended level of 12 percent protected land. However, the nonprofit Conservation Trust of Puerto Rico (Fideicomiso de Conservación de Puerto Rico) has been preserving and managing the island's rich natural resources since its creation in the 1970s by the governments of Puerto Rico and the United States.

The trust manages several properties and seeks to acquire sites that it considers to be of unique ecological, aesthetic, and historical value to present and future generations of Puerto Ricans. Its properties include the Las Cabezas de San Juan Nature Reserve wildlife habitat; the Hacienda Buena Vista, a 19th century coffee-processing farm; and Hacienda La Esperanza, a 19th century sugar plantation that features 2,200 acres of coastal lowlands, beaches, and unusual formations known as mogotes. The trust's activities in environmental education, land acquisition, reforestation programs, and other projects are spotlighting one of Puerto Rico's unique and vulnerable assets: the environment itself.

## Fishing

Although seafood and shellfish are popular food items in Puerto Rico, the fishing industry is relatively small, mostly due to the extreme depths of the waters surrounding the islands.

## Mining/Metals

The mining industry of Puerto Rico is small. Commonly mined materials in Puerto Rico include cement, stone, gravel, and sand.

## Agriculture

Agriculture accounts for an estimated seven percent of the GDP in Puerto Rico an employs just over one percent of the labor force (2013).

Common crops include sugarcane, pineapple, plantains, coffee, and bananas.

## Animal Husbandry

Chickens and cattle are the predominate forms of livestock in Puerto Rico.

## Tourism

Tourism is an integral party of the economy in Puerto Rico and, in the early 21st century, continues to be a fast-growing industry, accounting for roughly seven percent of the GDP. Approximately 3.1 million tourists visit the commonwealth each year.

*Izza Tahir, Susan Anderson*

## DO YOU KNOW?

- The word "criollo" (a variant of creole) is used by Puerto Ricans when discussing things native to the island and its culture, such as music, art, and architecture.

- Animal species introduced to Puerto Rico include the horse and the mongoose.

- The first governor of Puerto Rico was Ponce de Leon (1460–1521), the famed Spanish conquistador who explored the New World, particularly the modern-day area of Florida, searching for the Fountain of Youth.

## Bibliography

Acosta Cruz, Maria. *Dream Nation: Puerto Rican Culture and the Fictions of Independence*. New Brunswick, NJ: Rutgers University Press, 2014.

Ayala, Cesar J. and Rafael Bernabe. *Puerto Rico in the American Century: A History since 1898*. Charlotte, NC: University of North Carolina Press, 2009.

Flores, Juan. *Divided Borders: Essays on Puerto Rican Identity*. Houston, TX: Arte Publico Press, 1993.

Perez, Ramon Bosque and Jose Javier Colon Morera. *Puerto Rico under Colonial Rule*. Albany, NY: SUNY Press, 2006.

Rivera, Nelson. *Visual Arts and the Puerto Rican Performing Arts, 1950–1990s*. New York: Peter Lang Publishing, 1997.

Santiago, Roberto, ed. *Boricuas: Influential Puerto Rican Writings—An Anthology*. New York: One World, 1995.

Thompson, Hunter S. *The Rum Diary: The Long Lost Novel*. New York: Simon & Schuster, 1998.

## Works Cited

"Already Deep in Debt, Puerto Rico Now Faces a New Crisis". *Washington Post*. March 26, 2015. http://washingtonpost.com/news/wonkblog/wp/2015/05/25/

"Failure to Police Crimes of Violence and Sexual Assault in Puerto Rico". American Civil Liberties Union. http://aclu.org/failure_to_police_crimes_of_violence_and_sexual_assault_in_puerto_rico

Foster, David. *The Global Etiquette Guide to Mexico and Latin America*. New York: John Wiley & Sons, Inc., 2002.

"Forest Land (% of land area) in Puerto Rico". Trading Economics. http://tradingeconomics.com/puertorico/forest_area_percent_od_land_wb_data.html

"Global Health Facts". The Henry J. Kaiser FamilyFoundation. http://kff.org/global-indicator/urban-population/

Henderson, Helene, Ed. *Holidays, Festivals, and Celebrations of the World Dictionary*. Detroit: Omnigraphics, Inc., 2005.

*Institute of Puerto Rican Culture*. http://www.icp. gobierno.pr/

Otis, Ginger Adams. *Puerto Rico*. Oakland (CA): Lonely Planet Publications, 2005.

"Puerto Rico". *CIA World Factbook*. http://www.cia.gov/ library/publications/the-world-factbook/geos/rq.html

"Puerto Rico". *Nations of the World: A Political, Economic, and Business Handbook*. 14th ed. Amenia: NY: Grey House Publishing, 2014.

"Regions and Territories: Puerto Rico". *BBC News*. December 12, 2008. http://news.bbc.co.uk/2/hi/americas/ country_profiles/3593469.stm

Rivera, Magaly. *Welcome to Puerto Rico*. http://welcome. topuertorico.org/index.shtml

Roman, Shirley E. "The Future Status of Puerto Rico: Implications for U.S. Foreign Policy". *Naval Postgraduate School*. http://www.dtic.mil/cgi-bin/GetT RDoc?AD=ADA246205&Location=U2&doc=GetTRD oc.pdf

"Status of children". Kids Count Data Book, 2014. The Anne E. Curry Foundation. http://www.aecf. org/m/resourcedoc/aecf-2014kidscountdatabook-2014pdf#page=5

Villa, Antonio. *Puerto Rico: A Travel Guide*. New York: Modern Guides Company, 1982.

*Welcome to Puerto Rico*. http://www.topuertorico.org/tinfo. shtml

*Mas dancers in Basseterre on their way to a performance. iStock/Michael Turner*

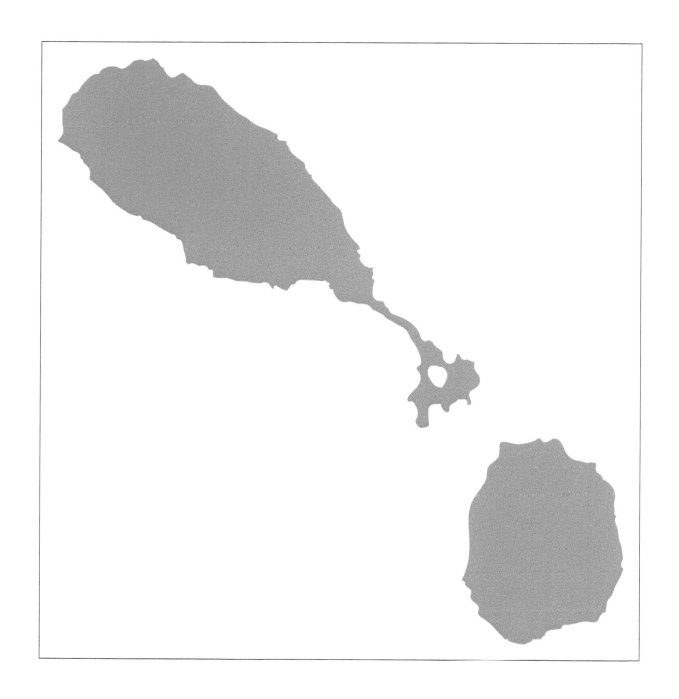

ST. KITTS & NEVIS

# Introduction

The Federation of Saint Kitts and Nevis (also known as the Federation of Saint Christopher and Nevis) is an island pair that forms part of the West Indies island group in the eastern Caribbean Sea. The culture in St. Kitts and Nevis is an amalgam of British, African and West Indian traditions. A former colony of Great Britain, the country gained its independence in 1983, and remains a Commonwealth Realm. The islands are a tropical tourist paradise, but they bear a bloody history of slavery as pawns in the struggle for power in the New World.

Basseterre is the capital of St. Kitts and Nevis, and is located on the island of St. Kitts. It grew from a French port in the 17th century to become the capital during the British colonial period in the 18th century. Basseterre was once an important link in the international sugar trade, until the collapse of the sugar industry in the 21st century. The city now exports a variety of commodities.

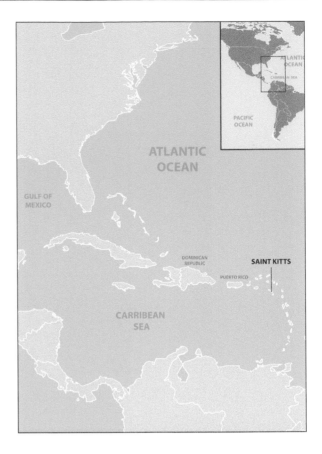

## GENERAL INFORMATION

**Official Language(s):** English
**Population:** 51,936 (2014 estimate)
**Currency:** Eastern Caribbean dollar
**Coins:** The Eastern Caribbean dollar comes in coin denominations of 1, 2, 5, 10, and 25; there is also a one-dollar coin.
**Land Area:** 261 square kilometers (101 square miles)

**National Motto:** "Country above Self"
**National Anthem:** "Oh Land of Beauty!"
**Capital:** Basseterre
**Time Zone(s):** GMT -4
**Flag Description:** The flag is divided by a black diagonal band edged in yellow that runs from the lower left (hoist) corner to the upper right corner. Situated on the black band are two white, five-pointed stars. The upper triangle of the flag is green, and the lower triangle is red.

## Population

It was estimated in 2014 that the population of St. Kitts and Nevis was 51,936. St. Kitts is the larger of the two islands and has an estimated population of 34,983. More than 90 percent of the population of St. Kitts and Nevis is descended from West African slaves who were brought there by 17th-century European colonial powers.

Another five percent are of mixed African and European ancestry, and approximately three percent are Indo-Pakistani. Whites account for

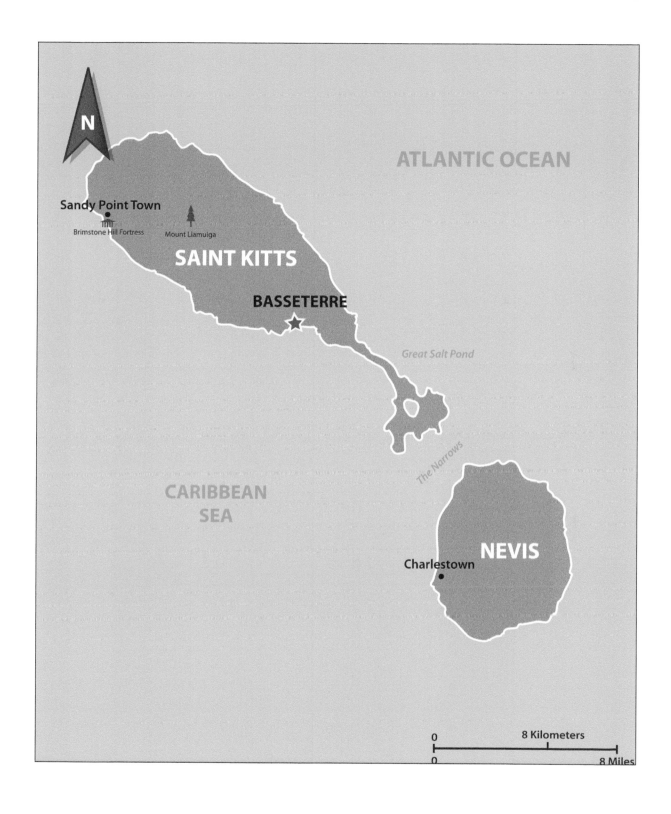

roughly one percent of the population. Less than one percent of the population consists of Portuguese, Lebanese, or other minority groups. English is the official language, and virtually everyone speaks it.

Approximately half the population lives near the coastlines and 68 percent lives in rural villages. The capital, Basseterre, which is located on the island of St. Kitts, has a population of about 14,000 and is the country's main urban center. Charlestown, the only large town on Nevis, has an estimated population of 1,538. Most of the population of Nevis is situated in and near the town of Charlestown.

## Languages

English is the official language, and virtually all the inhabitants speak it.

## Native People & Ethnic Groups

The earliest inhabitants of St. Kitts and Nevis were probably the Sibonay Indians, who arrived about 2,100 years ago from Central America. All that remains of this culture are tools made of stone and shells.

Later groups included the Arawaks and the Carib Indians from South America. Today, at least two dozen archaeological sites yield artifacts of the Arawaks and Caribs, including pottery, shells, flint tools, and occasionally (especially after a particularly hard rain) human remains.

British settlers arrived in 1623, quickly followed by the French. The last of the Caribs on the island of Nevis were massacred by British and French settlers at Bloody Point in 1626. As the sugarcane plantations were developed, the

Europeans brought in African slave labor. The descendants of these slaves comprise the majority of the modern population.

Today, the islands' mostly rural inhabitants work on small farms, sugarcane estates, and large coconut farms.

## Religions

Protestantism is the primary religion in St. Kitts and Nevis, and is practiced by over 80 percent of the population. The Anglican and Methodist churches are the country's largest, each claiming about one-quarter of the population. Small groups adhere to Rastafarianism, Hinduism, and other religions.

## Climate

The climate of St. Kitts and Nevis is tropical, with constant sea winds to temper the heat. Temperatures range from 17° to 33° Celsius (62° to 92° Fahrenheit). The average temperature is 25° Celsius (78° Fahrenheit), with high humidity.

The most rain falls between May and November. On average, St. Kitts receives about 1,400 millimeters (55 inches) of precipitation each year, whereas Nevis receives about 1,200 millimeters (48 inches). Natural hazards include hurricanes, which usually occur from July through October.

## ENVIRONMENT & GEOGRAPHY

## Topography

The twin Caribbean islands of St. Kitts and Nevis lie at the southern end of the Leeward Islands chain in the West Indies, about 310 kilometers (190 miles) east of Puerto Rico. To the northwest lie the islands of Sabah and St. Eustatius, of the Netherlands Antilles; to the northeast lies Barbuda, and Antigua lies to the southeast.

The capital, Basseterre, is located on the southwest coast of St. Kitts island.

St. Kitts is shaped vaguely like a baseball bat, and Nevis somewhat like a ball. They are separated by the Narrows, a strait three kilometers (2 miles) wide. Both islands are volcanic. The Great Salt Pond on the southeastern peninsula of St. Kitts attracts marsh and water birds. Both islands have narrow, fertile coastal plains, black volcanic sand beaches, and rolling landscapes.

The center of Nevis is dominated by Nevis Peak, rising to 985 meters (3,232 feet). St. Kitts is dominated by Mount Liamuiga (Mount Misery), rising 1,156 meters (3,792 ft.) above sea level. This extinct volcano, topped by a crater 1 mile in diameter, is the highest point in the country.

## Plants & Animals

Although it is a small country, St. Kitts and Nevis enjoys a great deal of biodiversity. The blossom of the Poinciana, or flamboyant tree, is the national flower. Common trees include the screw pine, coconut palm, kapok (silk cotton tree), bamboo, cilliment (West Indian bay tree), white cedar, joint wood, and tree fern.

More than 100 bird species are common to St. Kitts and Nevis. The national bird is the brown pelican. Other birds found on the islands include terns, doves, feral pigeons, the brown booby, frigate bird, cattle egret, grey kingbird, Bananaquit, purple-throated Carib bird and the Lesser Antillean bullfinch.

The islands' largest wild animal is the green vervet monkey. These primates live in extended family groups in the rainforests of the mountain slopes. Other mammals include mongooses, cats, dogs, goats, and donkeys. All of these are introduced species.

Native to St. Kitts and Nevis are several species of lizards, bats, frogs, several kinds of land crabs, and toads. In addition, the islands are home to about 60 types of butterflies, including several species of sulphur butterflies. Four species of sea turtles, including the 680–kilogram (1,500-pound) leatherback, come to the islands to lay their eggs.

Common marine life include sharks, rays, snappers, sea fans, lobsters, sea urchins, giant basket sponges, soft coral, and rare black coral. In the fall and spring, more than thirty species of dolphins and whales, including orcas, false orcas, humpbacks, melon-headed whales and short-finned pilot whales, visit the islands.

## CUSTOMS & COURTESIES

### Greetings

English is the official language of St. Kitts, and it is typically spoken with a heavy, West Indian accent and often blended with local slang. For example, the common greeting, "Hello" may be expressed as "How ya gwain," meaning, "How are you?" Although Kittitians and Nevisians are generally relaxed in conversation, formal greetings are customary in business settings and when greeting new people. In some parts of the country, residents speak a French patois, a remnant of the islands' French colonial period. French speakers may greet one another with "Salut" ("Hi"), or the more formal "Bon jour" ("Good day").

Kittitians and Nevisians shake hands in greeting, and there are no particular rules regarding the firmness or length of a handshake. Close friends and acquaintances may embrace when greeting, but this is usually reserved for women and family.

### Gestures & Etiquette

Kittitian and Nevisian citizens maintain a conservative style of etiquette; men dress in casual clothing, including slacks and short sleeve shirts, while women wear skirts and modest shirts in the city. Although the constitution of St. Kitts and Nevis allows freedom of expression and protects the rights of the media, using foul language in public is considered a crime in St. Kitts and Nevis and is punishable by fines of more than $200 (USD). While foreign visitors may be given a warning for this offense, locals are sometimes arrested for indecency and even given prison sentences for disturbing the public.

### Eating/Meals

Most Kittitians and Nevisians eat three meals each day. The morning meal is generally substantial, as it is local tradition to begin the day with a hearty meal. A typical breakfast may include a variety of fruits and pastries, fish and rice, or fried pork. Tea and coffee is also usually served in the morning. The islanders have maintained the British tradition of afternoon tea, which usually consists of tea or coffee with snacks.

The mid-day meal is generally light and may be eaten quickly before returning to work. Most Kittitians and Nevisians consume rice or other vegetables with the afternoon meal. In agricultural communities, the mid-day meal and morning meal may be combined to a single meal consumed in late morning, which better corresponds to the rigors of agricultural labor.

The evening meal is typically the most formal meal, and is more likely to be served in courses, including appetizers, entrees, and dessert. The evening meal is also considered the primary gathering time for families. Liquor, including wine, beer, and cane spirits, is most often served with the evening meal. A variety of seafood and roasted meat dishes are used as main courses and usually served with rice and vegetables.

As tourism has replaced agriculture as the primary industry on the islands, the development of the local cuisine has become a major industry. Islanders are proud of their reputation for serving excellent Caribbean food. The agricultural industry, which produces a wide variety of tropical fruits and sugarcane, fuels the development of native cuisine and plays a role in local custom. Traditional meals accompany every family, community, and national celebration.

### Visiting

When visiting a Kittitian and Nevisian home, gifts are not expected, but appreciated. Candies, pastries, and flowers are appropriate, though white flowers should be avoided as they are usually reserved for funerary customs, and roses should be avoided because they generally signify romantic intentions. While most families on St. Kitts and Nevis live in modest homes, hospitality is an important part of native tradition. Despite limited resources, most hosts will insist on giving guests food and drink. It is considered polite to sample any food or drink offered, though there

are no customs dictating that guests finish all their food and drink.

## LIFESTYLE

### Family

Scarcity of work has led to an increasing number of single-parent households, as men migrate to find jobs. Remittances to family from those working abroad account for more than 10 percent of the disposable income in many families. While the nuclear family is the basic unit of society on the islands, illegitimacy rates are high. Marriage is most common in the middle class, which constitutes a minority of the population on the islands.

Because of absentee fathers, matriarchal family structures are common in St. Kitts and Nevis. Young mothers will often live in close proximity to their mothers and other relatives for aid in raising children and handling domestic duties. The birth of illegitimate children, while discouraged under the islands' Christian traditions, is widely accepted in society. It is common for a child's maternal aunt or grandmother to care for young children in place of their birth mothers. It is also common for young women to have two or more children by different men before deciding to marry.

Childcare and domestic duties fall largely on women. Cultural norms surrounding divisions of labor have prevented the development of equality on the islands. Even when Kittitian and Nevisian couples establish two-parent households, it is common for couples to postpone or forgo marriage in order to save money on wedding expenses.

### Housing

Housing on St. Kitts and Nevis ranges from lavish wooden mansions, which have been preserved from the island's colonial period, to simple shack-like structures in rural areas. The nation's cities, which are small by comparison to many Caribbean cities, are often fashioned to appear as quaint colonial towns with wooden buildings constructed in the colonial style.

Rural homes on the islands are usually constructed of imported materials, including concrete, wood, brick, and stone. Many rural homes are constructed of wood planks enclosing between one and three rooms, including one or two bedrooms. Most islanders cook outside and many homes have wooden cooking sheds near the main house. Many families use bamboo poles for fencing and may also use bamboo or rattan furniture on the outside of the home.

It is uncommon for rural homes to have indoor running water. Many villagers share a common water system, with a shared reservoir and faucets located in a central part of the village. Residents visit the neighborhood faucet to obtain water for cooking and bathing. On St. Kitts, where sugarcane agriculture remains an important feature of the local economy, many houses are clustered into areas surrounding the sugarcane fields, where the families of agricultural workers live. On Nevis, where sugarcane production has been replaced by animal husbandry, small numbers of houses are often clustered around fields for grazing and keeping populations of goats, sheep, and cattle.

## Food

Kittitian and Nevisian cuisine is closely linked to ocean commerce and the fishing industry. Fish and marine invertebrates are major components of local cuisine. Kittitian and Nevisian cuisine is similar to that of other eastern Caribbean nations, including several varieties of curried meat and seafood and liberal use of cassava, yams, and rice. The cuisine of the islands blends elements of European, African, and West Indian culinary traditions.

Conch, a marine mollusk, is a common ingredient in Kittitian and Nevisian cooking. A typical preparation for conch is to cook strips of conch meat in a curry sauce and then serve the mix over rice. Kittitian and Nevisian curries are prepared in numerous varieties from mild to spicy and are also used with goat, pork, chicken, and fish. Conch is also used to prepare fritters, which are balls of fried dough containing spiced chunks of conch meat.

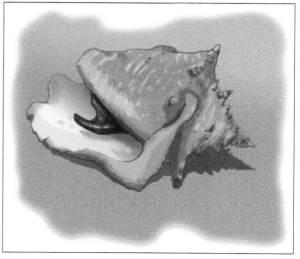

*Conch is a type of seafood featured in many dishes in St. Kitts and Nevis.*

Another popular preparation for conch and other types of meat is pelau, which is a stew-like mixture of rice and beans, usually pigeon peas, with various types of meat. Conch and goat are commonly used in pelau, sometimes mixed with other meats. Some pelau recipes call for tomatoes, which are used to create a base for the mixture. Other pelau recipes use stock made from boiled vegetables with bones and other scraps from whatever meat is used for the recipe.

One of the most popular dishes in Kittitian and Nevisian cuisine is goat water, a stew made from goat meat and various vegetables, often including cassava and yams, mixed with tomatoes and onions. The stew is very popular as a peasant dish, but is also served in restaurants specializing in local cuisine. Gourmet versions of goat water may include scallions, ginger, and other, more expensive spices and vegetables. Roti is a popular snack or appetizer made from meat and vegetables cooked in a flaky crust. There are several varieties of roti, and it is often served as an accompaniment to a meal, or as a meal itself. Popular fillings include ground goat with onion and cassava and conch with rice and curry.

There are a variety of drinks served on the islands, including dozens of fruit juices like mango, papaya, and pineapple juice. St. Kitts and Nevis also produce beer and a variety of cane liquor, which is popularly served in cocktails.

The Caribbean cane spirit is similar to that made in other sugar-producing nations, such as the guaro produced in Central American nations like Costa Rica and Nicaragua.

There are a variety of pastries produced locally on St. Kitts and Nevis, most of which have been developed from recipes left by the British. Chocolate cake is a popular dessert in restaurants and in Kittitian and Nevisian homes. Locally grown fruits such as papaya and coconut are also popular dessert items. Out of economic concerns, families that serve dessert usually choose simple items, like fruit sprinkled with sugar, in place of more elaborate delicacies.

## Life's Milestones

As a predominantly Christian population, most Kittitians and Nevisians follow Christian rights of passage, including baptism, communion, marriage, and funerary traditions. A child's baptism and first communion are occasions for family celebration and usually involve a family feast with music and dancing. There are several native dishes and desserts that are commonly served at baptism or communion ceremonies, to the extent that they have become exclusively associated with these observances. While marriage traditionally marks the transition from childhood to adulthood in Christian culture, declining marriage rates have indicated a shift in the importance of marriage to the native culture.

Funerals are very important in Kittitian and Nevisian culture. Family members living abroad will often pay high prices and sacrifice jobs to attend funerals, as it is often considered an insult to the family to fail to appear at funeral services. Similar to British tradition, Kittitian and Nevisian funerals are generally formal and somber affairs with family and friends gathering for a church service followed by a large meal.

Sociological analyses have shown that funerals in the Caribbean are an essential part of maintaining community and family bonds. Visitors to funerals often meet with distant kin and conduct business, and form and maintain alliances and cooperative relationships between families. Because of the importance of funerals in main-taining social structures, Kittitians and Nevisians living abroad are often subject to considerable pressure to attend them and/or the extended socialization period that surrounds them, which sometimes last for more than a week.

## CULTURAL HISTORY

### Art

The art of the native peoples of St. Kitts and Nevis has included pottery, usually fashioned from red clay and adorned with indigenous motifs and designs, as well as landscape paintings. Other art forms include rug weaving, glass art such as jewelry, and wood carving. St. Kitts and Nevis is also one of many Caribbean islands known for their batik fabrics, which is the art of using hot wax and dye to decorate cloth.

### Architecture

The architecture of St. Kitts and Nevis was influenced heavily by its European colonizers. The island nation is particularly known for its 18th-century architecture, when it was a British colony. (By the time of the American Revolution, St. Kitts was considered, in fact, the richest British colony.) Examples of British influence include its Circus, a roundabout in Basseterre modeled after Piccadilly Circus in England; urban architecture such as the 18th-century Georgian House, an elegantly constructed townhouse; and religious architecture such as St. George's Anglican Church, which was initially constructed by the French (and called Notre Dame), but restructured in the Georgian style by the British in 1869. Home to numerous plantations over the centuries, the island nation is also known for its colonial-influenced estate architecture. The Brimstone Hill Fortress, which dates back to the late 17th century, and which was given World Heritage status, also bears architectural significance as both a historical and military site.

### Drama

Over the years, many types of Kittitian and Nevisian theater have been integrated into the

Carnival tradition. One of the best-known Kittitian and Nevisian theatrical forms is the clown theater, which involves the performance of troupes of acrobatic actors. Local legend holds that the clown troupes were inspired by a French governor who lived near Basseterre. The governor is said to have engaged locals to perform amusing theatrical productions for his guests. Over the years, clown theater became more elaborate with the introduction of new music and costumes. In fact, local composers began writing songs specifically to accompany the clown performances.

Another popular play, which has become a sort of Christmas season tradition, is the bull play, a comic performance that is reportedly based on an actual event that occurred in the mid-1920s. According to legend, the owner of a sugar plantation bought a bull to impregnate his cattle, but found that the bull was unruly and aggressive. The plantation owner then stabbed the bull, thinking he had killed it. However, when he approached, the bull began to attack and run frantically. The plantation owner then called the vet who tended to the bull's wounds. The bull play, which includes actors portraying the bull and charging comically through the audience, has been performed continuously since the 1930s. Now part of the Carnival tradition, the bull play is one of the most characteristic performances in Kittitian and Nevisian theater.

## Music

The music scene in St. Kitts and Nevis has never received the same attention as the larger Caribbean islands such as Jamaica and Trinidad. Nonetheless, music is one of the central components of Kittitian and Nevisian culture and accompanies every cultural and social event. Musical traditions date back to the arrival of European colonists, who brought spiritual and classical music to the island. Over the years, these European traditions were altered by the inclusion of Amerindian musical traditions. When the colonists began bringing large numbers of slaves to the islands, African musical traditions were also included into the developing musical heritage of the island nation.

The slave population on St. Kitts and Nevis is perhaps the most important influence on the character of native music. The slaves created hundreds of spirituals and work songs that became part of the folklore and musical roots of the country. These songs often involved complex rhythms blended with melodic ideas more in keeping with European music. Eventually, musical styles were imported from elsewhere in the Caribbean, including calypso from Trinidad and reggae from Jamaica. Kittitians and Nevisians embraced the Afro-Caribbean stylings of calypso to such an extent that it is sometimes considered the national music. The calypso style itself is a blend of improvisational lyricism and complex rhythmic patterns. During the genre's early history, calypso musicians would gather and compete with one another for the crowd's favor. These competitions became popular in St. Kitts and Nevis in the early 1950s, and were later integrated into the Carnival celebration.

On St. Kitts and Nevis, December to January is the Carnival season, the culmination of musical and performance traditions on the islands. Hundreds participate in the celebration, marching in the streets in various parades, attending performances of calypso bands, and visiting beauty pageants. Carnival started before the establishment of Christianity as the dominant religion in Europe. As Christianity replaced pagan religions, the holiday, which was originally tied to the agricultural calendar, was linked to the Christian tradition of Lent. During the newly named Carnival, developed from the Italian term for "no meat," adherents would celebrate with food and drink before they swore off meat and liquor for Lent.

The colonists who settled St. Kitts and Nevis brought the Carnival tradition with them. The celebration of Carnival was permanently altered by an infusion of African and indigenous cultural characteristics. Carnival dance and music, while based on European forms, bear a distinctly African character. The African slave population on the islands embraced Carnival partially because it was one of the few times during the year that they were permitted to congregate in large numbers and to dance and sing openly.

Another tradition that developed alongside Carnival and still constitutes a major part of the December festivities is the "mas" celebration. Short for "masquerade," mas performances involve elaborate costumes, often decorated with feathers and bales of cloth. The mas performances embody some elements of indigenous traditions. For example, modern mas groups are still generally composed of a chief, a leader who is followed by between 10 to 15 dancers. Most performers are adorned with headpieces, usually lined with feathers, which are similar to those worn by the pre-Columbian Carib tribes during their spiritual ceremonies.

In the 21st century, St. Kitts and Nevis gained worldwide recognition for their music festivals, including the Carnival and the "Culturama," an annual weeklong festival of music and theater celebrated on the anniversary of the nation's independence. As St. Kitts and Nevis has become a popular tourist spot for visitors from North America and Europe, the government has aggressively invested in promoting the annual music festivals in hopes of attracting tourism revenue.

## Literature

Perhaps the most famous literary connection of the islands is that of British poet Robert Browning (1812–1889), whose grandfather owned a plantation on St. Kitts. Contemporary authors include Caryl Phillips (1958– ), who was born on St. Kitts and grew up in England. He is known for his 1993 novel *Crossing the River*, the theme of which is the African diaspora.

## CULTURE

## Arts & Entertainment

The arts occupy an important place in Kittitian and Nevisian culture, and form a part of the basic elementary school curriculum. Promotion of art and music in the primary school system is considered part of the government's commitment to child welfare and is intended to give children enrichment opportunities outside of the workforce. While many Kittitians and Nevisians engage in the arts in their youth, few opportunities for higher and more specialized training has prevented the development of a large professional artist community.

St. Kitts maintains a small gallery community where local artists can display their work. The islands have no national art gallery or showcase for music outside of the annual Carnival, but private institutions are highly active in promoting local artists. During the Carnival celebration, hundreds of local painters and sculptors gather in the cities to sell their works to the crowds gathered for the festivities.

Traditional Caribbean arts are popular in St. Kitts and Nevis, including sea island cottons and colorful batiks, wood carvings, and crafts made from coconut shells, coral, and seashells.

The islands' ten-day Carnival begins each year on December 24. Events include contests for the titles Calypso King, Calypso Queen, and Miss St. Kitts. Calypso contests and talent shows are presented in the evenings. Moko Jumbies (colorfully costumed stilt-walkers) perform throughout the event.

Other festivals include the St. Kitts Music Festival, which features a variety of musical styles, such as salsa, soca, samba, reggae, jazz, and soul. In July, the Nevis Culturama offers costumed troupes, arts and crafts, talent shows, beauty contests, calypso competitions, and a local food fair.

Popular sports in St. Kitts and Nevis include football (soccer), cricket, track and field, netball (similar to basketball), golf, and tennis. Outstanding athletes from the islands include Kim Collins, who won the 2003 World Championship in the 100-meter sprint. Tiandra Ponteen won the silver medal in the women's 400-meter sprint at the 20th Central American and Caribbean (CAC) Games in 2005.

## Cultural Sites & Landmarks

St. Kitts and Nevis is home to numerous cultural and natural sites. One of the more prestigious landmarks is the Brimstone Hill Fortress National Park, which was designated as a World Heritage Site by the United Nations Educational,

Scientific and Cultural Organization (UNESCO). One of the best-preserved examples of British military architecture in the New World, construction on the fort began around 1690 and continued, intermittently, until the late 18th century. The fort is arranged in a polygonal design and carved from the barren rock in the park's ancient volcanic hills.

Mount Liamuiga (Fertile Mountain), a dormant volcano, is the highest point on the island of St. Kitts, with a peak rising 1,156 meters (3792 feet) above sea level. Once known as Mount Misery, the mountain is a popular ecotourism destination. The open crater at the summit of the mountain is more than a kilometer in diameter and contains steaming pools of heated earth, known as fumaroles, and a volcanic lake. As most of the natural vegetation of St. Kitts and Nevis was cleared during the colonial period for agriculture, highland areas, such as the forests covering the sides of Mount Liamuiga, are the last refuges for many of the island's native plant species.

The island of Nevis has a much smaller tourism industry than the larger St. Kitts. There, visitors will find a more traditional island lifestyle, with small villages scattered across the island. In Charlestown, the capital of the island, visitors can find the Botanical Gardens of Nevis, a collection of hundreds of plant species representing tropical zones around the world. Of particular interest is the garden's collection of species native to the islands prior to colonization. The gardens also have an enclosed rainforest exhibit, consisting of a small model showing how plants colonize and eventually overtake structures built within the jungle.

In downtown Charlestown visitors can see the Cotton Ginnery, built on the site where local farmers once congregated to sell cotton crops to buyers. The shops and buildings at the ginnery are constructed in the historic colonial style, but now serve mainly as retail shops where visitors and tourists can buy local goods and crafts. Charlestown's small but active artist community has developed a gallery district similar to what visitors will find in Basseterre, but on a smaller scale. The most renowned of the gallery district's shops is the Café des Artes, a French style-gallery café where many of the most famous artists from St. Kitts and Nevis display and sell their work.

## Libraries & Museums

The National Museum of St. Kitts and Nevis, the nation's largest museum, is located in the capital of Basseterre. Dedicated to the history of the island from early Amerindian culture to independence, the museum contains dozens of exhibits and hundreds of artifacts significant to Caribbean history. Among the museum's exhibits are a collection of artifacts relating to the history of Carnival, from its early European roots to the modern Carnival with its flourishing of African and Caribbean traditions.

Museums on the island of Nevis include the Museum of Nevis History, the Horatio Nelson Museum, and the Alexander Hamilton Museum, which is located in Charlestown, the birthplace of Hamilton (1755–1804), who served as the first United States secretary of the treasury.

The government is also building a museum located in one of the nation's former sugar factories; it will contain artifacts related to the history of the sugar industry. The museum has been under construction since 2005, when the government suspended the state-run sugar industry.

A free public library system was instituted in St. Kitts and Nevis in 1890. Its headquarters, the Charles A. Halbert Public Library, is located in Basseterre; there are an additional four other library centers. The Clarence Fitzroy Bryant College also features a library.

## Holidays

Although St. Kitts and Nevis is a secular state, some Christian holidays are officially observed, including Christmas (December 25). In British countries, December 26 is known as Boxing Day. Traditionally, this was a day when British gentry gave presents to their servants and tradespeople.

Secular holidays include Carnival Last Lap, the end of the 10-day Carnival (January 2), Heroes Day (September 16), and Independence Day (September 19). As a Commonwealth

Realm, St. Kitts and Nevis also observe the birthday of the reigning British monarch as a national holiday.

## Youth Culture

High nationwide levels of poverty restrict the recreational and social options of Kittitian and Nevisian youth. Sports are one of the primary modes of youth recreation—the tropical weather on the island allows year-round participation in sports—with cricket and football (soccer) ranking as the most popular sports. Most urban areas and many rural settlements have set aside green spaces where children and adults can gather to play cricket and other games. These neighborhood green spaces are popular gathering spots for children and teenagers, and form part of the social hub for every community. In the 21st century, the government of St. Kitts and Nevis has developed a more aggressive program for improving the lives of children and women on the island and this has manifested in an increasing number of youth programs, including sports, arts, and music camps.

Teens in St. Kitts and Nevis enjoy music, dancing, video games, and gathering at local restaurants and cafés. Imported music is popular with teens, including calypso and reggae from other Caribbean nations and hip-hop and rock music from the United States and Europe. As St. Kitts and Nevis are relatively ethnically homogenous, in comparison to other Caribbean islands, teenagers tend to refrain from gathering in ethnic groups. Most social groups and networks represent the socioeconomic division common on the island. All children have access to free education up to the secondary level.

## SOCIETY

## Transportation

St. Kitts and Nevis has two international airports. On St. Kitts is the Robert L. Bradshaw International Airport, which offers flights to the United States and Canada, as well as to numerous airports throughout the Caribbean. On the island

of Nevis is the Vance W. Armory International Airport. Ferry transport from St. Kitts to Nevis is available for a modest fee. Ferries are privately owned and operate on fairly consistent schedules. The Seabridge is a car ferry service offering transport between Basseterre and Charlestown, which offers transport on a two-hour schedule every day.

On the islands there is a small system of public minivans offering transport within the cities and to many of the outlying towns. Visitors can recognize the public minivans by the letter "H" appearing on the license plates, whereas private taxis carry the letter "T" on their license plates. Taxis are available in Charlestown and Basseterre, but less frequently service other cities and towns.

Traffic moves on the left-hand side of the road in St. Kitts and Nevis.

## Transportation Infrastructure

There are approximately 383 kilometers (238 miles) of roadways on the islands, but only an estimated 163 kilometers (101 miles) are paved. Even paved roads are frequently in disrepair because of poorly funded maintenance systems.

## Media & Communications

The government of St. Kitts and Nevis provides for freedom of the press and freedom of expression among the populace. Agents of the press are permitted to publish reports critical of government practices and policy without fear of reprisal. According to media rights monitoring groups, the government does not monitor Internet traffic or communication and citizens may visit any Internet site without penalty.

Most of the primary political parties on the islands publish weekly or bi-weekly newssheets with information about party developments, policy notifications, and news. The privately owned and operated *Sun St. Kitts and Nevis* is the most popular publication in the nation providing daily news coverage. The *St. Kitts and Nevis Observer*, a weekly publication, is the second leading publication, providing news and entertainment articles.

There are 11 radio stations broadcasting on the islands, including the government-owned ZIZ Radio, which primarily concentrates on news broadcasts with some music and talk radio programming. Winn FM is one of the nation's most popular private radio networks, providing news shows and a variety of music broadcasts. Calypso and reggae programs are offered by most of the radio stations and are especially popular in the urban areas. In Basseterre and Charlestown, residents also have access to some international radio options, including British Broadcasting Corporation (BBC) News broadcasts.

The nation's only television station, ZIZ Television, is owned by the government. There were some reports that the government refused to allow broadcast licenses for groups that opposed government programs. ZIZ Television provides news and entertainment programming, including several popular drama and comedy series rebroadcast from nearby Caribbean islands.

According to a 2009 estimate, about one-third of the populations uses the Internet.

## SOCIAL DEVELOPMENT

### Standard of Living

In 2013, St. Kitts and Nevis ranked 73 out of 187 countries on the United Nations Human Development Index (HDI).

### Water Consumption

It is estimated that approximately 30 percent of the country's water comes from surface sources such as rivers and springs, with the remainder harvested from groundwater sources. The central mountain regions of each island provide freshwater springs, and both islands are considered to have considerable quantities of groundwater. In fact, in 2005, 41 wells were drilled and seven pumping stations were constructed on the islands. Rainwater is also harvested, particularly on Nevis, which is the drier of the two islands. Over 85% of inhabitants have access to improved sanitary facilities, and nearly 99 percent of the people have access to clean water.

### Education

School attendance in St. Kitts and Nevis is compulsory for children between the ages of five and 17. The country has approximately 30 state schools, as well as several private schools and denominational schools. Clarence Fitzroy Bryant College offers courses of study in education and health, as well as others. Recently, a private medical college, the Medical University of the Americas, was founded in Nevis.

The literacy rate was about 98 percent in a 2013 estimate, and students spend an average of 13 years in the education system. In 2007, education expenditures accounted for 4.2 percent of the country's gross domestic product (GDP).

### Women's Rights

Though the constitution of St. Kitts and Nevis guarantees equality between men and women and equal protection under the law, cultural norms, such as the permissive stigma of spousal abuse, make protecting the rights of women difficult. Spousal violence is covered under a special section of the penal code, which also contains provisions for emotional abuse. Penalties for domestic violence include fines and prison terms, with a maximum of six months in prison. Reports from the Ministry of Gender Affairs indicate that domestic abuse may be more common than indicated by the number of official reports and/or cases brought to trial. Reports from nongovernmental organizations (NGOs) indicate that women infrequently report domestic violence and that it is commonly believed that police and other authorities will do little to protect abused women.

While rape and domestic violence are specifically addressed in the penal code, the law has no special provisions covering spousal rape or molestation. Rape of any kind carries penalties ranging from two years to life imprisonment. The Ministry of Gender Affairs is responsible for administering counseling centers for women and families victimized by domestic abuse and for training police and other officials in the treatment of abuse victims.

Although women are guaranteed equal treatment, they are less likely than men to occupy management positions and are less likely offered opportunities for advancement. Women are most often employed in retail sales, nursing, education, and agricultural positions. However, despite no legal requirement for equal pay, men and women generally received equal or similar salaries in similar positions. The government and NGOs acknowledged persistent gender stereotypes and cultural norms as the primary factors preventing women from obtaining management and leadership positions in many industries.

## Health Care

Life expectancy for Kittitians and Nevisians is 78 years for women and 73 years for men (2015 estimate). The major causes of death are circulatory diseases and cancer. Prevalent infectious illnesses include gastroenteritis, sexually transmitted diseases, viral hepatitis, and dengue fever. Workers are covered for illness and injury by the country's Social Security system.

The government provides prenatal and postpartum care for mothers and infants. The infant mortality rate is seven deaths per 1,000 live births, about half of what is was just five years ago.

## GOVERNMENT

### Structure

Great Britain gained complete control of St. Kitts in 1713. Later, St. Kitts, Nevis, and Anguilla were administered as a single colony, which became an associated state of Britain in 1967. In 1980, Anguilla separated from the other two islands. St. Kitts and Nevis became the independent Federation of St. Kitts and Nevis in 1983.

The government is a constitutional monarchy with a unicameral legislature and universal adult suffrage at age 18. St. Kitts and Nevis is divided into 14 administrative districts, and is under the jurisdiction of the Caribbean Court of Appeals.

The chief of state is the British monarch, represented by an appointed governor general. The head of state is the prime minister, who is usually the leader of the party with the most seats in Parliament.

Parliament consists of the monarch and the 14-member National Assembly; eight members are from St. Kitts and three are from Nevis. They serve five-year terms unless a no-confidence vote is passed. Then, the prime minister dissolves the government and calls for new elections. In addition to the representatives, the governor general appoints three senators.

Nevis has its own legislature for all internal affairs. It also has the option of seceding from the federation. In 1998, Nevis a referendum for secession almost passed. A secession movement continues to this day.

### Political Parties

The two main political parties of St. Kitts are the Saint Kitts and Nevis Labour Party (SKNLP) and the People's Action Movement (PAM). The smaller island of Nevis also has two main political parties: the Nevis Reformation Party (NRP) and the Concerned Citizens' Movement (CCM).

In the 2015 general elections, the PAM won four seats in the National Assembly. The SKNLP won three seats in the assembly, only half of the total they held after the 2010 election. Also in the 2015 general elections, the CCM won two seats.

### Local Government

The island of St. Kitts, which is divided into 14 administrative districts or parishes, does not have a local government; the island of Nevis, however, has an eight-member assembly that handles local government. The Nevis Island Assembly has five elected members and three appointed.

### Judicial System

The country is a member of the Organisation of Eastern Caribbean States (OECS), and as such, its judicial system is administered by the Eastern Caribbean Supreme Court (ECSC), which is headquartered on St. Lucia and consists of a High Court of Justice and a Court of Appeal. A judge from the High Court is stationed on St. Kitts and Nevis. The country is also a member of the Caribbean Court of Justice.

## Taxation

There is no personal income tax, gift tax, or sales tax in St. Kitts and Nevis. A house tax is levied based on annual gross rental values, and a property tax is also levied, with rates varying by region.

## Armed Forces

The Saint Kitts and Nevis Defense Force comprises an infantry and coast guard. There is also a Saint Kitts and Nevis Police Force, which was established in 1960.

## Foreign Policy

Since gaining independence in 1983, the Federation of St. Kitts and Nevis has developed a functional international presence and is a member of numerous international groups, including the United Nations (UN) and the Caribbean Community and Common Market (CARICOM). St Kitts and Nevis is also a member of the Organization of American States (OAS) and the Organization of Eastern Caribbean States (OECS).

St. Kitts and Nevis has participated with the United States and other countries to monitor the flow of illegal drugs in the Caribbean and to develop prevention and alert systems for black-market transport in the nation's waters. St. Kitts and Nevis are popular tourist locations for American travelers, leading the U.S. government to become involved in promoting economic development on the islands. The United States is one of the largest annual donors to development projects on St. Kitts and Nevis, including donations to fund education rehabilitation programs and economic recovery.

One of the primary international concerns for St. Kitts and Nevis is to develop and maintain cooperative international conservation efforts. The government has engaged in aggressive programs to protect natural resources across the islands and in international waters. Efforts to protect fish stocks, among Eastern Caribbean states, have resulted in an increase in the populations of certain fish species commonly used as food on the islands. In the 21st century, St. Kitts has been working with international scientific organizations to develop a marine sanctuary off the coast, partially funded by tourist revenues from scuba diving enthusiasts.

## Human Rights Profile

International human rights law insists that states respect civil and political rights, and also promote an individual's economic, social, and cultural rights. The United Nations Universal Declaration on Human Rights (UDHR) is recognized as the standard for international human rights. Its authors sought the counsel of the world's great thinkers, philosophers, and religious leaders, and were careful to create a document that reflects the core values shared by every world culture. (To read this document or view the articles relating to cultural human rights, go to: http://www.udhr.org/UDHR/default.htm.)

The Federation of St. Kitts and Nevis has a strong record of protecting and ensuring the rights of its citizens. However, pressing human rights concerns include failure to adequately protect the safety of women and children and failure to ensure humane treatment of the nation's prison population.

Corporal punishment is legal in St. Kitts and Nevis, both for adults and children within the school system and at home. While some NGOs reported that child abuse was a problem and objected to the permissive attitude regarding corporal punishment, instances of serious abuse were rarely reported. The government has committed to United Nations standards on child welfare and protection and maintained a training program to instruct police and other officials in the proper treatment of children. NGOs report that the primary difficulty in addressing child abuse on the islands is that many islanders are reluctant to report instances of abuse.

Conditions within the nation's sole prison and auxiliary detention centers fail to meet international standards on the humane treatment of prisoners, a violation of Article 9 of the UDHR. Overcrowding is the most significant problem for the detention system, with an estimated 334 prisoners housed in two facilities meant to hold no more than 232 prisoners. In addition, prisoners have inadequate access to medical and sanitary facilities. Reports from NGOs working within the country indicate that police in St. Kitts and Nevis occasionally use excessive force in their treatment of criminals and those accused of crimes. Though instances are rare, the courts have the power to order that criminals be whipped for their crimes.

St. Kitts and Nevis have a history of committed labor organization and the law provides for a minimum wage within the needs of most families. In addition, the government provides protection from unfair or unsafe working conditions. Although there are no laws specifically addressing the right to organize in labor unions, the government respects the existence of unions, and many industries work collectively to bargain with employers.

## ECONOMY

### Overview of the Economy

Until the 1970s, sugar was the basis of St. Kitts and Nevis' economy. The state-sponsored sugarcane industry was abandoned in 2005, though sugarcane is still produced on farms across the country and remains one of the nation's largest export commodities. Tourism, export manufacture, and offshore banking now account for a large share of the gross domestic product (GDP). The service industry, which includes tourism, accounts for three-quarters of the GDP. As both sugar and tourism depend on the global economy, fluctuations in the world market often significantly affect unemployment in St. Kitts and Nevis.

In 2014, the per capita GDP was estimated at $21,100 (USD).

### Industry

The islands' main industries are tourism, sugar processing, manufacturing (primarily clothing and footwear), and the production of cotton, salt, beverages, and copra.

The manufacturing industry accounts for about a quarter of the nation's GDP; manufac-

tured products include textiles, clothing, and cotton. Mines and refineries are located in the valley near Basseterre, and the city serves as a major hub in the export industry. Agricultural and industrial products are often shipped to the United States, which receives almost half of the nation's exports. Canada and Azerbaijan are also major trading partners. St. Kitts and Nevis imports goods such as fuel and petroleum from the United States, the United Kingdom, and the islands of Trinidad and Tobago.

### Labor

St. Kitts and Nevis has a relatively minor unemployment rate of roughly four percent and low levels of poverty in comparison to other West Indian nations.

### Energy/Power/Natural Resources

The primary resource of St. Kitts and Nevis is arable land, accounting for nearly 20 percent of the country's area. Other major resources are the island's warm climate and scenery, which attract tourists.

### Fishing

The fishing industry of St. Kitts and Nevis is relatively small. Common catches include conch and lobster.

### Mining/Metals

Sand mining, although not a large industry in St. Kitts and Nevis, has led to the environmental degradation of some of the country's beaches.

### Agriculture

A total of 39 percent of the land is used for agriculture and permanent cultivation, with 17 percent of that total made up of tropical rainforest and three percent of meadows and pastures.

Sugarcane is the main crop raised on St. Kitts. The processing mill there is owned by the government. Agriculture on Nevis consists of small farms where vegetables, fruit, and cotton are grown. Other national agricultural products include rice, yams, bananas, coconuts, and fish.

## Animal Husbandry

Poultry (including egg production), pork, and dairy represent small industries in St. Kitts and Nevis. A few livestock operations on the islands are government owned and run.

## Tourism

In 2014, approximately 104,000 tourists visited St. Kitts and Nevis, by air alone. Tourism directly accounts for over six percent of the jobs on the two islands and helps to support many more indirectly.

Attractions include the islands' beaches, scenery, music, and sunny climate. In addition, ancient archeological sites and historic forts dating to the 17th century dot the country. Charlestown, on Nevis, boasts many historic sites and homes, including the birthplace of Alexander Hamilton (whose picture is on the United States $10 bill) and the Cottle Church, built by Methodists in 1824, the first integrated church in the West Indies.

Spas, beach resorts and restaurants throughout the islands cater to tourists. Eco-tourism is highly popular. Activities of ecotourists include hikes to the peaks of the dormant volcanoes, bird watching, and tours through lava formations and seaside lagoons.

*Micah Issitt, Ellen Bailey*

---

### DO YOU KNOW?

- Captain John Smith and his men are said to have visited Nevis for several days in 1607 on their way to found the colony of Virginia.

- The Caribbean islands of St. Kitts and Nevis were among the first in the region to be settled by Europeans.

- Nevis takes its name from the Spanish word "nieve" ("snow"), because of the snowy white cloud that surrounds the island's volcanic peak.

---

### Bibliography

Dyde, Brian. *St. Kitts: Cradle of the Caribbean.* New York: Macmillan, 1989.

Gordon, Joyce. *Nevis: Queen of the Caribees.* New York: Macmillan Caribbean, 2005.

Hubbard, Vincent K. *A History of St. Kitts: The Sweet Trade.* Northampton, MA: Interlink, 2002.

Kuss, Malena, ed. *Music in Latin America and the Caribbean: An Encyclopedic History.* Austin, TX: University of Texas Press, 2004.

Permenter, Paris and John Bigley. *Antigua, Barbuda, St. Kitts and Nevis Alive.* Walpole, MA: Hunter Publishing, 2001.

Sheridan, Richard B. *Sugar and Slavery: An Economic History of the British West Indies, 1623–1775.* Traverse City, MI: Canoe Press, 2000.

Ver Berkmoes, Ryan, et al. *Caribbean Islands.* Oakland, CA: Lonely Planet, 2013.

Whitten, Norman E. and Arlene Torres. *Blackness in Latin America and the Caribbean: Social Dynamics and Cultural Transformations.* Bloomington, IN: Indiana University Press, 1998.

### Works Cited

"St. Kitts and Nevis." Country Reports on Human Rights Practices. *U.S. Department of State Online.* http://www.state.gov/g/drl/rls/hrrpt/2000/wha/829.htm

"St. Kitts and Nevis." International Religious Freedom Report. *U.S. Department of State Online.* http://www.state.gov/j/drl/rls/irf/

"Human Rights in the Federation of St. Kitts and Nevis." *Amnesty International Online.* http://www.amnesty.org/en/region/st-kitts-and-nevis

"Country Profile: St. Kitts and Nevis." *BBC News Online.* http://news.bbc.co.uk/2/hi/americas/country_profiles/1202982.stm

"St. Kitts and Nevis." Bureau of Western Hemisphere Affairs. *U.S. Department of State Online.* http://www.state.gov/r/pa/ei/bgn/2341.htm

"St. Kitts and Nevis." *CIA World Factbook Online.* February 24, 2009. https://www.cia.gov/library/publications/the-world-factbook/geos/sc.html#Issues

"St. Kitts and Nevis." Permanent Mission of St. Kitts and Nevis to the United Nations. *United Nations.* http://www.stkittsnevis.org/

"Local News." *Sun St. Kitts Nevis Online.* http://sunstkitts. com/paper/?asknw=view

"St. Kitts and Nevis." *Lonely Planet Press Online.* Introducing St. Kitts and Nevis. http://www.lonelyplanet. com/st-kitts-and-nevis

"St. Kitts and Nevis: Country Specific Information." *State Department Online.* Bureau of Consular Affairs. (October 15, 2015). http://travel.state.gov/travel/cis_pa_ tw/cis/cis_1026.html

Epstein, Irving and Leslie Limage. "The Greenwood Encyclopedia of Children's Issues Worldwide." Westport, CT: Greenwood Publishing Group, 2008.

Whitten, Norman E. and Arlene Torres. *Blackness in Latin America and the Caribbean: Social Dynamics and Cultural Transformations.* Bloomington, IN: Indiana University Press, 1998.

Kuss, Malena. Ed. *Music in Latin America and the Caribbean: An Encyclopedic History.* Austin, TX: University of Texas Press, 2004.

Porter, Darwin and Danforth Prince. 3rd ed. *Frommer's Caribbean 2008.* Indianapolis, IN: Frommer's Press, 2007.

Rapp, Laura and Diane Rapp. *Cruising the Eastern Caribbean: A Passager's Guide to the Ports of Call.* 4th ed., Walpole, MA: Hunter Publishing, Inc., 2004.

Sheridan, Richard B. *Sugar and Slavery: An Economic History of the British West Indies, 1623–1775.* Traverse City, MI: Canoe Press, 2000.

Dyde, Brian. *St. Kitts: Cradle of the Caribbean.* New York: Macmillan, 1989.

Hubbard, Vincent K. *A History of St. Kitts: The Sweet Trade.* Northampton, MA: Interlink, 2002.

Gordon, Joyce. *Nevis: Queen of the Caribees.* New York: Macmillan Caribbean, 2005.

Ver Berkmoes, Ryan. *Caribbean Islands.* Oakland, CA: Lonely Planet Press, 2008.

Permenter, Paris and John Bigley. *Antigua, Barbuda, St. Kitts and Nevis Alive.* Walpole, MA: Hunter Publishing, 2001.

"Saint Kitts and Nevis—Largest Cities." *Geonames.* http:// www.geonames.org/KN/largest-cities-in-saint-kitts-and- nevis.html

"Saint Kitts and Nevis" *Prison Studies.* http://www. prisonstudies.org/country/st-kitts-and-nevis

"Travel & Tourism: St. Kitts and Nevis." *World Travel & Tourism Council.* http://www.wttc.org/-/media/files/ reports/economic%20impact%20research/country%20 reports/st_kitts_and_nevis2014.pdf

"St. Kitts and Nevis." *UNData.* http://data.un.org/ CountryProfile.aspx?crName=Saint%20Kitts%20 and%20Nevis

"St. Kitts and Nevis." *United Nations Development Programme.* http://hdr.undp.org/en/countries/profiles/ KNA

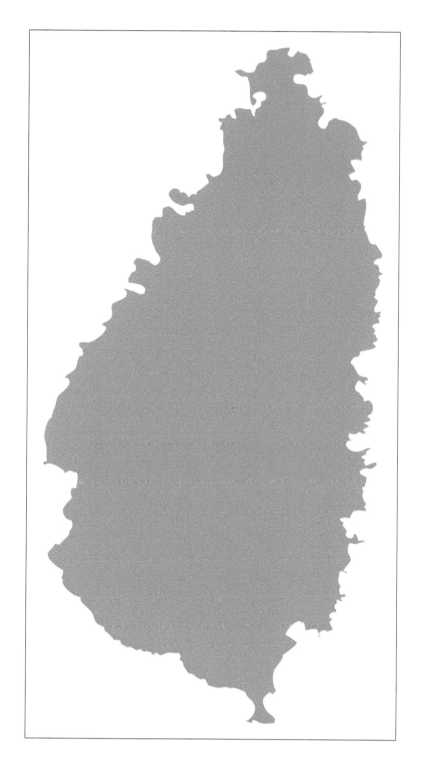

# SAINT LUCIA

# Introduction

A small island nation located in the West Indies, St. Lucia is the second-largest of the Windward Islands group. It is located in the Caribbean Sea between the islands of St. Vincent and Martinique. St. Lucia is known for its beach resorts and attracts many tourists. Originally inhabited by the Arawak Amerindian tribe, it is now a member of the British Commonwealth of Nations. Its people are known as St. Lucians.

## GENERAL INFORMATION

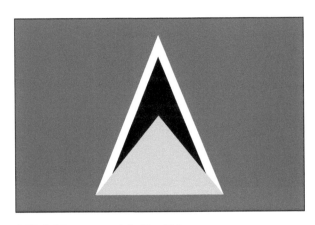

**Official Language(s):** English
**Population:** 163,922 (2015 est.)
**Currency:** East Caribbean dollar
**Coins:** The Eastern Caribbean dollar comes in coin denominations of 1, 2, 5, 10, and 25; there is also a one-dollar coin.
**Land Area:** 606 square kilometers (234 square miles)
**Water Area:** 10 square kilometers (4 square miles)
**National Motto:** "The Land, the People, the Light"
**National Anthem:** "The Sons and Daughters of St. Lucia"
**Capital:** Castries
**Time Zone(s):** GMT -4
**Flag Description:** The flag of St. Lucia features a light blue field (water and sky) with three triangles, centered and sharing the same base, superimposed on one another. The bottom triangle is a

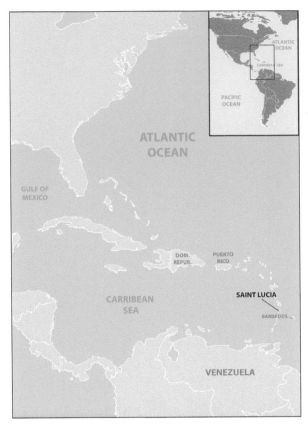

golden isosceles triangle, which is superimposed upon a larger and narrower black triangle, which itself is superimposed upon a slightly larger white triangle, so that it acts as a border along the sides. The triangles represent Caribbean sunshine and racial harmony.

## Population

Nearly all St. Lucians are descended from black Africans. France and Great Britain both made attempts to colonize St. Lucia in the 17th, 18th, and 19th centuries, and in the process, they transported large numbers of African slaves to the island. Nearly 90 percent of the current population is descended from this African group. The largest minorities in St. Lucia are East Indians (most of whom are black Caribs), whites from France and Great Britain, and people of mixed race.

Over 70 percent of St. Lucians live in the island's rural areas, which are mostly inland. The majority of the urban areas are along the coast,

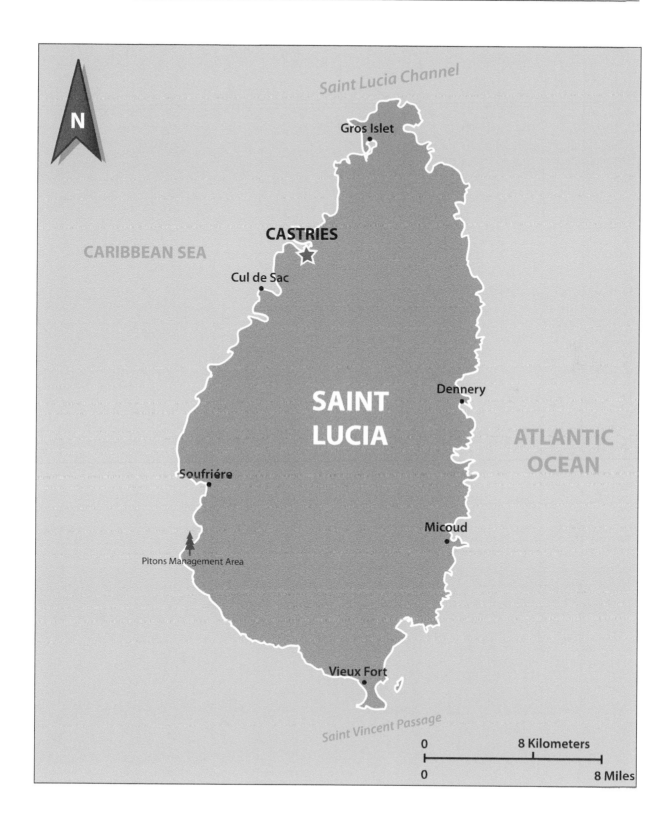

**Principal Cities by Population (2015):**

- Castries (20,000)
- Bisée (12,980)
- Vieux Fort (4,574)
- Micoud (3,406)
- Soufrière (2,918)
- Dennery (2,870)
- Gros Islet (2,362)

including Castries, the capital and largest city. With the island's largest port and best natural harbor, Castries is the commercial center of St. Lucia. It was rebuilt after most of its buildings were destroyed by fire in 1948. It accounts for nearly an eighth of the nation's population.

## Languages

English is the official language of St. Lucia, though many residents speak French Creole, or Kweyol. St. Lucian culture exhibits many French influences.

## Native People & Ethnic Groups

St. Lucia's earliest inhabitants were members of the Arawak tribe of Amerindians, who arrived in the third century. By the 14th century, the Caribs, another Amerindian group, had wiped out the Arawak living in St. Lucia. There are numerous Arawak heritage sites and artifacts in St. Lucia, but there are few Arawak people still living on the island. The Caribs are the oldest significant native population remaining in St. Lucia; they predate the arrival of the African population by centuries.

It is possible, though it is not known for certain, that Spain was the first European nation to visit St. Lucia. However, claims that Christopher Columbus discovered the island in 1502 have been refuted by historians. In addition to Great Britain and France, Spain and the Netherlands have attempted to colonize St. Lucia.

The majority of St. Lucians—between an estimated 80 and 85 percent—are descended from black Africans. There is a small population of mixed ethnicities, including those of French, British, and Carib ancestry, and East Indians make up fewer than three percent of the population.

## Religions

Christianity, which was brought to the island by European colonists, is the prevailing religion in St. Lucia practiced by nearly 80 percent of the population. Roman Catholics account for the majority of Christians, encompassing over 60 percent of the nation's people. Other Christian denominations include Seventh Day Adventists, Anglicans, Methodists, and Pentecostals. Non-Christian religions, such as Rastafarianism, are practiced by a small percentage of the population.

## Climate

With a tropical climate, the weather in St. Lucia remains warm throughout the year. The average temperature is 25° Celsius (77° Fahrenheit), but is slightly lower in the mountainous southwest. The dry season lasts from January to April, and the wet season from May through August. St. Lucia receives a high annual average rainfall of 254 centimeters (100 inches).

St. Lucia is susceptible to high winds and violent rain storms. It has been the victim of several major tropical storms and hurricanes, including Tropical Storm Debbie in 1994, Tropical Storm Iris in 1995, a large tropical wave in 1996, and Hurricane Tomas in 2010. Each of these events caused several deaths, numerous injuries, massive property damage, and widespread homelessness, flooding, and crop devastation. Hurricanes and volcanic activity are among the island's other natural hazards.

## ENVIRONMENT & GEOGRAPHY

## Topography

St. Lucia is volcanic in origin, and the island has a rocky terrain of mountains, valleys, and rivers. Most of its terrain is covered with rainforest vegetation. The island's coastline is indented with dozens of natural harbors, bays, and inlets.

St. Lucia's highest point is Morne Gimie, which reaches 950 meters (3,118 feet) at its peak. Other significant mountains include Gros Piton and Petit Piton, twin volcanic peaks at 798 meters (2,619 feet) and 750 meters (2,461 feet) above sea level, respectively. In addition to these, there are seven other major peaks, most of which are volcanoes.

## Plants & Animals

There are several nature reserves throughout St. Lucia, established to shelter many of the island's native plants and animals. These include the Fregate Islands Nature Reserve and the Savannes Bay Nature Reserve.

St. Lucia is characterized by dense tropical flora throughout the island. However, much of St. Lucia's original rainforest has been destroyed by deforestation since the island was colonized by the British. Still, it remains the home of more than 1,100 different species of plants, including orchids, anthoria, thornscrubs, and several varieties of cacti.

Palm trees grow in great numbers along St. Lucia's coast. Mangrove trees grow in the nation's swampy areas, particularly the Savannes Bay Nature Reserve. Savannes Bay is also the habitat of sea moss and a living reef.

Numerous reptiles and amphibians live in St. Lucia. Among them are the St. Lucian tree lizard, the pygmy gecko, the Maria Island ground lizard, the Maria Island grass snake, the Kouwes snake, the dangerous Fer de Lance snake, and numerous tree frogs. Small rodents, such as the agouti and the manicou, are also found on the island.

Many species of birds also nest on St. Lucia, including the St. Lucian parrot, the St. Lucian oriole, Semper's warbler, the white-breasted thrasher, the hummingbird, the vireo, the sisserou, the jacquot, and the St. Lucian black finch.

---

## CUSTOMS & COURTESIES

### Greetings

English is the official language of St. Lucia, but a majority of residents speak St. Lucian Creole, which borrows heavily from French. While native French speakers may understand many words in this patois, the language is significantly different and also contains elements of British English and African dialects. Generally, St. Lucians may say "Bonjou" ("Good day") in the morning and early day, and "Bonswa" ("Goodnight") in the evening. As an example of the differences between standard French and St. Lucian Creole, the phrase "How are you," pronounced "Comment allez vous" in standard French, is "Komon ou ye?" in St. Lucian Creole.

Most St. Lucians shake hands in greeting, while close friends and acquaintances may embrace or kiss each other on the cheek. Men should behave respectfully when greeting women for the first time, and allow the woman to lead the pace of conversation and interaction.

### Gestures & Etiquette

Many influences have combined to create a relatively conservative atmosphere in St. Lucia. While St. Lucians value hospitality and friendliness, indecency is taboo and may meet with social reprisal. St. Lucia has laws against using foul language in public and against nudity on public beaches. In addition, conservative dress, while loose and comfortable due to the climate, is the norm in areas other than beaches and resorts. For example, the national dress for women, called a jupe, is designed to cover the body while remaining loose and allowing air to flow around the body.

*Semper's warbler is one of several neotropical bird species found on St. Lucia.*

While the nation is largely conservative in morals and ethics, St. Lucians pride themselves on their hospitality. Strangers will often stop to give directions or help someone in need, and it is considered polite to provide small gratuities to anyone offering a service. Showing one's temper, particularly in public, is considered a sign of disrespect and may be met with hostility.

### Eating/Meals

Most St. Lucians eat three meals a day, corresponding to breakfast, lunch, and dinner. Breakfast is usually a substantial meal, with fish and other meats that may be served with vegetables, bread, and coffee. There are numerous varieties of fresh fruit grown on the island and these are commonly included in the morning and afternoon meals. Lunch is typically lighter than the evening meal and consists of lighter fare like sandwiches and soft drinks. Many St. Lucians eat lunch on the go, visiting any of the numerous restaurants and snack carts found throughout the cities. Fish and other roasted or fried meat dishes are also commonly served with the afternoon meal. Many business meetings are held over lunch, and it is a popular time to consume beer or other light alcoholic beverages.

The evening meal is the prime time for dating and gathering with friends and family. Seafood, roasted goat, or beef and a variety of vegetable dishes are served in the evening, often accompanied by fruit and followed by dessert. Many St. Lucians drink rum before or after the evening meal. In St. Lucian homes, most meals are served family style, with individuals serving themselves from communal dishes. In restaurants, meals are served in a more formal manner, including appetizers, entrees, and dessert.

### Visiting

When visiting a St. Lucian home, it is considered polite to bring a small gift for the host. Liquor, wine, candies, and flowers are acceptable gifts. However, as is common in European tradition, white flowers are usually reserved for situations of mourning and funerary traditions. Roses are often used to signify romantic intentions.

Many visitors to St. Lucia remark on the generosity of locals, who often spare little expense to offer food and drink to their guests. It is considered polite to sample any food or drink offered in a St. Lucian home, though guests are not required to finish all of the food or drink they are given. It is recommended to dress conservatively if invited to a St. Lucian home, as this is considered a sign of respect.

## LIFESTYLE

### Family

The nuclear family is the primary unit of St. Lucian society. However, an increasing number of St. Lucians choose to cohabitate and enter into common law unions rather than marry. The tradition of visiting unions, in which a man and woman have children but continue to live separately, is common in St. Lucia. Women may continue to live with their parents or other female relatives, while men visit their wives and children on a daily or less frequent schedule.

The tendency toward illegitimacy and visiting unions has contributed to the likelihood of women to live near and work with members of their families. While having children out of wedlock is generally permitted within society, social mores require that fathers contribute to the economic welfare of their children. As such, delinquent fathers are held in low regard in St. Lucian society.

### Housing

Housing in St. Lucia varies according to economic indicators. Many St. Lucians live in simple wooden or concrete homes with one or two bedrooms. There are also colonial-style mansions in some areas, largely located on the coast or near one of the urban centers. More than 30 percent of the population lives in or near the capital of Castries, and nearly 30 percent of the population lives in urbanized areas. Shared housing and apartments are increasingly popular, though most people continue to live in private homes.

The standard home design in St. Lucia is a rectangular wooden building with numerous windows, an angled slate or tin roof to protect from rain, and a small front or back porch. Traditional houses were often built with a cooking area located outside the home, usually in the back of the house. Several families may share a single cooking area or a common irrigation system located in a central location. However, most new houses are constructed with built-in running water.

It is common to find clusters of houses near productive grazing or agricultural fields. Houses are also grouped near naturally occurring sources of water, like springs, creeks, and rivers. Along the coast, St. Lucians often construct their houses on short stilts to protect from floodwaters. Wooden homes are more popular in coastal areas because timber withstands the changing climatic conditions of the coast and allows more natural circulation than concrete.

## Food

St. Lucian cuisine is a blend of cultural influences, including French, British, African, and Amerindian cuisine. From African cuisine, St. Lucian dishes use ginger, clove, and nutmeg, while European spices like onion, garlic, pepper, and thyme are also used in local dishes. Most dishes are served hot, with liberal use of hot pepper sauce and other spices. An unusual condiment found on the island is banana sauce, a mixture of ground banana with savory herbs, salt, and spices. Similar sauces, sweetened with banana rather than sugar, are found in Southeast Asia.

Seafood is often considered the cornerstone of St. Lucian cuisine. St. Lucians consume fish at every time of day and prepare and serve it in a variety of ways. Along the coast, the "fish fry," a form of barbecue, is popular. It typically features fish and pork cooked over an outdoor grill and usually served with spicy sauces. At many fish fries, St. Lucians serve tatiri, a small fish served deep-fried and eaten whole as a snack. Fish steaks, seasoned with curry, salt, and pepper are served with roasted vegetables. St. Lucians also serve blackfish, a variety of porpoise. The national dish of St. Lucia is saltfish, made from cod or other whitefish packed in salt. Saltfish is usually served boiled with slices of green banana

or breadfruit. St. Lucians also eat conch, a type of marine mollusk, during the prime fishing season from January to April. Other types of fish served in St. Lucia include snapper, tuna, and mahi mahi (dolphin fish).

As on other Caribbean islands, St. Lucians make pepperpot, a stew containing beef and pork meat and intestines flavored with hot peppers, onions, and tomatoes. Some pepperpot recipes call for callaloo leaves, once a colonial substitute for European greens like spinach and mustard green. Pepperpot is a traditional peasant dish, and therefore often contains leftover or discarded ingredients, including pigs' tails and ears and goat intestine. The St. Lucians have dozens of varieties of curry to flavor their dishes. A common combination of spices used in the West Indies, curries can be either spicy or mild and come in both red and green varieties. A common curry dish served in St. Lucia is curried goat, which uses chunks of goat meat cooked in a thick curry sauce and served with yams, corn, or cassava.

For dessert, many St. Lucians eat tropical fruits with sugar or coconut milk. Papaya, mango, banana, and coconut are grown on the island and used in both sweet and savory dishes. Chocolate cake with coconut is a common pastry while custard pies, using locally grown bananas, limes, and lemons, are also a popular dessert choice.

Rum is the national drink of St. Lucia. The island manufactures its own variety of rum through St. Lucia Distillery, located in the Roseau Valley, an area known for its numerous banana plantations. Rum is also mixed with fruit juices, including coconut milk, ground banana, and pineapple. St. Lucians consume rum with the afternoon and evening meals and take pride in their local varieties, which are also sold on the international market.

## Life's Milestones

More than 60 percent of St. Lucians are Catholic, and most celebrate the traditional Catholic rites of passage, including baptism, first communion, marriage, and funerary traditions. A child's baptism is accompanied by a family celebration that can last for an entire day, and includes dining, drinking, and dancing following the church services. Members of the extended family usually give small monetary donations or other gifts to the parents of the child.

While marriage is the traditional marker of the transition to adulthood in Catholic tradition, many choose to postpone marriage until their late twenties or thirties in St. Lucia. Weddings are generally simple, with a church service followed by a gathering of friends and family. Brides traditionally wear white at weddings while the groom wears a suit and tie. Guests at the wedding are expected to dress in formal attire and will usually bring a small gift for the couple.

The St. Lucian wake is an important part of local tradition and blends unique African and Amerindian traditions with Catholic rites. For example, it is traditional for each household of a village to send one member to a funeral. The funerary proceedings can last for more than 12 hours, as friends, family, and neighbors gather to pay their respect to the departed. While family and friends gather inside the home, neighbors and others from the community stage a festive event outside the family's home to celebrate the life of the deceased. This blend of somber and festive tradition is similar to other funeral customs in the Caribbean.

## CULTURAL HISTORY

### Art

Early art in St. Lucia dates back to the Arawaks, who most likely came from northern South America. The Arawaks were known for their crafts, particularly stone carving and ceramics. They were also adept weavers, and many of their folk arts are still in practice to some extent. By 800 CE, the Arawaks were replaced by the warlike Caribs, though a population of Arawaks still exists on St. Lucia. Following the advent of colonialism in the 17th century, the fine arts were slow to develop, and were mostly imitations of Western styles. Because St. Lucia is considered one of the most unspoiled nations of the Caribbean, many local and expatriated artists

focus on landscapes and native scenes, as well as portraits and watercolors.

St. Lucia's premier artist is perhaps Llewellyn Xavier (1945–), famous for a series of collages he created in 1993 that use recycled material. His art is represented in various European museums, as well as the Metropolitan Museum of Art and the Smithsonian Institution. For his contributions to art, Xavier was awarded the chivalrous Order of the British Empire (ODE) in 2004.

### Architecture

Because the history of the Caribbean is intricately linked with European colonialism, much of the architectural heritage of the region is a continuation of European styles imbued with a national artistic character, a style often regarded as Caribbean colonial. Both French and British colonial architecture can be found throughout St. Lucia. (In fact, St. Lucia's oldest intact building is a brick and stone building built by the French in 1769 to store gun powder.) French colonial architecture is prominently found in Soufrière, the island nation's oldest town, while British colonial architecture is evident in the estate homes that surround the capital of Castries. Another prominent example of British colonial architecture is the Government House, a Victorian structure that houses the governor general of St. Lucia. Elements of classic European architecture are also evident in St. Lucia's numerous historic churches and religious buildings, such as the Holy Trinity Anglican Church in Castries, one of the oldest churches in St. Lucia, dating back to the mid 19th century.

### Drama

The formal theatrical tradition of the island of St. Lucia dates back to the mid-20th century, when twin brothers Roderick Walcott (1930–2000) and famed author Derek Walcott (1930–) helped established the Saint Lucia Arts Guild. While the guild was later succeeded by other performing arts groups, both of the Walcott brothers would play an integral part of theatrical development in St. Lucia. A playwright himself, much of Roderick Walcott's work was based on the island's French Creole culture, a major theme of St. Lucia's local theatrical tradition. Caribbean influences and Creole farce continue to occupy the modern stage, and many plays now focus on current social issues and concerns.

## Music

The annual Carnival festival, held in the capital of Castries, brings together the various theatrical, musical, and artistic traditions of the country into a single, multi-day celebration. While Castries is the center of the St. Lucian Carnival, there are smaller celebrations in every town across the country. Carnival has its origins in pre-Christian pagan traditions and arose as a celebration closely linked to the island's agricultural calendar. As Christianity and Catholicism supplanted pagan religions in Europe, elements of pagan holidays were absorbed into Christianity. This assimilation gave birth to Carnival, originally associated with the observance of Lent. The name "Carnival" is taken from the Italian expression for "no meat," as Lent is traditionally a time when Catholics abstain from meat.

French and British colonists first celebrated Carnival in St. Lucia. As the culture changed and slavery was abolished, elements of African and Amerindian culture were added to the celebration. Traditionally, the festival began in February and extended to Ash Wednesday. In 1999, St. Lucia became one of a few Caribbean islands that moved the festival to June to avoid conflicting with Carnival celebrations on other islands. This way, the St. Lucian Carnival also coincides with dozens of calypso music concerts and festivals held across the island. It continues into July, culminating in a massive celebration in Castries with music, beauty pageants, and other performances.

Throughout the Carnival season, calypso, reggae, and soca (a form of dance music derived from calypso) concerts are held around the island. The traditional theater of St. Lucia is also performed almost exclusively during the Carnival. In the parades, which occur near the end of Carnival, marchers wear elaborate costumes constructed from wire, colorful cloth, and other decorations. As tourism has become one of the island's most important industries, the government has invested heavily in promoting the Carnival to encourage the tourism industry. The island is also famous for the St. Lucia Jazz, a jazz festival first established in 1992.

Some of St. Lucia's most recognized dances stem from the union of European and African folk culture. In fact, dances such as the French Creole Belair dance and the quadrille, a historic square dance featuring four couples, began as imitations or adaptations of European dances and movements, generally ballroom-style dances, blended with elements of African traditions. Traditional St. Lucian dance, and its accompanying folk tunes, also shares many similarities with Country and Western dance and music, brought over by American soldiers during World War II. (America had two military bases in St. Lucia). Shared dances include the polka and the waltz, and St. Lucians continue to celebrate country music, which is widely broadcasted throughout the island. Folk music and calypso also continue to be popular styles of dance music in the early 21st century, and cultural festivals and celebrations continue to provide an outlet for performers of traditional and modern St. Lucian dance.

## Literature

Derek Walcott (1930–) was the first St. Lucian writer to gain international fame. Born into a literary family, Walcott's father was an unpublished poet and his mother worked as an educator. Walcott began writing early in his life and had gained national attention for his poetry as he reached adulthood. In 1992, Walcott received the Nobel Prize in Literature in recognition of his achievements as a poet. The poetry collection *25 Poems* (1948) and the epic *Omeros* (1990) are considered his finest works.

Another notable St. Lucian author is Garth St. Omer (1931–), whose novels explore the difficulty of life on the island. Through his characters, St. Omer provides commentary on the various economic, political and social issues that face the St. Lucian population. The married couple Jane King (1952–) and Kendel Hippolyte (1952–) are both successful St. Lucian poets.

## CULTURE

### Arts & Entertainment

While few St. Lucian artists have gained a reputation outside of the island, such as renowned muralist Dunstan St. Omer (1927–), who designed the national flag, and painter Llewellyn Xavier, the arts play an important role in native culture, especially those connected to the annual Carnival. Painting, sculpture, and various crafts combine elements of native traditions, blended with modern techniques and materials. Each year, a limited number of government grants are available for artists and performers involved in Carnival.

Although there is no national fine arts gallery on the island, a number of private galleries help native artists promote and sell their work. The Modern Art Gallery in Castries, for instance, promotes the work of native artists and also collects modern art from across the Caribbean for sale to visitors. The Caribbean Art Gallery, in Rodney Bay, is another private gallery that helps to promote local artists and also contains a collection of historic maps and documents relating to the island's history.

The public school system offers basic art and music instruction as part of the general curriculum. However, there are few opportunities for young artists to study art or music at a higher level. Because of the island's strong literary history, writing and literary study programs form a large part of the higher education opportunities on the island.

Zouk, cadence, calypso, jazz, and reggae are all forms of popular music performed throughout the island. During celebrations and holidays such as Christmas, drumming groups perform with dancers and singers, who sing only in Creole.

In addition to traditional music played during holidays and celebrations, the island's resort hotels host live music and dance for the entertainment of tourists. Authentic entertainment venues include the Light House Theatre in Tapion, the Great House Theatre in the Cap Estate, and the Natural Culture Centre in Castries.

Popular sports in St. Lucia include golf, tennis, squash, horse racing, cycling, diving, rock climbing, football (soccer), and volleyball. Windsurfing and other water sports are popular as well, particularly in the Rodney Bay region.

### Cultural Sites & Landmarks

St. Lucia is home to a variety of cultural attractions, both in the island's urban centers and in more natural settings. The capital of Castries is known for its colorful atmosphere and quaint, colonial-style buildings. In the downtown area, near Derek Walcott Square, visitors can find one of the oldest buildings on the island, a 19th-century Roman Catholic Cathedral, known as the Cathedral of the Immaculate Conception. The cathedral was constructed in the Victorian Renaissance style from stone blocks. It is one of the largest churches in the West Indies and is famous for its frescoes.

Castries also has the island's largest market, where visitors can purchase food, crafts, and other goods. The entertainment district of Castries also features restaurants and cafés in the French and British style. Near the southern end of the city is the Morne Fortune (Hill of Good Luck), a famous battleground where British and French soldiers fought during the struggle for control of the island. Morne Fortune is now a military landmark, with a small memorial located near a burial ground containing the remains of soldiers who fought on the hill.

The Diamond Botanical Gardens is a small resort and botanical garden located near Soufrière, the second largest city on the island. The Botanical Gardens contain the Diamond Mineral Baths, a manmade cauldron of mud heated by steam rising from subterranean volcanic activity. The baths were constructed in 1784 under the direction of King Louis XVI (1754–1793) of France to provide therapy and relaxation for French soldiers fighting on the island. The botanical garden itself has a small collection of plants, most of which represent species important to the island. Near the baths is Diamond Waterfall, perhaps the most popular attraction of the gardens. Water emerging from the volcanic mountains spills into the small waterfall and leaves colorful traces of minerals on the surrounding earth. These minerals also stain the small pool with a colorful combination of gray, green, and blue, giving the waterfall its name.

Near the city of Soufrière, on the southern tip of the island, is the Pitons Management Area, a volcanic complex and World Heritage Site, as recognized by the United Nations Educational, Scientific and Cultural Organization (UNESCO). This conservation area occupies more than 2,909 hectares (7,188 acres) of moist tropical forest, dry forest, and marine habitat, including the Piton mountain range. This mountain range contains the island's two tallest peaks, Gros Piton and Petit Piton, which reach 770 and 743 meters (2,526 and 2,438 feet), respectively. The coastal marine habitat includes densely populated coral reefs, home to hundreds of species of fish and marine invertebrates.

## Libraries & Museums

The St. Lucian Folk Research Centre (FRC), established in 1973, is perhaps the primary cultural repository in the island nation. It houses numerous publications and audio and visual artifacts, and acts as the center of study for St. Lucia's history and folk heritage, including the Kweyol language. It is housed in a 19th-century colonial structure on Mount Pleasant. Another important cultural institution is the Pigeon Island Museum and Interpretive Center, located off of St. Lucia's western coast. Also housed in a colonial structure (a 19th-century British military mess building), it details the history of the island and St. Lucia's first settlers, the Carib Indians, as well as St. Lucia's colonial periods.

The Central Public Library of St. Lucia, located in Castries, dates back to 1924 and serves as the country's national library.

## Holidays

Independence Day, celebrated on February 22, is St. Lucia's national holiday. Carnival is held each year on July 11. As on other Caribbean islands, St. Lucia's Carnival is a festival involving music, dance, costumes, and colorful decorations. Other festivals held on the island include the Festival of Comedy in May, and the St. Lucia Jazz Festival.

Other holidays observed in St. Lucia include Jounen Kweyol (Creole Day) in October, and St. Cecilia's Day in November.

## Youth Culture

Poverty is widespread in St. Lucia, affecting an estimated 25 percent of the population. St. Lucian youth begin working at an early age to support their families. Many young children and teenagers are employed in the agricultural industry, while others find work in the retail and tourism sectors. Other challenges facing St. Lucian youth include HIV/AIDS, unemployment, and crime. Education is free and compulsory between the ages of five and 15. Postsecondary education is available through the Sir Arthur Lewis Community College and the Distance Education Centre of the University of the West Indies. On April 14, 1999, St. Lucia observed the first National Youth Day, an annual event that commemorates the establishment of the St. Lucia National Youth Council (NYC) and highlights youth empowerment in the island nation.

Music and sports are two of the most popular recreational activities for young St. Lucians. The island is a member of the British West Indies Cricket League, and cricket remains the most popular sport on the island. Other sports such as football (soccer) and softball are also popular, and many of the towns and settlements in St. Lucia have green spaces set aside for sports. Both local and imported music are available, largely through vendors in Castries. Hip-hop and rock music imported from the United States has become popular with teenagers, though the most popular genres in the nation are Caribbean styles such as reggae, calypso, and soca. The annual Carnival celebration is popular with youth, and includes special events aimed at young audiences, such as dancing and singing competitions and pageants.

## SOCIETY

## Transportation

The public transportation system in St. Lucia is a mixed public/private service involving vehicles operated by private contractors traveling along a pre-determined route established by the government. While the bus service is affordable, many minivans are crowded and take a considerable time to reach their destination because of frequent stops. Most public minivans travel along the broad circular road that runs along the perimeter of the island. In urban areas, bus stops are marked with signs and the buses will often carry signs indicating their route. Minivans also travel along direct routes between cities or from the cities to surrounding towns and villages. Taxis are widely available in St. Lucia, especially in the area surrounding Castries, Vieux Fort, and other cities. Taxis can be identified by their blue or red license plates, while public minivans have green license plates.

In St. Lucia, traffic moves on the left side of the road.

## Transportation Infrastructure

As of 2011, there were approximately 1,210 kilometers (752 miles) of roads on St. Lucia, most of which wind through the volcanic terrain, sometimes at sharp angles. Driving can be dangerous for the uninitiated and many roads are in disrepair because of a poorly funded public works department. There are two international airports in St. Lucia, Hewanorra International Airport, located near the city of Vieux Fort, and George Charles Airport near the capital of Castries.

## Media & Communications

The constitution of St. Lucia guarantees freedom of expression, and the government protects the rights of the media to express a variety of views. There are a number of privately owned broadcast and print media organizations that criticize government policy regularly without reprisal. In 2006, the government repealed the "false news" clause, which imposed penalties, including imprisonment, for individuals who knowingly published or broadcasted false information.

Most broadcasters and publishers are privately owned. The government operates a single radio station, Radio St. Lucia (RSL), which provides a mix of news and entertainment programming. There are three privately owned national radio stations. Hot FM and Radio 100 both broadcast music, news, and other programming

in English. Radio Caribbean International (RCI) broadcasts a mix of English and St. Lucian Creole music and news. There are also a number of smaller radio stations. There are no daily newspapers on St. Lucia and most publications are on a weekly schedule. The island's most popular newspapers, including *The Voice* and *The Star*, publish three times each week. Most publications found on the island are printed in English. There are few locally produced programs and most television shows are rebroadcast from the United States, the United Kingdom (UK), or elsewhere in the Caribbean.

The telecommunications infrastructure of the island nation is modern and efficient. St. Lucia serves as the headquarters for the Eastern Caribbean Telecommunications (ECTEL) authority, which is the telecommunications regulator for the region. As of 2009, there were an estimated 142,900 Internet users, representing 89.2 percent of the population.

## SOCIAL DEVELOPMENT

## Standard of Living

In 2013, St. Lucia was ranked 97 out of 187 countries on the United Nations Human Development Index (HDI), which measures quality of life indicators.

## Water Consumption

Due to a growing populous and tourism sector, water consumption has increased significantly in St. Lucia in recent decades. The issue made headlines in early 2010, when drought-like conditions began to affect the region, bringing about a water crisis in St. Lucia. In February of 2010, the country implemented conservation measures such as a water rationing system. Generally, the quality of St. Lucia's water is good, as St. Lucian water is believed to be one of the purest in the Caribbean region.

## Education

Primary schooling is free and compulsory for students between the ages of five and 15. Secondary education is available, but attendance rates are low. As of 2012, the gross enrollment ratio for primary and secondary education is less than 60 percent. Secondary education consists of five years of basic training, and students take a Common Entrance Examination (CEE) in seventh grade to determine their secondary schooling. The Sir Arthur Lewis Community College and the University of the West Indies (through the Distance Education Centre) are the nation's only institutions of higher learning. St. Lucia's average literacy rate, aged 15 and older, is approximately 88.6 percent.

## Women's Rights

Spousal rape and domestic sexual abuse are specifically addressed in the St. Lucian penal code with sentences ranging from one year to life imprisonment. Both police and non-governmental organizations (NGOs) investigations have revealed that victims are often reluctant to press charges in cases involving rape. This is mostly due to social stigmas surrounding rape and a widespread belief that the police will not address the issue effectively. Both police and NGOs have also reported that domestic violence is a significant issue in St. Lucia that is also complicated by a reluctance to contact authorities. The national police force contains a special division, the Vulnerable Persons Unit, to investigate domestic violence and child abuse issues, and the penal code contains special provisions for domestic abuse, including protection for abused women and sentencing for offenders that include both fines and imprisonment. However, a lack of funding prevented officers of the Vulnerable Persons Unit from investigating some claims of abuse.

The Women's Support Center (WSC) and the Caribbean Association for Feminist Research and Action (CAFRA) operates hotlines for women and abuse victims and also provides residential counseling visits and shelter for abused women and their families. In addition, the National Organization of Women (NOW) is active in Castries providing counseling, legal services, and educational services for abused women. In 2007, CAFRA and NOW cooperated to conduct an anti-violence campaign in Castries. This effort included lectures on women's rights and other educational programs to raise public awareness about counseling and government services.

St. Lucian women are guaranteed equality in property ownership and legal protection under the constitution. Investigations by NGOs, including CAFRA, revealed that, in most cases, women are given equal pay to male counterparts. Investigations also found that women participate in all national industries and are as likely as men to occupy management positions. As of 2013, more than 63 percent of women in St. Lucia were employed on a part- or full-time basis.

## Health Care

St. Lucia has a stable health-care system, and most residents of the island receive adequate attention and care. There are numerous health clinics, district hospitals, and general hospitals on the island.

St. Lucians are generally healthy and are at low risk for contracting communicable diseases. Many diseases have been eradicated by improvements in the nation's health care that have come since gaining independence.

Average life expectancy is 78 years; 80 for women and 75 for men (2015 estimate). The infant mortality rate is roughly 15 deaths per 1,000 live births (2013 estimate).

## GOVERNMENT

## Structure

The British attempted to colonize St. Lucia as early as 1638, but were thwarted by the island's Carib population. In 1642, France gained control of the island, spurring disputes with Great Britain. The disputes wrangled on nearly a dozen times before 1814, the year Great Britain wrested control of the colony under terms of the Treaty of Paris.

St. Lucia was granted full independence from Great Britain in 1979. Today, the independent state of St. Lucia is a parliamentary democracy. As a former British possession, it is a member of the Commonwealth of Nations. The head of state is the British monarch, whose power is represented on St. Lucia by the governor general. The chief executive is the prime minister, who oversees the executive cabinet, a 10-member council of ministers.

The bicameral legislature consists of a 17-member House of Assembly, whose members are directly elected by the electorate, and an 11-member Senate, six of whose members are appointed by the prime minister, three on the advice of the opposition leader, and two after the consultation of religious, economic, and social leaders. Representatives from both houses serve five year terms.

St. Lucia's judicial branch is the Eastern Caribbean Supreme Court, which has jurisdiction in several other Caribbean nations as well. The age of suffrage in St. Lucia is 18.

### Political Parties

St. Lucia has a two-party political system. The two dominant parties are the Saint Lucia Labour Party, a center-left party, and the United Workers Party, a conservative or center-right party. After the 2011 elections, the Saint Lucia Labour Party held the majority of seats in the House of Assembly—11 of 17. A minor party, the Lucian People's Movement (LPM), was formed in 2010 by two former members of the United Workers Party.

### Local Government

St. Lucia is divided into 10 administrative divisions. Overall, local governance consists of three town councils, six village councils, and the Castries City Council. There are 9 members each in the town and village councils. Mostly, the responsibilities of local governance have become centralized since 1980—solid waste disposal, for example, is a centralized service, and not localized—and falls under the Ministry of Physical Development, Housing, Urban Renewal and Local Government. This ministry is also responsible for collecting local taxes. Matters such as road and park maintenance, landscaping, and the granting of licenses and permits are still undertaken by local councils.

### Judicial System

St. Lucia maintains a mixed legal system, combining English common law and influences of the Napoleonic Code (old legal system of France). Its independent judiciary is made up of district (or magistrates) courts and a High Court (court of appeal), which is a part of the Eastern Caribbean Supreme Court (ECSC). The ECSC has jurisdiction in St. Lucia and applies the law in the six member states of the Organization of Eastern Caribbean States (OECS). Civil and criminal cases can be appealed to the ECSC and to the Judicial Committee of the Privy Council of the United Kingdom, which acts as the highest judicial organ (or final court of appeal). The ECSC is headquartered on St. Lucia and consists of a High Court of Justice and a Court of Appeal. St. Lucia is a member of the Caribbean Court of Justice (CCJ).

### Taxation

The top corporate tax rate in St. Lucia is 33.3 percent, while the top income tax rate is 30 percent. Property transfers and sales are also taxed. In 2009, a value-added tax (VAT) was implemented.

### Armed Forces

St. Lucia has no national armed forces, and internal security matters are handled by the Royal Saint Lucia Police Force (including the Coast Guard). The country belongs to the Eastern Caribbean's Regional Security System (RSS), a defense and security agreement among Eastern Caribbean states.

### Foreign Policy

St. Lucia is a member of the international community, active primarily through the Organization of Eastern Caribbean States (OECS) and the Caribbean Community and Common Market (CARICOM). St. Lucia is also an active member of the United Nations (UN), the Organization of American States (OAS), the Non-Aligned Movement (NAM), and the International Monetary Fund (IMF), among others. St. Lucia's overriding goal in foreign relations is to improve the country's economic standing through strategic partnerships. One of the government's primary diplomatic efforts has been to increase oil supplies and reduce petroleum prices through trade agreements.

The United States provides economic and development aid to St. Lucia through the U.S. Agency for International Development (USAID) and the World Bank. The United States is also one of the nation's primary trade partners. France and the United Kingdom are also significant trading partners and have contributed to aid programs operating on the island. St. Lucia also imports a number of commodities, including machinery, chemicals and electronics, from the United States, Brazil, and elsewhere in the Caribbean. In 2007, St. Lucia was denounced by China for severing foreign relations and establishing diplomatic ties with Taiwan, or Republic of China (ROC), one of only a handful of countries to do so.

From its strategic location within the Eastern Caribbean, St. Lucia has been an important hub in the ongoing effort to prevent drug trafficking in the Caribbean. The St. Lucian government has partnered with the United States to prevent drug shipments in nearby waters, and the United States has aided in training St. Lucian military personnel. St. Lucia is active in ongoing international efforts to promote environmental protection and has focused largely on marine environments, as fishing and marine explorations are essential components of economic stability. St. Lucia supports a number of international environmental treaties and conventions, including those related to marine dumping and pollution and the regulation of whaling. St. Lucia also supports the Kyoto Protocols, a series of regulatory measures designed to reduce global warming.

## Human Rights Profile

International human rights law insists that states respect civil and political rights and also promote an individual's economic, social, and cultural rights. The United Nations Universal Declaration on Human Rights (UDHR) is recognized as the standard for international human rights. Its authors sought the counsel of the world's great thinkers, philosophers, and religious leaders, and were careful to create a document that reflects the core values shared by every world culture. (To

read this document or view the articles relating to cultural human rights, go to: http://www.udhr. org/UDHR/default.htm.)

The parliamentary republic of St. Lucia has a positive record of protecting the rights of citizens in accordance with the principles of the UDHR. The principal human rights concerns in St. Lucia are poor prison conditions and insufficient oversight of the civilian police. In addition, there have been reports from human rights monitoring organizations that domestic abuse and child abuse are common and not sufficiently addressed by police.

The St. Lucian constitution supports the United Nations's resolutions on the rights of children. However, human rights organizations have criticized the government for having insufficient protections in place to ensure child welfare, a violation of Article 25 of the UDHR guaranteeing special treatment for women and children. The government provides counseling services for abused children and also engages in community outreach programs to educate parents about counseling services and anger management. In addition, CAFRA provides child protection services and aid to mothers of abused children. NGOs, including CAFRA, have reported that sexual abuse of minors is common and that many cases are not investigated because designated organizations are overwhelmed.

Some reports indicate that police abuse was a problem in St. Lucia and that police officers occasionally use unnecessary force when detaining subjects. Most reports of police abuse are not indicative of systematic corruption. The St. Lucian system for addressing police complaints involves an internal complaints department supervised by a civilian organization known as the Complaints Board. Investigations by NGOs revealed that the system was inefficient and that authorities failed to address a significant number of complaints.

NGO reports indicate that conditions are poor within Bordelais Correctional Facility, the island nation's sole adult detention center. Official investigations have indicated that conditions are within internationally established guidelines. Some NGO investigations revealed that juvenile offenders housed at the Boys Training Center were subject to abuse at the hands of fellow inmates and center employees. In 2007, the government began an investigation of conditions and procedures at the juvenile detention center. The St. Lucian court system has also been limited due to lack of resources, and detainees are often held for extended periods before being brought to trial. Nonetheless, NGO evaluations indicated that the national courts functioned appropriately in terms of providing representation and impartial trial conditions for the accused.

Lastly, human rights monitoring groups have criticized the St. Lucian government for failing to establish statutes calling for the protection of persons with disabilities and prohibiting discrimination. Individuals with physical disabilities often lacked access to state-sponsored rehabilitation, and few public buildings provide access and services for disabled persons. Some groups, including homosexuals and transgendered individuals, also suffered from discrimination. There are no laws in place to prevent discrimination based on sexual identity or creed.

## ECONOMY

### Overview of the Economy

St. Lucia's economy is largely focused on the agricultural sector, but like all Caribbean islands, revenues from tourism are essential to the nation's economic well-being. Because Latin American countries are exporting their bananas in increasing competition with St. Lucia, the government is under pressure to diversify the nation's economy. In 2014, St. Lucia's gross domestic product (GDP) was estimated at $1.356 billion (USD).

### Industry

St. Lucia's industrial sector is underdeveloped, and accounts for approximately 15 percent of GDP. Manufacturing includes the production of textiles, coconut items, electronic goods, bever-

ages, clothing, toys, sportswear, and diving gear. In addition to manufactured goods, the industrial sector also includes data processing and the managing of an oil shipping terminal. Offshore banking is also a significant industry. St. Lucia's major trading partners are other Caribbean nations, the United Kingdom, and the United States.

### Labor

In 2012, St. Lucia had an estimated labor force of approximately 79,700 and an estimated labor force participation rate of around 69.3 percent. The majority of the labor force is employed in the services industry. The unemployment rate in 2013 was estimated at 21 percent.

### Energy/Power/Natural Resources

St. Lucia's rainforests provide vast amounts of timber, the island's most significant natural resource. However, concerns over deforestation have limited exploitation of this resource.

Other natural resources found in St. Lucia include mineral springs and volcanic minerals such as pumice. Soufrière contains natural sulfur springs, with pools of boiling water. The area's potential for producing geothermal energy has been recognized, but St. Lucia has not yet developed the infrastructure necessary to exploit this resource.

### Fishing

The fishing industry of St. Lucia is an important part of the economy, providing food for the tourism sector and for domestic consumption. Primary fisheries include tuna, wahoo, mahi mahi, and dorado, as well as reef species such as conchs, mussels, and spiny lobsters. The government continues to support the fishing industry, which it perceived as the country's fastest growing economic sector in the early 21st century.

### Forestry

Domestic lumber production is minimal and commercially unimportant, though forests account for approximately three-quarters of the island's land. To meet the demand of the construction industry, large volumes of timber and pine wood products are imported.

## Agriculture

Subsistence farming is the focus of St. Lucia's agricultural sector. However, cash crops provide the bulk of the nation's revenue. Sugarcane was the staple crop of St. Lucia for many years, but has since been replaced by bananas, which now constitute 41 percent of the nation's exports. St. Lucia has the largest banana plantations in the Windward Islands.

Beside bananas, St. Lucia's most important cash crops are cocoa, coconuts (used in the production of coconut oil), mangoes, avocados, and citrus fruits.

The risks of an economy focused heavily in agriculture include lost revenues due to poor weather. In 1994, Tropical Storm Debbie destroyed 68 percent of St. Lucia's banana crop, causing major economic setbacks.

According to the St. Lucian 2007 Census of Agriculture, there were approximately 30,204 acres in agricultural holdings, representing a decrease of 41 percent since 1996. In addition, more than 70 percent of large farms (at least 100 operational acres) disappeared in that same time period; small farms, however, increased.

## Animal Husbandry

The livestock industry on St. Lucia consists primarily of pigs, poultry, sheep, goats, and cattle (though most red meat is imported). With the exception of poultry and pigs, all livestock species have seen a decrease in their total stock numbers since the mid-1990s.

## Tourism

St. Lucia benefits greatly from its tourism business. The services sector, accounting for over half of the GDP, is dominated by tourism-related activities. Annual revenue generated by tourists, most of who come from Europe and North America, is more than $200 million (USD).

Popular tourist activities include diving, deep sea fishing, yachting, water sports, and golf, most of which are available at the islands' many beach resorts. Most visitors to St. Lucia are interested in leisure and recreation rather than cultural attractions.

Other sites, such as Fond Latisab Creole Park in the village of Babonneau and the Pigeon Island National Landmark, are also popular tourist destinations, as are the Diamond Gardens and Sulphur Springs of Soufrière. Other attractions include botanical gardens, boat tours, and plantation tours.

*Micah Issitt, Richard Means*

## DO YOU KNOW?

- Throughout its history, St. Lucia has been named Iouanalao, Hiwanarau and Hewanorra. Iouanalao, the name given to the island by the Arawak Amerindians, is believed to mean "where the iguana are found." The island's English name is in honor of St. Lucy, the patron saint of sight.

- St. Lucia boasts two Nobel laureates among its natives: author Derek Walcott and economist Arthur Lewis. Due to the island's small size, it has the world's highest ratio of Nobel laureates to total population.

- Castries, the nation's capital, was named in 1756, for Commander Charles Eugene Gabriel de La Croix, marquis de Castries.

## Bibliography

Best, Curwen. *Culture @ the Cutting Edge: Tracking Caribbean Popular Music.* Jamaica, West Indies: University of the West Indies Press, 2004.

Ellis, Guy. *Macmillan St. Lucia: Helen of the West Indies.* 4th ed. New York: Macmillan Caribbean, 2006.

*Fodor's in Focus: Barbados & St. Lucia.* New York: Fodor's Press, 2013.

Higgins, Chris. *St. Lucia.* Berkeley, CA: Ulysses Press, 2001.

James, Louis. *Caribbean Literature in English.* White Plains, NY: Longman Press, 1999.

Luntta, Karl and Nick Agate. *The Rough Guide to St. Lucia.* 2nd ed. London, UK: Rough Guides, 2006.

Martinez-Vergne, Teresita. *Contemporary Caribbean Cultures and Societies in Global Context.* Durham, NC: The University of North Carolina Press, 2005.

Ver Berkmoes, Ryan, et al. *Caribbean Islands.* Oakland, CA: Lonely Planet, 2011.

## Works Cited

"Background Note: St. Lucia." Bureau of Western Hemisphere Affairs. *U.S. Department of State Online.* http://www.state.gov/r/pa/ei/bgn/2344.htm

"Census 2001: A Count for Everyone." *St. Lucia Government Statistics Office.* http://www.stats.gov.lc/cen2001.htm

"Country Profile: St. Lucia." *BBC News Online.* http://news.bbc.co.uk/2/hi/americas/country_profiles/1210491.stm

"Human Development Reports: St. Lucia." *United Nations Development Programme.* http://hdr.undp.org/en/countries/profiles/LCA

"Human Rights Report: St. Lucia." Bureau of Democracy, Human Rights and Labor. *U.S. Department of State Online.* http://www.state.gov/g/drl/rls/hrrpt/2008/wha/119172.htm

"Labor Force Participation." *The World Bank.* http://data.worldbank.org/indicator/SL.TLF.CACT.FE.ZS

"Media and Communications: St. Lucia." Portals to the World. *Library of Congress Online.* http://www.loc.gov/rr/international/hispanic/stlucia/resources/stlucia-media.html

"Ministry of Education and Culture." Official Site of the St. Lucia Government Online. http://www.education.gov.lc/

"St. Lucia." *Amnesty International Online.* http://www.amnesty.org/en/region/st-lucia

"St. Lucia." Country Profiles. *CIA World Factbook Online.* https://www.cia.gov/library/publications/the-world-factbook/geos/st.html

"St. Lucia Culture." *The St. Lucian Cultural Organization Online.* http://stluciaculture.com/

"Saint Lucia's History with Tropical Storms." *Hurricane City.* http://www.hurricanecity.com/city/saintlucia.htm

"St. Lucia." *Info Please Online.* http://www.infoplease.com/ipa/A0107931.html

"Saint Lucia—Largest Cities." *GeoNames.* http://www.geonames.org/LC/largest-cities-in-saint-lucia.html

"St. Lucia." Official Site. *St. Lucia Tourism Board Online.* http://www.stlucia.org/

"St. Lucia: Travel Information and Travel Guide." Introducing St. Lucia. *Lonely Planet Online.* http://www.lonelyplanet.com/st-lucia

"St. Lucia." *UN Data.* http://data.un.org/CountryProfile.aspx?crName=Saint%20Lucia

"Travel & Tourism Economic Impact 2014: St. Lucia." *World Travel & Tourism Council.* http://www.wttc.org/-/media/files/reports/economic%20impact%20research/country%20reports/st_lucia2014.pdf

# SAINT VINCENT &
# THE GRENADINES

# Introduction

The island of St. Vincent and the northern part of the Grenadines chain in the eastern Caribbean make up the nation of St. Vincent & the Grenadines. Once a British colony, the country achieved independence in 1979. It remains a part of the British Commonwealth of Nations.

The coastal waters off the Grenadines have long been prized by scuba divers for their diverse communities of fish and marine invertebrates. The islands' natural beauty has made tourism an important industry in the country's economy.

## GENERAL INFORMATION

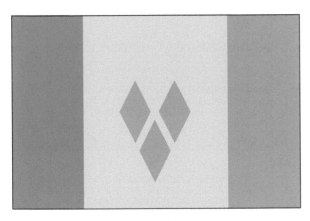

**Official Language(s):** English
**Population:** 102,627 (2015 estimate)
**Currency:** East Caribbean dollar
**Coins:** The Eastern Caribbean dollar comes in coin denominations of 1, 2, 5, 10, and 25; there is also a one-dollar coin.
**Land Area:** 389 square kilometers (150 square miles)
**National Motto:** "Pax et Justitia" (Latin, "Peace and Justice")
**National Anthem:** "St. Vincent! Land So Beautiful"
**Capital:** Kingstown
**Time Zone(s):** GMT -4
**Flag Description:** The flag of St. Vincent and the Grenadines features three vertical bands of blue (left), yellow (center), and green (right). The center yellow band is twice the width of the other

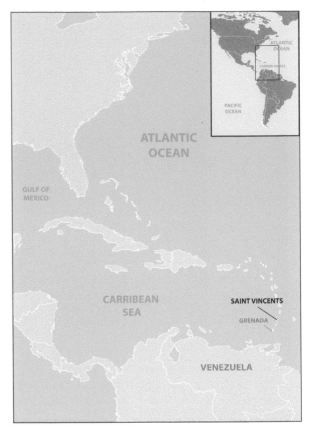

two bands. Three green lozenges, or diamonds, are centered in the middle yellow band, arranged in a "V" formation. The colors are representative of the island nation's beauty: blue for the clear waters, yellow for the golden sands, and green for the lush flora.

## Population

The majority of the population, over 90,000, resides on the island of Saint Vincent, while the remainder of the population lives on the Grenadines; between an estimated 40 and 50 percent of the population lives in urban areas. Roughly one-quarter of the population lives in Kingstown, the capital, and its suburbs. Located on the island of St. Vincent, the capital Kingstown is the country's only large town, with an estimated population of 26,721.

Most Vincentians are descendants of African slaves brought to the islands by European planters. Black Africans comprise the majority ethnic group, at 66 percent of the population. Another

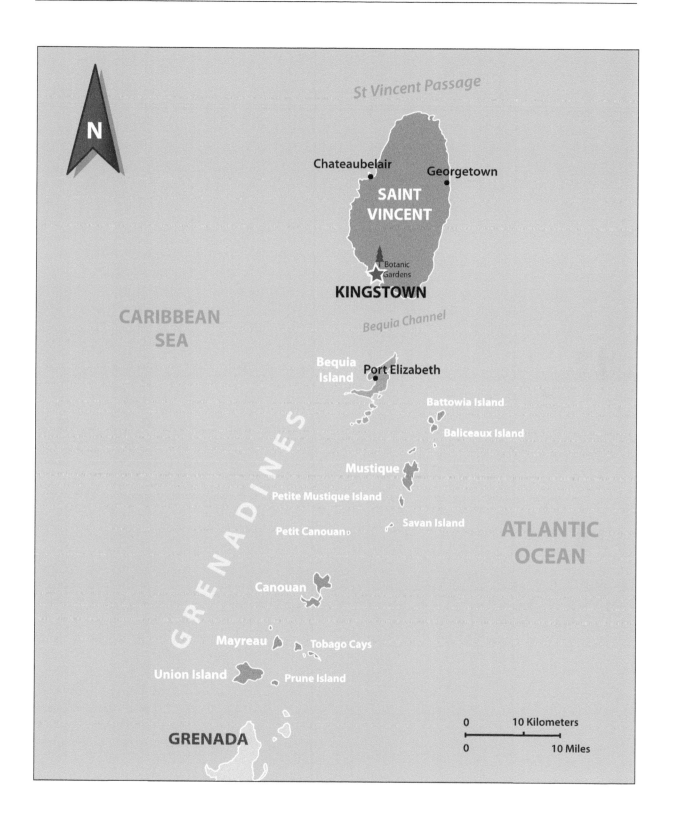

**Principal Districts by Population (2012):**

- Calliaqua (24,205)
- Suburbs of Kingstown (13,812)
- Kingstown (12,909)
- Marriaqua (7,798)
- Georgetown (7,061)

19 percent is of mixed African and European descent. Other minority groups include East Indians (six percent of the population) and Carib Amerindians (two percent of the population.)

## Languages

Although English is the official language, most people speak Vincentian Creole, also known as "Vincy English." A French patois is spoken on some of the smaller islands.

## Native People & Ethnic Groups

It is possible that St. Vincent's first inhabitants were the Ciboney. Little is known about these hunter-gatherers, beyond some shell and stone tool artifacts left on many Caribbean islands. After the Ciboney came the Arawak Indians, who arrived from Venezuela and spread north and west through the West Indies. A peaceful people, the Arawak were farmers and fishermen. Numerous sites throughout the Caribbean yield archaeological evidence of their culture.

Around 1300 CE, the Arawaks were displaced by the warlike Caribs, also from South America. The aggressiveness of the Caribs discouraged settlement of St. Vincent, but eventually the island was colonized.

The British gained control of St. Vincent in 1783, but a few years later Chatoyer, chief of the black Caribs (a mixture of Africans and Amerindians), began a rebellion against the British. The chief's forces were eventually defeated, and in 1796, he was forced to surrender. His people were exiled the next year. The Garifuna people of Belize have traced their roots to this event.

On March 14, 2002, Chief Chatoyer was declared the first National Hero of St. Vincent and the Grenadines. National Heroes Day, an official holiday in his honor, is observed on March 14.

## Religions

St. Vincent and the Grenadines is a secular state, with no established church. Estimates of membership percentages vary widely. The Methodist and Anglican churches count a large percentage of the inhabitants as members. Other religions include Roman Catholic, Hindu, and Muslim.

## Climate

The climate of St. Vincent and the Grenadines is tropical, with little seasonal variation. Temperatures range from 18° to 32° Celsius (64° to 90° Fahrenheit). The average annual temperature is 27° Celsius (81° Fahrenheit). Humidity is high throughout the year.

The annual rainfall, which occurs mostly from May to November, ranges from about 1,500 millimeters (60 inches) in the south to 3,750 millimeters (150 inches) in the mountains of St. Vincent.

St. Vincent and the Grenadines are somewhat vulnerable to hurricanes, though the islands are barely within the hurricane belt, and tropical storms are much more common. La Soufrière is an ever-present volcanic threat.

## ENVIRONMENT & GEOGRAPHY

## Topography

Part of the Windward Islands group of the West Indies, St. Vincent and the Grenadines lies 160 kilometers (100 miles) west of Barbados. St. Lucia lies 34 kilometers (21 miles) to the northeast. The small country has a coastline of 84 kilometers (52 miles). St. Vincent and the Grenadines is 320 kilometers (200 miles) north of Venezuela.

St. Vincent is the country's largest island, approximately 29 kilometers (18 miles) long and 18 kilometers (11 miles) wide. The country's capital and largest urban area, Kingstown, is located on the island's southern coast. The fertile Buccament River valley lies in the southwest corner of the island.

St. Vincent is volcanic and mountainous, with steep valleys and numerous waterfalls. La Soufrière, an active volcano, rises to 1,219 meters (4,040 feet) in the northern part of the island, and is the country's highest point. The volcano last erupted in 1979.

The largest of the 32 tiny Grenadine islands, or cays (pronounced "keys"), are Bequia, Mustique, Canouan, Mayreau, Isle D'Quatre, and Union Island.

## Plants & Animals

Tropical vegetation covers most of the islands' area. The biodiversity is impressive. Sea grass and mangroves are abundant throughout the islands. The blossom of the soufrière tree is the national flower.

In the Buccament River valley alone, numerous fruits and vegetables grow, including pineapples, plums, bananas, avocado, citrus fruits, wild yams, breadfruit, wild spinach, pigeon peas, pumpkins, and cucumbers.

Many plants in the same area are used for medicinal purposes. These include bwa kwabit, castor bean, broom, river senna, bird pepper, wild tamarind, mint, watergrass, black sage, mahoe, verveine, and wedelia.

Endemic birds, found only in St. Vincent and the Grenadines, include the Lesser Antillean tanager, whistling warbler, and the Grenada flycatcher. The protected St. Vincent parrot, the national bird, is the only parrot found on the islands.

Endangered animals of St. Vincent include the St. Vincent pygmy rice rat, leatherback and hawksbill turtles, and the humpback whale. A number of birds are on the endangered list, including the St. Vincent parrot, the whistling warbler, black hawk, cocoa thrush, crested hummingbird and red-capped green tanager, among others.

Several species of dolphins, including the spinner, spotted, and bottlenose, are found in the waters surrounding the islands. Pilot whales, orcas, and other whales are also seen. The coral reefs are filled with marine species, including grouper, herring, mackerel, marlin, sailfish, snapper, tuna, angelfish, and sharks.

St. Vincent and the Grenadines is also home to snakes, tree lizards, geckoes, and iguanas. Amphibians include tree frogs, piping frogs, and pond frogs. The Buccament valley is home to crustaceans such as crayfish and crabs, including a rare species of hermit crab.

## CUSTOMS & COURTESIES

### Greetings

English is the official language of St. Vincent and the Grenadines, but it is spoken with a distinct West Indian accent. The phrases "Good morning," "Good afternoon," and "Good evening" are the basic expressions used for greeting, though Vincentians tend to use liberal abbreviations and altered forms of English. The Vincentians also commonly use the expression "How it gwain," meaning, "How are you."

In some parts of St. Vincent and the Grenadines, residents speak a form of French patois, common to many Caribbean nations with a history of French colonization. Those who speak patois may use the expressions "Bon jour" ("Good day") and "Bonne nuit" ("Good night"). Informally, patois speakers say "Salut" ("Hi") to friends and friendly acquaintances.

Shaking hands is the most common form of greeting in Vincentian culture. Friends and relatives may embrace or kiss on greeting. While Vincentians tend to be friendly and informal in manner, men customarily display a reserved attitude when greeting women for the first time and allow the woman to initiate conversation.

### Gestures & Etiquette

Most activities in St. Vincent and the Grenadines are handled at a different pace than in Western culture. As with many island cultures, Vincentians tend to take a relaxed approach to scheduling and performing daily functions, and most schedules are seen as highly flexible. This pace of life has been ingrained into local culture to such an extent that attempts to rush Vincentians may be meet with surprise and annoyance.

Although Vincentians tend to take a relaxed attitude about some social customs, they have strong prohibitions against indecency. Most notably, they dress very conservatively. On Sunday, in particular, many Vincentians dress up for church and generally expect visitors to dress in decent or conservative attire when in town. For business meetings, Vincentians prefer modest, conservative suits and ties, though meetings taking place over lunch and at outdoor venues may call for more casual attire.

## Eating/Meals

Most Vincentians eat three meals a day, corresponding to breakfast, lunch and dinner. The morning meal is generally substantial and usually consists of baked goods, fruit, and some variety of meat, whether goat, pork, or fish. There are several varieties of coffee locally grown in St. Vincent and the Grenadines, and many residents drink coffee with their morning meal. Because Vincentians tend to eat large morning meals, the afternoon meal is typically light by comparison and may consist of leftovers from the morning meal or small fare like sandwiches and fruit. Before the evening meal, some Vincentians break from their activities to have afternoon tea, a tradition that was brought to the islands from Europe.

The evening meal is the primary time for family socialization. Many Vincentians invite guests to their homes for the evening meal, which is also the time of the day when islanders unveil their most complex dishes. A variety of roasted meat dishes, seafood dishes and curries are commonly served in the evening, as well as cocktails made with rum or cane spirits (rum is an important export of the island nation).

## Visiting

It is considered polite, but not expected, to bring small gifts when visiting a Vincentian home. Flowers, candies, and baked goods are appropriate gifts, as well as small toys for children of the house. When bringing flowers, it is important to note that white flowers, especially lilies, are commonly used for mourning and funerary ceremonies, while roses are often taken to signify romantic intentions.

Visitors often remark on the warm hospitality of the Vincentian people, who will typically spare little expense to make guests comfortable. Despite widespread poverty, guests to Vincentian homes will usually be offered something to eat and drink. It is considered polite to sample any food or drink offered, though guests are not required to finish their food and/or drink.

## LIFESTYLE

## Family

Extended family systems are an important part of Vincentian culture, especially given that illegitimacy and single-parent households have become increasingly common in the 21st century. It is estimated that more than 40 percent of Vincentian children are born to unwed mothers, and women tend to bear a majority of the domestic and child-rearing duties.

Young men in St. Vincent and Grenadines commonly engage in "visiting unions," in which men will temporarily stay with the mother of their children while maintaining their own residence. While the high cost of marriage is a contributing factor to the visiting family custom, it has been integrated into the basic social fabric and is an increasingly common practice. It is not uncommon for women to have children with more than one man and shift responsibility for child-rearing to older female members of her family.

Infrequent male participation in child-rearing has fostered the development of matrilineal family structures in Vincentian society. Young mothers frequently rely on the participation of grandparents, sisters, and aunts in caring for children and providing for household needs. When young couples choose to marry, they commonly settle near the wife's extended family.

## Housing

While there are some colonial era buildings and homes remaining on St. Vincent and the Grenadines, most islanders live in modest one- or two-bedroom homes constructed of wood or stone. Many homes are constructed of imported materials, and importing stone and brick has become a major industry. Bamboo fencing is common in rural areas and around some urban homes, giving the houses a unique, island appearance.

Many families decorate their homes with handcrafted wooden furniture, which is affordable through local vendors. In addition, most families have decorations similar to homes in parts of England and France. Rural homes rarely have central utilities or running water and many villages share a communal sewage and irrigation system located in the center of the village or town. Uneven terrain, owing to the nation's volcanic origin, makes housing difficult to establish in highland areas; as a result, most residents live in the low-lying zones. Many villages are located near the coast or along naturally occurring springs and rivers. Houses are also clustered in the areas immediately surrounding productive agricultural zones.

## Food

Food plays an important role in Vincentian culture and is part of every celebration and family event. The natives are proud of their local cuisine, which includes elements of African, European, and West Indian culinary traditions. Most native dishes are spicy and contain some variety of meat—either goat, fish, or chicken—and a starchy side dish or accompaniment. Locals refer to starchy foods such as rice, pasta, and bread as "provisions."

Like many Caribbean islands, seafood is one of the pillars of Vincentian nutrition and cuisine. A variety of fish are found near the islands, including red snapper, kingfish, and cod. Saltfish and peas is a popular dish on the islands, which is prepared by roasting chunks of fish and serving them with a mix of rice and pigeon peas. The dish may also be spiced with curry or hot peppers.

Like many Caribbean nations, Vincentians make extensive use of conch, a marine mollusk. One preparation for the mollusk is to make conch souse, a dish that uses boiled strips of conch meat, seasoned with salt and lime, and combined with a "pickled" preparation of parsley, peppers, onion, and cucumber.

The Vincentians also make extensive use of goat meat in their dishes. A popular presentation is to cook chunks of goat meat into a stew made with tomatoes and spices. To this mixture, Vincentians add various vegetables such as breadfruit (a vegetable that was imported to the islands and has become a popular replacement for starchy foods like rice and pasta). Breadfruit is very common on the islands and is also eaten alone, either roasted or fried, as a snack.

Another popular Caribbean dish often served in St. Vincent and the Grenadines is a soup made with callaloo, the leaves of a plant locally known as dasheen or taro. Though there are numerous recipes, most callaloo soups use coconut milk as the base, with crushed taro and onion providing the primary flavors. Some use spinach, kale, or other greens to replace the taro leaves, thereby giving the dish a different flavor. The leaves of the taro plant are also served steamed or fried to accompany various dishes and may also be mixed into salads.

For dessert, Vincentians enjoy simple fare, including some of the many varieties of tropical fruits available on the island. Among other fruits, Vincentian farms produce star fruit, papaya, coconut, and mango. One popular dessert is banana bread, which is created with a variety of short, fat bananas locally called "figs." Other local specialties include lime pie, which is made with tart limes mixed with sugar and custard.

## Life's Milestones

A majority of Vincentians are Christian and follow standard Christian rights of passage, including baptism, communion, marriage, and funerary rites. Baptism is a time to form bonds among extended family members, and mothers typically invite a large party to their homes for a post-baptism feast. While families also celebrate a child's first communion, the celebrations are typically smaller in scale.

While marriage traditionally marks the transition to adulthood in Christian culture, more Vincentians prefer cohabitation to marriage, and the importance of marriage has declined in recent years. When they do decide to marry, most Vincentians prefer modest ceremonies with a few friends and family members invited to their homes after a small church wedding. In the Rastafarian tradition, popular in some parts of the country, individuals may be married in their home with a Rastafarian priest conducting the ceremony.

As in many West Indian countries, funerals are an important occasion for networking and maintaining community bonds. The importance of funerary customs in West Indian culture is thought to be a remnant of African ancestor worship modified through Christian tradition. Vincentian funerals are similar to those held in British tradition, with a somber church service followed by a gathering of friends and family.

## CULTURAL HISTORY

### Art

Like many island natives, early Vincentian artisans tended to use supplies that were readily available on the island for their artistic endeavors. Palm fronds were woven into baskets and decorative artistic creations, shells and fish teeth were made into jewelry, and gourds and coconut husks were carved into wooden sculptures. Additionally, stemming from the whaling heritage of the island of Bequia is the art of scrimshaw (handicrafts created from the byproducts of whaling). These makeshift items eventually developed into artistic traditions passed from generation to generation.

One of the most popular folk arts on St. Vincent and the Grenadines is dressmaking. Fabrics taken from local livestock are woven into skirts and dresses and dyed to create colorful patterns and thematic decorations. The images of local birds and plants are a common motif for Vincentian dresses and decorated clothing. Many skilled dressmakers also contribute to the Vincy Mas celebration, creating Carnival dresses for attendees and dancers.

Painters and sculptors on the islands also tend to favor discarded material as a medium for their artwork. One self-trained artist, Nzimbu Browne (1955–), uses the refuse from the annual banana crop to create works of art. Browne uses ground plantain, fig, and other botanicals to create a palette of brown and tan paints. He has painted numerous landscapes and images of street life, but has also used his "banana art" to depict the inside of the St. Vincent courthouse and other unique subjects. Another native artist who has become well known throughout the Caribbean is Joseph Esquina, a former soldier who absorbed painting techniques from the people of Samoa and Tahiti during time spent abroad. Esquina concentrates on landscape-style oil paintings, usually depicting scenes of everyday island life in muted colors. He is one of the few local artists to gain international fame, selling his works to collectors in Europe and North America.

### Architecture

Colonial Kingston best exemplifies the varying architectural styles that have influenced Saint Vincent and the Grenadines over the centuries. The city is, in fact, nicknamed the "city of arches" due to the number of historic buildings that employ the European-influenced architectural structure, including the 19th-century, dark-bricked St. Mary's Roman Catholic Cathedral, whose architectural styles range from Romanesque to Moorish (as well as Gothic-inspired spires), and the historic Cobblestone Inn. Additionally, the Anglican cathedral of St. George's is known for its original stained glass ornamentation and Georgian-style architecture, while Fort Charlotte, on the outskirts of the capital, is a great example of British 19th-century military architecture. Lastly, the use of cobblestone, in streets and on frontal facades, also illustrates the prevalence of colonial-style influences.

### Music

The annual Carnival celebration, known as "Vincy Mas," brings together the island's dance, music, and theatrical traditions into a single, island-wide celebration. The Carnival tradition reaches back to pagan celebrations linked to the changing seasons. After Christianity became the dominant religion in Europe, the festivities were integrated into the Christian tradition of Lent (the period leading up to Easter). When the Carnival started on St. Vincent in the 1890s, it was celebrated as a pre-Lenten festival on the Tuesday prior to Ash Wednesday. The early Carnival celebrations, which involved community feasting, dancing, and music, were held only among the lower classes. Calypso music, an Afro-Caribbean style of music, was introduced to the island at the turn of the century and was quickly integrated into the festivities. Eventually, the festival grew to occupy the entire week before Lent.

In the 1960s, immigrants from Trinidad introduced the steel band concept at Vincy Mas. The steel band phenomenon, now recognized as a central element in Caribbean music, began as a street performance in which a percussionist would entertain crowds by playing various makeshift metal instruments, like pots and pans recycled from the kitchen. Eventually, more refined steel drums began to appear and the tradition spread throughout the Caribbean. The steel band became an integral part of Vincy Mas. By the mid-1970s, the various musical performances at Vincy Mas had been organized into competitions for, among other prizes, best performance, best new band, and best dancer. Among the more popular competitions are the annual calypso competition and the steel band competition. In addition, Vincy Mas was integrated with the local pageant scene and each year the state awards beauty pageant winners for "Miss St. Vincent and the Grenadines" and "Miss Carnival."

In 1977, in an effort to attract more tourists by setting Vincy Mas apart from other Caribbean Carnivals, the newly organized Carnival Development Committee (CDC) moved the celebration to June; most other Carnivals are held in December and January. The modern carnival still features traditional music and dance performances, but has integrated modern sounds such as electronica music at makeshift outdoor dance clubs.

## Literature

Few Vincentian writers have gained international attention for their work, as the literary community is still relatively young and emerging from a recent transition to independence. One of the first local writers to gain national impact was Horatio Nelson Huggins (1830–1895). He penned an epic poem entitled *Hiroona* in the mid-1880s about the struggle of the native Carib tribe against the colonial invaders. The poem was later published in 1930, but earlier works were published in the late 19th century, such as a protest poem about the pollution from a large sugar refinery.

H. Nigel Thomas (1947–), who relocated to Canada and became a teacher, was one of the few island natives to make a significant international impact as a novelist. His novels *Spirits of the Dark* (1993) and *Behind the Face of Winter* (2001) were both nominated for international literary awards. Thomas is also an important authority on Caribbean writing and has contributed to anthologies and scholarly evaluations of literature in the eastern Caribbean.

## CULTURE

## Arts & Entertainment

Although Vincentians are proud of their native arts and craft traditions, there is little funding available from the central government to promote arts education or to involve local artists in official functions. Elementary and secondary schools include art and music instruction as part of the basic curriculum, though instruction is limited to basic artistic skills. In addition, there are few organizations active in maintaining native folk arts and traditions. These traditions, such as potting, dressmaking, and woodcarving, have been maintained largely through informal apprenticeships with established artisans.

Government funding for the arts is available for theater groups, musical groups, and other participants in the annual Carnival celebration. Funding is distributed through a number of government organizations, and organized by the Ministry of Culture. In an effort to promote tourism and preserve native culture, the government also provides some limited funding for annual musical celebrations.

Music in St. Vincent reflects the nation's multi-ethnic heritage. Typical music heard on the islands includes steel pan, soca, calypso, and drum music. The islands also host annual blues and gospel festivals. The Carol Singing Competition and Nine Mornings festivals are held in December.

Both soccer and cricket are popular sports among Vincentians. St. Vincent has thirteen professional soccer clubs, and numerous Vincentian professional cricket players have represented the West Indies in international competition. Other popular sports include basketball and netball. Vincentians also enjoy snorkeling and diving, sailing, and windsurfing. The islands are also known for boat building.

## Cultural Sites & Landmarks

St. Vincent Island offers a wealth of historic cultural attractions for visitors, ranging from the colonial architecture of the island's administrative buildings and churches to modern museums and ecological parks. The Kingstown Market in downtown Kingstown is the social and commercial center of the island. Hundreds of residents gather each day to buy and sell goods, conduct business, and socialize with friends and associates.

Near the Kingstown market visitors can find two of the island's oldest buildings: St. George's Anglican Church and St. Mary's Catholic Cathedral. St. George's is a large white building originally constructed in the mid-1800s and repaired in the 1930s. The building is noted for its collection of stained glass appointments, a feature common to most Georgian-style churches of the period. One of the windows in the church was originally built for England's Queen Victoria

(1819–1901), but was later given to the bishop of St. Vincent and now hangs in the church. St. Mary's Cathedral was built in 1823 and refurbished in the 1930s under the supervision of a visiting Flemish monk. In addition to its architectural importance, a combination of early colonial and Flemish design, the building is notable for its materials, as it was constructed entirely from native volcanic rock.

Many of the historic homes of Kingstown were built during the 19th century, with bricks that were brought to the island by European trading vessels. The bricks were often used as ballast on the voyage to St. Vincent, which were then replaced with sugar and molasses for the return trip back to Europe.

In the Montrose area of Kingstown is the Botanic Gardens, founded in 1765, making them the oldest such gardens in the West Indies and the Western Hemisphere. Collections of tropical plants representing the island's original botanical complement are interspersed with collections of plants from around the world. Certain varieties of trees have been growing in the gardens for more than two centuries. One of the breadfruit trees in the park was reportedly grown from seeds brought by Captain William Bligh (1754–1817). A famous figure in Caribbean history, he is believed responsible for introducing numerous agricultural products such as breadfruit and cassava to the region. Bligh had previously survived the mutiny of the HMS Bounty in 1789 and returned to St. Vincent with these and other botanicals in later years.

The coastal waters off the Grenadines have long been prized by scuba divers for their diverse communities of fish and marine invertebrates. The Tobago Cays and Mayreau Island are two of the most popular spots for scuba diving expeditions. Thousands of species live in the coastal communities, which are protected by the government as a marine park and have been submitted to the United National Educational, Scientific, and Cultural Organization (UNESCO) as a possible World Heritage Site. The cays serve as a breeding ground for hundreds of species of tropical fish. At certain times of the year, they are filled with thousands of young fish feeding off the populations of plankton and small invertebrates that populate the nutrient-rich waters.

The Marriqua Valley is another popular location for visitors to the islands. Known for its natural beauty, the cultivated lowlands contain fields of planted trees, including nutmeg, coconut, and banana, while the surrounding hills are rich with native species. The valley leads to Grand Bonhomme Mountain, a 924-meter (3,129-foot) peak popular with mountain climbers and hikers. Hundreds of migrating birds visit the valley as well as many native species including hummingbirds, doves, and parrots.

Another popular natural attraction on the island is La Soufrière Volcano, the highest peak on St. Vincent at 1,234 meters (4,048 feet). "Soufrière" is French for "sulfur outlet." The sides of the mountain, with soil created by ancient lava flows, are covered with tropical vegetation, bamboo, and rainforest communities. As the volcano erupted in 1979, recently by geological standards, the mountain attracts hundreds of amateur and professional volcanologists each year and is the site of several ongoing geological studies.

## Libraries & Museums

The National Trust of St. Vincent and the Grenadines (SVG) is dedicated to preserving the historic and cultural heritage and biodiversity of the island nation. In the Old Carnegie Public Library in the capital of Kingstown—designated the first Protected National Heritage structure in 2009—is housed the National Inventory of Archaeological Resources, which features a permanent exhibition of ancient Amerindian culture. The archaeological museum is home to numerous pre-Columbian artifacts and other historical displays. Another unique museum is located on the island of Bequia, known for its whaling heritage. The Bequia Maritime Museum contains numerous whaling and maritime artifacts and displays, and focuses on the art of boat building as well. Other museums include permanent display about the history of Black Caribs, housed in the old barracks of Fort Charlotte, and an exhibition on

the history of the famed Botanical Gardens, displayed in the gardens' restored Curator's House.

## Holidays

Official holidays observed in St. Vincent and the Grenadines include National Heroes' Day (March 14), which honors Carib Chief Chatoyer, Labor Day (May 1), and Independence Day (October 27). Emancipation Day, marking the abolition of slavery in 1834, is celebrated on August 1. Carnival Monday is the first Monday in July, followed by Carnival Tuesday.

## Youth Culture

Youth in St. Vincent and the Grenadines enjoy a variety of recreational and social options. Young children generally gather into groups within their neighborhoods and villages to play games and socialize. Cricket and football (soccer) are the most popular sports, and most towns and villages have set aside a green space for matches. St. Vincent and the Grenadines is a member of the West Indies Cricket Association and many children follow the progress of their national team. Singing and dancing are also popular activities for youth, and young children develop improvisational songs in a competitive fashion, similar to adult Calypso musicians who improvise verses during contests.

Teenagers in St. Vincent and the Grenadines have been more affected by imported culture from North America and Europe. Clothing, music, and film from the United States are prized among teenagers, as these items are not widely available. Music from elsewhere in the Caribbean also plays an important role in teen culture. Reggae and hip-hop music are increasingly popular in St. Vincent and the Grenadines, and many teenagers form musical groups and perform at local venues.

Widespread poverty forces many pre-teens in St. Vincent and the Grenadines to begin work at a young age. Many children work in family businesses, especially in families living in agricultural areas. After time spent assisting in the family business, teenagers may migrate to the cities to find work. Education is free and compulsory for children until age 16, and enrollment rates have been estimated at close to 100 percent for primary education.

## SOCIETY

### Transportation
Urban transportation is mostly composed of small minivans that tend to be crowded and operate on inconsistent schedules. Bus travel is cheap, though most buses make frequent stops along their routes and there are no express bus lines. In the cities, visitors can also obtain passage from taxis and private minibuses, which provide travel within the islands. Few private vehicles provide metered fare.

For travel between the islands, a number of ferries offer affordable public transport, and some also transport cars for those owning or renting automobiles. Most ferries begin offering trips between St. Vincent and surrounding islands in the early morning and end in the evening, so travelers may need to arrange for sleeping quarters if visiting one of the islands in the evening.

Traffic moves on the left side of the road. Nighttime driving is discouraged in the islands' mountainous areas due to unsafe conditions such as steep inclines and lack of guardrails.

### Transportation Infrastructure
There are approximately 829 kilometers (515 miles) of roads of which 580 kilometers (360 miles) are surfaced or paved. The island nation has six airports, five of which are paved. ET Joshua International, located in Kingston, is the sole international airport in St. Vincent and the Grenadines. However, the airport is too small to accept jet aircraft and only serves smaller planes from nearby airports. International visitors from the United States and Europe are therefore forced to stop in another Caribbean location to switch to a smaller aircraft for access to the islands. Most connecting flights arrive in Barbados, St. Lucia, and Puerto Rico. The airport is set to be replaced by a state-owned international airport in Argyle;

however, the opening of Argyle International has been beset by delays. As of October 2015, the airport is slated to open by the end of the year.

### Media & Communications
The Vincentian constitution guarantees freedom of the press and there are no censorship restrictions governing the content of radio, television, or Internet broadcasts. Publications and broadcast media regularly criticize government policy without fear of reprisal.

In 2008, there were eight FM and one AM station in operation on the islands. NBC Radio, the nation's most popular network, is partially funded through government grants, and broadcasts news and official information in addition to entertainment programming. St. Vincent and the Grenadines has a single locally produced and privately-owned television station, SVG Television. It provides news and entertainment, including programs rebroadcast from elsewhere in the Caribbean. In addition to public television, Vincentians have access to cable television in the cities and surrounding areas.

The nation has a single daily newspaper, *The Herald,* and three weekly papers, *The News*, *Searchlight,* and *The Vincentian*, which are all privately owned. Local newspapers are printed in English, but merchants import a variety of international publications in French and Spanish in Kingstown and other urban areas.

Internet coverage continues to be in a state of expansion, with more than 100 providers increasing network coverage on all of the inhabited islands. High speed Internet is only available in Kingston and Georgetown though some smaller cities have begun to implement high speed Internet. As of 2009, there were an estimated 76,000 Internet users, 73 percent of the population.

## SOCIAL DEVELOPMENT

### Standard of Living
The country ranked 91 out of 187 nations on the 2013 United Nations Human Development Index (HDI), which measures quality of life indicators.

## Water Consumption

The island of Saint Vincent has a readily available source of water, extracted mostly from rivers and streams; outlying islands employ rain harvesting methods and desalination techniques, or may receive water from the main island. Approximately 90 percent of the population has access to a pipe-borne water supply. The water supply does not support the island nation's agricultural sector, and there are generally no official water policies or records of use and consumption.

## Education

Education in St. Vincent and the Grenadines is compulsory from ages five through 15. Public education is free at the primary and secondary levels, but parents must buy school uniforms and books, as well as supply bus fare. Textbooks and sports equipment are not always available. About one-quarter of students do not finish primary school because they have to work to help support their family. Students who complete secondary school may go on for two years of advanced studies. The government fully funds public schools and provides some financial support for private, church-related schools.

Recent educational reforms have allowed the use of Vincentian Creole in schools. Also, the curriculum now provides vocational courses as well as academic subjects. The average literacy rate is estimated at 96 percent for those 15 years or older. The primary school net enrollment rate is nearly 100 percent; however, an estimated 31 percent drop out before reaching the secondary level. Overall, school life expectancy is 13 years.

St. Vincent has polytechnics (technical and nursing schools) and the Kingstown Medical College, an affiliate campus of St. George's University of Grenada. It is estimated that three times as many Vincentian women as men attend college.

## Women's Rights

There are no laws in St. Vincent and the Grenadines specifically addressing domestic abuse. However, domestic battery and violence are considered criminal acts under laws governing assault. While there were no statistics available on the number of domestic assault cases handled in the courts, international NGOs and domestic organizations like the St. Vincent and the Grenadines Human Rights Association (SVGHRA) report that women are reluctant to report abuse and that few women decide to press charges in domestic violence cases. Some reports also indicate that police are reluctant to follow through on prosecuting domestic assault charges because women are not likely to testify against their spouses when the case comes to trial.

The state provides counseling and psychological services to abused women and their families through the Gender Affairs Division of the Ministry of National Mobilization. The Marion House, a non-profit welfare services organization headquartered in Kingston, provides shelter and counseling for women and children who are victims of abuse. In conjunction with SVGHRA, the Marion House also sent counselors to public venues to educate women regarding their legal rights. In 2008, the SVGHRA reported that some courts were imposing fines against victims who brought charges but refused to testify in court. Though the measure was intended to increase cooperation from victims, some NGOs were concerned that fines for failing to testify would further discourage women from taking action against abusive spouses.

Although women are guaranteed equal rights under the constitution and are guaranteed equal pay under the minimum wage laws, evidence suggests that women are often paid less than male counterparts. Laws provide equal ownership of property in cases of divorce, and the justice system regularly enforces these laws in divorce cases.

## Health Care

Medical care is free for children under the age of 17. Also, the government provides free family planning, prenatal, and postnatal services. Lower medical fees are charged for the unemployed, the elderly, and poorer families.

Average life expectancy among Vincentians is approximately 75 years; 73 years for men and

77 years for women (2015 estimate). The major causes of death are circulatory diseases, followed by cancer; disorders of the endocrine and metabolic systems; infectious and parasitic diseases; and respiratory disorders.

The infant mortality rate is 13 deaths per 1,000 live births (2015 estimate).

The island nation has six public hospitals and three that are privately-owned. There are nearly 40 outpatient clinics, which provide a range of health-related services such as midwifery and emergency care.

# GOVERNMENT

## Structure

St. Vincent and the Grenadines is a constitutional monarchy with a unicameral legislature and universal suffrage at age 18. The chief of state is the British monarch, represented in the islands by the governor general, who is appointed on advice of the prime minister (PM). The head of government is the prime minister, who must retain the support of a majority in the legislature. Parliament consists of the governor general and the 21 member House of Assembly. Fifteen representatives are directly elected for five-year terms, and the remaining six representatives are appointed by the governor general. The governor-general also appoints cabinet ministers; the cabinet is responsible to the House.

## Political Parties

There are two dominant political parties in St. Vincent and the Grenadines: the New Democratic Party (NDP) and the Unity Labour Party (ULP). Following the 2010 general election, the Unity Labour Party won eight parliamentary seats while the NDP won seven. Other political parties include the National Reform Party, the People's Progressive Movement, the Progressive Labor Party, the United People's Movement, and the Saint Vincent and the Grenadines Green Party, none of which enjoyed popular electoral support or were represented in parliament after the 2010 elections.

## Local Government

St. Vincent and the Grenadines, which is divided into the six parishes (administrative units) of Charlotte, Grenadines, St Andrew, St David, St George, and St Patrick, has no form of local governance. Considered units of the central government, these parishes are only responsible for a small number of activities and services.

## Judicial System

The Eastern Caribbean Supreme Court is the highest court, and has jurisdiction over several Caribbean countries. Two judges of the court reside in St. Vincent and the Grenadines. There are 11 local courts in three magisterial districts and a High Court. The country's legal system is based on English common law. Final appeal rests with the Privy Council in the United Kingdom.

## Taxation

The country, which implemented tax reforms in 2009, maintains a top personal income tax rate of 32.5 percent, as well as a corporate tax rate of 32.5. Other levied taxes include a value-added tax (VAT) and a property tax.

## Foreign Policy

St. Vincent and the Grenadines is an active member of the international community and belongs to, among other international organizations, the United Nations (UN), the Caribbean Community (CARICOM), the Organization of Eastern Caribbean States (OECS) and the Association of American States (OAS). The government's primary concern is to engage in international agreements to strengthen the country's economic position and facilitate trade.

Most of the nation's exports go to other Caribbean states or Europe. The nation also has strong economic relationship with Singapore, which provides many of the nation's imports, including machinery and electronics. After Singapore, other Caribbean states, China and the United States contribute the most imports to the country. St. Vincent and the Grenadines has cooperated closely with the United States in the international effort to prevent drug trafficking in the Caribbean. The United States also provides developmental aid to the nation through the World Bank.

St. Vincent and the Grenadines has been actively involved in the ongoing effort to preserve ecological diversity and animal populations in coastal waters. These efforts have included limits on fishing and commercial exploitation of littoral habitat. St. Vincent and the Grenadines is also one of the Caribbean nations that opposed Venezuela's effort to expand its maritime territory by claiming that the Aves Islands were capable of supporting human habitation.

## Human Rights Profile

International human rights law insists that states respect civil and political rights, and also promote an individual's economic, social, and cultural rights. The United Nations Universal Declaration on Human Rights (UDHR) is recognized as the standard for international human rights. Its authors sought the counsel of the world's great thinkers, philosophers, and religious leaders, and were careful to create a document that reflects the core values shared by every world culture. (To read this document or view the articles relating to cultural human rights, go to: http://www.udhr. org/UDHR/default.htm.)

Although the parliamentary democracy of St. Vincent and the Grenadines generally respects the rights of citizens in compliance with the UDHR, several human rights concerns remain, including violence against women and children, an overburdened prison system, and insufficient supervision of police.

The St. Vincent and Grenadines Human Rights Association (SVGHRA) reported in 2008 that police sometimes used unnecessary force and violence to coerce confessions from suspects, a violation of Article 5 guaranteeing freedom from inhumane treatment. The SVGHRA has further claimed that the nation has insufficient measures in place to monitor and control police activity. The SVGHRA and other foreign non-governmental organizations (NGOs) have reported that detainees are not given adequate access to counsel and other assistance. There

have been accusations of corruption within the judicial system, especially in cases where public officials or members of the police have been accused of crimes. Because of lack of personnel and funding, detainees were forced to wait for long periods before being brought to trial.

The United Nations has criticized the St. Vincent and the Grenadines government for failing to create specific laws to prohibit racial discrimination. The United Nations recommended, in 2003, that St. Vincent and the Grenadines amend its constitution to include statutes prohibiting discrimination on the basis of racial, ethnic, linguistic, and economic basis. Some NGOs have reported that persons with disabilities, persons of alternative sexual orientation, and persons suffering from HIV/AIDS are sometimes the victims of discrimination, a violation of Article 7 of the UDHR. Members of the Rastafarian religion in St. Vincent and the Grenadines complained to representatives of several NGOs that they were discriminated against in hiring practices.

Her Majesty's Prison, in Kingstown, was built in 1872 to hold approximately 150 inmates, but has regularly exceeded this limit. In 2014, the prison population was measured at 412. Overcrowding in the prison system exacerbated existing concerns regarding sanitary and medical care within the prison system. NGO investigations of the prison system reported that drug use, widespread violence, and institutional corruption were common. The SVGHRA also criticized the government for housing young and juvenile offenders with the adult population, a violation of Article 25 of the UDHR requiring special treatment for youth.

Although the island nation's penal code is in keeping with the recommendations made by the United Nations Committee on the Rights of the Child, some NGOs have reported that child abuse is common in rural areas and not adequately addressed by police. Traditional cultural norms permitting corporal punishment in the home was one of the primary factors preventing the government from addressing child abuse, as few incidents were reported to authorities.

## ECONOMY

### Overview of the Economy

The economy of St. Vincent and the Grenadines is based on tourism and agriculture. While hurricanes are rare, tropical storms are frequent and sometimes devastating. Crops suffered tremendous damage from storms in 1994, 1995, and 2002. St. Vincent is the world's leading producer of arrowroot, which is used to make starch.

Tourism is sensitive not only to the weather but also to world politics. Tourist traffic in the entire eastern Caribbean dropped off after the September 2001 terrorist attacks. The development of offshore banking services has helped to diversify the economy.

In 2014, the per capita gross domestic product (GDP) was estimated at $10,800 (USD). The unemployment rate is estimated at 18.8 percent. According to the Central Intelligence Agency (CIA), the island nations' GDP increased at an annual rate of nearly 1.1 percent between 2013 and 2014.

### Industry

The islands' major industries include the production and processing of copra, raw sugar, rum, and starch. Other industries include electricity production, food processing, and furniture and clothing manufacturing.

The country's exports generated an estimated $48.2 million (USD) in 2014. The biggest export is bananas, which account for almost half of the nation's exports. Arrowroot starch and taro are other important agricultural exports.

### Labor

The labor force of St. Vincent and the Grenadines is estimated at approximately 57,520. The unemployment rate in 2008 was about 18.8 percent. The majority of the labor force is employed in the services sector, primarily reliant on tourism.

### Energy/Power/Natural Resources

There are no native sources of coal, oil, and natural gas, and St. Vincent's major natural resources are fertile farmland and hydropower (generating more than 20 percent of the island nation's electricity). All petroleum products and refined oil—the Caribbean country has no oil refineries—are imported. Alternative energy such as wind power and geothermal power projects are currently being explored.

Pollution of the islands' coastal waters is an environmental concern, as discharge from yachts has made the water is some areas unsafe for swimming. Tourist hotels and resorts are also damaging to the coastal areas. In addition, timbering and "slash-and-burn" agriculture is causing deforestation.

### Fishing

Fishing is generally small-scale and provides food for domestic consumption. The catch includes sardinellas, anchovies, albacore, mackerel, and Patagonian squid. The hunting of whales—the International Whaling Commission allows a four whale per year quota using traditional methods for Bequia natives—remains a highly sensitive environmental issue.

### Forestry

The cultivation of bananas and the illegal cultivation of marijuana have been primary factors in the ongoing deforestation on St. Vincent and the Grenadines. Urban development has also threatened coastal woodlands. Local timber is used for furniture, as well as residential, commercial, and boat construction.

### Mining/Metals

Mining and quarrying, basically for the production of cement, accounts for only a small role in the island nation's economy.

### Agriculture

Farming is concentrated on St. Vincent, where roughly one-third of the land is cultivated. Bananas are the chief crop, with 46,000 metric tons (twice as much as any other crop) grown each year. Coconuts are second, at 24,000 metric tons. Other crops include taro, sugarcane, yams, sweet potatoes, plantains, corn, citrus fruits, apples, and mangoes.

## Animal Husbandry

Vincentian farmers keep small numbers of sheep, pigs, cattle, goats, and donkeys. Livestock products include pork, cows' milk and eggs.

## Tourism

In 2013, St. Vincent and the Grenadines welcomed over 200,000 visitors, for receipts of more than $70 million (USD).

Tourist attractions include yachting facilities in the Grenadines, Kingstown Market, historic churches and cathedrals, the Botanical Gardens, and Fort Charlotte. There are resorts on many of the smaller uninhabited islands.

Swimming in one of the many waterfalls on St. Vincent is a popular tourist activity. Divers may use snorkels or scuba tanks to explore the coral reefs. Sea kayaking and yachting are other favorite activities. At Easter, the Bequia Island Regatta is open to international sailors as well as locals. Races include all sizes and types of crafts, even models and children's coconut boats.

Natural attractions include the Old Hegg Turtle Sanctuary, Tobago Cays Marine Park, and Owia Salt Pond. Outdoor enthusiasts also enjoy whale, dolphin and bird watching, volcano tours, and backpacking and hiking.

*Micah Issitt, Ellen Bailey*

## DO YOU KNOW?

- The 2003 Walt Disney Pictures film *Pirates of the Caribbean: The Curse of the Black Pearl* was filmed entirely in St. Vincent and the Grenadines. The city of Kingstown served as the base of operations for the film crew and cast. Although some of the elaborate sets were torn down during post-production, others have remained to become landmarks for tourists.

- The Tobago Cays were sold by a private owner to the government of St. Vincent and the Grenadines on the condition that a national park would be established and commercial activity forbidden. Building is not allowed on the cays, and visitors are asked to take their trash with them when they leave.

- Fort Charlotte, built in 1806, was named for the wife of England's King George III.

- Breadfruit is not native to the Caribbean. British Captain William Bligh was commissioned to import breadfruit to St. Vincent from Tahiti in 1789. That mission was thwarted when his crew mutinied and stole his ship, the *Bounty*. Four years later, he successfully landed at St. Vincent with a cargo of breadfruit trees.

- The capital of Kingston is nicknamed the "city of arches" due to the fact that it features over 400 arches in its infrastructure and colonial buildings.

## Bibliography

Henke, Holger. *Modern Political Culture in the Caribbean.* Kingston, Jamaica: University of the West Indies Press, 2003.

Knight, Franklin M. *The Modern Caribbean.* Durham, NC: The University of North Carolina Press, 1989.

Kuss, Malena, ed. *Music in Latin America and the Caribbean: An Encyclopedic History.* Austin, TX: University of Texas Press, 2004.

Martin, Kathy. *St. Vincent and the Grenadines.* New York: Macmillan Caribbean, 2003.

Sheller, Mimi. *Consuming the Caribbean: From Arawaks to Zombies.* New York: Routledge, 2003.

Sheridan, Richard B. *Sugar and Slavery: An Economic History of the British West Indies, 1623–1775.* Traverse City, MI: Canoe Press, 2000.

Sutty, Leslie. *St. Vincent and the Grenadines.* New York: Macmillan Caribbean, 2002.

Whitten, Norman E. and Arlene Torres. *Blackness in Latin America and the Caribbean: Social Dynamics and Cultural Transformations.* Bloomington, IN: Indiana University Press, 1998.

## Works Cited

"Country Profile: St. Vincent and Grenadines." *BBC News* Online. November 12, 2008. http://news.bbc.co.uk/2/hi/americas/country_profiles/1210689.stm

"Gov VC." Official Website of St. Vincent and Grenadines Government. http://www.gov.vc/govt/index.asp

"Human Development Reports: St. Vincent and the Grenadines." *United Nations Development Programme*. http://hdr.undp.org/en/countries/profiles/VCT

"2008 Human Rights Report: St. Vincent and Grenadines." Bureau of Democracy Human Rights and Labor. *U.S. Department of State* Online. http://www.state.gov/g/drl/rls/hrrpt/2008/wha/119173.htm

"The Marion House." *Marion House* Online. http://marionhousesvg.org/

"Political Database of the Americas: St. Vincent and Grenadines." *Georgetown University* Online. http://pdba.georgetown.edu/Constitutions/Vincent/stvincent.html

"St. Vincent and the Grenadines." Bureau of Western Hemisphere Affairs. *U.S. Department of State* Online. http://www.state.gov/r/pa/ei/bgn/2345.htm

"St Vincent and the Grenadines." *Caribbean Elections*. http://www.caribbeanelections.com/vc/results/default.asp

"St. Vincent and the Grenadines." *CIA World Factbook* Online. https://www.cia.gov/library/publications/the-world-factbook/geos/vc.html#Issues

"St. Vincent and the Grenadines." *City Population*. http://www.citypopulation.de/StVincent.html

"St. Vincent and the Grenadines." Introducing St. Vincent and the Grenadines. *Lonely Planet Press* Online. http://www.lonelyplanet.com/st-vincent-and-the-grenadines

"St. Vincent and the Grenadines." United Nations Human Rights. *OHCHR* Online. http://www.ohchr.org/EN/countries/LACRegion/Pages/VCIndex.aspx

"St. Vincent and the Grenadines." *World Health Organization*. Country Profiles. (Accessed October 19, 2015). Online http://www.who.int/countries/vct/en/

"St. Vincent and the Grenadines." *World Prison Brief*. http://www.prisonstudies.org/country/st-vincent-and-grenadines

"St. Vincent and the Grenadines." *UN Data*. http://data.un.org/CountryProfile.aspx?crName=Saint%20Vincent%20and%20the%20Grenadines

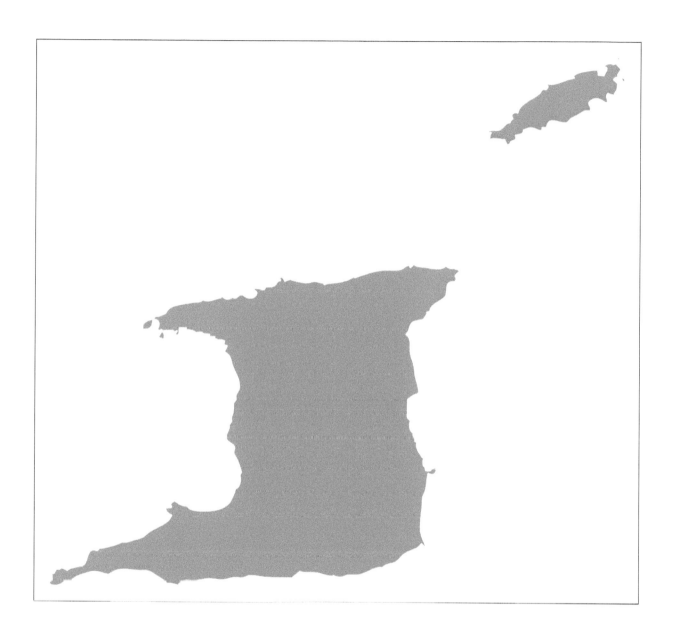

TRINIDAD & TOBAGO

# Introduction

Once a central point in the trading network of the Carib Indians, the twin island republic of Trinidad and Tobago is now a nation with a modern economy based on petroleum and tourism. Trinidad is the larger of the two islands, with an area about the size of the American state of Rhode Island. Together with its smaller and less-developed counterpart of Tobago, Trinidad has achieved a level of economic and political stability envied by many of its Caribbean neighbors.

Trinidad and Tobago is most famous for the musical traditions of calypso, soca, and steel pan music. Conversation is an important part of the culture, and the language of Trinidad & Tobago, known as Trini, is a mixture of English, the base language, and broken French, Hindu, Amerindian, and Spanish words and phrases, as well as dialects of African origin. The people of Trinidad & Tobago refer to themselves as Trinbagonians.

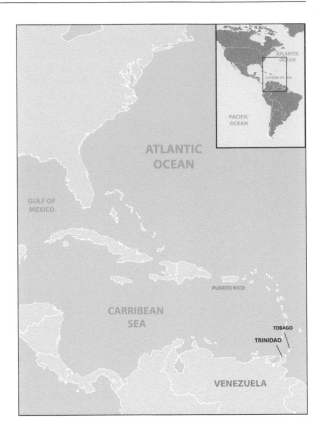

## GENERAL INFORMATION

**Official Language(s):** English
**Population:** 1,222,363 (2015 estimate)
**Currency:** Trinidad and Tobago dollar
**Coins:** The Trinidad and Tobago dollar comes in coin denominations of 1, 5, 10, 25, and 50.
**Land Area:** 5,128 square kilometers (1,978 square miles)
**National Motto:** "Together we aspire, together we achieve"

**National Anthem:** "Forged from the love of liberty"
**Capital:** Port of Spain
**Time Zone(s):** GMT -4
**Flag Description:** The flag of Trinidad and Tobago is red with a black diagonal band edged in white that runs from its upper-right side to its lower left.

## Population

The intertwined histories of European colonization, the slave trade, and indentured servitude have left Trinidad and Tobago with an astounding variety of inhabitants. It is estimated that about 35 percent of the country's residents are descended of South Asian, particularly Indian, immigrants. Another 34 percent are of African descent, 24 percent are mixed, and the remainder is from all over the globe.

The population of Trinidad and Tobago was estimated at 1,222,363 in 2015. The country's median age is 35 years old. At 13 births per 1,000, Trinidad and Tobago's birth rate is substantially

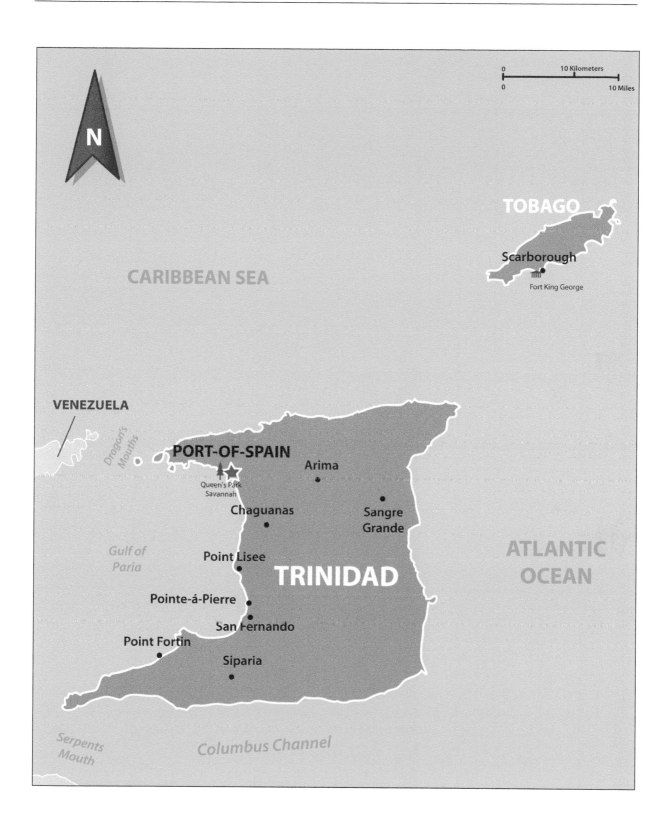

N

10 Kilometers
0

0
10 Miles

TOBAGO

Scarborough

Fort King George

CARIBBEAN SEA

VENEZUELA

PORT-OF-SPAIN

Arima

Queen's Park
Savannah

Chaguanas

Sangre
Grande

Gulf of
Paria

Point Lisee

TRINIDAD

Pointe-á-Pierre

San Fernando

Point Fortin

Siparia

ATLANTIC
OCEAN

Serpents
Mouth

Columbus Channel

**Principal Cities by Population (2011):**

- Chaguanas (83,516)
- San Fernando (48,838)
- Port of Spain (37,074)
- Arima (33,606)
- Point Fortin (20,235)
- Tunapuna (17,758)

higher than its death rate of nine deaths per 1,000 (2015 estimates). A fairly high immigration rate has kept the islands' population stable.

Life expectancy in Trinidad and Tobago is 70 years for men and 76 years for women according to 2015 estimates. Infant mortality is still fairly high at 24 deaths per 1,000 live births. The government estimates that HIV/AIDS was present in about 1.65 percent of the adult population as of 2013, with 14,000 people living with the virus and 700 deaths per year as a result of the disease.

The island of Trinidad is larger than the island of Tobago, which accounts for six percent of the entire country's land area and 4.7 percent of its population (2014). It was estimated in 2013 that only 14.3 percent of the entire country's population lived in urban areas.

## Languages

Languages on the island match the islands' cultural variety, and include Spanish, Castilian, Hindi, French, Chinese, and the official language, English.

## Native People & Ethnic Groups

The earliest known settlers on Trinidad and Tobago were Amerindian tribes like the Arawak. These people migrated throughout what we now call the Caribbean in canoes as part of an extensive trading network that seems to have originated near Venezuela. When Spanish explorer Christopher Columbus landed on Trinidad in 1498, earlier tribes had been almost entirely displaced by tribes of Carib Amerindians.

Historians estimate that the Carib tribes amounted to more than 40,000 people living on

Trinidad and Tobago when Columbus arrived. By the early part of the 16th century, Spanish traders were enslaving the Trinidadian Caribs for colonial work in South America. In spite of a number of armed revolts and well-sustained resistance against the Spanish, and later French, colonizers, the Carib population was decimated by the end of the 18th century. Only the small reservation of Arima was left to Carib peoples, who had by then been converted to Roman Catholicism. The town of Arima was founded by Capuchin monks in 1757.

Today, Arima is nominally led by a Carib Queen, chosen from among the women in the community. The Carib language has been irretrievably lost, along with most pre-colonial customs, but the Amerindian history of the island is evident in island foods, and place names. In the twenty years after the British Empire set up its colonial base on Trinidad in 1763, an estimated 10,000 African people were forcibly brought to the small island as slaves to work the sugar, cotton, and indigo plantations.

The two main ethnic groups are the Indo-Trinidadian and Tobagonians, who make up 35 percent of the total population, and the Afro-Trinidadian and Tobagonians, who make up 34 percent (2011 estimates).

## Religions

Christian Protestant groups, including Anglican, Baptist, Pentecostal, and Seventh Day Adventist churches, claim a total of 32 percent of the islands' populations as followers. Roman Catholics make up 22 percent, Hindus account for 18 percent, and Muslims constitute five percent.

## Climate

Northeast trade winds moderate Trinidad and Tobago's tropical climate. Temperatures throughout the year average 31° Celsius (87° Fahrenheit) during the day and 21° Celsius (69° Fahrenheit) at night.

Rainfall is heavier between June and December, with the exception of the annual September dry spell known as Petite Carême. During July, rainfall averages peak at six centimeters (two inches). January to May is the dry season, with a rainfall average of only one centimeter (less than 0.5 inches).

## ENVIRONMENT & GEOGRAPHY

### Topography

Trinidad and Tobago are both low, generally flat islands that are believed to have broken off from the South American continent. The two islands lie just northeast of Venezuela, forming the Gulf of Paria in between the islands and the mainland.

Tobago, with an area of 300 square kilometers (186 square miles), is 34 kilometers (21 miles) northeast of Trinidad. The larger island, Trinidad, is 81 kilometers (51 miles) long and 57 to 73 kilometers (35 to 45 miles) wide, with an area of 4,828 square kilometers (3,000 square miles). The nation's capital, Port of Spain, is located on the island of Trinidad.

Though far more developed than Tobago, Trinidad still has extensive woodlands and undeveloped forest covering approximately half of the island. Gorges, caves, river basins, waterfalls, mangrove swamps, and lagoons are found on both islands.

Trinidad's gentle hills and plains rise into two, low mountain ranges in the south and center of the island. In the northern section of the island, elevations are higher. Trinidad's highest point of elevation is on El Cerro del Aripo, at 940 meters (3,080 feet) above sea level.

Discharge into the Gulf of Paria from South America's rivers (especially the Orinoco) has colored Trinidad's coastal waters a characteristic green.

### Plants & Animals

Trinidad and Tobago's 2,300 species of flowering plants include 700 different varieties of orchid. The varied tropical climate and wetlands host nearly 400 bird species. Native trees include purpleheart, mora, and crappo.

Trinidad and Tobago's island habitats have a little more than 100 mammal species, 70 reptile varieties, and 620 types of butterfly. Among the islands' mammals, more than 50 species of bats thrive in forests and caves.

## CUSTOMS & COURTESIES

### Greetings

The language of Trinidad & Tobago, known as Trini, is a mixture of English, the base language, and broken French, Hindu, Amerindian, and Spanish words and phrases, as well as dialects of African origin. Trini is filled with double entendres and allusive language, and also tends to refer to the part instead of the whole, for example, referring to a leg as a foot. The official language is English, though there are some areas that may speak a native patois, which is a slang version of French.

Conversation is an important part of the culture, and people tend to take more time to talk during business interactions. In the countryside, people greet strangers with a head nod or by saying "good day" or "alright," though this is uncommon in cities. Customarily, simple English phrases that correspond to the time of day are common when greeting, such as "Good morning" or "Good evening" (though a good portion of people will refer to the afternoon as evening).

### Gestures & Etiquette

Trinbagonians are friendly and polite, and expect the same behavior from outsiders. Punctuality is not an important part of the culture, and it is common for people to arrive late for meetings, dates, or outings. Trinbagonians are conservative when it comes to public displays of affection, and obscene language is illegal (though the law is not enforced). Trinbagonians also dress conservatively when out in public, and bathing suits are restricted to beaches.

There are certain gestures for using transportation. For example, when hailing a route taxi, people typically point in the direction of the next turn-off where they want to go. Drivers also tend to use hand signals in traffic, moving their hand up and down to show that they are going to stop and putting their arm out the window when entering traffic. Additionally, honking a car horn in traffic is a way to say thank you and not to express annoyance.

### Eating/Meals

Food is an integral part of Trinbagonian culture, and eating is intertwined with social interaction and leisure. Meals are traditionally hearty and filling, and eating a full meal is considered essential before going out, whether to work or with friends.

Breakfast is customarily a large meal, eaten at home or from a street vendor. The meal is often accompanied by chocolate tea, a mixture of hot chocolate, cocoa, condensed milk, nutmeg, sugar, and cinnamon. There are several cold options, including banana bread, biscuits, hops (rolls), and fried bakes (rolls made without yeast and often mixed with coconut). Hot breakfasts are also popular, with many meat and fish options. Doubles is a popular take-out food, a sandwich made of fried bread, curry, cucumber, pepper sauce, and mango chutney. Other common breakfast foods include buljol, a mixture of boiled saltfish with vegetables, hot peppers, and lime juice, smoked herring with onions, and spicy smoked fish with vegetables.

Like breakfast, lunch and dinner also frequently consist of large meals. Seafood is commonly eaten, and dishes such as accra (fish fritters) and bake 'n' shark (sandwiches made from fried bread, shark meat, salad, and spicy sauce) are very popular. Oysters, crab, conch, and lobster are also eaten. Roti is one of the nation's most popular dishes and is made with stretchy bread and a variety of fillings. Macaroni pie is another option, which is made from pasta, eggs, and cheese.

Street food is very popular and found all over the country, which range from small snacks like salted peanuts to whole meals like roti. Doubles are often found at food vendor stands, as well as aloo pies, made with potatoes. Pholouri, made with split peas and tamarind sauce, and sahina (vegetable frit-

ters) are also common. Additionally, restaurant culture has grown in urban areas in the 21st century, though most are small and simple with inexpensive food.

### Visiting

Leisure is highly valued in Trinbagonian culture, especially spending time with friends and family. In fact, there is special vocabulary in Trini used to describe social interactions, and the term "liming," often referred to as the "art of idling," refers to spending time with friends, particularly in public places involving food and drink. Liming, which can also take place at home or around the city, is also a Caribbean expression for "hanging out." One of the most important rules of liming is not to leave when everyone is having fun, which is called "breaking a lime." It is considered in poor form, because it makes the other people feel guilty that they have things to do and should leave as well.

Food is an integral part of visiting, because preparing and serving food are important social activities. Hosts offer guests food upon arrival in their homes, and it is considered rude to refuse the offer.

---

## LIFESTYLE

### Family

Family structure varies by class and ethnicity. Black families often consist of a couple or a mother with several children. Legal marriage often takes place after years of common-law marriage and co-habitation among couples. However, nuclear families, with two parents and their children, are not as common. Poor families tend to be matriarchal, often with older relatives living in the same home. Middle- and upper-class families might hire nannies to take care of small children, while in lower-class families extended family members are entrusted to take care of children. East Indian families tend to have both parents with older generations living in the same house. Traditionally, East Indian couples move in with the husband's family, though this trend is changing.

## Housing

Most people in Trinidad and Tobago live in houses constructed of wood. In the rural areas, houses commonly have iron roofs, while urban dwellings are more modernized. Additionally, some rural sugar plantations are comprised of small wood houses with tin roofs. Houses congregated in neighborhoods and urban areas might have several stories, added on as families acquire more wealth; for example, some urban houses of the upper class are made of brick and are several stories high. Neighborhoods are often separated by ethnicity. Many cities also have shantytowns, which are informal settlements, typically with no basic sanitation or electricity, that consist of small shacks made out of discarded materials or wood boards. Also, in outdoor markets, many vendors live near their stalls in shantytowns.

The Ministry of Planning, Housing, and Environment is in charge of providing mortgages, subsidies for home improvements, and low-income housing. The government also introduced a plan at the turn of the 21st century to improve squatter settlements and dwellings. In the late 20th century, a program of land allocation—initially supported by the United Nations (UN) Centre for Human Settlements—was developed in which poor inhabitants could resettle agricultural estates cheaply and quickly. Known as the sou-sou land movement (sou-sou meaning "penny by penny"), it involved the formation of a non-profit organization, Sou-Sou Land Limited, which purchased the land on behalf of the poor, and was translated into state policy in 1987. (It has since been used as a case study illustrating the difficulty of implementing non-governmental programs into law or public policy.)

## Food

The cuisine of Trinidad and Tobago is a blend of African, Caribbean, European, East Indian, and Latin American influences. A prominent feature of the cuisine is creole food, based on African cooking. One of the most popular Creole dishes is pelau, made by cooking chicken, pigeon peas, and vegetables with garlic, spices, and coconut milk. The chicken is prepared using the "browning down" technique, which caramelizes the meat using heat and brown sugar. Other Creole dishes include Sunday baked chicken, which also uses browning down, callaloo (taro root leaves and okra cooked in coconut milk), and coocoo (cornmeal and okra). Oil down is a popular Creole side dish in which vegetables like cassava are cooked in coconut milk.

Meat dishes are common, including black pudding, made from blood sausage, and souse, a cold dish of pig or chicken feet soaked in lime and peppers. In rural areas, wild meats such as iguana, tattoo (armadillo) and agouti (a type of rodent) may be consumed. Despite the hot climate, soups are also popular dishes. They include corn soup, which is made from split-pea soup, vegetables, corn, and dumpling; cow heel soup, made with split peas and chunks of meat; san couche, made with lentils and pig tail; and fish broth, which mixes fish, bananas, and dumplings.

East Indian food is one of the main staples of Trinbagonian cuisine, though it has a distinctive Caribbean flavor. Roti is the country's most popular dish, eaten at any meal. It consists of stretchy bread stuffed with meat, fish, and vegetables. There are several types of roti bread, which include dhalpourri, which mixes split peas in the dough; sada, cooked on a griddle and usually served in the morning; buss-up-shut, which is thin, shredded bread; and paratha, which is plain. There are a multitude of fillings, such as beef, chicken, shrimp, conch, fish, goat, curried potato, and pumpkin. Curry dishes are also popular, though Trinidadian curry is made with hot peppers instead of chili paste (as in Indian cooking). The most common curry dish is curry duck lime. Chutneys are also popular.

There are many unique types of drinks, including deep cerise sorrel, a juice made from the sorrel flower; mauby, made from mauby tree bark and cloves; peanut punch milkshakes, made with milk, carrot juice, and cinnamon; and sea moss, a drink made from sea moss and milk. Trinidad is also a major rum producer.

## Life's Milestones

Demographically, the two largest religions in the island nation are Christianity (estimated at nearly 52 percent of the population) and Hinduism (estimated at about 18 percent of the population). Thus, most milestones are observed in these respective faiths, with weddings being one of the most important milestones. In general, weddings are very formal occasions. Weddings held in the capital, Port of Spain, might observe a particular tradition in which the bride and groom have their picture taken at the Botanical Gardens.

Christian Trinbagonians generally observe western-style wedding traditions, such as the bride wearing a long white gown and the groom donning a black tuxedo. Typically, there is a reception after the church ceremony that includes feasting and dancing.

Hindu Trinbagonians of Indian descent follow their own particular religious traditions. Many marriages are arranged by the families of the couple, and a bride is expected to marry someone of her social caste. The couple is permitted to meet each other before the wedding but the two are separated the week before the ceremony. The wedding is a three-day event: the first day is a procession and the bride's ritual to prepare for the ceremony, cleaning her skin with oils and herbs. The second day is "cooking night," where the bride and groom each prepare a large meal in separate homes to say goodbye to single life. The third day is the wedding ceremony, which takes place at a temple or the bride's home. The groom wears a long tunic and matching pants, and the bride wears a red sari and veil.

## CULTURAL HISTORY

### Art

Trinbagonian art echoes the multicultural make-up of the country, with influences from India, China, Africa, and Europe. The fine art of painting, in particular, has reflected the island nation's numerous historical movements, spanning from colonialism to nationalism to independence. Michel-Jean Cazabon (1813–1888) was one of Trinidad's most acclaimed painters. Born in Trinidad but educated in Europe, his work was representative of colonialism in the West Indies. After college in England, he went to Paris and trained with French academic painter Paul Delaroche (1797–1856), who was trained as a landscapist but was known for his historical works. Cazabon returned to Trinidad in 1850, where he produced paintings and lithographs and also taught art. Using watercolors and oils, he portrayed typical scenes of Trinbagonian life, one of the first local artists to do so. He is often considered the first great Trinbagonian artist.

Trinidad's first artistic movement, the Society of Trinidad Independents, emerged in the 1930s with the rise of nationalism. The movement gave rise to painters such as Hugh Strollmeyer (1913–1981), M.P. Alladin (1919–1980), and Alfred Codallo (1915–1970). These artists explored Trinbagonian themes and culture, including indigenous iconography, East Indian influences, and local folklore. When Trinidad and Tobago achieved independence in 1962, native artists began searching for a new united identity. The black consciousness movement of the 1970s also inspired artists to explore African themes.

Trinidad and Tobago claims several accomplished female artists. Theodora Walter (1869–1959), daughter of a British watercolorist, painted still life and landscapes and is one of the few female artists from the island nation during the late 19th century. Sybil Atteck (1911–1975) painted in an expressionist style and celebrated Trinidad's independence and the island nation's landscapes and newfound identity. She also helped form the first Trinbagonian painting school. The country continues to produce contemporary accomplished artists that celebrate their feminine identity while depicting cultural scenes from the islands. These include Lisa O'Connor (1965– ) known for using impressionism to show Trinbagonian architecture in great detail, and Irénée Shaw (1963–), who paints self-portraits and focuses on feminism and religion.

## Music

Trinidad and Tobago is most famous for the musical traditions of calypso, soca, and steel pan music. East Indian, Caribbean, and American influences helped create new genres in the mid-to-late 20th century. Calypso derived from the plantations of the 18th century, when slaves used songs as a means to communicate hidden messages and to aid them in their work. The songs, originally known as kaiso, were based on song-dances performed by the griots, roving West African poet-singers. Listening to chantuelles, as the kaiso singers were known, soon became a popular form of entertainment.

When slavery was abolished in 1838, the chantuelles brought their music to the country's Carnival celebration, a Christian European festival that occurs before Lent. However, the islands' British colonial rulers saw the celebrations as vulgar and banned African drumming and its associated dance traditions in 1884. Instead, drummers invented the tamboo bamboo, bamboo poles were used as percussion instruments until control over Carnival was loosened in the 1890s (and when the famous competition for the best band began).

Historically, calypso has been the most successful means of social commentary, and is known as the "poor man's newspaper." Calypso lyrics have always been analyzed by Trinbagonians, due to their use of double entendres (in which a phrase can be interpreted in two ways) and hidden meanings. Calypso has also effectively charted the history of Trinidad and showed the changes in government, development, and culture. Calypso's golden era came in the 1930s and lasted until the 1970s, with a large group of artists gaining success at home and abroad.

In the 1980s, when calypso temporarily lost popularity, soca music, which is a mixture of calypso, American disco, and electronic sounds, developed. Considered easier to dance to than calypso, it became increasingly popular. Steel pan music came about in the 1930s, when calypso Carnival performers used old saucepans for percussion instruments and discovered that discarded oil drums from the American troops stationed there could be used as well. Steel pans (pitched percussive instruments) were then designed not only to play Carnival music but a wide range of styles such as classical and reggae.

## Dance

The limbo dance actually comes from Trinidad and Tobago, though many mistakenly believe that it came from Hawaii or Polynesian culture. The limbo is believed to have derived from a ritualistic funerary dance performed at wakes beginning in the 1800s. Swaying the hips, the dancer moves underneath a pole that is gradually lowered. Dancers that touch the pole are eliminated until there is only one dancer left. Many believe the dance mimics being on a crowded slave ship coming from Africa to Trinidad, squirming to get through the packed crowd only to be pushed even further down to the bowels of the ship (similar to the Roman Catholic concept of Limbo, an afterlife state for unbaptized but innocent souls). Despite its origins, limbo is now a festive activity that is most often performed at celebrations and resorts.

Other dance traditions have a distinct West African, Hispanic, or European influence. These include stately waltzes and the English Maypole dance, introduced by Spanish migrants in the mid-20th century (though a similar folk tradition might have been preserved by the indigenous Caribs). The tradition involves dancing or galloping around a long pole with ribbons attached to the top held in the participants' hand.

## Literature

For an archipelagic state that has an estimated population of just over one million, Trinidad and Tobago has had a large number of critically acclaimed authors, including two Nobel Prize winners. A large part of this literary tradition began when several writers and intellectuals experimented with writing forms while publishing poems and short stories in a literary journal called *The Beacon* in the early 1930s. Many of the works were considered "yard literature," a genre of realistic tales of poverty in Trinidad. However, the nation is best known for its novelists, who gained an international reputation beginning in the 1950s.

Samuel Selvon (1923–1994) first wrote the light-hearted novel *A Brighter Sun* in 1952, followed by the dark tale *The Lonely Londoners* (1956) about Trinbagonian immigrants living in England. Earl Lovelace (1932–) is a novelist, playwright, and short story author. His best known novel is *The Dragon Can't Dance* (1979), which deals with colonialism as depicted through a character's preparations for the Trinidad Carnival. Trinidad's most famous literary native son is VS Naipaul (1932–). He studied at Oxford University in England and began writing in the 1950s, publishing his first book at age 23. Though he has written more than 20 works, his most famous novels are *A House for Mr. Biswas* (1961), which depicts life in a postcolonial society, and *The Middle Passage* (1962), an essay in book form about identity in the West Indies. He was awarded the Nobel Prize in Literature in 2001.

Derek Walcott (1930–) is a poet and playwright originally born in Saint Lucia who is often associated with Trinidad due to his residence on the island. In 1959, he established the Trinidad Theater Workshop, directing plays and helping local actors. He has written several plays, including *Dream on Monkey Mountain* (1967) and *Pantomine* (1978). His poems, based on Elizabethan poetry structures, discuss the beauty of the Caribbean and delve into his identity crisis between black and European cultures. He won the Nobel Prize in Literature in 1992. Two other acclaimed writers include Eintou Pearl Springer (1944–), a poet laureate and perhaps Trinidad's most acclaimed female poet, and historian and non-fiction writer Eric Williams (1911–1988), Trinidad and Tobago's first prime minister.

## CULTURE

### Arts & Entertainment

Due to its multicultural origins and centrality in popular and national holidays and celebrations, music plays an integral part in contemporary Trinbagonian society. Calypso continues to be one of the most popular forms of music, as well as a popular mode of social commentary. Calypso season runs in the months leading up to Carnival, when people listen to the bands and the songs they will use for the competition. Originally held in outdoor tents, the concerts have come to be called tents, even though they're now held in buildings. The first tent was held in 1921 to introduce songs for that year's Carnival festivities. Soca music, a blend of calypso and East Indian influences (later incorporating synthesizers), was invented in the 1970s after the stagnation of calypso. Native musician Ras Shorty I (1941–2000), who performed as Lord Shorty, is often credited with creating the genre, and is referred to as the "father of soca."

Since artists spend all year preparing to win the title for best artist during Carnival, music competitions are an important part of the local music scene. In 1956, the first Calypso King competition was held, and it is now a mainstay of the Trinbagonian Carnival tradition. The Soca Monarch competition is also held during Carnival for soca artists, as well as the Panorama contest for steel pan musicians, first held in 1963. The Chutney Soca Monarch competition honors the best of the East Indian music genre, first held in 1996. There's also a best band competition for Carnival bands.

Carnival was brought to Trinidad and Tobago by French aristocrats in the 1700s. They held masquerade balls with elaborate costumes, often dressing up like their slaves. The African slaves held their own parties outside, and after emancipation the two traditions merged into costume parades with drumming and music. The freed blacks reversed the French costume tradition, dressing up like the wealthy planters (where men would often dress up like women). They also introduced characters from African folklore, like jab jab (a demon) and moko jumbie (a stilt walker). Besides a musical performance, Carnival became an opportunity for political satire, in which residents imitated the French planters and later British sailors and local characters. Often, the parades are reflective of the times, and offer political statements on certain movements, such as the black power movement in the 1960s and the women's rights movement in the 1970s.

Carnival's official season begins in the summer, when bands release their designs for the parade. After Christmas, steel bands hold public rehearsals and calypso and soca artists perform at tents. At the tents, the artists focus on one or two songs to be used for the competition. As Carnival draws closer, the Soca Monarch and Panorama competitions are held before the official celebration. A parade is held the Sunday before Ash Wednesday, the same day as the King and Queen of the Bands and the Calypso Monarch competitions. Monday is the official celebration. Early in the morning, Jouvert (dirty mass) is held, when costumed or painted people parade through the streets. Later in the morning, another Carnival parade begins, with bands, masqueraded revelers, and dancers. The big parade is on Tuesday, when the bands use their themes and costumes and compete for Band of the Year.

After Carnival, reggae, dub, and rapso music seasons begin. Dub is Jamaican dancehall, an upbeat type of reggae. Rapso is a mixture of calypso, soca, African drumming, and American-style rapping, often with political lyrics. It developed in the 1970s during the black power movement, before American hip-hop was popularized. Rapso month is held each year in the spring. With reggae, dub, and rapso, outdoor concerts are popular, which are called fetes. Nightclubs are a common activity year-round and often run all night.

Steel band music is also enjoyed throughout the year and has a wide repertoire, ranging from European classical music to original, modern Trinbagonian pieces. Like calypso, this type of music also provides social commentary. Steel drum music was invented in the 1930s by Carnival percussionists who discovered the drums could be made from old oil drums to make a variety of sounds. There are a number of types of pans: the tenor/soprano pan, with the greatest range, guitar/cello pans, for background notes, and bass pans, for percussion. The steel band competition, Panorama, is very popular with

around 25,000 in attendance each year. There's also a World Steel Band Festival held in Trinidad each October.

## Cultural Sites & Landmarks

Many of the island country's important cultural landmarks are in and around the capital of Port of Spain, including the National Museum and Art Gallery. Of note is the Queen's Park Savannah (known as "the Savannah"), which serves as a public park and is one of largest traffic roundabouts (circles) in the world—it covers 105 hectares (260 acres). It was originally a sugar plantation that was sold to the city government in 1817, and now serves as a public leisure area with soccer and cricket fields, the oldest of its kind in the West Indies. The park also borders several important sites, including the Botanical Gardens, Emperor Valley Zoo, and the Queen's Hall performing arts center. The western side of the park is called the Magnificent Seven, a group of Victorian buildings in a variety of styles built in the early 1900s by plantation owners. One of the most notable buildings was modeled after Balmoral Castle in Scotland (a British royal residence).

There are several important religious sites in Trinidad and Tobago, including the Mount St. Benedict Abbey founded by exiled Brazilian monks in 1912. Considered the oldest Benedictine monastery in the Caribbean, the complex includes a chapel, monastery, farm, yogurt factory, and drug rehabilitation center, and is located outside of the capital in the mountains. Another religious site is the Temple in the Sea, located in Waterloo. The project was conceived by Sewdass Sadhu (1903–1970), an immigrant from India. He began building the Hindu temple in 1947, but it was torn down by the sugar company that owned the land. Sadhu was arrested and jailed, but when he was released he began rebuilding the temple in a place where no one could own the land: the sea. He worked on the temple for a quarter of a century, creating a rock embankment in the water, but he died before it was completed. In the 1990s, the temple was refurbished and completed with a bridge to the small man-made island and is now regarded as a national treasure. (The temple was severely vandalized in August 2007.)

Tobago also has several historical landmarks. Fort King George was built on the island in the 1770s by the British, though it was later captured by the French. The site includes a prison, a fort, an arts center, a powder magazine, and a history museum. In Crown Point is Crusoe's Cave, which is supposedly the location author Daniel Defoe (c. 1660–1731) had in mind for his fictional character in the classic novel *Robinson Crusoe* (1719).

### Libraries & Museums

The National Library and Information System and the Adult Library are both located in Port of Spain. The Trinity College Library is located in the Maraval Valley on Trinidad, and the library of the University of Augustine is located in St. Augustine. Additionally, the National Museum and Art Gallery is located in Port of Spain. Other museums include the Museum of Tobago History and the Indian Caribbean Museum, established in 2006.

### Holidays

Trinidad and Tobago's official Christian holidays include Good Friday, Easter Monday, Christmas, and Boxing Day. The government also recognizes other religions in the country with public holidays. Divali is the Hindu festival of lights, an international celebration of the triumph of light over darkness. Eid-al-Fitr is Islam's celebration to mark the end of the Ramadan month of fasting and prayer, and takes place in autumn according to the Muslim lunar calendar.

Trinidad and Tobago is best known for its Carnival. This traditional Roman Catholic day of parades, feasting, music, and dance marks the day before Ash Wednesday, when Roman Catholics begin their period of prayer and fasting in preparation for Easter. Trinidad traditionally hosts one of the most raucous and colorful Carnivals of any country in the Caribbean.

The country celebrates the arrival of East Indian immigrants brought by British colonizers on May 30, Emancipation Day on August 1, and Republic Day on September 24.

### Youth Culture

For teenagers, popular recreational activities include socializing with friends ("liming") and listening to music. Before Carnival, calypso and soca shows at tents are popular, and many teenagers frequent nightclubs that play hip-hop, reggae, and dancehall music. Urban youth enjoy more activities such as shopping. Religious activities are also a fundamental part of Trinbagonian life, and youth are often expected to attend religious services on weekends. The British Scout Movement also remains popular in Trinidad and Tobago among children, affording youth the opportunity to learn important skills as part of a troop.

## SOCIETY

### Transportation

The island nation has an extensive public bus system run by the Public Transport Service Corporation. In the early 21st century, service was extended to the countryside, providing a connection for rural inhabitants. The Priority Bus Route, which runs along the coast, is one of the fastest routes available. There are three types of taxis: maxi taxis, route taxis, and private taxis. Maxi taxis are actually small buses that hold between 10 and 20 people. These taxis are run by groups of private owners, and run on set routes with standardized prices. They are known for their decorative nature and loud music (though a law was passed requiring drivers to obtain a license to play music). Route taxis are similar to maxi taxis, but typically have a five-person capacity. They follow set routes and prices, and leave from taxi stands. Private taxis are unmetered and only go to one destination.

A ferry runs between Trinidad and Tobago, and small planes also offer domestic transportation. There are four airports on the islands, two with paved runways. In 2007, 353 out of 1,000 residents had a car—which is about one-third of the population. Drivers use the left-hand side of the road in Trinidad and Tobago, and the wearing of seat belts is mandatory in the front seats of vehicles. In rural areas, horse and ox-drawn carts are sometimes used, as are bicycles.

## Transportation Infrastructure
According to the United States State Department, the infrastructure of Trinidad and Tobago is considered adequate for its region. However, investment is needed to meet the increasing demands of a modernizing economy. To that end, the country is currently in the early stages of constructing a mass transit railway, the Trinidad Rapid Railway, to help alleviate increasing congestion. The government also implemented a water taxi service (four high-speed catamarans) connecting urban and industrial centers on Trinidad's western coast. The government also stated that a national highway network project, estimated to cost $2.44 billion (USD), would be prioritized in 2010.

## Media & Communications
The *Trinidad Guardian*, a conservative and well-established publication, is one of the largest national newspapers. Other newspapers include the *Express* and *Newsday*, known for their opinion columnists. Tabloid newspapers are also very popular, including *The Bomb, TnT Mirror*, and *Sunday Punch*, which include both gossip and political satire. Tobago only has one newspaper, *Tobago News*, published weekly.

Trinidad and Tobago has six television stations. TV6, which broadcasts the local news, also broadcasts the Gayelle show, which features domestic programming. Synergy is a music channel that shows music videos and local music shows. Radio is popular, a source of Trinbagonian music and news about events. The domestic music stations play soca and calypso, as well as reggae, hip-hop, and American music.

There is extensive telephone coverage in Trinidad and Tobago. In 2014, there were an estimated 290,000 landlines and approximately two million cell phones, with a ratio of 162 cell phones for every 100 people. The Internet has grown rapidly, with an estimated 779,900 users in 2014.

## SOCIAL DEVELOPMENT

### Standard of Living
Trinidad and Tobago ranked 64 of 187 on the United Nations' 2013 Human Development Index (HDI). In 2007, about 17 percent of Trinidadians and Tobagonians were living below the poverty line.

### Water Consumption
In 2014, about 95 percent of the country's population had access to clean drinking water. In 2014, some 91.5 percent of the population had access to an improved sanitation facility.

### Education
Trinidad and Tobago has more than 600 primary and secondary schools, run by eight education districts throughout the two islands. Children in the country attend kindergarten level education for one or two years prior to primary school, which is begun at age five. Primary school is followed by a standard examination to determine secondary school placement.

Trinidadian and Tobagonian students must complete five years of compulsory secondary education, referred to as Forms. Once a student has completed Forms 1 through 5 (ages 11 through 15), Lower and Upper Sixth Forms are optional.

In 2014, the World Economic Forum published the Gender Gap Report, which ranks countries according to gender equality in areas such as politics, health, and education. Trinidad and Tobago was ranked 49 out of 142 countries. In 2015, it was estimated that 99.2 percent of men and 98.7 percent of women were literate. The average school life expectancy for both men and women was 12 years (2013).

### Women's Rights
The promotion and creation of an egalitarian society for Trinbagonian women has its roots in the early 20th century. Audrey Jeffers (1898–1968) founded the Coterie of Social Workers in 1921 and became the first woman elected to the city council in Trinidad's capital in 1936. Other

pioneers soon followed, including trade unionist Clotil Walcott (1925–2007). She founded the National Union of Domestic Employees in 1974, a part of the Union of Ship Builders, Ship Repairers and Allied Workers, and fought for the rights of working-class women. She campaigned for and won legal protection for domestic workers. Women achieved suffrage in 1946.

At the turn of the 21st century, the law in Trinidad and Tobago guarantees women equal rights with men, specifically for employment, inheritance, and education. Also, government and public jobs generally pay men and women equally. However, Trinbagonian law does not guarantee equal wages for women, and in the private sector, many women earn less than their male counterparts, despite the fact that women tend to be more educated than men. There are also fewer women than men in government.

Domestic abuse and violence is one of the most serious issues affecting Trinbagonian women. Non-governmental organizations (NGOS) believe that 20 to 25 percent of all women are victims of abuse, especially domestic violence. Though domestic violence laws protect victims and assure jail time and penalties for abusers, not all incidents are reported. This is due in part to the traditional view that domestic abuse is a private issue. In the early 21st century, the media began to focus more on violence against women, which has caused a shift in this view. Nevertheless, some long-standing beliefs still remain prevalent, like the belief that women are expected to be solely responsible for their family, instead of having a job or an important role in society.

Rape carries serious legal consequences (life in prison), but the courts frequently give lighter punishment with less jail time. Like domestic abuse, nearly all cases of rape are not reported due to a combination of factors, including social stigma and mistrust of police. Sexual harassment, however, is not illegal. Though some efforts have made to curb harassment, such as sexual harassment clauses in labor contracts, very few cases are reported to the authorities, and harassment is believed to be widespread.

In response to these issues, the government has set aside a sector devoted to protecting women's rights called the Division of Gender Affairs (DGA), a part of the Ministry of Community Development, Culture, and Gender Affairs. This sector aims to create social programs for job training and income-generation for women, as well as programs for sensitizing men to women's issues. The DGA also has a hotline for female rape and abuse victims.

**Health Care**

In recent years, Trinidad and Tobago has restructured its national health care system, which now operates through a network of Regional Health Authorities (RHAs). Under Annual Service Agreements with the Ministry of Health, RHAs provide basic medical care to residents in their designated regions.

Much of this care is provided through public health clinics and centers. Patients who need advanced care are referred to three major hospitals: the Eric Williams Medical Science Complex, the General Hospital in Port-of-Spain, and the General Hospital in San Fernando. The government is in the process of building new hospitals and expanding existing hospitals and health centers.

Many residents have considered Trinidad and Tobago's public health services to be substandard, and those who can afford to use private providers. Private health care providers require patients to pay substantial fees, and wealthier residents often use employer-provided health insurance and supplemental insurance policies. The government has been exploring the possibility of introducing national health-care insurance.

## GOVERNMENT

**Structure**

The nation's capital, Port of Spain, was founded by Spanish explorers in 1560. Although the region became a Spanish colony, there was little Spanish settlement for the next century, due to the island's proximity to South America. The

British government then took control of the colony in 1797. Trinidad and Tobago received its independence from the British government on August 31, 1962, after almost 200 years of colonial rule and demands for reform from the islands' populations.

Politics in Trinidad and Tobago have been fairly stable since independence, with the notable exception of a 1990 coup, in which a minority group briefly gained control of the parliament building and held 45 hostages, including the prime minister.

Trinidad and Tobago remains a parliamentary democracy, with a president serving as head state and a prime minister who serves as head of government. An electoral college formed by members of the legislature elects the president to five-year terms. The bicameral legislature consists of the Senate and the House of Representatives. Of the Senate's 31 members, 16 are chosen by the ruling party, nine by the president, and six by the opposition party. Senators serve five-year terms. The 41 members of the House of Representatives are elected by popular vote, and also serve five-year terms.

## Political Parties

There are two main political parties in early 21st-century Trinidad and Tobago: the People's National Movement and the United National Congress. In the 2015 parliamentary elections, the People's National Movement won 23 seats, and the United National Congress won 18 seats.

Minor political parties include the National Alliance for Reconstruction, the Congress of the People Party, and the Democratic Action Congress.

## Local Government

The larger island of Trinidad is broken up into 14 municipalities, whereas the smaller island of Tobago is represented by one regional assembly. Trinidad's municipalities are governed by councils of elected councilors and aldermen. These councils elect the mayor (or, in some regions, chairperson) of the municipality. The Tobago House of Assembly comprises 12 elected assemblypersons who, by vote, determine a chief sec-

retary and deputy chief secretary. An additional four councilors are appointed to the assembly—three by the chief secretary and one by the leader of the opposition.

## Judicial System

Trinidad and Tobago's court system includes a House of Lords/Privy Council, a Court of Appeal, a High Court, and several low courts.

## Taxation

The corporate tax rate and the highest income tax rate in the country is 25 percent. The country also levies value-added taxes (VAT) and property taxes.

## Armed Forces

The Trinidad and Tobago Defence Force consists of a regiment, air guard, and coast guard, as well as a reserves unit. In 2013, there were approximately 6,500 active military personnel in the country.

## Foreign Policy

The foreign policy of Trinidad and Tobago is based on multilateralism, respect for sovereignty, non-interference and deference to international law. The country is a member of over 40 international organizations, the most important being the Caribbean Community and Common Market (CARICOM) and the Summit of the Americas (SOA). As the most developed English-speaking country in the Caribbean, it has taken a leadership role in the region.

CARICOM is a group of Caribbean nations that seek to integrate their economies and to forge regional cooperation on political and security measures. Established in 1973 with the signing of the Treaty of Chaguaramas in Trinidad and Tobago, there were 15 full members, five associate members, and eight observers as of 2015. Trinidad and Tobago, Barbados, Jamaica, and Guyana were the founding members, and Trinidad continues to have a leading role in the organization. Though it was originally a group of English-speaking countries, Suriname joined in 1995 followed by Haiti in 2002, adding Dutch and French to the official languages of the group. CARICOM's goal is to create a Caribbean Single Market and Economy (CSME) to further ease the flow of goods, capital, and people between the member nations. In 2006, Trinidad and Tobago helped found the CARICOM Single Market, the first step toward the CSME.

Trinidad and Tobago is also involved in the Summit of the Americas (SOA) organization that is part of the Organization of American States (OAS). The SOA organizes regional meetings to bring nations of the Americas together to discuss common issues such as security, economics, and the environment. Trinidad and Tobago was chosen to host the fifth Summit of the Americas in April 2009. The country has hosted similar meetings before, on energy, education, labor, and security. It was also chosen to host the Commonwealth Heads of Government Meeting in November 2009.

Trinidad and Tobago is also a member of the Association of Caribbean States (ACS), a regional organization that supports cooperation between the 25-member countries. The organization was founded in 1994, and Trinidad hosted the first meeting the following year. Port of Spain, Trinidad's capital, is home to the ACS headquarters. The island nation also holds membership in important international bodies, most notably the United Nations, the Organization of American States (OAS), and the Non-Aligned Movement (NAM), created to promote independence from the major power blocs. The majority of the member countries are in the developing world, and foster peace, sovereignty, and non-interference.

Though Trinidad and Tobago has friendly relations with its Latin American and North American neighbors, it has had several maritime disputes with nearby countries. In 2005, Trinidad and Barbados had a dispute about the northern limit of Trinidad's and Venezuela's maritime borders, because Barbados claimed it was extending into their territory. Trinidad and Barbados agreed to arbitration. Then, in 2006, a decision was reached to limit Trinidad's boundary, but forced Barbados to agree to limit fishing in a zone protected by Trinidad. Trinidad and Tobago also

has worked with neighboring countries regarding drug trafficking, since it is a strategic point between South America and the United States.

**Human Rights Profile**

International human rights law insists that states respect civil and political rights, and also promote an individual's economic, social, and cultural rights. The United Nations Universal Declaration on Human Rights (UDHR) is recognized as the standard for international human rights. Its authors sought the counsel of the world's great thinkers, philosophers, and religious leaders, and were careful to create a document that reflects the core values shared by every world culture. (To read this document or view the articles relating to cultural human rights, go to: http://www.udhr.org/UDHR/default.htm.)

Trinidad and Tobago's human rights violations are centered on the police, the judicial system, and the prison system. Police impunity has been a problem, and the police have been involved in the murder of citizens, many of whom eyewitnesses claim were innocent. The first time a police officer was convicted for murder while on duty was in 2004; it was the first since Trinidad's independence in 1962. From 2003 to 2007, 37 cases were reported, but few were brought to justice. From 1999 to 2007, only six percent of police killings went to trial. Also in 2007, six people were murdered by police, who claimed that several of the victims had opened fire on them first. By 2008, however, only one officer was charged with homicide.

There have also been abuses in the prisons. Prison conditions are very poor, with overcrowding, lack of adequate and basic sanitation, and minimal medical care. In August 2007, prisoners at the Golden Grove prison in Arouca rioted due to poor conditions and abuses by guards, and in November, police fired rubber bullets at a group of inmates accused of firing a weapon, injuring many. There have been widespread reports of torture and abuse by prison guards, like the case of Anton Cooper. In 2001, Cooper was detained as a suspect for abusing his cousin, and was beaten and murdered by prison guards. In 2006, both guards were acquitted.

There are also violations in the judicial system. Murder conviction rates are low, in part due to the intimidation of witnesses. As such, the witness protection program has been accused of failing to adequately care for witnesses, many of whom refuse to testify due to threats. Also, police officers frequently fail to participate in trials as witnesses to crimes, which have led to the dismissal of cases.

## ECONOMY

### Overview of the Economy

Trinidad and Tobago is the top exporter of oil and gas in the Caribbean region. Following the discovery of oil deposits, petroleum and petroleum products accounted for over 10 percent of the country's gross domestic product (GDP). In 2014, the per capita gross domestic product (GDP) was estimated at $32,100 (USD). The overall GDP in 2014 was $28.79 billion (USD).

From the capital in Port of Spain, the government sponsored massive investments in island infrastructure. The volatility of the worldwide oil market has caused painful contractions in the island economy, but overall growth rates have remained steady.

### Industry

Historically, the islands' most profitable industry has been in petroleum products and chemicals. Due to the abundance of cheap fuel, the steel, cement, and natural gas industries have all developed on the island, and massive port facilities have been constructed in Port of Spain harbor to transport these goods.

Government investment has also led to the development of a national airport in Port of Spain and the widening of the harbor to accommodate cruise ships, as tourism continues to be an important part of the country's economy. Other industries include food processing, beverage production, and cotton textiles manufacturing.

### Labor

The country's labor force was 623,500 in 2014; that same year, the unemployment rate was four percent.

### Energy/Power/Natural Resources

Trinidad and Tobago's natural resources include petroleum, natural gas, and asphalt, which have been responsible for much of the country's wealth since independence. The islands' temperate tropical climate, beaches, and location just outside the path of Atlantic hurricanes are significant factors in its thriving tourist industry.

### Agriculture

Trinidad and Tobago produces cocoa, sugarcane, rice, citrus, and coffee. Local farms also harvest vegetables and raise poultry. Most agricultural activity is concentrated on Tobago. However, agriculture accounts for less than one percent of the GDP.

### Animal Husbandry

In 2005, there were over 28.2 million poultry, 29,000 head of cattle, 5,700 water buffalo, 59,300 goats, 43,000 hogs, and 3,400 sheep in the country. Water buffalo are used as draft animals in the agricultural industry. Most dairy products in Trinidad and Tobago are imported from Europe.

### Tourism

Trinidad and Tobago's tourist industry, though a significant part of the national economy, is relatively small in comparison with other Caribbean island nations. The government undertook projects beginning in the 1980s to expand and update seaports and airports to facilitate cruise ship arrivals and increased air traffic. The industry has been growing at a modest pace throughout the end of the 20th century and the beginning of the 21st century.

*Rachel Glickhouse, Amy Witherbee,*
*Jeffrey Bowman*

## DO YOU KNOW?

- The island of Tobago contains the oldest protected rainforest in the Western Hemisphere.
- Italian explorer Christopher Columbus named Trinidad after the Catholic Trinity when he sighted the island in 1492.

### Bibliography

Brereton, Bridget. *A History of Modern Trinidad, 1783–1962*. Kingston, Jamaica: Heinemann, 1981.

Cowley, John. *Carnival, Canboulay, and Calypso: Traditions in the Making*. New York: Cambridge UP, 1996.

Mason, Peter. *Bacchanal!: The Carnival Culture of Trinidad*. Philadelphia: Temple University Press, 1998.

Regis, Louis. *The Political Calypso: True Opposition in Trinidad and Tobago, 1962–1987*. Gainsville, Florida: University Press of Florida, 1999.

Rohlehr, Gordon. *Calypso & Society in Pre-Independence Trinidad*. Port-of-Spain, Trinidad: G. Rohlehr, 1990.

Scher, Philip W. *Trinidad Carnival: The Cultural Politics of a Transnational Festival*. Ed. Garth L. Green. Bloomington: Indiana University Press, 2007.

Stuempfle, Stephen. *The Steelband Movement: The Forging of a National Art in Trinidad and Tobago*. Philadelphia: University of Pennsylvania Press, 1995.

Thomas, Polly, et al. *Rough Guide to Trinidad and Tobago*. London: Rough Guides, 2015.

### Works Cited

"About the ACS." *Association of Caribbean States*. http://www.acs-aec.org/about.htm.

Agostini, Keifel A. *Sunday Express* [Port-of-Spain] 21 Sept. 1997, sec. 2: 2–3. The National Library of Trinidad and Tobago. http://www.nalis.gov.tt/Places/Places_Queen%27sParkSav1.html.

Amnesty International, *Trinidad and Tobago: The Killing of Anton Cooper: "What I Saw Was Murder"*. AMR 49/003/2002. UNHCR Refworld. Online. http://www.unhcr.org/refworld/docid/3deb60b34.html.

"Animal Husbandry: Trinidad and Tobago." encyclopedia.com. http://www.encyclopedia.com/topic/Trinidad_and_Tobago.aspx

"Audrey Jeffers." *Trinidad Guardian* [Port-of-Spain] 1 Aug. 1998: 41–41. The National Library of Trinidad and Tobago. http://www.nalis.gov.tt/Biography/AudreyJeffers.html.

Brinkhoff, Thomas. "Trinidad and Tobago—Cities, Towns & Provinces–Statistics & Map." City Population: Trinidad and Tobago. http://www.citypopulation.de/Trinidad.html.

"The Caribbean Community." CARICOM Secretariat. http://www.caricom.org/jsp/community/community_index.jsp?menu=community.

"CIA—The World Factbook—Trinidad and Tobago." *Central Intelligence Agency World Factbook*. CIA. https://www.cia.gov/library/publications/the-world-factbook/geos/td.html.

Cudjoe, Selwyn R., ed. *Caribbean Women Writers: Essays from the First International Conference*. Boston: University of Massachusetts P, 1990.

De-Light, Dominique and Polly Thomas. *The Rough Guide to Trinidad & Tobago*. New York: Rough Guides, 2007.

"Emancipation Day: Trinidad and Tobago." The National Library of Trinidad and Tobago. http://library2.nalis.gov.tt/Default.aspx?PageContentID=441&tabid=216.

"The Foreign Policy of Trinidad & Tobago." Trinidad and Tobago Ministry of Foreign Affairs. 2007. http://foreign.gov.tt/pages/foreign-policy.php.

"Fort King George, Trinidad and Tobago." WCities Destination Guide. http://www.wcities.com/en/record/,285303/370/record.html.

"Gender Gap Index: Trinidad and Tobago." *World Econmic Forum*. http://reports.weforum.org/global-gender-gap-report-2014/economies/#economy=TTO

Gibbings, Wesley. "Walcott the Warrior." *Express* 15 May 2000. The National Library of Trinidad and Tobago. http://www.nalis.gov.tt/Biography/bio_ClotilWalcott_activist.htm.

Hernandez, Romel. *Trinidad & Tobago*. Philadelphia: Mason Crest Publishers, 2004.

Human Development Report 2007/2008: Women's Political Participation. Rep. 2007. United Nations Development Fund. http://hdrstats.undp.org/indicators/308.html.

"Human Development Reports: Trinidad and Tobago." *United Nations Development Programme*. http://hdr.undp.org/en/countries/profiles/TTO

"Jean Michel Cazabon." Profile of an Artist: Jean Michel Cazabon. The National Library of Trinidad and Tobago. http://www.nalis.gov.tt/Biography/bio_Cazabon.html.

"Limbo Dance." TnTisland.com. http://www.tntisland.com/limbo.html.

MacLean, Geoffrey. "History of Art of Trinidad & Tobago." 1998. Smithsonian Latino Center. http://latino.si.edu/rainbow/pages/History.html.

Mendes-Franco, Janine. "Trinidad & Tobago—Wedding Tradition." *Global Voices*. 4 Sept. 2007. Online. http://globalvoicesonline.org/2007/09/04/trinidad-tobago-wedding-tradition/.

"Ministry of Housing: About." MOH—Ministry Of Housing, Trinidad and Tobago. http://www.housing.gov.tt/moh.htm.

"Motor Vehicles (per 1,000 people)." *The World Bank*. http://web.archive.org/web/20140331072957/http://data.worldbank.org/indicator/IS.VEH.NVEH.P3?page=1

"Mount St. Benedict Monastery." PlanetWare Travel Guide. http://www.planetware.com/trinidad-north-range-and-north-coast/mount-st-benedict-monastery-tri-tri-mst.htm.

"NAM Background Information." *Non Aligned Movement, South Africa*. http://www.nam.gov.za/background/background.htm#4.4.

Nasta, Susheila. "Earl Lovelace." *Contemporary Writers in the UK. British Council*. http://www.contemporarywriters.com/authors/?p=auth63.

"Pearl Eintou Springer: Poet Laureate." *Profile*. National Library of Trinidad and Tobago. http://www.nalis.gov.tt/PSpringer/PSpringer.html.

*Population, Social & Vital Statistics*. Central Statistical Office of Trinidad and Tobago. http://www.cso.gov.tt/cso/statistics/population.aspx.

Reddock, Rhoda. "Clotil Wolcott 1925–2007: A Tribute." 20 Nov. 2007. Global Women Strike. http://www.globalwomenstrike.net/Trinidad/TributesToClotil.htm#Rhoda.

Reddock, Rhoda. *Reconciling Work and Family in Trinidad and Tobago*. Publication. July 2008. International Labor Organization. http://74.125.47.132/search?q=cache:vGMTqsdwCzYJ:www.amchamtt.com/Downloads/RECONCILING%2520WORK%2520AND%2520FAMILY.ppt+trinidad+%2B+family+structure&hl=en&ct=clnk&cd=8&gl=tt.

Reddock, Rhoda. "The Early Women's Movement in Trinidad and Tobago, 1900–1937." *Popline*. http://www.popline.org/docs/1218/128425.html.

Sheehan, Sean. *Cultures of the World: Trinidad & Tobago*. New York: Marshall Cavendish, 2001.

"Stages of a Hindu Wedding." *Trinidad Weddings*. http://www.trinidadweddings.com/Weddings/Traditional/HinduCeremony/tabid/100/Default.aspx.

"Summit of the Americas Process." *Summit of the Americas*. 2008. http://www.summit-americas.org/eng-2002/summit-process.htm.

"Trinidad and Tobago—Landmarks and Points of Interest." *Smithsonian Magazine*. 6 Nov. 2007. http://www.smithsonianmag.com/travel/destination-hunter/north-america/caribbean-atlantic/trinidad-tobago/trinidad-tobago-landmarks-points-of-interest.html.

"TRINIDAD & TOBAGO—Museums & Cultural Landmarks." *Go Trinidad and Tobago*. 2008. http://www.gotrinidadandtobago.com/information/museums_cultural_landmarks.php.

"Trinidad and Tobago." *Country Reports on Human Rights*. U.S. Department of State. http://www.state.gov/g/drl/rls/hrrpt/2006/78907.htm.

"Trinidad and Tobago: Information by Country: Human Rights—UNFPA." *Human Rights*. UNFPA—United Nations Population Fund. http://www.unfpa.org/derechos/trinidad-tobago_eng.htm.

"Trinidad and Tobago." *UN Data*. http://data.un.org/CountryProfile.aspx?crName=Trinidad%20and%20Tobago

"Trinidad and Tobago." *U.S. Department of State*. Bureau of Western Hemisphere Affairs. http://www.state.gov/r/pa/ei/bgn/35638.htm#people.

Vertovec, Steven. *Hindu Trinidad: Religion, Ethnicity, and Socio-Economic Change*. Basingstoke: Macmillan, 1992.

# Appendix One:
# World Governments

# Commonwealth

### Guiding Premise

A commonwealth is an organization or alliance of nations connected for the purposes of satisfying a common interest. The participating states may retain their own governments, some of which are often considerably different from one another. Although commonwealth members tend to retain their own sovereign government institutions, they collaborate with other members to create mutually agreeable policies that meet their collective interests. Some nations join commonwealths to enhance their visibility and political power on the international stage. Others join commonwealths for security or economic reasons. Commonwealth members frequently engage in trade agreements, security pacts, and other programs. Some commonwealths are regional, while others are global.

### Typical Structure

A commonwealth's structure depends largely on the nature of the organization and the interests it serves. Some commonwealths are relatively informal in nature, with members meeting on a periodic basis and participating voluntarily. This informality does not undermine the effectiveness of the organization, however—members still enjoy a closer relationship than that which exists among unaffiliated states. Commonwealths typically have a president, secretary general, or, in the case of the Commonwealth of Nations (a commonwealth that developed out of the British Empire), a monarch acting as the leader of the organization. Members appoint delegates to serve at summits, committee meetings, and other commonwealth events and programs.

Other commonwealths are more formal in structure and procedures. They operate based on mission statements with very specific goals and member participation requirements. These organizations have legislative bodies that meet regularly. There are even joint security operations involving members. The African Union, for example, operates according to a constitution and collectively addresses issues facing the entire African continent, such as HIV/AIDS, regional security, environmental protection, and economic cooperation.

One of the best-known commonwealths in modern history was the Soviet Union. This collective of communist states was similar to other commonwealths, but the members of the Soviet Union, although they retained their own sovereign government institutions, largely deferred to the organization's central leadership in Moscow, which in turn deferred to the Communist Party leadership. After the collapse of the Soviet Union, a dozen former Soviet states, including Russia, reconnected as the Commonwealth of Independent States. This organization features a central council in Minsk, Belarus. This council consists of the heads of state and heads of government for each member nation, along with their cabinet ministers for defense and foreign affairs.

Commonwealth structures and agendas vary. Some focus on trade and economic development, as well as using their respective members' collective power to address human rights, global climate change, and other issues. Others are focused on regional stability and mutual defense, including prevention of nuclear weapons proliferation. The diversity of issues for which commonwealths are formed contributes to the frequency of member meetings as well as the actions carried out by the organization.

### Role of the Citizen

Most commonwealths are voluntary in nature, which means that the member states must choose to join with the approval of their respective governments. A nation with a democratic government, therefore, would need the sanction of its popularly elected legislative and executive bodies in order to proceed. Thus, the role of the private citizen with regard to a commonwealth is indirect—the people may have the power to vote for or against a legislative or executive candidate based on his or her position concerning membership in a commonwealth.

Some members of commonwealths, however, do not feature a democratic government, or their respective governmental infrastructures are not yet in place. Rwanda, for instance, is a developing nation whose 2009 decision to join the Commonwealth of Nations likely came from the political leadership with very little input from its citizens, as Rwandans have very limited political freedom.

While citizens may not directly influence the actions of a commonwealth, they may work closely with its representatives. Many volunteer nonprofit organizations—having direct experience with, for example, HIV/AIDS, certain minority groups, or environmental issues—work in partnership with the various branches of a commonwealth's central council. In fact, such organizations are frequently called upon in this regard to implement the policies of a commonwealth, receiving financial and logistical support when working in impoverished and/or war-torn regions. Those working for such organizations may therefore prove invaluable to the effectiveness of a commonwealth's programs.

*Michael Auerbach*
*Marblehead, Massachusetts*

## Examples

African Union
Commonwealth of Independent States
Commonwealth of Nations
Northern Mariana Islands (and the United States)
Puerto Rico (and the United States)

### Bibliography

"About Commonwealth of Independent States." *Commonwealth of Independent States*. CIS, n.d. Web. 17 Jan. 2013.

"AU in a Nutshell." *African Union*. African Union Commission, n.d. Web. 17 Jan. 2013.

"The Commonwealth." *Commonwealth of Nations*. Nexus Strategic Partnerships Limited, 2013. Web. 17 Jan. 2013.

# Communist

## Guiding Premise

Communism is a political and economic system that seeks to eliminate private property and spread the benefits of labor equally throughout the populace. Communism is generally considered an outgrowth of socialism, a political and economic philosophy that advocates "socialized" or centralized ownership of the economy and the means of production.

Communism developed largely from the theories of Karl Marx (1818–83), who believed that a revolution led by the working class must occur before the state could achieve the even distribution of wealth and property and eliminate the class-based socioeconomic system of capitalist society. Marx believed that a truly equitable society required centralized control of credit, transportation, education, communication, agriculture, and industry, along with eliminating the rights of individuals to inherit or to own land.

Russia (formerly the Soviet Union) and China are the two largest countries to have been led by communist governments during the twentieth and twenty-first centuries. In both cases, the attempt to bring about a communist government came by way of violent revolutions in which members of the former government and ruling party were executed. Under Russian leader Vladimir Lenin (1870–1924) and Chinese leader Mao Zedong (1893–1976), strict dictatorships were instituted, curtailing individual rights in favor of state control. Lenin sought to expand communism into developing nations to counter the global spread of capitalism. Mao, in his form of communism, considered ongoing revolution within China a necessary aspect of communism. Both gave their names to their respective versions of communism, but neither Leninism nor Maoism managed to achieve the idealized utopia envisioned by Marx and other communist philosophers.

The primary difference between modern socialism and communism is that communist groups believe that a social revolution is necessary to create the idealized state without class structure, where socialists believe that the inequities of class structure can be addressed and eliminated through gradual change.

## Typical Structure

Most modern communist governments define themselves as "socialist," though a national communist party exerts control over all branches of government. The designation of a "communist state" is primarily an external definition for a situation in which a communist party controls the government.

Among the examples of modern socialist states operating under the communist model are the People's Republic of China, the Republic of Cuba, and the Socialist Republic of Vietnam. However, each of these governments in fact operates through a mixed system of socialist and capitalist economic policies, allowing private ownership in some situations and sharply enforcing state control in others.

Typically, a communist state is led by the national communist party, a political group with voluntary membership and members in all sectors of the populace. While many individuals may join the communist party, the leadership of the party is generally selected by a smaller number of respected or venerated leaders from within the party. These leaders select a ruling committee that develops the political initiatives of the party, which are thereafter distributed throughout the government.

In China, the Communist Party elects both a chairperson, who serves as executive of the party, and a politburo, a standing committee that makes executive decisions on behalf of the party. In Cuba, the Communist Party selects individuals who sit for election to the National Assembly of People's Power, which then serves directly as the state's sole legislative body.

In the cases of China, Cuba, and Vietnam, the committees and leaders chosen by the communist party then participate directly in electing leaders to serve in the state judiciary. In addition, the central committees typically appoint individuals to serve as heads of the military and to lower-level, provincial, or municipal government positions. In China, the populace elects individuals to local, regional, and provincial councils that in turn elect representatives to sit on a legislative body known as the National People's Congress (NPC), though the NPC is generally considered a largely ceremonial institution without any substantial power to enact independent legislation.

In effect, most modern communist states are controlled by the leadership of the national communist party, though this leadership is achieved by direct and indirect control of lesser legislative, executive, and judicial bodies. In some cases, ceremonial and symbolic offices created under the communist party can evolve to take a larger role in state politics. In China, for instance, the NPC has come to play a more important role in developing legislation in the twenty-first century.

### Role of the Citizen

In modern communist societies, citizens have little voice in selecting the leadership of the government. In many communist states, popular elections are held at local and national levels, but candidates are chosen by communist party leadership and citizens are not given the option to vote for representatives of opposing political parties.

In most cases, the state adopts policies that give the appearance of popular control over the government, while in actuality, governmental policies are influenced by a small number of leaders chosen from within the upper echelons of the party. Popularly elected leaders who oppose party policy are generally removed from office.

All existing communist states have been criticized for human rights violations in terms of curtailing the freedoms available to citizens and of enacting dictatorial and authoritarian policies. Cuba, Vietnam, and China, for instance, all have laws preventing citizens from opposing party policy or supporting a political movement that opposes the communist party. Communist governments have also been accused of using propaganda and misinformation to control the opinion of the populace regarding party leadership and therefore reducing the potential for popular resistance to communist policies.

*Micah Issitt*
*Philadelphia, Pennsylvania*

### Examples
China
Cuba
Laos
North Korea
Vietnam

### Bibliography
Caramani, Daniele. *Comparative Politics*. New York: Oxford UP, 2008. Print.
Priestland, David. *The Red Flag: A History of Communism*. New York: Grove, 2009. Print.
Service, Robert. *Comrades! A History of World Communism*. Cambridge: Harvard UP, 2007. Print.

# Confederation/Confederacy

## Guiding Premise

A confederation or confederacy is a loose alliance between political units, such as states or cantons, within a broader federal government. Confederations allow a central, federal government to create laws and regulations of broad national interest, but the sovereign units are granted the ultimate authority to carry out those laws and to create, implement, and enforce their own laws as well. Confederate governments are built on the notion that a single, central government should not have ultimate authority over sovereign states and populations. Some confederate governments were born due to the rise of European monarchies and empires that threatened to govern states from afar. Others were created out of respect for the diverse ideologies, cultures, and ideals of their respective regions. Confederations and confederacies may be hybrids, giving comparatively more power to a federal government while retaining respect for the sovereignty of their members. True confederate governments are rare in the twenty-first century.

## Typical Structure

Confederate governments are typically characterized by the presence of both a central government and a set of regional, similarly organized, and sovereign (independent) governments. For example, a confederate government might have as its central government structure a system that features executive, legislative, and judicial branches. Each region that serves as members of the confederation would have in place a similar system, enabling the efficient flow of lawmaking and government services.

In some confederations, the executive branch of the central government is headed by a president or prime minister, who serves as the government's chief administrative officer, overseeing the military and other government operations. Meanwhile, at the regional level, another chief executive, such as a governor, is charged with the administration of that government's operations.

Legislative branches are also similarly designed. Confederations use parliaments or congresses that, in most cases, have two distinct chambers. One chamber consists of legislators who each represent an entire state, canton, or region. The other chamber consists of legislators representing certain populations of voters within that region. Legislatures at the regional level not only have the power to create and enforce their own laws, but also have the power to refuse to enact or enforce any laws handed down by the national government.

A confederation's judiciary is charged with ensuring that federal and regional laws are applied uniformly and within the limits of the confederation's constitutional framework. Central and regional governments both have such judicial institutions, with the latter addressing those legal matters administered in the state or canton and the former addressing legal issues of interest to the entire country.

Political parties also typically play a role in a confederate government. Political leadership is achieved by a party's majority status in either the executive or the legislative branches. Parties also play a role in forging a compromise on certain matters at both the regional and national levels. Some confederations take the diversity of political parties and their ideologies seriously enough to create coalition governments that can help avoid political stalemates.

## Role of the Citizen

The political role of the citizen within a confederate political system depends largely on the constitution of the country. In some confederacies, for example, the people directly elect their legislative and executive leaders by popular vote. Some legislators are elected to open terms—they may technically be reelected, but this election is merely a formality, as they are allowed to stay in office until they decide to leave or they die—while others may be subject to term limits or other reelection rules. Popularly elected legislators and executives in turn draft, file, and pass new laws and regulations that ideally are favorable to the voters. Some confederate systems give popularly elected legislators the ability to elect a party leader to serve as prime minister or president.

Confederations are designed to empower the regional government and avoid the dominance of a distant national government. In this manner, citizens of a confederate government, in some cases, may enjoy the ability to put forth new legislative initiatives. Although the lawmaking process is expected to be administered by the legislators and executives, in such cases the people are allowed and even encouraged to connect and interact with their political representatives to ensure that the government remains open and accessible.

*Michael Auerbach*
*Marblehead, Massachusetts*

## Examples

European Union
Switzerland
United States under the Articles of Confederation (1781–89)

## Bibliography

"Government Type." *The World Factbook*. Central Intelligence Agency, n.d. Web. 17 Jan. 2013.

"Swiss Politics." *SwissWorld.org*. Federal Department of Foreign Affairs Presence Switzerland, n.d. Web. 17 Jan. 2013.

# Constitutional Monarchy

## Guiding Premise

A constitutional monarchy is a form of government in which the head of state is a monarch (a king or queen) with limited powers. The monarch has official duties, but those responsibilities are defined in the nation's constitution and not by the monarch. Meanwhile, the power to create and rescind laws is given to a legislative body. Constitutional monarchies retain the ceremony and traditions associated with nations that have long operated under a king or queen. However, the constitution prevents the monarch from becoming a tyrant. Additionally, the monarchy, which is typically a lifetime position, preserves a sense of stability and continuity in the government, as the legislative body undergoes periodic change associated with the election cycle.

## Typical Structure

The structure of a constitutional monarchy varies from nation to nation. In some countries, the monarchy is predominantly ceremonial. In such cases, the monarch provides a largely symbolic role, reminding the people of their heritage and giving them comfort in times of difficulty. Such is the case in Japan, for example; the emperor of that country was stripped of any significant power after World War II but was allowed to continue his legacy in the interest of ensuring that the Japanese people would remain peaceful. Today, that nation still holds its monarchical family in the highest regard, but the government is controlled by the Diet (the legislature), with the prime minister serving in the executive role.

In other countries, the sovereign plays a more significant role. In the United Kingdom, the king or queen does have some power, including the powers to appoint the prime minister, to open or dissolve Parliament, to approve bills that have been passed by Parliament, and to declare war and make peace. However, the monarch largely defers to the government on these acts. In Bahrain, the king (or, until 2002, emir or

hereditary ruler) was far more involved in government in the late twentieth and early twenty-first centuries than many other constitutional monarchs. In 1975, the emir of Bahrain dissolved the parliament, supposedly to run the government more effectively. His son would later implement a number of significant constitutional reforms that made the government more democratic in nature.

The key to the structure of this type of political system is the constitution. As is the case in the United States (a federal republic), a constitutional monarchy is carefully defined by the government's founding document. In Canada, for example, the king or queen of England is still recognized as the head of state, but that country's constitution gives the monarch no power other than ceremonial responsibilities. India, South Africa, and many other members of the Commonwealth of Nations (the English monarch's sphere of influence, spanning most of the former British colonies) have, since gaining their independence, created constitutions that grant no power to the English monarch; instead, they give all powers to their respective government institutions and, in some cases, recognize their own monarchs.

A defining feature of a constitutional monarchy is the fact that the monarch gives full respect to the limitations set forth by the constitution (and rarely seeks to alter such a document in his or her favor). Even in the United Kingdom itself—which does not have a written constitution, but rather a series of foundational documents—the king or queen does not step beyond the bounds set by customary rules. One interesting exception is in Bahrain, where Hamad bin Isa Al-Khalifa assumed the throne in 1999 and immediately implemented a series of reforms to the constitution in order to give greater definition to that country's democratic institutions, including resuming parliamentary elections in 2001. During the 2011 Arab Spring uprisings, Bahraini protesters called for further democratic reforms to be enacted, and tensions between the ruler and his opposition continue.

## Role of the Citizen

In the past, monarchies ruled nations with absolute power; the only power the people had was the ability to unify and overthrow the ruling sovereign. Although the notion of an absolute monarchy has largely disappeared from the modern political landscape, many nations have retained their respective kings, queens, emperors, and other monarchs for the sake of ceremony and cultural heritage. In the modern constitutional monarchy, the people are empowered by their nation's foundational documents, which not only define the rights of the people but the limitations of their governments and sovereign as well. The people, through their legislators and through the democratic voting process, can modify their constitutions to expand or shrink the political involvement of the monarchy.

For example, the individual members of the Commonwealth of Nations, including Canada and Australia, have different constitutional parameters for the king or queen of England. In England, the monarch holds a number of powers, while in Canada, he or she is merely a ceremonial head of state (with all government power centered in the capital of Ottawa). In fact, in 1999, Australia held a referendum (a general vote) on whether to abolish its constitutional monarchy altogether and replace it with a presidential republic. In that case, the people voted to retain the monarchy, but the proposal was only narrowly defeated. These examples demonstrate the tremendous power the citizens of a constitutional monarchy may possess through the legislative process and the vote under the constitution.

*Michael Auerbach*
*Marblehead, Massachusetts*

## Examples

Bahrain
Cambodia
Denmark
Japan
Lesotho
Malaysia
Morocco
Netherlands
Norway
Spain
Sweden
Thailand
United Kingdom

### Bibliography

Bowman, John. "Constitutional Monarchies." *CBC News.* CBC, 4 Oct. 2002. Web. 17 Jan. 2013.
"The Role of the Monarchy." *Royal.gov.uk.* Royal Household, n.d. Web. 17 Jan. 2013.

# Constitutional Republic

## Guiding Premise

A constitutional republic is a governmental system in which citizens are involved in electing or appointing leaders who serve according to rules formulated in an official state constitution. In essence, the constitutional republic combines the political structure of a republic or republican governmental system with constitutional principles.

A republic is a government in which the head of state is empowered to hold office through law, not inheritance (as in a monarchy). A constitutional republic is a type of republic based on a constitution, a written body of fundamental precedents and principles from which the laws of the nation are developed.

Most constitutional republics in the modern world use a universal suffrage system, in which all citizens of the nation are empowered to vote for or against individuals who attempt to achieve public office. Universal suffrage is not required for a nation to qualify as a constitutional republic, and some nations may only allow certain categories of citizens to vote for elected leaders.

A constitutional republic differs from other forms of democratic systems in the roles assigned to both the leaders and the citizenry. In a pure democratic system, the government is formed by pure majority rule, and this system therefore ignores the opinions of any minority group. A republic, by contrast, is a form of government in which the government's role is limited by a written constitution aimed at promoting the welfare of all individuals, whether members of the majority or a minority.

## Typical Structure

To qualify as a constitutional republic, a nation must choose a head of state (most often a president) through elections, according to constitutional law. In some nations, an elected president may serve alongside an appointed or elected individual who serves as leader of the legislature, such as a prime minister, often called the "head of government." When the president also serves as head of government, the republic is said to operate under a presidential system.

Typically, the executive branch consists of the head of state and the executive offices, which are responsible for enforcing the laws and overseeing relations with other nations. The legislative branch makes laws and has overlapping duties with the executive office in terms of economic and military developments. The judicial branch, consisting of the courts, interprets the law and the constitution and enforces adherence to the law.

In a constitutional republic, the constitution describes the powers allotted to each branch of government and the means by which the governmental bodies are to be established. The constitution also describes the ways in which governmental branches interact in creating, interpreting, and enforcing laws. For instance, in the United States, the executive and legislative branches both have roles in determining the budget for the nation, and neither body is free to make budgetary legislation without the approval of the other branch.

## Role of the Citizen

In a constitutional republic, the citizens have the power to control the evolution of the nation through the choice of representatives who serve on the government. These representatives can, generally through complicated means, create or abolish laws and even change the constitution itself through reinterpretations of constitutional principles or direct amendments.

Citizens in a republic are empowered, but generally not required, to play a role in electing leaders. In the United States, both state governments and the federal government function according to a republican system, and citizens are therefore allowed to take part in the election of leaders to both local and national offices. In addition, constitutional systems generally allow individuals to join political interest groups to further common political goals.

In a constitutional democratic republic such as Guatemala and Honduras, the president, who serves as chief of state and head of government, is elected directly by popular vote. In the United States, a constitutional federal republic, the president is elected by the Electoral College, whose members are selected according to the popular vote within each district. The Electoral College is intended to provide more weight to smaller states, thereby balancing the disproportionate voting power of states with larger populations. In all constitutional republics, the citizens elect leaders either directly or indirectly through other representatives chosen by popular vote. Therefore, the power to control the government is granted to the citizens of the constitutional republic.

*Micah Issitt*
*Philadelphia, Pennsylvania*

## Examples

Guatemala
Honduras
Iceland
Paraguay
Peru
United States
Uruguay

## Bibliography

Baylis, John, Steve Smith, and Patricia Owens. *The Globalization of World Politics: An Introduction to International Relations*. New York: Oxford UP, 2010. Print.

Caramani, Daniele. *Comparative Politics*. New York: Oxford UP, 2008. Print.

Garner, Robert, Peter Ferdinand, and Stephanie Lawson. *Introduction to Politics*. 2nd ed. Oxford: Oxford UP, 2009. Print.

Hague, Rod, and Martin Harrop. *Comparative Government and Politics: An Introduction*. New York: Palgrave, 2007. Print.

# Democracy

## Guiding Premise

Democracy is a political system based on majority rule, in which all citizens are guaranteed participatory rights to influence the evolution of government. There are many different types of democracy, based on the degree to which citizens participate in the formation and operation of the government. In a direct democratic system, citizens vote directly on proposed changes to law and public policy. In a representative democracy, individuals vote to elect representatives who then serve to create and negotiate public policy.

The democratic system of government first developed in Ancient Greece and has existed in many forms throughout history. While democratic systems always involve some type of majority rule component, most modern democracies have systems in place designed to equalize representation for minority groups or to promote the development of governmental policies that prevent oppression of minorities by members of the majority.

In modern democracies, one of the central principles is the idea that citizens must be allowed to participate in free elections to select leaders who serve in the government. In addition, voters in democratic systems elect political leaders for a limited period of time, thus ensuring that the leadership of the political system can change along with the changing views of the populace. Political theorists have defined democracy as a system in which the people are sovereign and the political power flows upward from the people to their elected leaders.

## Typical Structure

In a typical democracy, the government is usually divided into executive, legislative, and judicial branches. Citizens participate in electing individuals to serve in one or more of these branches, and elected leaders appoint additional leaders to serve in other political offices. The democratic system, therefore, involves a combination of elected and appointed leadership.

Democratic systems may follow a presidential model, as in the United States, where citizens elect a president to serve as both head of state and head of government. In a presidential model, citizens may also participate in elections to fill other governmental bodies, including the legislature and judicial branch. In a parliamentary democracy, citizens elect individuals to a parliament, whose members in turn form a committee to appoint a leader, often called the prime minister, who serves as head of government.

In most democratic systems, the executive and legislative branches cooperate in the formation of laws, while the judicial branch enforces and interprets the laws produced by the government. Most democratic systems have developed a system of checks and balances designed to prevent any single branch of government from exerting a dominant influence over the development of governmental policy. These checks and balances may be instituted in a variety of ways, including the ability to block governmental initiatives and the ability to appoint members to various governmental agencies.

Democratic governments generally operate on the principle of political parties, which are organizations formed to influence political development. Candidates for office have the option of joining a political party, which can provide funding and other campaign assistance. In some democratic systems—called dominant party or one-party dominant systems—there is effectively a single political party. Dominant party systems allow for competition in democratic elections, but existing power structures often prevent opposing parties from competing successfully. In multiparty democratic systems, there are two or more political parties with the ability to compete for office, and citizens are able to choose among political parties during elections. Some countries only allow political parties to be active at the national level, while other countries allow political parties to play a role in local and regional elections.

## Role of the Citizen

The citizens in a democratic society are seen as the ultimate source of political authority. Members of the government, by contrast, are seen as servants of the people, and are selected and elected to serve the people's interests. Democratic systems developed to protect and enhance the freedom of the people; however, for the system to function properly, citizens must engage in a number of civic duties.

In democratic nations, voting is a right that comes with citizenship. Though some democracies—Australia, for example—require citizens to vote by law, compulsory participation in elections is not common in democratic societies. Citizens are nonetheless encouraged to fulfill their voting rights and to stay informed regarding political issues. In addition, individuals are responsible for contributing to the well-being of society as a whole, usually through a system of taxation whereby part of an individual's earnings is used to pay for governmental services.

In many cases, complex governmental and legal issues must be simplified to ease understanding among the citizenry. This goal is partially met by having citizens elect leaders who must then explain to their constituents how they are shaping legislation and other government initiatives to reflect constituents' wants and needs. In the United States, citizens may participate in the election of local leaders within individual cities or counties, and also in the election of leaders who serve in the national legislature and executive offices.

Citizens in democratic societies are also empowered with the right to join political interest groups and political parties in an effort to further a broader political agenda. However, democratic societies oppose making group membership a requirement and have laws forbidding forcing an individual to join any group. Freedom of choice, especially with regard to political affiliation and preference, is one of the cornerstones of all democratic systems.

*Micah Issitt*
*Philadelphia, Pennsylvania*

## Examples

Denmark
Sweden
Spain
Japan
Australia
Costa Rica
Uruguay
United States

## Bibliography

Barington, Lowell. *Comparative Politics: Structures and Choices*. Boston: Wadsworth, 2012. Print.

Caramani, Daniele. *Comparative Politics*. New York: Oxford UP, 2008. Print.

Przeworski, Adam. *Democracy and the Limits of Self Government*, New York: Cambridge UP, 2010. Print.

# Dictatorship/Military Dictatorship

## Guiding Premise

Dictatorships and military dictatorships are political systems in which absolute power is held by an individual or military organization. Dictatorships are led by a single individual, under whom all political control is consolidated. Military dictatorships are similar in purpose, but place the system under the control of a military organization comprised of a single senior officer, or small group of officers. Often, dictatorships and military dictatorships are imposed as the result of a coup d'état in which the regime in question directly removes the incumbent regime, or after a power vacuum creates chaos in the nation. In both situations, the consolidation of absolute power is designed to establish a state of strict law and order.

## Typical Structure

Dictatorships and military dictatorships vary in structure and nature. Some come about through the overthrow of other regimes, while others are installed through the democratic process, and then become a dictatorship as democratic rights are withdrawn. Still others are installed following a complete breakdown of government, often with the promise of establishing order.

Many examples of dictatorships can be found in the twentieth century, including Nazi Germany, Joseph Stalin's Soviet Union, and China under Mao Tse-tung. A number of dictatorships existed in Africa, such as the regimes of Idi Amin in Uganda, Charles Taylor in Liberia, and Mu'ammar Gadhafi in Libya. Dictatorships such as these consolidated power in the hands of an individual leader. A dictator serves as the sole decision-maker in the government, frequently using the military, secret police, or other security agencies to enforce the leader's will. Dictators also have control over state institutions like legislatures. A legislature may have the ability to develop and pass laws, but if its actions run counter to the dictator's will, the latter can—and

frequently does—dissolve the body, replacing its members with those more loyal to the dictator's agenda.

Military dictatorships consolidate power not in the hands of a civilian but in an individual or small group of military officers—the latter of which are often called "juntas." Because military dictatorships are frequently installed following a period of civil war and/or a coup d'état, the primary focus of the dictatorship is to achieve strict order through the application of military force. Military dictatorships are often installed with the promise of an eventual return to civilian and/or democratic control once the nation has regained stability. In the case of North Korea, one-party communist rule turned into a communist military dictatorship as its leader, Kim Il-Sung, assumed control of the military and brought its leadership into the government.

In the late twentieth and early twenty-first centuries, dictatorships and military dictatorships are most commonly found in developing nations, where poverty rates are high and regional stability is tenuous at best. Many are former European colonies, where charismatic leaders who boast of their national heritage have stepped in to replace colonial governments. National resources are typically directed toward military and security organizations in an attempt to ensure security and internal stability, keeping the regime in power and containing rivals. Human rights records in such political systems are typically heavily criticized by the international community.

## Role of the Citizen

Dictatorships and military dictatorships are frequently installed because of the absence of viable democratic governments. There is often a disconnect, therefore, between the people and their leaders in a dictatorship. Of course, many dictatorships are identified as such by external entities and not by their own people. For example, the government of Zimbabwe is technically identified as a parliamentary democracy, with Robert Mugabe—who has been the elected leader of the country since 1980—as its president. However, the international community has long complained that Mugabe "won" his positions through political corruption, including alleged ballot stuffing. In 2008, Mugabe lost his first reelection campaign, but demanded a recount. While the recount continued, his supporters attacked opposition voters, utilizing violence and intimidation until his opponent, Morgan Tsvangirai, withdrew his candidacy, and Mugabe was restored as president.

By definition, citizens do not have a role in changing the course of a dictatorship's agenda. The people are usually called upon to join the military in support of the regime, or cast their vote consistently in favor of the ruling regime. Freedom of speech, the press, and assembly are virtually nonexistent, as those who speak out against the ruling regime are commonly jailed, tortured, or killed.

*Michael Auerbach*
*Marblehead, Massachusetts*

## Examples

Belarus (dictatorship)
Fiji (military dictatorship)
North Korea (military dictatorship)
Zimbabwe (dictatorship)

### Bibliography

Clayton, Jonathan. "China Aims to Bring Peace through Deals with Dictators and Warlords." *Times* [London]. Times Newspapers, 31 Jan. 2007. Web. 6 Feb. 2013.
"Robert Mugabe—Biography." *Biography.com.* A+E Television Networks, 2013. Web. 6 Feb. 2013.

# Ecclesiastical

## Guiding Premise

An ecclesiastical government is one in which the laws of the state are guided by and derived from religious law. Ecclesiastical governments can take a variety of forms and can be based on many different types of religious traditions. In some traditions, a deity or group of deities are considered to take a direct role in the formation of government, while other traditions utilize religious laws or principles indirectly to craft laws used to manage the state.

In many cultures, religious laws and tenets play a major role in determining the formation of national laws. Historically, the moral and ethical principles derived from Judeo-Christian tradition inspired many laws in Europe and North America. Few modern governments operate according to an ecclesiastical system, but Vatican City, which is commonly classified as a city-state, utilizes a modernized version of the ecclesiastical government model. All states utilizing an ecclesiastical or semi-ecclesiastical system have adopted a single state religion that is officially recognized by the government.

In some predominantly Islamic nations, including the Sudan, Oman, Iran, and Nigeria, Islamic law, known as sharia, is the basis for most national laws, and government leaders often must obtain approval by the leaders of the religious community before being allowed to serve in office. Most modern ecclesiastical or semi-ecclesiastical governments have adopted a mixed theocratic republic system in which individuals approved by religious authorities are elected by citizens to hold public office.

## Typical Structure

In an ecclesiastical government, the church or recognized religious authority is the source of all state law. In a theocracy, which is one of the most common types of ecclesiastical governments, a deity or group of deities occupies a symbolic position as head of state, while representatives are chosen to lead the government based on their approval by the prevailing religious authority. In other types of ecclesiastical governments, the chief of state may be the leading figure in the church, such as in Vatican City, where the Catholic Pope is also considered the chief of state.

There are no modern nations that operate on a purely ecclesiastical system, though some Islamic countries, like Iran, have adopted a semi-ecclesiastical form of republican government. In Iran, the popularly elected Assembly of Experts—comprised of Islamic scholars called mujtahids—appoints an individual to serve as supreme leader of the nation for life, and this individual has veto power over all other governmental offices. Iranian religious leaders also approve other individuals to run as candidates for positions in the state legislature. In many cases, the citizens will elect an individual to serve as head of government, though this individual must conform to religious laws.

In an ecclesiastical government, those eligible to serve in the state legislature are generally members of the church hierarchy or have been approved for office by church leaders. In Tibet, which functioned as an ecclesiastical government until the Chinese takeover of 1951, executive and legislative duties were consolidated under a few religious leaders, called lamas, and influential citizens who maintained the country under a theocratic system. Most modern nations separate governmental functions between distinct but interrelated executive, legislative, and judicial branches.

Many modern semi-ecclesiastical nations have adopted a set of state principles in the form of a constitution to guide the operation of government and the establishment of laws. In mixed constitutional/theocratic systems, the constitution may be used to legitimize religious authority by codifying a set of laws and procedures that have been developed from religious scripture.

In addition, the existence of a constitution facilitates the process of altering laws and governmental procedures as religious authorities reinterpret religious scriptures and texts.

## Role of the Citizen

Citizens in modern ecclesiastical and semi-ecclesiastical governments play a role in formulating the government though national and local elections. In some cases, religious authorities may approve more than one candidate for a certain position and citizens are then able to exercise legitimate choice in the electoral process. In other cases, popular support for one or more candidates may influence religious authorities when it comes time to nominate or appoint an individual to office.

In ecclesiastical governments, the freedoms and rights afforded to citizens may depend on their religious affiliation. Christians living in a Christian ecclesiastical government, for instance, may be allowed to run for and hold government office, while representatives of other religions may be denied this right. In addition, ecclesiastical governments may not recognize religious rights and rituals of other traditions and may not offer protection for those practicing religions other than the official state religion.

Though religious authority dominates politics and legislative development, popular influence is still an important part of the ecclesiastical system. Popular support for or against certain laws may convince the government to alter official policies. In addition, the populace may join local and regional religious bodies that can significantly affect national political developments. As local and regional religious groups grow in numbers and influence, they may promote candidates to political office, thereby helping to influence the evolution of government.

*Micah Issitt*
*Philadelphia, Pennsylvania*

## Examples

Afghanistan
Iran
Nigeria
Oman
Vatican City

## Bibliography

Barrington, Lowell. *Comparative Politics: Structures and Choices*. Boston: Wadsworth, 2012. Print.

Hallaq, Wael B. *An Introduction to Islamic Law*. New York: Cambridge UP, 2009. Print.

Hirschl, Ran. *Constitutional Theocracy*. Cambridge, MA: Harvard UP, 2010. Print.

# Failed State

## Guiding Premise

A failed state is a political unit that at one point had a stable government that provided basic services and security to its citizens, but then entered a period marked by devastating conflict, extreme poverty, overwhelming political corruption, and/or unlivable environmental conditions. Often, a group takes hold of a failed state's government through military means, staving off rivals to fill in a power vacuum. The nominal leadership of a failed state frequently uses its power to combat rival factions, implement extreme religious law, or protect and advance illicit activities (such as drug production or piracy). Failed states frequently retain their external borders, but within those borders are regions that may be dominated by a particular faction, effectively carving the state into disparate subunits, with some areas even attaining relative stability and security—a kind of de facto independence.

## Typical Structure

Failed states vary in appearance based on a number of factors. One such factor is the type of government that existed prior to the state's collapse. For example, a failed state might have originally existed as a parliamentary democracy, with an active legislature and executive system that developed a functioning legal code and administered to the needs of the people. However, that state may not have adequately addressed the needs of certain groups, fostering a violent backlash and hastening the country's destabilization. An ineffectual legislature might have been dissolved by the executive (a prime minister or president), and in the absence of leadership, the government as a whole ceased to operate effectively.

Another major factor is demographics. Many states are comprised of two or more distinct ethnic, social, or religious groups. When the ruling party fails to effectively govern and/or serve the interests of a certain segment of the population, it may be ousted or simply ignored by the marginalized faction within the state. If the government falls, it creates a power vacuum that rival groups compete to fill. If one faction gains power, it must remain in a constant state of vigilance against its rivals, focusing more on keeping enemies in check than on rebuilding crippled government infrastructure. Some also seek to create theocracies based on extreme interpretations of a particular religious doctrine. Frequently, these regimes are themselves ousted by rivals within a few years, leaving no lasting government and keeping the state in chaos.

Failed states are also characterized by extreme poverty and a lack of modern technology. Potable water, electricity, food, and medicine are scarce among average citizens. In some cases, these conditions are worsened by natural events. Haiti, for example, was a failed state for many years before the devastating 2010 earthquake that razed the capitol city of Port au Prince, deepening the country's poverty and instability. Afghanistan and Ethiopia—with their harsh, arid climates—are also examples of failed states whose physical environments and lack of resources exacerbated an already extreme state of impoverishment.

Most failed states' conditions are also worsened by the presence of foreigners. Because their governments are either unable or unwilling to repel terrorists, for example, failed states frequently become havens for international terrorism. Somalia, Afghanistan, and Iraq are all examples of states that failed, enabling terrorist organizations to set up camp within their borders. As such groups pose a threat to other nations, those nations often send troops and weapons into the failed states to engage the terrorists. In recent years, NATO, the United Nations, and the African Union have all entered failed states to both combat terrorists and help rebuild government.

## Role of the Citizen

Citizens of a failed state have very little say in the direction of their country. In most cases, when a faction assumes control over the government, it installs strict controls that limit the rights of citizens, particularly such rights as freedom of speech, freedom of assembly, and freedom of religion. Some regimes allow for "democratic" elections, but a continued lack of infrastructure and widespread corruption often negates the legitimacy of these elections.

Citizens of failed states are often called upon by the ruling regime (or a regional faction) to serve in its militia, helping it combat other factions within the state. In fact, many militias within failed states are comprised of people who were forced to join (under penalty of death) at a young age. Those who do not join militias are often drawn into criminal activity such as piracy and the drug trade.

Some citizens are able to make a difference by joining interest groups. Many citizens are able to achieve a limited amount of success sharing information about women's rights, HIV/AIDS and other issues. In some situations, these groups are able to gain international assistance from organizations that were unable to work with the failed government.

*Michael Auerbach*
*Marblehead, Massachusetts*

## Examples

Chad
Democratic Republic of the Congo
Somalia
Sudan
Zimbabwe

### Bibliography

"Failed States: Fixing a Broken World." *Economist*, 29 Jan. 2009. Web. 6 Feb. 2012.

"Failed States." Global Policy Forum, 2013. Web. 6 Feb. 2012.

"Somalia Tops Failed States Index for Fifth Year." *CNN.com*. Turner Broadcasting System, 18 June 2012. Web. 6 Feb. 2012.

Thürer, Daniel. (1999). "The 'Failed State' and International Law." *International Review of the Red Cross*. International Committee of the Red Cross, 31 Dec. 1999. Web. 6 Feb. 2012.

# Federal Republic

## Guiding Premise

A federal republic is a political system that features a central government as well as a set of regional subunits such as states or provinces. Federal republics are designed to limit the power of the central government, paring its focus to only matters of national interest. Typically, a greater degree of power is granted to the regional governments, which retain the ability to create their own laws of local relevance. The degree to which the federal and regional governments each enjoy authority varies from nation to nation, based on the country's interpretation of this republican form of government. By distributing authority to these separate but connected government institutions, federal republics give the greatest power to the people themselves, who typically vote directly for both their regional and national political representation.

## Typical Structure

A federal republic's structure varies from nation to nation. However, most federal republics feature two distinct governing entities. The first is a central, federal government, usually based in the nation's capital city. The federal government's task is to address issues of national importance. These issues include defense and foreign relations, but also encompass matters of domestic interest that must be addressed in uniform fashion, such as social assistance programs, infrastructure, and certain taxes.

A federal republic is comprised of executive, legislative, and judicial branches. The executive is typically a president or prime minister—the former selected by popular vote, the latter selected by members of the legislature—and is charged with the administration of the federal government's programs and regulations. The legislature—such as the US Congress, the Austrian Parliament, or the German Bundestag—is charged with developing laws and managing government spending. The judiciary is charged

with ensuring that federal and state laws are enforced and that they are consistent with the country's constitution.

The federal government is limited in terms of its ability to assert authority over the regions. Instead, federal republics grant a degree of sovereignty to the different states, provinces, or regions that comprise the entire nation. These regions have their own governments, similar in structure and procedure to those of the federal government. They too have executives, legislatures, and judiciaries whose foci are limited to the regional government's respective jurisdictions.

The federal and regional segments of a republic are not completely independent of one another, however. Although the systems are intended to distribute power evenly, federal and regional governments are closely linked. This connectivity ensures the efficient collection of taxes, the regional distribution of federal funds, and a rapid response to issues of national importance. A federal republic's greatest strength, therefore, is the series of connections it maintains between the federal, regional, and local governments it contains.

## Role of the Citizen

A federal republic is distinguished by the limitations of power it places on the national government. The primary goal of such a design was to place the power of government in the hands of the people. One of the ways the citizens' power is demonstrated is by participating in the electoral process. In a federal republic, the people elect their legislators. In some republics, the legislators in turn elect a prime minister, while in others, the people directly elect a president. The electoral process is an important way for citizens to influence the course of their government, both at the regional and federal levels. They do so by placing people who truly represent their diverse interests in the federal government.

The citizen is also empowered by participating in government as opposed to being subjected to it. In addition to taking part in the electoral process, the people are free to join and become active in a political party. A political party serves as a proxy for its members, representing their viewpoint and interests on a local and national level. In federal republics like Germany, a wide range of political parties are active in the legislature, advancing the political agendas of those they represent.

*Michael Auerbach*
*Marblehead, Massachusetts*

### Examples

Austria
Brazil
Germany
India
Mexico
Nigeria
United States

### Bibliography

"The Federal Principle." *Republik Österreich Parlament.* Republik Österreich Parlament, 8 Oct. 2010. Web. 6 Feb. 2013.

"The Federal Republic of Germany." *Deutscher Bundestag.* German Bundestag, 2013. Web. 6 Feb. 2013.

Collin, Nicholas. "An Essay on the Means of Promoting Federal Sentiments in the United States." *Friends of the Constitution: Writings of the "Other" Federalists, 1787–1788.* Ed. Colleen A. Sheehan and Gary L. McDowell. Online Library of Liberty, 2013. Web. 6 Feb. 2013.

# Federation

## Guiding Premise

A federation is a nation formed from the unification of smaller political entities. Federations feature federal governments that oversee nationwide issues. However, they also grant a degree of autonomy to the regional, state, or other local governments within the system. Federations are often formed because a collective of diverse regions find a common interest in unification. While the federal government is installed to address those needs, regions with their own distinct ethnic, socioeconomic, or political characteristics remain intact. This "separate but united" structure allows federations to avoid conflict and instability among their regions.

## Typical Structure

The primary goal of a federation is to unify a country's political subunits within a national framework. The federal government, therefore, features institutions comprised of representatives from the states or regions. The representatives are typically elected by the residents of these regions, and some federal systems give the power to elect certain national leaders to these representatives. The regions themselves can vary considerably in size. The Russian Federation, for example, includes forty-six geographically large provinces as well as two more-concentrated cities as part of its eighty-three constituent federation members.

There are two institutions in which individuals from the constituent parts of a federation serve. The first institution is the legislature. Legislatures vary in appearance from nation to nation. For example, the US Congress is comprised of two chambers—the House of Representatives and the Senate—whose directly elected members act on behalf of their respective states. The German Parliament, on the other hand, consists of the directly elected Bundestag—which is tasked with electing the German federal chancellor, among other things—and the state-appointed Bundesrat, which works on behalf of the country's sixteen states.

The second institution is the executive. Here, the affairs of the nation are administered by a president or similar leader. Again, the structure and powers of a federal government's executive institutions varies from nation to nation according to their constitutional framework. Federal executive institutions are charged with management of state affairs, including oversight of the military, foreign relations, health care, and education. Similarly diverse is the power of the executive in relation to the legislative branch. Some prime ministers, for example, enjoy considerably greater power than the president. In fact, some presidents share power with other leaders, or councils thereof within the executive branch, serving as the diplomatic face of the nation but not playing a major role in lawmaking. In India, for example, the president is the chief executive of the federal government, but shares power with the prime minister and the Council of Ministers, headed by the prime minister.

In order to promote continuity between the federal government and the states, regions, or other political subunits in the federation, those subunits typically feature governments that largely mirror that of the central government. Some of these regional governments are modified according to their respective constitutions. For example, whereas the bicameral US Congress consists of the Senate and House of Representatives, Nebraska's state legislature only has one chamber. Such distinctive characteristics of state/regional governments reflect the geographic and cultural interests of the region in question. It also underscores the degree of autonomy given to such states under a federation government system.

## Role of the Citizen

Federations vary in terms of both structure and distribution of power within government institutions. However, federal systems are typically democratic in nature, relying heavily on the participation of the electorate for installing representatives in those institutions. At the regional level, the people vote for their respective legislators and executives either directly or through political parties. The executive in turn appoints cabinet officials, while the legislators select a chamber leader. In US state governments, for example, such a leader might be a Senate president or speaker of the House of Representatives.

The people also play an important role in federal government. As residents of a given state or region, registered voters—again, through either a direct vote or through political parties—choose their legislators and national executives. In federations that utilize a parliamentary system, however, prime ministers are typically selected by the legislators and/or their political parties and not through a direct, national vote. Many constitutions limit the length of political leaders' respective terms of service and/or the number of times they may seek reelection, fostering an environment in which the democratic voting process is a frequent occurrence.

*Michael Auerbach*
*Marblehead, Massachusetts*

## Examples

Australia

Germany

India

Mexico

Russia

United States

## Bibliography

"Federal System of India." *Maps of India*. MapsOfIndia.com, 22 Sep. 2011. Web. 7 Feb. 2013.

"Political System." *Facts about Germany*. Frankfurter Societäts-Medien, 2011. Web. 7 Feb. 2013.

"Russia." *CIA World Factbook*. Central Intelligence Agency, 5 Feb. 2013. Web. 7 Feb. 2013.

# Monarchy

## Guiding Premise

A monarchy is a political system based on the sovereignty of a single individual who holds actual or symbolic authority over all governmental functions. The monarchy is one of the oldest forms of government in human history and was the most common type of government until the nineteenth century. In a monarchy, authority is inherited, usually through primogeniture, or inheritance by the eldest son.

In an absolute monarchy, the monarch holds authority over the government and functions as both head of state and head of government. In a constitutional monarchy, the role of the monarch is codified in the state constitution, and the powers afforded to the monarch are limited by constitutional law. Constitutional monarchies generally blend the inherited authority of the monarchy with popular control in the form of democratic elections. The monarch may continue to hold significant power over some aspects of government or may be relegated to a largely ceremonial or symbolic role.

In most ancient monarchies, the monarch was generally believed to have been chosen for his or her role by divine authority, and many monarchs in history have claimed to represent the will of a god or gods in their ascendancy to the position. In constitutional monarchies, the monarch may be seen as representing spiritual authority or may represent a link to the country's national heritage.

## Typical Structure

In an absolute monarchy, a single monarch is empowered to head the government, including the formulation of all laws and leadership of the nation's armed forces. Oman is one example of a type of absolute monarchy called a sultanate, in which a family of leaders, called "sultans," inherits authority and leads the nation under an authoritarian system. Power in the Omani sultanate remains within the royal family. In the event of the sultan's death or incapacitation, the Royal Family Council selects a successor by consensus from within the family line. Beneath the sultan is a council of ministers, appointed by the sultan, to create and disseminate official government policy. The sultan's council serves alongside an elected body of leaders who enforce and represent Islamic law and work with the sultan's ministers to create national laws.

In Japan, which is a constitutional monarchy, the Japanese emperor serves as the chief of state and symbolic representative of Japan's culture and history. The emperor officiates national ceremonies, meets with world leaders for diplomatic purposes, and symbolically appoints leaders to certain governmental posts. Governmental authority in Japan rests with the Diet, a legislative body of elected officials who serve limited terms of office and are elected through popular vote. A prime minister is also chosen to lead the Diet, and the prime minister is considered the official head of government.

The Kingdom of Norway is another example of a constitutional monarchy wherein the monarch serves a role that has been codified in the state constitution. The king of Norway is designated as the country's chief of state, serving as head of the nation's executive branch. Unlike Japan, where the monarch's role is largely symbolic, the monarch of Norway has considerable authority under the constitution, including the ability to veto and approve all laws and the power to declare war. Norway utilizes a parliamentary system, with a prime minister, chosen from individuals elected to the state parliament, serving as head of government. Though the monarch has authority over the executive functions of government, the legislature and prime minister are permitted the ability to override monarchical decisions with sufficient support, thereby providing a system of control to prevent the monarch from exerting a dominant influence over the government.

## Role of the Citizen

The role of the citizen in a monarchy varies depending on whether the government is a constitutional or absolute monarchy. In an absolute monarchy, citizens have only those rights given to them by the monarch, and the monarch has the power to extend and retract freedoms and rights at will. In ancient monarchies, citizens accepted the authoritarian role of the monarch, because it was widely believed that the monarch's powers were derived from divine authority. In addition, in many absolute monarchies, the monarch has the power to arrest, detain, and imprison individuals without due process, thereby providing a strong disincentive for citizens to oppose the monarchy.

In a constitutional monarchy, citizens are generally given greater freedom to participate in the development of governmental policies. In Japan, Belgium, and Spain, for instance, citizens elect governmental leaders, and the elected legislature largely controls the creation and enforcement of laws. In some countries, like the Kingdom of Norway, the monarch may exert significant authority, but this authority is balanced by that of the legislature, which represents the sovereignty of the citizens and is chosen to promote and protect the interests of the public.

The absolute monarchies of medieval Europe, Asia, and Africa held power for centuries, but many eventually collapsed due to popular uprisings as citizens demanded representation within the government. The development of constitutional monarchies may be seen as a balanced system in which the citizens retain significant control over the development of their government while the history and traditions of the nation are represented by the continuation of the monarch's lineage. In the United Kingdom, the governments of Great Britain and Northern Ireland are entirely controlled by elected individuals, but the continuation of the monarchy is seen by many as an important link to the nation's historic identity.

*Micah Issitt*
*Philadelphia, Pennsylvania*

## Examples

Belgium
Bhutan
Japan
Norway
Oman
United Kingdom

### Bibliography

Barrington, Lowell. *Comparative Politics: Structures and Choices*. Boston: Wadsworth, 2012. Print.
Dresch, Paul, and James Piscatori, eds. *Monarchies and Nations: Globalisation and Identity in the Arab States of the Gulf*. London: Tauris, 2005. Print.
Kesselman, Mark, et al. *European Politics in Transition*. New York: Houghton, 2009. Print.

# Parliamentary Monarchy

## Guiding Premise

A parliamentary monarchy is a political system in which leadership of the government is shared between a monarchy, such as a king or queen, and the members of a democratically elected legislative body. In such governments, the monarch's role as head of state is limited by the country's constitution or other founding document, preventing the monarch from assuming too much control over the nation. As head of state, the monarch may provide input during the lawmaking process and other operations of government. Furthermore, the monarch, whose role is generally lifelong, acts as a stabilizing element for the government, while the legislative body is subject to the periodic changes that occur with each election cycle.

## Typical Structure

Parliamentary monarchies vary in structure and distribution of power from nation to nation, based on the parameters established by each respective country's constitution or other founding document. In general, however, parliamentary monarchies feature a king, queen, or other sovereign who acts as head of state. In that capacity, the monarch's responsibilities may be little more than ceremonial in nature, allowing him or her to offer input during the lawmaking process, to approve the installation of government officials, and to act as the country's international representative. However, these responsibilities may be subject to the approval of the country's legislative body. For example, the king of Spain approves laws and regulations that have already been passed by the legislative branch; formally appoints the prime minister; and approves other ministers appointed by the prime minister. Yet, the king's responsibilities in those capacities are subject to the approval of the Cortes Generales, Spain's parliament.

In general, parliamentary monarchies help a country preserve its cultural heritage through their respective royal families, but grant the majority of government management and lawmaking responsibilities to the country's legislative branch and its various administrative ministries, such as education and defense. In most parliamentary monarchies, the ministers of government are appointed by the legislative body and usually by the prime minister. Although government ministries have the authority to carry out the country's laws and programs, they are also subject to criticism and removal by the legislative body if they fail to perform to expectations.

The legislative body itself consists of members elected through a democratic, constitutionally defined process. Term length, term limit, and the manner by which legislators may be elected are usually outlined in the country's founding documents. For example, in the Dutch parliament, members of the House of Representatives are elected every four years through a direct vote, while the members of the Senate are elected by provincial government councils every four years. By contrast, three-quarters of the members of Thailand's House of Representatives are elected in single-seat constituencies (smaller districts), while the remaining members are elected in larger, proportional representation districts; all members of the House are elected for four-year terms. A bare majority of Thailand's senators are elected by direct vote, with the remainder appointed by other members of the government.

## Role of the Citizen

While the kings and queens of parliamentary monarchies are the nominal heads of state, these political systems are designed to be democratic governments. As such, they rely heavily on the input and involvement of the citizens. Participating in legislative elections is one of the most direct ways in which the citizen is empowered. Because the governments of such systems are subject to legislative oversight, the people—through their respective votes for members of parliament—have influence over their government.

Political parties and organizations such as local and municipal councils also play an important role in parliamentary monarchies. Citizens' participation in those organizations can help shape parliamentary agendas and build links between government and the public. In Norway, for example, nearly 70 percent of citizens are involved in at least one such organization, and consequently Norway's Storting (parliament) has a number of committees that are tied to those organizations at the regional and local levels. Thus, through voting and active political involvement at the local level, the citizens of a parliamentary monarchy help direct the political course of their nation.

*Michael Auerbach*
*Marblehead, Massachusetts*

**Examples**

Netherlands
Norway
Spain
Sweden
Thailand
United Kingdom

**Bibliography**

"Form of Government." *Norway.org*. Norway–The Official Site in the United States, n.d. Web. 17 Jan. 2013.

"Issues: Parliament." *Governmentl.nl*. Government of the Netherlands, n.d. Web. 17 Jan. 2013.

"King, Prime Minister, and Council of Ministers." *Country Studies: Spain*. Lib. of Congress, 2012. Web. 17 Jan. 2013.

"Thailand." *International Foundation for Electoral Systems*. IFES, 2013. Web. 17 Jan. 2013.

# Parliamentary Republic

## Guiding Premise

A parliamentary republic is a system wherein both executive and legislative powers are centralized in the legislature. In such a system, voters elect their national representatives to the parliamentary body, which in turn appoints the executive. In such an environment, legislation is passed more quickly than in a presidential system, which requires a consensus between the executive and legislature. It also enables the legislature to remove the executive in the event the latter does not perform to the satisfaction of the people. Parliamentary republics can also prevent the consolidation of power in a single leader, as even a prime minister must defer some authority to fellow legislative leaders.

## Typical Structure

Parliamentary republics vary in structure from nation to nation, according to the respective country's constitution or other governing document. In general, such a system entails the merger of the legislature and head of state such as a president or other executive. The state may retain the executive, however. However, the executive's role may be largely ceremonial, as is the case in Greece, where the president has very little political authority. This "outsider" status has in fact enabled the Greek president to act as a diplomatic intermediary among sparring parliamentary leaders.

While many countries with such a system operate with an executive—who may or may not be directly elected, and who typically has limited powers—the bulk of a parliamentary republic's political authority rests with the legislature. The national government is comprised of democratically elected legislators and their appointees. The length of these representatives' respective terms, as well as the manner by which the legislators are elected, depend on the frameworks established by each individual nation. Some parliamentary republics utilize a constitution for this purpose, while others use a set of common laws or other legal precepts. In South Africa, members of the parliament's two chambers, the National Assembly and the National Council of Provinces, are elected differently. The former's members are elected directly by the citizens in each province, while the latter's members are installed by the provincial legislatures.

Once elected to parliament, legislators are often charged with more than just lawmaking. In many cases, members of parliament oversee the administration of state affairs as well. Legislative bodies in parliamentary republics are responsible for nominating an executive—typically a prime minister—to manage the government's various administrative responsibilities. Should the executive not adequately perform its duties, parliament has the power to remove the executive from office. In Ireland, for example, the Dail Eireann (the House of Representatives) is charged with forming the country's executive branch by nominating the Taoiseach (prime minister) and approving the prime minister's cabinet selections.

## Role of the Citizen

A parliamentary republic is a democratic political system that relies on the involvement of an active electorate. This civic engagement includes a direct or indirect vote for representatives to parliament. While the people do not vote for an executive as well, by way of their vote for parliament, the citizenry indirectly influences the selection of the chief executive and the policies he or she follows. In many countries, the people also indirectly influence the national government by their votes in provincial government. As noted earlier, some countries' parliaments include chambers whose members are appointed by provincial leaders.

Citizens may also influence the political system through involvement in political parties. Such organizations help shape the platforms of parliamentary majorities as well as selecting candidates for prime minister and other government positions. The significance of political parties varies from nation to nation, but such organizations require the input and involvement of citizens.

*Michael Auerbach*
*Marblehead, Massachusetts*

## Examples
Austria
Greece

Iceland
Ireland
Poland
South Africa

## Bibliography
"About the Oireachtas." *Oireachtas.ie*. Houses of the Oireachtas, n.d. Web. 7 Feb. 2013.
"Our Parliament." *Parliament.gov*. Parliament of the Republic of South Africa, n.d. Web. 7 Feb. 2013.
Tagaris, Karolina, and Ingrid Melander. "Greek President Makes Last Push to Avert Elections." *Reuters*. Thomson Reuters, 12 May 2012. Web. 7 Feb. 2013.

# Presidential

## Guiding Premise

A presidential system is a type of democratic government in which the populace elects a single leader—a president—to serve as both head of state and the head of government. The presidential system developed from the monarchic governments of medieval and early modern Europe, in which a royal monarch, holder of an inherited office, served as both head of state and government. In the presidential system, the president does not inherit the office, but is chosen by either direct or indirect popular vote.

Presidential systems differ from parliamentary systems in that the president is both the chief executive and head of state, whereas in a parliamentary system another individual, usually called the "prime minister," serves as head of government and leader of the legislature. The presidential system evolved out of an effort to create an executive office that balances the influence of the legislature and the judiciary. The United States is the most prominent example of a democratic presidential system.

Some governments have adopted a semi-presidential system, which blends elements of the presidential system with the parliamentary system, and generally features a president who serves only as head of state. In constitutional governments, like the United States, Mexico, and Honduras, the role of the president is described in the nation's constitution, which also provides for the president's powers in relation to the other branches of government.

## Typical Structure

In most modern presidential governments, power to create and enforce laws and international agreements is divided among three branches: the executive, legislative, and judicial. The executive office consists of the president and a number of presidential advisers—often called the cabinet—who typically serve at the president's discretion and are not elected to office. The terms of office for the president are codified in the state constitution and, in most cases, the president may serve a limited number of terms before he or she becomes ineligible for reelection.

The president serves as head of state and is therefore charged with negotiating and administering international treaties and agreements. In addition, the president serves as head of government and is therefore charged with overseeing the function of the government as a whole. The president is also empowered, in most presidential governments, with the ability to deploy the nation's armed forces. In some governments, including the United States, the approval of the legislature is needed for the country to officially declare war.

The legislative branch of the government proposes new laws, in the form of bills, but must cooperate with the executive office to pass these bills into law. The legislature and the executive branch also cooperate in determining the government budget. Unlike prime ministers under the parliamentary system, the president is not considered a member of the legislature and therefore acts independently as the chief executive, though a variety of governmental functions require action from both branches of government. A unique feature of the presidential system is that the election of the president is separate from the election of the legislature.

In presidential systems, members of the legislature are often less likely to vote according to the goals of their political party and may support legislation that is not supported by their chosen political party. In parliamentary systems, like the government of Great Britain, legislators are more likely to vote according to party policy. Presidential systems are also often marked by a relatively small number of political parties, which often allows one party to achieve a majority in the legislature. If this majority coincides with the election of a president from the same party, that party's platform or agenda becomes dominant until the next election cycle.

The judicial branch in a presidential system serves to enforce the laws among the populace. In most modern presidential democracies, the president appoints judges to federal posts, though in some governments, the legislature appoints judges. In some cases, the president may need the approval of the legislature to make judicial appointments.

## Role of the Citizen

In a democratic presidential system, citizens are empowered with the ability to vote for president and therefore have ultimate control over who serves as head of government and head of state. Some presidential governments elect individuals to the presidency based on the result of a popular vote, while other governments use an indirect system, in which citizens vote for a party or for individuals who then serve as their representatives in electing the president. The United States utilizes an indirect system called the Electoral College.

Citizens in presidential systems are also typically allowed, though not required, to join political parties in an effort to promote a political agenda. Some governmental systems that are modeled on the presidential system allow the president to exert a dominant influence over the legislature and other branches of the government. In some cases, this can lead to a presidential dictatorship, in which the president may curtail the political rights of citizens. In most presidential systems, however, the roles and powers of the legislative and executive branches are balanced to protect the rights of the people to influence their government.

In a presidential system, citizens are permitted to vote for a president representing one political party, while simultaneously voting for legislators from other political parties. In this way, the presidential system allows citizens to determine the degree to which any single political party is permitted to have influence on political development.

*Micah Issitt*
*Philadelphia, Pennsylvania*

## Examples

Benin
Costa Rica
Dominican Republic
Guatemala
Honduras
Mexico
United States
Venezuela

### Bibliography

Barington, Lowell. *Comparative Politics*: *Structures and Choices*. Boston: Wadsworth, 2012. Print.

Caramani, Daniele. *Comparative Politics*. New York: Oxford UP, 2008. Print.

Garner, Robert, Peter Ferdinand, and Stephanie Lawson. *Introduction to Politics*. 2nd ed. Oxford: Oxford UP, 2009. Print.

# Republic

**Guiding Premise**

A republic is a type of government based on the idea of popular or public sovereignty. The word "republic" is derived from Latin terms meaning "matters" and "the public." In essence, a republic is a government in which leaders are chosen by the public rather than by inheritance or by force. The republic or republican governmental system emerged in response to absolute monarchy, in which hereditary leaders retained all the power. In contrast, the republican system is intended to create a government that is responsive to the people's will.

Most modern republics operate based on a democratic system in which citizens elect leaders by popular vote. The United States and Mexico are examples of countries that use a democratic republican system to appoint leaders to office. However, universal suffrage (voting for all) is not required for a government to qualify as a republic, and it is possible for a country to have a republican government in which only certain categories of citizens, such as the wealthy, are allowed to vote in elections.

In addition to popular vote, most modern republics are further classified as constitutional republics, because the laws and rules for appointing leaders have been codified in a set of principles and guidelines known as a "constitution." When combined with universal suffrage and constitutional law, the republican system is intended to form a government that is based on the will of the majority while protecting the rights of minority groups.

**Typical Structure**

Republican governments are typically led by an elected head of state, generally a president. In cases where the president also serves as the head of government, the government is called a "presidential republic." In some republics, the head of state serves alongside an appointed or elected head of government, usually a prime minister.

This mixed form of government blends elements of the republic system with the parliamentary system found in countries such as the United Kingdom or India.

The president is part of the executive branch of government, which represents the country internationally and heads efforts to make and amend international agreements and treaties. The laws of a nation are typically created by the legislative branch, which may also be composed of elected leaders. Typically, the legislative and executive branches must cooperate on key initiatives, such as determining the national budget.

In addition to legislative and executive functions, most republics have a judiciary charged with enforcing and interpreting laws. The judicial branch may be composed of elected leaders, but in many cases, judicial officers are appointed by the president and/or the legislature. In the United States (a federal republic), the president, who leads the executive branch, appoints members to the federal judiciary, but these choices must be approved by the legislature before they take effect.

The duties and powers allotted to each branch of the republican government are interconnected with those of the other branches in a system of checks and balances. For instance, in Mexico (a federal republic), the legislature is empowered to create new tax guidelines for the public, but before legislative tax bills become law, they must first achieve majority support within the two branches of the Mexican legislature and receive the approval of the president. By creating a system of separate but balanced powers, the republican system seeks to prevent any one branch from exerting a dominant influence over the government.

**Role of the Citizen**

The role of the citizen in a republic depends largely on the type of republican system that the country has adopted. In democratic republics, popular elections and constitutional law give the public significant influence over governmental development and establish the people as the primary source of political power. Citizens in democratic republics are empowered to join political groups and to influence the development of laws and policies through the election of public leaders.

In many republican nations, a powerful political party or other political group can dominate the government, preventing competition from opposing political groups and curtailing the public's role in selecting and approving leaders. For instance, in the late twentieth century, a dominant political party maintained control of the Gambian presidency and legislature for more than thirty years, thereby significantly limiting the role of the citizenry in influencing the development of government policy.

In general, the republican system was intended to reverse the power structure typical of the monarchy system, in which inherited leaders possess all of the political power. In the republican system, leaders are chosen to represent the people's interests with terms of office created in such a way that new leaders must be chosen at regular intervals, thereby preventing a single

leader or political entity from dominating the populace. In practice, popular power in a republic depends on preventing a political monopoly from becoming powerful enough to alter the laws of the country to suit the needs of a certain group rather than the whole.

*Micah Issitt*
*Philadelphia, Pennsylvania*

## Examples
Algeria
Argentina
Armenia
France
Gambia
Mexico
San Marino
South Sudan
Tanzania
United States

### Bibliography
Caramani, Daniele. *Comparative Politics*. New York: Oxford UP, 2008. Print.
Przeworski, Adam. *Democracy and the Limits of Self-Government*. New York: Cambridge UP, 2010. Print.

# Socialist

## Guiding Premise

Socialism is a political and economic system that seeks to elevate the common good of the citizenry by allowing the government to own all property and means of production. In the most basic model, citizens cooperatively elect members to government, and the government then acts on behalf of the people to manage the state's property, industry, production, and services.

In a socialist system, communal or government ownership of property and industry is intended to eliminate the formation of economic classes and to ensure an even distribution of wealth. Most modern socialists also believe that basic services, including medical and legal care, should be provided at the same level to all citizens and not depend on the individual citizen's ability to pay for better services. The origins of socialism can be traced to theorists such as Thomas More (1478–1535), who believed that private wealth and ownership led to the formation of a wealthy elite class that protected its own wealth while oppressing members of lower classes.

There are many different forms of socialist philosophy, some of which focus on economic systems, while others extend socialist ideas to other aspects of society. Communism may be considered a form of socialism, based on the idea that a working-class revolution is needed to initiate the ideal socialist society.

## Typical Structure

Socialism exists in many forms around the world, and many governments use a socialist model for the distribution of key services, most often medical and legal aid. A socialist state is a government whose constitution explicitly gives the government powers to facilitate the creation of a socialist society.

The idealized model of the socialist state is one in which the populace elects leaders to head the government, and the government then oversees the distribution of wealth and goods among the populace, enforces the laws, and provides for the well-being of citizens. Many modern socialist governments follow a communist model, in which a national communist political party has ultimate control over governmental legislation and appointments.

There are many different models of socialist states, integrating elements of democratic or parliamentary systems. In these cases, democratic elections may be held to elect the head of state and the body of legislators. The primary difference between a socialist democracy and a capitalist democracy can be found in the state's role in the ownership of key industries. Most modern noncommunist socialist states provide state regulation and control over key industries but allow some free-market competition as well.

In a socialist system, government officials appoint leaders to oversee various industries and to regulate prices based on public welfare. For instance, if the government retains sole ownership over agricultural production, the government must appoint individuals to manage and oversee that industry, organize agricultural labor, and oversee the distribution of food products among the populace. Some countries, such as Sweden, have adopted a mixed model in which socialist industry management is blended with free-market competition.

## Role of the Citizen

All citizens in a socialist system are considered workers, and thus all exist in the same economic class. While some citizens may receive higher pay than others—those who work in supervisory roles, for instance—limited ownership of private property and standardized access to services places all individuals on a level field with regard to basic welfare and economic prosperity.

The degree to which personal liberties are curtailed within a socialist system depends upon the type of socialist philosophy adopted and the degree to which corruption and authoritarianism play a role in government. In most modern communist governments, for instance, individuals are often prohibited from engaging in any activity seen as contrary to the overall goals of the state or to the policies of the dominant political party. While regulations of this kind are common in communist societies, social control over citizens is not necessary for a government to follow a socialist model.

Under democratic socialism, individuals are also expected to play a role in the formation of their government by electing leaders to serve in key positions. In Sri Lanka, for instance, citizens elect members to serve in the parliament and a president to serve as head of the executive branch. In Portugal, citizens vote in multiparty elections to elect a president who serves as head of state, and the president appoints a prime minister to serve as head of government. In both Portugal and Sri Lanka, the government is constitutionally bound to promote a socialist society, though both governments allow private ownership and control of certain industries.

Citizens in a socialist society are also expected to provide for one another by contributing to labor and by forfeiting some ownership rights to provide for the greater good. In the Kingdom of Sweden, a mixed parliamentary system, all citizens pay a higher tax rate to contribute to funds that provide for national health care, child care, education, and worker support systems. Citizens who have no children and require only minimal health care benefits pay the same tax rate as those who have greater need for the nation's socialized benefits.

*Micah Issitt*
*Philadelphia, Pennsylvania*

## Examples

China

Cuba

Portugal

Sri Lanka

Venezuela

Zambia

### Bibliography

Caramani, Daniele. *Comparative Politics*. New York: Oxford UP, 2008. Print.

Heilbroner, Robert. "Socialism." *Library of Economics and Liberty*. Liberty Fund, 2008. Web. 17 Jan. 2013.

Howard, Michael Wayne. *Socialism*. Amherst, NY: Humanity, 2001. Print.

# Sultanate/Emirate

## Guiding Premise

A sultanate or emirate form of government is a political system in which a hereditary ruler—a monarch, chieftain, or military leader—acts as the head of state. Emirates and sultanates are most commonly found in Islamic nations in the Middle East, although others are found in Southeast Asia as well. Sultans and emirs frequently assume titles such as president or prime minister in addition to their royal designations, meshing the traditional ideal of a monarch with the administrative capacities of a constitutional political system.

## Typical Structure

A sultanate or emirate combines the administrative duties of the executive with the powers of a monarch. The emir or sultan acts as the head of government, appointing all cabinet ministers and officials. In Brunei, a sultanate, the government was established according to the constitution (set up after the country declared autonomy from Britain in 1959). The sultan did assemble a legislative council in order to facilitate the lawmaking process, but this council has consistently remained subject to the authority of the sultan and not to a democratic process. In 2004, there was some movement toward the election of at least some of the members of this council. In the meantime, the sultan maintains a ministerial system by appointment and also serves as the nation's chief religious leader.

In some cases, an emirate or sultanate appears similar to a federal system. In the United Arab Emirates (UAE), for example, the nation consists of not one but seven emirates. This system came into being after the seven small regions achieved independence from Great Britain. Each emirate developed its own government system under the leadership of an emir. However, in 1971, the individual emirates agreed to join as a federation, drafting a constitution that identified the areas of common interest to the entire

group of emirates. Like Brunei, the UAE's initial government structure focused on the authority of the emirs and the various councils and ministries formed at the UAE's capital of Abu Dhabi. However, beginning in the early twenty-first century, the UAE's legislative body, the Federal National Council, has been elected by electoral colleges from the seven emirates, thus further engaging various local areas and reflecting their interests.

Sultanates and emirates are at times part of a larger nation, with the sultans or emirs answering to the authority of another government. This is the case in Malaysia, where the country is governed by a constitutional monarchy. However, most of Malaysia's western political units are governed by sultans, who act as regional governors and, in many cases, religious leaders, but remain subject to the king's authority in Malaysia's capital of Kuala Lumpur.

## Role of the Citizen

Sultanates and emirates are traditionally non-democratic governments. Like those of other monarchs, the seats of emirs and sultans are hereditary. Any votes for these leaders to serve as prime minister or other head of government are cast by ministers selected by the emirs and sultans. Political parties may exist in these countries as well, but these parties are strictly managed by the sultan or emir; opposition parties are virtually nonexistent in such systems, and some emirates have no political parties at all.

As shown in the UAE and Malaysia, however, there are signs that the traditional sultanate or emirate is increasingly willing to engage their respective citizens. For example, the UAE, between 2006 and 2013, launched a series of reforms designed to strengthen the role of local governments and relations with the people they serve. Malaysia may allow sultans to continue their regional controls, but at the same time, the country continues to evolve its federal system, facilitating multiparty democratic elections for its national legislature.

*Michael Auerbach*
*Marblehead, Massachusetts*

## Examples
Brunei
Kuwait
Malaysia
Qatar
United Arab Emirates

**Bibliography**
"Brunei." *The World Factbook*. Central Intelligence Agency, 2 Jan. 2013. Web. 17 Jan. 2013.
"Malaysia." *The World Factbook*. Central Intelligence Agency, 7 Jan. 2013. Web. 17 Jan. 2013.
"Political System." *UAE Interact*. UAE National Media Council, n.d. Web. 17 Jan. 2013.
*Prime Minister's Office, Brunei Darussalam*. Prime Minister's Office, Brunei Darussalam, 2013. Web. 17 Jan. 2013.

# Theocratic Republic

## Guiding Premise

A theocratic republic is a type of government blending popular and religious influence to determine the laws and governmental principles. A republic is a governmental system based on the concept of popular rule and takes its name from the Latin words for "public matter." The defining characteristic of a republic is that civic leaders hold elected, rather than inherited, offices. A theocracy is a governmental system in which a supreme deity is considered the ultimate authority guiding civil matters.

No modern nations can be classified as pure theocratic republics, but some nations, such as Iran, maintain a political system largely dominated by religious law. The Buddhist nation of Tibet operated under a theocratic system until it was taken over by Communist China in the early 1950s.

In general, a theocratic republic forms in a nation or other governmental system dominated by a single religious group. The laws of the government are formed in reference to a set of religious laws, either taken directly from sacred texts or formulated by religious scholars and authority figures. Most theocratic governments depend on a body of religious scholars who interpret religious scripture, advise all branches of government, and oversee the electoral process.

## Typical Structure

In a typical republic, the government is divided into executive, legislative, and judicial branches, and citizens vote to elect leaders to one or more of the branches of government. In most modern republics, voters elect a head of state, usually a president, to lead the executive branch. In many republics, voters also elect individuals to serve as legislators. Members of the judiciary may be elected by voters or may be appointed to office by other elected leaders. In nontheocratic republics, the citizens are considered the ultimate source of authority in the government.

In a theocratic republic, however, one or more deities are considered to represent the ultimate governmental authority. In some cases, the government may designate a deity as the ultimate head of state. Typically, any individual serving as the functional head of state is believed to have been chosen by that deity, and candidates for the position must be approved by the prevailing religious authority.

In some cases, the religious authority supports popular elections to fill certain governmental posts. In Iran, for instance, citizens vote to elect members to the national parliament and a single individual to serve as president. The Iranian government is ultimately led by a supreme leader, who is appointed to office by the Assembly of Experts, the leaders of the country's Islamic community. Though the populace chooses the president and leaders to serve in the legislature, the supreme leader of Iran can overrule decisions made in any other branch of the government.

In a theocratic republic, the power to propose new laws may be given to the legislature, which works on legislation in conjunction with the executive branch. However, all laws must conform to religious law, and any legislation produced within the government is likely to be abolished if it is deemed by the religious authorities to violate religious principles. In addition, religious leaders typically decide which candidates are qualified to run for specific offices, thereby ensuring that the citizens will not elect individuals who are likely to oppose religious doctrine.

In addition, many modern nations that operate on a partially theocratic system may adopt a set of governmental principles in the form of a constitution, blended with religious law. This mixed constitutional theocratic system has been adopted by an increasing number of Islamic nations, including Iraq, Afghanistan, Mauritania, and some parts of Nigeria.

## Role of the Citizen

Citizens in a theocratic republic are expected to play a role in forming the government through elections, but they are constrained in their choices by the prevailing religious authority. Citizens are also guaranteed certain freedoms, typically codified in a constitution, that have been formulated with reference to religious law. All citizens must adhere to religious laws, regardless of their personal religious beliefs or membership within any existing religious group.

In many Middle Eastern and African nations that operate on the basis of an Islamic theocracy, citizens elect leaders from groups of candidates chosen by the prevailing religious authority. While the choices presented to the citizens are more limited than in a democratic, multiparty republic, the citizens nevertheless play a role in determining the evolution of the government through their voting choices.

The freedoms and rights afforded to citizens in a theocratic republic may depend, in part, on the individual's religious affiliation. For instance, Muslims living in Islamic theocracies may be permitted to hold political office or to aspire to other influential political positions, while members of minority religious groups may find their rights and freedoms limited. Religious minorities living in Islamic republics may not be permitted to run for certain offices, such as president, and must follow laws that adhere to Islamic principles but may violate their own religious principles. Depending on the country and the adherents' religion, the practice of their faith may itself be considered criminal.

*Micah Issitt*
*Philadelphia, Pennsylvania*

## Examples

Afghanistan
Iran
Iraq
Pakistan
Mauritania
Nigeria

### Bibliography

Cooper, William W., and Piyu Yue. *Challenges of the Muslim World: Present, Future and Past.* Boston: Elsevier, 2008. Print.

Hirschl, Ran. *Constitutional Theocracy.* Cambridge: Harvard UP, 2010. Print.

# Totalitarian

### Guiding Premise

A totalitarian government is one in which a single political party maintains absolute control over the state and is responsible for creating all legislation without popular referendum. In general, totalitarianism is considered a type of authoritarian government where the laws and principles used to govern the country are based on the authority of the leading political group or dictator. Citizens under totalitarian regimes have limited freedoms and are subject to social controls dictated by the state.

The concept of totalitarianism evolved in fascist Italy in the 1920s, and was first used to describe the Italian government under dictator Benito Mussolini. The term became popular among critics of the authoritarian governments of Fascist Italy and Nazi Germany in the 1930s. Supporters of the totalitarian philosophy believed that a strong central government, with absolute control over all aspects of society, could achieve progress by avoiding political debate and power struggles between interest groups.

In theory, totalitarian regimes—like that of Nazi Germany and modern North Korea—can more effectively mobilize resources and direct a nation toward a set of overarching goals. Adolf Hitler was able to achieve vast increases in military power during a short period of time by controlling all procedural steps involved in promoting military development. In practice, however, pure totalitarianism has never been achieved, as citizens and political groups generally find ways to subvert complete government control.

Totalitarianism differs from authoritarianism in that a totalitarian government is based on the idea that the highest leader takes total control in order to create a flourishing society for the benefit of the people. By contrast, authoritarian regimes are based on the authority of a single, charismatic individual who develops policies designed to maintain personal power, rather than promote public interest.

### Typical Structure

In a fully realized totalitarian system, a single leader or group of leaders controls all governmental functions, appointing individuals to serve in various posts to facilitate the development of legislation and oversee the enforcement of laws. In Nazi Germany, for instance, Adolf Hitler created a small group of executives to oversee the operation of the government. Governmental authority was then further disseminated through a complex network of departments, called ministries, with leaders appointed directly by Hitler.

Some totalitarian nations may adopt a state constitution in an effort to create the appearance of democratic popular control. In North Korea, the country officially operates under a multiparty democratic system, with citizens guaranteed the right to elect leaders to both the executive and legislative branches of government. In practice, the Workers' Party of North Korea is the only viable political party, as it actively controls competing parties and suppresses any attempt to mount political opposition. Under Supreme Leader Kim Il-sung, the Workers' Party amended the constitution to allow Kim to serve as the sole executive leader for life, without the possibility of being removed from office by any governmental action.

In some cases, totalitarian regimes may favor a presidential system, with the dictator serving officially as president, while other totalitarian governments may adopt a parliamentary system, with a prime minister as head of government. Though a single dictator generally heads the nation with widespread powers over a variety of governmental functions, a cabinet or group of high-ranking ministers may also play a prominent role in disseminating power throughout the various branches of government.

## Role of the Citizen

Citizens in totalitarian regimes are often subject to strict social controls exerted by the leading political party. In many cases, totalitarian governments restrict the freedom of the press, expression, and speech in an effort to limit opposition to the government. In addition, totalitarian governments may use the threat of police or military action to prevent protest movements against the leading party. Totalitarian governments maintain absolute control over the courts and any security agency, and the legal/judicial system therefore exists only as an extension of the leading political party.

Totalitarian governments like North Korea also attempt to restrict citizens' access to information considered subversive. For instance, North Korean citizens are not allowed to freely utilize the Internet or any other informational source, but are instead only allowed access to government-approved websites and publications. In many cases, the attempt to control access to information creates a black market for publications and other forms of information banned by government policy.

In some cases, government propaganda and restricted access to information creates a situation in which citizens actively support the ruling regime. Citizens may honestly believe that the social and political restrictions imposed by the ruling party are necessary for the advancement of society. In other cases, citizens may accept governmental control to avoid reprisal from the military and police forces. Most totalitarian regimes have established severe penalties, including imprisonment, corporal punishment, and death, for criticizing the government or refusing to adhere to government policy.

*Micah Issitt*
*Philadelphia, Pennsylvania*

## Examples

Fascist Italy (1922–1943)
Nazi Germany (1933–1945)
North Korea
Stalinist Russia (1924–1953)

### Bibliography

Barrington, Lowell. *Comparative Politics: Structures and Choices*. Boston: Wadsworth, 2012. Print.

Gleason, Abbot. *Totalitarianism: The Inner History of the Cold War*. New York: Oxford UP, 1995. Print.

McEachern, Patrick. *Inside the Red Box: North Korea's Post-Totalitarian Regime*. New York: Columbia UP, 2010. Print.

# Treaty System

## Guiding Premise

A treaty system is a framework within which participating governments agree to collect and share scientific information gathered in a certain geographic region, or otherwise establish mutually agreeable standards for the use of that region. The participants establish rules and parameters by which researchers may establish research facilities and travel throughout the region, ensuring that there are no conflicts, that the environment is protected, and that the region is not used for illicit purposes. This system is particularly useful when the region in question is undeveloped and unpopulated, but could serve a number of strategic and scientific purposes.

## Typical Structure

A treaty system of government is an agreement between certain governments that share a common interest in the use of a certain region to which no state or country has yet laid internationally recognized claim. Participating parties negotiate treaty systems that, upon agreement, form a framework by which the system will operate. Should the involved parties be United Nations member states, the treaty is then submitted to the UN Secretariat for registration and publication.

The agreement's founding ideals generally characterize the framework of a treaty. For example, the most prominent treaty system in operation today is the Antarctic Treaty System, which currently includes fifty nations whose scientists are studying Antarctica. This system, which entered into force in 1961, focuses on several topics, including environmental protection, tourism, scientific operations, and the peaceful use of that region. Within these topics, the treaty system enables participants to meet, cooperate, and share data on a wide range of subjects. Such cooperative activities include regional meetings, seminars, and large-scale conferences.

A treaty system is not a political institution in the same manner as state governments. Rather, it is an agreement administered by delegates from the involved entities. Scientists seeking to perform their research in Antarctica, for example, must apply through the scientific and/or government institutions of their respective nations. In the case of the United States, scientists may apply for grants from the National Science Foundation. These institutions then examine the study in question for its relevance to the treaty's ideals.

Central to the treaty system is the organization's governing body. In the case of the Antarctic Treaty, that body is the Antarctic Treaty Secretariat, which is based in Buenos Aires, Argentina. The Secretariat oversees all activities taking place under the treaty, welcomes new members, and addresses any conflicts or issues between participants. It also reviews any activities to ensure that they are in line with the parameters of the treaty. A treaty system is not a sovereign organization, however. Each participating government retains autonomy, facilitating its own scientific expeditions, sending delegates to the treaty system's main governing body, and reviewing the treaty to ensure that it coincides with its national interests.

## Role of the Citizen

Although treaty systems are not sovereign government institutions, private citizens can and frequently do play an important role in their function and success. For example, the Antarctic Treaty System frequently conducts large-scale planning conferences, to which each participating government sends delegates. These teams are comprised of qualified scientists who are nominated and supported by their peers during the government's review process. In the United States, for example, the State Department oversees American participation in the Antarctic

Treaty System's events and programs, including delegate appointments.

Another area in which citizens are involved in a treaty system is in the ratification process. Every nation's government—usually through its legislative branch—must formally approve any treaty before the country can honor the agreement. This ratification is necessary for new treaties as well as treaties that must be reapproved every few years. Citizens, through their elected officials, may voice their support or disapproval of a new or updated treaty.

While participating governments administer treaty systems and their secretariats, those who conduct research or otherwise take part in activities in the region in question are not usually government employees. In Antarctica, for example, university professors, engineers, and other private professionals—supported by a combination of private and government funding—operate research stations.

*Michael Auerbach*
*Marblehead, Massachusetts*

### Example
Antarctic Treaty System

### Bibliography
"Antarctic." *Ocean and Polar Affairs.* US Department of State, 22 Mar. 2007. Web. 8 Feb. 2013.
"About Us." *Antarctic Treaty System.* Secretariat of the Antarctic Treaty, n.d. Web. 8 Feb. 2013.
"United Nations Treaty Series." *United Nations Treaty Collection.* United Nations, 2013. Web. 8 Feb. 2013.
"Educational Opportunities and Resources." *United States Antarctic Program.* National Science Foundation, 2013. Web. 8 Feb. 2013.

# Appendix Two: World Religions

# African Religious Traditions

## General Description

The religious traditions of Africa can be studied both religiously and ethnographically. Animism, or the belief that everything has a soul, is practiced in most tribal societies, including the Dogon (people of the cliffs), an ethnic group living primarily in Mali's central plateau region and in Burkina Faso. Many traditional faiths have extensive mythologies, rites, and histories, such as the Yoruba religion practiced by the Yoruba, an ethnic group of West Africa. In South Africa, the traditional religion of the Zulu people is based on a creator god, ancestor worship, and the existence of sorcerers and witches. Lastly, the Ethiopian or Abyssinian Church (formally the Ethiopian Orthodox Union Church) is a branch of Christianity unique to the east African nations of Ethiopia and Eritrea.

## Number of Adherents Worldwide

Some 63 million Africans adhere to traditional religions such as animism. One of the largest groups practicing animism is the Dogon, who number about six hundred thousand. However, it is impossible to know how many practice traditional religion. In fact, many people practice animism alongside other religions, particularly Islam. Other religions have spread their adherence and influence through the African diaspora. In Africa, the Yoruba number between thirty-five and forty million and are located primarily in Benin, Togo and southwest Nigeria. The Zulu, the largest ethnic group in South Africa, total over eleven million. Like Islam, Christianity has affected the number of people who still hold traditional beliefs, making accurate predictions virtually impossible. The Ethiopian or Abyssinian Church has over thirty-nine million adherents in Ethiopia alone.

## Basic Tenets

Animism holds that many spiritual beings have the power to help or hurt humans. The traditional faith is thus more concerned with appropriate rituals rather than worship of a deity, and focuses on day-to-day practicalities such as food, water supplies, and disease. Ancestors, particularly those most recently dead, are invoked for their aid. Those who practice animism believe in life after death; some adherents may attempt to contact the spirits of the dead. Animists acknowledge the existence of tribal gods. (However, African people traditionally do not make images of God, who is thought of as Spirit.)

The Dogon divide into two caste-like groups: the inneomo (pure) and innepuru (impure). The hogon leads the inneomo, who may not sacrifice animals and whose leaders are forbidden to hunt. The inneomo also cannot prepare or bury the dead. While the innepuru can do all of the above tasks, they cannot take part in the rituals for agricultural fertility. Selected young males called the olubaru lead the innepuru. The status of "pure" or "impure" is inherited. The Dogon have many gods. The chief god is called Amma, a creator god who is responsible for creating other gods and the earth.

The Dogon have a three-part concept of death. First the soul is sent to the realm of the dead to join the ancestors. Rites are then performed to remove any ritual polluting. Finally, when several members of the village have died, a rite known as dama occurs. In the ritual, a sacrifice is made to the Great Mask (which depicts a large wooden serpent and which is never actually worn) and dancers perform on the housetops where someone has died to scare off any lingering souls. Often, figures of Nommo (a worshipped ancestral spirit) are put near funeral pottery on the family shrine.

The Yoruba believe in predestination. Before birth, the ori (soul) kneels before Olorun, the wisest and most powerful deity, and selects a destiny. Rituals may assist the person in achieving his or her destiny, but it cannot be altered. The Yoruba, therefore, acknowledge a need for ritual and sacrifice, properly done according to the oracles.

Among the Yoruba, the shaman is known as the babalawo. He or she is able to communicate with ancestors, spirits and deities. Training for this work, which may include responsibility as a doctor, often requires three years. The shaman is consulted before major life decisions. During these consultations, the shaman dictates the right rituals and sacrifices, and to which gods they are to be offered for maximum benefit. In addition, the Yoruba poetry covers right conduct. Good character is at the heart of Yoruba ethics.

The Yoruba are polytheistic. The major god is Olorun, the sky god, considered all-powerful and holy, and a father to 401 children, also gods. He gave the task of creating human beings to the deity Obatala (though Olorun breathed life into them). Olorun also determines the destiny of each person. Onlie, the Great Mother Goddess, is in some ways the opposite of Olorun. Olorun is the one who judges a soul following death. For example, if the soul is accounted worthy, it will be reincarnated, while the unworthy go to the place of punishment. Ogun, the god of hunters, iron, and war, is another important god. He is also the patron of blacksmiths. The Yoruba have some 1,700 gods, collectively known as the Orisa.

The Yoruba believe in an afterlife. There are two heavens: one is a hot, dry place with potsherds, reserved for those who have done evil, while the other is a pleasant heaven for persons who have led a good life. There the ori (soul) may choose to "turn to be a child" on the earth once more.

In the Zulu tradition, the king was responsible for rainmaking and magic for the benefit of the nation. Rainmakers were also known as "shepherds of heaven." They performed rites during times of famine, drought or war, as well as during planting season, invoking royal ancestors for aid. Storms were considered a manifestation of God.

The Zulu are also polytheistic. They refer to a wise creator god who lives in heaven. This Supreme Being has complete control of everything in the universe, and is known as Unkulunkulu, the Great Oldest One. The Queen of heaven is a virgin who taught women useful arts; light surrounds her, and her glory is seen in rain, mist, and rainbows.

The Ethiopian Church incorporates not only Orthodox Christian beliefs, but also aspects of Judaism. The adherents distinguish between clean and unclean meats, practice circumcision, and observe the seventh-day Sabbath. The Ethiopian (or Abyssinian) Church is monotheistic and believes in the Christian God.

## Sacred Text

Traditional religions such as animism generally have no written sacred texts. Instead, creation stories and other tales are passed down orally. The Yoruba do have some sacred poetry, in 256 chapters, known as odus. The text covers both right action in worship and ethical conduct. The Ethiopian Church has scriptures written in the ancient Ge'ez language, which is no longer used, except in church liturgy.

## Major Figures

A spiritual leader, or hogon, oversees each district among the Dogon. There is a supreme hogon for the entire country. Among the Yoruba, the king, or oba, rules each town. He is also considered sacred and is responsible for performing rituals. Isaiah Shembe is a prophet or messiah among the Zulu. He founded the Nazareth Baptist Church (also called the amaNazaretha Church or Shembe Church), an independent Zulu Christian denomination. His son, Johannes Shembe, took the title Shembe II. In the Ethiopian Church, now fully independent, the head of the church is the Patriarch. Saint Frumentius, the first bishop of Axum in northern Ethiopia, is credited with beginning the Christian tradition during the fourth century. King Lalibela, noted for authorizing construction of monolithic churches carved underground, was a major figure in the twelfth century.

## Major Holy Sites

Every spot in nature is sacred in animistic thinking. There is no division between sacred and profane—all of life is sacred, and Earth is Mother. Sky and mountains are often regarded as sacred space.

For the Yoruba of West Africa, Osogbo in Nigeria is a forest shrine. The main goddess is Oshun, goddess of the river. Until she arrived, the work done by male gods was not succeeding. People seeking to be protected from illness and women wishing to become pregnant seek Osun's help. Ilé-Ifè, an ancient Yoruba city in Nigeria, is another important site, and considered the spiritual hub of the Yoruba. According to the Yoruba creation myth, Olorun, god of the sky, set down Odudua, the founder of the Yoruba, in Ilé-Ifè. Shrines within the city include one to Ogun. The shrine is made of stones and wooden stumps.

Mount Nhlangakazi (Holy Mountain) is considered sacred to the Zulu Nazareth Baptist Church (amaNazaretha). There Isaiah Shembe built a High Place to serve as his headquarters. It is a twice-yearly site of pilgrimage for amaNazarites.

Sacred sites of the Ethiopian Church include the Church of St. Mary of Zion in Axum, considered the most sacred Ethiopian shrine. According to legend, the church stands adjacent to a guarded chapel which purportedly houses the Ark of the Covenant, a powerful biblical relic. The Ethiopian Church also considers sacred the eleven monolithic (rock-hewn) churches, still places of pilgrimage and devotion, that were recognized as a collective World Heritage Site by the United Nations Educational, Scientific and Cultural Organization.

## Major Rites & Celebrations

Most African religions involve some sacrifice to appease or please the gods. Among the Yoruba, for example, dogs, which are helpful in both hunting and war, are sacrificed to Ogun. In many tribes, including the Yoruba, rites of passage for youth exist. The typical pattern is three-fold: removal from the tribe, instruction, and return to the tribe ready to assume adult responsibilities. In this initiation, the person may be marked bodily through scarification or circumcision. The Yoruba also have a yearly festival re-enacting

the story of Obatala and Oduduwa (generally perceived as the ancestor of the Yorubas). A second festival, which resembles a passion play, re-enacts the conflict between the grandsons of these two legendary figures. A third festival celebrates the heroine Moremi, who led the Yoruba to victory over the enemy Igbo, an ethnicity from southeastern Nigeria, and who ultimately reconciled the two tribes.

Yoruba death rites include a masked dancer who comes to the family following a death, assuring them of the ancestor's ongoing care for the family. If the person was important in the village, a mask will be carved and named for them. In yearly festivals, the deceased individual will then appear with other ancestors.

Masks are also used in a Dogon funeral ritual, the dama ceremony, which is led by the Awa, a secret society comprised of all adult Dogon males of the innepuru group. During ceremonial times, the hogon relinquishes control and the Awa control the community. At the end of the mourning period the dama ceremony begins when the Awa leave the village and return with both the front and back of their heads masked. Through rituals and dances, they lead the spirit of the deceased to the next world. Control of the village reverts to the hogon at that point. The Wagem rites govern contact with the ancestors. Following the dama ceremony, the eldest male descendant, called the ginna bana, adds a vessel to the family shrine in the name of the deceased. The spirit of the ancestor is persuaded to return to the descendents through magic and sacrificial offerings, creating a link from the living to the first ancestors.

Ethiopian Christians observe and mark most typical Christian rites, though some occur on different dates because of the difference in the Ethiopian and Western calendars. For example, Christmas in Ethiopia is celebrated on January 7.

## ORIGINS

### History & Geography

The Dogon live along the Bandiagara Cliffs, a rocky and mountainous region. (The Cliffs of Bandiagara, also called the Bandiagara Escarpment, were recognized as a UNESCO World Heritage Site due to the cultural landscape, including the ancient traditions of the Dogon and their architecture.) This area is south of the Sahara in a region called the Sahel, another region prone to drought (though not a desert). The population of the villages in the region is typically a thousand people or less. The cliffs of the Bandiagara have kept the Dogon separate from other people.

Myths of origin regarding the Dogon differ. One suggestion is that the Dogon came from Egypt, and then lived in Libya before entering the the region of what is now Burkina Faso, Mauritania, or Guinea. Near the close of the fifteenth century, they arrived in Mali.

Among the Yoruba, multiple myths regarding their origin exist. One traces their beginnings to Uruk in Mesopotamia or to Babylon, the site of present-day Iraq. Another story has the Yoruba in West Africa by 10,000 BCE.

After the death of the Zulu messiah Isaiah Shembe in 1935, his son Johannes became the leader of the Nazareth Baptist Church. He lacked the charisma of his father, but did hold the church together. His brother, Amos, became regent in 1976 when Johannes died. Johannes's son Londa split the church in 1979 when Amos refused to give up power. Tangled in South African politics, Londa was killed in 1989.

The Ethiopian Orthodox Church is the nation's official church. A legend states that Menelik, supposed to have been the son of the Queen of Sheba and King Solomon, founded the royal line. When Jesuits arrived in the seventeenth century, they failed to change the church, and the nation closed to missionary efforts for several hundred years. By retaining independence theologically and not being conquered politically, Ethiopia is sometimes considered a model for the new religious movements in Africa.

## Founder or Major Prophet

The origins of most African traditional religions or faiths are accounted for through the actions of deities in creation stories rather than a particular founder. One exception, however, is Isaiah Shembe, who founded the Nazareth Baptist Church, also known as the Shembe Church or amaNazarite Church, in 1910 after receiving a number of revelations during a thunderstorm. Shembe was an itinerant Zulu preacher and healer. Through his influence and leadership, amaNazarites follow more Old Testament regulations than most Christians, including celebrating the Sabbath on Saturday rather than Sunday. They also refer to God as Jehovah, the Hebrew name for God. Shembe was regarded as the new Jesus Christ for his people, adapting Christianity to Zulu practice. He adopted the title Nkosi, which means king or chief.

The Ethiopian Orthodox church was founded, according to legend, by preaching from one of two New Testament figures—the disciple Matthew or the unnamed eunuch mentioned in Acts 8. According to historical evidence, the church began when Frumentius arrived at the royal court. Athanasius of Alexandria later consecrated Frumentius as patriarch of the church, linking it to the Christian church in Egypt.

## Creation Stories

The Dogon believe that Amma, the sky god, was also the creator of the universe. Amma created two sets of twins, male and female. One of the males rebelled. To restore order, Amma sacrificed the other male, Nommo, strangling and scattering him to the four directions, then restoring him to life after five days. Nommo then became ruler of the universe and the children of his spirits became the Dogon. Thus the world continually moves between chaos and order, and the task of the Dogon is to keep the world in balance through rituals. In a five-year cycle, the aspects of this creation myth are re-enacted at altars throughout the Dogon land.

According to the Yoruba, after one botched attempt at creating the world, Olorun sent his son Obatala to create earth upon the waters. Obatala tossed some soil on the water and released a five-toed hen to spread it out. Next, Olorun told Obatala to make people from clay. Obatala grew bored with the work and drank too much wine. Thereafter, the people he made were misshapen or defective (handicapped). In anger, Olorun relieved him of the job and gave it to Odudua to complete. It was Odudua who made the Yoruba and founded a kingdom at Ilé-Ifè.

The word *Zulu* means "heaven or sky." The Zulu people believe they originated in heaven. They also believe in phansi, the place where spirits live and which is below the earth's surface.

## Holy Places

Osun-Osogbo is a forest shrine in Nigeria dedicated to the Yoruba river goddess, Osun. It may be the last such sacred grove remaining among the Yoruba. Shrines, art, sculpture, and sanctuaries are part of the grove, which became a UNESCO World Heritage site in 2005.

Ilé-Ifè, regarded as the equivalent of Eden, is thought to be the site where the first Yoruba was placed. It was probably named for Ifa, the god associated with divination. The palace (Afin) of the spiritual head of the Yoruba, the oni, is located there. The oni has the responsibility to care for the staff of Oranmiyan, a Benin king. The staff, which is eighteen feet tall, is made of granite and shaped like an elephant's tusk.

Axum, the seat of the Ethiopian Christian Church, is a sacred site. The eleven rock-hewn churches of King Lalibela, especially that of Saint George, are a pilgrimage site. According to tradition, angels helped to carve the churches. More than 50,000 pilgrims come to the town of Lalibela at Christmas. After the Muslims captured Jerusalem in 1187, King Lalibela proclaimed his city the "New Jerusalem" because Christians could no longer go on pilgrimage to the Holy Land.

## AFRICAN RELIGIONS IN DEPTH

## Sacred Symbols

Because all of life is infused with religious meaning, any object or location may be considered or become sacred in traditional African religions. Masks, in particular, have special meaning and

may be worn during ceremonies. The mask often represents a god, whose power is passed to the one wearing the mask.

## Sacred Practices & Gestures

The Yoruba practice divination in a form that is originally Arabic. There are sixteen basic figures—combined, they deliver a prophecy that the diviner is not to interpret. Instead, he or she recites verses from a classic source. Images may be made to prevent or cure illness. For example, the Yoruba have a smallpox spirit god that can be prayed to for healing. Daily prayer, both morning and evening, is part of life for most Yoruba.

In the amaNazarite Church, which Zulu Isaiah Shembe founded, singing is a key part of the faith. Shembe himself was a gifted composer of hymns. This sacred music was combined with dancing, during which the Zulu wear their traditional dress.

## Rites, Celebrations & Services

The Dogon have three major cults. The Awa are associated with dances, featuring ornately carved masks, at funerals and on the anniversaries of deaths. The cult of the Earth god, Lebe, concerns itself with the agricultural cycles and fertility of the land; the hogon of the village guards the soil's purity and presides at ceremonies related to farming. The third cult, the Binu, is involved with communication with spirits, ancestor worship, and sacrifices. Binu shrines are in many locations. The Binu priest makes sacrifices of porridge made from millet and blood at planting time and also when the help of an ancestor is needed. Each clan within the Dogon community has a totem animal spirit—an ancestor spirit wishing to communicate with descendents may do so by taking the form of the animal.

The Dogon also have a celebration every fifty years at the appearing of the star Sirius B between two mountains. (Sirius is often the brightest star in the nighttime sky.) Young males leaving for three months prior to the sigui, as it is called, for a time of seclusion and speaking in private language. This celebration is rooted in the Dogon belief that amphibious creatures, the Nommo, visited their land about three thousand years ago.

The Yoruba offer Esu, the trickster god, palm wine and animal sacrifices. Because he is a trickster, he is considered a cheater, and being on his good side is important. The priests in Yoruba traditional religion are responsible for installing tribal chiefs and kings.

Among the Zulu, families determine the lobola, or bride price. They believe that a groom will respect his wife more if he must pay for her. Further gifts are then exchanged, and the bride's family traditionally gives the groom a goat or sheep to signify their acceptance of him. The groom's family provides meat for the wedding feast, slaughtering a cow on the morning of the wedding. The families assemble in a circle and the men, in costume, dance. The bride gives presents, usually mats or blankets, to members of her new family, who dance or sing their thanks. The final gift, to the groom, is a blanket, which is tossed over his head. Friends of the bride playfully beat him, demonstrating how they will respond if he mistreats his new wife. After the two families eat together, the couple is considered one.

In the traditional Zulu religion, ancestors three generations back are regarded as not yet settled in the afterlife. To help them settle, offerings of goats or other animals are made and rituals to help them settle into the community of ancestors are performed.

Christmas is a major celebration in Ethiopian Christianity. Priests rattle an instrument derived from biblical times, called the sistra, and chant to begin the mass. The festivities include drumming and a dance known as King David's dance.

*Judy A. Johnson, MTS*

**Bibliography**

A, Oladosu Olusegun. "Ethics and Judgement: A Panacea for Human Transformation in Yoruba Multireligious Society." *Asia Journal of Theology* 26.1 (2012): 88–104. Print.

Barnes, Trevor. *The Kingfisher Book of Religions*. New York: Kingfisher, 1999. Print.

Dawson, Allan Charles, ed. *Shrines in Africa: history, politics, and society*. Calgary: U of Calgary P, 2009. Print.

Doumbia, Adama, and Naomi Doumbia. *The Way of the Elders: West African Spirituality*. St. Paul: Llewellyn, 2004. Print.

Douny, Laurence. "The Role of Earth Shrines in the Socio-Symbolic Construction of the Dogon Territory: Towards a Philosophy of Containment." *Anthropology & Medicine* 18.2 (2011): 167–79. Print.

Friedenthal, Lora, and Dorothy Kavanaugh. *Religions of Africa*. Philadelphia: Mason Crest, 2007. Print.

Hayes, Stephen. "Orthodox Ecclesiology in Africa: A Study of the 'Ethiopian' Churches of South Africa." *International Journal for the Study of the Christian Church* 8.4 (2008): 337–54. Print.

Lugira, Aloysius M. *African Religion*. New York: Facts on File, 2004. Print.

Mbiti, John S. *African Religions and Philosophy*. 2nd ed. Oxford: Heinemann, 1991. Print.

Monteiro-Ferreira, Ana Maria. "Reevaluating Zulu Religion." *Journal of Black Studies* 35.3 (2005): 347–63. Print.

Peel, J. D. Y. "Yoruba Religion as a Global Phenomenon." *Journal of African History* 5.1 (2010): 107–8. Print.

Ray, Benjamin C. *African Religions*. 2nd ed. Upper Saddle River: Prentice, 2000. Print.

Thomas, Douglas E. *African Traditional Religion in the Modern World*. Jefferson: McFarland, 2005. Print.

# Bahá'í Faith

## General Description

The Bahá'í faith is the youngest of the world's religions. It began in the mid-nineteenth century, offering scholars the opportunity to observe a religion in the making. While some of the acts of religious founders such as Buddha or Jesus cannot be substantiated, the modern founders of Bahá'í were more contemporary figures.

## Number of Adherents Worldwide

An estimated 5 to 7 million people follow the Bahá'í faith. Although strong in Middle Eastern nations such as Iran, where the faith originated, Bahá'í has reached people in many countries, particularly the United States and Canada.

## Basic Tenets

The Bahá'í faith has three major doctrines. The first doctrine is that there is one transcendent God, and all religions worship that God, regardless of the name given to the deity. Adherents believe that religious figures such as Jesus Christ, the Buddha, and the Prophet Muhammad were different revelations of God unique to their time and place. The second doctrine is that there is only one religion, though each world faith is valid and was founded by a ""manifestation of God" who is part of a divine plan for educating humanity. The third doctrine is a belief in the unity of all humankind. In light of this underlying unity, those of the Bahá'í faith work for social justice. They believe that seeking consensus among various groups diffuses typical power struggles and to this end, they employ a method called consultation, which is a nonadversarial decision-making process.

The Bahá'í believe that the human soul is immortal, and that after death the soul moves nearer or farther away from God. The idea of an afterlife comprised of a literal "heaven" or "hell" is not part of the faith.

## Sacred Text

The Most Holy Book, or the Tablets, written by Baha'u'llah, form the basis of Bahá'í teachings. Though not considered binding, scriptures from other faiths are regarded as "Divine Revelation."

## Major Figures

The Bab (The Gate of God) Siyyad 'Ali Mohammad (1819–50), founder of the Bábí movement that broke from Islam, spoke of a coming new messenger of God. Mirza Hoseyn 'Ali Nuri (1817–92), who realized that he was that prophet, was given the title Baha'u'llah (Glory of God). From a member of Persia's landed gentry, he was part of the ruling class, and is considered the founder of the Bahá'í faith. His son, 'Abdu'l-Bahá (Servant of the Glory of God), who lived from 1844 until 1921, became the leader of the group after his father's death in 1892. The oldest son of his eldest daughter, Shogi Effendi Rabbani (1899–1957), oversaw a rapid expansion, visiting Egypt, America, and nations in Europe. Tahirih (the Pure One) was a woman poet who challenged stereotypes by appearing unveiled at meetings.

## Major Holy Sites

The Bahá'í World Center is located near Haifa, Israel. The burial shrine of the Bab, a pilgrimage site, is there. The Shrine of Baha'u'llah near Acre, Israel, is another pilgrimage site. The American headquarters are in Wilmette, Illinois. Carmel in Israel is regarded as the world center of the faith.

## Major Rites & Celebrations

Each year, the Bahá'í celebrate Ridvan Festival, a twelve-day feast from sunset on April 20 to sunset on May 2. The festival marks Baha'u'llah's declaration of prophethood, as prophesized by the Bab, at a Baghdad garden. (Ridvan means Paradise.) The holy days within that feast are the first (Baha'u'llah's garden arrival), ninth (the arrival of his family), and twelfth (his departure from Ridvan Garden)—on these days, the Bahá'í do not work. During this feast, people attend social events and meet for devotions. Baha'u'llah referred to it as the King of Festivals and Most Great Festival. The Bahá'í celebrate several other events, including World Religion Day and Race Unity Day, both founded by Bahá'í, as well as days connected with significant events in the life of the founder. Elections to the Spiritual Assemblies, and the national and local administrations; international elections are held every five years.

## ORIGINS

### History & Geography

Siyyad 'Ali Muhammad was born into a merchant family of Shiraz in 1819. Both his parents were descendents of the Prophet Muhammad, Islam's central figure. Like the Prophet, the man who became the Bab lost his father at an early age and was raised by an uncle. A devout child, he entered his uncle's business by age fifteen. After visiting Muslim holy cities, he returned to Shiraz, where he married a distant relative named Khadijih.

While on pilgrimage in 1844 to the black stone of Ka'bah, a sacred site in Islam, the Bab stood with his hand on that holy object and declared that he was the prophet for whom they had been waiting. The Sunni did not give credence to these claims. The Bab went to Persia, where the Shia sect was the majority. However, because Muhammad had been regarded as the "Seal of the Prophets," and the one who spoke the final revelation, Shia clergy viewed his claims as threatening, As such, nothing further would be revealed until the Day of Judgment. The authority of the clergy was in danger from this new movement.

The Bab was placed under house arrest, and then confined to a fortress on the Russian frontier. That move to a more remote area only increased the number of converts, as did a subsequent move to another Kurdish fortress. He

was eventually taken to Tabriz in Iran and tried before the Muslim clergy in 1848. Condemned, he was caned on the soles of his feet and treated by a British doctor who was impressed by him.

Despite his treatment and the persecution of his followers—many of the Bab's eighteen disciples, termed the "Letters of the Living," were persistently tortured and executed—the Bab refused to articulate a doctrine of jihad. The Babis could defend themselves, but were forbidden to use holy war as a means of religious conquest. In three major confrontations sparked by the Shia clergy, Babis were defeated. The Bab was sentenced as a heretic and shot by a firing squad in 1850. Lacking leadership and grief-stricken, in 1852 two young Babis fired on the shah in 1852, unleashing greater persecutions and cruelty against those of the Bahá'í faith.

A follower of the Bab, Mirza Hoseyn 'Ali Nuri, announced in 1863 that he was the one who was to come (the twelfth imam of Islam), the "Glory of God," or Baha'u'llah. Considered the founder of the Bahá'í Faith, he was a tireless writer who anointed his son, 'Abdu'l-Bahá, as the next leader. Despite deprivations and imprisonments, Baha'u'llah lived to be seventy-five years old, relinquishing control of the organization to 'Abdu'l-Bahá before the time of his death.

'Abdu'l-Bahá, whom his father had called "the Master," expanded the faith to the nations of Europe and North America. In 1893, at the Parliament of Religions at the Chicago World's Fair, the faith was first mentioned in the United States. Within a few years, communities of faith were established in Chicago and Wisconsin. In 1911, 'Abdu'l-Bahá began a twenty-eight month tour of Europe and North America to promote the Bahá'í faith. Administratively, he established the spiritual assemblies that were the forerunner of the Houses of Justice that his father had envisioned.

During World War I, 'Abdu'l-Bahá engaged in humanitarian work among the Palestinians in the Holy Land, where he lived. In recognition of his efforts, he was granted knighthood by the British government. Thousands of people, including many political and religious dignitaries, attended his funeral in 1921.

'Abdu'l-Bahá conferred the role of Guardian, or sole interpreter of Bahá'í teaching, to his eldest grandson, Shoghi Effendi Rabbani. To him, all questions regarding the faith were to be addressed. Shoghi Effendi Rabbani was a descendent of Baha'u'llah through both parents. He headed the Bahá'í faith from 1921 to 1963, achieving four major projects: he oversaw the physical development of the World Centre and expanded the administrative order; he carried out the plan his father had set in motion; and he provided for the translating and interpreting of Bahá'í teachings, as the writings of both the Bab and those of Baha'u'llah and 'Abdu'l-Bahá have been translated and published in more than eight hundred languages.

Beginning in 1937, Shoghi Effendi Rabbani began a series of specific plans with goals tied to deadlines. In 1953, during the second seven-year plan, the house of worship in Wilmette, Illinois, was completed and dedicated.

Although the beliefs originated in Shi'ite Islam, the Bahá'í Faith has been declared a new religion without connections to Islam. To followers of Islam, it is a heretical sect. During the reign of the Ayatollah Khomeini, a time when Iran was especially noted as intolerant of diverse views, the Bahá'í faced widespread persecution.

## Founder or Major Prophet

Mirza Husayn Ali Nuri, known as Baha'u'llah, was born into privilege in 1817 in what was then Persia, now present-day Iran. At twenty-two, he declined a government post offered at his father's death. Although a member of a politically prestigious family, he did not follow the career path of several generations of his ancestors. Instead, he managed the family estates and devoted himself to charities, earning the title "Father of the Poor."

At twenty-seven, he followed the Babis's movement within Shia Islam, corresponding with the Bab and traveling to further the faith. He also provided financial support. In 1848, he organized and helped to direct a conference that explained the Bab's teaching. At the conference, he gave symbolic names to the eighty-one followers who had attended, based on the spiritual qualities he had observed.

Although he managed to escape death during the persecutions before and after the Bab's death, a fact largely attributed to his upbringing, Baha'u'llah was imprisoned several times. During a four-month stay in an underground dungeon in Tehran, he realized from a dream that he was the one of whom the Bab had prophesied. After being released, he was banished from Persia and had his property confiscated by the shah. He went to Baghdad, refusing the offer of refuge that had come from Russia. Over the following three years a small band of followers joined him, including members of his family. When his younger brother attempted to take over the leadership of the Babis, Baha'u'llah spent two years in a self-imposed exile in the Kurdistan wilderness. In 1856, with the community near anarchy as a result of his brother's failure of leadership, Baha'u'llah returned to the community and restored its position over the next seven years.

Concerned by the growing popularity of the new faith, the shah demanded that the Babis move further away from Persia. They went to Constantinople where, in 1863, Baha'u'llah revealed to the whole group that he was "He Whom God Will Make Manifest." From there the Bahá'í were sent to Adrianople in Turkey, and at last, in 1868, to the town of Acre in the Holy Land. Baha'u'llah was imprisoned in Acre and survived severe prison conditions. In 1877, he moved from prison to a country estate, then to a mansion. He died in 1892 after a fever.

## Philosophical Basis

The thinking of Shia Muslims contributed to the development of Bahá'í. The writings incorporate language and concepts from the Qur'an (Islam's holy book). Like Muslims, the Bahá'í believe that God is one. God sends messengers, the Manifestations of God, to instruct people and benefit society. These have included Jesus Christ, the Buddha, the Prophet Muhammad, Krishna, and the Bab. Bahá'í also goes further than Islam in accepting all religions—not just Judaism, Christianity, and Islam—as being part of a divinely inspired plan.

Shia Muslims believe that Muhammad's descendents should lead the faithful community. The leaders, known as imams, were considered infallible. The Sunni Muslims believed that following the way (sunna) of Muhammad was sufficient qualification for leadership. Sunni dynastics regarded the imams as a threat and executed them, starting with two of Muhammad's grandsons, who became Shia martyrs.

In Persia, a state with a long tradition of divinely appointed rulers, the Shia sect was strong. When the Safavids, a Shia dynasty, came to power in the sixteenth century, the custom of the imamate was victorious. One tradition states that in 873, the last appointed imam, who was still a child, went into hiding to avoid being killed. For the following sixty-nine years, this twelfth imam communicated through his deputies to the faithful. Each of the deputies was called bab, or gate, because they led to the "Hidden Imam." Four babs existed through 941, and the last one died without naming the next bab. The Hidden Imam is thought to emerge at the end of time to bring in a worldwide reign of justice. From this tradition came the expectation of a Mahdi (Guided One) to lead the people.

During the early nineteenth century, many followers of both the Christian and Islamic faiths expected their respective messiahs to return. Shia teachers believed that the return of the Mahdi imam was near. In 1843, one teacher, Siyyid Kázim, noted that the Hidden Imam had disappeared one thousand lunar years earlier. He urged the faithful to look for the Mahdi imam.

The following year in Shiraz, Siyyad 'Ali Mohammad announced that he was the Mahdi. (*Siyyad* is a term meaning descended from Muhammad.) He referred to himself as the Bab, though he expanded the term's meaning. Eighteen men, impressed with his ability to expound the Qur'an, believed him. They became the Letters of the Living, and were sent throughout Persia (present-day Iran) to announce the dawning of the Day of God.

In 1853, Mirza Husayn Ali Nuri experienced a revelation that he was "He Whom God Shall Make Manifest," the one of whom the Bab prophesied. Accepted as such, he began writing the words that became the Bahá'í scriptures. Much of what is known of the early days of the faith comes from a Cambridge academic, Edward Granville Browne, who first visited Baha'u'llah in the 1890. Browne wrote of his meeting, introducing this faith to the West.

The emphasis of the Bahá'í faith is on personal development and the breaking down of barriers between people. Service to humanity is important and encouraged. Marriage, with a belief in the equality of both men and women, is also encouraged. Consent of both sets of parents is required prior to marrying.

## Holy Places

The shrine of the Bab near Haifa and that of Baha'u'llah near Acre, in Israel, are the two most revered sites for those of the Bahá'í faith. In 2008, the United Nations Educational, Scientific, and Cultural Organization (UNESCO) recognized both as World Heritage Sites. They are the first such sites from a modern religious tradition to be added to the list of sites. Both sites are appreciated for the formal gardens surrounding them that blend design elements from different cultures. For the Bahá'í, Baha'u'llah's shrine is the focus of prayer, comparable to the significance given to the Ka'bah in Mecca for Muslims or to the Western Wall for Jews.

As of 2013, there are seven Bahá'í temples in the world; an eighth temple is under construction in Chile. All temples are built with a center dome and nine sides, symbolizing both diversity and world unity. The North American temple is located in Wilmette, Illinois. There, daily prayer services take place as well as a Sunday service.

---

## THE BAHÁ'Í FAITH IN DEPTH

## Governance

Elected members of lay councils at international, national, and local levels administer the work of the faith. The Universal House of Justice in Haifa, Israel, is the location of the international nine-member body. Elections for all of these lay councils are by secret ballot, and do not include nominating, candidates, or campaigns. Those twenty-one and older are permitted to vote. The councils make decisions according to a process of collective decision-making called consultation. They strive to serve as a model for governing a united global society.

## Personal Conduct

In addition to private prayer and acts of social justice, those of the Bahá'í faith are encouraged to have a profession, craft, or trade. They are also asked to shun and refrain from slander and partisan politics. Homosexuality and sexual activity outside marriage are forbidden, as is gambling.

The Bahá'í faith does not have professional clergy, nor does it engage in missionary work. However, Bahá'í may share their faith with others and may move to another country as a "pioneer." Pioneers are unlike traditional missionaries, and are expected to support themselves through a career and as a member of the community.

## Avenues of Service

Those of the Bahá'í Faith place a high value on service to humanity, considering it an act of worship. This can be done through caring for one's own family or through one's choice of vocation. Within the local community, people may teach classes for children, mentor youth groups, host devotional programs, or teach adult study circles. Many are engaged in economic or social development programs as well. Although not mandated, a year or two of service is often undertaken following high school or during college.

## United Nations Involvement

Beginning in 1947, just one year after the United Nations (UN) first met, the Bahá'í Faith was represented at that body. In 1948, the Bahá'í International Community was accredited by the UN as an international nongovernmental organization (NGO). In 1970, the faith received special consultative status with the UN Economic and Social Council (ECOSOC). Following World War I, a Bahá'í office opened in Geneva, Switzerland, where the League of Nations was headquartered. Thus the Bahá'í Faith has a long tradition of supporting global institutions.

## Money Matters

The International Bahá'í Fund exists to develop and support the growth of the faith, and the Universal House of Justice oversees the distribution of the money. Contributions are also used to maintain the Bahá'í World Center. No money is accepted from non-Bahá'í sources. National and local funds, administered by National or Local Spiritual Assemblies, are used in supporting service projects, publishing endeavors, schools, and Bahá'í centers. For the Bahá'í, the size of the donation is less important than regular contributions and the spirit of sacrifice behind them.

## Food Restrictions

Bahá'í between fifteen and seventy years of age **fast** nineteen days a year, abstaining from food and drink from sunrise to sunset. Fasting occurs the first day of each month of the Bahá'í calendar, which divides the year into nineteen months of nineteen days each. The Bahá'í faithful do not drink alcohol or use narcotics, because these will deaden the mind with repeated use.

## Rites, Celebrations & Services

Daily prayer and meditation is recommended in the Bahá'í faith. During services there are mediations and prayers, along with the reading of Bahá'í scriptures and other world faith traditions. There is no set ritual, no offerings, and no sermons. Unaccompanied by musical instruments, choirs also sing. Light refreshments may be served afterwards.

Bahá'í place great stress on marriage, the only state in which sex is permitted. Referred to as "a fortress for well-being and salvation," a monogamous, heterosexual marriage is the ideal. To express the oneness of humanity, interracial marriages are encouraged. After obtaining the consent of their parents, the couple takes the following vow: "We will all, verily, abide by the will of God." The remainder of the service may be individually crafted and may also include dance, music, feasting, and ceremony. Should a couple choose to end a marriage, they must first complete a year of living apart while trying to reconcile differences. Divorce is discouraged, but permitted after that initial year.

*Judy A. Johnson, MTS*

**Bibliography**

Albertson, Lorelei. *All about Bahá'í Faith*. University Pub., 2012. E-book.

Bowers, Kenneth E. *God Speaks Again: an Introduction to the Bahá'í Faith*. Wilmette: Bahá'í, 2004. Print.

Buck, Christopher. "The Interracial 'Bahá'í Movement' and the Black Intelligentsia: The Case of W. E. B. Du Bois." *Journal of Religious History* 36.4 (2012): 542–62. Print.

Cederquist, Druzelle. *The Story of Baha'u'llah*. Wilmette: Bahá'í, 2005. Print.

Echevarria, L. *Life Stories of Bahá'í Women in Canada: Constructing Religious Identity in the Twentieth Century*. Lang, 2011. E-book.

Garlington, William. *The Bahá'í Faith in America*. Lanham: Rowman, 2008. Print.

Hartz, Paula R. *Bahá'í Faith*. New York. Facts on File, 2006. Print.

Hatcher, William S. and J. Douglas Martin. *The Bahá'í Faith: The Emerging Global Religion*. Wilmette: Bahá'í, 2002. Print.

Karlberg, Michael. "Constructive Resilience: The Bahá'í Response to Oppression." *Peace & Change* 35.2 (2010): 222–57. Print.

Lee, Anthony A. *The Bahá'í Faith in Africa: Establishing a New Religious Movement, 1952–1962*. Brill NV, E-book.

Momen, Moojan. "Bahá'í Religious History." *Journal of Religious History* 36.4 (2012): 463–70. Print.

Momen, Moojan. *The Bahá'í Faith: A Beginner's Guide*. Oxford: Oneworld, 2007. Print.

Smith, Peter. *The Bahá'í Faith*. Cambridge: Cambridge UP, 2008. Print.

Wilkinson, Philip. *Religions*. New York: DK, 2008. Print.

# Buddhism

## General Description

Buddhism has three main branches: Theravada (Way of the Elders), also referred to as Hinayana (Lesser Vehicle); Mahayana (Greater Vehicle); and Vajrayana (Diamond Vehicle), also referred to as Tantric Buddhism. Vajrayana is sometimes thought of as an extension of Mahayana Buddhism. These can be further divided into many sects and schools, many of which are geographically based. In Buddhism, these different divisions or schools are regarded as alternative paths to enlightenment (Wilkinson 2008).

## Number of Adherents Worldwide

An estimated 474 million people around the world are Buddhists. Of the major sects, Theravada Buddhism is the oldest, developed in the sixth century BCE. Its adherents include those of the Theravada Forest Tradition. From Mahayana Buddhism, which developed in the third to second centuries BCE, came several offshoots based on location. In what is now China, Pure Land Buddhism and Tibetan Buddhism developed in the seventh century. In Japan, Zen Buddhism developed in the twelfth century, Nichiren Buddhism developed a century later, and Soka Gakkai was founded in 1937. In California during the 1970s, the Serene Reflection Meditation began as a subset of Sōtō Zen. In Buddhism, these different divisions or schools are regarded as alternative paths to enlightenment.

## Basic Tenets

Buddhists hold to the Three Universal Truths: impermanence, the lack of self, and suffering. These truths encompass the ideas that everything is impermanent and changing and that life is not satisfying because of its impermanence and the temporary nature of all things, including contentment. Buddhism also teaches the Four Noble Truths: All life is suffering (Dukkha). Desire and attachment cause suffering (Samudaya). Ceasing to desire or crave conceptual attachment ends suffering and leads to release (Nirodha). This release comes through following the Noble Eightfold Path—right understanding (or view), right intention, right speech, right conduct, right occupation, right effort, right mindfulness, and right concentration (Magga).

Although Buddhists do not believe in an afterlife as such, the soul undergoes a cycle of death and rebirth. Following the Noble Eightfold Path leads to the accumulation of good karma, allowing one to be reborn at a higher level. Karma is the Buddhist belief in cause-effect relationships; actions taken in one life have consequences in the next. Ultimately, many refer to the cessation or elimination of suffering as the primary goal of Buddhism.

Buddhists do not believe in gods. Salvation is to be found in following the teachings of Buddha, which are called the Dharma (law or truth). Buddhism does have saint-like bodhisattvas (enlightened beings) who reject ultimate enlightenment (Nirvana) for themselves to aid others.

## Sacred Text

Buddhism has nothing comparable to the Qur'an (Islam's holy book) or the Bible. For Theravada Buddhists, an important text is the Pāli Canon, the collection of Buddha's teachings. Mahayana Buddhists recorded their version of these as sutras, many of them in verse. The Lotus Sutra is among the most important. The Buddhist scriptures are written in two languages of ancient India, Pali and Sanskrit, depending on the tradition in which they were developed. Some of these words, such as karma, have been transliterated into English and gained common usage.

## Major Figures

Siddhartha Gautama (ca. 563 to 483 BCE) is the founder of Buddhism and regarded as the Buddha or Supreme Buddha. He is the most highly regarded historical figure in Buddhism.

He had two principle disciples: Sariputta and Mahamoggallana (or Maudgalyayana). In contemporary Buddhism, the fourteenth Dalai Lama, Tenzin Gyatso, is a significant person. Both he and Aung San Suu Kyi, a Buddhist of Myanmar who was held as a political prisoner for her stand against the oppressive regime of that nation, have been awarded the Nobel Peace Prize.

## Major Holy Sites

Buddhist holy sites are located in several places in Asia. All of those directly related to the life of Siddhartha Gautama are located in the northern part of India near Nepal. Lumbini Grove is noted as the birthplace of the Buddha. He received enlightenment at Bodh Gaya and first began to teach in Sarnath. Kusinara is the city where he died.

In other Asian nations, some holy sites were once dedicated to other religions. Angkor Wat in Cambodia, for example, was constructed for the Hindu god Vishnu in the twelfth century CE. It became a Buddhist temple three hundred years later. It was once the largest religious monument in the world and still attracts visitors. In Java's central highlands sits Borobudur, the world's largest Buddhist shrine. The name means "Temple of Countless Buddhas." Its five terraces represent what must be overcome to reach enlightenment: worldly desires, evil intent, malicious joy, laziness, and doubt. It was built in the eighth and ninth centuries CE, only to fall into neglect at about the turn of the millennium; it was rediscovered in 1815. The complex has three miles of carvings illustrating the life and teachings of the Buddha. In Sri Lanka, the Temple of the Tooth, which houses what is believed to be one of the Buddha's teeth, is a popular pilgrimage site.

Some of the holy sites incorporate gifts of nature. China has four sacred Buddhist mountains, symbolizing the four corners of the universe. These mountains—Wŭtái Shān, Émĕi Shān, Jiŭhuá Shān, and Pŭtuó Shān—are believed to be the homes of bodhisattvas. In central India outside Fardapur, there are twenty-nine caves carved into the granite, most of them with frescoes based on the Buddha's life. Ajanta, as the site is known, was created between 200 BCE and the fifth century CE. Five of the caves house temples.

The Buddha's birthday, his day of death, and the day of his enlightenment are all celebrated, either as one day or several. Different traditions and countries have their own additional celebrations, including Sri Lanka's Festival of the Tooth. Buddhists have a lunar calendar, and four days of each month are regarded as holy days.

---

## ORIGINS

### History & Geography

Buddhism began in what is now southern Nepal and northern India with the enlightenment of the Buddha. Following his death, members of the sangha, or community, spread the teachings across northern India. The First Buddhist Council took place in 486 BCE at Rajagaha. This council settled the Buddhist canon, the Tipitaka. In 386 BCE, a little more than a century after the Buddha died, a second Buddhist Council was held at Vesali. It was at this meeting that the two major schools of Buddhist thought—Theravada and Mahayana—began to differ.

Emperor Asoka, who ruled most of the Indian subcontinent from around 268 to 232 BCE, converted to Buddhism. He sent missionaries across India and into central parts of Asia. He also set up pillars with Buddhist messages in his own efforts to establish "true dharma" in the kingdom, although he did not create a state church. His desire for his subjects to live contently in this life led to promoting trade, maintaining canals and reservoirs, and the founding a system of medical care for both humans and animals. Asoka's son Mahinda went to southern Indian and to Sri Lanka with the message of Buddhism.

Asoka's empire fell shortly after his death. Under the following dynasties, evidence suggests Buddhists in India experienced persecution. The religion continued to grow, however, and during the first centuries CE, monasteries and monuments were constructed with support from local rulers. Some additional support came from women within the royal courts. Monastic centers also grew in number. By the fourth century CE, Buddhism had become one of the chief religious traditions in India.

During the Gupta dynasty, which lasted from about 320 to 600 CE, Buddhists and Hindus began enriching each other's traditions. Some Hindus felt that the Buddha was an incarnation of Vishnu, a Hindu god. Some Buddhists showed respect for Hindu deities.

Also during this era, Mahavihara, the concept of the "Great Monastery," came to be. These institutions served as universities for the study and development of Buddhist thinking. Some of them also included cultural and scientific study in the curriculum.

Traders and missionaries took the ideas of Buddhism to China. By the first century CE, Buddhism was established in that country. The religion died out or was absorbed into Hinduism in India. By the seventh century, a visiting Chinese monk found that Huns had invaded India from Central Asia and destroyed many Buddhist monasteries. The religion revived and flourished in the northeast part of India for several centuries.

Muslim invaders reached India in the twelfth and thirteenth centuries. They sacked the monasteries, some of which had grown very wealthy. Some even paid workers to care for both the land they owned and the monks, while some had indentured slaves. Because Buddhism had become monastic rather than a religion of the laity, there was no groundswell for renewal following the Muslim invasion.

Prominent in eastern and Southeast Asia, Buddhism is the national religion in some countries. For example, in Thailand, everyone learns about Buddhism in school. Buddhism did not begin to reach Western culture until the nineteenth century, when the Lotus Sutra was translated into German. The first Buddhist temple in the United States was built in 1853 in San Francisco's Chinatown.

Chinese Communists took control of Tibet in 1950. Nine years later, the fourteenth Dalai Lama left for India, fearing persecution. The Dalai Lama is considered a living teacher (lama) who is to instruct others. (The term *dalai* means "great as the ocean.") In 1989, he received the Nobel Peace Prize.

Buddhism experienced a revival in India during the twentieth century. Although some of this new beginning was due in part to Tibetan immigrants seeking safety, a mass conversion in 1956 was the major factor. The year was chosen to honor the 2,500th anniversary of the Buddha's death year. Buddhism was chosen as an alternative to the strict caste structure of Hinduism, and hundreds of thousands of people of the Dalit caste, once known as untouchables, converted in a ceremony held in Nagpur.

**Founder or Major Prophet**

Siddhartha Gautama, who became known as the "Enlightened One," or Buddha, was a prince in what is now southern Nepal, but was then northern India during the sixth century BCE. The name Siddhartha means "he who achieves his aim." He was a member of the Sakya tribe of Nepal, belonging to the warrior caste. Many legends have grown around his birth and early childhood. One states that he was born in a grove in the woods, emerging from his mother's side able to walk and completely clean.

During Siddhartha's childhood, a Brahmin, or wise man, prophesied that he would grow to be a prince or a religious teacher who would help others overcome suffering. Because the life of a sage involved itinerant begging, the king did not want this life for his child. He kept Siddhartha in the palace and provided him with all the luxuries of his position, including a wife, Yashodhara. They had a son, Rahula.

Escaping from the palace at about the age of thirty, Gautama first encountered suffering in the form of an old man with a walking stick. The following day, he saw a man who was ill. On the third day, he witnessed a funeral procession. Finally he met a monk, who had nothing, but who radiated happiness. He determined to leave his privileged life, an act called the Great Renunciation. Because hair was a sign of vanity in his time, he shaved his head. He looked for enlightenment via an ascetic life of little food or sleep. He followed this path for six years, nearly starving to death. Eventually, he determined on a Middle Way, a path neither luxurious as he had known in the palace, nor ascetic as he had attempted.

After three days and nights of meditating under a tree at Bodh Gaya, Siddhartha achieved his goal of enlightenment, or Nirvana. He escaped fear of suffering and death.

The Buddha began his preaching career, which spanned some forty years, following his enlightenment. He gave his first sermon in northeast India at Sarnath in a deer park. The first five followers became the first community, or sangha. Buddha died around age eighty, in 483 BCE after he had eaten poisoned food. After warning his followers not to eat the food, he meditated until he died.

Buddhists believe in many enlightened ones. Siddhartha is in one tradition regarded as the fourth buddha, while other traditions hold him to have been the seventh or twenty-fifth buddha.

His disciples, who took the ideas throughout India, repeated his teachings. When the later Buddhists determined to write down the teachings of the Buddha, they met to discuss the ideas and agreed that a second meeting should occur in a century. At the third council, which was held at Pataliputta, divisions occurred. The two major divisions—Theravada and Mahayana—differ over the texts to be used and the interpretation of the teachings. Theravada can be translated as "the Teachings of the Elders," while Mahayana means "Great Vehicle."

Theravada Buddhists believe that only monks can achieve enlightenment through the teachings of another buddha, or enlightened being. Thus they try to spend some part of their lives in a monastery. Buddhists in the Mahayana tradition, on the other hand, feel that all people can achieve enlightenment, without being in a monastery. Mahayanans also regard some as bodhisattvas, people who have achieved the enlightened state but renounce Nirvana to help others achieve it.

## Philosophical Basis

During Siddhartha's lifetime, Hinduism was the predominant religion in India. Many people, especially in northern India, were dissatisfied with the rituals and sacrifices of that religion. In addition, as many small kingdoms expanded and the unity of the tribes began to break down, many people were in religious turmoil and doubt. A number of sects within Hinduism developed.

The Hindu belief in the cycle of death and rebirth led some people to despair because they could not escape from suffering in their lives. Siddhartha was trying to resolve the suffering he saw in the world, but many of his ideas came from the Brahmin sect of Hinduism, although he reinterpreted them. Reincarnation, dharma, and reverence for cows are three of the ideas that carried over into Buddhism.

In northeast India at Bodh Gaya, he rested under a bodhi tree, sometimes called a bo tree. He meditated there until he achieved Nirvana, or complete enlightenment, derived from the freedom of fear that attached to suffering and death. As a result of his being enlightened, he was known as Buddha, a Sanskrit word meaning "awakened one." Wanting to help others, he began teaching his Four Noble Truths, along with the Noble Eightfold Path that would lead people to freedom from desire and suffering. He encouraged his followers to take Triple Refuge in the Three Precious Jewels: the Buddha, the teachings, and the sangha, or monastic community. Although at first Buddha was uncertain about including women in a sangha, his mother-in-law begged for the privilege.

Greed, hatred, and ignorance were three traits that Buddha felt people needed to conquer. All three create craving, the root of suffering. Greed and ignorance lead to a desire for things that are not needed, while hatred leads to a craving to destroy the hated object or person.

To the Four Noble Truths and Eightfold Path, early devotees of Buddhism added the Five Moral Precepts. These are to avoid taking drugs and alcohol, engaging in sexual misconduct, harming others, stealing, and lying.

The precepts of the Buddha were not written down for centuries. The first text did not appear for more than 350 years after the precepts were first spoken. One collection from Sri Lanka written in Pāli during the first century BCE is known as Three Baskets, or Tipitaka. The three baskets include Buddha's teaching (the Basket of Discourse), commentary on the sayings (the Basket of Special Doctrine), and the rules for monks to follow (the Basket of Discipline). The name Three Baskets refers to the fact that the sayings were first written on leaves from a palm tree that were then collected in baskets.

## Holy Places

Buddhists make pilgrimages to places that relate to important events in Siddhartha's life. While Lumbini Grove, the place of Siddhartha's birth, is a prominent pilgrimage site, the primary site for pilgrimage is Bodh Gaya, the location where Buddha received enlightenment. Other pilgrimage sites include Sarnath, the deer park located in what is now Varanasi (Benares) where the Buddha first began to teach, and Kusinara, the city where he died. All of these are in the northern part of India near Nepal.

Other sites in Asia that honor various bodhisattvas have also become pilgrimage destinations. Mountains are often chosen; there are four in China, each with monasteries and temples built on them. In Japan, the Shikoku pilgrimage covers more than 700 miles and involves visits to eighty-eight temples along the route.

## BUDDHISM IN DEPTH

## Sacred Symbols

Many stylized statue poses of the Buddha exist, each with a different significance. One, in which the Buddha has both hands raised, palms facing outward, commemorates the calming of an elephant about to attack the Buddha. If only the right hand is raised, the hand symbolizes friendship and being unafraid. The teaching gesture is that of a hand with the thumb and first finger touching.

In Tibetan Buddhism, the teachings of Buddha regarding the cycle of rebirth are symbolized in the six-spoke wheel of life. One may be reborn into any of the six realms of life: hell, hungry spirits, warlike demons called Asuras, animals, humans, or gods. Another version of the wheel has eight spokes rather than six, to represent the Noble Eightfold Path. Still another wheel has twelve spokes, signifying both the Four Noble Truths and the Noble Eightfold Path.

Tibetan Buddhists have prayer beads similar to a rosary, with 108 beads representing the number of desires to be overcome prior to reaching enlightenment. The worshipper repeats the Triple Refuge—Buddha, dharma, and sangha—or a mantra.

The prayer wheel is another device that Tibetan Buddhists use. Inside the wheel is a roll of paper on which the sacred mantra—Hail to the jewel in the lotus—is written many times. The lotus is a symbol of growing spiritually; it grows in muddied waters, but with the stems and flowers, it reaches toward the sun. By turning the wheel and spinning the mantra, the practitioner spreads blessings. Bells may be rung to wake the hearer out of ignorance.

In Tantric Buddhism, the mandala, or circle, serves as a map of the entire cosmos. Mandalas may be made of colored grains of sand, carved or painted. They are used to help in meditation and are thought to have a spiritual energy.

Buddhism recognizes Eight Auspicious Symbols, including the banner, conch shell, fish, knot, lotus, treasure vase, umbrella, and wheel. Each has a particular significance. A conch shell, for example, is often blown to call worshippers to meetings. Because its sound travels far, it signifies the voice of Buddha traveling throughout the world. Fish are fertility symbols because they have thousands of offspring. In Buddhist imagery, they are often in facing pairs and fashioned of gold. The lotus represents spiritual growth, rooted in muddy water but flowering toward the sun. The umbrella symbolizes protection, because servants once used them to protect royalty from both sun and rain.

## Sacred Practices & Gestures

Two major practices characterize Buddhism: gift-giving and showing respect to images and relics of the Buddha. The first is the transaction between laity and monks in which laypersons present sacrificial offerings to the monks, who in return share their higher state of spiritual being with the laity. Although Buddhist monks are permitted to own very little, they each have a begging bowl, which is often filled with rice.

Buddhists venerate statues of the Buddha, bodhisattvas, and saints; they also show respect to his relics, housed in stupas. When in the presence of a statue of the Buddha, worshippers have a series of movements they repeat three times, thus dedicating their movements to the Triple Refuge. It begins with a dedicated body: placing hands together with the palms cupped slightly and fingers touching, the devotee raises the hands to the forehead. The second step symbolizes right speech by lowering the hands to just below the mouth. In the third movement, the hands are lowered to the front of the chest, indicating that heart—and by extension, mind—are also dedicated to the Triple Refuge. The final movement is prostration. The devotee first gets on all fours, then lowers either the entire body to the floor or lowers the head, so that there are five points of contact with the floor.

Statues of the Buddha give a clue to the gestures held important to his followers. The gesture of turning the hand towards the ground indicates that one is observing Earth. Devotees assume a lotus position, with legs crossed, when in meditation.

Allowing the left hand to rest in the lap and the right hand to point down to Earth is a gesture used in meditation. Another common gesture is to touch thumb and fingertips together while the palms of both hands face up, thus forming a flat triangular shape. The triangle signifies the Three Jewels of Buddhism.

## Food Restrictions

Buddhism does not require one to be a vegetarian. Many followers do not eat meat, however, because to do so involves killing other creatures. Both monks and laypersons may choose not to eat after noontime during the holy days of each month.

## Rites, Celebrations, & Services

Ancient Buddhism recognized four holy days each month, known as *uposatha*. These days included the full moon and new moon days of each lunar month, as well as the eighth day after each of these moons appeared. Both monks and members of the laity have special religious duties during these four days. A special service takes place in which flowers are offered to images of the Buddha, precepts are repeated, and a sermon is preached. On these four days, an additional three precepts may be undertaken along with the five regularly observed. The three extra duties are to refrain from sleeping on a luxurious bed, eating any food after noon, and adorning the body or going to entertainments.

In Theravada nations, three major life events of the Buddha—birth, enlightenment, and entering nirvana—are celebrated on Vesak, or Buddha Day. In temples, statues of Buddha as a child are ceremonially cleaned. Worshippers may offer incense and flowers. To symbolize the Buddha's enlightenment, lights may be illuminated in trees and temples. Because it is a day of special kindness, some people in Thailand refrain from farm work that could harm living creatures. They may also seek special merit by freeing captive animals.

Other Buddhist nations that follow Mahayana Buddhism commemorate these events on three different days. In Japan, Hana Matsuri is the celebration of Buddha's birth. On that day, people create paper flower gardens to recall the gardens of Lumbini, Siddhartha's birthplace. Worshippers also pour perfumed tea over statues of Buddha; this is because, according to tradition, the gods provided scented water for Siddhartha's first bath.

Poson is celebrated in Sri Lanka to honor the coming of Buddhism during the reign of Emperor Asoka. Other holy persons are also celebrated in the countries where they had the greatest influence. In Tibet, for instance, the arrival of

Padmasambhava, who brought Buddhism to that nation, is observed.

Buddhists also integrate their own special celebrations into regular harvest festivals and New Year activities. These festivities may include a performance of an event in the life of any buddha or bodhisattva. For example, troupes of actors in Tibet specialize in enacting Buddhist legends. The festival of the Sacred Tooth is held in Kandy, Sri Lanka. According to one legend, a tooth of Buddha has been recovered, and it is paraded through the streets on this day. The tooth has been placed in a miniature stupa, or sealed mound, which is carried on an elephant's back.

Protection rituals have been common in Buddhism from earliest days. They may be public rituals meant to avoid a collective danger, such as those held in Sri Lanka and other Southeast Asia nations. Or they may be designed for private use. The role of these rituals is greater in Mahayana tradition, especially in Tibet. Mantras are chanted for this reason.

Customs surrounding death and burial differ between traditions and nations. A common factor, however, is the belief that the thoughts of a person at death are significant. This period may be extended for three days following death, due to a belief in consciousness for that amount of time after death. To prepare the mind of the dying, another person may read sacred texts aloud.

*Judy A. Johnson, MTS*

## Bibliography

Armstrong, Karen. *Buddha*. New York: Penguin, 2001. Print.

Barnes, Trevor. *The Kingfisher Book of Religions*. New York: Kingfisher, 1999. Print.

Chodron, Thubten. *Buddhism for Beginners*. Ithaca: Snow Lion, 2001. Print.

Eckel, Malcolm David. *Buddhism*. Oxford: Oxford UP, 2002. Print.

Epstein, Ron. "Application of Buddhist Teachings in Modern Life." *Religion East & West* Oct. 2012: 52–61. Print.

Harding, John S. *Studying Buddhism in Practice*. Routledge, 2012. E-book. Studying Religions in Practice.

Harvey, Peter. *An Introduction to Buddhism: Teachings, History and Practices*. 2nd ed. Cambridge UP, 2013. E-book.

Heirman, Ann. "Buddhist Nuns: Between Past and Present." *International Review for the History of Religions* 58.5/6 (2011): 603–31. Print.

Langley, Myrtle. *Religion*. New York: Knopf, 1996. Print.

Low, Kim Cheng Patrick. "Three Treasures of Buddhism & Leadership Insights." *Culture & Religion Review Journal* 2012.3 (2012): 66–72. Print.

Low, Patrick Kim Cheng. "Leading Change, the Buddhist Perspective." *Culture & Religion Review Journal* 2012.1 (2012): 127–45. Print.

McMahan, David L. *Buddhism in the Modern World*. Routledge, 2012. E-book.

Meredith, Susan. *The Usborne Book of World Religions*. London: Usborne, 1995. Print.

Morgan, Diane. *Essential Buddhism: A Comprehensive Guide to Belief and Practice*. Praeger, 2010. E-book.

Wilkinson, Philip. *Buddhism*. New York: DK, 2003. Print.

Wilkinson, Philip. *Religions*. New York: DK, 2008. Print.

# Christianity

## General Description

Christianity is one of the world's major religions. It is based on the life and teachings of Jesus of Nazareth, called the Christ, or anointed one. It is believed that there are over thirty thousand denominations or sects of Christianity worldwide. Generally, most of these sects fall under the denominational families of Catholicism, Protestant, and Orthodox. (Anglican and Oriental Orthodox are sometimes added as separate branches.) Most denominations have developed since the seventeenth-century Protestant Reformation.

## Number of Adherents Worldwide

Over 2.3 billion people around the world claim allegiance to Christianity in one of its many forms. The three major divisions are Roman Catholicism, Eastern Orthodox, and Protestant. Within each group are multiple denominations. Roman Catholics number more than 1.1 billion followers, while the Eastern Orthodox Church has between 260 and 278 million adherents. An estimated 800 million adherents follow one of the various Protestant denominations, including Anglican, Baptist, Lutheran, Presbyterian, and Methodist. Approximately 1 percent of Christians, or 28 million adherents, do not belong to one of the three major divisions

There are a number of other groups, such as the Amish, with an estimated 249,000 members, and the Quakers, numbering approximately 377,000. Both of these churches—along with Mennonites, who number 1.7 million—are in the peace tradition (their members are conscientious objectors). Pentecostals have 600 million adherents worldwide. Other groups that are not always considered Christian by more conservative groups include Jehovah's Witnesses (7.6 million) and Mormons (13 million) (Wilkinson, p. 104-121).

## Basic Tenets

The summaries of the Christian faith are found in the Apostles Creed and Nicene Creed.

In addition, some churches have developed their own confessions of faith, such as Lutheranism's Augsburg Confession. Christianity is a monotheistic tradition, although most Christians believe in the Trinity, defined as one God in three separate but equal persons—Father, Son, and Holy Spirit. More modern, gender-neutral versions of the Trinitarian formula may refer to Creator, Redeemer, and Sanctifier. Many believe in the doctrine of original sin, which means that the disobedience of Adam and Eve in the Garden of Eden has been passed down through all people; because of this sin, humankind is in need of redemption. Jesus Christ was born, lived a sinless life, and then was crucified and resurrected as a substitute for humankind. Those who accept this sacrifice for sin will receive eternal life in a place of bliss after death. Many Christians believe that a Second Coming of Jesus will inaugurate a millennial kingdom and a final judgment (in which people will be judged according to their deeds and their eternal souls consigned to heaven or hell), as well as a resurrected physical body.

## Sacred Text

The Bible is the sacred text of Christianity, which places more stress on the New Testament. The canon of the twenty-six books of the New Testament was finally determined in the latter half of the fourth century CE.

## Major Figures

Christianity is based on the life and teachings of Jesus of Nazareth. His mother, Mary, is especially revered in Roman Catholicism and the Eastern Orthodox tradition, where she is known as Theotokos (God-bearer). Jesus spread his teachings through the twelve apostles, or disciples, who he himself chose and named. Paul (Saint Paul or Paul the Apostle), who became the first missionary to the Gentiles—and whose writings comprise a bulk of the New Testament—is a key figure for the theological treatises embedded in his letters to early churches. His conversion occurred after Jesus' crucifixion. All of these figures are biblically represented.

Under the Emperor Constantine, Christianity went from a persecuted religion to the state religion. Constantine also convened the Council of Nicea in 325 CE, which expressed the formula defining Jesus as fully God and fully human. Saint Augustine (354–430) was a key thinker of the early church who became the Bishop of Hippo in North Africa. He outlined the principles of just war and expressed the ideas of original sin. He also suggested what later became the Catholic doctrine of purgatory.

In the sixth century, Saint Benedict inscribed a rule for monks that became a basis for monastic life. Martin Luther, the monk who stood against the excesses of the Roman Catholic Church, ignited the seventeenth-century Protestant Reformation. He proclaimed that salvation came by grace alone, not through works. In the twentieth century, Pope John XXIII convened the Vatican II Council, or Second Vatican Council, which made sweeping changes to the liturgy and daily practice for Roman Catholics.

## Major Holy Sites

The key events in the life of Jesus Christ occurred in the region of Palestine. Bethlehem is honored as the site of Jesus's birth; Jerusalem is especially revered as the site of Jesus's crucifixion. The capital of the empire, Rome, also became the center of Christianity until the Emperor Constantine shifted the focus to Constantinople. Rome today is the seat of the Vatican, an independent city-state that houses the government of the Roman Catholic Church. Canterbury, the site of the martyrdom of Saint Thomas Becket and seat of the archbishop of the Anglican Communion, is a pilgrimage site for Anglicans. There are also many pilgrimage sites, such as Compostela and Lourdes, for other branches of Christianity. In Ethiopia, Lalibela is the site of eleven churches carved from stone during the twelfth century. The site serves as a profound testimony to the vibrancy of the Christian faith in Africa.

## Major Rites & Celebrations

The first rite of the church is baptism, a water-related ritual that is traditionally administered to infants or adults alike through some variant of sprinkling or immersion. Marriage is another rite of the church. Confession is a major part of life for Roman Catholics, although the idea is also present in other branches of Christianity.

The celebration of the Eucharist, or Holy Communion, is a key part of weekly worship for the liturgical churches such as those in the Roman Catholic or Anglican traditions. Nearly all Christians worship weekly on Sunday; services include readings of scripture, a sermon, singing of hymns, and may include Eucharist. Christians honor the birth of Jesus at Christmas and his death and resurrection at Easter. Easter is often considered the most significant liturgical feast, particularly in Orthodox branches.

Many Christians follow a calendar of liturgical seasons. Of these seasons, perhaps the best known is Lent, which is immediately preceded by Shrove Tuesday, also known as Mardi Gras. Lent is traditionally a time of fasting and self-examination in preparation for the Easter feast. Historically, Christians gave up rich foods. The day before Lent was a time for pancakes—to use up the butter and eggs—from which the term Mardi Gras (Fat Tuesday) derives. Lent begins with Ash Wednesday, when Christians are marked with the sign of the cross on their foreheads using ashes, a reminder that they are dust and will return to dust.

## ORIGINS

## History & Geography

Christianity was shaped in the desert and mountainous landscapes of Palestine, known as the Holy Land. Jesus was driven into the wilderness following his baptism, where he remained for forty days of fasting and temptation. The Gospels record that he often went to the mountains for solitude and prayer. The geography of the deserts and mountains also shaped early Christian spirituality, as men and women went into solitude to pray, eventually founding small communities of the so-called desert fathers and mothers.

Christianity at first was regarded as a sect within Judaism, though it differentiated itself early in the first century CE by breaking with the code of laws that defined Judaism, including the need for circumcision and ritual purity. Early Christianity then grew through the missionary work of the apostles, particularly Paul the Apostle, who traveled throughout the Mediterranean world and beyond the Roman Empire to preach the gospel (good news) of Jesus. (This is often called the Apostolic Age.)

Persecution under various Roman emperors only served to strengthen the emerging religion. In the early fourth century, the Emperor Constantine (ca. 272-337) made Christianity the official religion of the Roman Empire. He also convened the Council of Nicea in 325 CE to quell the religious controversies threatening the Pax Romana (Roman Peace), a time of stability and peace throughout the empire in the first and second centuries.

In 1054 the Great Schism, which involved differences over theology and practice, split the church into Eastern Orthodox and Roman Catholic branches. As Islam grew stronger, the Roman Catholic nations of Europe entered a period of Crusades—there were six Crusades in approximately 175 years, from 1095-1271—that attempted to take the Holy Land out of Muslim control.

A number of theologians became unhappy with the excesses of the Roman church and papal authority during the fifteenth and sixteenth centuries. The Protestant Reformation, originally an attempt to purify the church, was led by several men, most notably Martin Luther (1483-1546), whose ninety-five theses against the Catholic Church sparked the Reformation movement. Other leaders of the Protestant Reformation include John Knox (ca. 1510-1572), attributed as the founder of the Presbyterian denomination, John Calvin (1509-1564), a principle early developer of Calvinism, and Ulrich Zwingli (1484-1531), who initially spurred the Reformation in Switzerland. This period of turmoil resulted in the founding of a number of church denominations: Lutherans, Presbyterians, and Anglicans. These groups were later joined by the Methodists and the Religious Society of Friends (Quakers).

During the sixteenth and seventeenth centuries, the Roman Catholic Church attempted to stem this wave of protest and schism with the Counter-Reformation. Concurrently, the Inquisition, an effort to root out heresy and control the rebellion, took place. There were various inquisitions, including the Spanish Inquisition, which was led by Ferdinand II of Aragon and Isabella I of Castile in mid-fifteenth century and sought to "guard" the orthodoxy of Catholicism in Spain. There was also the Portuguese Inquisition, which began in 1536 in Portugal under King John III, and the Roman Inquisition, which took place in the late fifteenth century in Rome under the Holy See.

During the modern age, some groups became concerned with the perceived conflicts between history (revealed through recent archaeological findings) and the sciences (as described by Charles Darwin and Sigmund Freud) and the literal interpretation of some biblical texts. Fundamentalist Christianity began at an 1895 meeting in Niagara Falls, New York, with an attempt to define the basics (fundamentals) of Christianity. These were given as the inerrant nature of the Bible, the divine nature of Jesus, his literal virgin birth, his substitutionary death and literal physical resurrection, and his soon return. Liberal Christians, on the other hand, focused more on what became known as the Social Gospel, an attempt to relieve human misery.

Controversies in the twenty-first century throughout Christendom focused on issues such as abortion, homosexuality, the ordination of women and gays, and the authority of the scriptures. An additional feature is the growth of Christianity in the Southern Hemisphere. In Africa, for example, the number of Christians grew from 10 million in 1900 to over 506 million a century later. Initially the result of empire-building and colonialism, the conversions in these nations have resulted in a unique blend of native religions and Christianity. Latin America has won renown for its liberation theology, which was first articulated in 1968 as God's call for justice and God's preference for the poor, demonstrated in the ministry and teachings of Jesus Christ. Africa, Asia, and South America are regions that are considered more morally and theologically conservative. Some suggest that by 2050, non-Latino white persons will comprise only 20 percent of Christians.

## Founder or Major Prophet

Jesus of Nazareth was born into a peasant family. The date of his birth, determined by accounts in the Gospels of Matthew and Luke, could be as early as 4 or 5 BCE or as late as 6 CE. Mary, his mother, was regarded as a virgin; thus, Jesus' birth was a miracle, engendered by the Holy Spirit. His earthly father, Joseph, was a carpenter.

At about age thirty, Jesus began an itinerant ministry of preaching and healing following his baptism in the Jordan River by his cousin, John the Baptist. He selected twelve followers, known as apostles (sent-ones), and a larger circle of disciples (followers). Within a short time, Jesus' ministry and popularity attracted the negative attention of both the Jewish and Roman rulers. He offended the Jewish leaders with his emphasis on personal relationship with God rather than obedience to rules, as well as his claim to be coequal with God the Father.

For a period of one to three years (Gospel accounts vary in the chronology), Jesus taught and worked miracles, as recorded in the first four books of the New Testament, the Gospels of Matthew, Mark, Luke, and John. On what has become known as Palm Sunday, he rode triumphantly into Jerusalem on the back of a donkey while crowds threw palm branches at his feet. Knowing that his end was near, at a final meal with his disciples, known now to Christians as the Last Supper, Jesus gave final instructions to his followers.

He was subsequently captured, having been betrayed by Judas Iscariot, one of his own twelve apostles. A trial before the Jewish legislative body, the Sanhedrin, led to his being condemned for blasphemy. However, under Roman law, the Jews did not have the power to put anyone to death. A later trial under the Roman governor, Pontius Pilate, resulted in Jesus being crucified, although Pilate tried to prevent this action, declaring Jesus innocent.

According to Christian doctrine, following the crucifixion, Jesus rose from the dead three days later. He appeared before many over a span of forty days and instructed the remaining eleven apostles to continue spreading his teachings. He then ascended into heaven. Ultimately, his followers believed that he was the Messiah, the savior who was to come to the Jewish people and deliver them. Rather than offering political salvation, however, Jesus offered spiritual liberty.

## Philosophical Basis

Jesus was a Jew who observed the rituals and festivals of his religion. The Gospels reveal that he attended synagogue worship and went to Jerusalem for celebrations such as Passover. His teachings both grew out of and challenged the religion of his birth.

The Jews of Jesus' time, ruled by the Roman Empire, hoped for a return to political power. This power would be concentrated in a Messiah, whose coming had been prophesied centuries before. There were frequent insurrections in Judea, led in Jesus' time by a group called the Zealots. Indeed, it is believed that one of the twelve apostles was part of this movement. Jesus, with his message of a kingdom of heaven, was viewed as perhaps the one who would usher in a return to political ascendancy.

When challenged to name the greatest commandment, Jesus answered that it was to love God with all the heart, soul, mind, and strength. He added that the second was to love one's neighbor as one's self, saying that these two commands summarized all the laws that the Jewish religion outlined.

Jewish society was concerned with ritual purity and with following the law. Jesus repeatedly flouted those laws by eating with prostitutes and tax collectors, by touching those deemed unclean, such as lepers, and by including

Gentiles in his mission. Women were part of his ministry, with some of them providing for him and his disciples from their own purses, others offering him a home and a meal, and still others among those listening to him teach.

Jesus's most famous sermon is called the Sermon on the Mount. In it, he offers blessings on those on the outskirts of power, such as the poor, the meek, and those who hunger and thirst for righteousness. While not abolishing the law that the Jews followed, he pointed out its inadequacies and the folly of parading one's faith publicly. Embedded in the sermon is what has become known as the Lord's Prayer, the repetition of which is often part of regular Sunday worship. Much of Jesus' teaching was offered in the form of parables, or short stories involving vignettes of everyday life: a woman adding yeast to dough or a farmer planting seeds. Many of these parables were attempts to explain the kingdom of heaven, a quality of life that was both present and to come.

## Holy Places

The Christian church has many pilgrimage sites, some of them dating back to the Middle Ages. Saint James is thought to have been buried in Compostela, Spain, which was a destination for those who could not make the trip to the Holy Land. Lourdes, France, is one of the spots associated with healing miracles. Celtic Christians revere places such as the small Scottish isle of Iona, an early Christian mission. Assisi, Italy, is a destination for those who are attracted to Saint Francis (1181-1226), founder of the Franciscans. The Chartres Cathedral in France is another pilgrimage destination from the medieval period.

Jerusalem, Rome, and Canterbury are considered holy for their associations with the early church and Catholicism, as well as with Anglicanism. Within the Old City of Jerusalem is the Church of the Holy Sepulchre, an important pilgrimage site believed to house the burial place of Jesus. Another important pilgrimage site is the Church of the Nativity in Bethlehem. It is built on a cave believed to be the birthplace of Jesus, and is one of the oldest operating churches in existence.

## CHRISTIANITY IN DEPTH

### Sacred Symbols

The central symbol of Christianity is the cross, of which there are many variant designs. Some of them, such as Celtic crosses, are related to regions of the world. Others, such as the Crusader's cross, honor historic events. The dove is the symbol for the Holy Spirit, which descended in that shape on the gathered disciples at Pentecost after Jesus's ascension.

Various symbols represent Jesus. Candles allude to his reference to himself as the Light of the World, while the lamb stands for his being the perfect sacrifice, the Lamb of God. The fish symbol that is associated with Christianity has a number of meanings, both historic and symbolic. A fish shape stands for the Greek letters beginning the words Jesus Christ, Son of God, Savior; these letters form the word *ichthus*, the Greek word for "fish." Fish also featured prominently in the scriptures, and the early apostles were known as "fishers of man." The crucifixion symbol is also a popular Catholic Christian symbol.

All of these symbols may be expressed in stained glass. Used in medieval times, stained glass often depicted stories from the Bible as an aid to those who were illiterate.

### Sacred Practices & Gestures

Roman Catholics honor seven sacraments, defined as outward signs of inward grace. These include the Eucharist, baptism, confirmation, marriage, ordination of priests, anointing the sick or dying with oil, and penance. The Eastern Orthodox Church refers to these seven as mysteries rather than sacraments.

Priests in the Roman Catholic Church must remain unmarried. In the Eastern Orthodox, Anglican, and Protestant denominations, they may marry. Both Roman Catholic and Eastern Orthodox refuse to ordain women to the priesthood.

The Orthodox Church practices a rite known as chrismation, anointing a child with oil following its baptism. The "oil of gladness," as it is known, is placed on the infant's head, eyes, ears, and mouth. This is similar to the practice of confirmation in some other denominations. Many Christian denominations practice anointing the sick or dying with oil, as well as using the oil to seal those who have been baptized.

Many Christians, especially Roman Catholics, use a rosary, or prayer beads, when praying. Orthodox believers may have icons, such as small paintings of God, saints or biblical events, as part of their worship. There may be a font of water that has been blessed as one enters some churches, which the worshippers use to make the sign of the cross, touching fingers to their forehead, heart, right chest, and left chest. Some Christians make the sign of the cross on the forehead, mouth, and heart to signify their desire for God to be in their minds, on their lips, and in their hearts.

Christians may genuflect, or kneel, as they enter or leave a pew in church. In some churches, particularly the Catholic and Orthodox, incense is burned during the service as a sweet smell to God.

In some traditions, praying to or for the dead is encouraged. The rationale for this is known as the communion of saints—the recognition that those who are gone are still a part of the community of faith.

Catholic, Orthodox, and some branches of other churches have monastic orders for both men and women. Monks and nuns may live in a cloister or be engaged in work in the wider world. They generally commit to a rule of life and to the work of prayer. Even those Christians who are not part of religious orders sometimes go on retreats, seeking quiet and perhaps some spiritual guidance from those associated with the monastery or convent.

### Food Restrictions

Historically, Christians fasted during Lent as preparation for the Easter celebration. Prior to the Second Vatican Council in 1962,

Roman Catholics did not eat meat on Fridays. Conservative Christians in the Evangelical tradition tend to eliminate the use of alcohol, tobacco, and drugs.

### Rites, Celebrations & Services

For churches in the liturgical tradition, the weekly celebration of the Eucharist is paramount. While many churches celebrate this ritual feast with wine and a wafer, many Protestant churches prefer to use grape juice and crackers or bread.

Church services vary widely. Quakers sit silently waiting for a word from God, while in many African American churches, hymns are sung for perhaps an hour before the lengthy sermon is delivered. Some churches have a prescribed order of worship that varies little from week to week. Most services, however, include prayer, a sermon, and singing, with or without musical accompaniment.

A church's architecture often gives clues as to the type of worship one will experience. A church with the pulpit in the center at the front generally is a Protestant church with an emphasis on the Word of God being preached. If the center of the front area is an altar, the worship's focus will be on the Eucharist.

Christmas and Easter are the two major Christian celebrations. In liturgical churches, Christmas is preceded by Advent, a time of preparation and quiet to ready the heart for the coming of Christ. Christmas has twelve days, from the birth date of December 25 to the Epiphany on January 6. Epiphany (to show) is the celebration of the arrival of the Magi (wise men) from the East who came to worship the young Jesus after having seen his star. Their arrival is believed to have been foretold by the Old Testament prophet Isaiah, who said "And the Gentiles shall come to thy light, and kings to the brightness of thy rising" (Isaiah 60:3). Epiphany is the revealing of the Messiah to the Gentiles.

In the early church, Easter was preceded by a solemn period of fasting and examination, especially for candidates for baptism and penitent sinners wishing to be reconciled. In Western churches, Lent begins with Ash Wednesday, which is six and half weeks prior to Easter. By excluding Sundays from the fast, Lent thus gives a forty-day fast, imitating that of Jesus in the wilderness. Historically forbidden foods during the fast included eggs, butter, meat, and fish. In the Eastern Church, dairy products, oil, and wine are also forbidden.

The week before Easter is known as Holy Week. It may include extra services such as Maundy Thursday, a time to remember Jesus's new commandment (*maundy* is etymologically related to *mandate*) to love one another. In some Catholic areas, the crucifixion is reenacted in a Passion play (depicting the passion—trial, suffering, and death—of Christ). Some churches will have an Easter vigil the Saturday night before or a sunrise service on Easter morning.

*Judy A. Johnson, MTS*

## Bibliography

Bakker, Janel Kragt. "The Sister Church Phenomenon: A Case Study of the Restructuring of American Christianity against the Backdrop of Globalization." *International Bulletin of Missionary Research* 36.3 (2012): 129–34. Print.

Bandak, Andreas and Jonas Adelin Jørgensen. "Foregrounds and Backgrounds—Ventures in the Anthropology of Christianity." *Ethos: Journal of Anthropology* 77.4 (2012): 447–58. Print.

Barnes, Trevor. *The Kingfisher Book of Religions*. New York: Kingfisher, 1999. Print.

Chandler, Daniel Ross. "Christianity in Cross-Cultural Perspective: A Review of Recent Literature." *Asia Journal of Theology* 26.2 (2012): 44–57. Print.

Daughrity, Dyron B. "Christianity Is Moving from North to South—So What about the East?" *International Bulletin of Missionary Research* 35.1 (2011): 18–22. Print.

Kaatz, Kevin. *Voices of Early Christianity: Documents from the Origins of Christianity*. Santa Barbara: Greenwood, 2013. E-book.

Langley, Myrtle. *Religion*. New York: Alfred A. Knopf, 1996.

Lewis, Clive Staples. *Mere Christianity*. New York: Harper, 2001. Print.

McGrath, Alistair. *Christianity: An Introduction*. Hoboken, New Jersey: Wiley, 2006. Print.

Meredith, Susan. *The Usborne Book of World Religions*. London: Usborne, 1995. Print.

Ripley, Jennifer S. "Integration of Psychology and Christianity: 2022." *Journal of Psychology & Theology* 40.2 (2012): 150–54. Print.

Stefon, Matt. *Christianity: History, Belief, and Practice*. New York: Britannica Educational, 2012. E-book.

Wilkinson, Philip. *Christianity*. New York: DK, 2003. Print.

Wilkinson, Philip. *Religions*. New York: DK, 2008. Print.

Zoba, Wendy Murray. *The Beliefnet Guide to Evangelical Christianity*. New York: Three Leaves, 2005. Print.

# East Asian Religions

## General Description

East Asian religious and philosophical traditions include, among others, Confucianism, Taoism, and Shintoism. Confucianism is a philosophy introduced by the Chinese philosopher Confucius (Kongzi; 551–479 BCE) in the sixth century BCE, during the Zhou dynasty. Taoism, which centers on Tao, or "the way," is a religious and philosophical tradition that originated in China about two thousand years ago. Shinto, "the way of the spirits," is a Japanese tradition of devotion to spirits and rituals.

## Number of Adherents Worldwide

Between 5 and 6 million people, the majority of them in China, practice Confucianism, once the state religion of China. About 20 million people identify as Taoists. Most of the Taoist practitioners are in China as well. In Japan, approximately 107 million people practice Shintoism, though many practitioners also practice Buddhism. Sects of Shinto include Tenrikyo (heavenly truth), founded in 1838, with nearly 2 million devotees. Shukyo Mahikari (divine light) is another, smaller sect founded in the 1960s. Like other sects, it is a blend of different religious traditions (Wilkinson 332–34).

## Basic Tenets

Confucianism is a philosophy of life and does concerns itself not with theology but with life conduct. Chief among the aspects of life that must be tended are five key relationships, with particular focus on honoring ancestors and showing filial piety. Confucianism does not take a stand on the existence of God, though the founder, Confucius, referred to "heaven." Except for this reference, Confucianism does not address the question of life after death.

Taoists believe that Tao (the way or the flow) is in everything. Taoism teaches that qi, or life energy, needs to be balanced between yin and yang, which are the female and male principles of life, respectively. With its doctrine of the evil of violence, Taoism borders on pacifism, and it also preaches simplicity and naturalness. Taoists believe in five elements—wood, earth, air, fire and water—that need to be in harmony. The five elements lie at the heart of Chinese medicine, particularly acupuncture. In Taoism, it is believed that the soul returns to a state of nonbeing after death.

Shinto emphasizes nature and harmony, with a focus on lived experience rather than doctrine. Shinto, which means "the way of the gods," is a polytheistic religion; Amaterasu, the sun goddess, is the chief god. At one point in Japan's history, the emperor was believed to be a descendant of Amaterasu and therefore divine. In Tenrikyo Shinto, God is manifested most often as Oyakami, meaning "God the parent."

Shinto teaches that some souls can become kami, a spirit, following death. Each traditional home has a god-shelf, which honors family members believed to have become kami. An older family member tends to the god-shelf, placing a bit of food and some sake (rice wine) on the shelf. To do their work, kami must be nourished. The Tenrikyo sect includes concepts from Pure Land Buddhism, such as an afterlife and the idea of salvation.

## Sacred Texts

Five classic texts are sacred to the Confucians. These include the I Ching, or Book of Changes; the Book of Odes; the Book of History; the Book of Rites; and the Annals of Spring and Autumn. The Analects, a collection of Confucius's sayings, is another revered classic. The Tao Te Ching (The Way of Power) is the most sacred book of the Taoists. Those who practice Shinto hold sacred two works: the Kojiki (Record of Ancient Matters) and the Nihon-gi (Chronicles of Japan). Both texts, which contain legends and creation myths, were written during the eighth century.

## Major Figures

Confucius, who lived during the sixth century, was the first great philosopher of China. Mengzi (Meng-tzu; 371–289 BCE), known in the West as Mencius, developed Confucius's teachings about the higher power guiding human life. Another ancient Chinese philosopher, Laozi(or Lao-tzu), is the founder of Taoism. He is believed to have been a contemporary of Confucius's in the central region of China. Modern scholars are not certain he ever existed, though one account includes the story of Confucius visiting Laozi. Chuang Tzu wrote of Laozi and his ideas during the fourth and third centuries BCE. Shinto's major figures include Ō no Yasumaro (d. 723), the compiler of the Kokiji who acted under the orders of Empress Gemmei and consulted a bard known to have an infallible memory; the scholar Motoori Norinaga (1730–1800), whose work led to a revived interest in ancient Shinto texts; and Nakayama Miki (1798–1887), the farmer's wife who founded Tenrikyo.

## Major Holy Sites

Most Confucian sacred places are located within private homes, where an ancestral shrine and an altar to gods and spirits are maintained. In China's Shandong Province is Qufu, the site of Confucius's family mansion, temple, and cemetery. The temple was built in 478 BCE, only a year after Confucius's death, and has been maintained and enlarged. In addition to its status as a holy site, the United Nations Educational, Scientific, and Cultural Organization (UNESCO) has placed it on their World Heritage List.

Taoists regard mountains as a way to communicate with Earth's primeval powers and with those who are immortal. Five of the nine sacred mountains in China are associated with Taoism: Hengshan in both the north and the south, Songshan in the south, Taishan in the east, and Huashan in the west. The holiest of the five is Taishan, which symbolizes stability, prevents natural disasters, and ensures fertility.

Shintoism has a high regard for natural beauty. As such, Shinto shrines are everywhere, particularly in mountains or near waterfalls.

Mountains in particular are regarded as homes of the gods. Mount Fuji is the holiest Shinto mountain, and climbing it to reach the shrine on its peak is an act of worship. More than forty thousand shrines are dedicated to Inari, the rice god.

Shinto was formalized during the Yamato period (the name for ancient Japan), and because the emperor of the imperial dynasty was from the Yamato area and was considered divine, the whole region is revered. At Ise, located near the coast in Mie Prefecture, southeast of Nara, the shrine has been rebuilt every twenty years for at least fourteen centuries. This rebuilding ensures that Toyouke-Ōmikami (the harvest goddess) and Amaterasu (the sun goddess) are renewed in vigor, which in turn invigorates both the rice crop and the imperial line. Those who have died in war are revered as kami in Japan. In Tokyo, a shrine called Yasukuni is dedicated to them. However, there is controversy surrounding the place because of its association with Japan's extreme nationalism prior to World War II.

## Sacred Texts

Five classic texts are sacred to the Confucians. These include the I Ching, or Book of Changes; the Book of Odes; the Book of History; the Book of Rites; and the Annals of Spring and Autumn. The Analects, a collection of Confucius's sayings, is another revered classic. The Tao te Ching (The Way of Power) is the most sacred book of the Taoists. Those who practice Shinto hold sacred two works: the Kojiki (Record of Ancient Matters) and the Nihon-gi (Chronicles of Japan). Both texts, which contain legends and creation myths, were written during the eighth century.

## Major Figures

Confucius, who lived during the sixth century, was the first great philosopher of China. Mengzi (Meng-tzu; 371–289 BCE), known in the West as Mencius, developed Confucius's teachings about the higher power guiding human life. Another ancient Chinese philosopher, Laozi,(or Lao-tzu) is the founder of Taoism. He is believed to have been a contemporary of Confucius in the central region of China. Modern scholars are not certain he ever existed, though one account includes the story of Confucius visiting Laozi. Chuang Tzu wrote of Laozi and his ideas during the fourth and third centuries BCE. Shinto's major figures include Ō no Yasumaro, the compiler of the Kokiji who acted under the orders of Empress Gemmei and consulted a bard known to have an infallible memory; the scholar Motoori Norinaga (1730–1800), whose work led to a revived interest in ancient Shinto texts; and Nakayama Miki (1798–1887), the farmer's wife who founded Tenrikyo.

## Major Holy Sites

Most Confucian sacred places are located within private homes, where an ancestral shrine and an altar to gods and spirits are maintained. In China's Shandong Province is Qufu, the site of Confucius's family mansion, temple and cemetery. The temple was built in 478 BCE, only a year after Confucius's death, and has been maintained and enlarged. In addition to being a holy site, the United Nations Educational, Scientific, and Cultural Organization (UNESCO) has placed it on their World Heritage List.

Taoists consider mountains as a way to communicate with Earth's primeval powers and with those who are immortal. Five of the nine sacred mountains in China are associated with Taoism. They are Hengshan in both the north and south, Songshan in the south, Taishan in the east, and Huashan in the west. The holiest of the five is Taishan, which symbolizes stability, prevents natural disasters, and ensures fertility.

Shintoism has a high regard for natural beauty. As such, Shinto shrines are everywhere, particularly in mountains or near waterfalls. Mountains in particular are regarded as homes of the gods. Mount Fuji is the holiest Shinto mountain, and climbing it to reach the shrine on its peak is an act of worship. More than forty thousand shrines are dedicated to Inari, the rice god.

Shinto was formalized during the Yamato period (the name for ancient Japan), and because the emperor of the imperial dynasty is from the Yamato area, and was considered divine, the whole region is revered. At Ise, located near the coast in the Mie prefecture southeast of Nara, the shrine has been rebuilt every twenty years for at least fourteen centuries. This rebuilding ensures that Toyouke-Ōmikami (the harvest goddess) and Amaterasu (the sun goddess) are renewed in vigor, which in turn invigorates both the rice crop and the imperial line. Those who have died in war are revered as kami in Japan. In Tokyo, a shrine called Yasukuni is dedicated to them. However, there is controversy surrounding the place because of its association with Japan's extreme nationalism prior to World War II.

## Major Rites & Celebrations

Confucian celebrations have to do with honoring people rather than gods. At Confucian temples, the philosopher's birthday is celebrated each September. In Taiwan, this day is called "Teacher's Day." Sacrifices, music and dance are part of the event.

Taoism has a jiao (offering) festival near the winter solstice. It celebrates the renewal of the yang force at this turning of the year. During the festival priests, who have been ritually purified, wear lavish clothing. The festival includes music and dancing, along with large effigies of the gods which are designed to frighten away the evil spirits. Yang's renewal is also the focus of New Year celebrations, which is a time for settling debts and cleaning house. Decorations in the yang warm colors of gold, orange and red abound.

Many of the Shinto festivals overlap with Buddhist ones. There are many local festivals and rituals, and each community has an annual festival at the shrine dedicated to the kami of the region. Japanese New Year, which is celebrated for three days, is a major feast. Since the sixteenth century, the Gion Festival has taken place in Kyoto, Japan. Decorated floats are part of the celebration of the shrine.

---

## ORIGINS

---

## History & Geography

During the Zhou dynasty (1050–256 BCE) in China, the idea of heaven as a force that controlled events came to the fore. Zhou rulers believed that they ruled as a result of the "Mandate of Heaven," viewing themselves as morally superior to those of the previous dynasty, the Shang dynasty (1600-1046 BCE). They linked virtue and power as the root of the state.

By the sixth century the Zhou rulers had lost much of their authority. Many schools of thought developed to restore harmony, and were collectively known as the "Hundred Schools." Confucius set forth his ideas within this historical context. He traveled China for thirteen years, urging rulers to put his ideas into practice and failing to achieve his goals. He returned home to teach for the rest of his life and his ideas were not adopted until the Han dynasty (206 BCE–220 CE). During the Han period, a university for the nation was established, as well as the bureaucratic civil service that continued until the twentieth century. When the Chinese Empire fell in 1911, the Confucian way became less important.

Confucianism had influenced not only early Chinese culture, but also the cultures of Japan, Korea, and Vietnam. The latter two nations also adopted the bureaucratic system. In Japan, Confucianism reached its height during the Tokugawa age (1600–1868 CE). Confucian scholars continue to interpret the philosophy for the modern period. Some regard the ideas of Confucius as key to the recent economic booms in the so-called "tiger" economies of East Asia (Hong Kong, Singapore, South Korea, Taiwan, and Thailand). Confucianism continues to be a major influence on East Asian nations and culture.

Taoism's power (te) manifests itself as a philosophy, a way of life, and a religion. Philosophically, Taoism is a sort of self-help regimen, concerned with expending power efficiently by avoiding conflicts and friction, rather than fighting against the flow of life. In China, it is known as School Taoism. As a way of life, Taoism is concerned with increasing the amount of qi available through what is eaten and through meditation, yoga, and tai chi (an ancient Chinese martial art form). Acupuncture and the use of medicinal herbs are outgrowths of this way of

life. Church Taoism, influenced by Buddhism and Tao Chiao (religious Taoism), developed during the second century. This church looked for ways to use power for societal and individual benefit.

By the time of the Han dynasty (206–220 CE), Laozi had been elevated to the status of divine. Taoism found favor at court during the Tang dynasty (618–917 CE), during which the state underwrote temples. By adapting and encouraging people to study the writings of all three major faiths in China, Taoism remained relevant into the early twentieth century. During the 1960s and 1970s, Taoist books were burned and their temples were destroyed in the name of the Cultural Revolution (the Great Proletarian Cultural Revolution). Taoism remains popular and vital in Taiwan.

Shinto is an ancient religion, and some of its characteristics appeared during the Yayoi culture (ca. 300 BCE–300 CE). The focus was on local geographic features and the ancestry of local clan leaders. At first, women were permitted to be priests, but that equality was lost due to the influence of Confucian paternalism. The religion declined, but was revived in 1871 following the Meiji Restoration of the emperor. Shoguns (warlords) had ruled Japan for more than 250 years, and Shinto was the state religion until 1945. It was associated with the emperor cult and contributed to Japan's militarism. After the nation's defeat in World War II, the 1947 constitution forbade government involvement in any religion. In contemporary Shinto, women are permitted to become priests and girls, in some places, are allowed to carry the portable shrines during festivals.

## Founder or Major Prophet

Confucius, or Kongzi ("Master Kong"), was a teacher whose early life may have included service in the government. He began traveling throughout the country around age fifty, attempting and failing to interest rulers in his ideas for creating a harmonious state. He returned to his home state after thirteen years, teaching a group of disciples who spread his ideas posthumously.

According to legend, Taoism's founder, Laozi, lived during the sixth century. Laozi may be translated as "Grand Old Master," and may be simply a term of endearment. He maintained the archives and lived simply in a western state of China. Weary of people who were uninterested in natural goodness and perhaps wanting greater solitude in his advanced years, he determined to leave China, heading for Tibet on a water buffalo. At the border, a gatekeeper wanted to persuade him to stay, but could not do so. He asked Laozi to leave behind his teachings. For three days Laozi transcribed his teachings, producing the five-thousand-word Tao Te Ching. He then rode off and was never heard of again. Unlike most founders of religions, he neither preached nor promoted his beliefs. Still, he was held with such regard that some emperors claimed descent from him.

No one is certain of the origin of Shinto, which did not have a founder or major prophet. Shinto—derived from two Chinese words, *shen* (spirit) and *dao* (way)—has been influenced by other religions, notably Confucianism and Buddhism.

## Philosophical Basis

Confucianism sought to bring harmony to the state and society as a whole. This harmony was to be rooted in the Five Constant Relationships: between parents and children; husbands and wives; older and younger siblings; older and younger friends; and rulers and subjects. Each of these societal relationships existed to demonstrate mutual respect, service, honor, and love, resulting in a healthy society. The fact that three of the five relationships exist within the family highlights the importance of honoring family. Ritual maintains the li, or rightness, of everything, and is a way to guarantee that a person performed the correct action in any situation in life.

Taoism teaches that two basic components—yin and yang—are in all things, including health, the state, and relationships. Yin is the feminine principle, associated with soft, cold, dark, and moist things. Yang is the masculine principle,

and is associated with hard, warm, light, and dry things. By keeping these two aspects of life balanced, harmony will be achieved. Another concept is that of wu-wei, action that is in harmony with nature, while qi is the life force in all beings. The Tao is always in harmony with the universe. Conflict is to be avoided, and soldiers are to go as if attending a funeral, solemnly and with compassion. Taoism also teaches the virtues of humility and selflessness.

Shinto is rooted in reverence for ancestors and for the spirits known as kami, which may be good or evil. By correctly worshipping the kami, Shintoists believe that they are assisting in purifying the world and aiding in its functioning.

## Holy Places

Confucianism does not always distinguish between sacred and profane space. So much of nature is considered a holy place, as is each home's private shrine. In addition, some Confucian temples have decayed while others have been restored. Temples do not have statues or images. Instead, the names of Confucius and his noted followers are written on tablets. Like the emperor's palace, temples have the most important halls placed on the north-south axis of the building. Temples are also internally symmetrical, as might be expected of a system that honors order. In Beijing, the Temple of Heaven, just south of the emperor's palace, was one of the holiest places in imperial China.

Taoism's holy places are often in nature, particularly mountains. The holiest of the five sacred mountains in China is Taishan, located in the east. Taoism also reveres grottoes, which are caves thought to be illuminated by the light of heaven.

In the Shinto religion, nature is often the focus of holy sites. Mount Fuji is the most sacred mountain. Near Kyoto the largest shrine of Inari, the rice god, is located. The Grand Shrines at Ise are dedicated to two divinities, and for more than one thousand years, pilgrims have come to it. The Inner Shrine (Naiku) is dedicated to Amaterasu, the sun goddess, and is Shinto's most holy location. The Outer Shrine (Geku) is dedicated to

Toyouke, the goddess of the harvest. Every twenty years, Ise is torn down and rebuilt, thus renewing the gods. Shinto shrines all have torii, the sacred gateway. The most famous of these is built in the sea near the island of Miyajima. Those going to the shrine on this island go by boat through the torii.

---

## EAST ASIAN RELIGIONS IN DEPTH

### Sacred Symbols

Water is regarded as the source of life in Confucianism. The water symbol has thus become an unofficial symbol of Confucianism, represented by the Japanese ideogram or character for water, the Mizu, which somewhat resembles a stick figure with an extra leg. Other sacred symbols include the ancestor tablets in shrines of private homes, which are symbolic of the presence of the ancestor to whom offerings are made in hopes of aid.

While not a sacred symbol as the term is generally used, the black and white symbol of yin and yang is a common Taoist emblem. Peaches are also of a symbolic nature in Taoism, and often appear in Asian art. They are based on the four peaches that grew every three thousand years and which the mother of the fairies gave to the Han emperor Wu Ti (140–87 BCE). They are often symbolic of the Immortals.

The Shinto stylized sun, which appears on the Japanese flag, is associated with Amaterasu, the sun goddess. The torii, the gateway forming an entrance to sacred space, is another symbol associated with Shinto.

### Sacred Practices & Gestures

Confucian rulers traditionally offered sacrifices honoring Confucius at the spring and autumnal equinoxes. Most of the Confucian practices take place at home shrines honoring the ancestors.

Taoists believe that one can reach Tao (the way) through physical movements, chanting, or meditation. Because mountains, caves, and springs are often regarded as sacred sites, pilgrimages are important to Taoists. At a Taoist

funeral, a paper fairy crane is part of the procession. After the funeral, the crane, which symbolizes a heavenly messenger, is burned. The soul of the deceased person is then thought to ride to heaven on the back of the crane.

Many Shinto shrines exist throughout Japan. Most of them have a sacred arch, known as a torii. At the shrine's entrance, worshippers rinse their mouths and wash their hands to be purified before entering the prayer hall. Before praying, a worshipper will clap twice and ring a bell to let the kami know they are there. Only priests may enter the inner hall, which is where the kami live. During a festival, however, the image of the kami is placed in a portable shrine and carried in a procession through town, so that all may receive a blessing.

### Rites, Celebrations & Services

Early Confucianism had no priests, and bureaucrats performed any rituals that were necessary. When the Chinese Empire fell in 1911, imperial ceremonies ended as well. Rituals have become less important in modern times. In contemporary times the most important rite is marriage, the beginning of a new family for creating harmony. There is a correct protocol for each aspect of marriage, from the proposal and engagement to exchanging vows. During the ceremony, the groom takes the bride to his family's ancestor tablets to "introduce" her to them and receive a blessing. The couple bows to the ancestors during the ceremony.

After a death occurs, mourners wear coarse material and bring gifts of incense and money to help defray the costs. Added to the coffin holding are food offerings and significant possessions. A willow branch symbolizing the deceased's soul is carried with the coffin to the place of burial. After the burial, family members take the willow branch to their home altar and perform a ritual to add the deceased to the souls at the family's shrine.

Confucians and Taoists celebrate many of the same Chinese festivals, some of which originated before either Confucianism or Taoism began and reflect aspects of both traditions. While some festivals are not necessarily Taoist, they may be led by Taoist priests. During the Lantern Festival, which occurs on the first full moon of the New Year, offerings are made to the gods. Many of the festivals are tied to calendar events. Qingming (Clear and Bright) celebrates the coming of spring and is a time to remember the dead. During this time, families often go to the family gravesite for a picnic. The Double Fifth is the midsummer festival that occurs on the fifth day of the fifth month, and coincides with the peak of yang power. To protect themselves from too much of the male force, people don garments of the five colors—black, blue, red, white, and yellow—and with the five "poisons"—centipede, lizard, scorpion, snake, and toad—in the pattern of their clothes and on amulets. The gates of hell open at the Feast of the Hungry Ghosts. Priests have ceremonies that encourage the escaped evil spirits to repent or return to hell.

Marriage is an important rite in China, and thus in Taoism as well. Astrologers look at horoscopes to ensure that the bride and groom are well matched and to find the best day for the ceremony. The groom's family is always placed at the east (yang) and the bride's family to the west (yin) to bring harmony. When a person dies, the mourners again sit in the correct locations, while the head of the deceased points south. White is the color of mourning and of yin. At the home of the deceased, white cloths cover the family altar. Mourners may ease the soul's journey with symbolic artifacts or money. They may also go after the funeral to underground chambers beneath the temples to offer a sacrifice on behalf of the dead.

In the Shinto religion, rites exist for many life events. For example, pregnant women ask at a shrine for their children to be born safely, and the mother or grandmother brings a child who is thirty-two or thirty-three-days-old to a shrine for the first visit and blessing. A special festival also exists for children aged three, five or seven, who go to the shrine for purifying. In addition, a bride and groom are purified before the wedding, usually conducted by Shinto priests. Shinto priests may also offer blessings for a new car or building. The New Year and the Spring Festival are among the most important festivals, and shrine virgins, known as miko girls, may dance to celebrate life's renewal. Other festivals include the Feast of the Puppets, Boys' Day, the Water Kami Festival, the Star Feast, the Festival of the Dead, and the autumnal equinox.

*Judy A. Johnson, MTS*

## Bibliography

Barnes, Trevor. *The Kingfisher Book of Religions*. New York: Kingfisher, 1999. Print.

Bell, Daniel A. "Reconciling Socialism and Confucianism? Reviving Tradition in China." *Dissent* 57.1 (2010): 91–99. Print.

Chang, Chung-yuan. *Creativity and Taoism: A Study of Chinese Philosophy, Art and Poetry*. London: Kingsley, 2011. E-book.

Coogan, Michael D., ed. *Eastern Religions*. New York: Oxford UP, 2005. Print.

Eliade, Mircea, and Ioan P. Couliano. *The Eliade Guide to World Religions*. New York: Harper, 1991. Print.

Lao Tzu. *Tao Te Ching*. Trans. Stephen Mitchell. New York: Harper, 1999. Print.

Li, Yingzhang. *Lao-tzu's Treatise on the Response of the Tao*. Trans. Eva Wong. New Haven: Yale UP, 2011. Print.

Littlejohn, Ronnie. *Confucianism: An Introduction*. New York: Tauris, 2011. E-book.

Littleton, C. Scott. *Shinto*. Oxford: Oxford UP, 2002. Print.

Mcvay, Kera. *All about Shinto*. Delhi: University, 2012. Ebook.

Merton, Thomas. *The Way of Chuang Tzu*. New York: New Directions, 1965. Print.

Oldstone-Moore, Jennifer. *Confucianism*. Oxford: Oxford UP, 2002. Print.

Poceski, Mario. *Chinese Religions: The EBook*. Providence, UT: Journal of Buddhist Ethics Online Books, 2009. E-book.

Van Norden, Bryan W. *Introduction to Classical Chinese Philosophy*. Indianapolis: Hackett, 2011. Print.

Wilkinson, Philip. *Religions*. New York: DK, 2008. Print.

# Hinduism

## General Description

Hinduism; modern Hinduism is comprised of the devotional sects of Vaishnavism, Shaivism, and Shaktism (though Smartism is sometimes listed as the fourth division). Hinduism is often used as umbrella term, since many point to Hinduism as a family of different religions.

## Number of Adherents Worldwide

Between 13.8 and 15 percent of the world's population, or about one billion people, are adherents of Hinduism, making it the world's third largest religion after Christianity and Islam. The predominant sect is the Vaishnavite sect (Wilkinson, p. 333).

## Basic Tenets

Hinduism is a way of life rather than a body of beliefs. Hindus believe in karma, the cosmic law of cause and effect that determines one's state in the next life. Additional beliefs include dharma, one's religious duty.

Hinduism has no true belief in an afterlife. Rather, it teaches a belief in reincarnation, known as samsara, and in moksha, the end of the cycle of rebirths. Different sects have different paths to moksha.

Hinduism is considered a polytheist religion. However, it is also accurate to say that Hinduism professes a belief in one God or Supreme Truth that is beyond comprehension (an absolute reality, called Brahman) and which manifests itself in many forms and names. These include Brahma, the creator; Vishnu, the protector; and Shiva, the re-creator or destroyer. Many sects are defined by their belief in multiple gods, but also by their worship of one ultimate manifestation. For example, Shaivism and Vaishnavism are based upon the recognition of Shiva and Vishnu, respectively, as the manifestation. In comparison, Shaktism recognizes the Divine Mother (Shakti) as the Supreme Being, while followers of Smartism worship a particular deity of their own choosing.

## Major Deities

The Hindu trinity (Trimurti) is comprised of Brahma, the impersonal and absolute creator; Vishnu, the great preserver; and Shiva, the destroyer and re-creator. The goddesses corresponding to each god are Sarasvati, Lakshimi, and Parvati. Thousands of other gods (devas) and goddesses (devis) are worshipped, including Ganesha, Surya, and Kali. Each is believed to represent another aspect of the Supreme Being.

## Sacred Texts

Hindus revere ancient texts such as the four Vedas, the 108 Upanishads, and others. No single text has the binding authority of the Qur'an (Islam's holy book) or Bible. Hindu literature is also defined by Sruti (revealed truth), which is heard, and Smriti (realized truth), which is remembered. The former is canonical, while the latter can be changing. For example, the Vedas and the Upanishads constitute Sruti texts, while epics, history, and law books constitute the latter. The Bhagavad Gita (The Song of God) is also considered a sacred scripture of Hinduism, and consists of a philosophical dialogue.

## Major Figures

Major figures include: Shankara (788–820 CE), who defined the unity of the soul (atman) and absolute reality (Brahman); Ramanuja (1077–1157 CE), who emphasized bhakti, or love of God; Madhva (1199–1278 CE), scholar and writer, a proponent of dualism; Ramprahsad Sen (1718–1775 CE), composer of Hindu songs of devotion, poet, and mystic who influenced goddess worship in the; Raja Rammohun Roy (1772–1833 CE), abolished the custom of suttee, in which widows were burned on the funeral pyres of their dead husbands, and decried polygamy, rigid caste systems, and dowries; Rabindranath Tagore (1861–1941 CE), first Asian to win the Nobel Prize in Literature; Dr. Babasaheb R. Ambedkar (1891–1956 CE), writer of India's constitution and leader of a mass conversion to Buddhism; Mohandas K. Gandhi (1869–1948 CE), the "great soul" who left a legacy of effective use of nonviolence.

## Major Holy Sites

The major holy sites of Hinduism are located within India. They include the Ganges River, in whose waters pilgrims come to bathe away their sins, as well as thousands of tirthas (places of pilgrimage), many of which are associated with particular deities. For example, the Char Dham pilgrimage centers, of which there are four—Badrinath (north), Puri (east), Dwarka (west) and Rameshwaram (south)—are considered the holy abodes or sacred temples of Vishnu. There are also seven ancient holy cities in India, including Ayodhya, believed to be the birthplace of Rama; Varanasi (Benares), known as the City of Light; Dwarka; Ujjian; Kanchipuram; Mathura; and Hardwar.

## Major Rites & Celebrations

Diwali, the Festival of Lights, is a five-day festival that is considered a national holiday in India. Holi, the Festival of Colors, is the spring festival. Krishna Janmashtmi is Krishna's birthday. Shivaratri is Shiva's main festival. Navaratri, also known as the Durga festival or Dasserah, celebrates one of the stories of the gods and the victory of good over evil. Ganesh Chaturthi is the elephant-headed god Ganesha's birthday. Rathayatra, celebrated at Puri, India, is a festival for Jagannath, another word for Vishnu.

## ORIGINS

## History & Geography

Hinduism, which many people consider to be the oldest world religion, is unique in that it has no recorded origin or founder. Generally, it developed in the Indus Valley civilization several thousand years before the Common Era. The faith blends the Vedic traditions of the Indus Valley civilization and the invading nomadic tribes of the Aryans (prehistoric Indo-Europeans). Most of what is known of the Indus Valley civilization comes from archaeological excavations at Mohenjo-Daro (Mound of the Dead) and Harappa. (Because Harappa was a chief city of the period, the Indus Valley civilization is also referred to as the Harappan civilization.) The Vedas, a collection of ancient hymns, provides information about the Aryan culture.

The ancient Persian word *hind* means Indian, and for centuries, to be Indian was to be Hindu. Even now, about 80 percent of India's people consider themselves Hindu. The root word alludes to flowing, as a river flows. It is also etymologically related to the Indus River. At first, the term Hindu was used as an ethnic or cultural term, and travelers from Persia and Greece in the sixteenth century referred to those in the Indus Valley by that name. British writers coined the term *Hinduism* during the early part of the nineteenth century to describe the culture of India. The Hindus themselves often use the term Sanatana Dharma, meaning eternal law.

The Rigveda, a collection of hymns to various gods and goddesses written around 1500 BCE, is the first literary source for understanding Hinduism's history. The Vedas were chanted aloud for centuries before being written down around 1400 CE. The Rigveda is one of four major collections of Vedas, or wisdom: Rigveda, Yajurveda, Samaveda, and Atharvaveda. Together these four are called Samhitas.

Additionally, Hinduism relies on three other Vedic works: the Aranyakas, the Brahamans, and the Upanishads. The Upanishads is a philosophical work, possibly written down between 800 and 450 BCE, that attempts to answer life's big questions. Written in the form of a dialogue between a teacher (guru) and student (chela), the text's name means "to sit near," which describes the relationship between the two. Along with the Samhitas, these four are called Sruti (heard), a reference to their nature as revealed truth. The words in these texts cannot be altered.

Remaining works are called Smriti, meaning "remembered," to indicate that they were composed by human writers. The longer of the Smriti epics is the Mahabharata, the Great Story of the Bharatas. Written between 300 and 100 BCE, the epic is a classic tale of two rival, related families, including teaching as well as story. It is considered the longest single poem in existence, with about 200,000 lines. (A film made of it lasts for twelve hours.)

The Bhagavad Gita, or Song of the Lord, is the sixth section of the Mahabharata, but is often read as a stand-alone narrative of battle and acceptance of one's dharma. The Ramayana is the second, shorter epic of the Mahabharata, with about fifty thousand lines. Rama was the seventh incarnation, or avatar, of Vishnu. The narrative relates the abduction of his wife, Sita, and her rescue, accomplished with the help of the monkey god, Hanuman. Some have regarded the Mahabharata as an encyclopedia, and the Bhagavad Gita as the Bible within it.

Although many of the practices in the Vedas have been modified or discontinued, sections of it are memorized and repeated. Some of the hymns are recited at traditional ceremonies for the dead and at weddings.

Hinduism has affected American life and culture for many years. For example, the nineteenth-century transcendental writers Margaret Fuller and Ralph Waldo Emerson were both influenced by Hindu and Buddhist literature, while musician George Harrison, a member of the Beatles, adopted Hinduism and explored his new faith through his music, both with and without the Beatles. In 1965, the International Society for Krishna Consciousness (ISKCON), or the Hare Krishna movement, came to the Western world. In addition, many people have been drawn to yoga, which is associated with Hinduism's meditative practices.

## Founder or Major Prophet

Hinduism has no founder or major prophet. It is a religion that has developed over many centuries and from many sources, many of which are unknown in their origins.

## Philosophical Basis

Hinduism recognizes multiple ways to achieve salvation and escape the endless cycle of rebirth. The way of devotion is the most popular. Through worship of a single deity, the worshipper hopes to attain union with the divine. A second path is the way of knowledge, involving the use of meditation and reason. The third way is via action, or correctly performing religious observances in hope of receiving a blessing from the gods by accomplishing these duties.

Hinduism is considered the world's oldest religion, but Hindus maintain that it is also a way of living, not just a religion. There is great diversity as well as great tolerance in Hinduism. While Hinduism does not have a set of dogmatic formulations, it does blend the elements of devotion, doctrine, practice, society, and story as separate strands in a braid.

During the second century BCE, a sage named Patanjali outlined four life stages, and the fulfilled responsibilities inherent in each one placed one in harmony with dharma, or right conduct. Although these life stages are no longer observed strictly, their ideas still carry weight. Traditionally, these codes applied to men, and only to those in the Brahman caste; members of the warrior and merchant classes could follow them, but were not obligated. The Shudra and Dalit castes, along with women, were not part of the system. Historically, women were thought of as protected by fathers in their childhood, by husbands in their youth and adulthood, and by sons in old age. Only recently have women in India been educated beyond the skills of domestic responsibility and child rearing.

The earliest life stage is the student stage, or brahmacharya, a word that means "to conduct oneself in accord with Brahman." From ages twelve to twenty-four, young men were expected to undertake learning with a guru, or guide. During these twelve years of studying the Veda they were also expected to remain celibate.

The second stage, grihastha, is that of householder. A Hindu man married the bride that his parents had chosen, sired children, and created a livelihood on which the other three stages depended.

Vanaprastha is the third stage, involving retirement to solitude. Historically, this involved leaving the house and entering a forest dwelling.

A man's wife had the option to go with him or to remain. This stage also involved giving counsel to others and further study.

At the final stage of life, sannyasis, the Hindu renounces material goods, including a home of any sort. He may live in a forest or join an ashram, or community. He renounces even making a fire, and lives on fruit and roots that can be foraged. Many contemporary Hindus do not move to this stage, but remain at vanaprastha.

Yoga is another Hindu practice, more than three millennia old, which Patanjali codified. The four forms of yoga corresponded to the Hindu avenues of salvation. Hatha yoga is the posture yoga seeking union with god through action. Jnana yoga is the path to god through knowledge. Bhakti yoga is the way of love to god. Karma yoga is the method of finding god through work. By uniting the self, the practitioner unites with God. Yoga is related etymologically to the English word *yoke*—it attempts to yoke the individual with Brahman. All forms of yoga include meditation and the acceptance of other moral disciplines, such as self-discipline, truthfulness, nonviolence, and contentment.

Aryan society was stratified, and at the top of the social scale were the priests. This system was the basis for the caste system that had long dominated Hinduism. Caste, which was determined by birth, affected a person's occupation, diet, neighborhood, and marriage partner. Vedic hymns allude to four varnas, or occupations: Brahmins (priests), Kshatriyas (warriors), Vaishyas (merchants and common people), and Shudras (servants). A fifth class, the Untouchables, later known as Dalit (oppressed), referred to those who were regarded as a polluting force because they handled waste and dead bodies. The belief was that society would function properly if each group carried out its duties. These varnas later became wrongly blended with castes, or jatis, which were smaller groups also concerned with a person's place in society.

The practice of Hinduism concerns itself with ritual purity; even household chores can be done in a ritualistic way. Some traditions demand ritual purity before one can worship. Brahmin priests, for example, may not accept water or food from non-Brahmins. Refusal to do so is not viewed as classism, but an attempt to please the gods in maintaining ritual purity.

Mohandas Gandhi was one of those who refused to use the term *Untouchable*, using the term *harijan*(children of God), instead. Dr. Babasaheb R. Ambedkar, who wrote India's constitution, was a member of this class. Ambedkar and many of his supporters became Buddhists in an attempt to dispel the power of caste. In 1947, following India's independence from Britain, the caste system was officially banned, though it has continued to influence Indian society.

Ahimsa, or dynamic harmlessness, is another deeply rooted principle of Hinduism. It involves six pillars: refraining from eating all animal products; revering all of life; having integrity in thoughts, words, and deeds; exercising self-control; serving creation, nature, and humanity; and advancing truth and understanding.

## Holy Places

In Hinduism, all water is considered holy, symbolizing the flow of life. For a Hindu, the Ganges River is perhaps the most holy of all bodies of water. It was named for the goddess of purification, Ganga. The waters of the Ganges are said to flow through Shiva's hair and have the ability to cleanse sin. Devout Hindus make pilgrimages to bathe in the Ganges. They may also visit fords in the rivers to symbolize the journey from one life to another.

Pilgrimages are also made to sites associated with the life of a god. For example, Lord Rama was said to have been born in Ayodhya, one of the seven holy cities in India. Other holy sites are Dwarka, Ujjian, Kanchipuram, Mathura, Hardwar, and Varanasi, the City of Light.

After leaving his mountain home, Lord Shiva was thought to have lived in Varanasi, or Benares, considered the holiest city. Before the sixth century, it became a center of education for Hindus. It has four miles of palaces and temples along the river. One of the many pilgrimage circuits covers thirty-five miles, lasts for five days, and includes prayer at 108 different shrines. Because of the river's sacred nature, Hindus come to bathe from its many stone steps, called ghats, and to drink the water. It is also the place where Hindus desire to be at their death or to have their ashes scattered. Because Varanasi is regarded as a place of crossing between earth and heaven, dying there is thought to free one from the cycle of rebirth.

The thirty-four Ellora Caves at Maharashtra, India, are known for their sculptures. Built between 600 and 1000 CE, they were cut into a tufa rock hillside on a curve shaped like a horse-shoe, so that the caves go deeply into the rock face. Although the one-mile site includes temples for Buddhist, Jain, and Hindu faiths, the major figure of the caves is Shiva, and the largest temple is dedicated to Shiva.

Lastly, Hindu temples, or mandirs, are regarded as the gods' earthly homes. The buildings themselves are therefore holy, and Hindus remove their shoes before entering.

## HINDUISM IN DEPTH

### Sacred Symbols

The wheel of life represents samsara, the cycle of life, death and rebirth. Karma is what keeps the wheel spinning. Another circle is the hoop of flames in which Shiva, also known as the Lord of the Dance, or Natraja, is shown dancing creation into being. The flames signify the universe's energy and Shiva's power of both destruction and creation. Shiva balances on his right foot, which rests on a defeated demon that stands for ignorance.

The lotus is the symbol of creation, fertility, and purity. This flower is associated with Vishnu because as he slept, a lotus flower bloomed from his navel. From this lotus Brahma came forth to create the world. Yoga practitioners commonly assume the lotus position for meditation.

Murtis are the statues of gods that are found in both temples and private homes. They are often washed with milk and water, anointed with oil, dressed, and offered gifts of food or flowers. Incense may also be burned to make the air around the murti sweet and pure.

One of Krishna's symbols is the conch shell, a symbol of a demon he defeated. A conch shell is blown at temples to announce the beginning of the worship service. It is a visual reminder for followers of Krishna to overcome ignorance and evil in their lives.

For many years, the Hindus used the swastika as a holy symbol. (*Swastika* is a Sanskrit word for good fortune and well-being.) The four arms meet at a central point, demonstrating that the universe comes from one source. Each arm of the symbol represents a path to God and is bent to show that all paths are difficult. It is used at a time of new beginnings, such as at a wedding, where it is traditionally painted on a coconut using a red paste called kum kum. The symbol appears as a vertical gash across the horizontal layers on the southern face of Mount Kailas, one of the Himalayas's highest peaks, thought to have been the home of Shiva. The mountain is also near the source of the Ganges and the Indus Rivers. The use of the swastika as a symbol for Nazi Germany is abhorrent to Hindus.

Some Hindus use a mala, or rosary, of 108 wooden beads when they pray. As they worship, they repeat the names of God.

### Sacred Practices & Gestures

Many homes have private altars or shrines to favorite gods. Statues or pictures of these deities are offered incense, flowers and food, as well as prayers. This daily devotion, known as puja, is generally the responsibility of women, many of whom are devoted to goddesses such as Kali or Sita. A rich family may devote an entire room of their house to the shrine.

Om, or Aum, a sacred syllable recorded first in the Upanishads, is made up of three Sanskrit letters. Writing the letter involves a symbol resembling the Arabic number three. Thus, it is a visual reminder of the Trimurti, the three major Hindu gods. The word is repeated at the beginning of all mantras or prayers.

Each day the Gayatri, which is perhaps the world's oldest recorded prayer, is chanted during the fire ritual. The prayer expresses gratitude to the sun for its shining and invokes blessings of prosperity on all. The ritual, typically done at large consecrated fire pits, may be done using burning candles instead.

Holy Hindu men are known as sadhus. They lead ascetic lives, wandering, begging, and living in caves in the mountains. Regarded as having greater spiritual power and wisdom, they are often consulted for advice.

## Food Restrictions

Many Hindus are vegetarians because they embrace ahimsa (reverence for and protection of all life) and oppose killing. In fact, Hindus comprise about 70 percent of the world's vegetarians. They are generally lacto-vegetarians, meaning that they include dairy products in their diets. However, Hindus residing in the cold climate of Nepal and Tibet consume meat to increase their caloric intake.

Whether a culture practices vegetarianism or not, cows are thought to be sacred because Krishna acted as a cowherd as a young god. Thus cows are never eaten. Pigs are also forbidden, as are red foods, such as tomatoes or red lentils. In addition, garlic and onions are also not permitted. Alcohol is strictly forbidden.

Purity rituals before eating include cleaning the area where the food is to be eaten and reciting mantras or praying while sprinkling water around the food. Other rituals include Annaprasana, which celebrates a child's eating of solid food—traditionally rice—for the first time. In addition, at funerals departed souls are offered food, which Hindus believe will strengthen the soul for the journey to the ancestors' world.

Serving food to those in need also generates good karma. Food is offered during religious ceremonies and may later be shared with visiting devotees of the god.

To show their devotion to Shiva, many Hindus fast on Mondays. There is also a regular fast, known as agiaras, which occurs on the eleventh day of each two-week period. On that day, only one meal is eaten. During the month of Shravan, which many consider a holy month, people may eat only one meal, generally following sunset.

## Rites, Celebrations & Services

Many Hindu celebrations are connected to the annual cycle of nature and can last for many days. In addition, celebrations that honor the gods are common. Shiva, one of the three major gods, is honored at Shivaratri in February or March. In August or September, Lord Krishna is honored at Krishnajanmashtmi. Prayer and fasting are part of this holiday.

During the spring equinox and just prior to the Hindu New Year, Holi is celebrated. It is a time to resolve disputes and forgive or pay debts. During this festival, people often have bonfires and throw objects that represent past impurity or disease into the fire.

Another festival occurs in July or August, marking the beginning of the agricultural year in northern India. Raksha Bandhan (the bond of protection) is a festival which celebrates sibling relationships. During the festivities, Hindus bind a bauble with silk thread to the wrists of family members and friends.

To reenact Rama's defeat of the demon Ravana, as narrated in the Ramayana, people make and burn effigies. This festival is called Navaratri in western India, also known as the Durgapuja in Bengal, and Dasserah in northern India. It occurs in September or October each year as a festival celebrating the victory of good over evil. September is also time to celebrate the elephant-headed god Ganesha's birthday at the festival of Ganesh Chaturthi.

Diwali, a five-day festival honoring Lakshmi (the goddess of good fortune and wealth), occurs in October or November. This Festival of Lights is the time when people light oil lamps and set off fireworks to help Rama find his way home after exile. Homes are cleaned in hopes that Lakshmi will come in the night to bless it. People may use colored rice flour to make patterns on their doorstep. Competitions for designs of these patterns, which are meant to welcome God to the house, frequently take place.

Jagannath, or Vishnu, is celebrated during the festival Rathayatra. A large image of Jagannath rides in a chariot pulled through the city of Puri.

The temple for Hindus is the home of the god. Only Brahmin priests may supervise worship there. The inner sanctuary of the building is called the garbhagriha, or womb-house; there the god resides. Worshippers must be ritually pure before the worship starts. The priest recites the mantras and reads sacred texts. Small lamps are lit, and everyone shares specially prepared and blessed food after the service ends.

*Judy A. Johnson, MTS*

**Bibliography**

Barnes, Trevor. *The Kingfisher Book of Religions*. New York: Kingfisher, 1999. Print.

Harley, Gail M. *Hindu and Sikh Faiths in America*. New York: Facts on File, 2003. Print.

Iyengar, B. K. S. and Noelle Perez-Christiaens. *Sparks of Divinity: The Teachings of B. K. S. Iyengar from 1959 to 1975*. Berkeley: Rodmell, 2012. E-book.

"The Joys of Hinduism." *Hinduism Today* Oct./Dec. 2006: 40–53. Print.

Langley, Myrtle. *Religion*. New York: Knopf, 1996. Print.

Meredith, Susan. *The Usborne Book of World Religions*. London: Usborne, 1995. Print.

Rajan, Rajewswari. "The Politics of Hindu 'Tolerance.'" *Boundary 2* 38.3 (2011): 67–86. Print.

Raman, Varadaraja V. "Hinduism and Science: Some Reflections." *Journal of Religion & Science* 47.3 (2012): 549–74. Print.

Renard, John. *Responses to 101 Questions on Hinduism*. Mahwah: Paulist, 1999. Print.

Siddhartha. "Open-Source Hinduism." *Religion & the Arts* 12.1–3 (2008): 34–41. Print.

Shouler, Kenneth and Susai Anthony. *The Everything Hinduism Book*. Avon: Adams, 2009. Print.

Soherwordi, Syed Hussain Shaheed. "'Hinduism'—A Western Construction or an Influence?" *South Asian Studies* 26.1 (2011): 203–14. Print.

Theodor, Ithamar. *Exploring the Bhagavad Gita: Philosophy, Structure, and Meaning*. Farnham and Burlington: Ashgate, 2010. E-book.

Whaling, Frank. *Understanding Hinduism*. Edinburgh: Dunedin, 2010. E-book.

Wilkinson, Philip. *Religions*. New York: DK, 2008. Print.

# Islam

## General Description

The word *Islam* derives from a word meaning "submission," particularly submission to the will of Allah. Muslims, those who practice Islam, fall into two major groups, Sunni and Shia (or Shi'i,) based on political rather than theological differences. Sunni Muslims follow the four Rightly Guided Caliphs, or Rashidun and believe that caliphs should be elected. Shia Muslims believe that the Prophet's nearest male relative, Ali ibn Abi Talib, should have ruled following Muhammad's death, and venerate the imams (prayer leaders) who are directly descended from Ali and the Prophet's daughter Fatima.

## Number of Adherents Worldwide

Approximately 1.6 billion people, or 23 percent of the world's population, are Muslims. Of that total, between 87 and 90 percent of all Muslims are Sunni Muslims and between 10 and 13 percent of all Muslims are Shia. Followers of the Sufi sect, noted for its experiential, ecstatic focus, may be either Sunni or Shia.

## Basic Tenets

Islam is a monotheistic faith; Muslims worship only one God, Allah. They also believe in an afterlife and that people are consigned to heaven or hell following the last judgment.

The Islamic faith rests on Five Pillars. The first pillar, Shahadah is the declaration of faith in the original Arabic, translated as: "I bear witness that there is no god but God and Muhammad is his Messenger." The second pillar, Salah, are prayers adherents say while facing Mecca five times daily at regular hours and also at the main service held each Friday at a mosque. Zakat, "the giving of a tax," is the third pillar and entails giving an income-based percentage of one's wealth to help the poor without attracting notice. The fourth pillar is fasting, or Sawm, during Ramadan, the ninth month of the Islamic calendar. Certain groups of people are excused from the fast, however. The final pillar is the Hajj, the pilgrimage to Mecca required of every able-bodied Muslim at least once in his or her lifetime.

## Sacred Text

The Qur'an (Koran), meaning "recitation," is the holy book of Islam.

## Major Figures

Muhammad, regarded as the Prophet to the Arabs—as Moses was to the Jews—is considered the exemplar of what it means to be a Muslim. His successors—Abu Bakr, Umar, Uthman, and Ali—were known as the four Rightly Guided Caliphs.

## Major Holy Sites

Islam recognizes three major holy sites: Mecca, home of the Prophet; Medina, the city to which Muslims relocated when forced from Mecca due to persecution; and the Dome of the Rock in Jerusalem, believed to be the oldest Islamic building in existence. Muslims believe that in 621 CE Muhammad ascended to heaven (called the Night Journey) from a sacred stone upon which the Dome was constructed. Once in heaven, God instructed Muhammad concerning the need to pray at regular times daily...

There are also several mosques which are considered primary holy sites. These include the al-Aqsa Mosque in the Old City of Jerusalem, believed by many to be the third holiest site in Islam. The mosque, along with the Dome of the Rock, is located on Judaism's holiest site, the Temple Mount, where the Temple of Jerusalem is believed to have stood. Muslims also revere the Mosque of the Prophet (Al-Masjid al-Nabawi) in Medina, considered the resting place of the Prophet Muhammad and the second largest mosque in the world; and the Mosque of the Haram (Masjid al-Haram or the Sacred or Grand Mosque) in Mecca, thought to be the largest mosque in the world and site of the Ka'bah, "the sacred house," also known as "the Noble Cube," Islam's holiest structure.

## Major Rites & Celebrations

Two major celebrations mark the Islamic calendar. 'Id al-Adha, the feast of sacrifice—including animal sacrifice—held communally at the close of the Hajj (annual pilgrimage), commemorates the account of God providing a ram instead of the son Abraham had been asked to sacrifice. The second festival, 'Id al-Fitr, denotes the end of Ramadan and is a time of feasting and gift giving.

---

## ORIGINS

### History & Geography

In 610 CE, a forty-year-old businessman from Mecca named Muhammad ibn Abdullah, from the powerful Arab tribe Quraysh, went to Mount Hira to meditate, as he regularly did for the month of Ramadan. During that month, an entire group of men, the hanif, retreated to caves. The pagan worship practiced in the region, as well as the cruelty and lack of care for the poor, distressed Muhammad. As the tribe to which he belonged had become wealthy through trade, it had begun disregarding traditions prescribed by the nomadic code.

The archangel Jibra'il (Gabriel) appeared in Muhammad's cave and commanded him to read the words of God contained in the scroll that the angel showed him. Like most people of his time, Muhammad was illiterate, but repeated the words Jibra'il said. Some followers of Islam believe that this cave at Jebel Nur, in what is now Saudi Arabia, is where Adam, the first human Allah created, lived.

A frightened Muhammad told only his wife, Khadija, about his experience. For two years, Muhammad received further revelations, sharing them only with family and close friends. Like other prophets, he was reluctant about his calling, fearing that he was—or would be accused of being—possessed by evil spirits or insane. At one point, he tried to commit suicide, but was stopped by the voice of Jibra'il affirming his status as God's messenger.

Muhammad recalled the words spoken to him, which were eventually written down. The Qur'an is noted for being a book of beautiful language, and Muhammad's message reached many. The Prophet thus broke the old pattern of allegiance to tribe and forged a new community based on shared practice.

Muhammad considered himself one who was to warn the others of a coming judgment. His call for social justice and denunciation of the wealthy disturbed the powerful Arab tribe members in Mecca. These men stood to lose the status and income derived from the annual festival to the Ka'bah. The Prophet and his followers were persecuted and were the subject of boycotts and death threats. In 622 CE, Muslim families began a migration (hijrah) to Yathrib, later known as Medina. Two years earlier, the city had sent envoys seeking Muhammad's leadership for their own troubled society. The hijrah marks the beginning of the Islamic calendar.

The persecutions eventually led to outright tribal warfare, linking Islam with political prowess through the victories of the faithful. The Muslims moved from being an oppressed minority to being a political force. In 630 CE, Muhammad and ten thousand of his followers marched to Mecca, taking the city without bloodshed. He destroyed the pagan idols that were housed and worshipped at the Ka'bah, instead associating the hajj with the story of Abraham sending his concubine Hagar and their son Ishmael (Ismail in Arabic) out into the wilderness. With this victory, Muhammad ended centuries of intertribal warfare.

Muhammad died in 632, without designating a successor. Some of the Muslims believed that his nearest male relative should rule, following the custom of the tribes. Ali ibn Abi Talib, although a pious Muslim, was still young. Therefore, Abu Bakr, the Prophet's father-in-law, took the title khalifah, or caliph, which means successor or deputy. Within two years Abu Bakr had stabilized Islam. He was followed by three additional men whom Muhammad had known. Collectively, the four are known as the Four Rightly Guided Caliphs, or the Rashidun. Their rule extended from 632 until 661. Each of the final three met a violent death.

Umar, the second caliph, increased the number of raids on adjacent lands during his ten-year rule, which began in 634. This not only increased wealth, but also gave Umar the authority he needed, since Arabs objected to the idea of a monarchy. Umar was known as the commander of the faithful. Under his leadership, the Islamic community marched into present-day Iraq, Syria, and Egypt and achieved victory over the Persians in 637.

Muslims elected Uthman ibn Affan as the third caliph after Umar was stabbed by a Persian prisoner of war. He extended Muslim conquests into North Africa as well as into Iran, Afghanistan, and parts of India. A group of soldiers mutinied in 656, assassinating Uthman.

Ali, Muhammad's son-in-law, was elected caliph of a greatly enlarged empire. Conflict developed between Ali and the ruler in Damascus whom Uthman had appointed governor of Syria. The fact that the governor came from a rival tribe led to further tensions. Increasingly, Damascus rather than Medina was viewed as the key Muslim locale. Ali was murdered in 661 during the internal struggles.

Within a century after Muhammad's death, Muslims had created an empire that stretched from Spain across Asia to India and facilitated the spread of Islam. The conquerors followed a policy of relative, though not perfect, tolerance toward adherents of other religions. Christians and Jews received special status as fellow "People of the Book," though they were still required to pay a special poll tax in exchange for military protection. Pagans, however, were required to convert to Islam or face death. Later, Hindus, Zoroastrians, and other peoples were also permitted to pay the tax rather than submit to conversion. Following the twelfth century, Sufi mystics made further converts in Central Asia, India, sub-Saharan Africa, and Turkey. Muslim traders also were responsible for the growth of Islam, particularly in China, Indonesia, and Malaya.

The Muslim empire continued to grow until it weakened in the fourteenth century, when it was replaced as a major world power by European states. The age of Muslim domination ended with the 1683 failure of the Ottoman Empire to capture Vienna, Austria.

Although lacking in political power until recent years, a majority of nations in Indonesia, the Middle East, and East and North Africa are predominately Islamic. The rise of Islamic fundamentalists who interpret the Qur'an literally and seek victory through acts of terrorism began in the late twentieth century. Such extremists do not represent the majority of the Muslim community, however.

Like Judaism and Christianity, Islam has been influenced by its development in a desert climate. Arabia, a region three times the size of France, is a land of steppe and desert whose unwelcoming climate kept it from being mapped with any precision until the 1950s. Because Yemen received monsoon rains, it could sustain agriculture and became a center for civilization as early as the second millennium BCE. In the seventh century CE, nomads roamed the area, guarding precious wells and oases. Raiding caravans and other tribes were common ways to obtain necessities.

Mecca was a pagan center of worship, but it was located not far from a Christian kingdom, Ethiopia, across the Red Sea. Further north, followers of both Judaism and Christianity had influenced members of Arab tribes. Jewish tribes inhabited Yathrib, the city later known as Medina. Neither Judaism nor Christianity was especially kind to those they considered pagans. According to an Arabian tradition, in 570 the Ethiopians attacked Yemen and attempted an attack on Mecca. Mecca was caught between two enemy empires—Christian Byzantine and Zoroastrian Persia—that fought a lengthy war during Muhammad's lifetime.

The contemporary clashes between Jews and Muslims are in part a result of the dispersion of Muslims who had lived in Palestine for centuries. More Jews began moving into the area under the British Mandate; in 1948, the state of Israel was proclaimed. Historically, Jews had been respected as a People of the Book.

## Founder or Major Prophet

Muslims hold Allah to be the founder of their religion and Abraham to have been the first Muslim. Muhammad is God's prophet to the Arabs. The instructions that God gave Muhammad through the archangel Jibra'il and through direct revelation are the basis for the Islamic religion. These revelations were given over a period of twenty-one years. Because Muhammad and most of the Muslims were illiterate, the teachings were read publicly in chapters, or suras.

Muhammad did not believe he was founding a new religion. Rather, he was considered God's final Prophet, as Moses and Jesus had been prophets. His task was to call people to repent and to return to the straight path of God's law, called Sharia. God finally was sending a direct revelation to the Arab peoples, who had sometimes been taunted by the other civilizations as being left out of God's plan.

Muhammad, who had been orphaned by age six, was raised by an uncle. He became a successful businessman of an important tribe and married Khadija, for whom he worked. His integrity was such that he was known as al-Amin, the trusted one. He and Khadija had six children; four daughters survived. After Khadija's death, Muhammad married several women, as was the custom for a great chief. Several of the marriages were political in nature.

Muhammad is regarded as the living Qur'an. He is sometimes referred to as the perfect man, one who is an example of how a Muslim should live. He was ahead of his time in his attitudes toward women, listening to their counsel and granting them rights not enjoyed by women in other societies, including the right to inherit property and to divorce. (It should be noted that the Qur'an does not require the seclusion or veiling of all women.)

Islam has no religious leaders, especially those comparable to other religions. Each mosque has an imam to preach and preside over prayer at the Friday services. Although granted a moral authority, the imam is not a religious leader with a role comparable to that of rabbis or priests.

## Philosophical Basis

Prior to Muhammad's receiving the Qur'an, the polytheistic tribes believed in Allah, "the god." Allah was far away and not part of worship rituals, although he had created the world and sustained it. He had three daughters who were goddesses.

Islam began pragmatically—the old tribal ways were not working—as a call for social justice, rooted in Muhammad's dissatisfaction with the increasing emphasis on accumulating wealth and an accompanying neglect of those in need. The struggle (jihad) to live according to God's desire for humans was to take place within the community, or the ummah. This effort was more important than dogmatic statements or beliefs about God. When the community prospered, this was a sign of God's blessing.

In addition, the revelation of the Qur'an gave Arab nations an official religion. The Persians around them had Zoroastrianism, the Romans and Byzantines had Christianity, and the Jews of the Diaspora had Judaism. With the establishment of Islam, Arabs finally could believe that they were part of God's plan for the world.

Four principles direct Islam's practice and doctrine. These include the Qur'an; the traditions, or sunnah; consensus, or ijma'; and individual thought, or ijtihad. The term sunnah, "well-trodden path," had been used by Arabs before Islam to refer to their tribal law.

A fifth important source for Islam is the Hadith, or report, a collection of the Prophet's words and actions, intended to serve as an example. Sunni Muslims refer to six collections made in the ninth century, while Shia Muslims have a separate Hadith of four collections.

## Holy Places

Mecca was located just west of the Incense Road, a major trade route from southern Arabia to Palestine and Syria. Mecca was the Prophet's home and the site where he received his revelations. It is also the city where Islam's holiest structure, the Ka'bah, "the sacred house," was located. The Ka'bah was regarded as having been built by Abraham and his son Ishmael. This forty-three-foot gray stone cube was a center for pagan idols in the time of Muhammad. In 628 the Prophet removed 360 pagan idols—one for each day of the Arabic lunar year—from inside the Ka'bah.

When the followers of Muhammad experienced persecution for their beliefs, they fled to the city of Medina, formerly called Yathrib. When his uncle Abu Talib died, Muhammad lost the protection from persecution that his uncle had provided. He left for Ta'if in the mountains, but it was also a center for pagan cults, and he was driven out. After a group of men from Yathrib promised him protection, Muhammad sent seventy of his followers to the city, built around an oasis about 215 miles north. This migration, called the hijra, occurred in 622, the first year of the Muslim calendar. From this point on, Islam became an organized religion rather than a persecuted and minority cult. The Prophet was buried in Medina in 632, and his mosque in that city is deeply revered.

Islam's third holiest site is the Dome of the Rock in Jerusalem. Muslims believe that the Prophet Muhammad ascended to heaven in 621 from the rock located at the center of this mosque. During this so-called night journey, Allah gave him instructions about prayer. In the shrine at the Dome of the Rock is a strand of hair that Muslims believe was Muhammad's.

Shia Muslims also revere the place in present-day Iraq where Ali's son, Husayn, was martyred. They regard the burial place of Imam Ali ar-Rida in Meshed, Iran, as a site of pilgrimage as well.

---

## ISLAM IN DEPTH

### Sacred Symbols

Muslims revere the Black Stone, a possible meteorite that is considered a link to heaven. It is set inside the Ka'bah shrine's eastern corner. The Ka'bah is kept covered by the kiswa, a black velvet cloth decorated with embroidered calligraphy in gold. At the hajj, Muslims walk around it counterclockwise seven times as they recite prayers to Allah.

Muslim nations have long used the crescent moon and a star on their flags. The crescent moon, which the Ottomans first adopted as a symbol during the fifteenth century, is often placed on the dome of a mosque, pointing toward Mecca. For Muhammad, the waxing and waning of the moon signified the unchanging and eternal purpose of God. Upon seeing a new moon, the Prophet confessed his faith in God. Muslims rely on a lunar calendar and the Qur'an states that God created the stars to guide people to their destinations.

Islam forbids the making of graven images of animals or people, although not all Islamic cultures follow this rule strictly. The decorative arts of Islam have placed great emphasis on architecture and calligraphy to beautify mosques and other buildings. In addition, calligraphy, floral motifs, and geometric forms decorate some editions of the Qur'an's pages, much as Christian monks once decorated hand-copied scrolls of the Bible. These elaborate designs can also be seen on some prayer rugs, and are characteristic of Islamic art in general.

### Sacred Practices & Gestures

When Muslims pray, they must do so facing Mecca, a decision Muhammad made in January 624 CE. Prior to that time, Jerusalem—a holy city for both Jews and Christians—had been the geographic focus. Prayer involves a series of movements that embody submission to Allah.

Muslims sometimes use a strand of prayer beads, known as subhah, to pray the names of God. The beads can be made of bone, precious stones, or wood. Strings may have twenty-five, thirty-three or 100 beads.

### Food Restrictions

Those who are physically able to do so fast from both food and drink during the daylight hours of the month Ramadan. Although fasting is not required of the sick, the aged, menstruating or pregnant women, or children, some children attempt to fast, imitating their parents' devotion. Those who cannot fast are encouraged to do so the following Ramadan. This fast is intended to concentrate the mind on Allah. Muslims recite from the Qur'an during the month.

All meat must be prepared in a particular way so that it is halal, or permitted. While slaughtering the animal, the person must mention the name of Allah. Blood, considered unclean, must be allowed to drain. Because pigs were fed garbage, their meat was considered unclean. Thus Muslims eat no pork, even though in modern times, pigs are often raised on grain.

In three different revelations, Muslims are also forbidden to consume fermented beverages. Losing self-control because of drunkenness violates the Islamic desire for self-mastery.

## Rites, Celebrations, and Services

The **mosque** is the spiritual center of the Muslim community. From the minaret (a tower outside the mosque), the call to worship occurs five times daily—at dawn, just past noon, at midafternoon, at sunset, and in the evening. In earliest times, a muezzin, the official responsible for this duty, gave the cry. In many modern countries, the call now comes over a speaker system. Also located outside are fountains to provide the necessary water for ritual washing before prayer. Muslims wash their face, hands, forearms, and feet, as well as remove their shoes before beginning their prayers. In the absence of water, ritual cleansing may occur using sand or a stone.

Praying involves a series of movements known as rak'ah. From a standing position, the worshipper recites the opening sura of the Qur'an, as well as a second sura. After bowing to demonstrate respect, the person again stands, then prostrates himself or herself to signal humility. Next, the person assumes a sitting posture in silent prayer before again prostrating. The last movement is a greeting of "Peace be with you and the mercy of Allah." The worshipper looks both left and right before saying these words, which are intended for all persons, present and not.

Although Muslims stop to pray during each day when the call is given, Friday is the time for communal prayer and worship at the mosque. The prayer hall is the largest space within the mosque. At one end is a niche known as the mihrab, indicating the direction of Mecca, toward which Muslims face when they pray. At first, Muhammad instructed his followers to pray facing Jerusalem, as the Jewish people did. This early orientation was also a way to renounce the pagan associations of Mecca. Some mosques serve as community centers, with additional rooms for study.

The hajj, an important annual celebration, was a custom before the founding of Islam. Pagan worship centered in Mecca at the Ka'bah, where devotees circled the cube and kissed the Black Stone that was embedded in it. All warfare was forbidden during the hajj, as was argument, speaking crossly, or killing even an insect.

Muslims celebrate the lives of saints and their death anniversaries, a time when the saints are thought to reach the height of their spiritual life. Mawlid an-Nabi refers to "the birth of the Prophet." Although it is cultural and not rooted in the Qur'an, in some Muslim countries this is a public holiday on which people recite the Burdah, a poem that praises Muhammad. Muslims also celebrate the night that the Prophet ascended to heaven, Lailat ul-Miraj. The Night of Power is held to be the night on which Allah decides the destiny of people individually and the world at large.

Like Jews, Muslims practice circumcision, a ceremony known as khitan. Unlike Jews, however, Muslims do not remove the foreskin when the male is a baby. This is often done when a boy is about seven, and must be done before the boy reaches the age of twelve.

Healthy adult Muslims fast between sunrise and sunset during the month of Ramadan. This commemorates the first of Muhammad's revelations. In some Muslim countries, cannons are fired before the beginning of the month, as well as at the beginning and end of each day of the month. Some Muslims read a portion of the Qur'an each day during the month.

*Judy A. Johnson, MTS*

## Bibliography

Al-Saud, Laith, Scott W. Hibbard, and Aminah Beverly. *An Introduction to Islam in the 21st Century*. Wiley, 2013. E-book.

Armstrong, Lyall. "The Rise of Islam: Traditional and Revisionist Theories." *Theological Review* 33.2 (2012): 87–106. Print.

Armstrong, Karen. *Islam: A Short History*. New York: Mod. Lib., 2000. Print.

Aslan, Reza. *No god but God: The Origins, Evolution, and Future of Islam*. New York: Random, 2005. Print.

Badawi, Emran El-. "'For All Times and Places': A Humanistic Reception of the Qur'an." *English Language Notes* 50.2 (2012): 99–112. Print.

Barnes, Trevor. *The Kingfisher Book of Religions*. New York: Kingfisher, 1999. Print.

Ben Jelloun, Tahar. *Islam Explained*. Trans. Franklin Philip. New York: New, 2002. Print.

Esposito, John L. *Islam: the Straight Path*. New York: Oxford UP, 1988. Print.

Glady, Pearl. *Criticism of Islam*.Library, 2012. E-book.

Holland, Tom. "Where Mystery Meets History." *History Today* 62.5 (2012): 19–24. Print.

Langley, Myrtle. *Religion*. New York: Knopf, 1996. Print.

Lunde, Paul. *Islam: Faith, Culture, History*. London: DK, 2002. Print.

Nasr, Seyyed Hossein. *Islam: Religion, History, and Civilization*. New York: Harper, 2002. Print.

Pasha, Mustapha Kamal. "Islam and the Postsecular." *Review of International Studies* 38.5 (2012): 1041–56. Print.

Sayers, Destini and Simone Peebles. *Essence of Islam and Sufism*. College, 2012. E-book.

Schirmacher, Christine. "They Are Not All Martyrs: Islam on the Topics of Dying, Death, and Salvation in the Afterlife." *Evangelical Review of Theology* 36.3 (2012): 250–65. Print.

Wilkinson, Philip. *Islam*. New York: DK, 2002. Print.

Wilkinson, Philip. *Religions*. New York: DK, 2008. Print.

# Jainism

## General Description

Jainism is one of the major religions of India. The name of the religion itself is believed to be based on the Sanskrit word *ji*, which means "to conquer or triumph," or *jina*, which means "victor or conqueror." The earliest name of the group was Nirgrantha, meaning bondless, but it applied to monks and nuns only. There are two sects: the Svetambaras (the white clad), which are the more numerous and wear white clothing, and the Digambaras (the sky clad), the most stringent group; their holy men or monks do not wear clothing at all.

## Number of Adherents Worldwide

Jainism has about five million adherents, most of them in India (in some estimates, the religion represents approximately 1 percent of India's population). Because the religion is demanding in nature, few beyond the Indian subcontinent have embraced it. Jainism has spread to Africa, the United States, and nations in the Commonwealth (nations once under British rule) by virtue of Indian migration to these countries.

## Basic Tenets

The principle of nonviolence (ahimsa) is a defining feature of Jainism. This results in a pacifist religion that influenced Mohandas Gandhi's ideas on nonviolent resistance. Jains believe that because all living creatures have souls, harming any of those creatures is wrong. They therefore follow a strict vegetarian diet, and often wear masks so as to not inhale living organisms. The most important aspect of Jainism is perhaps the five abstinences: ahimsa, satya (truthfulness), asteya (refrain from stealing), brahmacarya (chaste living), and aparigraha (refrain from greed).

A religion without priests, Jainism emphasizes the importance of the adherents' actions. Like Buddhists and Hindus, Jainists believe in karma and reincarnation. Unlike the Buddhist and Hindu idea of karma, Jainists regard karma as tiny particles that cling to the soul as mud clings to shoes, gradually weighing down the soul. Good deeds wash away these particles. Jainists also believe in moksha, the possibility of being freed from the cycle of death and rebirth. Like many Indian religions, Jainism does not believe in an afterlife, but in a cycle of death and rebirth. Once freed from this cycle, the soul will remain in infinite bliss.

While Jains do not necessarily believe in and worship God or gods, they believe in divine beings. Those who have achieved moksha are often regarded by Jains in the same manner in which other religions regard deities. These include the twenty-four Tirthankaras (ford makers) or jinas (victors), those who have escaped the cycle of death and rebirth, and the Siddhas, the liberated souls without physical form. The idea of a judging, ruling, or creator God is not present in Jainism.

Jainists believe that happiness is not found in material possessions and seek to have few of them. They also stress the importance of environmentalism. Jainists follow the Three Jewels: Right Belief, Right Knowledge, and Right Conduct. To be completely achieved, these three must be practiced together. Jainists also agree to six daily obligations (avashyaka), which include confession, praising the twenty-four Tirthankaras (the spiritual leaders), and calm meditation.

## Sacred Text

The words of Mahavira were passed down orally, but lost over a few centuries. During a famine in the mid-fourth century BCE, many monks died. The texts were finally written down, although the Jain sects do not agree as to whether they are Mahavira's actual words. There are forty-five sacred texts (Agamas), which make up the Agam Sutras, Jainism's canonical literature. They were probably written down no earlier than 300 BCE. Two of the primary texts are the Akaranga

Sutra, which outlines the rule of conduct for Jain monks, and the Kalpa Sutra, which contains biographies of the last two Tirthankara. The Digambaras, who believe that the Agamas were lost around 350 BCE, have two main texts and four compendia written between 100 and 800 CE by various scholars.

## Major Figures

Jainism has no single founder. However, Mahavira (Great Hero) is one of the Tirthankaras or jinas (pathfinders). He is considered the most recent spiritual teacher in a line of twenty-four. Modern-day Jainism derives from Mahavira, and his words are the foundation of Jain scriptures. He was a contemporary of Siddhartha Gautama, who was revered as the Buddha. Both Mahavira and Rishabha (or Adinatha), the first of the twenty-four Tirthankaras, are attributed as the founder of Jainism, though each Tirthankara maintains founding attributes.

## Major Holy Sites

The Jain temple at Ranakpur is located in the village of Rajasthan. Carved from amber stone with marble interiors, the temple was constructed in the fifteenth century CE. It is dedicated to the first Tirthankara. The temple has twenty-nine large halls and each of the temple's 1,444 columns has a unique design with carvings.

Sravanabegola in Karnataka state is the site of Gomateshwara, Lord Bahubali's fifty-seven-foot statue. It was constructed in 981 CE from a single chunk of gneiss. Bahubali is considered the son of the first Tirthankara. The Digambara sect believes him to have been the first human to be free from the world.

Other pilgrimage sites include the Palitana temples in Gujarat and the Dilwara temples in Rajasthan. Sometimes regarded as the most sacred of the many Jain temples, the Palitana temples include 863 marble-engraved temples. The Jain temples at Dilwara were constructed of marble during the eleventh and thirteenth centuries CE. These five temples are often considered the most beautiful Jain temples in existence.

## Major Rites & Celebrations

Every twelve years, the festival of Mahamastakabhisheka (anointing of the head) occurs at a statue of one of Jain's holy men, Bahubali, the second son of the first Tirthankara. The statue is anointed with milk, curd, and ghee, a clarified butter. Nearly a million people attend this rite. Jainists also observe Diwali, the Hindu festival of lights, as it symbolizes Mahavira's enlightenment.

The solemn festival of Paryusana marks the end of the Jain year for the Svetambaras (also spelled Shvetambaras). During this eight-day festival, all Jains are asked to live as an ascetic (monk or nun) would for one day. Das Laxana, a ten-day festival similar to that of Paryusana, immediately follows for the Digambara sect. During these special religious holidays, worshippers are involved in praying, meditating, fasting, forgiveness, and acts of penance. These holy days are celebrated during August and September, which is monsoon season in India. During the monsoons, monks prefer to remain in one place so as to avoid killing the smallest insects that appear during the rainy season. The Kalpa Sutra, one of the Jain scriptures, is read in the morning during Paryusana.

The feast of Kartaki Purnima follows the four months of the rainy season. It is held in the first month (Kartik) according to one calendar, and marked by a pilgrimage to the Palitana temples. Doing so with a pure heart is said to remove all sins of both the present and past life. Those who do so are thought to receive the final salvation in the third or fifth birth.

## ORIGINS

## History & Geography

In the eastern basin of the Ganges River during the seventh century BCE, a teacher named Parshvanatha (or Parshva) gathered a community founded on abandoning earthly concerns. He is considered to be the twenty-third Tirthankara (ford-maker), the one who makes a path for salvation. During the following century, Vardhamana, called Mahavira (Great Hero), who was considered the twenty-fourth and final spiritual teacher of the age, formulated most Jain doctrine and practice. By the time of Mahavira's death, Jains numbered around 36,000 nuns and 14,000 monks.

A division occurred within Jainism during the fourth century CE. The most extreme ascetics, the Digambaras (the sky-clad), argued that even clothing showed too great an attachment to the world, and that laundering them in the river risked harming creatures. This argument applied only to men, as the Digambaras denied that a soul could be freed from a woman's body. The other group, the Svetambaras (the white-clad), believed that purity resided in the mind.

In 453 or 456 CE, a council of the Svetambara sect at Saurashtra in western India codified the canon still used. The split between the Digambaras, who did not take part in the meeting, and Svetambaras thus became permanent. Despite the split, Jainism's greatest flowering occurred during the early medieval age. After that time, Hindu sects devoted to the Hindu gods of Vishnu and Shiva flourished under the Gupta Empire (often referred to as India's golden age), slowing the spread of Jainism. Followers migrated to western and central India and the community became stronger.

The Digambaras were involved in politics through several medieval dynasties, and some Jain monks served as spiritual advisers. Royalty and high-ranking officials contributed to the building and maintenance of temples. Both branches of Jainism contributed a substantial literature. In the late medieval age, Jain monks ceased to live as ascetic wanders. They chose instead to don orange robes and to live at temples and other holy places.

The Muslims invaded India in the twelfth century. The Jains lost power and fractured over the next centuries into subgroups, some of which repudiated the worship of images. The poet and Digambara layman Banarsidas (1586-1643) played a significant role in a reform movement during the early 1600s. These reforms focused on the mystical side of Jainism, such as spiritual exploration of the inner self (meditation),

and denounced the formalized temple ritual. The movement, known as the Adhyatma movement, resulted in the Digambara Terapanth, a small Digambara sect.

The Jainists were well positioned in society following the departure of the British from India. Having long been associated with the artisan and merchant classes, they found new opportunities. As traditional Indian studies grew, spurred by Western interest, proponents of Jainism began to found publications and places of study (In fact, Jain libraries are believed to be the oldest in India.) The first Jain temple outside India was consecrated in Britain during the 1960s after Jains had gone there in the wake of political turmoil.

The Jains follow their typical profession as merchants. They publish English-language periodicals to spread their ideas on vegetarianism, environmentalism, and nonviolence (ahimsa). The ideas of ahimsa were formative for Mohandas Gandhi, born a Hindu. Gandhi used nonviolence as a wedge against the British Empire in India. Eventually, the British granted independence to India in 1947.

Virchand Gandhi (1864–1901) is believed to be the first Jain to arrive in America when he came over in 1893. He attended the first Parliament of World Religions, held in Chicago. Today North America has more than ninety Jain temples and centers. Jains in the West often follow professions such as banking and business to avoid destroying animal or plant life.

**Founder or Major Prophet**

Mahavira was born in India's Ganges Basin region. By tradition, he was born around 599 BCE, although some scholars think he may have lived a century later. His story bears a resemblance to that of the Buddha, with whom he was believed to have been a contemporary. His family was also of the Kshatriya (warrior) caste, and his father was a ruler of his clan. One tradition states that Mahavira's mother was of the Brahman (priestly) caste, although another places her in the Kshatriya.

Because he was not the eldest son, Mahavira was not in line for leadership of the clan.

He married a woman of his own caste and they had a daughter. Mahavira chose the life of a monk, with one garment. Later, he gave up wearing even that. He became a wandering ascetic around age thirty, with some legends stating that he tore out his hair before leaving home. He sought shelter in burial grounds and cremation sites, as well as at the base of trees. During the rainy season, however, he lived in towns and villages.

He followed a path of preaching and self-denial, after which he was enlightened (kevala). He spent the next thirty years teaching. Eleven disciples, all of whom were of the Brahman caste, gathered around him. At the end of his life, Mahavira committed Santhara, or ritual suicide through fasting.

### Philosophical Basis

Like Buddhists and the Brahmin priests, the Jains believe in human incarnations of God, known as avatars. These avatars appear at the end of a time of decline to reinstate proper thinking and acting. Such a person was Mahavira. At the time of Mahavira's birth, India was experiencing great societal upheaval. Members of the warrior caste opposed the priestly caste, which exercised authority based on its supposed greater moral purity. Many people also opposed the slaughter of animals for the Vedic sacrifices.

Jainists share some beliefs with both Hinduism and Buddhism. The Hindu hero Rama, for example, is co-opted as a nonviolent Jain, while the deity Krishna is considered a cousin of Arishtanemi, the twenty-second Tirthankara. Like Buddhism, Jainism uses a wheel with twelve spokes; however, Jainism uses the wheel to explain time. The first half of the circle is the ascending stage, in which human happiness, prosperity, and life span increase. The latter half of the circle is the descending stage, involving a decrease of life span, prosperity, and happiness. The wheel of time is always in motion.

For Jainists, the universe is without beginning or ending, and contains layers of both heaven and hell. These layers include space beyond, which is without time, matter, or soul. The cosmos is depicted in art as a large human. The cloud layers surrounding the upper world are called universe space. Above them is the base, Nigoda, where lowest life forms live. The netherworld contains seven hells, each with a different stage of punishment and misery. The middle world contains the earth and remainder of the universe—mankind is located near the waist. There are thirty heavens in the upper world, where heavenly beings reside. In the supreme abode at the apex of the universe, liberated souls (siddha) live.

Jainism teaches that there are six universal entities. Only consciousness or soul is a living substance, while the remaining five are non-living. They include matter, medium of rest, medium of motion, time, and space. Jainism also does not believe in a God who can create, destroy, or protect. Worshipping goddesses and gods to achieve personal gain or material benefit is deemed useless.

Mahavira outlined five basic principles (often referred to as abstinences) for Jainist life, based on the teachings of the previous Tirthankara. They are detachment (aparigraha); the conduct of soul, primarily in sexual morality (brahmacharya); abstinence from stealing (asteya); abstinence from lying (satya); and nonviolence in every realm of the person (ahimsa).

Like other Indian religions, Jainism perceives life as four stages. The life of a student is brahmacharya-ashrama; the stage of family life is gruhasth-ashrama; in vanaprasth-ashrama, the Jainist concentrates on both family and aiding others through social services; and the final stage is sanyast-ashrama, a time of renouncing the world and becoming a monk.

Like many religions, Jainism has a bias toward males and toward the rigorous life of monks and nuns. A layperson cannot work off bad karma, but merely keeps new bad karma from accruing. By following a path of asceticism, however, monks and nuns can destroy karma. Even members of the laity follow eight rules of behavior and take twelve vows. Physical austerity is a key concept in Jainism, as a saint's highest ideal is to starve to death.

## Holy Places

There are four major Jain pilgrimage sites: the Dilwara temples near Rajasthan; the Palitana temples; the Ranakpur temple; and Shravan Begola, the site of the statue of Lord Bahubali. In addition, Jains may make pilgrimages to the caves of Khandagiri and Udayagiri, which were cells for Jain monks carved from rock. The spaces carved are too short for a man to stand upright. They were essentially designed for prayer and meditation. Udayagiri has eighteen caves and Khandagiri has fifteen. The caves are decorated with elaborate carvings.

## JAINISM IN DEPTH

## Sacred Symbols

The open palm (Jain Hand) with a centered wheel, sometimes with the word *ahimsa* written on it, is a prominent Jain symbol. Seen as an icon of peace, the open palm symbol can be interpreted as a call to stop violence, and also means "assurance." It appears on the walls of Jain temples and in their publications. Jainism also employs a simple swastika symbol, considered to be the holiest symbol. It represents the four forms of worldly existence, and three dots above the swastika represent the Three Jewels. The Jain emblem, adopted in 1975, features both the Jain Hand (the open palm symbol with an inset wheel) and a swastika. This year was regarded as the 2,500th anniversary of Mahavira being enlightened.

## Sacred Practices & Gestures

Jains may worship daily in their homes at private shrines. The Five Supreme Beings stand for stages in the path to enlightenment. Rising before daybreak, worshippers invoke these five. In addition, devout Jainists set aside forty-eight minutes daily to meditate.

To demonstrate faithfulness to the five vows that Jains undertake, there are four virtuous qualities that must be cultivated. They are compassion (karuna), respect and joy (pramoda), love and friendship (maitri), and indifference toward and noninvolvement with those who are arrogant (madhyastha). Mahavira stressed that Jains must be friends to all living beings. Compassion goes beyond mere feeling; it involves offering both material and spiritual aid. Pramoda carries with it the idea of rejoicing enthusiastically over the virtues of others. There are contemplations associated with these virtues, and daily practice is suggested to attain mastery.

Some Jainists, both men and women, wear a dot on the forehead. This practice comes from Hinduism. During festivals, Jains may pray, chant, fast, or keep silent. These actions are seen as removing bad karma from the soul and moving the person toward ultimate happiness.

## Food Restrictions

Jainists practice a strict vegetarian way of life (called Jain vegetarianism) to avoid harming any creature. They refuse to eat root vegetables, because by uprooting them, the entire plant dies. They prefer to wait for fruit to drop from trees rather than taking it from the branches. Starving to death, when ready, is seen as an ideal.

## Rites, Celebrations & Services

Some festivals are held annually and their observances are based on a lunar calendar. Mahavir Jayanti is an example, as it celebrates Mahavira's birthday.

Jains may worship, bathe, and make offerings to images of the Tirthankaras in their home or in a temple. Svetambaras Jains also clothe and decorate the images. Because the Tirthankaras have been liberated, they cannot respond as a deity granting favors might. Although Jainism rejects belief in gods in favor of worshipping Tirthankaras, in actual practice, some Jainists pray to Hindu gods.

When Svetambara monks are initiated, they are given three pieces of clothing, including a small piece of white cloth to place over the mouth. The cloth, called a mukhavastrika, is designed to prevent the monk from accidentally eating insects.

Monks take great vows (mahavratas) at initiation. These include abstaining from lying, stealing, sexual activity, injury to any living thing, and personal possessions. Monks own a broom to sweep in front of where they are going to walk so that no small creatures are injured, along with an alms bowl and a robe. The Digambara monks practice a more stringent lifestyle, eating one meal a day, for which they beg.

Nuns in the Svetambaras are three times more common than are monks, even though they receive less honor, and are required to defer to the monks. In Digambara Jainism, the nuns wear robes and accept that they must be reborn as men before progressing upward.

The observance of Santhara, which is religious fasting until death, is a voluntary fasting undertaken with full knowledge. The ritual is also known as Sallekhana, and is not perceived as suicide by Jains, particularly as the prolonged nature of the ritual provides ample time for reflection. It is believed that at least one hundred people die every year from observing Santhara.

*Judy A. Johnson, MTS*

## Bibliography

Aristarkhova, Irina. "Thou Shall Not Harm All Living Beings: Feminism, Jainism, and Animals." *Hypatia* 27.3 (2012): 636–50. Print.

Aukland, Knut. "Understanding Possession in Jainism: A Study of Oracular Possession in Nakoda." *Modern Asian Studies* 47.1 (2013): 103–34. Print.

Barnes, Trevor. *The Kingfisher Book of Religions*. New York: Kingfisher, 1999. Print.

Langley, Myrtle. *Religion*. New York: Knopf, 1996. Print.

Long, Jeffery. *Jainism: An Introduction*. London: I. B. Tauris, 2009. Print.

Long, Jeffrey. "Jainism: Key Themes." *Religion Compass* 5.9 (2011): 501–10. Print.

Rankin, Aidan. *The Jain Path*. Berkeley: O Books, 2006. Print.

Shah, Bharat S. *An Introduction to Jainism*. Great Neck: Setubandh, 2002. Print.

Titze, Kurt. *Jainism: A Pictorial Guide to the Religion of Non-Violence*. Delhi: Motilal Banarsidass, 2001. Print.

Tobias, Michael. *Life Force: the World of Jainism*. Berkeley:Asian Humanities, 1991. E-book, print.

Wiley, Kristi L. *The A to Z of Jainism*. Lanham: Scarecrow, 2009. Print.

Wiley, Kristi L. *Historical Dictionary of Jainism*. Lanham: Scarecrow, 2004. Print.

Wilkinson, Philip. *Religions*. New York: DK, 2008. Print.

# Judaism

## General Description

In modern Judaism, the main denominations (referred to as movements) are Orthodox Judaism (including Haredi and Hasidic Judaism); Conservative Judaism; Reform (Liberal) Judaism; Reconstructionist Judaism; and to a lesser extent, Humanistic Judaism. In addition, the Jewry of Ethiopia and Yemen are known for having distinct or alternative traditions. Classical Judaism is often organized by two branches: Ashkenazic (Northern Europe) and Sephardic Jews (Spain, Portugal, and North Africa).

## Number of Adherents Worldwide

Judaism has an estimated 15 million adherents worldwide, with roughly 41 percent living in Israel and about 41 percent living in the United States. Ashkenazi Jews represent roughly 75 percent, while Sephardic Jews represent roughly 25 percent, with the remaining 5 percent split among alternative communities. Within the United States, a 2000-01 survey stated that 10 percent of American Jews identified as Orthodox (with that number increasing), 35 percent as Reform, 26 percent as Conservative, leaving the remainder with an alternative or no affiliation. [Source: Wilkinson, 2008]

Orthodox Judaism, which was founded around the thirteenth century BCE, has 3 million followers. Members of Reform Judaism, with roots in nineteenth-century Germany, wanted to live peacefully with non-Jews. Therefore, they left the laws that prevented this vision of peace and downplayed the idea of a Jewish state. Reform Judaism, also known as Progressive or Liberal Judaism, allows women rabbis and does not require its adherents to keep kosher. About 1.1 million Jews are Reform; they live primarily in the United States. When nonkosher food was served at the first graduation ceremony for Hebrew Union College, some felt that the Reform movement had gone too far. Thus the Conservative movement began in 1887. A group of rabbis founded the Jewish Theological Seminary in New York City, wanting to emphasize biblical authority above moral choice, as the Reform tradition stressed. Currently about 900,000 Jews practice this type of Judaism, which is theologically midway between Orthodox and Reform. The Hasidim, an ultra-conservative group, began in present-day Ukraine around 1740. There are 4.5 million Hasidic Jews.

## Basic Tenets

Though there is no formal creed (statement of faith or belief), Jews value all life, social justice, education, generous giving, and the importance of living based on the principles and values espoused in the Torah (Jewish holy book). They believe in one all-powerful and creator God, Jehovah or Yaweh, a word derived from the Hebrew letters "YHWH," the unpronounceable name of God. The word is held to be sacred; copyists were required to bathe both before and after writing the word. Jews also believe in a coming Messiah who will initiate a Kingdom of Righteousness. They follow a complex law, composed of 613 commandments or mitzvot. Jews believe that they are God's Chosen People with a unique covenant relationship. They have a responsibility to practice hospitality and to improve the world.

The belief in the afterlife is a part of the Jewish faith. Similar to Christianity, this spiritual world is granted to those who abide by the Jewish faith and live a good life. Righteous Jews are rewarded in the afterlife by being able to discuss the Torah with Moses, who first received the law from God. Furthermore, certain Orthodox sects believe that wicked souls are destroyed or tormented after death.

## Sacred Text

The complete Hebrew Bible is called the Tanakh. It includes the prophetic texts, called the Navi'im, the poetic writings, the Ketubim, and the Torah, meaning teaching, law, or guidance. Torah may refer to the entire body of Jewish law or to the first five books of the Hebrew Bible, known as the Pentateuch (it is the Old Testament in the Christian Bible). Also esteemed is the Talmud, made up of the Mishnah, a written collection of oral traditions, and Gemara, a commentary on the Mishnah. The Talmud covers many different subjects, such as law, stories and legends, medicine, and rituals.

## Major Figures

The patriarchs are held to be the fathers of the faith. Abraham, the first patriarch, was called to leave his home in the Fertile Crescent for a land God would give him, and promised descendents as numerous as the stars. His son Isaac was followed by Jacob, whom God renamed Israel, and whose twelve sons became the heads of the twelve tribes of Israel. Moses was the man who, along with his brother Aaron, the founder of a priestly line, and their sister Miriam led the chosen people out of slavery in Egypt, where they had gone to escape famine. The Hebrew Bible also details the careers of a group of men and women known as judges, who were really tribal rulers, as well as of the prophets, who called the people to holy lives. Chief among the prophets was Elijah, who confronted wicked kings and performed many miracles. Several kings were key to the biblical narrative, among them David, who killed the giant Goliath, and Solomon, known for his wisdom and for the construction of a beautiful temple.

## Major Holy Sites

Most of Judaism's holy sites are within Israel, the Holy Land, including Jerusalem, which was the capital of the United Kingdom of Israel under kings David and Solomon; David captured it from a Canaanite tribe around 1000 BCE. Within the Old City of Jerusalem is the Temple Mount (where the Temple of Jerusalem was built), often considered the religion's holiest site, the Foundation Stone (from which Judaism claims the world was created), and the Western (or Wailing) Wall. Other sites include Mount Sinai

in Egypt, the mountain upon which God gave Moses his laws.

## Major Rites & Celebrations

The Jewish calendar recognizes several important holidays. Rosh Hashanah, literally "first of the year," is known as the Jewish New Year and inaugurates a season of self-examination and repentance that culminates in Yom Kippur, the Day of Atonement. Each spring, Passover commemorates the deliverance of the Hebrew people from Egypt. Shavuot celebrates the giving of the Torah to Moses, while Sukkot is the harvest festival. Festivals celebrating deliverance from enemies include Purim and Hanukkah. Young adolescents become members of the community at a bar or bat mitzvah, held near the twelfth or thirteenth birthday. The Sabbath, a cessation from work from Friday at sundown until Saturday when the first star appears, gives each week a rhythm.

## ORIGINS

## History & Geography

Called by God perhaps four thousand years ago, Abraham left from Ur of the Chaldees, or the Fertile Crescent in Mesopotamia in present-day Iraq, to go the eastern Mediterranean, the land of Canaan. Several generations later, the tribe went to Egypt to escape famine. They were later enslaved by a pharaoh, sometimes believed to have been Ramses II (ca. 1279–1213 BCE), who was noted for his many building projects. The Israelites returned to Canaan under Moses several hundred years after their arrival in Egypt. He was given the law, the Ten Commandments, plus the rest of the laws governing all aspects of life, on Mount Sinai about the thirteenth century BCE. This marked the beginning of a special covenant relationship between the new nation, known as Israel, and God.

Following a period of rule by judges, kings governed the nation. Major kings included David, son-in-law to the first king, Saul, and David's son, Solomon. The kingdom split at the beginning of the reign of Solomon's son

Rehoboam, who began ruling about 930 BCE. Rehoboam retained the ten northern tribes, while the two southern tribes followed a military commander rather than the Davidic line.

Rehoboam's kingdom was known as Israel, after the name Jehovah gave to Jacob. Judah was the name of the southern kingdom—one of Jacob's sons was named Judah. Prophets to both nations warned of coming judgment unless the people repented of mistreating the poor and other sins, such as idolatry. Unheeding, Israel was taken into captivity by the Assyrians in 722 BCE. and the Israelites assimilated into the nations around them.

The Babylonians captured Judah in 586 BCE. After Babylon had been captured in turn by Persians, the Jewish people were allowed to return to the land in 538 BCE. There they began reconstructing the temple and the walls of the city. In the second century BCE, Judas Maccabeus led a rebellion against the heavy taxes and oppression of the Greek conquerors, after they had levied high taxes and appointed priests who were not Jewish. Judas Maccabeus founded a new ruling dynasty, the Hasmoneans, which existed briefly before the region came under the control of Rome.

The Jewish people revolted against Roman rule in 70 CE, leading to the destruction of the second temple. The final destruction of Jerusalem occurred in 135 under the Roman Emperor Hadrian. He changed the city's name to Aelia Capitolina and the name of the country to Palaestina. With the cultic center of their religion gone, the religious leaders developed new methods of worship that centered in religious academies and in synagogues.

After Christianity became the official state religion of the Roman Empire in the early fourth century, Jews experienced persecution. They became known for their scholarship, trade, and banking over the next centuries, with periods of brutal persecution in Europe. Christians held Jews responsible for the death of Jesus, based on a passage in the New Testament. The Blood Libel, begun in England in 1144, falsely accused Jews of killing a Christian child to bake

unleavened bread for Passover. This rumor persisted for centuries, and was repeated by Martin Luther during the Protestant Reformation. England expelled all Jews in 1290; they were not readmitted until 1656 under Oliver Cromwell, and not given citizenship until 1829. Jews were also held responsible for other catastrophes—namely poisoning wells and rivers to cause the Black Death in 1348—and were often made to wear special clothing, such as pointed hats, or badges with the Star of David or stone tablets on them.

The relationship between Muslims and Jews was more harmonious. During the Muslim Arab dominance, there was a "golden age" in Spain due to the contributions of Jews and Muslims, known as Moors in Spain. This ideal and harmonious period ended in 1492, when both Moors and Jews were expelled from Spain or forced to convert to Christianity.

Jews in Russia suffered as well. An estimated two million Jews fled the country to escape the pogroms (a Russian word meaning devastation) between 1881 and 1917. The twentieth-century Holocaust, in which an estimated six million Jews perished at the hands of Nazi Germany, was but the culmination of these centuries of persecution. The Nazis also destroyed more than six hundred synagogues.

The Holocaust gave impetus to the creation of the independent state of Israel. The Zionist movement, which called for the founding or reestablishment of a Jewish homeland, was started by Austrian Jew Theodor Herzl in the late nineteenth century, and succeeded in 1948. The British government, which had ruled the region under a mandate, left the area, and Israel was thus established. This ended the Diaspora, or dispersion, of the Jewish people that had begun nearly two millennia before when the Romans forced the Jews to leave their homeland.

Arab neighbors, some of whom had been removed forcibly from the land to create the nation of Israel, were displeased with the new political reality. Several wars have been fought, including the War of Independence in 1948, the Six-Day War in 1967, and the Yom Kippur War in 1973. In addition, tension between Israel and its neighboring Arab states is almost constant.

When the Jewish people were dispersed from Israel, two traditions began. The Ashkenazi Jews settled in Germany and central Europe. They spoke a mixture of the Hebrew dialect and German called Yiddish. Sephardic Jews lived in the Mediterranean countries, including Spain; their language, Ladino, mixed Hebrew and old Spanish.

### Founder or Major Prophet

Judaism refers to three major patriarchs: Abraham, his son Isaac, and Isaac's son Jacob. Abraham is considered the first Jew and worshipper in Judaism, as the religion began through his covenant with God. As the forefather of the religion, he is often associated as the founder, though the founder technically is God, or Yahweh (YHWH). Additionally, the twelve sons of Jacob, who was also named Israel, became the founders of the twelve tribes of Israel.

Moses is regarded as a major prophet and as the Lawgiver. God revealed to Moses the complete law during the forty days that the Jewish leader spent on Mount Sinai during the wilderness journey from Egypt to Canaan. Thus, many attribute Moses as the founder of Judaism as a religion.

### Philosophical Basis

Judaism began with Abraham's dissatisfaction with the polytheistic worship of his culture. Hearing the command of God to go to a land that would be shown to him, Abraham and his household obeyed. Abraham practiced circumcision and hospitality, cornerstones of the Jewish faith to this day. He and his descendents practiced a nomadic life, much like that of contemporary Bedouins. They migrated from one oasis or well to another, seeking pasture and water for the sheep and goats they herded.

The further development of Judaism came under the leadership of Moses. A Jewish child adopted by Pharaoh's daughter, he was raised and educated in the palace. As a man, he identified with the Jewish people, killing one of the Egyptians who was oppressing a Jew. He subsequently fled for his life, becoming a shepherd in the wilderness, where he remained for forty years. Called by God from a bush that burned but was not destroyed, he was commissioned to lead the people out of slavery in Egypt back to the Promised Land. That forty-year pilgrimage in the wilderness and desert of Arabia shaped the new nation.

### Holy Places

The city of Jerusalem was first known as Salem. When King David overcame the Jebusites who lived there, the city, already some two thousand years old, became the capital of Israel. It is built on Mount Zion, which is still considered a sacred place. David's son Solomon built the First Temple in Jerusalem, centering the nation's spiritual as well as political life in the city. The Babylonians captured the city in 597 BCE and destroyed the Temple. For the next sixty years, the Jews remained in exile, until Cyrus the Persian conqueror of Babylon allowed them to return. They rebuilt the temple, but it was desecrated by Antiochus IV of Syria in 167 BCE. In 18 BCE, during a period of Roman occupation, Herod the Great began rebuilding and expanding the Temple. The Romans under the general Titus destroyed the Temple in 70 CE, just seven years after its completion.

The city eventually came under the rule of Persia, the Muslim Empire, and the Crusaders before coming under control of Britain. In 1948 an independent state of Israel was created. The following year, Jerusalem was divided between Israel, which made the western part the national capital, and Jordan, which ruled the eastern part of the city. The Western or Wailing Wall, a retaining wall built during Herod's time, is all that remains of the Second Temple. Devout Jews still come to the Wailing Wall to pray, sometimes placing their petitions on paper and folding the paper into the Wall's crevices. The Wall is known as a place where prayers are answered and a reminder of the perseverance of the Jewish people and faith. According to tradition, the Temple will be rebuilt when Messiah comes to inaugurate God's Kingdom.

The Temple Mount, located just outside Jerusalem on a natural acropolis, includes the Dome of the Rock. This shrine houses a rock held sacred by both Judaism and Islam. Jewish tradition states that it is the spot from which the world was created and the spot on which Abraham was asked to sacrifice his son Isaac. Muslims believe that from this rock Muhammad ascended for his night journey to heaven. Much of Jerusalem, including this holy site, has been and continues to be fought over by people of three faiths: Judaism, Islam, and Christianity.

Moses received the law from God on Mount Sinai. It is still regarded as a holy place.

---

## JUDAISM IN DEPTH

### Sacred Symbols

Observant Jewish men pray three times daily at home or in a synagogue, a center of worship, from the word meaning "meeting place." They wear a tallis, or a prayer shawl with tassles, during their morning prayer and on Yom Kippur, the Day of Atonement. They may also cover their heads as a sign of respect during prayer, wearing a skullcap known as a kippah or yarmulka. They find their prayers and blessings in a siddur, which literally means "order," because the prayers appear in the order in which they are recited for services. Jewish daily life also includes blessings for many things, including food.

Tefillin or phylacteries are the small black boxes made of leather from kosher animals that Jewish men wear on their foreheads and their left upper arms during prayer. They contain passages from the Torah. Placing the tefillin on the head reminds them to think about the Torah, while placing the box on the arm puts the Torah close to the heart.

The Law of Moses commands the people to remember the words of the law and to teach them to the children. A mezuzah helps to fulfill that command. A small box with some of the words of the law written on a scroll inside, a mezuzah is hung on the doorframes of every door in the house. Most often, the words of the Shema,

the Jewish recitation of faith, are written on the scroll. The Shema is repeated daily. "Hear, O Israel: the Lord your God, the Lord is one. . . . Love the Lord your God with all your heart, and with all your soul, and with all your might."

Jews adopted the Star of David, composed of two intersecting triangles, during the eighteenth century. There are several interpretations of the design. One is that it is the shape of King David's shield. Another idea is that it stands for daleth, the first letter of David's name. A third interpretation is that the six points refer to the days of the work week, and the inner, larger space represented the day of rest, the Sabbath, or Shabot. The Star of David appears on the flag of Israel. The flag itself is white, symbolizing peace and purity, and blue, symbolizing heaven and reminding all of God's activity.

The menorah is a seven-branch candlestick representing the light of the Torah. For Hanukkah, however, an eight-branched menorah is used. The extra candle is the servant candle, and is the one from which all others are lit.

Because the Torah is the crowning glory of life for Jewish people, a crown is sometimes used on coverings for the Torah. The scrolls of Torah are stored in a container, called an ark, which generally is covered with an ornate cloth called a mantle. The ark and mantle are often elaborately decorated with symbols, such as the lion of Judah. Because the Torah scroll, made of parchment from a kosher animal, is sacred and its pages are not to be touched, readers use a pointed stick called a yad. Even today, Torahs are written by hand in specially prepared ink and using a quill from a kosher bird. Scribes are trained for seven years.

A shofar is a ram's horn, blown as a call to repentance on Rosh Hashanah, the Jewish New Year. This holiday is the beginning of a ten-day preparation for the Day of Atonement, which is the most holy day in the Jewish calendar and a time of both fasting and repentance.

### Sacred Practices & Gestures

Sacred practices can apply daily, weekly, annually, or over a lifetime's events. Reciting the Shema, the monotheistic creed taken from the

Torah, is a daily event. Keeping the Sabbath occurs weekly. Each year the festivals described above take place. Circumcision and bar or bat mitzvah are once-in-a-lifetime events. Each time someone dies, the mourners recite the Kaddish for seven days following death, and grieve for a year.

### Food Restrictions

Kosher foods are those that can be eaten based on Jewish law. Animals that chew the cud and have cloven hooves, such as cows and lamb, and domestic poultry are considered kosher. Shellfish, pork, and birds of prey are forbidden. Keeping kosher also includes the method of preparing and storing the food. This includes animals which are slaughtered in a way to bring the least amount of pain and from which all blood is drained. In addition, dairy and meat products are to be kept separate, requiring separate refrigerators in the homes of the Orthodox.

### Rites, Celebrations & Services

Sabbath is the weekly celebration honoring one of the Ten Commandments, which commands the people to honor the Sabbath by doing no work that day. The practice is rooted in the Genesis account that God rested on the seventh day after creating the world in six days. Because the Jewish day begins at sundown, the Sabbath lasts from Friday night to Saturday night. Special candles are lit and special food—included the braided egg bread called challah—for the evening meal is served. This day is filled with feasting, visiting, and worship.

Boys are circumcised at eight days of age. This rite, B'rit Milah, meaning "seal of the covenant," was first given to Abraham as a sign of the covenant. A trained circumciser, or mohel, may be a doctor or rabbi. The boy's name is officially announced at the ceremony. A girl's name is given at a special baby-naming ceremony or in the synagogue on the first Sabbath after she is born.

A boy becomes a "son of the commandment," or bar mitzvah, at age thirteen. At a special ceremony, the young man reads a portion of

Torah that he has prepared ahead of time. Most boys also give a speech at the service. Girls become bat mitzvah at age twelve. This ceremony developed in the twentieth century. Not all Orthodox communities will allow this rite. Girls may also read from the Torah and give a sermon in the synagogue, just as boys do.

When a Jewish person dies, mourners begin shiva, a seven-day mourning period. People usually gather at the home of the deceased, where mirrors are covered. In the home, the Kaddish, a collection of prayers that praise God and celebrate life, is recited. Traditionally, family members mourn for a full year, avoiding parties and festive occasions.

The Jewish calendar offers a series of feasts and festivals, beginning with Rosh Hashanah, the Jewish New Year. At this time, Jews recall the creation. They may also eat apples that have been dipped into honey and offer each other wishes for a sweet New Year. The next ten days are a time of reflection on the past year, preparing for Yom Kippur.

This Day of Atonement once included animal sacrifice at the Temple. Now it includes an all-day service at the synagogue and a twenty-five-hour fast. A ram's horn, called a shofar, is blown as a call to awaken to lead a holier life. The shofar reminds Jewish people of the ram that Abraham sacrificed in the place of his son, Isaac.

Passover, or Pesach, is the spring remembrance of God's deliverance of the people from slavery in Egypt. In the night that the Jewish people left Egypt, they were commanded to sacrifice a lamb for each household and sprinkle the blood on the lintels and doorposts. A destroying angel from God would "pass over" the homes with blood sprinkled. During the first two nights of Passover, a special meal is served known as a Seder, meaning order. The foods symbolize different aspects of the story of deliverance, which is told during the meal by the head of the family.

Shavuot has its origins as a harvest festival. This celebration of Moses receiving the Torah on Mount Sinai occurs fifty days after the second day of Passover. To welcome the first fruits of the season, the synagogue may be decorated with fruit and flowers. Traditionally, the Ten Commandments are read aloud in the synagogue.

Purim, which occurs in February or March, celebrates the deliverance of the Jews during their captivity in Persia in the fifth century BCE. The events of that experience are recorded in the Book of Esther in the Hebrew Bible (Tanakh). The book is read aloud during Purim.

Sukkot, the feast celebrating the end of the harvest, occurs in September or October. Jews recall God's provision for them in the wilderness when they left Egypt to return to Canaan. Traditionally, huts are made and decorated with flowers and fruits. The conclusion of Sukkot is marked by a synagogue service known as Simchat Torah, or Rejoicing in the Law. People sing and dance as the Torah scrolls are carried and passed from person to person.

Hanukkah, known as the Festival of Lights, takes place over eight days in December. It celebrates the rededicating of the Temple under the leader Judas Maccabeus, who led the people in recapturing the structure from Syria in 164 BCE. According to the story, the Jews had only enough oil in the Temple lamp to last one day, but the oil miraculously lasted for eight days, after which Judas Maccabeus re-dedicated the Temple. On each day of Hanukkah, one of the eight candles is lit until all are burning. The gift-giving custom associated with Hanukkah is relatively new, and may derive from traditional small gifts of candy or money. The practice may also have been encouraged among those integrated with communities that exchange gifts during the Christmas season.

*Judy A. Johnson, MTS*

**Bibliography**

Barnes, Trevor. *The Kingfisher Book of Religions*. New York: Kingfisher, 1999. Print.

"A Buffet to Suit All Tastes." *Economist* 28 Jul. 2012: Spec. section 4–6. Print.

Charing, Douglas. *Judaism*. London: DK, 2003. Print.

Coenen Snyder, Saskia. *Building a Public Judaism: Synagogues and Jewish Identity in Nineteenth-Century Europe*. Cambridge: Harvard UP, 2013. E-book.

Diamant, Anita. *Living a Jewish Life*. New York: Collins, 1996. Print.

Exler, Lisa and Rabbi Jill Jacobs. "A Judaism That Matters." *Journal of Jewish Communal Service* 87.1/2 (2012): 66–76. Print.

Gelernter, David Hillel. *Judaism: A Way of Being*. New Haven: Yale UP, 2009. E-book.

Kessler, Edward. *What Do Jews Believe?* New York: Walker, 2007. Print.

Krieger, Aliza Y. "The Role of Judaism in Family Relationships." *Journal of Multicultural Counseling & Development* 38.3 (2010): 154–65. Print.

Langley, Myrtle. *Religion*. New York: Knopf, 1996. Print.

Madsen, Catherine. "A Heart of Flesh: Beyond 'Creative Liturgy.'" *Cross Currents* 62.1 (2012): 11–20. Print.

Meredith, Susan. *The Usborne Book of World Religions*. London: Usborne, 1995. Print.

Schoen, Robert. *What I Wish My Christian Friends Knew About Judaism*. Chicago: Loyola, 2004. Print.

Stefon, Matt. *Judaism: History, Belief, and Practice*. New York: Britannica Educational, 2012. E-book.

Wertheimer, Jack. "The Perplexities of Conservative Judaism." *Commentary* Sept. 2007: 38–44. Print.

Wilkinson, Philip. *Religions*. New York: DK, 2008. Print.

# Sikhism

### General Description

The youngest of the world religions, Sikhism has existed for only about five hundred years. Sikhism derives from the Sanskrit word *sishyas*, which means "disciple"; in the Punjabi language, it also means "disciple."

### Number of Adherents Worldwide

An estimated 24.5 million people follow the Sikh religion. Most of the devotees live in Asia, particularly in the Punjab region of India (Wilkinson, p. 335).

### Basic Tenets

Sikhism is a monotheistic religion. The deity is God, known as Nam, or Name. Other synonyms include the Divine, Ultimate, Ultimate Reality, Infinity, the Formless, Truth, and other attributes of God.

Sikhs adhere to three basic principles. These are hard work (kirt kao), worshipping the Divine Name (nam japo), and sharing what one has (vand cauko). Meditating on the Divine Name is seen as a method of moving toward a life totally devoted to God. In addition, Sikhs believe in karma, or moral cause and effect. They value hospitality to all, regardless of religion, and oppose caste distinctions. Sikhs delineate a series of five stages that move upward to gurmukh, total devotion to God. This service is called Seva. Sahaj, or tranquility, is practiced as a means of being united with God as well as of generating external good will. Sikhs are not in favor of external routines of religion; they may stop in their temple whenever it is convenient during the day.

Sikhism does not include a belief in the afterlife. Instead, the soul is believed to be reincarnated in successive lives and deaths, a belief borrowed from Hinduism. The goal is then to break this karmic cycle, and to merge the human spirit with that of God.

### Sacred Text

The Guru Granth Sahib (also referred to as the Aad Guru Granth Sahib, or AGGS), composed of Adi Granth, meaning First Book, is the holy scripture of Sikhism. It is a collection of religious poetry that is meant to be sung. Called shabads, they were composed by the first five gurus, the ninth guru, and thirty-six additional holy men of northern India. Sikhs always show honor to the Guru Granth Sahib by carrying it above the head when in a procession.

A second major text is the Dasam Granth, or Tenth Book, created by followers of Guru Gobind Singh, the tenth guru. Much of it is devoted to retelling the Hindu stories of Krishna and Rama. Those who are allowed to read and care for the Granth Sahib are known as granthi. Granthi may also look after the gurdwara, or temple. In the gurdwara, the book rests on a throne with a wooden base and cushions covered in cloths placed in a prescribed order. If the book is not in use, it is covered with a cloth known as a rumala. When the book is read, a fan called a chauri is fanned over it as a sign of respect, just as followers of the gurus fanned them with chauris. At Amritsar, a city in northwestern India that houses the Golden Temple, the Guru Granth Sahib is carried on a palanquin (a covered, carried bed). If it is carried in the city, a kettle drum is struck and people welcome it by tossing rose petals.

### Major Figures

Guru Nanak (1469–1539) is the founder of Sikhism. He was followed by nine other teachers, and collectively they are known as the Ten Gurus. Each of them was chosen by his predecessor and was thought to share the same spirit of that previous guru. Guru Arjan (1581–1606), the fifth guru, oversaw completion of the Golden Temple in Amritsar, India. Guru Gobind Singh (1675–1708) was the tenth and last human guru. He decreed that the True Guru henceforth would be the Granth Sahib, the scripture of the Sikhs. He also founded the Khalsa, originally a military order of male Sikhs willing to die for the faith; the term is now used to refer to all baptized Sikhs.

## Major Holy Sites

Amritsar, India, is the holy city of Sikhism. Construction of the city began under Guru Ram Das (1574–1581), the fourth guru, during the 1570s. One legend says that the Muslim ruler, Emperor Akbar, gave the land to the third guru, Guru Amar Das (1552–74). Whether or not that is true, Amar Das did establish the location of Amritsar. He chose a site near a pool believed to hold healing water.

When construction of the Golden Temple began, only a small town existed. One legend says that a Muslim saint from Lahore, India, named Mian Mir laid the foundation stone of the first temple. It has been demolished and rebuilt three times. Although pilgrimage is not required of Sikhs, many come to see the shrines and the Golden Temple. They call it Harmandir Sahib, God's Temple, or Darbar Sahib, the Lord's Court. When the temple was completed during the tenure of the fifth guru, Arjan, he placed the first copy of the Guru Granth Sahib inside.

Every Sikh temple has a free kitchen attached to it, called a langar. After services, all people, regardless of caste or standing within the community, sit on the floor in a straight line and eat a simple vegetarian meal together. As a pilgrimage site, the langar serves 30,000–40,000 people daily, with more coming on Sundays and festival days. About forty volunteers work in the kitchen each day.

## Major Rites & Celebrations

In addition to the community feasts at temple langars, Sikhs honor four rites of passage in a person's life: naming, marriage, initiation in Khalsa (pure) through the Amrit ceremony, and death.

There are eight major celebrations and several other minor ones in Sikhism. Half of them commemorate events in the lives of the ten gurus.

The others are Baisakhi, the new year festival; Diwali, the festival of light, which Hindus also celebrate; Hola Mahalla, which Gobind Singh created as an alternative to the Hindu festival of Holi, and which involves military parades; and the installing of the Guru Granth Sahib.

---

## ORIGINS

### History & Geography

The founder of Sikhism, Nanak, was born in 1469 CE in the Punjab region of northeast India, where both Hinduism and Islam were practiced. Both of these religions wanted control of the region. Nanak wanted the fighting between followers of these two traditions to end and looked for solutions to the violence.

Nanak blended elements of both religions and also combined the traditional apparel of both faiths to construct his clothing style. The Guru Granth Sahib further explains the division between Sikhs and the Islamic and Muslim faiths:

Nanak would become the first guru of the Sikh religion, known as Guru Nanak Dev. A Muslim musician named Bhai Mardana, considered the first follower, accompanied Nanak in his travels around India and Asia. Guru Nanak often sang, and singing remains an important part of worship for Sikhs. Before his death, Nanak renamed one of his disciples Angad, a word meaning "a part of his own self." He became Guru Angad Dev, the second guru, thus beginning the tradition of designating a successor and passing on the light to that person.

Guru Baba Ram Das, the fourth guru, who lived in the sixteenth century, began constructing Amritsar's Golden Temple. The structure was completed by his successor, Guru Arjan Dev, who also collected poems and songs written by the first four gurus and added his own. He included the work of Kabir and other Hindu and Muslim holy men as well. This became the Adi Granth, which he placed in the Golden Temple.

Guru Arjan was martyred in 1606 by Jehangir, the Muslim emperor. His son Hargobind became the sixth guru and introduced several important practices and changes. He wore two swords, representing both spiritual and worldly authority. Near the Golden Temple he had a building known as Akal Takht, or Throne of the Almighty, erected. In it was a court of justice as well as a group of administrators. Even today, orders and decisions enter the community from Akal Takht. Guru Hargobind was the last of the gurus with a direct link to Amritsar. Because of conflict with the Muslim rulers, he and all subsequent gurus moved from the city.

The tenth guru, Gobind Singh, created the Khalsa, the Community of the Pure, in 1699. The members of the Khalsa were to be known by five distinctive elements, all beginning with the letter *k*. These include kes, the refusal to cut the hair or trim the beard; kangha, the comb used to keep the long hair neatly combed in contrast to the Hindu ascetics who had matted hair; kaccha, shorts that would allow soldiers quick movement; kara, a thin steel bracelet worn to symbolize restraint; and kirpan, a short sword not to be used except in self-defense. Among other duties, members of this elite group were to defend the faith. Until the middle of the nineteenth century, when the British created an empire in India, the Khalsa remained largely undefeated.

In 1708, Guru Gobind Singh announced that he would be the final human guru. All subsequent leadership would come from the Guru Granth Sahib, now considered a living guru, the holy text Arjan had begun compiling more than a century earlier.

Muslim persecution under the Mughals led to the defeat of the Sikhs in 1716. The remaining Sikhs headed for the hills, re-emerging after decline of Mughal power. They were united under Ranjit Singh's kingdom from 1820 to 1839. They then came under the control of the British.

The British annexed the Punjab region, making it part of their Indian empire in 1849, and recruited Sikhs to serve in the army. The Sikhs remained loyal to the British during the Indian Mutiny of 1857–1858. As a result, they were given many privileges and land grants, and with peace and prosperity, the first Singh Sabha was founded in 1873. This was an educational and religious reform movement.

During the early twentieth century, Sikhism was shaped in its more modern form. A group known as the Tat Khalsa, which was more progressive, became the dominant way of understanding the faith.

In 1897, a group of Sikh musicians within the British Army was invited to attend the Diamond Jubilee of Queen Victoria in England. They also traveled to Canada and were attracted by the nation's prairies, which were perfect for farming. The first group of Sikhs came to Canada soon after. By 1904, more than two hundred Sikhs had settled in British Columbia. Some of them later headed south to Washington, Oregon, and California in the United States. The first Sikh gurdwara in the United States was constructed in Stockton, California, in 1912. Sikhs became farmers, worked in lumber mills, and helped to construct the Western Pacific railroad. Yuba City, California, has one of the world's largest Sikh temples, built in 1968.

Sikh troops fought for Britain in World War I, achieving distinction. Following the war, in 1919, however, the British denied the Sikhs the right to gather for their New Year festival. When the Sikhs disobeyed, the British troops fired without warning on 10,000 Sikhs, 400 of whom were killed. This became known as the first Amritsar Massacre.

The British government in 1925 did give the Sikhs the right to help manage their own shrines. A fragile peace ensued between the British and the Sikhs, who again fought for the British Empire during World War II.

After the war ended, the Sikh hope for an independent state was dashed by the partition of India and Pakistan in 1947. Pakistan was in the Punjab region; thus, 2.5 million Sikhs lived in a Muslim country where they were not welcome. Many of them became part of the mass internal migration that followed Indian independence.

In 1966, a state with a Sikh majority came into existence after Punjab boundaries were redrawn. Strife continued throughout second half of twentieth century, however, as a result of continuing demands for Punjab autonomy. A second massacre at Amritsar occurred in 1984, resulting in the death of 450 Sikhs (though some estimates of the death toll are higher). Indian troops, under orders from Indian Prime Minister Indira Gandhi, fired on militant leaders of Sikhs, who had gone to the Golden Temple for refuge. This attack was considered a desecration of a sacred place, and the prime minister was later assassinated by her Sikh bodyguards in response. Restoration of the Akal Takht, the administrative headquarters, took fifteen years. The Sikh library was also burned, consuming ancient manuscripts.

In 1999, Sikhs celebrated the three-hundredth anniversary of the founding of Khalsa. There has been relative peace in India since that event. In the United States, however, Sikhs became the object of slander and physical attack following the acts of terrorism on September 11, 2001, as some Americans could not differentiate between Arab head coverings and Sikh turbans.

## Founder or Major Prophet

Guru Nanak Dev was born into a Hindu family on April 15, 1469. His family belonged to the merchant caste, Khatri. His father worked as an accountant for a Muslim, who was also a local landlord. Nanak was educated in both the Hindu and Islamic traditions. According to legends, his teachers soon realized they had nothing further to teach him. After a direct revelation from Ultimate Reality that he received as a young man, Nanak proclaimed that there was neither Muslim nor Hindu. God had told Nanak "Rejoice in my Name," which became a central doctrine of Sikhism.

Nanak began to preach, leaving his wife and two sons behind. According to tradition, he traveled not only throughout India, but also eventually to Iraq, Saudi Arabia, and Mecca. This tradition and others were collected in a volume known as Janamsakhis. A Muslim servant of the family, Mardana, who also played a three-stringed musical instrument called the rebec, accompanied him, as did a Hindu poet, Bala Sandhu, who had been a friend from childhood

(though the extent of his importance or existence is often considered controversial).

Nanak traveled as an itinerant preacher for a quarter century and then founded a village, Kartarpur, on the bank of Punjab's Ravi River. Before his death he chose his successor, beginning a tradition that was followed until the tenth and final human guru.

## Philosophical Basis

When Guru Nanak Dev, the first guru, began preaching in 1499 at about age thirty, he incorporated aspects of both Hinduism and Islam. From Hinduism, he took the ideas of karma and reincarnation. From Islam, he borrowed the Ultimate as the name of God. Some scholars see the influence of the religious reformer and poet Kabir, who lived from 1440 until 1518. Kabir merged the Bhakti (devotional) side of Hinduism with the Islamic Sufis, who were mystics.

Within the Hindu tradition in northern India was a branch called the Sants. The Sants believed that God was both with form and without form, unable to be represented concretely. Most of the Sants were illiterate and poor, but created poems that spoke of the divine being experienced in all things. This idea also rooted itself in Sikhism.

Guru Nanak Dev, who was raised as a Hindu, rejected the caste system in favor of equality of all persons. He also upheld the value of women, rejecting the burning of widows and female infanticide. When eating a communal meal, first begun as a protest against caste, everyone sits in a straight line and shares karah prasad (a pudding), which is provided by those of all castes. However, Sikhs are expected to marry within their caste. In some cases, especially in the United Kingdom, gurdwaras (places of worship) for a particular caste exist.

## Holy Places

Amritsar, especially the Golden Temple, which was built in the sixteenth century under the supervision of the fifth guru, Guru Arjan, is the most sacred city.

Ram Das, the fourth guru, first began constructing a pool on the site in 1577. He called it

Amritsar, the pool of nectar. This sacred reflecting pool is a pilgrimage destination. Steps on the southern side of the pool allow visitors to gather water in bottles, to drink it, to bathe in it, or to sprinkle it on themselves.

---

## SIKHISM IN DEPTH

### Sacred Symbols

The khanda is the major symbol of Sikhism. It features a two-edged sword, representing justice and freedom, in the center. It is surrounded by a circle, a symbol of both balance and of the unity of God and humankind. A pair of curved swords (kirpans) surrounds the circle. One sword stands for religious concerns, the other for secular concerns. The khanda appears on Sikh flags, which are flown over every temple.

Members of the Khalsa have five symbols. They do not cut their hair, and men do not trim their beards. This symbol, kes, is to indicate a harmony with the ways of nature. To keep the long hair neat, a comb called a kangha is used. The third symbol is the kara, a bracelet usually made of steel to represent continuity and strength. When the Khalsa was first formed, soldiers wore loose-fitting shorts called kaccha. They were worn to symbolize moral restraint and purity. The final symbol is a short sword known as a kirpan, to be used only in self-defense. When bathing in sacred waters, the kirpan is tucked into the turban, which is worn to cover the long hair. The turban, which may be one of many colors, is wound from nearly five yards of cloth.

### Sacred Practices & Gestures

Sikhs use Sat Sri Akal (truth is timeless) as a greeting, putting hands together and bowing toward the other person. To show respect, Sikhs keep their heads covered with a turban or veil. Before entering a temple, they remove their shoes. Some Sikhs may choose to wear a bindhi, the dot on the forehead usually associated with Hinduism.

When Guru Gobind Singh initiated the first men into the Khalsa, he put water in a steel bowl and added sugar, stirring the mixture with his sword and reciting verses from the Guru Granth as he did so. He thus created amrit (immortal), a holy water also used in baptism, or the Amrit ceremony. The water represents mental clarity, while sugar stands for sweetness. The sword invokes military courage, and the chanting of verses brings a poetic spirituality.

The Sikh ideal of bringing Ultimate Reality into every aspect of the day is expressed in prayers throughout the day. Daily morning prayer (Bani) consists of five different verses, most of them the work of one of the ten gurus; there are also two sets of evening prayers. Throughout the day, Sikhs repeat the Mul Mantra, "Ikk Oan Kar" (There is one Being). This is the first line of a brief creedal statement about Ultimate Reality.

### Food Restrictions

Sikhs are not to eat halal meat, which is the Muslim equivalent of kosher. Both tobacco and alcohol are forbidden. Many Sikhs are vegetarians, although this is not commanded. Members of the Khalsa are not permitted to eat meat slaughtered according to Islamic or Hindu methods, because they believe these means cause pain to the animal.

### Rites, Celebrations, & Services

The Sikhs observe four rite of passage rituals, with each emphasizing their distinction from the Hindu traditions. After a new mother is able to get up and bathe, the new baby is given a birth and naming ceremony in the gurdwara. The child is given a name based on the first letter of hymn from the Guru Granth Sahib at random. All males are additionally given the name Singh (lion); all females also receive the name Kaur (princess).

The marriage ceremony (anand karaj) is the second rite of passage. Rather than circle a sacred fire as the Hindus do, the Sikh couple walks four times around a copy of the Guru Granth Sahib, accompanied by singing. The bride often wears red, a traditional color for the Punjabi.

The amrit initiation into the Khalsa is considered the most important rite. It need not take place in a temple, but does require that five

Sikhs who are already Khalsa members conduct the ceremony. Amrit initiation may occur any time after a child is old enough to read the Guru Granth and understand the tenets of the faith. Some people, however, wait until their own children are grown before accepting this rite.

The funeral rite is the fourth and final rite of passage. A section of the Guru Granth is read. The body, dressed in the Five "K's," is cremated soon after death.

Initiation into the Khalsa is now open to both men and women. The earliest gurus opposed the Hindu custom of sati, which required a widow to be burned on her husband's funeral pyre. They were also against the Islamic custom of purdah, which required women to be veiled and covered in public. Women who are menstruating are not excluded from worship, as they are in some religions. Women as well as men can be leaders of the congregation and are permitted to read from the Guru Granth and recite sacred hymns.

The Sikh houses of worship are known as gurdwaras and include a langar, the communal dining area. People remove their shoes and cover their heads before entering. They touch their foreheads to the floor in front of the scripture to show respect. The service itself is in three parts. The first segment is Kirtan, singing hymns (kirtans) accompanied by musical instruments, which can last for several hours. It is followed by a set prayer called the Ardas, which has three parts. The first and final sections cannot be altered. In the first, the virtues of the gurus are extolled. In the last, the divine name is honored. In the center of the Ardas is a list of the Khalsa's troubles and victories, which a prayer leader recites in segments and to which the congregation responds with Vahiguru, considered a word for God. At the end of the service, members eat karah prasad, sacred food made of raw sugar, clarified butter, and coarse wheat flour. They then adjourn for a communal meal, Langar, the third section of worship.

Sikhism does not have a set day for worship similar to the Jewish Sabbath or Christian Sunday worship. However, the first day of the month on the Indian lunar calendar, sangrand, and the darkest night of the month, masia, are considered special days. Sangrand is a time for praying for the entire month. Masia is often considered an auspicious time for bathing in the holy pool at the temple.

Four of the major festivals that Sikhs observe surround important events in the lives of the gurus. These are known as gurpurabs, or anniversaries. Guru Nanak's birthday, Guru Gobind Singh's birthday, and the martyrdoms of the Gurus Arjan and Tegh Bahadur comprise the four main gurpurabs. Sikhs congregate in the gurudwaras to hear readings of the Guru Granth and lectures by Sikh scholars.

Baisakhi is the Indian New Year, the final day before the harvest begins. On this day in 1699, Guru Gobind Singh formed the first Khalsa, adding even more importance to the day for Sikhs. Each year, a new Sikh flag is placed at all temples.

Diwali, based on a word meaning string of lights, is a Hindu festival. For Sikhs, it is a time to remember the return of the sixth guru, Hargobind, to Amritsar after the emperor had imprisoned him. It is celebrated for three days at the Golden Temple. Sikhs paint and whitewash their houses and decorate them with candles and earthenware lamps.

Hola Mohalla, meaning attack and place of attack, is the Sikh spring festival, which corresponds to the Hindu festival Holi. It is also a three-day celebration and a time for training Sikhs as soldiers. Originally, it involved military exercises and mock battles, as well as competitions in archery, horsemanship, and wrestling. In contemporary times, the festival includes athletic contests, discussion, and singing.

*Judy A. Johnson, MTS*

**Bibliography**

Barnes, Trevor. *The Kingfisher Book of Religions*. New York: Kingfisher, 1999. Print.

Dhanjal, Beryl. *Amritsar*. New York: Dillon, 1993. Print.

Dhavan, Purnima. *When Sparrows Became Hawks: The Making of the Sikh Warrior Tradition, 1699–1799*. Oxford: Oxford UP, 2011. Print.

Eraly, Abraham, et. al. *India*. New York: DK, 2008. Print.

Harley, Gail M. *Hindu and Sikh Faiths in America*. New York: Facts on File, 2003. Print.

Jakobsh, Doris R. *Sikhism and Women: History, Texts, and Experience*. Oxford, New York: Oxford UP, 2010. Print.

Jhutti-Johal, Jagbir. *Sikhism Today*. London, New York: Continuum, 2011. Print.

Langley, Myrtle. *Religion*. New York: Knopf, 1996. Print.

Mann, Gurinder Singh. *Sikhism*. Upper Saddle River: Prentice, 2004. Print.

Meredith, Susan. *The Usborne Book of World Religions*. London: Usborne, 1995. Print.

Sidhu, Dawinder S. and Neha Singh Gohil. *Civil Rights in Wartime: The Post-9/11 Sikh Experience*. Ashgate, 2009. E-book.

Singh, Nikky-Guninder Kaur. *Sikhism*. New York: Facts on File, 1993. Print.

Singh, Nikky-Guninder Kaur. *Sikhism: An Introduction*. Tauris, 2011. E-book.

Singh, Surinder. *Introduction to Sikhism and Great Sikhs of the World*. Gurgaon: Shubhi, 2012. Print.

Wilkinson, Philip. *Religions*. New York: DK, 2008. Print.

# Index